Statistical Concepts
for the
Behavioral Sciences

The fourth edition of *Statistical Concepts for the Behavioral Sciences* emphasizes contemporary research problems to better illustrate the relevance of statistical analysis in scientific research. All statistical methods are introduced in the context of a realistic problem, many of which are from contemporary published research. These studies are fully referenced so students can easily access the original research. The uses of statistics are then developed and presented in a conceptually logical progression for increased comprehension by using the accompanying workbook and the problem sets. Several forms of practice problems are available to students and presented in a manner that assists students in mastering component pieces before integrating them together to tackle more complicated, real-world problems.

Harold O. Kiess is Professor Emeritus, Framingham State University, and received his Ph.D. in Experimental Psychology from the University of Illinois, Urbana–Champaign, USA. While at Framingham, Kiess developed and taught courses in research methodology and statistical analysis, as well as the historical foundations of psychology. He has also authored three editions of *Statistical Concepts for the Behavioral Sciences* before joining with Bonnie A. Green as co-author for the fourth edition.

Bonnie A. Green is Professor of Psychology at East Stroudsburg University and received her Ph.D. in Psychology from Lehigh University, USA. As a fellow of the Eastern Psychological Association, Green presents research on student success and effective teaching. She also actively mentors undergraduate students in research, statistics, and psychometrics. Both Kiess and Green have co-authored the book *Measuring Humans: Fundamentals of Psychometrics for Selecting and Interpreting Tests.*

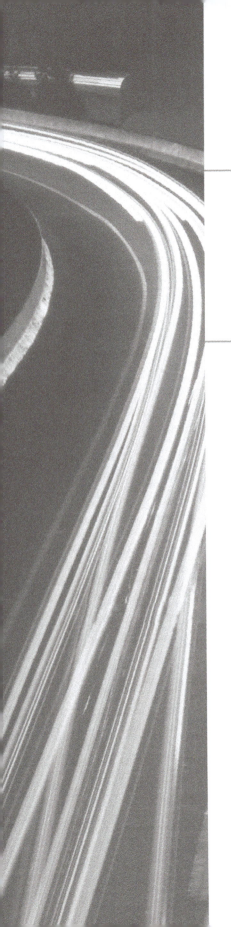

Statistical Concepts for the Behavioral Sciences

FOURTH EDITION

Harold O. Kiess
Framingham State University

Bonnie A. Green
East Stroudsburg University of Pennsylvania

CAMBRIDGE
UNIVERSITY PRESS

CAMBRIDGE
UNIVERSITY PRESS

University Printing House, Cambridge CB2 8BS, United Kingdom

One Liberty Plaza, 20th Floor, New York, NY 10006, USA

477 Williamstown Road, Port Melbourne, VIC 3207, Australia

314-321, 3rd Floor, Plot 3, Splendor Forum, Jasola District Centre, New Delhi - 110025, India

79 Anson Road, #06-04/06, Singapore 079906

Cambridge University Press is part of the University of Cambridge.

It furthers the University's mission by disseminating knowledge in the pursuit of education, learning and research at the highest international levels of excellence.

www.cambridge.org
Information on this title: www.cambridge.org/9781108733014
DOI: 10.1017/9781108774604

This book was previously published by Pearson Education, Inc., publishing as Allyn & Bacon 1989, 1996, 2002, 2010

This fourth edition reissued by Cambridge University Press 2020

First paperback edition 2020

A catalogue record for this publication is available from the British Library

ISBN 978-1-108-73301-4 Paperback

Additional resources for this publication at www.cambridge.org/SCBS4

Why Do You Need this New Edition?

5 good reasons why you should buy this new edition of *Statistical Concepts for the Behavioral Sciences!*

- **Numerous new examples and problems** have been added that students will find relevant to their everyday lives. Many of the examples introducing statistical techniques have been revised with contemporary behavioral science research.

- All chapters have been **substantially revised** to improve the conceptual flow of the material. Any extraneous information not central to understanding statistical methods has been removed.

- **New chapter introductions** provide a better frame of reference to build new knowledge and pose interesting behavioral science questions that require statistical methods for their solution.

- **New feature** called *Integrating Your Knowledge* asks students to apply the knowledge they have acquired over several chapters to solve a practical problem in statistics.

- **New discussion of research methods** and their relation to statistics includes a discussion of research ethics.

Brief Contents

Contents

8   Is There Really a Difference? Introduction to Statistical Hypothesis Testing   159

9   The Basics of Experimentation and Testing for a Difference Between Means   191

10 One-Factor Between-Subjects Analysis of Variance   238

13   Correlation: Understanding Covariation   369

14   Regression Analysis: Predicting Linear Relationships   409

Preface

Statistics teaches us that there is little of which we can be absolutely certain. Nonetheless, we very much suspect that most behavioral science majors do not relish the thought of taking a course in statistics. Too often, statistics is taught as a series of formulas with a "here's how you do it" approach, with little emphasis on either the context in which the formulas are used or the conceptual basis for what is being done. This text is thus an attempt to provide a conceptual development of basic statistical methods in the context of their use in behavioral science. Statistics are introduced conceptually in the context of a realistic problem so that students may understand what the statistic does with data. This fourth edition carries with it the goals of the past editions, using up-to-date research to illustrate the relevance of statistical analysis in scientific research in a nonthreatening way.

A major addition to this edition is a coauthor, Bonnie A. Green, PhD, associate professor in the Psychology Department of East Stroudsburg University of Pennsylvania. Dr. Green began her professional career as a teacher of mathematics and science to fifth and sixth graders. Since earning her PhD in experimental psychology, she has experienced success teaching applied statistics and research methods to reluctant college students. Her research focus has been applying statistical procedures to further understand cognitive processes. Thus, she brings to this edition both practical experience and a formal understanding of how to apply research in cognitive development to maximize student learning without sacrificing the rigor of the discipline of applied statistics and research methods in the behavioral sciences.

Organization of the Text

The organization of this edition is designed for continuity in the concepts presented. The uses of statistics are developed and presented in a conceptually logical progression. The first five chapters introduce the need for statistics, the measurement of behavior, displaying scores in frequency distributions graphically, and measures of central tendency and variability. Chapters 6 and 7 introduce the normal distribution, probability, sampling distributions, and using statistics for estimation of parameters. The basics of statistical hypothesis testing are introduced with the z test and the one-sample t test in Chapter 8. Chapters 9 to 12 deal with hypothesis testing for the difference between means using parametric tests. The analysis of variance is emphasized, for it is among the most widely used statistical tests in the behavioral sciences and students clearly need to be familiar with its use. A thorough introduction is provided for the one-factor between-subjects, one-factor within-subjects, and the factorial between-subjects analyses of variance, including the use of multiple comparison tests and effect size measures. In addition, considerable attention is given to the interpretation of an interaction in a factorial design. Chapters 13 and 14 present correlation and regression. The first of these chapters introduces both the Pearson and Spearman correlation coefficients. Statistical hypothesis testing with each correlation coefficient is also developed. Chapter 14 then provides an overview of the basics of simple linear regression, building from the discussion of correlation in Chapter 13. The placement of these chapters near the end of the text is somewhat unusual, for many texts place these chapters following a discussion of descriptive statistics. But we believe this common placement poses conceptual difficulties for students. Descriptive statistics, such as the mean and standard deviation, lead naturally to a discussion of statistical tests for the difference between sample means. Interposition of correlation and regression between descriptive statistics and statistical hypothesis testing interrupts this continuity of thought. We elected to maintain the continuity of conceptual development and place the correlation and regression material after the presentation of parametric statistical tests. Chapter 15 concludes the text with a discussion of three nonparametric statistical tests, the chi-square, Mann–Whitney U, and the Wilcoxon signed-ranks tests.

Features

Students attempting to grasp the sometimes difficult conceptual basis of statistics often encounter many problems. To help overcome these problems, the text uses a variety of features to keep the material tied to actual research problems and to permit students to assess their understanding of the material as they proceed through a chapter.

Realistic Problems

All statistical methods are introduced in the context of a problem from behavioral research. Many problems are based on studies drawn from contemporary published research. These studies are referenced fully so that the interested student may read the original research. Other studies are based upon undergraduate student-designed research. We have found that students often find research designed by other students to be both relevant and interesting.

Conceptual Development of Statistics

The various statistics are introduced conceptually. Each chapter begins with a realistic example to help students get mentally prepared to better understand the material that will follow. Definitional formulas are provided to aid in conceptual understanding. An example problem is then worked using this conceptual approach so that students may see what the statistic does with the data. Using this format, we have tried not to overwhelm students mathematically when introducing a statistic. The mathematics required for elementary statistics is simple, yet many students are intimidated by a first chapter that reviews basic mathematics with no immediate connection to the statistics that use them. Thus, we begin the textbook by helping students focus on methods to be successful in the class and by providing an overview of statistics in the context of behavioral research. We save the introduction and explanation of the necessary mathematical concepts for when they are needed. For those who need a more complete review of basic mathematical operations, however, a review is provided in Appendix A.

Testing Your Knowledge and Review Questions

Each chapter contains interspersed Testing Your Knowledge sections and end-of-chapter Review Questions. The questions in these sections provide an opportunity for students to review and test their understanding of the text material. Many of the questions are based on actual research problems. Thus, not only do these questions provide a review, but they also give examples of the uses of the various statistical methods. A number of new questions and problems have been added for the fourth edition, with careful attention paid to ensuring that students practice component parts of the calculation before being asked to integrate what they have learned. We strongly encourage students to complete these exercises whenever they are encountered before continuing on in the chapter or to the next chapter.

Integrating Your Knowledge

To aid students in being able to apply what they are learning in class to real research problems, new to this edition is an Integrating Your Knowledge section that follows every second or third chapter. These sections require students to integrate information learned from previous chapters to solve a realistic problem. Integrating Your Knowledge sections are arranged in a manner that guides students through the evaluation of a study, the selection of the right statistical tools, and the implementation and interpretation of the statistics. Not only will this section aid students in applying information in a more realistic fashion, it should serve to demonstrate to students how statistics can really be useful in answering important questions in the behavioral sciences.

Sample Journal Formats

For many statistical tests, a sample journal report of a statistical analysis is presented with an explanation of the information contained in the report. The sample is followed by exercises on extracting information from journal presentations of the results of a study. For this edition, we have included a discussion of the recommendations of the American Psychological Association Task Force on Statistical Inference (Wilkinson & Task Force on Statistical Inference, 1999) as well as the requirements of the *Publication Manual of the American Psychological Association* (2001).

Marginal Definitions and Terms Glossary

Marginal definitions of important terms and a glossary of these terms are included in this edition. Important terms are boldfaced and defined in the text material. These definitions are supplemented by marginal definitions to reinforce learning of the material. A glossary of all these terms is provided in Appendix F.

Symbols Glossary

It is easy to become overwhelmed by the variety of symbols used in statistics. To aid in learning the language of statistics, Appendix B provides a glossary of all the symbols used in this text. Thus, students may easily refresh themselves on the meaning of symbols that they encounter.

Readability

Each chapter begins with a conversational tone, placing what is to be learned into the context of the real world. Moreover, the text is written so that it may be read and studied without interruption by boxed features or optional reading. Each section of the text follows from the previous material.

New for the Fourth Edition

Our goal for this revision was to update many of the problems and examples without changing the basic approach of the text. Given that almost all statistical analysis is now done with computer software, all computational formulas have been removed from the book. A majority of the example and practice problems have been updated to include new research on contemporary topics of interest to college students. In addition, more practice problems and review questions have been added to ensure students master the component pieces before having to apply their knowledge in the Integrating Your Knowledge practice problems. Based upon feedback from students and professors, Chapter 5 has been rewritten and reorganized to provide a clearer explanation of measures of variability. Finally, the introductory sections of most chapters have been rewritten to provide an example of the need for the statistical method introduced in the chapter.

Ultimately, we hope that you will find that this text leads to an interesting and rewarding study of statistics, one that provides you with the fundamental understanding of how statistics can be used to answer challenging questions in the behavior sciences, not just for the sake of a grade in this class, but for greater understanding throughout your student and professional career in the behavioral sciences. If you have any comments, suggestions, or you would like to share with us a study you have conducted that we may mention in the next edition, please email us at bgreen@po-box.esu.edu (Bonnie Green) or hkiess@verizon.net (Hal Kiess).

Supplements

Additional Instructor Supplements

The Supplements package for qualified instructors includes an Instructor's Manual, a computerized test bank, and PowerPoint lectures. You can download any or all of these resources from the Publisher's website: www.cambridge.org/SCBS4

Instructor's Manual

The **Instructor's Manual** provides:

▶ A general introduction of ideas and suggestions for teaching behavioral statistics, including discussions of:

   ▶ **Activities and Demonstrations**

   ▶ **Interteaching** covering a review of this pedagogical technique

   ▶ **Writing About Statistics**

   ▶ **The Controversy Over Statistical Hypothesis Testing**

   ▶ **Definitional vs. Computation Formulas** discussion to assist professors in maximizing student learning

   ▶ **Using the Internet in Teaching Statistics** including discussions on:

      ▶ **Just-in-time Teaching** pedagogical technique

      ▶ **Online Resources for Instructors and Students**

▶ Specific recommendations and information for each chapter include:

   ▶ **Overview and Suggestions** regarding methods for covering the material from each chapter

   ▶ **Goals and Objectives**

   ▶ **Chapter Outline**

   ▶ **Summary** providing the critical information covered in each chapter

   ▶ **Key Terms and Symbols**

   ▶ **Discussion Questions** that align with the objectives and material covered in each chapter

▶ The **Assignments and Exercises for Student** supplementary material provides chapter specific assignments that:

   ▶ Cover the most critical objectives of the chapter

   ▶ Assist students in using terminology and concepts

   ▶ Provide students with additional calculation practice

   ▶ Are based on targeted areas that often require additional practice

   ▶ Can be used with students as they are learning the material or reviewing for exams

   ▶ Were written by the authors of the textbook to complement **Testing Your Knowledge, Chapter Review,** and **Integrating Your Knowledge** questions found in the text

Computerized Test Bank

In addition to the Instructor's Manual for qualified instructors, there is a computerized test bank. The "MyTest" program allows instructors to select from hundreds of multiple-choice items, modify or write new items, and construct examinations. The Test Bank that accompanies this text allows instructors to assess objectives, and cover knowledge, application, and evaluation type questions. Questions come in three levels of difficulty: easy, moderate, and challenging, and all test questions were written by the authors of the textbook. MyTest is a web-based program that you can access from either Mac or PC computer.

PowerPoint Presentation

Finally, a complete set of PowerPoint lectures are available for downloading from the Publisher's website. These lectures include critical terms and their definitions and general statistical concepts that instructors can use if desired.

Acknowledgments

Many people have contributed to this edition of the text. Michelle Limoges, Acquisitions Editor at Pearson Allyn & Bacon, suggested the preparation of a fourth edition to a somewhat reluctant first author. After Bonnie joined as a second author, Michelle enthusiastically mentored her throughout the process of writing a textbook. Michelle has expertly guided the project through reviews and revisions. Her careful analysis of the reviews and numerous suggestions have led to a variety of revisions in the text, clearly improving the quality of this book. We express our sincere appreciation to her. Also, many thanks to others at Pearson Allyn & Bacon for their assistance and answers to our many questions: Christina Manfroni, Editorial Assistant; Robert Tonner, Copyright and Permissions Manager; Sarah Bylund, Copyright and Permissions Assistant; and Patty Bergin, Production Supervisor, as well as those many people behind the scenes whose names are unknown to us. We would also like to thank our copy editor, Jane Loftus, for her conscientious review of our manuscript, her many improvements to our writing, and her patience in dealing with us. Gary Kliewer, of The Book Company, pulled all of the myriad details of producing a textbook together. Also many thanks to Charlene Squibb and the team at Nesbitt Graphics for their work on editorial production.

Various professional colleagues have also contributed to the development of this edition of this text. Their careful scrutiny helped immensely in clarifying the presentation and avoiding conceptual and mathematical errors. Of course, any inaccuracies remaining are our responsibility alone. We are grateful to the following for their assistance:

Eric L. Bruns	Campbellsville University
Sarah Cavanaugh	Tufts University
Jackie Koch	Hofstra University
Julie Heberle	Albright College
Donald Kendrick	Middle Tennessee State University
Elizabeth Krupinski	University of Arizona
Jeffrey Lorentz	University of Houston, Clear Lake
Diane K. Martichuski	University of Colorado
John Petrocelli	Wake Forest University
John Pittenger	University of Arkansas at Little Rock
Jane Thompson	University of Hawaii at Hilo
Brian Uldall	University of Hawaii at Hilo
Deanne Westerman	State University of New York, Binghamton

A number of Bonnie Green's students have made contributions by suggesting example studies and preparing supplementary materials. We give a special thank you to Joshua Sandry for his efforts on the supplemental material and to Joshua Sandry and Christopher

Pohorence for their careful review and thoughtful suggestions for various sections within the textbook.

Ashley Adams, Nicole Deptula, Edwin Henriquez, Elizabeth Lambert, Joseph Perriera, Christopher Pohorence, Lisa Rieks, Deborah Ritter, Joshua Sandry, and Dina Sapp helped to develop the example in Chapter 3 regarding the relationship of one's implicit view of intelligence to academic success.

Charlene Conklin and Lisa Alexander, assisted by Kevin Holmes, Ryan Love, and Dennis Maldonado, completed research on the problem of parking on a college campus and its impact on student learning. Portions of this study were used as the example to introduce the one-sample t-test in Chapter 8.

Liane Domowicz, Josef Faturos, Ben Grieco, Yvonne Marfo, and Maxine Wheeler designed a study to determine how people read emotion into text messaging based on the gender of the sender. Their study is used in Review Question 3 in Chapter 9.

Paul Green, Allyssa Homschek, Steven Oberman, Amanda Reese, and Nealiani Rosario completed research on the effects of stress on pronunciation, which served as the basis for Review Question 5 in Chapter 9 and Review Question 2 in Chapter 12.

Ashley Bergholtz, Anna Governali, Kristen Stachina, Daniel Marx, and Crystal Williams conducted the research on the effect of different types of professor humor on student attention and memory that served as the basis for a similar example used at the beginning of Chapter 13 and carried over into Chapter 14.

Two groups of students examined the effects of visual images of "perfect" bodies on the self-esteem of others that served as the basis for a similar example used for Example Problem 9.3 and Review Question 6 in Chapter 9. Ashley Herbert, Eric Kresge, Meghan Johnson, Lindsay Sadawski, Joanna Spinelli, and Stacy Waldon worked together on this research, as did Heather Fagan, Amanda Iorio, Nikki Matthews, Tamara Rivera, Wylie Schweers, and Claes Wyckoff.

We are also grateful to the Biometrika Trustees for permission to reprint several tables from *Biometrika Tables for Statisticians*.

Each of the authors also has special acknowledgments to express.

Hal Kiess.   I would like to express my appreciation to Bonnie Green, without whom this edition would not exist. Comfortably ensconced in retirement, I had no intention of revising the previous edition of this text until I received an email from Bonnie saying, "I'll be your coauthor." That email was the beginning of this edition. I must also acknowledge the person affected most by the work required to write a book, my wife, Sandra. She has been through this process four times with me and is still supportive and encouraging. Without her understanding, tolerance, encouragement, and love over many years, this book would never have been completed.

Bonnie Green.   I must acknowledge both my husband and my students, who for many years have said, "Write a statistics book," and to my statistics mentor, Marty Richter, who said, "You're writing a statistics book?" And though my children have grown to hate "Mommy's stinking book," I must also thank them for allowing me to make sure that at least one more set of students gets to read the well-articulated words of Harold Kiess, to whom I owe the greatest gratitude. Lastly, to the students who will read this book and toil over its pages, may your efforts always bear fruit and may you use your skills in behavioral statistics for making the world a better place to live!

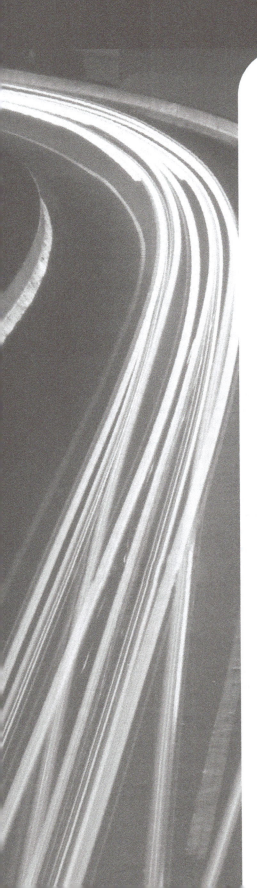

Making Sense of Variability: An Introduction to Statistics

"Oh that blasted alarm," you mutter as you push the snooze button for a second time. What a short night! As you stumble out of bed, you realize that only a quick shower and a fast breakfast will let you be on time for your 8:00 A.M. class. As you walk to your car, you notice what a pleasant, warm day seems to be in store for this early spring day, much nicer than yesterday's cold rain and drizzle. As you pull onto the expressway, the traffic is heavier than usual, and it's not moving as fast as you had expected. Will you be late for your class? Fortunately, you make your class on time; the lecture today is one of the best of the semester. But you dread your 9:00 A.M. science lab; often it runs so long you don't have time for lunch. Yet, today is different. Everything goes smoothly, and you get out in time to have a leisurely, fun lunch with two of your best friends, as well as time to respond to a few text messages. After lunch, it's off to work at the Big Bargain Department Store. The customers today seem very pleasant in contrast to yesterday—you think maybe it's because of the nice weather. The pleasant customers make the afternoon pass quickly, and soon you are again on the expressway heading for home. Traffic now is lighter than most days; maybe everyone left work earlier today. You have a great deal of schoolwork to do, so after dinner you settle at your desk, hoping for a productive night of studying. But first you read your e-mail. Surprisingly, only few messages are spam in comparison to the typical number you receive each day. Your studying seems to go well, at least compared to many of your attempts to study after dinner. You really feel prepared for that statistics exam coming up at the end of the week. To reward yourself, you text a few friends and then go to bed. Maybe if you go to bed a bit earlier, the night will seem longer.

Perhaps this short vignette represents a typical day in your life, perhaps it does not. In any event, you are probably wondering what this vignette has to do with statistics. Well, for one, it illustrates that you have recognized certain regularities or consistencies in the events of your life: the typical amount of time you have for a shower or breakfast, the normal weather for an early spring day, the characteristic amount of traffic on your drive to college and how long it takes you to get there, the general interest level of a class, the average length of a science lab, the normal amount of fun you have at lunch, the typical behavior of a department store customer, the average number of spam e-mail messages you receive each day, and the normal productivity of a night of studying. The fact that you recognize there are consistencies or regularities in the occurrences of your life indicates you also recognize that there is variability or variation in these regularities. Some nights seem longer than others, showers and breakfasts vary in length from day to day, the weather rarely is normal for the time of the year, traffic may be lighter or heavier, classes vary in interest level from day to day (and from course to course), science labs are sometimes longer and other times shorter than average, the behavior of shoppers is quite variable from person to person, and some study sessions are more productive than others.

This variation among events implies the existence of variables in the environment. A **variable** is any environmental condition or event, stimulus, personal characteristic or attribute, or behavior that can take on different values at different times or with different people. The amount of sleep you obtain, the length of your shower, the amount of traffic on the expressway, the interest level of a class, the length of a science lab, the mood of shoppers, and the productivity of study sessions are all variables. Statistics is the discipline that quantifies the consistency found in a variable and the variability about this consistency. Although this definition of statistics is informal and incomplete, it will serve for the moment.

You, of course, are not the only person to note the regularity of events in the world. Lambert Adolphe Jacques Quetelet (1796–1874), a Belgian professor with wide-ranging

Variable ▶ Any environmental condition or event, stimulus, personal characteristic or attribute, or behavior that can take on different values at different times or with different people.

TABLE 1.1	Conviction rates in French courts as a function of year and the ability of the defendant to read and write.			

| Ability of Accused to Read or Write | Year | | | Average |
	1828	1829	1830	
Unable to read or write	0.63	0.63	0.62	0.627
Able to read and write imperfectly	0.62	0.60	0.58	0.600
Able to read and write well	0.56	0.55	0.52	0.543
Has a superior education	0.35	0.48	0.37	0.400

Source: After data of Quetelet. Adapted from Table 5.2, p. 176, *The History of Statistics: The Measurement of Uncertainty before 1900* by S. M. Stigler. Copyright 1986 by the President and Fellows of Harvard College.

interests, believed that such regularities in variables have causes and that if he could identify the regularities, he could then identify their causes. He thus set out to identify these regularities. His initial work was to characterize what he called an "average man." To do so, he obtained anthropometric data (that is, bodily measurements) on variables such as height and weight from a large number of French soldiers (Stigler, 1986). His hope was that by characterizing an average person, he could find regularities in human attributes and then compare these averages between males and females or across nationalities, localities, ages, or races. Quetelet's interest in the average person extended also to what he called "moral statistics," regularities in variables such as suicide rates or crime and conviction rates. For example, Quetelet studied conviction rates in French courts over a period of years and categorized the rate of conviction by the accused's ability to read and write. His results are presented in Table 1.1. The numerical values in Table 1.1 represent probabilities. For example, if you were being tried in a French court in 1829 and you were able to read and write only imperfectly, the probability of your being convicted would be 0.60 (or 6 chances out of 10). Notice there appears to be a clear relationship between the accused's reading and writing abilities and the likelihood that he or she would be convicted of a crime. Quetelet often is called the father of social science for initiating these statistical studies (Dudycha & Dudycha, 1972).

Studying Statistics: How to Use This Text

As the introduction illustrates, the study of statistics deals with both the regularities and variability of events that all of us have noticed in our lives. Thus, in one sense, although we are new to the study of statistics, we are all experienced statisticians finding consistency in variability. Nevertheless, many people are intimidated by the idea of statistics and dread the thought of an entire course in the subject. This fear need not be the case, however. Learning statistics is similar to learning a new language. The language of statistics is composed of words, symbols, and formulas. As with any new language, statistics requires time and effort to master its components. Throughout this text, we will provide you with information about how to maximize your success in understanding statistics. With practice and experience, statistics will become as natural to you as your native language. Several features of this text will help you with your study of statistics to achieve that goal.

Important Terms and Symbols

Terms and symbols that are especially important for understanding the concepts of a chapter are **boldfaced** in the text. The most important terms are also highlighted in a marginal definition. When you encounter a boldfaced term, you should recognize that it is important for your understanding of statistics. We suggest you come up with a plan for how to learn and understand the definitions of terms and the meaning of symbols, not merely memorize them. It often helps if after reading a section, you immediately attempt to define terms without looking at the definition provided in the book. Many students have also found that writing down the symbols, what they are called, and their definition helps them become more comfortable with the symbols. Other students have found that flash cards are helpful for learning terms and symbols. Regardless of your plan, it is important that you learn the terms and symbols as soon as they are introduced and that you continue to review them throughout the semester. If you cannot recall the meaning of a term or statistical symbol, a glossary of terms is provided in Appendix F and a glossary of statistical symbols is provided in Appendix B.

Self-Testing Questions

Self-testing is critical for success in understanding statistics. To help you test your knowledge of the material covered in the text, we have provided three types of self-test questions.

Testing Your Knowledge. Each chapter contains several Testing Your Knowledge sections. These sections provide an opportunity for you to review and test your understanding of the material you have just studied before you move on to the next section of the chapter. Many of the questions focus on actual research problems and provide examples of how the statistical methods you are studying are used. Answers for many of the Testing Your Knowledge questions are given in Appendix E, "Answers for Computational Problems."

Review Questions. Review questions are provided at the end of each chapter. These questions provide a review of the material presented in the chapter. As with the Testing Your Knowledge questions, we encourage you to complete the chapter review questions and then compare your answers to those given in Appendix E, "Answers for Computational Problems."

Integrating Your Knowledge. Many of the questions in Testing Your Knowledge and Review Questions are structured to help you focus on pieces of the statistical information presented in the chapter. The real world, however, is not going to present you with nice, compartmentalized statistical challenges. Integrating Your Knowledge problems are designed to assist you in practicing integrating information across multiple topics and chapters. Answers to Integrating Your Knowledge also appear in Appendix E, "Answers for Computational Problems." The first Integrating Your Knowledge occurs in Chapter 3.

Mathematics Review

The mathematics used in this text is elementary, requiring only the operations of addition, subtraction, multiplication, and division. Mathematical symbols and operations are explained as they are needed. If you encounter difficulties with any of the mathematical operations, a mathematics review is provided in Appendix A. This review provides a summary of basic mathematical symbols and operations.

Before You Begin

You Hold the Key to Success

You hold the key to your own success in this course because two of the most important predictors of your success are linked to your attitude and your behavior. Psychologists know that attitudes can affect behavior and that certain attitudes and behaviors are associated with mastery of information such as statistics. This book uses that knowledge in its design, and we will also pass this knowledge on to you. Thus, as you study this text, you will learn about the attitudes and behaviors that will help maximize your success in understanding statistics. Before you read further, please think carefully about the statement below. Then, select the number that best corresponds to the way you feel about the statement.

Some people are simply born smart, others are not so lucky.					
1	2	3	4	5	6
Strongly Agree					Strongly Disagree

Research by Dweck (1999, 2006) has found that students who strongly disagree with a statement similar to this example believe that intelligence is changeable. These students are also more likely to (1) attend class, (2) think about what the professor is presenting during class, (3) complete all homework assignments, (4) seek out study groups, and (5) seek out help from the professor when needed. Students who strongly agree with the above statement, however, believe that intelligence is fixed and cannot be changed. These students are (1) more likely to say things like, "I was never good in math anyway, I'm not going to be good in this class"; (2) less likely to attend class; (3) less likely to try to solve problems when they do attend class; (4) less likely to complete all homework assignments; and (5) less likely to seek out help when struggling in the class. Building upon these findings, several undergraduate students designed and completed a series of studies demonstrating that students who believe that they cannot become smarter do not do as well in class as students who believe that, with effort, they can become smarter. We will be discussing more about the relationship of attitudes and behaviors in future chapters. For now, recognize that if you adopt a "growth mindset," that is, if you believe your intellectual skills can grow, you are more likely to behave in a manner that will cause you to improve in statistics. However, if you do not believe that you can grow intellectually, why would you act as if you were able to improve your performance in statistics? So, start thinking about having an attitude of success for this class and putting into place the types of behaviors that will lead to that success. Believe that, with the right effort, you can learn statistics and be successful in this course.

Some Further Suggestions for Achieving Success

We have a few other tips to help you maximize your success with statistics.

Do not look ahead in the text. The material in the text can look scary and confusing, just like listening to someone speak in a foreign language that you do not know. No benefit will come from looking ahead in the text to see how difficult the material appears to be. As a woman who had five children once said when asked how she handled the challenges of her children, "I got used to one child at a time. Since each child came one at a time, with some chance for me to get acclimated before the next child arrived, it really wasn't that difficult." The material in this class will come at you one piece at a time. You will have a chance to become acclimated before you progress to the next piece. Before you know it, you'll be at the end of the book. There is no benefit in rushing it.

Read and study the textbook. It is critical that you read and study this book because it will help you understand the material when it is presented in class. Students who have anxiety related to statistics sometimes adopt the practice of ignoring the textbook as a method of decreasing anxiety. This approach may decrease your anxiety temporarily, but this short-term fix will hurt you in the long term. If you find reading the text to be anxiety provoking, seek a pleasant internal state (e.g., eat comfort food) and an external state (e.g., a comfortable chair and clean desk) that will improve your mood and decrease your anxiety. It often helps to start by just reading the headings and the terms in a section. Get comfortable with that information, then begin to read the entire chapter. It will be well worth your time.

Studying the textbook is critical, but how you study is equally critical. When you study, try to rid yourself of other distractions. Turn off the music, the TV, and the videogame. Unplug the iPod. Don't read your email, text your friends, or try to study with friends around. And give up the Internet for the duration of your studying. All these activities, enticing as they may be, have been shown to be related to lower exam performance (Gurung, 2005). Time is a precious commodity; make your study time effective!

Complete the various self-testing questions. Self-testing will help you discern whether you truly understand the material you are studying. This testing will help you target your studying and become more efficient. Moreover, there is real benefit in the act of self-testing, as it increases your understanding and long-term memory of the material. There is even reason to believe that self-testing will help decrease math or test anxiety that may otherwise interfere with your performance in this class. We understand that you have a limited amount of time to spend on academic pursuits. Skipping the self-testing questions in this book, however, is not a wise way to save time.

Be intellectually engaged. You hold the power of your mind. Use it to think about what is being covered in this book and in your class. Actively begin to examine results and conclusions of reported research studies. Do you agree? Does it make sense? Is there a flaw in the method or interpretation? Try to think of examples from your own experience. Often, forming study groups is a good way to become more intellectually engaged with this material, as you will find talking about statistics helpful for increasing your understanding. A study group is a particularly helpful strategy for someone who is experiencing some anxiety related to this material, because being around other people often decreases that fear while increasing positive emotions related to the material; but be sure it's a study group and not just a bunch of friends hanging out.

Finally, attend class and take careful notes. Be prepared for class, and ask questions about material that you do not understand. Study your class notes, and compare them to the material in the text. This recommendation may seem like a "no-brainer," but preparation for class and intellectual engagement in class activities and discussion is strongly related to academic success. In the hurry of our everyday lives, it's sometimes easy to forget this fact.

What Is Statistics?

Data ▶ The scores or measurements of behavior or characteristics obtained from observations of people or animals.

Following in the footsteps of Quetelet, behavioral scientists attempt to understand and explain human and animal behavior. They do so by collecting data. **Data** (*data* is plural, *datum* is singular) are the scores or measurements of behavior or characteristics obtained

Statistics ▷ The methods or procedures used to summarize, analyze, and draw conclusions from data.

from observations of people or animals. To identify both the consistencies and variability in these data, procedures called *statistics* are applied to it. **Statistics** thus refers to the methods or procedures used to summarize, analyze, and reach conclusions from a set of data.

Using Statistics: Four Examples

Statistical procedures are used in many different ways in behavioral science. The remainder of this chapter provides examples of four uses of statistical methods in behavioral science. A number of terms are introduced, and you should study and learn these terms, for you will encounter them throughout the text. Don't worry, however, if you don't understand all the details of the examples provided; the use of each approach is discussed more fully in later chapters.

Plain yet Mighty: Descriptive Statistics

There are probably many questions you have about the statistics class in which you are now enrolled. One of them may be how much time will you have to study each week? While we can't answer this question for you, many studies have been done on the amount of time college students spend studying. For example, Adams (2005) found that students believed that 6.2 hours of study per week indicated superior effort in a course, whereas faculty members believed that 8.5 hours per week of studying were indicative of superior effort. These numerical values illustrate the use of descriptive statistics. A **descriptive statistic**, often simply called a *statistic*, is a single number that may be used to describe or analyze a set of data from a sample. A sample is a small part of anything. In statistics, a **sample** is a subset, or subgroup, selected from a population. A **population** is a complete set of people, animals, objects, or events that share a common characteristic. For example, all students who are taking a college-level statistics class this semester could be considered a population. The common characteristic of this population is that all the individuals included in it are taking a similar class at the same time. They share something in common. Other examples of populations are all the college students in Canada, all the households in Bermuda, all the adult females in North Carolina, all the farmers in Nebraska, and all the people who have at least one bank credit card; each set comprises a population. Any group of individuals may be thought of as a population as long as all those possessing the characteristic common to the population are included in the group. For our example on study time, the numerical values were obtained from a sample of 159 college students from a population of college students and a sample of 59 faculty members from a population of college professors.

Descriptive statistic or statistic ▷ A single number used to describe data from a sample.

Sample ▷ A subset, or subgroup, selected from a population.

Population ▷ A complete set of people, animals, objects, or events that share a common characteristic.

We encounter such descriptive statistics every day in our reading or from the media. For example, it was reported that married mothers currently spend 14.1 hours a week on child care, whereas in 1965 married mothers typically spent 10.1 hours per week on child care (St. George, 2007). Again, these descriptive statistics were obtained from a sample of married mothers and are intended to be typical of the amount of time that the married mothers in that sample devote to child care.

Descriptive statistics help provide basic information about the sample from which you have collected data. Most likely, you are already familiar with some common descriptive statistics such as the mode, the median, or the mean, which we will discuss in following chapters. Descriptive statistics, however, have limitations; they cannot give you a cause or an explanation for what was observed. Why do married mothers currently spend more time on child care per week in comparison to 1965? Did they cut back on other activities? Do they perceive child care as being more important than did the mothers of 1965? Does society place a greater emphasis on child care now than it did in 1965? Are mothers of today more likely to overestimate how much time they spend with their children? Simple descriptive statistics such as those we have presented here cannot provide answers for these questions. We do not know what caused the difference in amount of time devoted to child care just from looking at the descriptive statistics. Yet, descriptive statistics are important for they provide us with an objective summary of information that has been collected.

Testing Your Knowledge 1.1

1. Define: data, descriptive statistic, population, sample, statistic, statistics, variable.

2. On the first day of statistics class, a professor conducted a brief survey asking students to rate their level of math anxiety. She determined that 24 percent of her class could be classified as possessing a high level of math anxiety, whereas 39 percent could be classified as having some math anxiety. The remainder of the class had either low or very low levels of math anxiety.

   a. What data were collected in this example?

   b. Was there variability in the data collected?

   c. Explain why descriptive statistics are necessary to summarize the results of this research.

   d. What percentage of the class had low or very low levels of math anxiety?

   e. Although the professor could determine what percentage of her class experiences math anxiety, what couldn't she determine from the percentages?

Making Sense of the World from a Little Piece: Inferential Statistics

Descriptive statistics tell us what is going on with the measurements we gather from a sample of people. However, as we have indicated, scientists often want to reach conclusions that go beyond the sample to the population from which the sample was selected. Behavioral scientists often want to characterize populations with statements such as "the typical married working mother devotes 14.1 hours per week to child care." It should be obvious that in most instances these characterizations cannot be obtained from measuring all members of the population; we cannot measure all married working mothers. Rather, scientists typically use information obtained from only a sample of the population to reach these conclusions.

Often, but not always, samples are selected from a population by following a set of rules to ensure that the sample is representative of the population. One common form of selecting a sample is random sampling. In a simple **random sample**, individuals are selected in such a way that each member of the population has an equal chance of being selected for the sample, and the selection of one member is independent of the selection of any other member of the population. Data are then obtained from members of the sample, and a descriptive statistic is calculated to describe the data. This descriptive statistic is then used to infer a characteristic of the population. The word *infer* implies reasoning from something known to something unknown. Thus, **statistical inference** is

Random sample ▶ A sample in which individuals are selected so that each member of the population has an equal chance of being selected for the sample and the selection of one member is independent of the selection of any other member of the population.

Statistical inference ▶ Estimating population values from statistics obtained from a sample.

Parameter ▶ A number that describes a characteristic of a population.

the process of reaching conclusions about unknown population values (e.g., how much time does the typical married working mother devote to child care per week?) called **parameters** from descriptive statistics obtained from a sample (e.g., the typical married working mother in the sample devoted 14.1 hours per week to child care). Characteristics of populations are called *parameters* rather than *statistics* to distinguish them from the statistics calculated on data from a sample.[1]

There are numerous common examples of descriptive statistics used to infer characteristics of populations. For example, the U.S. Census Bureau collects a variety of information about life in the United States and each year publishes summaries of some of this information in the *Statistical Abstract of the United States*. The 2007 *Statistical Abstract* revealed that

▶ 25.1 percent of the population played cards within the last 12 months.

▶ the typical female commuter spent 23.1 minutes traveling to work each day.

▶ the average family income was $56,194.

▶ 60.4 percent of males and 56.9 percent of females were married.

Each of these numerical values is a parameter estimated from a descriptive statistic obtained from a sample. Realize that it is impossible to ask every person whether or not he or she played cards within the past year or to ask each female commuter how much time she spends in traveling to work each day. Thus, each of these values is an estimate of a population value. How well these individual descriptive statistics estimate population values depends on how the sample was chosen and how representative it is of the population. The procedures involved in the selection and description of samples and inference to a population are discussed more fully in Chapters 3 through 7.

Testing Your Knowledge 1.2

1. Define: parameter, random sample, statistical inference.

2. In a recent election, 600 potential voters of a congressional district were polled to discover whom they planned to vote for in an upcoming election. The results indicated that 312 voters, or 52 percent of the sample, planned to vote for candidate A, 240 voters, or 40 percent, planned to vote for candidate B, and 48 voters, or 8 percent, said they did not plan to vote or had no preference among the candidates. Based on the results of the poll, the researchers estimated that candidate A would win the election with about 52 percent of the total vote.

   a. Explain why descriptive statistics are necessary to summarize the results of this research.

   b. What inferences to a population were made from the statistics obtained?

   c. What type of statistic helps us make generalizations from the sample to the population?

   d. Thinking ahead: although we haven't discussed the selection of samples in detail, what aspects of selecting this sample would make you trust the results of the poll that candidate A is going to win the election?

   e. What aspects of selecting this sample would make you distrust this result?

[1]Of course, not all statisticians adhere to this usage, and some use the term *statistic* to refer to both samples and populations. In this text, however, we will use the term *statistic* to refer to values obtained from a sample and *parameter* to refer to values obtained from a population.

More than a Chance Difference: Statistical Hypothesis Testing

Behavioral scientists are interested not only in describing and characterizing samples and populations, but they also want to find the causes for individual or group behaviors. One approach to this task is to perform an experiment. To conduct an experiment, a researcher identifies a variable, called an **independent variable**, that he or she thinks affects a person's behavior. The behavior that is expected to be affected by this independent variable is called the **dependent variable**.

For example, we might expect alcohol consumption to affect a person's response to violence: People under the influence of alcohol are expected to be more accepting of violence than people who are not under the influence of alcohol (Gustafson, 1987). In this instance, alcohol consumption is the independent variable. An experimenter has control over whether a person does or does not consume alcohol, and he or she expects it to affect the acceptance of violence. A measure of the person's acceptance of violence is the dependent variable. Acceptance of violence is presumed to depend on whether or not a person has consumed alcohol. The statement of the researcher's expectation that alcohol consumption will affect the acceptance of violence is called a *research hypothesis*. A **research hypothesis** is a statement of an expected, or predicted, relationship between two or more variables. In an experiment, a research hypothesis is a predicted relationship between an independent variable and a dependent variable.

The simplest experiment that could be performed to test a research hypothesis relating alcohol consumption to acceptance of violence begins by creating two equivalent groups of people. Scientists refer to the people who participate in research studies as **subjects** or **participants**. Although these terms are sometimes used interchangeably, we will use *subjects* in the chapters that follow. **Equivalent groups** are groups of subjects that are not expected to differ in any consistent or systematic way prior to receiving the independent variable of the experiment. Notice that we are saying the groups are equivalent, but we are not saying that the groups are equal. Subjects differ, so groups of subjects will also differ. However, psychologists have a technique called *random assignment* to obtain equivalent groups. **Random assignment** requires that all subjects selected for an experiment have an equal chance of being in any of the treatment groups and the assignment of one subject to a treatment group is independent of the assignment of any of the other subjects. If all subjects have been randomly assigned to the treatment groups, then there is no reason to believe one group will be different from another group in a consistent or systematic manner before the treatment is given. As such, we have equivalent, though not equal, groups. Random assignment and the creation of equivalent groups is discussed more fully in Chapter 9.

An experiment in which two or more groups are created is called a **between-subjects design**. After equivalent groups are created, the researcher manipulates or varies the independent variable and measures the dependent variable, while controlling all other variables that may affect the dependent variable. In this example, the experimenter might give people in the first group 0.8 milliliter of alcohol per kilogram of body weight mixed with an equal amount of orange juice. Subjects in the second group might be given 1.6 milliliters of plain orange juice per kilogram of body weight. The difference in the drink is the only way in which the two groups are allowed to vary. The dependent variable may be measured by having the subjects watch a violent movie and then rate the movie on the acceptability of the violence shown. A score on the rating task is obtained for each person. A **score** is the measurement obtained on the subject's performance of a task. This score is the dependent variable, for we expect it to depend on whether or not the person had consumed

---

Independent variable ▶ A variable manipulated in an experiment to determine its effect on the dependent variable.

Dependent variable ▶ The variable in an experiment that depends on the independent variable. In most instances, the dependent variable is some measure of a behavior.

Research hypothesis ▶ A statement of an expected or predicted relationship between two or more variables. In an experiment, a research hypothesis is a predicted relationship between an independent variable and a dependent variable.

Subject or participant ▶ The person who participates in an experiment.

Equivalent groups ▶ Groups of subjects that are not expected to differ in any consistent or systematic way prior to receiving the independent variable of the experiment.

Random assignment ▶ A method of assigning subjects to treatment groups so that any individual selected for the experiment has an equal probability of assignment to any of the groups and the assignment of one person to a group does not affect the assignment of any other individual to that same group.

Between-subjects design ▶ A research design in which two or more groups are created.

Score ▶ The measurement obtained on the subject's performance of a task.

Raw data ▷ The scores obtained from all the subjects before the scores have been analyzed statistically.

alcohol prior to watching the movie. The scores obtained from all the subjects provide the **raw data** for the experiment. From these raw data, the researcher must decide if the independent variable of alcohol consumption affected the rating of the acceptability of violence in the movie.

There are several steps involved in the process the experimenter uses to decide if the independent variable had an effect or not. The first step is to describe the ratings of each of the two groups by calculating descriptive statistics presenting the typical ratings of subjects in each group. This step is identical to the description of data process discussed earlier in this chapter. The second step involves deciding if any observed difference in the descriptive statistics for the two groups of scores is large enough to be attributed to the effect of the independent variable. This step requires using **statistical hypothesis testing**. The purpose of statistical hypothesis testing is to determine the anticipated size of chance differences between the groups.

Statistical hypothesis testing ▷ Procedures used to determine the anticipated size of chance differences between groups.

Chance difference ▷ A difference between equivalent groups due to random variation.

In an experiment, equivalent groups will always differ in some unpredictable way that we will call a **chance difference**. Chance differences occur between groups in an experiment even if the independent variable has no effect on the dependent variable. In statistical hypothesis testing, the difference actually observed between the two groups in the experiment is compared to expected chance differences between the groups. If the possibility of obtaining a chance difference as large as the actual difference found is small enough, then the researcher decides that the observed difference is not a chance difference. Rather, the observed difference is attributed to the effect of the independent variable.

As an example of experimentation and statistical hypothesis testing, consider the following question. Do the background conditions under which you learn some material affect how well you later recall this material? Cassaday, Bloomfield, and Hayward (2002) investigated this question with an experiment requiring students to learn and recall a list of words. Forty subjects were randomly assigned to create two equivalent groups of 20 subjects each. Subjects in both groups were asked to learn a list of 20 words and then were tested for recall of the list a short time later. The dependent variable was the number of errors made in recalling the words. The independent variable was the background learning condition under which the students learned the words, either relaxed or neutral. In the experimental condition, the students learned the list while sitting in a room with relaxing conditions: dim lights, a scent of lavender, and soft music. Subjects in the neutral control condition learned the same words while in a room with normal lighting, no lavender scent, and no music. After a brief duration, all subjects were asked to recall as many of the 20 words as they could in a setting typical of classroom testing, without lavender scent or music.

Cassaday et al. (2002) hypothesized that students in the experimental condition who learned the list in the relaxed background condition should make fewer recall errors than students in the neutral background control condition. They found that students in the relaxed background learning condition made an average of only 5.4 errors, whereas students who learned the words in a neutral control condition made an average of 9.1 errors in recalling the words. To determine if the number of errors made by the two groups differed by more than just chance, Cassady et al. used a statistical test called the *analysis of variance*. This test indicated that the number of errors made by the two groups differed by more than expected from chance differences alone. The students in the relaxed-background learning group made fewer errors than students in the neutral control group, a result in agreement with the research hypothesis. We can better remember some materials when we are relaxed during learning.

There are two types of between-subjects designs: experiments, which require creating equivalent groups as we have described here, and quasi-experiments, which use existing groups of subjects. These designs are discussed in more detail in Chapter 2. Chapter 9 will also introduce an additional type of research design called a *within-subjects design*, in which the same subjects are tested in two or more treatment conditions.

Statistical hypothesis testing is used widely in the behavioral sciences. Understanding the concepts involved, however, requires building on knowledge of descriptive statistics and statistical inference and estimation, topics discussed in Chapters 3 to 7. We discuss statistical hypothesis testing in Chapters 8 to 12.

Testing Your Knowledge 1.3

1. Define: between-subjects design, chance difference, dependent variable, equivalent groups, independent variable, participant, random assignment, raw data, research hypothesis, score, subject.

2. Answer the following based on the research example from Cassaday, Bloomfield, and Hayward (2002) described in the section above:

   a. What is the research hypothesis that was tested?

   b. Explain why this study is an experiment.

   c. What is the independent variable?

   d. What is the dependent variable?

   e. Who were the subjects in the sample?

   f. What are the two types of statistics used in this study?

Finding Associations Between Variables: Correlation and Regression

Subject variable ▷ A characteristic or attribute of a subject that can be measured, but not manipulated, by the researcher.

In many instances of behavioral science research, an experimenter does not want to or cannot manipulate an independent variable. Variables that cannot be manipulated but can be measured are called *subject variables*. **Subject variables** are characteristics or attributes of a subject, such as gender, age, handedness, anxiety level, weight, height, physical fitness, income level, amount of schooling, drug use or nonuse, smoking habits, or level of depression. Behavioral scientists are often interested in finding whether two or more subject variables covary. Two variables are said to **covary** if a change in one variable is related to a consistent change in the other variable. For example, if a person's typical level of anxiety is related to his or her use of alcohol, such that high levels of anxiety are related to high use of alcohol and low levels of anxiety are related to low use of alcohol, then anxiety and alcohol usage covary.

Covary ▷ Two variables covary when a change in one variable is related to a consistent change in the other variable.

To find if two variables covary, we measure a sample of people and obtain two scores from each person, for example, an anxiety score and an alcohol use score. Then a *correlation coefficient* is calculated. A **correlation coefficient** is a statistic that provides a numerical description of the extent of the relatedness of two sets of scores and the direction of the relationship. Values of this coefficient may range from −1.00 to 1.00.

Correlation coefficient ▷ A statistic that provides a numerical description of the extent of the relatedness of two sets of scores and the direction of the relationship.

Statistical hypothesis testing also enters into use with the correlation coefficient. There will always be some chance relationship between scores on two different variables. Thus, the question arises of whether an observed relation given by the numerical value of the correlation coefficient is greater than would be expected from chance alone. A statistical test on the correlation coefficient provides an answer for this question.

If the two sets of scores are related beyond chance occurrence, then we may be interested in attempting to predict one score from the other. If you knew a person's anxiety score, could you predict his or her use of alcohol score? And, if you could predict the use of alcohol score, how accurate would your prediction be? Predicting a score on one variable from a score on a second variable involves using **regression analysis**.

Regression analysis ▷ The use of statistical methods to predict one set of scores from a second set of scores.

Correlation and regression analysis techniques are widely used in many areas of behavioral science. For example, one area where behavioral scientists have attempted to find a relationship between subject variables is that of characteristics of an individual that are associated with academic success. Green, Deptula, and Agnew (2006) found a correlation between a person's math anxiety and his or her math performance. This correlation was found to be −0.50, indicating that higher math anxiety was associated with lower math performance. A statistical hypothesis test was performed, and this correlation was found to be greater than would be predicted by chance differences. Of course, we don't know if having weak math performance causes increased math anxiety or if high math anxiety causes weak math performance; the correlation only tells us that the two subject variables are related.

Testing Your Knowledge 1.4

1. Define: correlation coefficient, covary, regression analysis, subject variable.

2. Many people believe in paranormal phenomena such as precognition, extrasensory perception, and psychokinesis. Is the extent of belief in such phenomena related to the type of high school courses taken by such individuals? Tobacyk, Miller, and Jones (1984) measured the belief in paranormal phenomena of 193 11th-grade high school students. They also recorded the total number of science courses each student had taken. When relating the number of science courses to belief in paranormal phenomena, they discovered an inverse relationship. The more science courses a student had taken, the weaker the belief in paranormal phenomena.

   a. Explain why correlational statistics are needed in this study.

   b. What are the two subject variables used in this study?

Why Are Statistics Necessary?

We have presented four common uses of statistical analysis in behavioral science research. Nagging at you, however, may be the discomforting question of why statistical methods are necessary in the behavioral sciences in the first place. The answer is quite straightforward and the same for each statistical procedure we have presented. It is a delightful fact of life that people differ on many characteristics in varying degrees. It would be a tiresome world if every person were identical to every other person, but such an environment would possess the advantage of requiring no need for statistical techniques. Why? Consider the various uses of statistics that we have introduced.

Descriptive statistics describes numerical measurements obtained from individuals in a sample. If all people were alike, then a measurement taken on any one person would describe all other people. Everyone in the United States, for example, would earn the same income and play the same amount of cards. To make an inference to a population, we would need to measure only one person. There would be no need for descriptive statistics to represent a typical score for members of the sample, and there would be no problem of making an inference to a population. But as we are well aware, people are not all the same, and if we wish to describe a group using the typical amount of a characteristic possessed, such as age, weight, or years of schooling, descriptive statistics are needed.

Statistical hypothesis testing deals with answering the question of whether an independent variable has an effect on behavior. Think how easy it would be to decide if an independent variable has an effect on behavior if every person's behavior were identical to every other person's. Suppose, for example, that you wanted to know if a particular drug lowers heart rate. Without the drug, everyone's heart rate is 60 beats per minute, and with the drug, everyone's heart rate is 55 beats per minute. Is there any question of whether the drug lowers heart rate? Because there is no chance variation from person to person, there would be no doubt that the drug lowered the heart rate. Statistical hypothesis testing would be unnecessary. Again, however, chance variations exist between people and groups of people. Thus, we need statistical hypothesis testing to objectively determine whether differences between groups are larger than we expect by chance alone.

Finally, correlation and regression analysis asks if two behaviors are related. If so, can we predict the occurrence of one behavior from the occurrence of the other? These questions arise only because people are different from one another and behave differently in the same situation. If every person were identical to every other person on all behaviors, then all behaviors would be perfectly predictable. Because there would be no variability in behaviors among people, we could predict all behaviors perfectly without using correlation and regression statistics.

An environment with no variability among people and animals would eliminate the need for statistical analysis, but what a boring place it would be. People-watching would be monotonous. Fortunately, we do not have such a world. Instead, we have a life with both regularities and variability among its peoples, requiring statistical techniques to describe, explain, and predict behavior.

 ## Summary

▶ Statistics refers to the methods or procedures used to summarize, analyze, and draw inferences from data.

▶ A descriptive statistic is a number that may be used to describe the scores from a sample.

▶ A descriptive statistic may also be used to infer the value of a population parameter.

▶ Statistical hypothesis testing is used to determine if an observed difference between two groups in an experiment is large enough to be attributed to the effect of an independent variable rather than to chance.

▶ Correlational statistics are used to determine if two sets of scores are related.

▶ Regression statistics are used to predict one set of scores from another set of scores.

 ## Key Terms and Symbols

between-subjects design (10)
chance difference (11)
correlation coefficient (12)
covary (12)

data (6)
dependent variable (10)
descriptive statistic (7)
equivalent groups (10)

independent variable (10)
parameter (9)
participant (10)
population (7)

random assignment (10)   sample (7)   statistical inference (8)
random sample (8)   score (10)   subject (10)
raw data (11)   statistic (7)   subject variable (12)
regression analysis (13)   statistical hypothesis testing (11)   variable (2)
research hypothesis (10)

 ## Review Questions

1. Identify four events or occurrences in your life that possess regularity (e.g., the amount of sleep you obtain or the number of hours you work each day). Is there variability as well as regularity in these events?

2. Think of three different populations. What is the common characteristic possessed by the members of each population?

3. A recent research study reported that for males, anger levels and blood pressure are related. Higher levels of anger were related to higher blood pressures.
   a. Which statistical method discussed in this chapter was used in this study?
   b. Explain why correlational statistics were needed in this study.
   c. What two sets of measures were used in this study?

4. After reading Martin's (2002) article on the potential benefits of laughter, a group of student researchers decided to test the hypothesis that laughter increases pain tolerance. To test this hypothesis, they randomly assigned 60 subjects to one of two conditions. In the "laughter" condition, subjects watched a humorous videotape. The control group watched an action adventure videotape. While watching the videotape, subjects were asked, one at a time, to keep their hands in a bucket of ice water for as long as they could. The students recorded the amount of time each subject kept his or her hands in the ice water.
   a. Which statistical methods discussed in this chapter were used in this study?
   b. Identify the independent variable manipulated by the student researchers.
   c. Identify the dependent variable measured.
   d. Explain why this study is an experiment.
   e. Explain why statistical hypothesis testing is necessary in this experiment.

5. Jacoby (2000) reports that in a nationwide telephone survey of Americans, 72 percent of the males indicated a desire to be wealthy, whereas only 58 percent of females did so. Nineteen percent of the respondents indicated money can buy happiness, and 56 percent believed that more money would lead to a less stressful life.
   a. Which statistical method discussed in this chapter was used in this study?
   b. Explain why descriptive statistics were necessary to summarize the results of this research.
   c. What descriptive statistic was used in this study?

6. A professor conducted a survey of a sample of students in her behavioral statistics class for the purpose of making generalizations to the entire population of students majoring in behavioral science at her college. Identify whether the professor was

using a descriptive statistic or inferential statistic for each component of the study listed below.

   a. Seventeen percent of the students said their plans were to obtain a master's degree in social work.

   b. Using the information from the class survey, the professor concluded that for all people majoring in the behavioral sciences at her college, significantly more students want to become counseling psychologists than research psychologists.

   c. Seventy-two percent of the people answering the survey were female.

   d. The professor found that students who said they enjoy helping others also saw themselves working in a nonprofit agency upon graduation. She found this correlation was due to more than just chance variation in students' responses. As such, she concluded that, in general, students who envision themselves working in a nonprofit agency upon graduation also enjoy helping others.

7. For each of the following statements, indicate whether it describes raw data, a descriptive statistic, or an inference to a population parameter.

   a. Linda commutes 36 minutes to her work each day.

   b. The average male commuter in the United States spends 42 minutes commuting each day.

   c. A sample of 75 commuters gave an average daily commuting time of 46 minutes.

   d. Benjamin and Anita Houston have $5126 in their bank savings account.

   e. The typical American adult has $6024 in a bank savings account.

   f. A random sample of 50 residents of a small southwestern town provided an average bank savings account of $5692.

8. a. Identify three variables that a researcher can manipulate and as such can be independent variables.

   b. Identify three variables that a researcher either cannot or should not manipulate and as such must be subject variables.

   c. Think of an instance in which your score on one variable is used to predict your score on a second variable (e.g., your cholesterol level, which is used to predict the chance of heart disease).

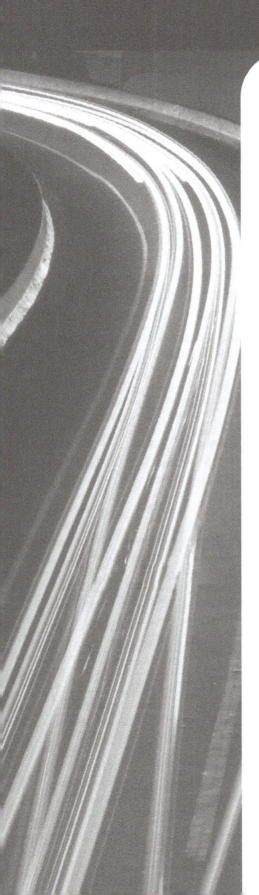

Statistics in the Context of Scientific Research

H ave you ever watched an 18-month-old child? They are fascinating to watch as they replicate an action over and over again. They often look like little scientists trying to unlock the mysteries of gravity or human behavior as they drop their plastic cup to the floor, yet again, watching to see where it goes and if it will bounce, then waiting to see if Mommy will pick it up. When you were that age, you were busy researching ideas, too. What happens if I jump off the couch and onto the cushion on the floor? Then you would try it and repeat it again and again, sometimes identically, other times with slight modifications to see how changes in one variable would alter the outcome. As you have become older, your questions have become more sophisticated. Over time, you have developed your own set of hypotheses about human behavior after making a series of observations; for example, it is best to ask to borrow the car when Dad is in a good mood. With additional observations, you honed your hypothesis: it is best to ask Dad to borrow the car when he is in a good mood, but not when he is watching football.

From childhood on, you have often thought like a scientist, attempting to answer questions through careful observation of your environment and deliberate attempts at collecting data. Now, as you enter into the field of behavioral science, you are going to need a tool to assist you in making sense of that data. That tool is statistics.

Statistical methods have developed over several thousand years to solve practical problems. In fact, the word *statistics* derives from the Latin *status* or state, for the earliest uses of statistics were for obtaining knowledge of the state or empire. Roman emperors always had a census taken whenever a new territory was conquered. Information from the census, which provided statistics about the population and the valuation of property, was used to levy taxes on the population. Although statistics are still used in this way, their use today has expanded to be an important component in analyzing the data obtained in the scientific study of human and animal behavior. Thus, to be able to use statistical methods, you need to understand the context in which they are used. The purpose of this chapter is to provide you with the basics of research to help you understand the context in which statistics are used and applied.

What Is Science?

Science is a method for the acquisition of knowledge. The scientific method involves identifying a question, proposing a tentative answer to the question in the form of a research hypothesis, formulating a research design to empirically test the hypothesis, collecting data, analyzing the data, and then reaching a conclusion about the hypothesis from the analyzed data.

Scientific Questions

A scientific question is one that allows an answer to be obtained by the collection of empirical data. The word *empirical* refers to sensory experience or observation; thus, **empirical data** are scores or measurements based on systematic observation and sensory experience. Each example in Chapter 1 presented research based on a scientific question; each example allowed an answer to be obtained by collecting empirical data.

Often an experimenter will offer a tentative answer to the question in the form of a research hypothesis. In Chapter 1, a **research hypothesis** was defined as a statement of an expected or predicted relationship between two or more variables. For example, Karpicke and Roediger (reviewed in Roediger & Karpicke, 2006) hypothesized that a person who

Empirical data ▶ Scores or measurements based on observation and sensory experience.

Research hypothesis ▶ A statement of an expected or predicted relationship between two or more variables.

studies a set of words and then immediately takes a test on those words will remember more of them at a later point than someone who simply studies the words without being tested on them. Because a research hypothesis identifies the variables and indicates how they are expected to be related, it guides the researcher in a number of areas, including selecting a research method, identifying the population from which the sample will be selected, defining the type of data that will be collected, and choosing the type of statistical analysis that will be used. Thus, a research hypothesis is the driving force in scientific exploration.

Research Methods

Research method ▶ An approach scientists take to collect data in order to develop or evaluate a research hypothesis.

Collecting empirical data to test a research hypothesis requires using a research method. A **research method** is an approach the scientist uses to collect data in order to develop or evaluate a research hypothesis. A variety of methods is used in the behavioral sciences; here we provide only a brief overview of six basic methods. For all but one of these methods, statistics are used to summarize and analyze the data collected.

Case Study

Case study ▶ Research involving the study of a single person, animal, or situation.

A **case study** is the most basic of research methods in which the researcher selects a single example, such as a person, an animal, or a situation, to fully investigate. Although statistics are often not needed to understand a sample of size one, case studies are an important tool in scientific discovery, particularly when investigating a new or rare condition or situation. Case studies cannot be used for research hypothesis testing, but they are very useful in research hypothesis building.

An example of a case study is that of H. M., a man who had untreatable epilepsy and who, in the 1950s, had a surgery to remove his medial temporal lobes[1] from both hemispheres of his brain (Scoville & Milner, 1957). An unexpected outcome of the surgery was that it destroyed a type of H. M.'s memory that researchers now call *explicit memory*. Memory researchers have evaluated H. M. in an attempt to determine the role the medial temporal lobes have on cognitive functioning and memory. For example, H. M.'s performance on crossword puzzles was compared to people who were of similar age but with no known brain damage (Skotko et al., 2004). H. M. did not perform as well as the others, but why he didn't could not be determined. Could it be that we need a functioning explicit memory to complete crossword puzzles? Is it that H. M. experienced life differently from most people? Could it be the decades of long exposure to epileptic medicine damaged other parts of his brain? Could it be H. M.'s educational background prior to his surgery? We simply cannot answer these questions from this case study alone. Consequently, case studies often result in more questions than answers. Because questions are at the heart of good research hypotheses, however, case studies are an important part of developing research.

Naturalistic Observation

Naturalistic observation ▶ Research involving the observation of behaviors occurring in natural settings.

Naturalistic observation refers to observing behaviors occurring in natural settings without intruding into the situation. In an example of naturalistic observation, Trinkaus (1982, 1983, 1988, 1993, 1997, 1999, 2001) systematically observed the behavior of drivers at one intersection over a 20-year period. One of his findings is that compliance with a stop

---

[1]The temporal lobes are at the sides of the brain. The medial portion of these lobes is closer to the center of the brain.

sign has decreased over the observation period. In these observations, the experimenter remained unobtrusive; drivers were not aware that their compliance with a stop sign was being observed. Had the drivers been aware of this observation, they likely would have altered their behavior.

Similar to the case study, naturalistic observations are useful in devising research hypotheses. One can even test some research hypotheses. For example, Trinkaus (1999, 2001) wanted to identify which drivers were most likely to violate traffic laws at the intersection being observed. He found that women driving vans were most likely to not come to a stop at the stop sign and to violate other driving rules. This observation, however, cannot determine what is causing this behavior. As such, although Trinkaus found that women driving vans were more likely to ignore some driving rules, he cannot determine what caused these drivers to do so.

Archival Records

Archival records ▶ Research using existing records.

Archival records research involves answering questions by using existing records. Societies typically collect a variety of information about their members: birth, marriage, and death records; crime reports; census records; and so on. These existing records may provide the data necessary to answer a scientific question. For example, John Graunt (1620–1674), a London shopkeeper, used existing records on births and deaths to identify differences in the causes of death for men and women. Similarly, Zusne (1986–1987), interested in the question of whether dying individuals may attempt to delay their deaths until after an approaching birthday, examined the birthday and death day records for over 3000 people. These records indicated that such a relationship may exist, but it differs for males and females.

In another example, O'Brien and Stockard (2006) examined suicide rates in the United States from the 1930s to 2000. This research indicated that between the years 1930 and 2000 there was a decrease in the suicide rate in people ages 25 and older. During this same time period, however, there was an increase in suicide rates in children and young adults between the ages of 10 and 25.

The results of archival records studies are often summarized using descriptive statistics. Such results often allow us to find relationships among variables, but they do not allow us to find the cause of these relationships. We may find that suicide rates are decreasing among people who are 25 and older and increasing among people who are 10 to 25, but this finding alone does not indicate the cause for this occurrence.

Survey Research

Survey research ▶ Research involving obtaining data from either oral or written interviews with people.

Survey research involves obtaining data from either oral or written interviews with people. Survey research is widespread in society. If you have ever filled out a course evaluation rating a professor, or if you have ever completed a product warranty card that asked questions about your income, marital status, and hobbies, then you have participated in survey research.

Survey research often can provide a great deal of information about people very quickly. This information can be used to answer some hypotheses. For example, some college campuses have experienced an increase in student gambling. Understanding what causes a student to gamble to the point of creating problems is an important question to answer. Although survey research cannot answer what is causing serious gambling in college students, it can, however, identify traits that are seen in people who develop gambling problems. For example, Gupta, Deverensky, and Ellenbogen (2006) surveyed high school students and their rate of gambling. They found that students who reported being susceptible to boredom are also more likely to experience problems with gambling. Finding associations between variables such as susceptibility to boredom and gambling problems is important in understanding behavior, yet results from a survey study cannot tell us what causes this relationship to occur.

Both descriptive and inferential statistics are often used in survey research. For example, depending on how the sample was selected, we may be able to generalize our descriptive statistics from the sample to a larger population. Survey research, however, is open to many pitfalls; people may not truthfully answer questions asked of them, questions may be worded so the researcher is guiding people's answers, and conclusions drawn about a population from the results of a survey will depend on how the sample was selected.

For now, remember that survey research may be an easy way to collect data to test a hypothesis, but is challenging to do well. Moreover, the conclusions that you can draw from the results of survey research cannot determine that one variable is causing another to change.

Experiment

Experiment ▷ A controlled situation in which one or more independent variables are manipulated to observe the effects on the dependent variable.

In Chapter 1 we learned that an **experiment** is a carefully controlled situation in which a scientist creates two or more equivalent groups and then manipulates an independent variable to observe its effect on the dependent variable. The research of Cassaday et al. (2002) described in Chapter 1 provides an example of an experiment. The independent variable was the type of background learning condition during the study of the word lists, either relaxed or neutral. The dependent variable was the number of errors made during a recall situation. If the two groups of subjects make a different number of errors greater than expected by chance, then the cause for this difference must be the independent variable, the type of background learning condition. We discuss experiments more fully in Chapter 9, in which the statistical methods needed to analyze an experiment are introduced. The experiment is the only type of research method that enables us to test what is causing changes in the dependent variable. Because the experimenter has control over the independent variable and all other variables are held constant, we know that changes in the independent variable are what is causing any changes in the dependent variable. This ability to determine causal relationships between the independent and dependent variable makes the experiment a very powerful research method for scientists.

Quasi-Experiment

Quasi-experiment ▷ Research involving the use of subject variables as independent variables.

A **quasi-experiment** uses subject variables as the independent variables. *Quasi* means "resemble," so a quasi-experiment is a type of research method that resembles an experiment, but is not a true experiment because groups are not created by random assignment. A true experiment requires an independent variable be actively manipulated so that an experimenter can randomly assign subjects to each condition. Without random assignment, you cannot have an experiment. But many variables of interest to behavioral scientists cannot be actively manipulated because they are subject variables; that is, they are attributes or characteristics that individuals possess. Quasi-experiments permit the study of these variables. For example, a behavioral scientist may be interested in comparing people with Alzheimer's disease to people without Alzheimer's on the capability of memorizing a list of common grocery items. Here, the disease state of the individual, with or without Alzheimer's, is a subject variable because subjects cannot be randomly assigned into an Alzheimer's or non-Alzheimer's condition. Instead of randomly assigning a person to a disease state, a researcher must select individuals who possess the appropriate level of the subject variable. Essentially, the "manipulation" of the independent variable of disease state took place before the individual was selected as a subject in the research. The experimenter's use of the subject variable as an independent variable occurs after the variable has already been manipulated in nature. Thus, it is more difficult to determine causal relationships from a quasi-experiment than from a true experiment. The groups created in a quasi-experiment may systematically differ in ways other than the subject variable used to create the groups. For example, the two groups in our example of disease state, Alzheimer's or non-Alzheimer's, may differ not only in disease state, but the Alzheimer's subjects may generally be older than the non-Alzheimer's patients, the two groups may differ in the amount of sleep obtained nightly, or they may differ on nutritional status. If a difference in ability to remember a common grocery list occurs, it may be due to one of the other variables and not the subject variable of interest. Yet, understanding issues surrounding topics involving subject variables is important, and quasi-experimental designs are widely used. Quasi-experiments can help get us closer to understanding causal relationships between variables, but the path is more difficult than with a true experiment.

Operational Definitions

Scientific knowledge gained from application of the various research methods must be repeatable and subject to agreement among different observers. Scientific knowledge of a behavior gains strength and generality when other scientists can replicate the behavior in different settings and locations with different subjects. For knowledge to be scientific, there must be full communication of ideas and results so that findings can be replicated, criticized, and extended by others. A crucial step in this communication process is to provide an **operational definition** of the procedures used to make observations, to manipulate independent variables, or to measure the dependent variable. For example, Cassaday et al. (2002) operationally defined a relaxed study state as one having dim lighting, the smell of lavender, and the playing of music composed by Mozart. Thus, if another scientist wants to extend this research, he or she will know how Cassaday et al. defined a relaxed learning state.

Operational definition ▶ A specification of the operations used to make observations, to manipulate an independent variable, or to measure the dependent variable.

Ethics in Research

Just as we cannot discuss behavioral statistics without first understanding principles of research, we cannot begin conducting research on human or animal subjects without first understanding the ethics surrounding research and data collection. The relationship between a research scientist and the individuals who participate in his or her research often is unusual. Typically, a researcher is in a position of power over the subjects, may be perceived as a person with unique knowledge and powers of control over human behaviors, and may conduct research involving a subject's physical or mental well-being. Consequently, there are important ethical considerations for any research involving humans as well as animals. For an example of these ethical concerns, consider a study designed to evaluate the efficacy of the drug risperidone on the treatment of acute mania.

The study used a between-subjects design with two treatment conditions to evaluate the effectiveness of risperidone for reducing mania. Mania is a psychological disorder in which a person's thoughts, actions, beliefs, and behaviors can often be extreme, placing the person at risk of harming themselves or others. In this study, individuals with acute mania were falsely told their current treatment was no longer available to them, and they were randomly assigned to either a treatment condition with the drug risperidone or to a control group with a placebo drug treatment. The subjects were either not informed that they were a part of a study or only partially and unclearly informed about the aspects of the study (Weyzig & Schipper, 2006).

This example illustrates several important ethical deficiencies. The particularly vulnerable subjects were mistreated in three major ways. Firstly, they were deceived. Their current treatment was withheld from them, and they were falsely told it wasn't available. Because they were falsely told the treatment they had been receiving was no longer available, they may have felt pressured to participate in a study in which they might not have otherwise participated if they thought their regular treatment was available. Secondly, although it was appropriate to randomly assign subjects to one of two conditions, the control group should not have had a placebo treatment, but instead should have been provided with the standard treatment. Thirdly, all subjects in a research study or their guardians should be fully informed about the study's purpose, duration, and risks. Moreover, it should be made clear that participation is always voluntary, subjects are free to withdraw from the study at any time, and all information obtained will be kept confidential. This policy is called *informed consent*. **Informed consent** is a legal requirement of research that requires a researcher to inform a potential subject of all aspects of the research that might influence that person's willingness to participate in it.

To avoid the ethical failures illustrated in this example, everyone who is preparing to conduct research on human or animal subjects must first undergo training and become knowledgeable about all federal, state, and professional requirements governing ethics in research (e.g., American Psychological Association Ethics Code, 2003; American Sociological Association Code of Ethics, 1997; Human Subjects Research Issues, 2008). All training must include information on informed consent, confidentiality of data, dealing with vulnerable populations, the ethics of denying treatment and placing undue pressure on subjects, and institutional review board regulations.

An **institutional review board** (IRB) is a group of at least five people experienced in research issues who must review and approve all research involving human or animal subjects being conducted in an organization such as a college, hospital, or research laboratory. Each institution has its own IRB for reviewing all research. Typically, there is one group of people who examines proposed human subject research and another group who examines proposed animal subject research. In almost all situations, before researchers can begin collecting data, they must have their research approved through their institution's IRB. The IRB looks for documentation regarding the confidentiality of the data collected and the informed consent and ethical treatment of subjects, weighing potential risks to the subject participating in the study against the benefit that the information from the study will provide.

Informed consent ▶ Informing a subject of all aspects of a research study, including the study's purpose, duration, and potential risk, that might influence a person's willingness to participate in the research.

Institutional review board ▶ A group of at least five people experienced in research issues who must review and approve all research involving human or animal subjects occurring in an institution.

Testing Your Knowledge 2.1

1. Define: archival records, case study, empirical data, experiment, informed consent, institutional review board, IRB, naturalistic observation, operational definition, quasi-experiment, research hypothesis, research method, survey research.

2. Make a table of the six types of research methods discussed in this chapter, with a column defining each type of research. Make another column stating whether this type of research method can best be used for: (a) hypothesis building, (b) hypothesis testing, or (c) causal hypothesis testing.

3. For each of the following questions, name the type of research method that you would expect to be used to find an answer to the question asked.

   a. What is the opinion of a community concerning the siting of a hazardous waste-processing plant within its boundaries?

   b. What is the effect of the type of message, either fear inducing or factual, on attitude change?

   c. What is the average age of fathers of firstborn children in Arizona?

   d. How often do 4-year-old children play in groups of three in a nursery school?

   e. Do students in private colleges engage in more social drinking than students in public colleges?

   f. Following an industrial accident, a man has a complete change in behavior, going from a dedicated employee and family man to an impulsive, aggressive man. Was it damage to his frontal lobe that caused this dramatic change in behavior?

4. Answer the following questions regarding ethics in research.

   a. Who needs to go through ethics training before beginning research with human or animal subjects?

   b. What information must be provided to the subject for informed consent to be valid?

   c. What is the purpose of the IRB?

Measurement

Measurement ▷ Assigning numbers to variables following a set of rules.

Have you ever had a task to complete that required a special tool? For example, if the lens of your glasses falls out, you need a tiny screwdriver in order to put the lens back in. Without the tiny screwdriver, you cannot accomplish the task; the task determines what tool will work and what tool will not. Statistics, too, are like tools in a toolbox. Each statistic has a special job to do, and it is important to select the correct statistic for the task at hand. Two important factors affect the choice of a statistic: the research hypothesis and the type of measurement you have obtained for your data. **Measurement** is a process of assigning numbers to variables following a set of rules. Typically, measurements are classified into one of four scales or levels: nominal, ordinal, interval, or ratio measurements. The rest of this chapter is dedicated to understanding measurement to help in selecting the right statistical tool.

Scales of Measurement

Nominal Measurement

Nominal measurement ▷ A classification of the measured variable into different categories.

Nominal measurement is a classification of the measured variable into different categories. For example, with a nominal measure of the variable of ethnic origin, people may be categorized as Native American, Asian American, African American, White, or

Hispanic. A number is then assigned to name the category (hence, the term *nominal*, which means "to name"), such as 1 = Native American, 2 = Asian American, 3 = African American, 4 = White, and 5 = Hispanic. Each individual assigned to the same category will be assigned the same number. The number, however, conveys no numerical information; a letter could have been used to identify the category as easily as a number. Many behavioral scientists do not regard nominal measures as actual measurements because the numbers assigned serve the purpose of identification only; they do not provide quantitative information about the variable measured. As such, nominal measures are considered to provide **qualitative data**, that is, data that provides information on kind or quality of the variable instead of on the amount of the variable.

Qualitative data ▶ Data obtained from a nominal measurement indicating the kind or the quality of a variable.

Ordinal Measurement

When the amount of a variable is placed in order of magnitude along a dimension, then an **ordinal measurement** scale is used. For example, people may be asked to arrange a series of cartoons on a funniness scale from most to least funny. Often, a numerical value of 1 is assigned to the stimulus or individual possessing the greatest amount of the characteristic being measured, a value of 2 to that person or stimulus that exhibits the next greatest amount, and so forth. If, for example, anxiety is measured with an ordinal scale, then the person exhibiting the most anxiety is assigned a 1, the person showing the next largest amount of anxiety a 2, the next a 3, and so on, to the person possessing the least amount of anxiety, producing an ordering of people from most to least anxious.

Ordinal measurement ▶ The amount of a variable is placed in order of magnitude along a dimension.

Ordinal scales essentially produce a ranking in which someone or something assigned a rank of 1 possesses more of a variable than one given a rank of 2. Ordinal measures do not, however, permit determining how much difference exists in the measured variable between ranks. A small difference in the variable being measured may exist between ranks 1 and 2, but a large difference may exist between ranks 2 and 3. For example, the times for the first three runners of a marathon may be 2 hours 27 minutes, 2 hours 28 minutes, and 2 hours 32 minutes, respectively. The rank order of the finish of these runners is 1, 2, and 3. But the time difference between the first and second finisher is 1 minute, whereas it is 4 minutes between the second- and third-place contestants.

Ordinal scales do not indicate how much of the measured variable exists; they provide information only about the order of individuals or objects on the variable measured. A rank of 1 does not necessarily correspond to a large amount of the variable being measured, and the lowest-ranked object or person does not necessarily possess little of the property being measured. A person who is asked to rank order cartoons from most to least funny may find no humor in any of them. Yet a rank of 1 assigned to a cartoon by this individual conveys the same information as a rank of 1 assigned to a cartoon by another person who may regard all the cartoons as very funny.

Despite their deficiencies, however, ordinal measures are widely reported in popular sources. As an illustration, a ranking of cities on the quality of nightlife available ranks New Orleans, first; Las Vegas, second; New York City, third; and Austin, Texas, fourth. Atlanta, Georgia is ranked sixteenth (*Travel + Leisure*, 2007). Clearly, if you are in search of a city based on its nightlife, you should probably choose New Orleans rather than Atlanta. But this ranking itself gives you no indication of the quality of nightlife in any of the cities ranked or how much they may differ from each other on this dimension.

Testing Your Knowledge 2.2

1. Define: measurement, nominal measurement, ordinal measurement.
2. Identify one deficiency of nominal measurements.
3. What information is provided by a rank of 2 assigned to an individual on a ranking of motivation to achieve?
4. On a rank ordering of 13 people for depression proneness from most to least, Jennifer was ranked 1; Debbi, 2; Ena, 12; and Marty, 13.
   a. Explain why you cannot conclude that Jennifer is very prone to depression and Marty is not at all depression prone.
   b. Is it appropriate to conclude that the difference in depression proneness between Jennifer and Debbi is the same as the difference in depression proneness between Ena and Marty? Explain your answer.

Interval Measurement

If the requirements for ordinal measurement are met and, in addition, the differences between the assigned numbers represent equal amounts in the magnitude of the variable measured, then an **interval measurement** is created. An interval measurement, however, has no true zero point for which a value of zero represents the complete absence of the variable measured. A zero value on an interval measurement is an arbitrary starting point that could be replaced by any other value as a starting point.

Interval measurement ▶ The amount of a variable is ordered along a dimension, and the differences between the assigned numbers represent equal amounts in the magnitude of the variable measured. The zero point of an interval scale is an arbitrary starting point.

The Fahrenheit and Celsius temperature scales are examples of interval measurements. Zero degrees does not represent an absence of temperature for either scale. Neither scale contains a true zero point because measured temperatures may fall below zero degrees. It is accurate to state that the difference in temperature between 20°C and 40°C is equivalent to the difference in temperature between 40°C and 60°C, but it is not appropriate to say that 40°C is twice as high a temperature as 20°C. We can see why this difficulty arises by comparing several equivalent Celsius and Fahrenheit temperatures, as follows:

Equivalent Temperatures	
°C	°F
20	68
40	104
60	140

Notice that a difference of 20°C is always equal to a difference of 36°F, but because each scale starts with an arbitrary zero point, adjacent scores on one scale do not form ratios equal to adjacent scores on the other scale. For example, a ratio of 40°C/20° = 2.0, whereas a corresponding temperature ratio for the Fahrenheit scale is 104°F/68°F = 1.5.

Examples of measurements in the behavioral sciences that definitely achieve an interval level are infrequent. But rating scales, which frequently are used to measure attributes of people, such as personality characteristics, attitudes, marital happiness, fear of objects, motivation to achieve, or leadership ability, are often treated as yielding interval measurement. Rating scales generally present a statement and then a response scale with two extremes and several points between the extremes. For example, in attitude measurement, a person may be asked to respond to a statement such as "strong gun control laws reduce crime" by making a check mark on the scale:

Strongly agree	Agree	Uncertain	Disagree	Strongly disagree

Other forms of rating scales may ask you to rate a person on a continuum with two polar adjectives, such as

Dishonest _____ : _____ : _____ : _____ : _____ : _____ : _____ Honest

Attractive _____ : _____ : _____ : _____ : _____ : _____ : _____ Unattractive

Cold _____ : _____ : _____ : _____ : _____ : _____ : _____ Warm

Rating scales may have any number of categories between the extremes, and the scales may be referred to as 5-point, 6-point, or 9-point scales, depending on the number of categories provided. Often the favorability of the adjectives at the end points of the scale is reversed for half the items. Thus, half the favorable adjectives are at the left of the scale and half at the right. This reversal helps to avoid problems of response set, such as checking only the items on the right side of the scale.

After a person has responded on the scale, a numerical value is assigned to each category on the scale, such as

Dishonest _____ : _____ : _____ : _____ : _____ : _____ : _____ Honest
　　　　　　1　　　2　　　3　　　4　　　5　　　6　　　7

Attractive _____ : _____ : _____ : _____ : _____ : _____ : _____ Unattractive
　　　　　　7　　　6　　　5　　　4　　　3　　　2　　　1

Cold _____ : _____ : _____ : _____ : _____ : _____ : _____ Warm
　　　　1　　　2　　　3　　　4　　　5　　　6　　　7

In many instances, a series of scales is presented, and the scores on the separate scales are added to yield one score for a person. These scales are called *summated rating scales*. For example, in Chapter 1 you were asked to rate your belief of the changeability of intelligence on the scale below.

Some people are simply born smart, others are not so lucky.					
1	2	3	4	5	6
Strongly Agree					Strongly Disagree

The numbers on this scale correspond to beliefs about intelligence. Responses closer to 6 indicate a belief in an incremental view of intelligence, a belief that with effort, you can get smarter, whereas responses closer to 1 indicate a belief that intelligence is fixed and cannot change (Dweck, 1999, 2006). The entire scale consists of eight statements similar to the one above. For each statement, a person indicates agreement or disagreement by choosing a number between 1 (strongly agree) to 6 (strongly disagree). Higher numbers indicate a belief that intelligence can be changed, and lower numbers indicate a belief that intelligence cannot be changed. A score is then obtained by summing over the eight statements to yield a total score for the rating scale. The possible range of scores is from 8 (obtained by responding with a 1 to all eight statements) to 48 (obtained by responding with a 6 to all eight statements). Notice that the range of scores that this scale can assume is arbitrary; if the anchor points for each statement ranged from 0 to 10, then the range of the summated rating scale would be 0 to 80.

We will refer to this scale as the Implicit View of Intelligence scale, for it is designed to measure a person's implied but not directly expressed understanding of intelligence. What level of measurement is represented by scores on this scale and other similar rating scales? It should be clear that the rating for each statement represents at least ordinal measurement. A score of 4 indicates more of a particular characteristic described by the statement than does a 3, and a 3 reflects more than a 2; however, we cannot be certain that the difference between a 4 and 3 represents the same difference in a characteristic as that between 3 and 2. Such ratings do seem to provide more than merely ordinal information; however, we might expect that a respondent subjectively divides the categories into roughly equal intervals between the ends of the scale. Moreover, if the ratings obtained from a person on a number of separate scales are summed, then it seems reasonable to assume that the resulting score provides more than just ordinal information. Gardner (1975) argues that scores from summated scales are in a gray region between ordinal and interval. Thus, a measurement may not necessarily fit neatly into one of the four measurement scales. For statistical analysis, however, researchers often treat rating scales as representing interval measurement.

Ratio Measurement

Ratio measurement ▶ The amount of a variable is ordered along a dimension, the differences between the assigned numbers represent equal amounts in the magnitude of the variable measured, and a true zero point exists, which represents the absence of the characteristic measured.

A **ratio measurement** scale replaces the arbitrary zero point of the interval scale with a true zero starting point that corresponds to the absence of the variable being measured. With a ratio scale, it is possible to state that one thing (e.g., a stimulus, an event, or an individual) has twice, or half, or three times as much of the variable measured than another. Ratio measurement is used in the behavioral sciences when measures such as reaction time or the amount of time spent on a task are measured. These measures have a true zero point, and the intervals between the units of measurement are equal. For example, if the amount of time a person spends solving a puzzle is measured, the difference between 15 seconds and 25 seconds (i.e., 10 seconds) is equal to the difference between 50 seconds and 60 seconds (again 10 seconds). Furthermore, someone who spends 60 seconds solving a puzzle spends twice as long as someone who spends only 30 seconds.

The magnitude of perceptual illusions may often be measured with a ratio scale. An illusion occurs when our perception of a stimulus does not correspond to its physical characteristics; we misperceive what actually exists. A familiar example is the Müller-Lyer illusion, illustrated in Figure 2.1. Here you may perceive line A to be longer than line B. Both lines are physically equal in length, however. Your perception is in error. The magnitude of this illusion can be measured by finding how much the perceived length of the stimulus differs from its actual length. Perceptual error measured in millimeters represents a ratio measurement. It is possible for a person to have an error of 0 millimeters (i.e., no error) when the perceived length of the stimulus does not differ from the actual length. The difference between an error of 5 millimeters and an error of 8 millimeters is the same as the difference between errors of 10 millimeters and 13 millimeters; in each case the difference is 3 millimeters. Moreover, an error of 10 millimeters represents an illusion magnitude that is twice as great as an error of 5 millimeters.

Quantitative data ▶ Data obtained from ordinal, interval, or ratio measurements indicating how much of a variable exists.

Ordinal, interval, and ratio measurements provide **quantitative data**, the numbers assigned to a variable express the amount or quantity of the variable measured. However,

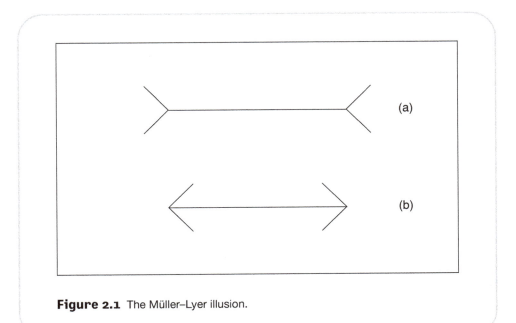

Figure 2.1 The Müller–Lyer illusion.

behavioral scientists prefer to use interval and ratio measurements because these measures allow more precise quantification of the underlying attribute or characteristic being measured than do ordinal measurements. Furthermore, interval and ratio measures allow the use of mathematical procedures such as addition, subtraction, multiplication, and division. Consequently, many of the statistical techniques presented in this text are for scores measured on an interval or ratio scale.

Testing Your Knowledge 2.3

1. Define: interval measurement, quantitative data, ratio measurement.

2. The following scores were obtained on an interval measure of leadership ability: Rosana, 84; Eva, 78; Pierce, 71; Victoria, 65; Nancy, 42; and William, 0.

   a. Is it accurate to conclude that the difference in leadership ability between Rosana and Eva is the same as the difference between Pierce and Victoria? Explain your answer.

   b. Is it accurate to conclude that Rosana possesses twice as much leadership ability as Nancy? Explain your answer.

   c. Is it accurate to conclude that, because of his score of zero, William totally lacks leadership ability? Explain your answer.

3. Several college students participated in a study on sleep in which the amount of time (in minutes) spent in rapid eye movement sleep (REM sleep, the dream sleep stage) was measured using an electroencephalogram. On one night, the durations of REM sleep were Dominic, 204 minutes; Greta, 194 minutes; Andre, 175 minutes; Jody, 165 minutes; and Carmen, 102 minutes.

a. Is it appropriate to conclude that the difference in the amount of REM sleep between Dominic and Greta is the same as the difference between Andre and Jody? Explain your answer.

b. Is it appropriate to conclude that Dominic spent twice as much time in REM sleep as Carmen? Explain your answer.

c. Suppose another student, Megan, spent zero minutes in REM sleep. Is it appropriate to conclude that she had no REM sleep that night? Explain your answer.

Discrete and Continuous Variables

Variables may also be characterized as discrete or continuous.

Discrete Variables

Discrete variable ▷ A variable that can take on only a finite or countable set of values within its limits.

A **discrete variable** is one that can take on only a finite or countable set of values within its limits. For example, the population of a town is a discrete variable; there may be 5652 or 5653 people living in a town, but not 5652.34. There is a restricted set of values the population may take on. The number of residents may increase or decrease by one whole person, but not one-half or one-third person. Thus, variables whose possible values can be counted are discrete variables: the number of students at your college, the number of children in a family, the number of automobiles registered in a state, and the number of runs scored in a baseball game are all examples of discrete variables.

Continuous Variables

Continuous variable ▷ A variable that can take on an infinite set of values between the limits of the variable.

A **continuous variable** is one that can take on an infinite set of values between the limits of the variable. A continuous variable, thus, has an unlimited set of values in the range within which it varies. A measurement of your weight is an example, because you may weigh 135.6 pounds or 135.64 pounds. Your weight is not restricted to discrete values such as 135 pounds or 136 pounds, although it is possible that you may have a scale that indicates your weight only in whole pounds. Yet your weight is not limited to these specific values. It may take on any value between 135 and 136 pounds. Similarly, many psychological variables, such as anxiety or intelligence, exist as continuous variables, although they may be measured by scales that assign whole number scores to a person.

Real Limits of a Measurement

When measurements are made of a continuous variable, specific numerical values are assigned to the amount of the variable present. But the assigned measures only approximate the actual amount of the variable. Consequently, we must be aware of the accuracy of our measurements, regardless of the scale of measurement that we are using. And the accuracy of measurement of a continuous variable is contained in the *real limits* of the number assigned.

Real limits of a measurement are easily understood using measurements of the variable of time. Suppose that you are measuring the amount of time that a person can hold his or her hand in a tub of 40°F water. This task may be used to induce pain safely in experiments dealing with relaxation strategies to increase pain tolerance. Suppose for one subject that you measured a time of 37 seconds by observing the second hand on a stopwatch. How accurate is this measurement? Because you measured to the nearest whole second, the time could not have been 36 or 38 seconds. But might the actual duration have been

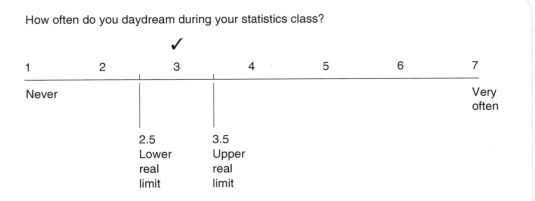

Figure 2.2 Upper and lower real limits for a response (indicated by the ✓) on a 7-point rating scale.

37.2 seconds or 36.7 seconds? The answer is yes, for you may have rounded either 36.7 seconds or 37.2 seconds to 37 seconds. The accuracy of this measurement of 37 seconds is given by the real limits of this number. The **real limits of a number** are the points that are midway between the number and the next lower and the next higher numbers on the scale used to make the measurements. For a measured value of 37 seconds, then, the **lower real limit** is 36.5 seconds and the **upper real limit** is 37.5 seconds. The lower real limit of 36.5 seconds is midway between 36 seconds, the next lower measured value on the scale used, and 37 seconds. The upper real limit of 37.5 seconds is midway between 37 seconds and 38 seconds, the next higher measured value on the scale used.

Suppose now that you had measured the duration with an electronic stopwatch that provided measurements to the nearest one-hundredth of a second, such as 37.21 seconds. What are the upper and lower real limits of this measurement? Again, the rule is to find the midpoint between the next lower and the next higher value on the measuring scale used. Thus, the lower real limit is the midpoint between 37.20 (the next lower number) and 37.21 seconds, or 37.205 seconds. The upper real limit is the midpoint between 37.21 seconds and 37.22 seconds (the next upper value), or 37.215 seconds.

Every numerical measurement of a continuous variable has upper and lower real limits associated with it. For example, suppose that we are using the 7-point rating scale illustrated in Figure 2.2. Assume that a person checked a response of 3 on this scale. Following the rules presented earlier, the upper and lower real limits for this score are 2.5 and 3.5, respectively. We will need the real limits of a measurement when creating frequency distributions in Chapter 3.

Real limits of a number ▷ The points midway between the number and the next lower and the next higher numbers on the scale used to make the measurements.

Lower real limit of a number ▷ The point midway between a number and the next lower number.

Upper real limit of a number ▷ The point midway between a number and the next higher number.

Testing Your Knowledge 2.4

1. Define: continuous variable, discrete variable, real limits of a number, lower real limit, upper real limit.

2. Identify each of the following variables being measured as discrete or continuous.

   a. A person's handgrip strength measured in pounds.

   b. The eye contact of an accuser with a defendant in a courtroom measured in seconds.

    c. The number of stotts (leaping vertically with four legs off the ground simultane-ously) made by a Thompson's gazelle in a one-hour period.

    d. The length of song (in seconds) by a male songbird during courtship.

    e. The funniness of a set of cartoons measured by the amount of time (in seconds) subjects laugh at them.

    f. The number of altruistic behaviors observed in nursery school children in a one-day period.

    g. The number of friends a child has.

    h. The number of items correct on a statistics examination with multiple choice questions.

3. Provide the lower real and upper real limits for each of the scores presented.

    a. A height of 152.4 centimeters.

    b. A duration of eye contact of 17.3 seconds.

    c. An assigned rating of 4 on a 7-point scale.

    d. A reaction time of 0.437 second.

    e. An error of 6.9 millimeters on the Müller–Lyer illusion.

    f. A handgrip strength of 67.81 pounds.

Summary

▶ Statistics are tools used to summarize and analyze data in the scientific study of behavior.

▶ Scientific research begins by asking a question that can be answered by obtaining empirical data.

▶ A research method is an approach used to collect data. The six types of research methods are case studies, naturalistic observation, archival records, survey research, experiments, and quasi-experiments.

▶ A case study selects a single example, such as a person, an animal, or a situation, to fully investigate.

▶ Naturalistic observation is research involving the observation of behaviors occurring in natural settings.

▶ Archival records research uses existing records.

▶ Survey research involves obtaining data from either oral or written interviews with people.

▶ An experiment is a carefully controlled situation in which a scientist manipulates one or more independent variables to observe their effect on the dependent variable.

▶ A quasi-experiment uses subject variables rather than manipulated variables as the independent variable.

▶ An operational definition identifies the operations or steps followed to make an observation or to manipulate a variable.

▶ Selecting the appropriate statistic depends upon the research hypothesis and the level of measurement used.

▶ Measurement is a process of assigning numbers to variables according to a set of rules.

▶ Nominal measurement is a classification of the measured variable into different categories. The numbers assigned each category serve the purpose of identification only.

▶ Ordinal measurement scales place a variable in an ordered set along a dimension.

▶ Interval scales create equal increments in the magnitude of the variable measured, but they do not have a true zero.

▶ Ratio scales possess the properties of the interval scale plus a true zero point.

▶ Qualitative data provides information on the kind or quality of a variable, whereas quantitative data provides information on the amount of a variable.

► A discrete variable is one that can take on only a finite or countable set of values within its limits.

► A continuous variable can take on an infinite set of values between any two levels of the variable.

► The real limits of a number are the points that are midway between the number and the next lower and the next higher numbers on the scale used to make the measurements.

Key Terms and Symbols

archival records (20)
case study (19)
continuous variable (30)
discrete variable (30)
empirical data (18)
experiment (21)
informed consent (23)
institutional review board (23)

interval measurement (26)
lower real limit of a number (31)
measurement (24)
naturalistic observation (19)
nominal measurement (24)
operational definition (22)
ordinal measurement (25)
qualitative data (25)

quantitative data (28)
quasi-experiment (21)
ratio measurement (28)
real limits of a number (31)
research hypothesis (18)
research method (19)
survey research (20)
upper real limit of a number (31)

Review Questions

1. Suppose that you were asked to collect data to answer each of the following questions. For each question, indicate what type of research design you would choose and why.

   a. What is the typical amount of time spent on homework by the members of your statistics class?

   b. How often does a basketball player make a free shot when a time-out is called immediately before the shot is made?

   c. Does a sales-training program increase the amount of sales by people who have completed the program? People will be randomly assigned to either be trained or not to be trained.

   d. What are the common behaviors of a young child in the checkout line of a supermarket?

   e. Why did a young man suddenly break off all contact with his friends and not leave his apartment?

   f. Is there a difference in the ability to solve anagrams (i.e., scrambled words) between 25- and 60-year-old males?

2. Suppose that you were asked to measure job stress in a group of employees. How would you operationally define your measure of job stress?

3. The career orientation of police officers was measured by having police officers order four paragraphs describing various career orientations from 1, the paragraph closest to the individual's career orientation, to 4, the paragraph furthest from the individual's career orientation.

   a. What is the variable being measured in this study?

   b. What level of measurement is achieved by the measure used?

4. Professional female golfers were weighed to determine if body weight was related to their game.

    a. What is the variable being measured in this study?

    b. What level of measurement is achieved by the measure used?

    c. The weight of one golfer was reported as 134.6 pounds. What are the upper and lower real limits of this measurement?

5. Parents of first-grade children were measured on a personality trait of emotional stability using a rating scale.

    a. What is the variable being measured in this study?

    b. What level of measurement is achieved by the measure used?

    c. Suppose that a person assigned a rating of 8 on a 9-point rating scale for agreement or disagreement with a statement. What are the upper and lower real limits of this measurement?

6. You are investigating how much time students spend doing homework each day. Kelly reported she spent 98 minutes working on chemistry last night, whereas Zach reported spending 49 minutes on his chemistry homework.

    a. What level of measurement is achieved by the measure used?

    b. What are the upper and lower real limits of the 98 minutes Kelly reported spending on homework?

    c. Is it appropriate to say that Kelly spent twice as much time on her chemistry homework when compared to Zach? Explain your answer.

7. Interpersonal values of an individual were measured by having the person order 12 value statements from most to least important. What level of measurement is achieved by the measure used?

8. The behavioral interactions of children at a nursery school were categorized as agonistic (i.e., argumentative or fighting), neutral (i.e., not interacting), or altruistic (i.e., helpful). What level of measurement is achieved by the measure used?

9. Identify each of the following measured variables as discrete or continuous.

    a. The number of students in your statistics class.

    b. The weight loss in pounds by people who have completed a diet and exercise workshop.

    c. The number of left-handed people in a group of 100.

    d. A person's blood pressure measured in millimeters of mercury.

10. Provide the lower and upper real limits for each of the scores presented.

    a. A weight of 141.3 pounds.

    b. A duration of 34 minutes playing a video game.

    c. A golf drive of 175.6 yards.

    d. A body temperature of 98.2°F.

    e. A systolic blood pressure of 109 millimeters of mercury.

11. A restaurant leaves cards for its patrons to complete after finishing a meal. Each card asks patrons to rate the restaurant on the quality of food, friendliness of service, speed of service, and cleanliness on 5-point scales ranging from poor to excellent. An overall score from 4 to 20 is obtained from each card. What level of measurement is used here? Explain your answer.

12. A psychologist studied how well people could tolerate pain by placing their hand in 40°F water and measuring how long they could keep their hand in the water. She performed two studies.

    a. In study 1, subjects were ranked on the duration that they could hold their hand in the water as follows: Lisa, 1; Stacia, 2; Maritza, 3; Valeria, 4; and Sophia, 5. What level of measurement is used here?

    b. In study 2, the duration of tolerance was measured in seconds, with the following results: Lisa, 111.3 seconds; Stacia, 97.8 seconds; Maritza, 71.3 seconds; Valeria, 18.7 seconds; and Sophia, 13.6 seconds. What level of measurement is used here?

13. In a ranking of the world's top tourist destinations (*World Tourism*, 2006), the top destination was France, followed by Spain. The United States ranked third, Italy was ranked fifth, and Austria ranked tenth .

    a. How much more popular is France as a tourist destination in comparison to Spain?

    b. Is Italy twice as popular as Austria as a tourist destination? Explain your answer.

    c. What does knowing that the United States ranked third tell you about the United States as a tourist destination?

Looking at Data: Frequency Distributions and Graphs

Think back to some of the people with whom you attended high school, not necessarily just your friends but also the minor players in your life. We bet most of you recall at least one person who was far more serious about working on cars and listening to music than working on schoolwork. We know a student who was like that in high school, graduating with an unimpressive C average, who took some classes at the community college, again amassing an unimpressive C average. Then, one day, he heard about the benefits of adopting a "growth mindset." His belief in his own abilities and behavior toward college changed. He graduated with a 4.0 and headed to graduate school. Recall in Chapter 1 we discussed the idea that students who have a growth mindset, who believe that their intellectual skills can grow, are more likely to engage in behaviors that will lead to success in statistics. To measure this mindset, we illustrated an Implicit View of Intelligence rating scale based on the work of Dweck (1999, 2006):

		Some people are simply born smart, others are not so lucky.			
1	2	3	4	5	6
Strongly Agree					Strongly Disagree

The numbers on this scale correspond to beliefs about intelligence. Responses closer to 6 indicate a belief in an incremental view of intelligence (a belief that, with effort, you can get smarter), whereas responses closer to 1 indicate a belief that intelligence is fixed and cannot change. As we indicated in Chapter 2, the entire scale consists of eight statements similar to the one above. For each statement, a person indicates agreement or disagreement with the statement by choosing a number between 1 (strongly agree) to 6 (strong disagree). A score is then obtained by summing over the eight statements to yield a total score for the rating scale. The possible range of scores is from 8 (obtained by responding with a 1 to all eight statements) to 48 (obtained by responding with a 6 to all eight statements). Higher scores indicate a belief that intelligence can be changed, and lower scores indicate a belief that intelligence cannot be changed. Scores from summated rating scales, such as this scale, are often treated as representing interval measurements. We follow this custom with the following example.

Suppose a college professor administers the Implicit View of Intelligence scale to a sample of 20 students in her class. The scores obtained are portrayed in Table 3.1. Such scores are

TABLE 3.1

Hypothetical Implicit View of Intelligence scores from 20 students

33	29
39	27
35	31
32	31
34	31
39	36
31	37
32	34
40	31
36	32

Raw data or raw scores ▶ The scores obtained from subjects before the scores have been analyzed statistically.

N ▶ The total number of scores in a set of scores.

called **raw data** or **raw scores**, for they are exactly as collected and have not been subjected to statistical analysis. The letter N is used to indicate the total number of scores obtained; thus, N for this example is 20.

Consider a student who obtains a score of 32 on this scale. What does this score tell us about that student's belief in the changeability of intelligence? Is it higher or lower than that of the other students completing the scale? Are you able to answer these questions knowing only this score? The answer to this last question is no, for as with many measures in behavioral science, an individual score is meaningful only in comparison to other scores. So, look at the 20 scores in Table 3.1. Notice, however, that it is difficult to compare one score to all the other scores in this table. Now look at the same 20 scores organized in a frequency distribution in Table 3.2. Which way of organizing data makes it easier to tell how a score of 32 compares to other scores?

Organizing your data is often the first step in helping you see what is going on with your data. A frequency distribution, such as that of Table 3.2, is one way to organize data. We will now discuss how to present quantitative data from interval or ratio measurements using a frequency distribution.

Frequency Distributions with Ungrouped Scores

Simple Frequencies

Frequency distribution ▶ A count of the number of times that each score occurs in a set of scores.

A **frequency distribution** provides a count of the number of times that each score occurs in a set of scores. Often, a frequency distribution is presented as a table that orders a set of scores from highest to lowest and indicates how often each score occurs. Table 3.2 illustrates an ungrouped frequency distribution for the Implicit View of Intelligence scale scores presented in

TABLE 3.2 Ungrouped frequency distribution for Implicit View of Intelligence scores of Table 3.1.

(a) Score	(b) Tally	(c) Frequency (*f*)	(d) Relative Frequency (*rf*)	(e) Percentage Frequency (%*f*)
40	/	1	.05	5
39	//	2	.10	10
38		0	.00	0
37	/	1	.05	5
36	//	2	.10	10
35	/	1	.05	5
34	//	2	.10	10
33	/	1	.05	5
32	///	3	.15	15
31	/////	5	.25	25
30		0	.00	0
29	/	1	.05	5
28		0	.00	0
27	/	1	.05	5

Ungrouped frequency distribution
▶ A frequency distribution constructed by listing all possible score values between the lowest and highest scores obtained and then placing a tally mark (/) beside a score each time it occurs.

f ▶ The simple frequency of occurrence of each score in a frequency distribution.

Table 3.1. This **ungrouped frequency distribution** was constructed by listing all possible score values between the lowest and highest scores obtained (27 and 40, respectively; column a of Table 3.2) and then placing a tally mark (/) beside a score each time it occurred (shown in column b of Table 3.2). All possible score values in the range from the lowest to the highest score obtained are included in column a, even if the score did not occur. The number of tally marks for each score was counted and entered into column c as the **simple frequency of occurrence of each score** (symbolized by *f*). Notice that this distribution lets us see that an Implicit View of Intelligence score of 32 is about in the middle of the distribution of scores; about one-half of the scores are less, and about one-half are more. We can also easily see that the most frequently occurring score is 31, with a total of five occurrences.

The information from a simple frequency distribution is not always easily interpreted, however. For example, if you are simply told that the most frequently occurring Implicit View of Intelligence score is 31, with a frequency of occurrence of 5, you cannot know if 31 occurs relatively often or not without knowing the total number of scores obtained. If only 10 scores were collected and 5 of them were 31, then half the scores would be 31. But if 100 scores were collected and the most frequently occurring score of 31 occurred only 5 times, then 31, although the most frequent score, occurs only occasionally among the 100 scores. Thus, scientists prefer to present frequency distributions in which the frequencies represent a proportion of the total number of scores obtained as either relative or percentage frequencies.

Relative Frequencies

Relative frequency (*rf*) ▶ The frequency of a score divided by the total number of scores obtained.

The relative frequency of a score is obtained by dividing the frequency of each score by the total number of scores in the distribution. Thus, a **relative frequency** (symbolized by *rf*) is expressed as

$$rf \text{ of a score} = f \text{ of a score}/N.$$

Relative frequencies are also often called *proportions*. For example, the relative frequency of occurrence of the score of 32 in Table 3.2 is found by dividing its frequency ($f = 3$) by the total number of scores ($N = 20$), which equals .15.[1] The relative frequency of the Implicit View of Intelligence scores is presented in column d of Table 3.2.

Percentage Frequencies

Percent ▶ A relative frequency expressed as a proportion of 100.

A **percent** or **percentage** (symbolized by the % sign) is a relative frequency expressed as a proportion of 100. Thus, to obtain a percent or percentage value for a score, the relative frequency of the score is multiplied by 100. For example, in Table 3.2 the most frequent score of 31 occurs 5 times out of the 20 scores collected. Thus, 31 represents $5/20 \times 100$ or 25% of the scores in Table 3.1. Accordingly the **percentage frequency** of a score (symbolized by %*f*) is found by multiplying the relative frequency of a score by 100, or

Percentage frequency (%*f*) ▶ The relative frequency of a score multiplied by 100.

$$\% f \text{ of a score} = (rf \text{ of score}) \times 100.$$

The percentage frequency of scores is presented in column e of Table 3.2. Notice that columns d and e of this table present equivalent information about the distribution of scores in Table 3.1. The advantage of having frequencies presented as relative or percentage

---

[1]When presenting decimal fractions in this text, we will follow the guidelines of the *Publication Manual of the American Psychological Association* (2001), which indicate that if a decimal fraction cannot be greater than 1, a zero is not used before the decimal point. Thus, relative frequencies are reported without a zero before the decimal point.

frequencies is that these values are independent of the total number of scores obtained. Thus, if you had a second sample of 35 scores ($N = 35$) from another group of students, it would be easier to compare the frequency distributions from the two different size samples if the frequency distributions were expressed as either relative or percentage frequencies rather than as simple frequencies alone.

Obtaining Information from a Frequency Distribution

The simple frequencies, relative frequencies, or percentage frequencies presented in Table 3.2 allow us to easily notice that

- ▶ the lowest score is 27;
- ▶ the highest score is 40;
- ▶ the most frequently occurring score is 31; and
- ▶ fifteen of the scores fall in the interval from 31 to 37.

These characteristics of the distribution of scores are not easily seen in the raw scores of Table 3.1.

EXAMPLE PROBLEM

3.1

Constructing Ungrouped Frequency Distributions

Problem: Psychologists are interested in the perception of ambiguous figures, for they believe that understanding how we perceive these figures will provide knowledge about our perception of the everyday world. The Mach pyramid shown in Figure 3.1 is an example of

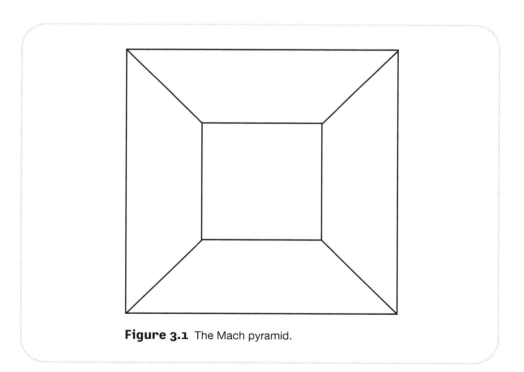

Figure 3.1 The Mach pyramid.

an ambiguous figure, for it is reversible in perspective. You may see this figure either as a pyramid, with the small square appearing to project out of the page toward you, or as a room in perspective, with the small square being the far wall. Suppose you timed 25 people over a 1-minute period to see how long each person could see the figure as a pyramid and found the following times (to the nearest whole second):

2, 7, 10, 5, 5, 3, 9, 11, 5, 8, 2, 4, 7, 6, 10, 7, 3, 9, 7, 11, 4, 6, 3, 1, and 8.

Construct an ungrouped simple frequency distribution including relative and percentage frequencies for these scores. What conclusions about the scores may you reach from these distributions?

Solution: The requested frequency distributions are shown in the following table.

Score	Tally	f	rf	%f
11	//	2	.08	8
10	//	2	.08	8
9	//	2	.08	8
8	//	2	.08	8
7	////	4	.16	16
6	//	2	.08	8
5	///	3	.12	12
4	//	2	.08	8
3	///	3	.12	12
2	//	2	.08	8
1	/	1	.04	4

Conclusions: The scores range from 1 to 11 seconds, and the most frequently occurring score is 7 seconds. With the exception of the most frequently occurring score of 7, the scores occur about equally throughout their range.

Testing Your Knowledge 3.1

1. Define: f, frequency distribution, N, percent, percentage, percentage frequency, $\%f$, raw data, raw scores, relative frequency, rf, ungrouped frequency distribution.

2. The ability to adapt to differing social situations is a characteristic often found in effective leaders. Suppose you measured 20 people on a scale of adaptability in which scores can range from 0 to 25 and obtained the following scores: 6, 13, 4, 19, 3, 12, 9, 8, 5, 11, 6, 8, 15, 5, 8, 10, 9, 14, 4, and 8.

   a. Construct an ungrouped simple frequency distribution including relative and percentage frequencies for these scores.

   b. What are the lowest and highest scores obtained?

   c. What is the most frequently occurring score?

Grouped Frequency Distributions

Grouped frequency distribution
▶ A frequency distribution in which scores are grouped together in class intervals and the frequency of scores occurring within each class is tabulated.

If a large number of scores is collected or if there is a wide range of score values in the data, an ungrouped frequency distribution, as illustrated in Table 3.2, can become spread out, making it difficult to see clear patterns in the data. It is useful, then, to construct a **grouped frequency distribution**, in which scores are grouped together in class intervals. To illustrate grouped frequency distributions, suppose the professor decided to measure the Implicit View of Intelligence in a randomly selected sample of 100 students and obtained the scores in Table 3.3.

Constructing Grouped Frequency Distributions

Class interval ▶ The width of the interval used to group raw scores in a grouped frequency distribution. The size or width of the interval is represented by *i*.

A grouped frequency distribution places raw scores into class intervals. A **class interval** is a range of score values into which the raw scores are grouped. Using a class interval of size 3, Table 3.4 presents several grouped frequency distributions of the scores in Table 3.3. The class intervals are arranged from highest to lowest, and the frequency of scores occurring within each class is tallied and tabulated. Constructing grouped frequency distributions, such as Table 3.4, requires two decisions: (1) the number of class intervals to be used and (2) the size (or width) of the class interval.

Number of Class Intervals

The number of class intervals to be used is determined by the range of the scores, with 10 to 20 class intervals ordinarily used. The number of intervals usually is chosen so that the size of the class interval is 1, 2, 3, 5, or a multiple of 5. The scores in Table 3.3 vary from 16 (the lowest score) to 48 (the highest score). With this range of scores, 10 intervals appear sufficient to group the data.

TABLE

3·3

Hypothetical Implicit View of Intelligence scores from 100 students.

28	16	32	33	31	34
31	38	46	35	26	29
19	37	27	31	28	36
38	28	32	26	43	27
28	34	36	30	17	38
32	25	30	22	33	47
39	35	18	34	40	26
38	32	39	29	40	48
25	26	31	35	28	43
29	28	28	26	30	34
27	41	29	34	27	39
36	23	27	37	42	30
28	28	32	22	31	42
33	29	36	32	26	36
30	32	27	18	33	40
34	20	45	38	28	37
29	35	26	33		

TABLE **3.4**	Grouped frequency distributions for the Implicit View of Intelligence scores of Table 3.3.									
(a)	(b) Real Limits		(c)	(d)	(e)	(f)	(g)	(h)	(i)	(j)
Class Interval	Lower	Upper	Midpoint of Interval	Tally	f	rf	%f	cf	crf	c%f
48–50	47.5–50.5		49	/	1	.01	1	100	1.00	100
45–47	44.5–47.5		46	///	3	.03	3	99	.99	99
42–44	41.5–44.5		43	////	4	.04	4	96	.96	96
39–41	38.6–41.5		40	///////	7	.07	7	92	.92	92
36–38	35.5–38.5		37	/////////////	13	.13	13	85	.85	85
33–35	32.5–35.5		34	///////////////	15	.15	15	72	.72	72
30–32	29.5–32.5		31	///////////// //////	17	.17	17	57	.57	57
27–29	26.5–29.5		28	//////////// ////////////	22	.22	22	40	.40	40
24–26	23.5–26.5		25	/////////	9	.09	9	18	.18	18
21–23	20.5–23.5		22	///	3	.03	3	9	.09	9
18–20	17.5–20.5		19	////	4	.04	4	6	.06	6
15–17	14.5–17.5		16	//	2	.02	2	2	.02	2

Size of Class Intervals

After the number of intervals is determined, the size or width of the interval is found by dividing the difference between the largest and smallest score by the number of class intervals to be used. In statistics, the letter X is often used to symbolically represent a score. Hence, the **size of the class interval**, represented by i, is found by

X ▶ A symbol used to represent an individual score.

i ▶ The size or width of the class interval in a grouped frequency distribution.

$$i = \frac{X_{\text{highest}} - X_{\text{lowest}}}{\text{number of intervals}}$$

where X_{highest} indicates the highest score and X_{lowest} the lowest score in the distribution. Using the raw data of Table 3.3, with $X_{\text{highest}} = 48$ and $X_{\text{lowest}} = 16$ and 10 class intervals, the size of the class interval equals

$$i = \frac{48 - 16}{10} = \frac{32}{10} = 3.2.$$

If this formula leads to a decimal value, such as 3.2, we round to the nearest recommended class size (i.e., 1, 2, 3, 5, or a multiple of 5). For the example, we round i to 3. Should scores be decimals less than 1.0, then we do not round the interval to a whole number. Rather, a decimal interval such as 0.3, 0.5, 0.03, or 0.05 is used.

Constructing the Class Intervals

Two guidelines are used to construct class intervals for the frequency distribution:

▶ The lowest interval must contain the lowest score.

▶ The lower limit of the first interval, that is, the lowest possible score value in the first interval, should be evenly divisible by the size of the class interval.

For the scores of Table 3.3, the lowest score is 16. Accordingly, the lowest class interval in column a of Table 3.4 begins with a lower limit of 15, because 15 is the first score less than 16 that is evenly divisible by the class interval of 3. The first class interval is then from 15 to 17. Notice that it is possible for three score values to fall into this interval: 15, 16, and 17; thus, its size or width is 3. The next class interval is 18 to 20. Additional class intervals are calculated up to the point needed to include the highest score, in the example, a class interval of 48 to 50.

Stated Limits and Real Limits of a Class Interval.   Each interval in column a of Table 3.4 has upper and lower stated and real limits. The **upper stated limit of a class interval** and the **lower stated limit of a class interval** (also called *apparent limits*) are the highest and lowest scores, respectively, that could fall into that class interval. For example, for the class interval of 42 to 44, the lower stated limit is 42 and the upper stated limit is 44. A numerical score of 42 is the lowest score that may be placed in the interval, and a score of 44 is the highest that may be placed in the interval. Figure 3.2 illustrates the lower and upper stated limits for the class interval of 42 to 44.

The real limits of a number were defined in Chapter 2 as the points that are midway between the number and the next lower and higher numbers on the scale used to make the measurements. Real limits exist for the intervals of a grouped frequency distribution also, and these real limits are found in a manner similar to those of the real limits of a number.

Stated limits of a class interval
▶ The highest and lowest scores that could fall into that class interval.

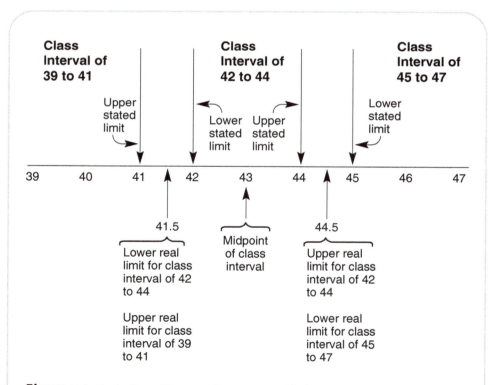

Figure 3.2 Illustration of lower and upper stated limits, lower and upper real limits, and the midpoint of a class interval of a grouped frequency distribution.

Real limit of a class interval ▷
The point midway between the
stated limit of a class interval and
the stated limit of the next lower or
upper class interval.

The **lower real limit of a class interval** is the point midway between the lower stated limit of the class interval and the upper stated limit of the next lower class interval. For example, for the class interval of 42 to 44 in Table 3.4, the lower stated limit is 42. The upper stated limit of the next lower class interval (i.e., the interval of 39 to 41) is 41. Accordingly, the real lower limit of the class interval of 42 to 44 is the midpoint between 41 and 42, or 41.5. This lower real limit is also illustrated in Figure 3.2.

Similarly, the **upper real limit of a class interval** is the point midway between the upper stated limit of that class interval and the lower stated limit of the next higher class interval. The upper real limit of the class interval of 42 to 44 is found by obtaining the midpoint of the upper stated limit of the interval of 42 to 44 (i.e., 44) and the lower stated limit of the next higher class interval, 45 to 47. The lower stated limit of this interval is 45; thus, the upper real limit of the class interval of 42 to 44 is the midpoint of 44 and 45, or 44.5. This upper real limit is also shown in Figure 3.2. Notice that the upper real limit for the class interval of 42 to 44 is also the lower real limit for the next class interval of 45 to 47. The upper and lower real limits of the class intervals are presented in column b of Table 3.4.

Midpoint of a class interval ▷
The point midway between the real
limits of the class interval.

Midpoints of Class Intervals.   Each class interval also has a midpoint. The **midpoint of a class interval** is the point midway between the real limits of the class interval. Midpoints of a class interval can be found by adding the values of the real limits of a class interval and dividing the sum by 2. For the class interval of 42 to 44, the midpoint is found by

$$\frac{41.5 + 44.5}{2} = \frac{86}{2} = 43.$$

The midpoints of each class interval are shown in column c of Table 3.4. Although we included both the real upper and lower limits and the midpoint of the class interval in Table 3.4, grouped frequency distributions often are presented with only the class intervals of column a.

Grouped Simple Frequency Distribution

A grouped simple frequency distribution is obtained by tallying scores into the class interval in which they fall (see column d of Table 3.4). For example, a score of 35 is tallied into the class interval of 33 to 35, and a score of 40 is tallied into the class interval of 39 to 41. The tallies in an interval are then summed to obtain the simple frequency (f) for that interval (given in column e of Table 3.4).

Grouped Relative and Percentage Frequencies

Relative frequencies and percentage frequencies may also be obtained for grouped frequency distributions. The procedures are similar to those used for an ungrouped frequency distribution.

**Grouped relative frequency
distribution** ▷ A grouped
frequency distribution in which the
frequency of scores in an interval is
divided by the total number of
scores in the distribution.

Grouped Relative Frequencies.   **Grouped relative frequencies** are found by dividing the frequency of scores in an interval by the total number of scores in the distribution. Thus

$$rf \text{ of scores in an interval} = \frac{f \text{ of scores in interval}}{N}.$$

Grouped relative frequencies for the Implicit View of Intelligence scores are presented in column f of Table 3.4.

Grouped percentage frequency distribution ▶ A grouped frequency distribution obtained by multiplying the relative frequency values by 100 to obtain percentages.

Grouped Percentage Frequencies. Grouped percentage frequencies are obtained by

$$\%f \text{ of scores in an interval} = rf \text{ of scores in interval} \times 100.$$

Grouped percentage frequencies of the Implicit View of Intelligence scale scores are presented in column g of Table 3.4.

Cumulative Grouped Frequency Distributions

Cumulative frequency of a score ▶ The frequency of occurrence of that score plus the sum of the frequencies of all the scores of lower value.

Cumulative frequency of a class interval ▶ The frequency of occurrence of scores in that interval plus the sum of the frequencies of scores of lower class intervals.

Cumulative Grouped Simple Frequency Distribution. Each form of frequency distribution discussed may also be presented as a cumulative frequency distribution. The **cumulative frequency of a score** (symbolized as *cf* or *cum f*) is the frequency of that score's occurrence plus the sum of the frequencies of all the scores of lower value. In a grouped distribution, the **cumulative frequency of a class interval** is the frequency of occurrence of scores in that interval plus the sum of the frequencies of scores of lower class intervals. For example, the cumulative frequency of the class interval of 21 to 23 in Table 3.4 is 9, because a total of 9 scores occur in the intervals 15 to 17 (2 scores), 18 to 20 (4 scores), and 21 to 23 (3 scores). The simple cumulative frequency of each class interval is shown in column h of Table 3.4.

Cumulative grouped relative frequency of a class interval ▶ The relative frequency of the scores in that interval plus the sum of the relative frequencies of class intervals of lower value.

Cumulative grouped percentage frequency of a class interval ▶ The percentage frequency of the scores in that interval plus the sum of the percentage frequencies of all the class intervals of lower value.

Cumulative Grouped Relative and Percentage Frequencies. Relative frequencies and percentage frequencies may also be presented as cumulative frequencies. The **cumulative grouped relative frequency of a class interval** (symbolized as *crf* or *cum rf*) is the relative frequency of the scores in that interval plus the sum of the relative frequencies of scores of lower class intervals.

Similarly, the **cumulative grouped percentage frequency of a class interval** (symbolized as *c%f* or *cum %f*) is the percentage frequency of the scores in that interval plus the sum of the percentage frequencies of scores of all lower class intervals. The cumulative grouped relative frequencies and percentage frequencies for each class interval of Table 3.4 are presented in columns i and j, respectively.

Obtaining Information from a Grouped Frequency Distribution

The several grouped frequency distributions in Table 3.4 indicate that the majority of scores are between 27 and 38. We can also see that the interval containing the most scores is from 27 to 29. However, the exact numerical value of scores is lost in Table 3.4. We cannot determine the exact lowest or highest scores or the most frequently occurring score. But this loss of information is often offset by the greater ease with which we can perceive the general shape of the distribution.

Percentile Ranks and Percentiles

Percentile rank of a score ▶ The percentage of scores in a distribution that are equal to or less than that score.

Frequency distributions, such as those illustrated in Tables 3.2 and 3.4, provide information concerning the highest and lowest scores and the most frequently occurring scores among a set of scores. Such distributions also allow us to compare a score in relation to other scores in the distribution. For example, if you obtained a score of 40 on the Implicit View of Intelligence scale, then by looking at Table 3.4, you would know you were in the upper 15 percent of the scores obtained in the sample. But, we can only make this determination if we have the entire distribution available for our inspection. Often, however, we would like to know the specific location of a score with respect to the other scores in the distribution without having to present the entire distribution. A statistic that provides this information is the percentile rank. The **percentile rank of a score** indicates the percentage of scores in the distribution that are equal to or less than that score. Thus, for example, if the percentile rank of a history test score of 70 is 35, then 35 percent of the scores in the distribution are equal to or less than 70. The benefit of providing a percentile or the percentile rank for a score is that it provides specific information about the score presenting the distribution itself. Suppose, for example, you were one of the 100 students who completed the Implicit View of Intelligence scale, and your score was 34. Simply knowing your score does not give you any information about your performance on the scale. Is 34 high or low compared to other students? You could only make a judgment if you saw the entire distribution of scores. But if you were told that the percentile rank for a score of 34 was 65, then you would know that 65 percent of the scores were equal to or less than 34 and that your score is in the upper 35 percent of the scores in the distribution.

Finding the Percentile Rank of a Score

Cumulative frequency distributions are frequently used to find percentile ranks. Suppose we want to find the percentile rank of a score of 34 in the distribution portrayed in Table 3.4. This score falls into the class interval of 33 to 35. The cumulative percentage of scores up to the lower real limit of this interval is 57 (from column j, the $c\%f$), and the cumulative percentage of scores to the upper real limit of this interval is 72 (from column j). Thus, the percentile rank of 34 will be between 57 and 72. To find the exact percentile rank, we must interpolate the value of 34 in the interval of 33 to 35. The following formula provides this interpolation and calculates the percentile rank of a score:

$$\text{Percentile rank} = P_X = \frac{cf_L + [(X - X_L)/i]f_i}{N} \times 100,$$

where

P_X = percentile rank of a score of X.

cf_L = cumulative frequency of scores up to the lower real limit of the interval containing X.

X = the score for which the percentile rank is being found.

X_L = lower real limit of the interval containing X.

i = size of the class interval.

f_i = frequency of scores in the interval containing X.

N = total number of scores in the distribution.

For a score of 34 in Table 3.4, the values for this formula are

$P_X = P_{34}$
$cf_L = 57$ (from column h of Table 3.4),
$X = 34$
$X_L = 32.5$ (from column b of Table 3.4),
$i = 3$
$f_i = 15$ (from column e of Table 3.4),
$N = 100.$

Substituting these values into the formula, we obtain

$$P_{34} = \frac{57 + [(34 - 32.5)/3]15}{100} \times 100$$

$$= \frac{57 + [(1.5/3)(15)]}{100} \times 100$$

$$= \frac{57 + [(.5)(15)]}{100} \times 100$$

$$= \frac{57 + 7.5}{100} \times 100$$

$$= \frac{64.5}{100} \times 100$$

$$= .645 \times 100 = 64.5.$$

Typically, a percentile rank is rounded to a whole number; thus

$$P_{34} = 65.$$

The percentile rank of a score of 34 is 65; 65 percent of the scores in Table 3.4 are equal to or less than 34. This formula may also be applied to an ungrouped frequency distribution by using $i = 1$.

Finding a Percentile of a Distribution

Percentile ▶ The score at or below which a specified percentage of scores in a distribution falls.

We have seen that the percentile rank of a score indicates the percentage of scores in the distribution that are equal to or less than that score. Consider now a second problem, that of having a distribution and wanting to find a score that corresponds to a specified percentile in that distribution. A **percentile** is the score at or below which a specified percentage of scores in a distribution fall. For example, if the 35th percentile on an examination is 70, then 35 percent of the scores on the examination are equal to or less than 70. To return to our example of the distribution of Implicit View of Intelligence scores in Table 3.4, suppose that we want to find the 75th percentile of this distribution. We notice that this percentile is a score in the class interval of 36 to 38, for 72 percent of the scores fall below the lower real limit of this interval and 85 percent of the scores fall below the upper real limit. Again, we must interpolate to find the exact score that is the 75th percentile. The following formula provides this interpolation and calculates the percentile:

$$\text{Percentile} = X_P = X_L + \left(\frac{P(N) - cf_L}{f_i} \right) i,$$

where

X_P = score at a specified percentile (i.e., the score we want to find).
X_L = lower real limit of the interval containing the specified percentile.
P = required percentile given as a proportion between 0 to 1.00.
N = total number of scores in the distribution.
cf_L = cumulative frequency of scores up to the lower real limit of the interval containing X_P.
f_i = frequency of scores in the interval containing X_P.
i = size of the class interval.

For the 75th percentile, these values are

$X_P = X_{75}$
$X_L = 35.5$ (from column b of Table 3.4),
$P = .75$
$N = 100,$
$cf_L = 72$ (from column h of Table 3.4),

$$f_i = 13 \qquad \text{(from column e of Table 3.4),}$$
$$i = 3.$$

Substituting these values into the formula, we obtain

$$X_{75} = 35.5 + \left(\frac{.75(100) - 72}{13}\right)3$$

$$= 35.5 + \left(\frac{75 - 72}{13}\right)3$$

$$= 35.5 + \left(\frac{3}{13}\right)3$$

$$= 35.5 + 0.7$$

$$= 36.2.$$

Rounding this value to a whole number, $X_{75} = 36$. The 75th percentile is a score of 36. Seventy-five percent of the scores in the distribution are equal to or less than 36. This formula may also be used with an ungrouped distribution by using $i = 1$.

EXAMPLE PROBLEM

3.2

Grouped Frequency Distributions

Problem: Suppose that we investigated the problem of perception of ambiguous figures discussed in example problem 3.1 and measured the duration that subjects could see the pyramid in the Mach pyramid figure. We used 50 subjects and obtained the following scores (to the nearest whole second): 18, 2, 7, 23, 16, 10, 5, 30, 5, 15, 17, 3, 31, 9, 11, 13, 5, 13, 8, 19, 16, 2, 14, 4, 7, 7, 6, 2, 10, 6, 7, 24, 3, 8, 9, 7, 19, 7, 11, 9, 4, 7, 6, 1, 3, 10, 1, 26, 8, and 5.

    a. Construct the following grouped distributions for these scores: simple frequency, relative frequency, percentage frequency, simple cumulative frequency, cumulative relative frequency, and cumulative percentage frequency distribution. Include the lower and upper real limits of the class intervals and the midpoint of each class interval.

    b. What conclusions about the scores may you reach from these distributions?

    c. Find the percentile rank of a score of 16 seconds.

    d. What is the 25th percentile for this distribution?

Solution: **a.** The solution requires choosing the number of class intervals to be used, finding the size of the class interval, and then constructing a grouped frequency distribution using these class intervals.

Number of Class Intervals: The range of scores is from 1 to 31 seconds, or 30 seconds. Ten class intervals seem sufficient to group the data.

Size of Class Intervals: $i = (31 - 1)/10 = 3.0$.

Constructing the Distribution: The lowest score obtained is 1 second, and the class interval to be used is 3 seconds. The first class interval then is

0 to 2. This interval contains the lowest score, and the lower stated limit of this interval (i.e., 0) is divisible evenly by the size of the class interval (i.e., 3). The class intervals of the grouped frequency distribution are presented in column a of the following table. The upper and lower real limits for each interval are obtained by finding the points midway between adjacent class intervals. For example, upper and lower real limits for the class interval of 24 to 26 are the points midway between 23 and 24 (lower real limit) and midway between 26 and 27 (upper real limit), respectively. The real limits of each class interval are shown in column b of the table. Midpoints for each class interval are presented in column c. The scores are tallied in column d, and the grouped frequency distributions are presented in columns e through j of the table.

(a)	(b) Real Limits		(c)	(d)	(e)	(f)	(g)	(h)	(i)	(j)
Class Interval	Lower	Upper	Midpoint of Interval	Tally	f	rf	$\%f$	cf	crf	$c\%f$
30–32	29.5–32.5		31	//	2	.04	4	50	1.00	100
27–29	26.5–29.5		28		0	.00	0	48	.96	96
24–26	23.5–26.5		25	//	2	.04	4	48	.96	96
21–23	20.5–23.5		22	/	1	.02	2	46	.92	92
18–20	17.5–20.5		19	///	3	.06	6	45	.90	90
15–17	14.5–17.5		16	////	4	.08	8	42	.84	84
12–14	11.5–14.5		13	///	3	.06	6	38	.76	76
9–11	8.5–11.5		10	////////	8	.16	16	35	.70	70
6–8	5.5–8.5		7	/////////////	13	.26	26	27	.54	54
3–5	2.5–5.5		4	ued/////	9	.18	18	14	.28	28
0–2	−0.5–2.5		1	/////	5	.10	10	5	.10	10

b. Conclusions: From the simple frequencies (column e), relative frequencies (column f), or percentage frequencies (column g), we see that scores in the interval of 6 to 8 seconds occurred most frequently. The cumulative frequency distributions indicate that .70 or 70 percent of the scores were durations of 11 seconds or less.

c. The percentile rank of a score is found using the formula

$$P_X = \frac{cf_L + [(X - X_L)/i]f_i}{N} \times 100.$$

The values needed to find the percentile rank of a score of 16 are

$$P_X = P_{16},$$
$$cf_L = 38,$$
$$X = 16,$$
$$X_L = 14.5,$$
$$i = 3,$$
$$f_i = 4,$$
$$N = 50.$$

Substituting these values, we obtain

$$P_{16} = \frac{38 + [(16 - 14.5)/3]4}{50} \times 100$$

$$= \frac{38 + (1.5/3)4}{50} \times 100$$

$$= \frac{38 + (.5)4}{50} \times 100$$

$$= \frac{38 + 2}{50} \times 100$$

$$= \frac{40}{50} \times 100$$

$$= .80 \times 100 = 80.$$

The percentile rank of a score of 16 seconds is 80. Eighty percent of the durations are equal to or less than 16 seconds.

d. The 25th percentile is found using the formula

$$X_P = X_L + \left(\frac{P(N) - cf_L}{f_i} \right) i.$$

The values needed to find the 25th percentile are

$$X_p = X_{25,}$$
$$X_L = 2.5,$$
$$P = .25,$$
$$N = 50,$$
$$cf_L = 5,$$
$$f_i = 9,$$
$$i = 3.$$

Substituting these values, we obtain

$$P_{16} = 2.5 + \left(\frac{.25(50) - 5}{9} \right) 3$$

$$= 2.5 + \left(\frac{12.5 - 5}{9} \right) 3$$

$$= 2.5 + \left(\frac{7.5}{9} \right) 3$$

$$= 2.5 + 2.5$$

$$= 5.0.$$

A score of 5 seconds is the 25th percentile.

Testing Your Knowledge 3.2

1. Define: class interval, cumulative frequency of a class interval, cumulative frequency of a score, cumulative grouped percentage frequency of a class interval, cumulative grouped relative frequency of a class interval, *cf, c%f, crf, cum f, cum %f, cum rf*, grouped frequency distribution, lower real limit of a class interval, lower stated limit of a class interval, midpoint of a class interval, percentile, percentile rank of a score, upper real limit of a class interval, upper stated limit of a class interval.

2. What is the recommended number of class intervals to use when constructing a grouped frequency distribution?

3. The largest score in a distribution is 88 and the smallest is 14. You plan to construct a grouped distribution with 15 intervals. What will be the size of your class interval?

4. The largest score in a distribution is 95 and the smallest is 62. You want the class interval to be 3. How many intervals will you use?

5. What are the two guidelines for constructing grouped distributions?

6. A grouped frequency distribution has class intervals of 120 to 122, 123 to 125, 126 to 128, 129 to 131, and 132 to 134.

   a. Identify the lower and upper stated limits for the class interval of 123 to 125.

   b. Identify the lower and upper stated limits for the class interval of 129 to 131.

   c. Identify the lower and upper real limits for the class interval of 123 to 125.

   d. Identify the lower and upper real limits for the class interval of 129 to 131.

   e. Find the midpoint of the class interval of 120 to 122.

   f. What is the value of *i* for this distribution?

7. When approached by a predator, Thompson's gazelles leap straight up with all four feet simultaneously off the ground. This behavior, known as stotting, appears costly to the gazelle, for it delays the onset of flight from the predator. To learn more about stotting, Caro (1986) used naturalistic observation to study gazelles in Serengeti National Park, Tanzania. One measure obtained was the estimated distance of a predator, such as a cheetah, from a gazelle before the first stott occurred. Suppose that he observed 50 instances of a cheetah approaching a gazelle and recorded the following estimated distances (in meters) between the cheetah and the gazelle before the first stott occurred: 47, 61, 72, 63, 56, 54, 67, 75, 91, 72, 83, 140, 31, 37, 25, 38, 57, 62, 49, 205, 66, 39, 43, 81, 66, 72, 42, 29, 190, 64, 76, 54, 38, 67, 61, 33, 48, 55, 59, 68, 18, 49, 37, 83, 70, 154, 91, 50, 58, and 66.

   a. Construct the following grouped distributions for these scores: simple frequency, relative frequency, percentage frequency, cumulative simple frequency, cumulative relative frequency, and cumulative percentage frequency distribution. Include the lower and upper real limits of the class intervals and the midpoint of each class interval. Use 20 class intervals.

   b. What conclusions about stotting distances are you able to reach from the information in the grouped frequency distributions?

   c. Find the percentile rank of a distance of 68 meters.

   d. What is the 50th percentile for this distribution?

Presenting Frequency Distributions Graphically

Frequency distributions such as those in Tables 3.2 and 3.4 provide a systematic way of looking at data to understand their characteristics. To further this understanding, the information contained in a frequency distribution is often displayed in the form of a graph, such as a histogram or a frequency polygon. There are several common rules for constructing such graphs.

▶ The two axes of the graph are drawn at right (90°) angles to each other. The horizontal axis is identified as the *x axis* or the *abscissa*. The vertical axis is called the *y axis* or *ordinate*.

▶ The possible scores, or the class intervals of the possible scores in a grouped frequency distribution, are located along the *x* axis. The measure of frequency (e.g., simple frequency, relative frequency, percentage frequency, cumulative frequency, etc.) is placed on the *y* axis.

▶ Lower value scores are always placed to the left of the *x* axis and increasing values to the right.

▶ Each axis is labeled so that the reader knows what information is being graphed.

▶ The origin of each axis is normally at zero. If a part of the scale between the zero origin and the first recorded score or frequency of a score is left off the axis, then a break, indicated by / /, is inserted into the axis.

▶ A scale should be chosen for the *y* axis such that the maximum height of the frequency measure is about two-thirds to three-fourths of the width of the *x* axis.

▶ All graphs must have a caption identifying the scores contained in the graph.

Histograms

Histogram ▶ A form of bar graph in which the frequency of occurrence of scores in a class interval is given by the height of the bar, and the size of each class interval is represented by the width of the bar on the abscissa.

A **histogram** uses the height of a vertical bar to show the frequency of occurrence for scores in a class interval. The size of each class interval is represented by the width of the bar on the abscissa. Histograms are usually drawn only for grouped frequency distributions, and the measure of frequency typically used is either the simple frequency tabulation or the relative frequency for a class interval (columns e and f of Table 3.4, respectively). A histogram of the grouped simple frequency of the Implicit View of Intelligence scores from Table 3.4 is presented in Figure 3.3. To construct a histogram, the midpoints of the class intervals or the class intervals themselves are plotted on the abscissa. The bar that represents the frequency of each interval is centered on the midpoint of the class interval, and the vertical sides of each bar are drawn at the real limits of each class interval. Scores on the abscissa are usually indicated by the numerical value of the midpoint of each class interval, as illustrated in Figure 3.3 (and see also Figure 3.5). The frequency of occurrence of scores is plotted on the ordinate, and the height of each bar is drawn to the frequency of the class interval it represents.

Frequency Polygons

Frequency polygon ▶ A graph constructed by placing the midpoints of each class interval of a frequency distribution on the abscissa and indicating the frequency of a class interval by placing a dot at the appropriate frequency above the midpoint. The dots are connected with straight lines.

A **frequency polygon** is constructed by placing the midpoints of each class interval on the abscissa and indicating the frequency of a class interval by placing a dot at the appropriate frequency above the midpoint. The dots are then connected by straight lines. Figure 3.4 portrays a frequency polygon of the grouped Implicit View of Intelligence scores of Table 3.4.

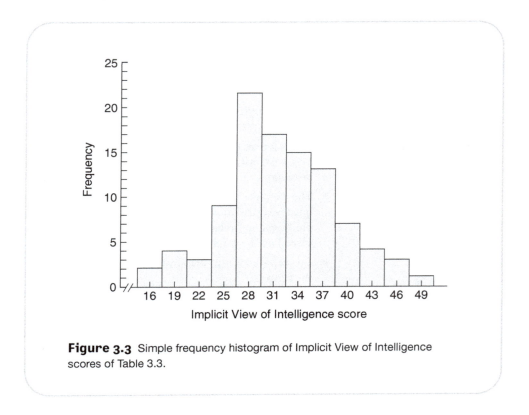

Figure 3.3 Simple frequency histogram of Implicit View of Intelligence scores of Table 3.3.

The frequency measure used is the simple frequency tabulation in column e of the table. Notice in Figure 3.4 that one extra class interval containing no scores has been included at each end of the distribution and the frequency polygon has been brought to zero at each end of the graph (at the midpoints of 13 and 52). This practice is commonly followed in the construction of frequency polygons.

Relative Frequency Histograms and Polygons

Histograms and frequency polygons may be constructed using relative frequencies in place of the simple frequencies used in Figures 3.3 and 3.4. A histogram and a frequency polygon of the Implicit View of Intelligence scores using relative frequencies (from column f of Table 3.4) are presented in Figures 3.5 and 3.6, respectively.

The benefit of using relative frequencies for a histogram or frequency polygon is that the relative frequency values indicate the proportion of scores falling in the various class intervals. Thus, if two different frequency distributions, each based on a different total number of scores, are being compared, relative frequencies make direct comparison easier than do simple frequencies.

Obtaining Information from a Histogram or a Frequency Polygon

The histogram and frequency polygon present the same information as does a frequency distribution. The advantage of histograms and frequency polygons is that this visual

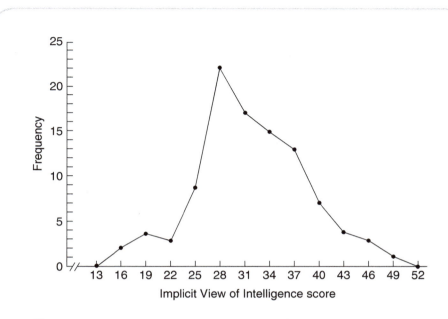

Figure 3.4 Simple frequency polygon of Implicit View of Intelligence scores of Table 3.3.

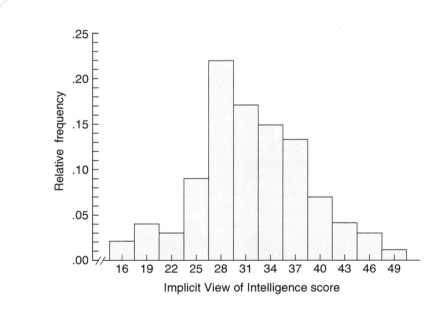

Figure 3.5 Relative frequency histogram of Implicit View of Intelligence scores of Table 3.3.

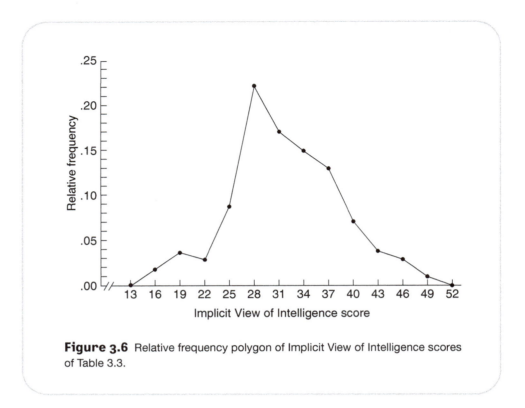

Figure 3.6 Relative frequency polygon of Implicit View of Intelligence scores of Table 3.3.

presentation of information may be more easily understood. By referring to any one of Figures 3.3, 3.4, 3.5, and 3.6, you can see that the peak of the distribution of the scores is in the high 20s and that the majority of scores are in the range from 25 to 40.

Graphic Presentation of Qualitative Data

Qualitative data ▷ Data obtained from a nominal measurement indicating the kind or the quality of a variable.

To this point, the discussion of graphing has dealt with the graphic presentation of quantitative data where numbers assigned to a variable express the amount or quantity of the variable measured. When measurements are at the nominal level, however, responses are simply categorized, and any number assigned to the category merely names the category. Recall from Chapter 2 that we indicated that nominal measurements represent **qualitative data**, the measured variables differ only in quality, not in quantity. For example, Trinkaus, in a series of studies using naturalistic observation (1982, 1983, 1988, 1993, 1997, 1999), categorized drivers' behavior at a highway stop sign into one of three categories: 1, coming to a full stop; 2, coming to a rolling stop; and 3, not stopping at all. These categories differ qualitatively; they label the behavior, but they do not tell us how it differs in amount. Trinkaus counted the number of occurrences of each behavior and found the percentage frequencies of occurrence of each category. These percentage frequencies can be presented graphically in the form of a **bar graph**, as shown in Figure 3.7, which presents data representative of those reported by Trinkaus.

Bar graph ▷ A graph used to present a frequency distribution when the variable measured is qualitative in nature. The frequency of occurrence of scores in a category is given by the height of the bar.

A bar graph is similar to a histogram, except the bars are separated on the *x* axis to indicate that the categories do not represent a continuous measurement. The distance

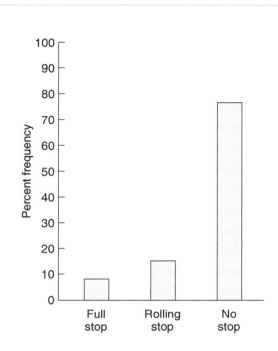

Figure 3.7 Percentage frequency of occurrence of three categories of stop sign behavior representative of that reported by Trinkaus (1982, 1983, 1988, 1993, 1997, 1999).

between the bars is arbitrary but is the same for each bar. Either simple frequencies, relative frequencies, or percentage frequencies (as illustrated in Figure 3.7) may be used to indicate the frequency of occurrence of each category. From this graph we easily note that the most frequently occurring behavior at the intersections observed was category 3, not stopping at all.

Shapes of Frequency Distributions

A distribution of scores may take on any of a variety of shapes. Thus, there usually is no simple way to describe precisely the shape of a frequency distribution in a word or two. There are, however, some general descriptive terms that apply to the shape of a distribution. To illustrate, Figure 3.8 presents examples of several different frequency polygon shapes.

Symmetrical Frequency Distributions

Symmetrical frequency distribution ▸ A frequency distribution that, when folded at a midpoint, produces two halves identical in shape.

A **symmetrical frequency distribution**, if it were folded in half, would produce two halves identical in shape. One side of the distribution is a mirror image of the other. Distributions (a), (b), and (c) in Figure 3.8 are symmetrical distributions, but distributions

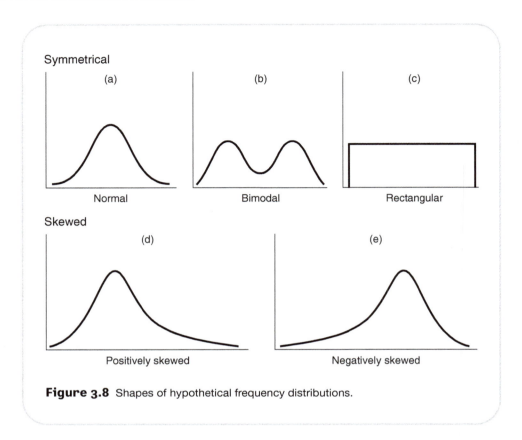

Figure 3.8 Shapes of hypothetical frequency distributions.

(d) and (e) are not symmetrical; they are **asymmetrical**. The symmetrical bell-shaped or normal distribution shown in Figure 3.8a is of special importance in the behavioral sciences. We discuss it more fully in Chapter 6.

Skewness

Skewed distribution ▸ A frequency distribution in which scores are clustered at one end of the distribution, with scores occurring infrequently at the other end of the distribution.

It is rare to obtain a perfectly symmetrical distribution of raw data for a given measure. Instead, a frequency distribution is likely to be asymmetrical or skewed. In a **skewed distribution**, scores are clustered at one end of the distribution, with scores occurring infrequently at the other end (or tail) of the distribution. A distribution is described as **positively skewed** if the tail occurs for the high scores at the right of the distribution (Figure 3.8d) or **negatively skewed** if the tail occurs for the low scores at the left of the distribution (Figure 3.8e).

Modality

Mode ▸ The most frequently occurring score in a distribution of scores.

Distributions are also described in terms of the number of modes possessed. The **mode** is the most frequently occurring score in a distribution of scores. A **unimodal distribution** has just one most frequently occurring score (see Figures 3.8a, d, and e). A frequency distribution that has two modes is described as **bimodal** (illustrated in Figure 3.8b). Many behavioral scientists consider a distribution bimodal if it has two distinct peaks, even if the peaks do not represent scores with equal frequencies of occurrence. A **multimodal distribution** has three or more score values that are the most frequently occurring scores. Again, a distribution may be considered multimodal if it has three or more peaks, even if the frequencies of occurrence of each peak are not equal. There is no mode in the flat rectangular distribution illustrated in Figure 3.8c; in such distributions, each score occurs an equal number of times, or nearly so. We discuss the mode more fully in Chapter 4.

Misleading Graphs

It should come as no surprise that something as useful for displaying data as a graph can also be used to mislead others. There are several commonly used approaches to misrepresenting data graphically, and we review several of them in this section.

Look at Figure 3.9a. Which political candidate, Abby Good or Kristin Brown, would you judge to be more liberal in her voting record? Abby would like you to believe that she is much less liberal than Kristin and thus shows you the graph of her voting record in Figure 3.9a. And if you said that Kristin is much more liberal than Abby, then Abby's trick worked. Notice in Figure 3.9a the starting point of the scale on the ordinate is not at zero, but at an arbitrary 80 percent. If you examine the graph carefully, you will see that there is only a 6 percentage point difference in the voting record of the two candidates, but this small difference is difficult to discern without noting that the ordinate scale begins at 80 instead of zero. Figure 3.9b presents the same voting record with the scale on the ordinate beginning at zero. Now it is easy to see that the voting records differ by very little.

Leaving the scale off the ordinate axis can also be used to try to create the impression that there is little difference between two things. Suppose that an automobile manufacturer wants you to believe that its Flying 8 sports car gets almost as good gas mileage as its competitor's Pokey 4 city car and presents the graph shown in Figure 3.9c. At first glance it appears that both cars get almost the same gas mileage. Then you notice there is no scale given on the ordinate. If a scale had been given, as shown in Figure 3.9d, then it's easy to see that Figure 3.9c is very misleading. The scale used to draw this figure covers a range of gas mileages that no car today actually obtains and thus makes it appear that the two cars differ little in gas mileage. A more appropriate graph is that shown in Figure 3.9e. Here the scale on the ordinate corresponds much more closely to the reality of actual gas mileages, and it is clear the Pokey 4 is 50 percent more fuel efficient than the Flying 8. The important point that arises from these two examples is that you should always carefully examine the ordinate scale on any graph. Using a misleading scale can create the appearance of large differences where only small ones exist or can visually minimize larger differences.

For another example of how graphing may create a visually misleading impression, consider the following example. A group of 100 psychology majors were asked in their first year and then again in their senior year what specialization within psychology they hoped to enter in the future. The following responses were obtained:

	Area of Specialization			
	Clinical or Counseling	School or Guidance	Applied or Organizational	Experimental
First-year students	80	12	6	2
Senior student	54	18	18	10

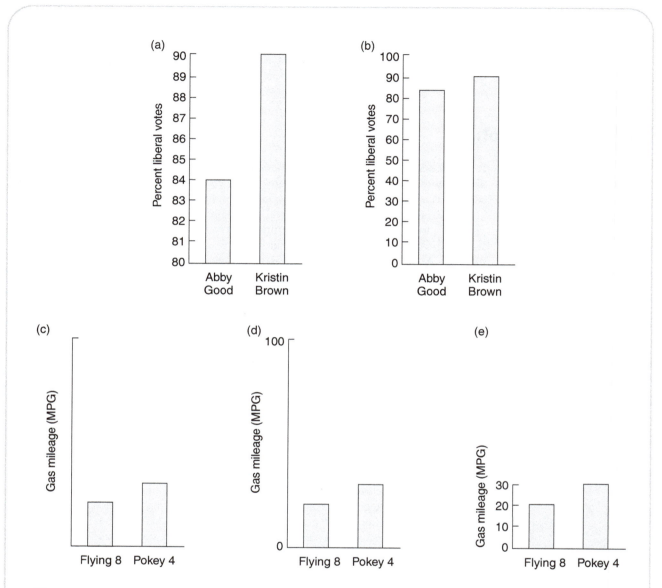

Figure 3.9 (a) Percent liberal votes for Abby Good and Kristin Brown. (b) Percent liberal votes for Abby Good and Kristin Brown. (c) Gas mileage of Flying 8 sports car and Pokey 4 city car. (d) Gas mileage of Flying 8 sports car and Pokey 4 city car. (e) Gas mileage of Flying 8 sports car and Pokey 4 city car. (*continued*)

You would like to present a graph that shows this change in specialization plans between the first and senior years. One way would be a graph of the percentage change for each area of specialization from the first to senior year. Such a graph is shown in Figure 3.9f. Notice the graph shows a 400 percent increase in the number of students planning to specialize in experimental psychology and a 33 percent decrease in those planning to specialize in clinical or counseling psychology. From this graph you might think that four years of being a psychology major makes most students want to become experimental psychologists and only

(f)

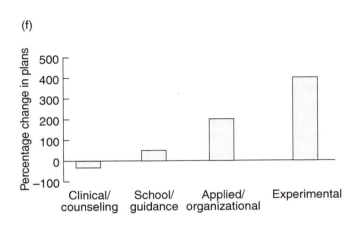

(g)

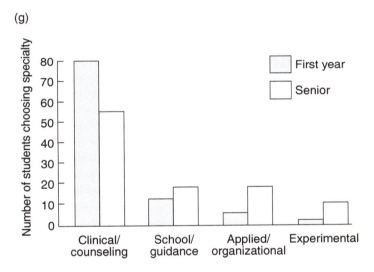

Figure 3.9 (*continued*) (f) Percentage change in career plans from first-year to senior-year psychology majors. (g) Career plans for first-year and senior-year psychology majors.

a few become counseling or clinical psychologists. In reality, only two first-year students plan to become experimental psychologists, thus even an increase of one or two students wanting this specialty in the senior year causes a large percentage change in the choice of this specialty. The majority of first-year students want counseling or clinical psychology, and the majority of senior-level students still want this specialty, although the total number has decreased from the first-year. But we don't get that impression from this graph.

Figure 3.9g is a better representation of these results. Here the ordinate indicates the number of students choosing a particular specialty for both the first year and the senior year rather than a percentage change. We can clearly see that the number of students choosing experimental psychology has increased by eight students; nevertheless, it is still the least popular of the specialties represented. And, we can clearly see that although the number of students choosing counseling or clinical psychology has dropped from the first to the senior year, it is still the most frequent choice of specialization among seniors.

It has been said that a picture is worth a 1000 words; however, no matter how nice it looks or how compelling it appears to be, a graph is only as good as the quality of the measures, research design, and data that are represented in it. Accordingly, don't just rely on graphs to convey information to you. Critically evaluate the research method, measurement, and data collection techniques. Be particularly critical when the person illustrating the graph has a motivation to present information in a less than accurate manner. And, when you are presenting information of your own, always try to accurately represent what is occurring with your data. Ultimately, as a scientist, it is your job to present the information as accurately as possible.

Testing Your Knowledge 3.3

1. Define: asymmetrical distribution, bar graph, bimodal distribution, frequency polygon, histogram, mode, multimodal distribution, negatively skewed distribution, positively skewed distribution, qualitative data, skewed distribution, symmetrical frequency distribution, unimodal distribution.

2. Question 7a of Testing Your Knowledge 3.2 required you to construct a frequency distribution of the estimated distance of a predator from a gazelle when the gazelle first stotted. Use that frequency distribution to answer question 2a and b.

   a. Construct a histogram and a frequency polygon for the estimated distances using the simple frequencies of a grouped distribution with a class interval of 10 meters.

   b. Construct a relative frequency histogram and a relative frequency polygon from the grouped distribution of question 2a.

   c. What conclusions do you reach about stotting distances from the graphs that you have constructed?

3. Describe the frequency distributions in Figure 3.10 with respect to symmetry, skewness, and modality.

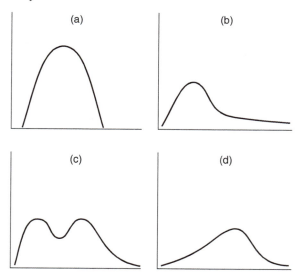

Figure 3.10 Frequency distributions for question 3.

Summary

▶ A frequency distribution shows each score in a set of scores and how frequently each score occurs.

▶ Frequency distributions are used to organize raw data.

▶ An ungrouped frequency distribution may be used when there is not a large number of scores in the data set.

▶ Grouped frequency distributions are used when the number of scores becomes large or the scores extend over a wide range of values.

▶ Ungrouped or grouped frequency distributions may be portrayed as simple, relative, or percentage frequencies.

▶ The percentile rank of a score indicates the percentage of scores in the distribution that are equal to or less than that score.

▶ A percentile is the score at or below which a specified percentage of scores in a distribution fall.

▶ Frequency distributions may be presented graphically as histograms or frequency polygons.

▶ Qualitative data may be presented graphically in a bar graph.

▶ Shapes of frequency distributions are described in terms of their symmetry, skewness, and modality.

 ## Key Terms and Symbols

asymmetrical frequency distribution (58)

bar graph (56)

bimodal distribution (58)

class interval (42)

cumulative frequency of a class interval (46)

cumulative frequency of a score (*cf* or *cum f*) (46)

cumulative grouped percentage frequency of a class interval (*c%f* or *cum%f*) (46)

cumulative grouped relative frequency of a class interval (*crf* or *cum rf*) (46)

f (39)

frequency distribution (38)

frequency polygon (53)

grouped frequency distribution (42)

grouped percentage frequency distribution (46)

grouped relative frequency distribution (45)

histogram (53)

i (43)

lower real limit of a class interval (45)

lower stated limit of a class interval (44)

midpoint of a class interval (45)

mode (58)

multimodal distribution (59)

N (38)

negatively skewed distribution (58)

percent (39)

percentage (39)

percentage frequency (*%f*) (39)

percentile (48)

percentile rank of a score (46)

positively skewed distribution (58)

qualitative data (56)

raw data (38)

raw scores (38)

real limits of a class interval (45)

relative frequency (*rf*) (39)

skewed distribution (58)

size of class interval (43)

stated limits of a class interval (upper and lower) (44)

symmetrical frequency distribution (57)

ungrouped frequency distribution (39)

unimodal distribution (58)

upper real limit of a class interval (45)

upper stated limit of a class interval (44)

X (43)

Review Questions

1. Jansz and Tanis (2007) conducted an online survey of 50 people, asking them to report how much time they spend a day playing video games to the nearest half hour. Suppose that the following scores, in hours, were reported: 4.0, 0.5, 2.0, 0.0, 1.5, 0.5, 1.5, 1.0, 6.0, 0.0, 2.0, 4.5, 1.0, 1.5, 0.0, 0.0, 2.0, 5.5, 0.0, 0.5, 3.0, 0.0, 2.5, 4.5, 1.0, 2.0, 0.0, 1.5, 1.0, 3.5, 3.0, 1.5, 2.0, 5.0, 2.5, 0.0, 1.0, 2.5, 4.0, 3.5, 0.5, 1.0, 2.5, 3.5, 1.0, 0.5, 0.0, 0.0, 2.0, 3.0.

    a. Construct a simple frequency distribution including relative and cumulative relative frequencies for these scores.

    b. What are the lowest and highest scores in this distribution?

    c. What is the most frequently occurring score?

    d. Find the 50th percentile of this distribution.

    e. What is the percentile rank of a score of 2.0 hours?

    f. Construct a histogram using simple frequencies from the distribution that you found in question 1a.

    g. Describe the shape of the distribution in terms of its skewness and modality.

2. A professor was interested in getting a sense of how much time her students spend preparing for class by studying and completing assignments. She asked students to provide her with the average number of hours they spend a week preparing for her class. She collected the following scores for 25 students: 7, 6, 5, 8, 6, 11, 8, 12, 7, 7, 4, 11, 10, 9, 9, 8, 11, 9, 9, 5, 6, 10, 8, 10, and 9.

    a. Construct a simple frequency distribution including relative and cumulative relative frequencies for these scores.

    b. If Miguel studies 10 hours a week, how does he compare to other students in the class using the information you just calculated?

    c. Many professors have an unspoken expectation that students should put in three hours of work outside of class for every one hour in class. This professor's class is 3 hours long, thus she expects students to be completing 9 or more hours of work preparation outside of class. What is the percentile rank for 9 hours? What does this mean with respect to the number of students who are satisfying this professor's expectation of work outside of the classroom?

    d. What is the score at the 50th percentile?

3. Suppose that you observed male and female drivers in a mall parking lot and counted the frequency with which they illegally parked in handicapped parking areas. Over a three-day period you observed that 12 of every 100 male drivers and 7 of every 100 female drivers parked illegally. Construct a bar graph of the relative frequency of illegal parking in handicapped spaces by male and female drivers.

4. Sturgeon and Beer (1990) report that an attendance policy of rewarding students who attend school regularly by exempting them from semester tests increases attendance in comparison to no such policy. Suppose that you compare attendance at two high schools, one that has a reward policy in effect and one that does not, and you obtain the following simple frequency distribution of absences:

Number of Days Absent	Reward Policy School	No Reward Policy School
More than 25	2	6
24–25	0	6
22–23	2	1
20–21	0	8
18–19	1	0
16–17	0	4
14–15	2	22
12–13	0	10
10–11	3	18
8–9	8	20
6–7	4	3
4–5	13	14
2–3	23	34
0–1	42	54
Total	100	200

a. Construct a relative frequency distribution for each school.

b. What is the 50th percentile for each school?

c. What is the percentile rank for four absences at each school?

d. Do the schools appear to differ in absence rates? Describe the distributions.

5. As the pace of life becomes more hectic, it seems there is more and more for each of us to remember each day. As part of a study of memory under natural conditions, a psychologist asked 120 college students to keep a record of the things they had to remember to do on a typical weekday. Suppose the psychologist presented the results in the following frequency polygon.

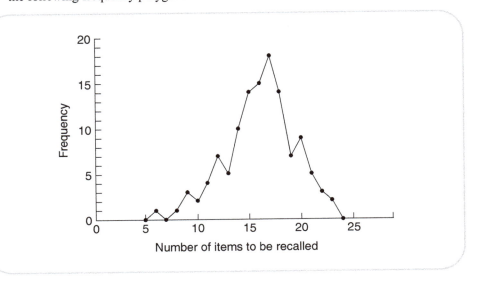

a. What is the lowest and the highest score reported?

b. What is the most frequently occurring score?

c. How many students gave responses of between 14 to 19 things to remember?

6. As a class project, members of a social psychology class interviewed 100 women ages 25 to 54 and asked them to estimate the amount of time they watched TV per day. Their estimates in minutes are shown in the following grouped frequency distribution.

Class Interval	Tally
510–539	/
480–509	
450–479	//
420–449	/////
390–419	//////
360–389	/////
330–359	/////////
300–329	////////
270–299	/////////
240–269	//////////
210–239	/////////
180–209	///
150–179	///////
120–149	//
90–119	////////
60–89	/////
30–59	///////
0–29	////

a. What is the width (i) of the class interval used in the preceding table?

b. What are the lower and upper real limits for the class interval of 210 to 239?

c. What is the midpoint of the class interval of 210 to 239?

d. Construct a grouped simple frequency and cumulative frequency distribution for these scores.

e. What is the 75th percentile of this distribution?

f. What is the percentile rank for a score of 264 minutes spent watching TV?

7. Twenty-five patrons of a health club were asked to estimate how long they exercised each day. The estimates given in minutes were 67, 73, 79, 78, 50, 80, 98, 88, 79, 71, 57, 81, 41, 65, 50, 71, 91, 75, 60, 79, 79, 71, 65, 85, and 64.

a. Using a class width of $i = 5$, construct a grouped relative frequency and a cumulative relative frequency distribution for the scores. What should be the lower stated limit of the first class interval? Why?

b. Describe the shape of the distribution.

c. What is the percentile rank of a score of 78 minutes?

d. Suppose a person would like to exercise sufficiently long each day so that she is among the top 25 percent of the people in the distribution. What would be the minimum amount of time she would need to exercise to achieve this goal?

8. Building upon the Cassaday et al. (2002) study of the effect of background conditions on learning material discussed in Chapter 1, suppose we wanted to see what effect a different operational definition for relaxation during studying would have. Instead of using a dimly lit room, the scent of lavender, and soft music, suppose we had students select their own light level, scent, and music in which to study, encouraging them to select whatever would help them to relax. We then measured the number of errors each student in this condition made on a recall of material learned under these conditions and obtained the following errors for 50 students: 5, 2, 2, 1, 0, 4, 2, 1, 1, 0, 3, 3, 0, 0, 0, 1, 0, 2, 1, 7, 5, 0, 2, 4, 0, 5, 3, 6, 0, 1, 3, 5, 2, 4, 2, 0, 5, 1, 3, 6, 4, 1, 0, 3, 4, 2, 0, 1, 3, 6.

   a. Construct the following frequency distributions for these scores: simple, relative, percentage, simple cumulative, cumulative relative, and cumulative percentage.

   b. What conclusions about the scores may you reach from these distributions?

   c. Find the percentile rank for a score of 3 errors.

   d. What is the 50th percentile for this distribution?

knowledge

Periodically, throughout this text we will present a section called Integrating Your Knowledge. These sections will be divided into three parts. Part A, A Look at a Problem, will provide you with information from a published research study. Your job will be to read the summary of the article in order to understand what is being reported and answer the questions that follow. Part B, Your Turn: Selecting Your Research Tools, will require you to expand on the research that was reported and design a study of your own. You will often have to determine what type of research design you will use, what type of data you will need to collect, and what statistical calculations you will need to provide answers to the questions asked. There are no necessarily "right" answers to this part, for there are always many ways to research a problem. Part C, Using Your Statistical Tools, will provide you some data from a hypothetical study and ask you to apply statistical methods to it.

You will need to apply information from all previous chapters in the text in the Integrating Your Knowledge section, not merely the chapter you have just completed. You may also be asked to think about questions that will be addressed in later chapters. As with many academic pursuits, you may find this task challenging the first time you complete it, but with practice over the course of the semester, you will soon find yourself thinking like a behavioral scientist!

PART A

A Look at a Problem   At a recent meeting of research psychologists, one psychologist suggested in a talk that parenting children does not make people happy. This suggestion was based partially on research findings by Kahneman, Krueger, Schkade, Schwartz, and Stone (2004). In their research, Kahneman et al. used a method called the *day reconstruction method (DRM)*. With this method, a person is asked to reconstruct their previous day as a series of episodes or events. For example, an episode might be "discussing a new project at work with a colleague," or "helping my daughter with homework." Kahneman et al. asked 909 working women to complete the DRM for the previous day. After the women had reconstructed the episodes of the previous day, they were asked to evaluate how they felt about the episodes by rating each on a series of 12 descriptive terms such as *happy, enjoying myself*, and *warm/friendly*. Each episode was rated on each term on a scale from zero ("not at all," e.g., not at all enjoying myself) to 6 ("very much," e.g., very much enjoying myself). The scores for the terms *happy, enjoying myself*, and *warm/friendly* were then summed and averaged for each episode to give a positive affect score for the episode. The word *affect* refers to feelings or emotions, thus a positive feelings or emotions score was obtained for each episode.

1. Based on the types of research methods presented in Chapter 2, which method was used in this research?
2. How did Kahneman et al. operationally define positive affect?
3. What level of measurement was used in measuring positive affect?
4. Does this measurement provide qualitative or quantitative data?
5. Name the type of measuring scale used.
6. Kahneman et al. identified 16 types of episodes that were generally reported by the subjects. Suppose you were told that the episode "taking care of children" ranked 12th

on positive affect, "commuting" ranked 16th, and "intimate relations" ranked 1 on positive affect. What conclusion could you reach about how women in the sample viewed taking care of children in relation to other activities?

7. From this ranking alone, can you conclude that episodes categorized as "taking care of children" were not a source of positive affect for the mothers? Explain your answer.

PART B

Your Turn Selecting Your Research Tools   Sitting in the audience with her parents during this talk was Elizabeth, who firmly believes that she is a continuing source of positive affect to her parents. Elizabeth was somewhat distressed upon hearing the suggestion that taking care of children does not make parents happy, and she decided she would like to investigate this question more fully for a science project for her school. Your job is to help Elizabeth test her hypothesis that being a mom or dad does make a parent happy much of the time, even though some individual tasks (e.g., diaper changes or talking with mouthy teenagers) may not be viewed as fun.

1. What type of a research method would you select for your study?

2. Who would you select to participate in the study?

3. How many people do you think you would need to have participate so that you could be confident of your results?

4. How would you measure how happy a parent is because of their children? Provide an operational definition of this measurement. What might a person's score be, for example, would it be a number on a rating scale, a rank ordering, or something else?

5. What level of measurement does your measure achieve? Is it a qualitative or quantitative measure?

6. After you completed your study, supposed you were asked to give a presentation of it to your classmates. How would you present your results to them so they could understand what you had found?

    a. Would your results lend themselves to a ranking?

    b. Would you be able to put your results into a frequency distribution? Explain your answer.

PART C

Using Your Statistical Tools   Assume you developed a measure of happiness about being a parent and you collected the following scores from 25 parents. The higher the score, the greater the happiness reported. Organize these scores in a manner that will help you understand what is going on with these data. Describe the distribution in as much detail as possible.

15	7	15	15	17
16	8	14	16	12
11	13	17	9	18
19	18	16	16	18
13	14	17	17	16

Looking at Data: Measures of Central Tendency

C hances are that you took an exam recently either in this class or another one. When grades were returned, you probably wanted to know how the class as a whole did on the exam. Most likely, the professor indicated what the typical grade was and how much the grades varied from one another. In this instance, the professor provided you with some descriptive statistics to help you better understand your grade in the context of the other grades on the exam. In the last chapter, we introduced how to organize data by using frequency distributions and graphs. Although frequency distributions and graphs present a great deal of information about the shape of a distribution of scores and the range of scores, a scientist often needs to describe a distribution of scores with only one number. These plain but mighty numbers are called **descriptive statistics** for they describe the raw data with a single number. There are two types of descriptive statistics that are commonly used. One type, called **measures of central tendency**, indicates the typical score obtained, and the other type, called **measures of variability** or *measures of dispersion*, indicates the amount of variation or dispersion around the typical score. By having both a measure of central tendency and a measure of variability, you can have a good idea of what is going on with your data, just as knowing what the typical exam score was and how varied the scores were helped you to understand how students performed on an exam.

Measures of central tendency and variability have two uses. The first is to describe the scores of a sample, which is why they are called *descriptive statistics*. The second use is to estimate or infer characteristics of the population from which the sample was selected. For example, the researcher of Chapter 3 may be interested in estimating the typical Implicit View of Intelligence score in the population of students at her college. One way to do so would be to base this estimate on a descriptive statistic obtained from the scores of her sample of 100 students.

The remainder of this chapter is concerned with a discussion of three measures of central tendency commonly used: the mean, median, and mode. Measures of variability and the use of descriptive statistics for inferring population characteristics are introduced in Chapters 5 and 7, respectively.

Descriptive statistics ▶ Statistical procedures used to summarize and describe the data from a sample.

Measures of central tendency ▶ Numbers that represent the average or typical score obtained from measurements of a sample.

Measures of variability ▶ Numbers that indicate how much scores differ from each other and the measure of central tendency in a set of scores.

Sample Mean

Sample mean ($\overline{X}$) ▶ The sum of a set of scores divided by the number of scores summed.

The most familiar measure of central tendency is the sample mean. The **sample mean**, often called the **arithmetic mean**, or simply the **mean**, is the sum of a set of scores divided by the number of scores summed. Stated in statistical notation,

$$\text{Sample mean} = \overline{X} = \frac{\Sigma X}{N}$$

where $\overline{X}$ = mean (pronounced "X-bar").
Σ = summation sign (the Greek capital letter sigma); it indicates summing or adding up a set of numbers.
X = score for any individual.
N = number of scores in the sample.

The notation ΣX, called the *sum of X*, is simply statistical notation for obtaining the sum for a set of scores. For example, the ΣX for the scores 2, 4, and 6 is 12.

Calculating the Sample Mean

Assume that we obtained the following six Implicit View of Intelligence scores: 34, 23, 31, 28, 26, and 32. The sample mean for this set of scores is obtained as follows.

First, we find the sum of the scores, or

$$\Sigma X = 34 + 23 + 31 + 28 + 26 + 32 = 174.$$

The number of scores, N, equals 6. To find the mean of the scores, we divide the sum, 174, by 6, or

$$\overline{X} = \frac{\Sigma X}{N} = \frac{174}{6} = 29.0^1.$$

The mean of the 100 Implicit View of Intelligence scores in Table 3.3 is found by summing the 100 scores and then dividing the sum by 100. In notation,

$$\overline{X} = \frac{28 + 31 + 19 + \cdots + 36 + 40 + 37}{100}$$

$$= \frac{3176}{100} = 31.76 = 31.8.$$

EXAMPLE PROBLEM

4.1

Calculating the Mean

Problem: Studies investigating visual perception of real-world scenes sometimes present an individual with a picture of a scene for study and then asks the person to recall details of the scene. Suppose that you followed this procedure with 18 people and found the following number of details recalled by each person: 7, 3, 7, 9, 6, 10, 14, 3, 6, 9, 14, 9, 8, 5, 4, 6, 9, 13. Find the mean of these scores.

Statistic to Be Used: $\overline{X} = \dfrac{\Sigma X}{N}.$

Solution: The first step is to obtain ΣX, which equals

$$7 + 3 + 7 + 9 + 6 + 10 + 14 + 3 + 6 + 9 + 14 + 9 + 8 + 5 + 4 + 6 + 9 + 13 = 142.$$

N is the number of scores added, or 18 in this example. Accordingly,

$$\overline{X} = \frac{\Sigma X}{N} = \frac{142}{18} = 7.89 = 7.9.$$

Characteristics of the Sample Mean

Calculating the mean requires the numerical value of every score in the distribution. Thus, any change of a score in a distribution will necessarily change the value of the mean for that distribution. For example, consider six Implicit View of Intelligence scores: 28, 30, 34, 35, 37, 40. The mean of this distribution is 34.0. If only one score, for example, 34, changes to a 43, the mean is now 35.5. Because the mean depends on the magnitude of

---

[1]We will follow the convention of rounding the final value of a computation to one decimal place beyond the value to which the original scores were measured. If computations require a number of steps prior to obtaining the final answer, then, depending on the accuracy needed for the final answer, we will carry intermediate numerical values to two or three decimal places beyond the number of decimal places needed for the final answer. Additional guidelines for rounding are given in Appendix A.

Outlier ▶ An extreme score in a distribution.

each score, *outliers* in a distribution may affect the value of the mean and distort its value as a measure of central tendency. An **outlier** is an extreme score that is not typical of the other scores in the distribution. For example, suppose that the 34 in the distribution of six Implicit View of Intelligence scores changes not to a 40 but to a 13. In comparison to the other scores in the distribution, 13 is an outlier; it is considerably different from the other scores. The mean now decreases to 30.5. Accordingly, if a distribution includes a few outliers, the mean may not be a representative typical score.

A second characteristic of the mean is that the differences of a set of scores from the mean of those scores sum to zero. The difference of a score from the mean of a set of scores, that is, $X - \overline{X}$, is often called a **deviation**. Notationally,

Deviation ▶ The difference of a score in a set of scores from the mean of that set of scores.

$$\Sigma(X - \overline{X}) = 0.$$

This notation indicates that if we obtain the deviation of each score in a set of scores and then sum the deviations, the sum of the deviations will be zero. Table 4.1 illustrates this relation. Column a of Table 4.1 portrays seven Implicit View of Intelligence scores with a mean of 35.0. The numerical value of the mean is subtracted from each of the seven scores in column b of the table. The sum of column b, $\Sigma(X - \overline{X})$, is zero.

For any set of scores, the value of $\Sigma(X - \overline{X})$ will always be zero. But the value of $\Sigma(X - \overline{X})^2$ will not be zero unless each score in the distribution is equal to the mean. This value is calculated in column c of the table, where each deviation of a score from the mean is squared (i.e., multiplied by itself). For example, the score of 22 differs from $\overline{X}$ by -13, and $(-13)^2 = 169$. The total of the scores in column c, $\Sigma(X - \overline{X})^2$, is 264. The value of $\Sigma(X - \overline{X})^2$ is used frequently in statistical calculations and is called a **sum of squares** (abbreviated *SS*). Thus,

Sum of squares (SS) ▶ A numerical value obtained by subtracting the mean of a distribution from each score in the distribution, squaring each difference, and then summing the differences.

$$\textbf{Sum of squares} = \textbf{SS} = \Sigma(X - \overline{X})^2.$$

It can be demonstrated mathematically that, for a set of scores, the sum of squares is smaller than the squared deviation of the scores from any other statistic, such as the median or the mode of the scores. The sum of squares will be used in Chapter 5 as part of a measure of the variability of scores.

TABLE 4.1	Set of seven scores (column a) with a mean of 35.0. Column b shows the value of $X - \overline{X}$ for each score. In column c, the $X - \overline{X}$ deviation is squared for each score.

(a) X	(b) $X - \overline{X}$	(c) $(X - \overline{X})^2$
22	$22 - 35 = -13$	169
34	$34 - 35 = -1$	1
35	$35 - 35 = 0$	0
35	$35 - 35 = 0$	0
37	$37 - 35 = +2$	4
38	$38 - 35 = +3$	9
44	$44 - 35 = +9$	81
$\overline{X}$ 35.0	$\Sigma(X - \overline{X}) = 0$	$SS = 264$

Population Mean

Population mean (μ) ▶ The sum of all the scores in a population divided by the number of scores summed.

A mean for a population of scores is calculated in a manner similar to that of the mean for a sample of scores, except N represents the number of scores in the population and the value of the mean is represented symbolically by the Greek letter μ (mu, the 12th letter of the Greek alphabet, pronounced "mew") rather than $\overline{X}$. Thus, a **population mean** is given by

$$\text{Population mean} = \mu = \frac{\Sigma X}{N_{\text{population}}}.$$

In most instances μ will be estimated from $\overline{X}$ because we cannot measure all the scores in a population. We discuss the characteristics of the sample mean as an estimator of the population mean more fully in Chapter 7.

Testing Your Knowledge 4.1

1. Define: arithmetic mean, descriptive statistics, deviation, M, measures of central tendency, measures of variability, μ, N, outlier, population mean, Σ, sample mean, sum of squares, SS, ΣX, $\overline{X}$.

2. Identify two uses of descriptive statistics.

3. Assume you obtained the following exam scores from six students: 97, 90, 86, 93, 76, and 86.

   a. Find the mean for the scores.

   b. Demonstrate that $\Sigma(X - \overline{X}) = 0$ for these scores.

   c. Find the value of $\Sigma(X - \overline{X})^2$ for these scores.

4. Assume that a researcher measured self-esteem in 10 seventh-grade girls and obtained the scores 49, 53, 67, 20, 27, 36, 49, 27, 61, and 28.

   a. Find the mean of these scores.

   b. Suppose that the experimenter measured one additional seventh-grader and obtained a score of 17. Include this score in the previous distribution and find the mean of the distribution.

   c. Suppose that the score of 67 was changed to 27 so that the scores obtained were 49, 53, 27, 20, 27, 36, 49, 27, 61, and 28. What is the mean of this new set of scores?

   d. Compare your answers for questions 4a, b, and c. What characteristic of the mean is illustrated by your answers?

Median

Median (Mdn) ▶ A score value in the distribution with an equal number of scores above and below it. The median is the 50th percentile in a distribution.

The **median** (abbreviated **Mdn**) corresponds to a score value in the middle of a frequency distribution such that one-half of the scores have values above the median and one-half of them have values below the median. The median, thus, has an equal number of scores above and below it and represents the 50th percentile in a distribution. For most distributions of scores, there are simple ways of finding the median.

Calculating the Median with an Odd Number of Scores

For an odd number of scores in a distribution with no tied scores near the median, the median is usually determined by finding the middle score in the frequency distribution. For example, for seven Implicit View of Intelligence scores of 22, 27, 34, 36, 37, 38, 44, the median is 36. This value is the fourth score and falls in the middle of the distribution of the seven scores. Three scores are less than 36 and three scores are greater than 36. Notice that once the scores are ordered from least to greatest, a counting procedure is used to determine a median. The numerical values of the scores that go into the count are not used in determining the value of the median.

Calculating the Median with an Even Number of Scores

With an even number of scores in a distribution and no tied scores near the median, the median is conventionally taken as the value that lies midway between the two middle scores in the frequency distribution. Consider, for example, six Implicit View of Intelligence scores: 28, 34, 36, 37, 38, 44. The median for these scores is 36.5, a value that falls halfway between 36 (the third score) and 37 (the fourth score). One-half of the six scores lie below a value of 36.5 and one-half lie above it.

EXAMPLE PROBLEM 4.2   **Finding the Median**

Problem: Suppose that you obtained the following 18 scores in a picture recall task, as discussed in Example Problem 4.1: 7, 3, 7, 9, 6, 10, 14, 3, 6, 9, 14, 9, 8, 5, 4, 6, 9, 13. Find the median.

Solution: Eighteen scores are given in the distribution; thus, the median is the score with nine scores on either side of it. Accordingly, the median is midway between the ninth and tenth scores when the scores are placed in a simple frequency distribution, as shown next.

Score	f
14	2
13	1
12	0
11	0
10	1
9	4
8	1
7	2
6	3
5	1
4	1
3	2
2	0
1	0
0	0

9 Scores (scores 14 through 8)

Median $= (7 + 8)/2 = 7.5$

9 Scores (scores 7 through 0)

The ninth score is 7 and the tenth score is 8; thus, the median is 7.5, midway between the scores of 7 and 8.

When there are identical (i.e., tied) scores in the region of the median, the simple methods for obtaining the median will not work. In this instance the percentile formula for the 50th percentile from Chapter 3 may be applied to obtain the median.

Characteristics of the Median

The median essentially is obtained by counting scores, ignoring numerical values except for the score that is the median. Therefore, the median is not influenced by the numerical value of outliers in a distribution. For example, consider distributions A and B below. For both distributions, most of the scores are in the range from 25 to 45, but distribution B contains an outlier score of 114. The median for each distribution is 37; the median ignores the 114 in the tail of distribution B. The means for the distributions, however, differ considerably; the outlier raises the value of the mean by a considerable amount. Both the mean and the median of distribution A are representative of the other scores in the distribution, but the mean of 47.0 for distribution B is larger than any of the scores in the distribution except for the outlier of 114. This mean is not very representative of the scores in the distribution.

A	B
26	26
34	34
35	35
37	37
39	39
44	44
44	114
$Mdn = 37$	$Mdn = 37$
$\overline{X} = 37.0$	$\overline{X} = 47.0$

The fact that the median is not affected by outliers makes it a desirable measure of central tendency for a skewed distribution, that is, a distribution that contains outliers. For example, the median is often reported for the typical income for a population because incomes are heavily positively skewed. There are only a few people who have incomes in the many millions of dollars (i.e., outliers). If the numerical values of these incomes were included in the measure of typical income, it would be too high to represent an average person. The median, however, is not affected by these few large incomes and, thus, provides a measure of central tendency representative of a typical income. As another example, the typical sale price for houses in a community is usually reported as a median, for the sale of one very expensive house in a community of more modest houses might considerably skew the distribution of sale prices.

The median is also often used as a measure of central tendency when not all entries in a distribution have a numerical value. For example, for teams in the National Football League, it typically takes a median of 8 years after being purchased by a new owner to win a championship (Healy, 2008). This median, however, is based only on the 11 teams that have won a Super Bowl since being purchased by a new owner. The other 21 teams in the league have never won the Super Bowl, so there is no numerical value to attach to the number of years before winning the Super Bowl for these teams. Thus the median is used as a measure of central tendency for this distribution.

Mode

Mode ▶ The most frequently occurring score in a distribution of scores.

Unimodal ▶ A distribution with one mode.

Bimodal ▶ A distribution with two modes.

Multimodal ▶ A distribution with more than two modes.

The **mode** is the most frequently occurring score in a distribution of scores. The mode is found by inspecting a simple frequency distribution and finding which score occurs most often. For example, in Table 3.2 (page 38), the most frequently occurring Implicit View of Intelligence score is 31, with five occurrences. Accordingly, the mode for this distribution is 31. Because there is only one mode for this set of scores, this distribution is said to be **unimodal**. A distribution of scores may be **bimodal** (i.e., have two modes) or even **multimodal** (i.e., have more than two modes). Recall from Chapter 3 that one way of describing the shape of a frequency distribution is on the basis of modality. Unimodal and bimodal distributions are shown in Figure 3.8.

Although the mode is found easily from a frequency distribution, it is not often used or reported as a measure of central tendency in behavioral science research. One reason for this rarity of use is that a distribution may have more than one mode. And, if more than one mode exists, which is a more typical score? Thus, the mode may not provide one typical score to characterize a distribution.

A second reason for the infrequent use of the mode is that a change in only one score in a distribution may change the mode dramatically. Suppose, for example, that you gave individuals a test of short-term memory by asking a person to repeat as many as possible of 10 digits from a list. Assume that you obtained the following numbers of digits repeated by six people:

Person	Number of Digits
Sofia	9
Adrian	8
Cesar	7
Alondra	7
Jade	6
Thomas	5

The mode of this distribution is 7, for two people repeated back 7 digits. Suppose, however, that Alondra repeated back only 5 digits instead of 7. Now the mode of the distribution is 5 rather than 7. The change of only one score shifted the mode considerably. As another instance, suppose Cesar had recalled 10 digits instead of 7. Now the distribution possesses no mode, for each score occurs an equal number of times. Because the mode is so dependent on only a few scores, it is not a very stable measure of central tendency for a distribution.

There are instances, however, when the mode is useful. If you want to know the typical age of a first-semester college student, then the modal age would be most representative of central tendency for this distribution. Similarly, if you ran a clothing boutique and could carry only a limited quantity of each size for an item of clothing, then you would want to carry the largest quantity of any style in the modal size.

Testing Your Knowledge 4.2

1. Define: bimodal distribution, *Mdn*, median, mode, multimodal distribution, unimodal distribution.

2. Assume that a researcher measured self-esteem in 25 seventh-grade girls. The girls rated their self-esteem on a scale ranging from 10 (lowest self-esteem) to 70 (highest self-esteem). The scores obtained were 49, 53, 67, 20, 27, 36, 49, 27, 61, 17, 49, 50, 29, 56, 65, 27, 48, 24, 49, 15, 32, 66, 46, 24, and 38.

   a. Find the mode for this distribution.

   b. Is this distribution unimodal, bimodal, or multimodal?

3. Assume that one of the girls with a score of 49 in question 2 had instead obtained a score of 27.

   a. Find the mode for this distribution.

   b. Is this distribution unimodal, bimodal, or multimodal?

4. Assume that one of the girls with a score of 49 in question 2 had instead obtained a score of 24.

   a. Find the mode for this distribution.

   b. Is this distribution unimodal, bimodal, or multimodal?

5. What limitation of the mode as a descriptive statistic is illustrated by your answers to questions 3 and 4?

6. Find the median for the set of scores in question 2.

7. Assume that the experimenter measured one additional seventh-grader in question 2 and obtained a score of 28. Include this score in the distribution and find the median of the distribution.

8. Assume the original distribution of 25 scores in question 2. Suppose, however, that the scores of 61, 65, 66, and 67 were changed to 51, 55, 56, and 57, respectively. What is the median of this new distribution of scores?

9. Compare your answers to questions 6 and 7 and to questions 6 and 8. What limitations of the median as a measure of central tendency are illustrated by your answers?

Journal Presentation of Measures of Central Tendency

M ▶ The symbol used for the sample mean in publications following the editorial style of the *Publication Manual of the American Psychological Association* (2001).

In journal articles following the style of the *Publication Manual of the American Psychological Association* (5th ed., 2001), the sample mean is often represented by the symbol *M* rather than $\overline{X}$. The median is represented by *Mdn*. There is no abbreviation or symbol for the mode; if it is reported, it is simply identified as the mode. If a population mean is reported, it is represented by μ. The total number of subjects in a sample is represented by N. When three or fewer descriptive statistics are given, the presentation will usually be simply a sentence or two. If four or more descriptive statistics are presented, then the presentation will likely use either a table or a figure. Thus, for example, if a researcher were reporting measures of central tendency for the 100 Implicit View of Intelligence scores of Table 3.3, the three measures of central tendency might be reported as:

> For the 100 Implicit View of Intelligence scores we obtained, $M = 31.8$, $Mdn = 31.5$, and the modal score was 28 with a frequency of 10.

Comparing Measures of Central Tendency

Which is the "best" average score? There is no simple answer to this question. Which measure of central tendency is best depends on the intended use for the statistic. Measures of central tendency have both descriptive and inferential uses.

Descriptive Uses of Measures of Central Tendency

The choice of which measure of central tendency to use as a descriptive statistic depends on the scale of measurement realized in the scores and the shape of the frequency distribution of the scores.

Scale of Measurement of the Scores

Nominal Scale.   A nominal measurement merely places responses into categories; a response occurred in a category or it did not occur. The only measure of central tendency that may be used with a nominal measurement is the mode—the category that occurs most frequently.

Ordinal Scale.   Ordinal measurement provides a ranking of a variable. For example, for the winter of 2006–2007, the ranking of the five cities in New York with the most snowfall was Syracuse, first; Rochester, second; Buffalo, third; Binghamton, fourth; and Albany, fifth. In this instance, no measure of central tendency is needed; each city simply possesses a rank. In other instances, however, we may have several sets of rankings for a variable, and for these the median is often used to describe the typical rank of the variable. For example, suppose you asked nine hockey fans to rank order their favorite teams in the Western Division of the National Hockey League. Of the 15 teams in the conference, the Calgary Flames received rankings of 2, 4, 4, 6, 7, 8, 9, 11, and 13. If you then wanted to provide a typical rank for the Flames, the median of 7 would usually be given.

Interval and Ratio Scales.   In both interval and ratio measures, the intervals between adjacent scores are assumed to represent equal intervals on the variable being measured. Thus, it is appropriate to compute a mean on either interval or ratio measurements. It is also appropriate to find the median and the mode for scores at this level.

Shape of the Distribution of Scores

How well a measure of central tendency characterizes a distribution also depends on the shape of the distribution. Figure 3.8 presented shapes of several typical distributions of scores. If a distribution is unimodal and symmetric, such as the normal distribution of Figure 3.8a, then the mode, median, and mean are identical values. Each statistic characterizes the distribution of scores equally well. Often, however, obtained distributions are not unimodal and symmetric; they may be either positively or negatively skewed. Think of a skewed distribution as having been pulled either up or down by outliers. Thus, in a skewed distribution, the median and mean will differ from each other. Because the mean is responsive to the extreme scores of a skewed distribution, it will be pulled in the direction of the extreme scores (i.e., the outliers) away from the median. Thus, the direction of the difference between the mean and median will reveal whether the distribution is positively or negatively skewed. In a negatively skewed distribution, the mean will be pulled down by the outlier(s) and have a lower value than the median; similarly, a few outliers in a positively skewed distribution will pull the mean up so the value of the mean will be higher than the median. Figure 4.1 illustrates the relative locations of the median and mean in positively and negatively skewed distributions. As you can see from this figure, if a distribution

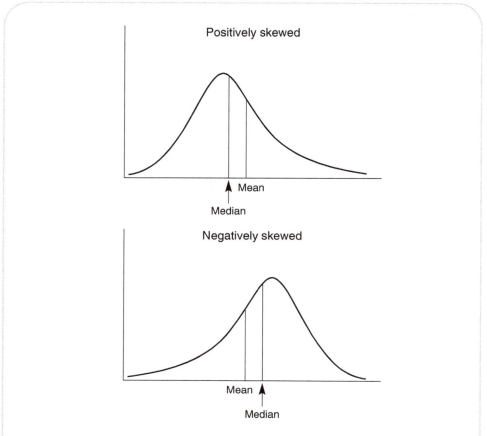

Figure 4.1 The relative locations of the median and mean in positively and negatively skewed distributions.

is seriously skewed, with a large difference between the mean and median values, the median usually provides a better measure of central tendency than does the mean. A distribution of the salaries of NBA basketball players illustrates this point. For the 2006–2007 basketball season, the range of annual salaries was from $197,087 to $21,000,000 (*USA Today*, 2007). The mean of this distribution is $4,176,241, but the median is $2,625,698 and the mode is $412,718. This distribution is severely positively skewed; 65% of the players earned less than the mean (see Figure 4.2). Thus, characterizing the typical salary of the players by the mean of $4,176,241 provides a misleading representation, for half the NBA players earn less than $2,625,698 and the most frequently occurring salary is $412,718.

Whenever description is important, we recommend presentation of all three measures of central tendency for a distribution of scores. As you read behavioral sciences literature, however, you will find that the mean is the most widely presented descriptive measure of central tendency, and the mode is provided only rarely. This choice of the mean often is not based on its superior descriptive characteristics; rather, the mean is the most useful of the

Figure 4.2 The impact of a player making $21,000,000 on the NBA salary distribution.

three measures of central tendency as an inferential statistic. And, as you will see, inference is an important aspect of statistical analysis.

Do Some Distributions Not Have a Central Tendency?

Bimodal distributions cannot be adequately described by a single measure of central tendency, especially when the modal scores are widely separated. Suppose, for example, that a researcher obtains a distribution of Implicit View of Intelligence scores such as that shown in Table 4.2. This distribution is clearly bimodal, with a mode at 21 and another at 45. The median of the distribution is 32.5, and the mean is 32.8. But no one obtained scores near either the median or the mean. Neither the median nor the mean represents the score of a typical person in this sample. In this instance, the modes of 21 and 45 present the best description of typical scores.

Consider another example. In 2006, the per capita consumption for cigarette use in the United States was 1691 cigarettes, or about 85 packs per year (Infoplease, 2008). Does this statistic describe you? If you do not smoke cigarettes, this number certainly doesn't describe you. However, if you do smoke cigarettes, this number is probably far too low. The distribution of the number of cigarettes smoked in a year is bimodal. In 2006, only 20.9% of adults were smokers, and their consumption was considerably in excess of 85 packs per year. The majority of the population does not smoke cigarettes, and their modal use is zero cigarettes per year.

Inferential Uses of Measures of Central Tendency

The choice of a measure of central tendency is determined in part by whether the statistic is to be used for inferential purposes. In Chapter 1, we indicated that population parameters are often estimated by statistics obtained from a sample. The sample mean, $\overline{X}$, is the

TABLE 4.2 Bimodal distribution of 26 Implicit View of Intelligence scores.

Score	Tally	f	
48	/	1	
47			
46	//	2	
45	/////	5	Mode
44	///	3	
43	/	1	
42	/	1	
41			
40			
39			
38			
37			
36			
35			
34			
33			
32			$\overline{X} = 32.8$ $Mdn = 32.5$
31			
30			
29			
28			
27			
26			
25			
24			
23	/	1	
22	///	3	
21	/////	5	Mode
20	//	2	
19	/	1	
18	/	1	

best estimator of a population mean, μ. Consequently, the sample mean enters into a number of important statistical tests. Because the mean is so useful for inference, behavioral scientists often use the mean to describe their data. We discuss the characteristics of the sample mean as an estimator of the population mean more fully in Chapter 7.

Testing Your Knowledge 4.3

1. Which measure of central tendency would you choose in order to achieve each of the following?

   a. Provide a value that is the 50th percentile in a distribution.

   b. Minimize the sum of the squared difference of each score in the distribution from the measure of central tendency.

   c. Describe the most frequently occurring score in a distribution.

   d. Use the numerical value of each score in its computation.

2. A distribution is severely negatively skewed. Would you expect the mean to be smaller than, equal to, or larger than the median? Explain your answer.

3. The mean of a distribution is considerably larger than the median. Do you expect the distribution to be symmetrical, negatively skewed, or positively skewed? Why?

4. A psychologist obtained a sample of 35 first-year undergraduate students who had joined an Internet social networking community on the first day of the semester. After three days, she asked each student how many friends he or she had developed in the community. She found that the mean number of friends was 38, the median, 25, and the mode, 24 with a frequency of 7 occurrences.

   a. Report these results in the form that would be used for a journal presentation.

   b. Do your think the distribution of friends reported is skewed? What aspects of the descriptive statistics lead you to this conclusion?

 ## Summary

▶ Measures of central tendency may be used for both descriptive and inferential purposes.

▶ The sample mean, median, and mode are the three commonly used measures of central tendency.

▶ The sample mean, $\overline{X}$, is found from $\Sigma X/N$.

▶ An outlier is an extreme score in a distribution.

▶ The population mean, μ is found from $\Sigma X/N_{\text{population}}$.

▶ The mean is the most used measure of central tendency for inferential purposes.

▶ The sum of squares (*SS*) provides a way to calculate how far each individual score deviates from the mean of the distribution of scores.

▶ The median is a score in the distribution with an equal number of scores above and below it.

▶ The mode is the most frequently occurring score in a distribution of scores.

▶ The appropriate use of each statistic for descriptive purposes depends on the scale of measurement achieved and the shape of the frequency distribution of the scores.

 ## Key Terms and Symbols

arithmetic mean (71)
bimodal distribution (77)
descriptive statistics (71)
deviation (73)
mean (71)
measures of central tendency (71)

measures of variability (71)
median (*Mdn*) (74)
mode (77)
multimodal distribution (77)
outlier (73)
population mean (μ) (74)

sample mean (*M* or $\overline{X}$) (71)
Σ (summation) (71)
sum of squares (*SS*) (73)
unimodal distribution (77)
$\Sigma(X - \overline{X})^2$ (73)

Review Questions

1. Ogletree, Turner, Vieira, and Brunotte (2005) developed a seven-item scale called Attitude Toward Housecleaning Scale to measure a person's attitude on housecleaning. Scores on this scale may range from 7 to 35, with 7 representing an attitude that housecleaning isn't at all important and a 35 representing that housecleaning is extremely important. For one sample of college males they report a mean of 24.9 and a median of 25.0. From this information, would you judge the distribution of scores to be approximately symmetrical or skewed? Why?

2. In a report in the *Los Angeles Business Journal* (2005), in 2004, for 19,850 actors in the entertainment industry, the mean hourly income was $22.01, whereas the median hourly income was $9.98. Do you think this distribution of incomes is skewed? If so, in which direction is it skewed? Why? This same report indicated that for floral designers in the entertainment industry, the mean hourly income was $11.40 and the median hourly income was $11.30. Do you think this distribution of incomes is skewed? Why?

3. Jansz and Tanis (2007) surveyed 751 people regarding the time they spend playing video games. The results revealed that the individuals played a mean of 2.6 hours per day, with a median of 2.5 hours per day. By looking at the mean and median, does it seem the distribution of hours played per week is skewed? If you think it is skewed, in which direction is it skewed? Why?

4. Jansz and Tanis (2007) recruited subjects for their survey on time spent playing video games from a "gaming" web site. If you used the same survey with students in your statistics class, would you be more likely to get a unimodal or bimodal distribution? Do you think the distribution would be negatively or positively skewed? Explain your answer.

5. Researchers in behavioral medicine are interested in psychological methods of controlling pain. To induce pain safely in their subjects, they may use the cold pressor task. One form of this task involves having a person immerse a hand in cold water and then timing how long the person can tolerate the pain induced. Suppose that an experimenter had each of 17 people place a hand in a tub of water and then timed how long the person could hold his or her hand in the water before the pain became too intense to endure. The experimenter replicated the study four times and obtained the following four sets of scores (the scores represent time in seconds):

Set 1:   35, 39, 38, 30, 37, 43, 30, 38, 41, 52, 25, 44, 33, 41, 38, 56, and 37.

Set 2:   20, 28, 26, 29, 60, 21, 37, 30, 28, 57, 29, 25, 63, 26, 32, 30, and 28.

Set 3:   45, 23, 57, 50, 47, 52, 20, 53, 50, 30, 52, 60, 52, 49, 52, 49, and 53.

Set 4:   52, 23, 40, 60, 52, 21, 20, 52, 50, 23, 55, 26, 28, 53, 26, 49, and 26.

For each set of scores:

a. Construct a simple frequency distribution. Use this frequency distribution to make a judgment about the shape of the distribution of the scores.

b. Calculate the mode, median, and mean.

c. Compare the measures of central tendency. Is the distribution skewed? Explain how you reached a decision. Does your answer from this comparison agree with your judgment from the frequency distribution constructed for question a?

d. Do you think one of the measures of central tendency describes the scores better than the others? If so, which measure and why?

6. Your statistics professor plans to grade you on the basis of five examinations each worth 100 points. She informs you that your grade will be based on the central tendency of your scores and that you will have to choose whether you want your grade based on the modal, median, or mean score. Suppose the grades of three students in the class are as follows:

	Exam				
	1	2	3	4	5
Roberto	35	40	65	90	90
Dimitrios	10	50	65	80	85
Karen	56	56	67	78	98

If you were each of these students, which measure of central tendency would you choose to determine your course grade? Explain the reason for your choice for each student.

7. A survey of graduate student credit card debt was conducted in 2000, 2003, and 2006 (Nelliemae, 2007). The following amount of credit card debt for graduate students was found.

Year	2000	2003	2006
Mean	$4,776	$7,831	$8,612
Median	$3,068	$3,730	$3,874

   a. How does having both information about the means and the medians for each year the survey was conducted aid your understanding of credit card use in graduate students? Specifically, do you think the distribution of the amount of credit card debt is skewed? If so, in which direction?

   b. Which measure of central tendency do you think may be a better measure to use in this instance?

8. Simple reaction time, the amount of time it takes to respond to a simple stimulus such as a light or tone, is a measure of a person's recovery from general anesthesia. Suppose that you measured nine surgery patients two hours after they received general anesthesia for minor surgery and found the following reaction times in milliseconds for eight of them: 782, 793, 793, 817, 832, 847, 866, 893. The ninth patient was not sufficiently recovered to provide a reaction time; thus, this patient was assigned an infinite reaction time.

   a. If you wanted to include the scores of all nine patients, which measure or measures of central tendency could you calculate?

   b. What is the numerical value of that measure?

9. The U.S. Census Bureau (U.S. Census Bureau, 2006) reports that the median age at first marriage for males in the United States in 2005 was 27.1 years. Explain why the median rather than the mean was reported for this statistic.

Looking at Data: Measures of Variability

e opened Chapter 4 with an example of a professor returning an exam and students asking for information on how well the class did. Suppose you obtained an 87 on the exam, and the class mean was 82. Is this sufficient information to let you know how well you performed on the exam with respect to other members of the class? You now know that if there were a few students with very low grades on the exam, the distribution of grades might be negatively skewed and the mean may not be a very good indicator of typical performance on the exam. On the other hand, there may be very little variability in the grades, and the highest and lowest grades differ by very little. Sometimes knowing a measure of central tendency, such as the mean, isn't enough to help you completely understand your grade; you would like to know something about the variability of grades. Measures of central tendency tell only part of the story about the scores obtained from a sample or a population. The mean, median, or mode alone does not indicate how much dispersion or variability there is among the scores in the distribution. Hence, in addition to understanding measures of central tendency that provide us with information about what the typical data are, we must also understand how varied the data are. Accordingly, we turn to a class of statistics called *measures of variability*.

Variability ▶ How much scores differ from each other and the measure of central tendency in a distribution.

Variability refers to how much scores in a distribution differ from each other and, thus, from the measure of central tendency in the distribution. The more the scores differ from each other, the more they will also differ from the measure of central tendency and the more variability there is in the distribution. Conversely, the less the scores differ from each other, the less they will differ from the measure of central tendency and the less variability there is in the distribution.

To illustrate the concept of variability, suppose that a researcher measured three different groups of nine subjects each on the amount of time they laughed while reading a book of cartoons. The scores obtained, in seconds, are portrayed in Table 5.1. The mean, median, and mode for each group is 41.0. But it should be apparent that the distributions are very different, and the measures of central tendency are not equally representative of the scores in each group. In group 1, each score is equal to 41; thus, there is no variability among the scores. Consequently, each measure of central tendency perfectly represents the

---

TABLE

5.1

Duration-of-laughter scores in seconds for three groups
of nine subjects each

	Group		
	1	2	3
	41	38	21
	41	39	26
	41	40	33
	41	41	41
	41	41	41
	41	41	41
	41	42	50
	41	43	51
	41	44	65
Mode	41	41	41
Mdn	41	41	41
$\overline{X}$	41	41	41

scores in the distribution. Clearly, the scores in group 1 would be a rare outcome if actual duration-of-laughter scores were obtained from nine people. In group 2, there is little variability among the scores. The scores are clustered closely around the measure of central tendency; no score differs more than 3 seconds from the 41 second score. Thus, each measure of central tendency is reasonably representative of all individuals in this group, for there is little variability among the individual scores.

The situation is different in group 3. Here there is more variability in the amount of laughter. The scores differ considerably from each other, and some scores differ by as much as 24 seconds from the measures of central tendency of 41 seconds. Clearly, any measure of central tendency for this set of scores is not as representative of the scores as are the measures of central tendency for groups 1 and 2.

As with measures of central tendency, the variability of scores must be quantified. Accordingly, there are several statistics to describe the variability of scores in a distribution.

Range as a Measure of Variability

Range ▶ The numerical difference between the lowest and highest scores in a distribution.

The **range** of a set of scores is found by

$$\text{Range} = X_{\text{highest URL}} - X_{\text{lowest LRL}}$$

where $X_{\text{highest URL}}$ represents the upper real limit for the highest score and $X_{\text{lowest LRL}}$ the lower real limit for the lowest score in a distribution. Thus, the range provides an interval containing 100% of the observed scores in a distribution. For group 3 of Table 5.1, $X_{\text{highest URL}} = 65.5$ and $X_{\text{lowest LRL}} = 20.5$, thus the range for this group is $65.5 - 20.5$, or 45. The range for scores in group 2 is $44.5 - 37.5$, or 7, and the range of scores for group 1 is $41.5 - 40.5$, or 1. For the 100 Implicit View of Intelligence scores that we saw in Chapter 3 (Table 3.3), the highest score is 48 and the lowest score is 16. Thus, the range for this distribution is $48.5 - 15.5$, or 33 rating scale points.

Characteristics of the Range

The range describes the overall spread between the highest and lowest scores from a distribution, taking into account their respective real limits. Any change in either the highest or lowest score will affect the range, even though all other scores may remain unchanged. Thus, because only two scores determine the value of the statistic, the range is a relatively unstable measure of variability. Moreover, the larger the size of the sample, the more likely the distribution could contain an outlier that would serve to inflate the value of the range. The virtue of the range is that it is easy to calculate, but because of its lack of stability, it is not a frequently reported measure of variability.

Testing Your Knowledge 5.1

1. Define: range, variability, $X_{\text{highest URL}}$, $X_{\text{lowest LRL}}$.
2. The highest score on a class test is 98 and the lowest is 54.
   a. Find the range of these scores.
   b. What information about the scores is given by this range?
3. On a test of complex reaction time, the longest score is 929 milliseconds (ms) and the shortest score is 642 ms. Find the range for these scores.
4. Explain why the range is a relatively unstable measure of variability.

Measures of Variability About the Sample Mean

The range provides an interval containing 100 percent of the scores in a distribution. But the range makes use of only two scores out of the distribution. A more stable measure of variability would take into account all of the scores in the distribution. The two most commonly used measures of variability, the *variance* and the *standard deviation,* do just that by using all of the scores to calculate the variability about the mean.

In Chapter 4, we obtained the *deviation* or difference of each score in a distribution from the mean of the distribution (see Table 4.1). That is, we calculated $X - \overline{X}$ for each score. This deviation provides a measure of how much a single score differs from the mean. If a score is equal to the mean, then $X - \overline{X}$ will be zero. But if the score is not equal to the mean, then $X - \overline{X}$ will take on a numerical value, and the more that X differs from $\overline{X}$, the larger $X - \overline{X}$ will become. We might then propose to obtain a measure of variability by adding up the deviations of all the scores in a distribution and dividing the sum by the number of scores. But as illustrated in column b of Table 4.1, the sum of the deviations, that is, $\Sigma(X - \overline{X})$, for a distribution of scores will always equal zero; that is, $\Sigma(X - \overline{X}) = 0$. Thus, although each of the individual deviations will provide an indication of how far an individual score is from the mean, when you add them together, the sum provides no information on the variability of the distribution because it will always be zero. This problem can be avoided by squaring each deviation value [i.e., $(X - \overline{X})^2$] before summing the deviations and obtaining the sum of the squared deviations, $\Sigma(X - \overline{X})^2$. Recall from Chapter 4 that we call $\Sigma(X - \overline{X})^2$ the *sum of squares* (*SS*) and that the value of $\Sigma(X - \overline{X})^2$ will be zero only if each $X - \overline{X}$ value is zero.

The sum of squares is useful in obtaining a measure of how much the scores in a distribution differ from the mean, but there is one problem. In general, unless all the scores in a distribution are the same and thus equal to the mean of the distribution, the value of *SS* will increase as the number of scores in the distribution gets larger. To illustrate this problem, look at Table 5.2.

Each set of scores in Table 5.2 is equally variable: the scores in data set 2 are the same as those in data set 1, except there are twice as many; data set 1 has 5 observations and data set 2 has 10 observations. Consequently, data set 2 has a sum of squares that is twice as large as data set 1. In general, the more scores in a data set, the larger the sum of squares will be. Thus, the sum of squares alone will not help us with understanding how variable the data are. We can overcome this problem, however, by finding the average of the sum of squares of a data set. This step of finding the average sum of squares will produce a statistic called the *variance,* which is presented in the next section.

Variance

Population Variance

The population variance is represented by σ^2 (the Greek letter *sigma,* squared) to indicate that this variance represents a population parameter rather than a statistic obtained from a sample. If we know μ, the mean of a population, and each score X in the population, then we can find the **population variance** by

Population variance (σ^2) ▶ The variance obtained by measuring all scores in a population.

$$\text{Population variance} = \sigma^2 = \frac{\Sigma(X - \mu)^2}{N_{\text{population}}}$$

TABLE								
5.2	Data sets illustrating that the value of *SS* increases with the number of scores in a distribution.							

	Data Set 1				Data Set 2			
(a)	(b)	(c)	(d)	(a)	(b)	(c)	(d)
X	$\overline{X}$	$(X - \overline{X})$	$(X - \overline{X})^2$	X	$\overline{X}$	$(X - \overline{X})$	$(X - \overline{X})^2$
1	3	-2	4	1	3	-2	4
4	3	1	1	3	3	0	0
5	3	2	4	5	3	2	4
2	3	-1	1	1	3	-2	4
3	3	0	0	2	3	-1	1
	$\Sigma(X - \overline{X}) = 0$		$SS = 10$	3	3	0	0
				5	3	2	4
				2	3	-1	1
				4	3	1	1
				4	3	1	1
					$\Sigma(X - \overline{X}) = 0$		$SS = 20$

where $\quad X =$ the individual scores of members of the population.

$\mu =$ the population mean of the scores.

$N_{population} =$ the total number of scores in the population.

Notice this formula obtains the sum of squares for the entire population and then divides by $N_{population}$, the total number of observations in the population. Let's go through a few examples of how to calculate a population variance using the data from Table 5.2. Assume that the data in this table represent two complete populations. To find the variance, we first find the sum of squares and then divide it by $N_{population}$.

Thus, for data set 1,

$$\sigma^2 = \frac{\Sigma(X - \mu)^2}{N} = \frac{10}{5} = \frac{10}{5} = 2$$

and for data set 2,

$$\sigma^2 = \frac{\Sigma(X - \mu)^2}{N} = \frac{20}{10} = \frac{20}{10} = 2.$$

Notice that each data set has the same variance, reflecting the fact that each data set is equally variable even though there are differing numbers of scores in the two data sets. As we have pointed out, however, in actual research a population would be much larger than only 5 or 10 members, and it usually is impractical to measure all members of a population; thus μ is usually not known. Consequently, σ^2 is typically not calculated from a population, but is estimated from a sample, as we discuss next.

Estimated Population Variance

It is rare for us to have a score from every member of a population. Thus, most often, we estimate the population variance, σ^2, from a sample selected from the population. The **estimated population variance**, often simply called the **variance**, is represented in notation as s^2 and defined as

$$\text{Estimated population variance} = s^2 = \frac{\Sigma(X - \overline{X})^2}{N - 1},$$

or using sum of squares notation,

$$\text{Estimated population variance} = s^2 = \frac{SS}{N - 1}.$$

Estimated population variance (s^2) ► The variance obtained from a sample of scores that is used to estimate the population variance for those scores.

Notice that this formula uses the sample mean, $\overline{X}$, to determine the sum of squares, and then divides these sum of squares by $N - 1$. You may wonder why $N - 1$ is used in place of N here. Consider the following analogy to help understand why $N - 1$ is used.

Imagine that you are at a large party where the host is serving an incredible fruit salad with kiwi, grapes, cherries, watermelon, cantaloupe, pineapple, apples, pears, strawberries, blueberries, and fruits you never even knew existed. Never have you seen such a fruit salad. Think of this large bowl of fruit salad as a population of a variety of fruits. You notice, however, as each guest gets a small bowl, or a sample of the fruit salad, some guests have grapes, others do not. Some guests have pineapple, others do not. In fact, while looking at the samples of fruit salad, it becomes clear they are each less varied in the variety of fruit than the large bowl, or population. Suppose you were now asked to identify all the varieties of fruit in the large bowl from only one sample in a small bowl. Because it would be unlikely for a small bowl to contain all the varieties of fruit in the entire salad, it is likely you would underestimate the varieties of fruit in the large bowl. Using the sample bowls to provide an idea of how varied the population fruit salad is becomes problematic, as the sample will usually be less varied than the population. A similar problem arises when we try to estimate the variability of any population from a sample; the scores in the sample will usually be less variable than the scores in the population, and we will likely underestimate the variability of the population. It is for this reason that we do not calculate the estimated population variance by dividing the sum of squares by N. Though using this kind of formula will give a measure of the variance of the sample, it will provide a biased estimate that will always underestimate the actual population variance. Though you may see a variance calculated using N rather than $N - 1$, this variance is used as a descriptive statistic to capture what is going on in the sample and not to estimate a population variance, σ^2. For most purposes, however, we calculate the variance of a sample to provide an estimated population variance. Thus, the bias is corrected by using $N - 1$ instead of N as the denominator in the formula for s^2. From this point on, when we discuss the variance, we will be using s^2 unless we specifically state otherwise.

To calculate s^2:

1. Subtract the mean from each score [i.e., $(X - \overline{X})$].
2. Square each resulting difference [i.e., $(X - \overline{X})^2$].
3. Add all the squared difference values [i.e., $\Sigma(X - \overline{X})^2$].
4. Divide the sum by $N - 1$, the number of scores in the sample minus one.

Standard Deviation

Population Standard Deviation

Population standard deviation (σ) ▸ The square root of the population variance.

If N is equal to the population and the population mean, μ, is known, then the **population standard deviation**, represented by σ, is given by

$$\text{Population standard deviation} = \sigma = \sqrt{\sigma^2} = \sqrt{\frac{\Sigma(X - \mu)^2}{N_{\text{population}}}}.$$

However, μ typically is unknown, and the value of σ is usually estimated from the sample.

Estimated Population Standard Deviation

Estimated population standard deviation (s) ▸ The square root of the estimated population variance.

The **estimated population standard deviation**, s, often simply called the **standard deviation**, is the square root of the estimated population variance, or

$$\text{Estimated population standard deviation} = s = \sqrt{s^2} = \sqrt{\frac{\Sigma(X - \overline{X})^2}{N - 1}} = \sqrt{\frac{SS}{N - 1}}.$$

To calculate s:

1. Subtract the mean from each score [i.e., $(X - \overline{X})$].
2. Square each resulting difference [i.e., $(X - \overline{X})^2$].
3. Add all the squared difference values [i.e., $\Sigma(X - \overline{X})^2$].
4. Divide the sum by $N - 1$, the number of scores in the sample minus one.
5. Take the square root of the resulting quotient.

EXAMPLE PROBLEM

5.1

Calculating the Estimated Population Variance and Standard Deviation

Problem: Find the estimated population variance and standard deviation of the nine duration-of-laughter scores of group 2 in Table 5.1.

Statistic to be used: $\quad s^2 = \dfrac{\Sigma(X - \overline{X})^2}{N - 1}$

Solution: The steps necessary in the calculation of s^2 and s are illustrated in the following table. We first find s^2

▸ The formula requires obtaining the sum of squares, SS or $\Sigma(X - \overline{X})^2$. The nine scores are given in column a. The mean for these scores is 41, and this value is presented in column b.

▸ The next step is to subtract this mean from each score as illustrated in column c.

▸ Next, square the difference for each score as shown in column d. The squared differences are added together, and this sum, given at the bottom of column d, is 28. This sum is the $\Sigma(X - \overline{X})^2$, or SS, needed for the numerator of s^2.

▶ The last step is to divide the SS by $N - 1$. Because nine scores were used, $N = 9$ and $N - 1 = 8$. Accordingly, $s^2 = \frac{28}{8} = 3.5$. Notice that, because the deviation of each score from the mean is squared, s^2 must always be either zero or a positive number. A negative s^2 indicates a mistake in calculations.

(a)	(b)	(c)	(d)
X	$\overline{X}$	$(X - \overline{X})$	$(X - \overline{X})^2$
38	41	−3	9
39	41	−2	4
40	41	−1	1
41	41	0	0
41	41	0	0
41	41	0	0
42	41	+1	1
43	41	+2	4
44	41	+3	9
		$\sum(X - \overline{X}) = 0$	$SS = 28$

The estimated population standard deviation, s, is the square root of s^2. Thus, $s = \sqrt{3.5} = 1.87$ seconds, which is rounded to 1.9 seconds. Notice that the units attached to s, in this case, seconds, are the same as those of the raw scores. It is important to remember to take the square root of s^2 when finding s; a common error in calculating s is failing to take the square root of s^2.

Summary of Computational Steps

1. Find the mean of the scores in column a and then list this value in column b as shown.
2. Subtract the mean in column b from each score in column a. The difference is shown in column c.
3. Square each difference in column c. The result of this squaring is shown in column d.
4. Sum the squared differences of column d.
5. Divide the sum of column d by $N - 1$. The resulting value is s^2.
6. Take the square root of s^2 to obtain s.

Computational Formulas

You have just learned the definitional formulas for the variance and standard deviation. These definitional formulas best convey conceptually what s^2 and s are, and they are easy to use with small data sets. When a large number of scores are involved, however, the definitional formulas become more cumbersome and prone to arithmetic errors. Then, it is often easier to calculate s^2 or s with computer-based statistical programs such as SPSS or Minitab, or hand-held calculators. Most calculators have functions for s^2 and s, and all statistical software programs provide these statistics.

Review of Symbols and Formulas

We have introduced a number of symbols and formulas up to this point. They are reviewed here.

s^2 The estimated population variance obtained from a sample of scores. This statistic is used to estimate a population variance, σ^2.

s The estimated population standard deviation obtained from a sample of scores. This statistic is used to estimate a population standard deviation, σ.

σ^2 The population variance, a parameter calculated on all scores in a population.

σ The population standard deviation, a parameter calculated on all scores in a population.

Table 5.3 presents the definitional and sum of squares formulas for both s^2 and s.

Interpreting the Variance and the Standard Deviation

In published reports of research, the standard deviation is presented as a descriptive statistic more often than the variance. One reason for this greater use is that, because the standard deviation is the square root of the variance, it provides a measure of the variability of scores using the scores' original units. In Example Problem 5.1, s^2 is 3.5 seconds squared, a value not easily interpreted. The value of s, however, is 1.9 seconds, the same units (i.e., seconds) that the raw scores were measured in. Thus, the focus in this section is on the interpretation of s. The variance, however, is used in several statistical hypothesis testing methods and is discussed more fully in Chapter 10.

The standard deviation provides a measure of the *average* of how much the scores in a distribution differ from the mean. If all the scores in a distribution are equal to the mean, such as those of group 1 of Table 5.1, then s will equal zero. Thus, the average amount by which the scores in group 1 differ from the mean is zero. In this case, if you use $\overline{X}$ to predict any of the scores in the distribution, there will be zero error in your prediction. If you see a value of s equal to zero, then you know that all scores in the distribution are equal to the sample mean, and the mean is a perfect predictor of all the scores.

TABLE 5·3   Definitional and sum of squares formulas for the estimated population variance and standard deviation.

	Formula	
	Definitional	Sum of Squares
Variance, s^2	$\dfrac{\Sigma(X-\overline{X})^2}{N-1}$	$\dfrac{SS}{N-1}$
Standard deviation, $s=\sqrt{s^2}$	$\sqrt{\dfrac{\Sigma(X-\overline{X})^2}{N-1}}$	$\sqrt{\dfrac{SS}{N-1}}$

On the other hand, if at least one score in the distribution is not equal to the mean, then s will take on a value greater than zero. And the value of s will increase as the variability of the scores increases. You can see this increase in s with increasing variability of scores by comparing the distributions of groups 2 and 3 of Table 5.1. Notice that the scores of group 3 are more variable about the mean of 41 than are the scores in group 2. For scores in group 2, $s = 1.9$ seconds, whereas in group 3, s is 13.4 seconds. Thus, for group 2 the average amount by which scores differ from $\overline{X}$ is 1.9 seconds, and in group 3 it is 13.4 seconds. If you use $\overline{X} = 41$ seconds to predict any of the scores in group 2, your prediction will be in error by about 1.9 seconds, whereas for group 3 such a prediction will be in error by about 13.4 seconds.

A second interpretation of s involves describing scores in terms of how many standard deviations they are away from the mean of a distribution. For many distributions, a majority of the scores are within one standard deviation of the mean. For example, the mean for the 100 Implicit View of Intelligence scores of Table 3.3 is 31.8, and the standard deviation for this distribution is 6.6. The scores within one standard deviation of $\overline{X}$ are scores from 25.2 to 38.4. These values are the distance encompassed by one standard deviation below the mean (i.e., $\overline{X} - 1s = 31.8 - 6.6 = 25.2$) to one standard deviation above the mean (i.e., $\overline{X} + 1s = 31.8 + 6.6 = 38.4$). If we round this interval (25.2 to 38.4) to 25 to 38 and count the scores of Table 3.3, we find that 76 of the 100 scores fall into this interval. If the distribution is normally shaped (as in Chapter 3, Figure 3.5a), then knowledge of the standard deviation provides even more information about the scores in the distribution. This interpretation of s is discussed in Chapter 7.

This analysis can be applied to an example from behavioral sciences literature. McGarva, Ramsey, and Shear (2006) wanted to see if cell phone use while driving increased the aggression levels of other drivers. One of the experimenters pulled up to an intersection with a red light while talking on a cell phone. When the light turned green, the driver sat there for one minute. A video camera was focused on the car behind the experimenter. McGarva et al. were looking for signs of any aggressive behaviors exhibited by the driver of the car behind the experimenter. One type of behavior they recorded was the number of times the driver blew his horn. They found that when male drivers were behind the experimenter, the drivers were more likely to honk if the experimenter was talking on a cell phone ($M = 2.6$, $SD = 1.5$) than when the experimenter was not talking on a cell phone ($M = 0.9$, $SD = 1.4$).

If we state from these descriptive statistics that the typical number of honks a male driver makes when sitting behind a driver on a cell phone while the traffic light is green is 2.6, we will be in error by an average of 1.5 honks. But we can anticipate the number of honks that the majority of men in this situation will make by finding the values that are one standard deviation below and one standard deviation above the mean, or between 1.1 honks (i.e., $2.6 - 1.5$) to 4.1 honks (i.e., $2.6 + 1.5$). It is unlikely that many of the men sitting behind the driver using a cell phone honked 10 times, for if they had honked that much, then such large differences from the mean of 2.6 honks would have increased the value of the standard deviation. On the other hand, when looking at the descriptive statistics for the men who were sitting behind the experimenter who was not on a cell phone, the standard deviation was larger than the mean. If we take the range of honks within one standard deviation of this mean, we obtain a range of -0.5 honks ($0.9 - 1.4$) to 2.3 honks ($0.9 + 1.4$). Obviously, a negative number of honks is impossible; thus, the implication of this relationship is that the data for the number of honks must have been positively skewed. At least one driver blew his horn a large number of times.

Notice also that a score can be described by indicating how many standard deviations it is above or below the mean. For example, if a distribution of scores on an exam has a mean of 80 and a standard deviation of 6, then a score of 86 is one standard deviation above the mean and a score of 74 is one standard deviation below the mean. Chapter 6 explains this use of the standard deviation more fully.

What Is a Large Amount of Variability?

No simple rule is used to determine whether a value for any measure of variability reflects a small or large amount of variability in a distribution of scores. Whether the variability is extensive or not is relative to the possible range of scores that can be obtained on the variable and the mean of the scores. For example, Senders (1958) points out that a standard deviation of 3 inches in the length of 100 electric utility poles would not be unusual, for the mean length of a utility pole is very long. If you were measuring the length of people's noses, however, a standard deviation of 3 inches would be alarming! You might expect you had found a new species. In relation to the average length of a person's nose, a standard deviation of 3 inches would be very large.

Journal Presentation of Measures of Variability

The estimated population standard deviation, s, is the measure of variability commonly presented in journal presentations of research. Journals that follow the editorial style of the *Publication Manual of the American Psychological Association* (American Psychological Association, 2001) use an italicized *SD* to indicate this standard deviation. Thus, in a journal publication or a laboratory report you may expect to find a presentation such as:

> The mean duration of laughter to the cartoons was 41.0 seconds (*SD* = 1.9 seconds).[1] The range of the scores was 7 seconds.

Testing Your Knowledge 5.2

1. Define: estimated population standard deviation, estimated population variance, sum of squares, s, s^2, SS, σ, σ^2.

2. Explain the difference between: s and s^2, SS and s^2, σ and σ^2.

3. A great deal of attention has been placed recently upon the safety of cell phone use while driving. Consequently, some states have adopted a policy that only hands-free cell phone conversations are permitted while driving. The contention is that if you don't have to hold the phone, then you can drive better than if you are holding a phone. Strayer and Drews (2007) found that even when drivers were using a hands-free cell phone, they were more likely to remember what they experienced in a driving simulation when they were not talking on the cell phone than when they were. Suppose you decided to conduct a similar study by having a subject watch a videotape of a person driving down a busy road. In one condition, subjects talked to a researcher on a hands-free cell phone, in the other condition, they did not. After watching the video, you asked subjects to complete a memory task where they checked off items they

---

[1]The editorial style of the *Publication Manual of the American Psychological Association* (2001) uses a lowercase s as the abbreviation for seconds. We did not use this abbreviation for seconds here to prevent any confusion with the symbol *s* used to represent the standard deviation.

recalled seeing in the videotape. Suppose you found the following number of items recalled by six subjects in each group. The minimum score that could be obtained was zero items recalled, and the maximum was 10 items recalled

Group	
Talking on Cell Phone	Not Talking on Cell Phone
3	8
4	10
5	6
5	7
4	9
3	8

a. Find $\overline{X}$, s^2, s, and the range for each group of scores.

b. From the values of s and s^2 obtained, which group has more variable scores?

c. If you use $\overline{X}$ to predict a typical score for the drivers who are using hands-free cell phones, what would be the average error in your prediction?

4. Many psychologists are interested in the concept of personal space, the idea that each person has an invisible boundary or space around him or her that the individual does not want strangers to encroach upon. One approach to the investigation of this phenomenon has been to invade a person's personal space in a public place, such as a college library or cafeteria, by having an experimenter sit in an empty chair next to the person. An accomplice of the experimenter then covertly times how long the person remains seated next to the experimenter who has invaded his or her personal space. Suppose that a male experimenter invaded the personal space of five college-aged males and five college-aged females while they were seated in a library. The amount of time (in minutes) that each person stayed seated next to the experimenter was recorded as follows:

Gender of Person	
Male	Female
9.6	8.6
19.8	4.7
4.3	8.1
20.6	6.2
15.7	2.4

a. Find $\overline{X}$, s^2, and s for each group.

b. From the values of s and s^2 obtained, which group has more variable scores?

c. What is the average error in describing a male as taking 14.0 minutes to move after his personal space was invaded?

d. If you use the mean of a group to predict the typical behavior of a subject, will you make more accurate predictions for males or females? Explain your answer.

The Choice of Descriptive Statistics

We have discussed a variety of statistics used to describe the average score and the variability of scores from a sample. Researchers, however, usually select only one measure of central tendency and one measure of variability to summarize their data from a study. The choice of which descriptive statistic to use to summarize data depends principally on three considerations: (1) the scale of measurement represented by the scores, (2) the shape of the frequency distribution of the scores, and (3) the intended use of the descriptive statistics for further statistical analysis. Table 5.4 summarizes the recommended measures depending on the scale of measurement and the shape of the distribution.

Scale of Measurement

Nominal Measurement

With nominal measurement, responses are classified into categories, and all responses within a category are equated behaviorally. Consequently, nominal data usually are described only in terms of frequencies (i.e., how many individuals in a group were assigned to one category or another) or percentages. Thus, the mode or most frequently occurring category may be used as a measure of central tendency. There is no measure of variability associated with the mode.

Ordinal Measurement

In Chapter 4, we indicated that when a measure of the typical rank is needed for a variable, the median is often used. If the median is used, then, of the measures of variability presented in this book, the range is used as a measure of variability. For the example we used in Chapter 4 of nine hockey fans asked to rank order their favorite teams in the Western Division of the National Hockey League, we found the median rank of 7 for the Calgary Flames with a range of 12 in the rankings.

Interval and Ratio Measurement

When the frequency distribution of scores is approximately symmetric, the mean is the preferred measure of central tendency for interval and ratio measures. The estimated population standard deviation is the measure of variability commonly used with the mean.

| TABLE 5.4 | Recommended measures of central tendency and variability given scales of measurement of the scores and the shape of the frequency distribution. |

| | Shape of the Frequency Distribution | | | |
| | Approximately Symmetrical Unimodal | | Skewed Unimodal | |
Scale of Measurement	Measure of Central Tendency	Measure of Variability	Measure of Central Tendency	Measure of Variability
Nominal	Mode	None	Mode	None
Ordinal	Mdn	Range	Mdn	Range
Interval or ratio	$\overline{X}$	s	Mdn	Range

Shape of the Frequency Distribution

The shape of the frequency distribution determines the choice of the descriptive statistics only when the dependent variable is measured with an interval or ratio scale of measurement. If the distribution of scores is approximately symmetrical, then the sample mean and standard deviation are the preferred statistics. But if the distribution of scores is considerably skewed, then the median and range may be the descriptive statistics of choice.

Further Data Analysis

The choice of measures of central tendency and variability is also determined by whether the descriptive statistics are to be used for statistical inference. For inferential purposes, the mean, estimated population standard deviation, and estimated population variance are used because they are related to the known characteristics of the normal distribution. These relationships are discussed in Chapter 6. Hence, behavioral scientists may use the sample mean and standard deviation to summarize their data when considerations of level of measurement and shape of the frequency distribution might dictate against it. The issue of making inferences from the data sometimes overrides these other considerations. For this reason, you will find that the mean and standard deviation are the most frequently used descriptive statistics in behavioral research.

Testing Your Knowledge 5.3

1. For each of the following distributions of scores, indicate the measure of central tendency and variability that would provide the most appropriate description of the scores.
   a. The scores represent interval measurement, and the distribution is heavily negatively skewed.
   b. The scores represent ordinal measurement, and the distribution is approximately symmetric.
   c. The scores represent ratio measurement, and the distribution is approximately symmetric.
   d. The scores represent ordinal measurement, and the distribution is heavily positively skewed.
   e. The scores represent interval measurement, and the distribution is approximately symmetric.
   f. The scores represent interval measurement, and the distribution is heavily positively skewed.
   g. The scores represent ratio measurement, and the distribution is heavily negatively skewed.

Summary

▶ Measures of variability quantify how much scores differ from each other and the measure of central tendency of a distribution.

▶ The range is found by $X_{\text{highest URL}} - X_{\text{lowest LRL}}$.

▶ The population variance, σ^2 is defined as $\Sigma(X - \mu)^2/N_{\text{population}}$.

▶ The estimated population variance, s^2 is defined as $\Sigma(X - \overline{X})^2/(N - 1)$.

▶ The square root of the variance provides the standard deviation. The square root of σ^2 provides the population standard deviation, and the square root of s^2 provides the estimated population standard deviation.

▶ The estimated population variance and standard deviation are the most frequently used measures of variability.

▶ The choice of a measure of variability depends on the scale of measurement represented in the scores, the shape of the frequency distribution of the scores, and what further data analysis is intended.

Key Terms and Symbols

estimated population standard deviation (s) (92)
estimated population variance (s^2) (91)

measures of variability (87)
population standard deviation (σ) (92)
population variance (σ^2) (89)
range (88)

sum of squared deviations (89)
sum of squares (SS) (89)
variability (87)

Review Questions

1. Is the amount of effort a student puts into a class related to the professor's gender? Suppose that you had 11 female college juniors complete a survey on the amount of effort they put forth in a course taught by a female professor. The 10-question survey has questions on topics such as class attendance, staying awake during class, and reading the book before coming to class. Scores can range from zero, indicating that the student is putting forth no effort in class, to 70, indicating that the student is putting forth extreme effort (Heckert, Latier, Ringwald-Burton, & Drazen, 2006). The 11 scores you obtained were 30, 54, 57, 53, 56, 55, 54, 55, 57, 54, and 58.

   a. Find the *Mdn*, $\overline{X}$, *range*, s^2, and s for this distribution.

   b. From a purely descriptive view, does the *Mdn* or $\overline{X}$ appear to be a better measure of central tendency for these scores? Explain your answer.

2. Suppose now that you had 11 female college juniors complete a survey on their effort in the same course as in question 1, but now taught by a male professor. You obtained the following effort scores: 30, 35, 40, 45, 31, 51, 32, 58, 57, 50, and 55.

   a. Find the *Mdn*, $\overline{X}$, *range*, s^2, and s for this distribution.

   b. From a purely descriptive view, does the *Mdn* or $\overline{X}$ appear to be a better measure of central tendency for these scores? Explain your answer.

   c. The value of s was higher in this set of scores compared with the value of s for question 1. Yet, the range did not change. Explain this outcome.

3. For each of the following statements, which measure of variability is described?

   a. It provides an interval that contains 100 percent of the scores.

   b. Its value is found by dividing the sum of squares by N − 1.

   c. Its value is found from $X_{\text{highest URL}} - X_{\text{lowest LRL}}$.

   d. It provides an estimate for the population of the average squared deviation of a score from the mean of a distribution.

e. It provides an estimate for the population of the square root of the average squared deviation of a score from the mean of a distribution.

f. Its value depends on only two scores in the distribution.

g. Its value is found by the formula $\Sigma(X - \overline{X})^2/(N - 1)$.

h. Its value is found by the formula $\sqrt{\Sigma(X - \overline{X})^2/(N - 1)}$.

i. Its value is found by the formula $\sqrt{\Sigma(X - \mu)^2/N_{population}}$.

j. Its value is found by the formula $\Sigma(X - \mu)^2/N_{population}$.

k. Its value is found by the formula $SS/(N - 1)$.

l. Its value is found by the formula $\sqrt{SS/(N - 1)}$.

4. Question 7 of the Review Questions for Chapter 4 presented partial results of a survey by Nelliemae (2007) on the credit card debt experienced by graduate students in 2000, 2003, and 2006. Assume that the standard deviations associated with these means were $2357 in 2000, $2987 in 2003, and $4127 in 2006.

   a. If you predicted that the typical graduate student had $8612 worth of credit card debt in 2006, what would be the average error of your prediction?

   b. Would you judge these standard deviations to indicate a large or small amount of variation in the amount of credit card debt?

   c. What information do these standard deviations give you about the appropriateness of the mean as a measure of central tendency for the distributions of scores obtained in this survey?

5. Ogletree, Turner, Vieira, and Brunotte (2005) found that college-aged women prefer cleaner apartments than college-aged men. Deciding you would like to replicate that finding with adults in their fifties, you use their Attitude Toward House Cleaning Scale that was discussed in Review Question 1 of Chapter 4. Nine men and eight women between the ages of 50 to 59 agree to participate in your study. Suppose you obtained the scores in the table to the left:

   a. Find the Mdn, $\overline{X}$, $range$, s^2, and s for both distributions.

   b. Compare the median to the mean for the data for the men. What does the difference between these values tell you about the shape of the distribution for these scores? Which measure of central tendency best represents the typical score for the men? Why?

   c. Is there a score in the data for the men that you would identify as an outlier? Why? Is there a score in the data for the women that you would identify as an outlier? Why?

   d. If an outlier exists in a set of scores, what effect will it have on the mean and median for those scores? What effect will it have on the range? What effect will it have on the variance or standard deviation?

   e. Are the women or men more variable in their responses? What information did you use to reach this conclusion?

Men	Women
28	27
26	26
30	30
23	31
29	24
19	28
10	28
31	30
29	

knowledge

A Look at a Problem Most college professors are aware of the Dead Grandmother Problem, which was identified by Adams (1990; p. 1) in an amusing article as "A student's grandmother is far more likely to die suddenly just before the student takes an exam, than at any other time of year." Now there isn't anything funny about dying relatives; however, most professors have often seen an increase in the reported deaths of students' relatives, especially grandmothers, just prior to an upcoming exam. But most reports of this phenomenon are anecdotal; there is little evidence to empirically support these reports. Thus, Adams collected data on the number of reported deaths of student's family members (the family death rate, FDR) over the course of 20 years. He recorded these reports by his students in relation to whether there was no exam scheduled, a midterm exam was scheduled, or a final exam was scheduled. His measurement was the FDR, the rate of reported deaths per 100 students. For example, if the FDR was 1, then for every 100 students Adams received one student reporting the death of a family member (most often his or her grandmother). The following table summarizes Adam's results as a function of the student's grade in the course at the time of the reported death and whether or not an exam was scheduled when the death was reported. The numerical values refer to the mean number of family deaths per 100 students (the FDR). Refer to this table as you answer the following questions.

Student's Current Grade at Time of Reported Death						
	A	B	C	D	F	Mean
No Exam Scheduled	0.04	0.07	0.05	0.05	0.06	0.054
Midterm Exam Next Week	0.06	0.21	0.49	0.86	1.25	0.574
Final Exam Next Week	0.09	0.41	0.96	1.57	2.18	1.042

Source: Adapted from Dr. Mike Adams, *The Dead Grandmother/Exam Syndrome and the Potential Downfall of American Society.* Used by permission of Dr. Mike Adams. Available from http://www.easternct.edu/personal/faculty/adams/Resources/Grannies.pdf.

1. What is the operational definition for the death of a relative that was used by Adams? (*Hint:* How did Adams find out if a student's relative died?)

2. For students with a D average, the FDR in the week before the final exam was 1.57. How many students out of 100 in this condition reported the death of a relative?

3. Suppose that for a total of 600 students in one year, Adams received 36 reports of a death in the family. What is the FDR for these students?

4. What is the scale of measurement represented by the FDR?

5. Why did Adams record information based on the number of deaths per 100 students instead of just the number of deaths?

6. Adams reports a mean FDR over all levels of a student's grade of 0.574 in the week prior to a midterm exam. What numerical values were used to calculate this mean?

7. Compare the mean family death rates over the three exam conditions. Do you see any patterns or trends in the FDR for these three conditions?

8. Calculate the mean FDR for each level of the student's grade in the course. Does the FDR appear to vary with current student performance in the course?

9. Adams' tongue-in-cheek explanation of these findings is that family members are worrying themselves to death about the student's college performance, particularly when students' current grades are low. Although a specific breakdown by relative is not given in the table, Adams found that by and large, the reported death was that of a grandmother. Adams believes this occurs because grandmothers are often the designated worriers of a family, and as such, they are worrying themselves to death during exam times. Behavioral scientists often talk of "alternative rival hypotheses," which are other hypotheses to explain possible outcomes. Clearly, there are explanations other than that offered by Adams for the phenomenon he reports. Can you think of an alternative explanation for why relatives of students, particularly students who are not doing well in a course, are so prone to die just before course exams?

PART B

Your Turn: Selecting Your Research Tools   We suspect that your alternative explanation focuses on the truthfulness of the student reports of the death of a relative. Suppose you suspect that by using a different operational definition of the death of a student's relative, you would find results different from those reported by Adams. Write a brief description of the study you might like to conduct. In your description, answer the following questions.

1. What is your operational definition of the death of a family member of a student?

2. What level of measurement does your measure achieve?

3. How many reports of deaths of a family member do you think you would need so that you could be confident of your results?

4. What descriptive statistic(s) would you use? Are they measures of variability or central tendency?

5. Fill in a table similar to that given above with numbers (i.e., family death rates) that you believe would demonstrate support for your hypothesis.

PART C

Using Your Statistical Tools   Let's say that you asked 12 professors to keep track of reports of all students' verified attendance at a funeral for a relative over the course of a year. Verification was from a published obituary. You asked the professors to take note of whether funeral attendance would result in students missing an exam, an assignment, or both. Suppose you obtained the following results. The numerical values represent the FDR for verified deaths.

| | Exam Condition | | |
Professor	No Missed Exam or Assignments	Missed Assignment No Missed Exam	Missed Exam No Missed Assignment
1	0.02	0.02	0.02
2	0.03	0.01	0.02
3	0.00	0.01	0.02
4	0.00	0.01	0.01
5	0.01	0.02	0.01
6	0.00	0.03	0.02
7	0.02	0.01	0.03
8	0.00	0.01	0.01
9	0.02	0.02	0.03
10	0.00	0.00	0.02
11	0.02	0.00	0.03
12	0.00	0.01	0.02

1. Suppose you were asked to find the most frequently occurring FDR for each exam condition. What statistic would you use? What is the value of this statistic for each exam condition? How would you describe each exam condition with respect to this statistic?

2. What is the range of the FDR for each exam condition? Do these ranges differ from each other?

3. Find the mean and standard deviation for each exam condition. Notice that the means differ slightly from each other. Do you think they differ enough from each other to indicate a difference among the exam conditions in the FDR? Explain how you reached this decision.

4. Write a brief paragraph summarizing these findings following the style of the *Publication Manual of the American Psychological Association* (American Psychological Association, 2001).

5. Which hypothesis do these data seem to better support: the "family members are worrying themselves to death" hypothesis humorously proposed by Adams (1990), or your alternative hypothesis that student reports of a family member's death may often be an excuse to avoid taking an exam? Explain your answer.

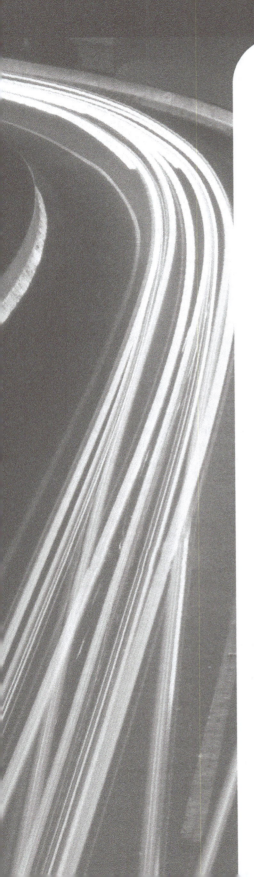

The Normal Distribution, Probability, and Standard Scores

Normal Distribution
  The Normal Distribution and the Behavioral Sciences
  Properties of the Normal Distribution
  Area Under the Normal Distribution

Standard Normal Distribution
  Using a Table of the Standard Normal Distribution
  An Example of the Use of z Scores

Probability
  Properties of Discrete Probability Distributions
  Theoretical and Empirical Probability
  The Standard Normal Distribution as a Probability Distribution

Standard Scores

Summary

Key Terms and Symbols

Review Questions

Can you think of someone who is off-the-charts physically attractive? What about someone at the opposite extreme? A humorous Super Bowl commercial for Planters nuts featured a woman whose hair and dress was unkempt, whose teeth prevented her mouth from completely closing, and who possessed a very furry unibrow—one big eyebrow! This combination of unusual physical attributes typically would result in this person being viewed as very physically unattractive. What made this commercial funny and memorable was that despite her appearance, the woman was found to be irresistible due to the aroma from the nuts she used as "perfume." The judgment of attractiveness of individuals, such as the woman in the commercial, has a long history in the behavioral sciences. Sir Francis Galton (1822–1911), a pioneer in the development of statistics, judged the attractiveness of all the women he met. Ultimately, he concluded that the women of London were the most attractive in all of Great Britain. Of course, Galton could not judge the attractiveness of all the women in Great Britain, he had to reach his conclusions based on only the women he met. Galton faced a problem common to modern behavioral science research; he wanted to reach conclusions about a population, but he could only measure a sample.

Population ▶ A complete set of people, animals, objects, or events that share a common characteristic.

In Chapter 1, we defined a **population** as a complete set of people, animals, objects, or events that possess a common characteristic. Populations that are of interest to behavioral scientists can come in many sizes. Sometimes a researcher may be interested in a population in which all the members can be easily identified, such as the students in a particular college. Most often, however, behavioral scientists are interested in populations in which all of the members cannot be as easily identified, such as all the daily commuters to Chicago, all the iPod owners in North America, or all the women in Great Britain. As a result, most frequently researchers will work with data obtained from a sample selected from a population.

Sample ▶ A subset, or subgroup, selected from a population.

A **sample** is some subset or subgroup selected from a population. To understand what information is contained in the sample data requires that we organize the data and use descriptive statistics to summarize it. This is why the focus in Chapters 3 to 5 has been on organizing and describing scores in samples. However, researchers are usually interested in more than just describing the sample; their goal is often to understand or draw inferences about what is going on with every member of the population. Thus, we now turn to a discussion of populations and their characteristics, with emphasis on a very special population distribution, the normal distribution.

In previous chapters, we introduced terms and symbols used to identify and characterize populations and samples. To indicate when we are measuring an entire population, we symbolize the population mean as μ and the standard deviation as σ. The values obtained for the population mean and standard deviation are called *parameters*. Thus, a **parameter** is a number, such as a mean or standard deviation, that characterizes a population. For samples, however, we use $\overline{X}$ and s to represent the mean and standard deviation, respectively, and refer to their values as *descriptive statistics*. The purpose of using different terms and symbols for populations and samples is to ensure that it is clear whether we are discussing a sample or a population. It is important to understand this distinction, for the normal distribution that we discuss next is a population distribution, and it is characterized by μ and σ rather than by $\overline{X}$ and s. This difference in notation for samples and populations is summarized in Table 6.1.

Parameter ▶ A number that describes a characteristic of a population.

Normal Distribution

Normal distribution ▶ A theoretical mathematical distribution that specifies the relative frequency of a set of scores in a population.

One population distribution of importance to the behavioral sciences is the normal distribution. The **normal distribution** is a theoretical mathematical distribution that specifies the relative frequency of a population of scores. The frequency distribution for a normally distributed set of scores can be described completely by knowing only the

TABLE 6.1	Notation for samples and populations		
		Sample	**Population**
Descriptive characteristics		Statistics	Parameters
Mean		$\overline{X}$	μ
Standard deviation		s	σ
Variance		s^2	σ^2

mean (μ) and the standard deviation (σ) of the distribution. A normal distribution with $\mu = 70$ and $\sigma = 10$ is illustrated in Figure 6.1. The distribution shown is a mathematical distribution that does not represent any actually measured population of scores. No real population of scores is distributed so precisely that it will be exactly normal, but it will be useful at times to assume that some populations of scores are approximately normally distributed. In this chapter, however, we focus on the normal distribution as a theoretical mathematical distribution.

The Normal Distribution and the Behavioral Sciences

The normal distribution developed from the work of Jakob Bernoulli (1654–1705), Abraham de Moivre (1667–1754), Pierre Remond de Montmort (1678–1719), Karl Friedrich Gauss (1777–1855), and others. Their interests were in developing mathematical approximations for probabilities encountered in various games of chance or in the distribution of errors to be expected in observations, such as in astronomy or physics. The normal distribution soon became an important distribution to statisticians because many problems in statistics can be solved only if a normal distribution is assumed.

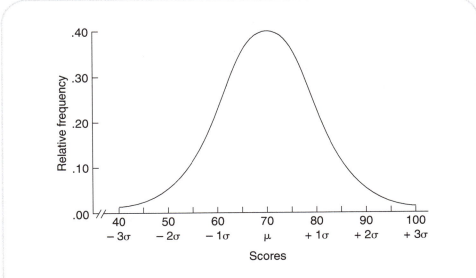

Figure 6.1 A normal distribution with $\mu = 70$ and $\sigma = 10$.

The normal distribution also gained importance for behavioral scientists because it is reasonable to assume that any behavioral measures determined by a large number of independent variables will be approximately normally distributed for a population. Many human capabilities, such as mathematical ability or verbal skills, are determined by a number of independent factors—genetic heritage, parental encouragement, schooling, a particular teacher, social class, cultural forces, and so forth. Consequently, measurements of such abilities are likely to be approximately normally distributed in a population. Similarly, some physical characteristics of people, such as attractiveness, are also determined by many independent factors and thus may be approximately normally distributed in a population. We stress the word *approximately*, for no actual set of scores of any ability or characteristic, such as mathematical ability or physical attractiveness, is exactly normally distributed, but it will often be useful to us to assume that it is. This point becomes clearer later in the chapter. First, however we discuss the normal distribution more fully.

Properties of the Normal Distribution

The normal distribution possesses the properties of being symmetrical, unimodal, asymptotic, and continuous.

Symmetrical

Symmetrical distribution ▷ A frequency distribution that, when folded in half, produces two halves identical in shape.

A theoretical normal distribution is **symmetrical** about its mode, median, and mean. In a normal distribution, then, the mode, median, and mean are equal to each other.

Unimodal

Unimodal distribution ▷ A distribution with one mode.

Figure 6.1 illustrates there is only one most frequently occurring score in the theoretical normal distribution, thus it is **unimodal**.

Asymptotic

Asymptotic distribution ▷ A distribution for which the tails of the distribution never touch the *X* axis.

Notice from Figure 6.1 that the tails of the normal distribution approach closer to the base line, or abscissa, as they get farther away from μ. The distribution, however, is **asymptotic**; the tails never touch the base line, regardless of the distance from μ.

Continuous

Continuous distribution ▷ A distribution for which, if any two scores in the distribution are chosen, another score that lies between them can always be found.

The normal distribution is **continuous** for all scores between plus and minus infinity. It is not a discrete distribution. This means that for any two scores, we can always obtain another score that lies between them.

Area Under the Normal Distribution

The normal distribution is a theoretical relative frequency distribution. Recall from Chapter 3 that the relative frequency of a score is the frequency of occurrence of the score divided by the total number of scores in a distribution. Thus, relative frequency is expressed as a proportion, and the total cumulative relative frequency in a distribution is 1.0 (see, for example, column i of Table 3.4). Because the normal distribution is a relative frequency distribution, the total area under the distribution is equal to 1.0; that is, the relative frequencies of the scores in a normal distribution sum to 1.0.

In all normal distributions, specific proportions of scores are within certain intervals about the mean. In any normally distributed population, .3413 of the scores is in an interval between μ and μ plus one standard deviation (i.e., between μ and $\mu + 1\sigma$). The

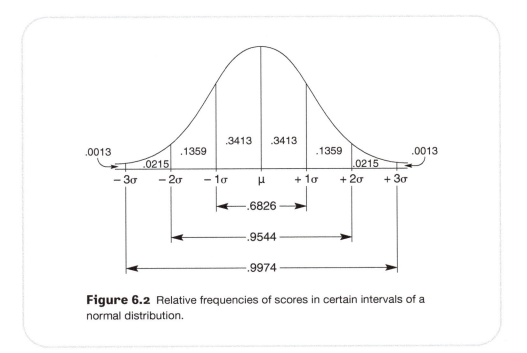

Figure 6.2 Relative frequencies of scores in certain intervals of a normal distribution.

proportion .3413 can be expressed as a percent by multiplying by 100; thus .3413 equals 34.13 percent. Hence, we can say that 34.13 percent of the scores in a normal distribution are in an interval between μ and μ plus one standard deviation. Because the distribution is symmetrical, the same proportion of scores is within an interval between μ and μ minus one standard deviation (i.e., between μ and $\mu - 1\sigma$). This relationship is shown in Figure 6.2. The interval from one to two standard deviations above the mean (i.e., the interval from $\mu + 1\sigma$ to $\mu + 2\sigma$) contains .1359 or 13.59 percent of the scores. Similarly, an interval from one to two standard deviations below the mean (i.e., the interval from $\mu - 1\sigma$ to $\mu - 2\sigma$) also contains .1359 of the scores. Because the normal distribution is symmetrical, corresponding intervals above and below the mean always contain equal areas. Notice from Figure 6.2 that scores more than two standard deviations above μ occur only .0228 of the time (i.e., .0215 + .0013 = .0228), as do scores more than two standard deviations below μ. These relationships hold for any normal distribution regardless of the specific values of μ and σ.

Notice that these relationships are in agreement with many of our everyday observations of the world around us. Most of us hover around the average with respect to physical attractiveness. As physical attractiveness either increases or decreases from the average, the number of instances occurring drops off with greater deviation from the mean. Finally there are very few instances of either the off-the-charts attractiveness or unattractiveness that we discussed in the chapter opening. Few people are as unattractive as the unibrowed woman of the Super Bowl commercial.

The areas under the normal distribution may also be added so that, for example, the interval from the mean minus one standard deviation to the mean plus one standard deviation (i.e., from $\mu - 1\sigma$ to $\mu + 1\sigma$) contains .3413 + .3413 or .6826 of the scores. Similarly, within plus or minus two standard deviations around the mean (the interval from

$\mu - 2\sigma$ to $\mu + 2\sigma$), $.1359 + .3413 + .3413 + .1359$, or $.9544$, of the scores occur. Extending the range to three standard deviations around the mean (the interval from $\mu - 3\sigma$ to $\mu + 3\sigma$) encompasses $.0215 + .1359 + .3413 + .3413 + .1359 + .0215$, or $.9974$, of the scores. These relationships also are illustrated in Figure 6.2. Again, the proportions remain the same regardless of the values of μ and σ.

To illustrate these relationships, suppose that a population of scores is normally distributed with $\mu = 100$ and $\sigma = 15$. A score of 85 is one standard deviation below the mean (i.e., $\mu - 1\sigma = 100 - 15 = 85$), and a score of 115 is one standard deviation above the mean (i.e., $\mu + 1\sigma = 100 + 15 = 115$) in this distribution. Accordingly, $.6826$ of the scores in this distribution will have values between 85 and 115. Similarly, $.9544$ of the scores will have values between 70 and 130 (the interval from $\mu - 2\sigma$ to $\mu + 2\sigma$), and $.9974$ of the scores will have values between 55 and 145 (the interval from $\mu - 3\sigma$ to $\mu + 3\sigma$).

As another example, suppose that we have a second normally distributed population of scores with $\mu = 50$ and $\sigma = 5$. In this distribution, $.6826$ of the scores will have values between 45 and 55 (the interval from $\mu - 1\sigma$ to $\mu + 1\sigma$), $.9544$ of the scores will have values between 40 and 60 (the interval from $\mu - 2\sigma$ to $\mu + 2\sigma$), and $.9974$ of the scores will have values between 35 and 65 (the interval from $\mu - 3\sigma$ to $\mu + 3\sigma$).

To summarize, in a normal distribution the following relations hold between μ, σ, the proportion of scores, and the percentage of scores contained in certain intervals about the mean:

Interval	Proportion of Scores in Interval	Percentage of Scores in Interval
$\mu - 1\sigma$ to $\mu + 1\sigma$	.6826	68.26
$\mu - 2\sigma$ to $\mu + 2\sigma$	.9544	95.44
$\mu - 3\sigma$ to $\mu + 3\sigma$	.9974	99.74

In the next section, you will learn to use a table to look up the proportion of scores that falls in certain intervals about the mean of a normal distribution; thus, the values given here do not have to be memorized. It is useful to remember approximate values, however, so that when solving problems, you can estimate answers to check on the correctness of your calculations. Thus, it is helpful to remember the following approximations:

▶ The interval $\mu - 1\sigma$ to $\mu + 1\sigma$ contains approximately 68 percent of the scores.

▶ The interval $\mu - 2\sigma$ to $\mu + 2\sigma$ contains slightly more than 95 percent of the scores.

▶ The interval $\mu - 3\sigma$ to $\mu + 3\sigma$ contains over 99 percent of the scores.

Testing Your Knowledge 6.1

1. Define: asymptotic, continuous distribution, μ, normal distribution, parameter, population, sample, symmetrical, σ, statistic.

2. Identify four properties of the normal distribution.

3. Why may scores obtained from an actual population of people never be exactly normally distributed? *Hint:* Think of the properties of the normal distribution.

4. Assume that you have a normally distributed population of scores with $\mu = 200$ and $\sigma = 20$. Indicate the proportions of scores that will be contained within each of the following intervals (use Figure 6.2).

Interval

a. 200 to 220   **g.** 180 to 260

b. 200 to 240   **h.** 160 to 240

c. 200 to 260   **i.** 140 to 260

d. 180 to 200   **j.** 220 to 240

e. 160 to 200   **k.** 220 to 260

f. 140 to 200   **l.** 140 to 160

Standard Normal Distribution

Knowing the mean and standard deviation of a normal distribution provides precise information about the proportion of scores contained within certain intervals on that distribution. Because the normal distribution is defined by a mathematical equation, we can determine the exact relative frequency for any interval of scores on the distribution. A problem faced, however, is that we have to use a complex mathematical equation employing the value of μ and σ for the distribution of scores of interest. Fortunately, there is a simple way around this problem. The solution is to transform a normal distribution with mean μ and standard deviation σ (e.g., $\mu = 20$, $\sigma = 2$) into a standard form with $\mu = 0$ and $\sigma = 1$. Then, if we use only this standard normal distribution with $\mu = 0$ and $\sigma = 1$, we can solve the equation for score values and create a table with the relative frequencies found. Subsequently, we could simply look up the relative frequency or cumulative relative frequency of scores in a table, rather than using the equation of the normal distribution.

Standard normal distribution ▷
A normal distribution with $\mu = 0$ and $\sigma = 1$.

The **standard normal distribution** (also called the *unit normal distribution*) has a mean of zero ($\mu = 0$) and a standard deviation of one ($\sigma = 1$). A score from a normally distributed variable with any μ and σ may be transformed into a z score on the standard normal distribution by employing the relation

$$z = \frac{X - \mu}{\sigma}$$

where $z =$ standardized score.
$X =$ raw score from the population.
$\mu =$ mean of the normal distribution from which the score X was obtained.
$\sigma =$ standard deviation of the normal distribution from which the score X was obtained.

When numerical values are substituted into the formula, we will refer to the value of z obtained as z_{obs}, where the subscripted *obs* refers to the value of z observed from the value of X. We use this terminology so that it is clear whether we are discussing a value of z obtained from substituting scores into the formula (z_{obs}) or the values of z found in Appendix C.1, which are explained in the next section. z is often called a **standard normal deviate** because it expresses the value of a score on the standard normal distribution. A standard normal

Standard normal deviate ▷ The value of z_{obs} when a score is transformed into a score on the standard normal distribution.

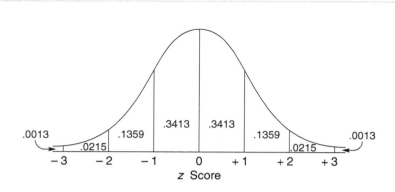

Figure 6.3 The standard normal distribution with μ = 0 and σ = 1.0. The proportion of scores between the identified z values is shown.

distribution is illustrated in Figure 6.3. The figure includes the proportion of scores between the illustrated z scores. Notice that because $z = +1$ indicates a score one standard deviation above the mean, the proportion of scores between $z = 0$ and $z = +1$ is .3413, the same as the proportion of scores between μ and μ + 1σ on Figure 6.2.

To demonstrate the use of the standard normal distribution, suppose that a score of 115 (i.e., $X = 115$) is obtained from a normally distributed set of scores with μ = 100 and σ = 15. This score is converted to a z_{obs} by

$$z_{obs} = \frac{X - \mu}{\sigma}$$

$$= \frac{115 - 100}{15}$$

$$= \frac{15}{15} = +1.0.$$

For the original score of 115, the transformed standard normal score is +1.0. The z_{obs} score of +1.0 indicates that the original score of 115 is one standard deviation (i.e., 15) above the mean (i.e., 100) of the normal distribution from which it was obtained.

The transformation of a score to a z score on the standard normal distribution locates the original score (i.e., X) in terms of how many standard deviations the score is away from the mean. The score of 115 that we used as an example is +1.0σ units away from the mean of its distribution. Consider the scores in Table 6.2 and their corresponding z_{obs} values. These scores were obtained from a normal distribution with μ = 75 and σ = 10. Attempt to calculate some of the z_{obs} scores given. Notice that the z_{obs} value for any score is simply how many standard deviation units the score is above or below the mean of zero on the standard normal distribution.

A note of caution is in order here. Transforming a score, X, into a z score precisely locates the original score on the standard normal distribution only if the score is from a normally distributed set of scores. If the score is from a nonnormal distribution, such as

TABLE **6.2**	Transformation of scores from a normal distribution with $\mu = 75$ and $\sigma = 10$ to z scores on a standard normal distribution.

Score (X)	z
105	+3.0
100	+2.5
95	+2.0
90	+1.5
85	+1.0
80	+0.5
75	0.0
70	−0.5
65	−1.0
60	−1.5
55	−2.0
50	−2.5
45	−3.0

a rectangular distribution or a bimodal distribution, then converting the score, X, into a z score cannot provide information about the location of the score on a normal distribution because the z score does not make the original set of scores normally distributed.

Using a Table of the Standard Normal Distribution

The advantage of transforming scores into z scores on a standard normal distribution is that the proportion of scores occurring between values of z is known and tabled. These proportions are presented in Appendix C.1. A portion of Appendix C.1 is illustrated in Table 6.3. Column a lists values of z. Column b presents the area between $z = 0$ and the value of z listed in column a. The shaded area in the small figure at the top of the column illustrates this area. Column c provides the area beyond the value of z in column a to infinity. Again, the small figure at the top of the column illustrates this area. Because the normal distribution is symmetrical, negative values of z encompass areas identical to positive values of z. Thus, negative values of z are not tabled.

To demonstrate how to use this table, consider a normally distributed set of scores with $\mu = 100$ and $\sigma = 15$. Suppose a score of 115 is obtained from this distribution. What proportion of scores is equal to or less than 115? To solve this problem we convert the score of 115 to a z score as follows:

$$z_{obs} = \frac{X - \mu}{\sigma} = \frac{115 - 100}{15} = +1.0.$$

Notice that because this value of z is obtained from a raw score of 115, it is identified as z_{obs} to distinguish it from the values of z given in Table 6.3. To help visualize the solution to the problem, it is useful to draw a figure of the standard normal distribution and indicate on it the raw scores and the z_{obs} values of those scores, as shown in Figure 6.4. The answer to the

TABLE

6.3

Proportion of area under the normal distribution between $z = 0.95$ and $z = 1.10$. Column a lists values of z; column b presents the area between $z = 0$ and the value of z listed in column a; column c provides the area beyond the value of z in column a to infinity.

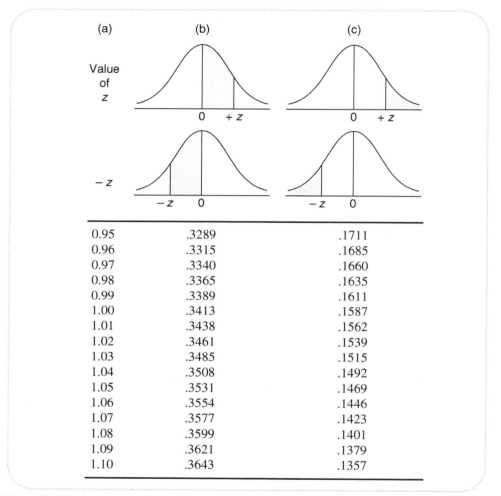

(a) Value of z	(b)	(c)
0.95	.3289	.1711
0.96	.3315	.1685
0.97	.3340	.1660
0.98	.3365	.1635
0.99	.3389	.1611
1.00	.3413	.1587
1.01	.3438	.1562
1.02	.3461	.1539
1.03	.3485	.1515
1.04	.3508	.1492
1.05	.3531	.1469
1.06	.3554	.1446
1.07	.3577	.1423
1.08	.3599	.1401
1.09	.3621	.1379
1.10	.3643	.1357

Source: Values calculated by the authors using Microsoft Excel Normsdist(value) − .5 (column a); 1 − Normsdist(value) (column b). All values rounded to four decimal places.

problem requires that we obtain the area of the distribution from $z = -\infty$ to $z = +1.0$. One-half (or .5000) of the scores in the distribution are below $z = 0$. Column b of Table 6.3 indicates that .3413 of the scores are between $z = 0$ and $z = +1.0$ (see the axis labeled c on Figure 6.4). Thus, the answer to the problem is the proportion of scores from $z = -\infty$ to $z = 0$ (i.e., .5000) plus the proportion of scores from $z = 0$ to $z = +1.0$ (.3413 from column b of Appendix C.1), or .8413. The proportion of scores equal to or less than 115 is .8413 or, expressed as a percentage, 84.13 percent.

Suppose that we now want to know the proportion of scores equal to or greater than 115. We may obtain this proportion in one of two ways. First, because we have already

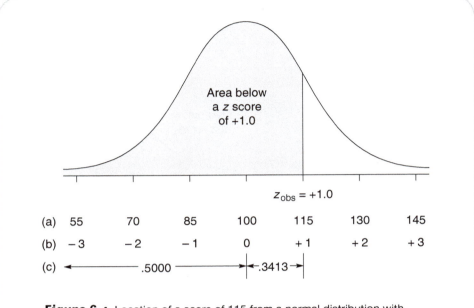

Figure 6.4 Location of a score of 115 from a normal distribution with $\mu = 100$ and $\sigma = 15$ on the standard normal distribution. The labels on the X axis show (a) the raw scores, (b) z_{obs} scores corresponding to the raw scores, and (c) the proportion of scores from $z = -\infty$ to $z = 0$ and from $z = 0$ to $z = +1$.

found that 84.13 percent of the scores will be equal to or less than 115, the remaining area under the normal distribution must indicate the number of scores that will be equal to or greater than 115. We find this proportion by subtracting .8413 from 1.000, the total area of the distribution. Accordingly, $1.000 - .8413 = .1587$, the proportion of scores equal to or greater than 115.

If we had not previously found that .8413 of the scores is equal to or less than 115, then we could solve the problem by recognizing that the proportion requested is the area of the distribution beyond $z = +1.00$. Using Table 6.3, we find the value of $z = 1.00$ in column a. We then read across to column c, which presents the proportion of scores beyond z. For $z = +1.0$, this value is .1587. Thus, .1587 of the scores, or 15.87 percent, is equal to or greater than 115.

Consider another problem from this distribution. What proportion of scores in this distribution is equal to or less than 82? To solve the problem we convert 82 to a z score, $z_{obs} = (82 - 100)/15 = -1.2$. This z_{obs} indicates that a score of 82 is 1.2 standard deviations below the mean of the distribution. The raw scores of the distribution and the $z_{obs} = -1.2$ are shown in Figure 6.5. We then obtain the proportion of scores below z equal to -1.2. Notice that from the figure alone we can estimate that this proportion will be very small. Because the standard normal distribution is symmetrical, as many scores lie beyond $z = -1.2$ as lie beyond $z = +1.2$, we look up $z = +1.2$. This value is not included in Table 6.3, however; thus, we use the complete table of proportions of area under the normal distribution given in Appendix C.1. We find $z = 1.2$ in column a and

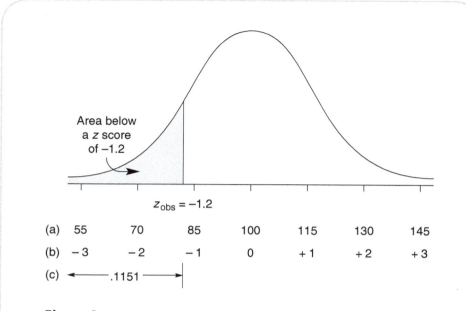

Figure 6.5 Location of a score of 82 from a normal distribution with $\mu = 100$ and $\sigma = 15$ on the standard normal distribution. The labels on the X axis show (a) the raw scores, (b) z_{obs} scores corresponding to the raw scores, and (c) the proportion of scores from $z = -\infty$ to $z = -1.2$.

read across to the value of .1151 in column c. Thus, .1151 of the scores or 11.51 percent is equal to or less than 82. Other uses of the standard normal distribution are given in Example Problem 6.1.

EXAMPLE PROBLEM

6.1

Using the Standard Normal Distribution

Assume a normally distributed population with $\mu = 80$ and $\sigma = 5$.

Problem: What proportion of scores in this distribution is equal to or greater than 88?

Statistic to Be Used: $z = \dfrac{\overline{X} - \mu}{\sigma}$

Solution: The score of 88 must be converted into z_{obs}. Then Appendix C.1 is used to obtain the proportion of scores equal to or greater than z_{obs}. Substituting numerical values into the formula for z, we obtain

$$z_{obs} = \frac{88 - 80}{5} = \frac{8}{5} = +1.6.$$

Column c of Appendix C.1 indicates that the area of the standard normal distribution equal to or greater than $z = +1.6$ is .0548. Hence, the proportion of scores equal to or greater than 88 is .0548. Thus, out of every 100 scores in the population, 5.48 are equal to or greater than 88.

Problem: What proportion of scores in this distribution is between 83 and 87?

Solution: Both 83 and 87 must be converted to z_{obs} scores. Then we obtain the area of the standard normal distribution between the two values of z_{obs}. Substituting numerical values, we obtain

$$z_{obs} \text{ for } 83 = \frac{83 - 80}{5} = \frac{3}{5} = +0.6,$$

$$z_{obs} \text{ for } 87 = \frac{87 - 80}{5} = \frac{7}{5} = +1.4.$$

The raw scores and the corresponding z_{obs} scores are shown in Figure 6.6. From column b of Appendix C.1, for $z_{obs} = +0.6$, the proportion of scores between $z = 0$ and $z = +0.6$ is .2257. For $z_{obs} = +1.4$, the proportion of scores between $z = 0$ and $z = +1.4$ is .4192. The area of the distribution between these two values of z provides the proportion of scores between 83 and 87. To obtain this area, we subtract .2257 from .4192. The result is .1935 (see the axis labeled c in Figure 6.6). Thus, the proportion of scores that is in the interval from 83 to 87 is .1935. For every 1000 scores, 193.5 are between scores of 83 to 87.

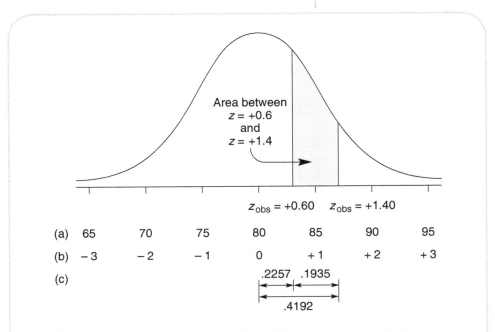

Figure 6.6 Location of scores of 83 and 87 from a normal distribution with $\mu = 80$ and $\sigma = 5$ on the standard normal distribution. The labels on the X axis show (a) the raw scores, (b) z_{obs} scores corresponding to the raw scores, and (c) the proportion of scores from $z = 0$ to $z = +0.6$ and from $z = 0$ to $z = +1.4$.

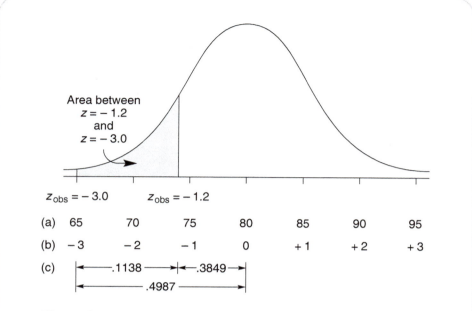

Area between
$z = -1.2$
and
$z = -3.0$

$z_{obs} = -3.0$　　　$z_{obs} = -1.2$

(a) 65　　70　　75　　80　　85　　90　　95

(b) −3　　−2　　−1　　0　　+1　　+2　　+3

(c) |◄——.1138——►|◄—.3849—►|
　　　|◄————— .4987 —————►|

Figure 6.7 Location of scores of 65 and 74 from a normal distribution with $\mu = 80$ and $\sigma = 5$ on the standard normal distribution. The labels on the X axis show (a) the raw scores, (b) z_{obs} scores corresponding to the raw scores, and (c) the proportion of scores from $z = 0$ to $z = -3.0$ and from $z = 0$ to $z = -1.2$.

Problem: What proportion of scores is between 65 and 74?

Solution: This problem is solved identically to the previous problem. Both 65 and 74 must be converted to z_{obs} scores. Then we find the area of the standard normal distribution between the values of z_{obs} for the two scores. Substituting numerical values, we obtain

$$z_{obs} \text{ for } 65 = \frac{65 - 80}{5} = \frac{-15}{5} = -3.0,$$

$$z_{obs} \text{ for } 74 = \frac{74 - 80}{5} = \frac{-6}{5} = -1.2.$$

The raw scores and the corresponding z_{obs} scores are shown in Figure 6.7. Column b of Appendix C.1 indicates that .4987 of the scores is between $z = 0$ and $z = -3.0$. For $z_{obs} = -1.2$, .3849 of the scores is between $z = 0$ and $z = -1.2$. We obtain the proportion of scores between $z = -3.0$ and $z = -1.2$ by subtracting .3849 from .4987. This value is .1138 (see the axis labeled c in Figure 6.7). The proportion of scores in the interval from 65 to 74 is .1138. For every 1000 scores in the population, 113.8 are between 65 and 74.

Problem: What range of scores includes the middle 80 percent of the scores on the distribution?

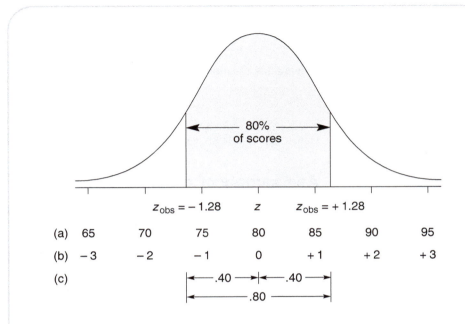

Figure 6.8 Illustration of finding scores that include the middle 80 percent of the scores from a normal distribution with $\mu = 80$ and $\sigma = 5$ on the standard normal distribution. The labels on the X axis show (a) the raw scores, (b) z_{obs} scores corresponding to the raw scores, and (c) the proportion of scores from $z = 0$ to $z = -1.28$ and from $z = 0$ to $z = +1.28$.

Solution: This problem is solved by finding areas in column b of Appendix C.1 that include a proportion of .40 or 40 percent of the scores on each side of the mean, determining the z value for these scores, and then solving the formula for z to obtain values of X. Figure 6.8 illustrates the proportions and scores that we need. To find the z that includes .40 of the scores between $z = 0$ and its value, we read down column b until we find the proportion closest to .40. This area is .3997, which corresponds to a z of 1.28. Thus, scores that result in z values between 0 and +1.28 occur with a relative frequency of .3997, and scores that result in z values between 0 and −1.28 also occur with a relative frequency of .3997. The total area encompassed by scores between $z = -1.28$ and $z = +1.28$ is .3997 + .3997 = .7994, or approximately .80. The last step is to obtain the values of X that correspond to $z = -1.28$ and $z = +1.28$. To find these values, we substitute numerical values of z, μ, and σ into the formula $z = (X - \mu)/\sigma$ and solve for X.

For $z_{obs} = +1.28$,

$$+1.28 = \frac{X - 80}{5}.$$

Solving this equation for X,

$$(+1.28)5 = X - 80$$
$$X = 5(1.28) + 80 = 86.4.$$

For $z_{obs} = -1.28$,

$$-1.28 = \frac{X - 80}{5}.$$

Solving this equation for X,

$$(-1.28)5 = X - 80$$
$$X = 5(-1.28) + 80 = 73.6.$$

Hence, the middle 80 percent of the scores is between 73.6 and 86.4.

An Example of the Use of z Scores

Many human phenomena and characteristics, such as height and weight, are approximately normally distributed. Hack et al. (2003) were interested in the question of the growth of very low birth weight infants through childhood and adolescence. Consequently, they followed the growth of 103 male and 92 female very low birth weight infants from birth to age 20 years. Many of their results were presented as z scores so they could be compared to the growth of other infants. For example, at birth, the mean z score for height of both the males and females in this study was -1.2. From column c of Appendix C.1, we find that only about .12 (the actual value from the table is .1151, and we rounded to .12) of the values of z on a standard normal distribution is equal to or less than $z = -1.2$. Thus, these infants were in the 12th percentile for height at birth. At age 40 weeks, both the males ($z = -2.6$) and the females ($z = -2.4$) were in the 1st percentile for height. By age 20 years, however, both males and females were closer to the average, with $z = -0.4$ for males and $z = -0.3$ for females. These z values place the males in the 34th percentile and females in the 38th percentile for height.

Testing Your Knowledge 6.2

1. Define: standard normal deviate, standard normal distribution, z, z_{obs}.

2. For each of the following values of X, μ, and σ, obtain the value of z_{obs}. Then use Appendix C.1 to find the area between $z = 0$ and z_{obs} and the area beyond z_{obs}.

	μ	σ	X
a.	73	4.2	81
b.	127	11.6	121
c.	17	1.3	18
d.	50	6.0	39
e.	5	0.4	5.7
f.	256	35.0	212

3. Solve the following problems using the approach illustrated in example problem 6.1. You have conducted a large-scale testing project measuring students on a test of reasoning with verbal analogies. Assume that the test scores are normally distributed with $\mu = 72$ and $\sigma = 8$.

a. What proportion of scores in the distribution is equal to or greater than 86?

b. What proportion of scores in the distribution is between 80 and 90?

c. What proportion of scores in the distribution is between 60 and 70?

d. What range of scores includes the middle 90 percent of scores on the test?

Probability

We have discussed the normal distribution as a theoretical relative frequency distribution, but it also is a probability distribution of a continuous variable. The concepts associated with probability represent an important component of statistics; however, only some very fundamental aspects of probability are needed to understand the following chapters. In this section, we introduce the basics of probability needed to understand probability distributions and their use in statistics.

The daily activities of living provide an intuitive sense of probability. For example, have you ever received a letter similar to the following?

> Urgent Notification—Reply Immediately. You are the lucky winner of one of the following prizes:
>
>   A Brand-New Luxury Sports Car, Value $42,000
>   A Two-Week, All-Expenses-Paid Vacation in Hawaii, Value $6500
>   A Large Screen Plasma TV Home Theater System, Value $1995
>   An Easy-Use Microwave Oven, Value $125
>   A Top-Quality, Digital Camera, Value $49
>   A Whiz-Bang Home Computer, Value $529
>
> All you need to do to claim your prize is visit beautiful LAZY ACRES VACATION RESORT and see the MAGNIFICENT home sites available for your purchase. You will definitely win one of the above prizes when you visit our STUNNING resort.

Visions of a luxurious sports car or a delightful two-week vacation may begin to fill your thoughts. Those beautiful visions are shattered, however, when you read the small print on the second page of the letter. Here you find your chances of winning each gift and often they are expressed as follows:

Prize	Number of Awards/1,000,000 Visitors
Car	1
Vacation	20
TV	34
Microwave	66
Camera	999,845
Computer	34

Assuming that each visitor has an equal chance of winning one prize, which prize do you think it is most likely you will win? Which prize do you think it is least likely that you will win? Even if you haven't studied probability formally, you likely will say, "Forget the sports car, I'll take a picture of it with my camera." Only one visitor out of a million wins a car, whereas 999,845 visitors out of a million win a camera. Obviously, the chances are that you will win the camera, not the car.

Suppose that you are asked what is the probability that you will win a TV. It's likely you will answer something similar to "I have 34 chances in a million." In effect, what you have indicated is that the probability of winning a specific prize is found by dividing the numbers of the prize to be awarded by the total number of prizes to be given, or

$$\text{Probability of winning a specific prize} = \frac{\text{Number of the specific prize to be awarded}}{\text{Total number of prizes awarded}}.$$

Applying this formula to the TV prize, we obtain the probability of winning a TV as 34/1,000,000, or .000034. If we apply this formula to each of the prizes, we obtain the following probability distribution for the prizes:

Prize	Number of Awards/1,000,000 Visitors	Probability of Winning
Car	1	.000001
Vacation	20	.000020
TV	34	.000034
Microwave	66	.000066
Camera	999,845	.999845
Computer	34	.000034

Outcome ▷ Each possible occurrence in a probability distribution.

Event ▷ The occurrence of a specified set of outcomes in a probability distribution.

You may notice that the formula for the probability of a prize looks much like the formula for relative frequency given in Chapter 3. In fact, this probability formula is a specific application of the relative frequency formula. If we call each possible occurrence in this distribution of prizes an **outcome**, then there are 1,000,000 possible outcomes for the distribution. Each outcome is equally probable, for each has a probability of occurrence of 1/1,000,000 or .000001. An **event** is the occurrence of a set of outcomes of interest. For example, if we consider the event of winning a camera, then there are 999,845 outcomes that compose this event. If the event of interest is winning either the TV or the microwave, then there are 34 outcomes for the TV and 66 outcomes for the microwave, for a total of 100 outcomes that compose the event. Notice that the event of winning a camera is much more probable than the event of winning a vacation, for there are 999,845 outcomes out of a possible 1,000,000 that compose the event of winning the camera, whereas there are only 20 outcomes out of a possible 1,000,000 that compose the event of winning a vacation. In a more general sense, if the occurrence of each outcome in a distribution is equally likely, then the **probability (p) of occurrence of an event** is defined as

Probability of occurrence of an event (p) ▷

$$p(\text{event}) = \frac{\text{Number of outcomes composing the event}}{\text{Total number of possible outcomes}}$$

$$p(\text{event}) = \frac{\textbf{Number of outcomes composing the event}}{\textbf{Total number of possible outcomes}}.$$

The letter p is used to indicate the probability of occurrence of an event. The result of applying this formula usually is expressed as a decimal, for example,

$$p(\text{microwave}) = .000066,$$

Discrete outcomes ▷ Outcomes in a distribution that have a countable set of values.

although probabilities may also be expressed as percentages or fractions. This formula provides the probability for **discrete outcomes**, outcomes that have a countable set of values, such as the number of computers to be awarded per one million visitors. Thus, the probabilities associated with the awarding of each prize constitute a discrete probability distribution.

As another example of a discrete probability distribution, consider the frequency distribution of the 100 Implicit View of Intelligence scores in Table 3.4. Suppose we were to randomly select one score from this set of scores, what is the probability it would be between 36 and 38? This question asks for the probability of an event of a score occurring between 36 and 38. Thus, the outcomes that are included in this event are scores of 36, 37, and 38. To find the probability of this event, we must find the total number of outcomes associated with these scores. We can find these outcomes by examining the frequency distribution of these scores in column e of Table 3.4. This column indicates that 13 scores are included in the interval of 36 to 38. Given there are 100 total scores in the distribution, the probability that a score is between 36 and 38 is

$$p(\text{score between 36 and 38}) = \frac{13}{100} = .13.$$

We may also state this probability as

$$p(36 \leq X \leq 38) = .13,$$

where $\leq$ = "less than or equal to" symbol. The number preceding the $\leq$ is less than or equal to the number following the $\leq$.
          $X =$ score selected.

This statement is read "the probability that X is equal to or greater than 36 (i.e., $36 \leq X$) and equal to or less than 38 (i.e., $X \leq 38$) is .13." We can go directly to this probability in Table 3.4 by using the relative frequency for these scores given in column f, which indicates that the relative frequency of scores between 36 and 38 is .13. Notice that this probability could also be found using the relative frequency histogram and the relative frequency polygon of the Implicit View of Intelligence scores, Figures 3.5 and 3.6, respectively.

Properties of Discrete Probability Distributions

Probability distributions possess several properties of which you likely are aware already; they have been introduced in the two examples we have discussed. The first is that for any probability distribution, the probability of an event must be between .00 and 1.00. An event with $p(\text{event}) = .00$ is certain not to occur, and an event with $p(\text{event}) = 1.00$ is certain to occur. Few events are absolutely certain in life and possess a probability equal to 1.00, and few are absolutely impossible and possess a probability equal to .00. This range of probability from .00 to 1.00 corresponds to the characteristic of a relative frequency distribution that the cumulative relative frequencies (*crf*) range from 0 to 1.00 (see column i of Table 3.4).

The second property is that the individual probabilities associated with the total number of outcomes in a probability distribution add to 1.00. This characteristic of probability distributions can be easily seen in Table 3.4 by noting that the cumulative relative frequency of the Implicit View of Intelligence scores adds to 1.00 (see column i). If you visit the Lazy Acres Vacation Resort, then the probability of winning a prize is 1.00.

The third property is that the probability of an event comprising mutually exclusive outcomes can be found by adding the probabilities of the outcomes composing the event.

Mutually exclusive outcomes are outcomes that cannot occur at the same time. In the example, the outcomes of a person winning both a vacation and a computer are mutually exclusive. A person can win one prize or the other, but not both. Similarly, a person cannot have scores of both 25 and 42 on the Implicit View of Intelligence scale. These outcomes are mutually exclusive. For example, suppose we were to randomly select one score from the set of Implicit View of Intelligence scores in Table 3.3. What is the probability it would be 39 or greater? This question can be answered by examining the simple frequency distribution in column e of Table 3.4. Notice that there are 15 scores that are 39 or more. We obtain this value simply by adding the frequencies of scores in column e that are 39 or more (i.e., $7 + 4 + 3 + 1 = 15$). Thus, the probability of selecting a score of 39 or more is $15 \div 100$ or .15. Using probability notation,

$$p(X \geq 39) = .15.$$

We could also obtain this probability from Table 3.4 by adding the relative frequencies of column f for scores of 39 or greater (i.e., $.07 + .04 + .03 + .01 = .15$).

This example illustrates the concept that if two or more outcomes are mutually exclusive, then to find the probability of the event of one of those outcomes occurring we add the probability associated with each outcome. In probability terminology, if A and B represent two mutually exclusive outcomes from a probability distribution, then the probability of either A or B occurring is the probability of A plus the probability of B, or

$$p(A \text{ or } B) = p(A) + p(B).$$

This relationship is known as the **additivity rule** for the probability of mutually exclusive outcomes.

As another example of the application of this formula, suppose we again randomly sample one Implicit View of Intelligence score and want to know the probability of it being either between 21 and 23 or between 36 and 38. These outcomes are mutually exclusive because one score cannot be both between 21 and 23 and 36 and 38. Using the frequency distribution shown in Table 3.4, the probability of randomly selecting a score either between 21 and 23 or between 36 and 38 is the relative frequency for scores in the class interval 21 and 23 (i.e., .03) plus the relative frequency for scores in the class interval 36 and 38 (i.e., .13), or a total probability of .16. In probability notation,

$$p(\text{selecting a score between 21 and 23 or 36 and 38}) = p(21 \text{ to } 23) + p(36 \text{ to } 38)$$
$$= .03 + .13 = .16.$$

This additivity rule becomes very important later in this chapter and in following chapters on hypothesis testing.

Theoretical and Empirical Probability

There are two ways in which we can determine the probability of an outcome, *theoretically* and *empirically*. For certain outcomes, we can reason the probability of occurrence of that outcome and determine a **theoretical probability distribution**. As a simple example, the probability of the toss of a fair coin resulting in a head showing can be determined theoretically. There are two possible outcomes of a coin toss, a head or a tail. If the coin is fair, then each is equally likely. Hence, the probability of a single toss resulting in a head showing is one outcome out of the two possible, or $p(\text{head showing}) = 1/2 = .5$. Theoretical probability models often are more complex than this, however. An example occurs in the next section in which we discuss the standard normal distribution as a theoretical probability distribution.

For other outcomes, however, such as what is the probability that if you are a female you will live to be 60 years old, we cannot reason a theoretical probability. To obtain this probability we use actual occurrences of the event to determine an **empirical probability distribution**. For example, suppose you were at a Major League Baseball game in 2006 and wanted to know the probability of a home run occurring for any plate appearance by a batter. To find this probability, you need to know how many plate appearances occurred in a season and how many home runs were hit in a season. For 2006, these rates were 188,052 plate appearances by batters in the major leagues and 5386 home runs (Edes, 2007). Thus, the probability of a home run occurring for a plate appearance is:

Empirical probability distribution
▶ A probability distribution found by counting actual occurrences of an event.

$$p(\text{home run for a plate appearance}) = \frac{5386}{188052} = .029.$$

Of course, this value of p will change from season to season, depending on the number of plate appearances by batters and the number of home runs hit. Likewise, we can only determine the probability of specific Implicit View of Intelligence scores by actually measuring people with this scale. Behavioral scientists have occasion to use both theoretical and empirical probabilities, but the emphasis in this text is on theoretical distributions such as the standard normal distribution.

In the following chapters, we will be concerned with problems of statistical inference—reaching conclusions about populations based on measures obtained from samples drawn from those populations. In doing so, however, we will never be absolutely sure of the correctness of our conclusions; thus, our inferences will use probability statements.

The Standard Normal Distribution as a Probability Distribution

The normal distribution is a theoretical relative frequency distribution. Thus, it is also a probability distribution. But it is a slightly different probability distribution from the discrete probability distribution just introduced. A score, X, in a normal distribution is a continuous variable, one that can take on an unlimited set of values in the range within which it varies. For example, suppose that the scores to which a theoretical normal distribution is being applied are body weights. What is the probability of finding a person who weighs exactly 123 pounds? Weight is a continuous variable, however, and some people may weigh 123.3 pounds, or perhaps 123.36, or even 123.364 pounds. Conceptually, at least, we might find someone weighing 123.3642193 pounds if we could measure so precisely. Is a weight of 123.3 pounds to be considered 123 pounds? What of a weight of 123.00001 pounds? In principle, we can never obtain a weight of exactly 123 pounds, for we could always measure weight to a greater degree of accuracy and find that it was not exactly 123 pounds.

Following this line of reasoning, the probability of occurrence of an exact value of a continuous score is zero. But the probability of the score falling within a certain interval is not zero. Although we cannot obtain a weight of exactly 123 pounds, we can obtain a weight in the interval between 122.5 and 123.5 pounds. For example, regardless of the number of decimal places to which we may carry our measurements, a weight of 123.36 (or even 123.3642193) will always fall into the interval between 122.5 and 123.5 pounds. Thus, the probability function specified by the normal distribution does not provide probabilities for discrete values of X; rather, it provides probabilities that the value of X will fall within a certain interval. The probability is provided by the area under the distribution encompassed by the interval.

As an example of the normal distribution used as a probability distribution, consider the following problem. Suppose you know that a set of scores is normally distributed with $\mu = 150$ and $\sigma = 8$. If you were to randomly select a score from this distribution, what is the probability of obtaining a score between 150 and 158? To answer this question, we first transform the distribution into the standard normal distribution with $\mu = 0$ and $\sigma = 1$ using $z = (X - \mu)/\sigma$. Thus, the score of 150 becomes $z = 0$, and the score of 158 becomes $z = +1.0$. The question then resolves to what is the probability of obtaining a score with a value between $z = 0$ and $z = +1.0$? The answer is the area under the standard normal distribution between $z = 0$ and $z = +1.0$, or .3413 (obtained from column b of Appendix C.1). Accordingly, the probability of obtaining a score between 150 and 158 is .3413 or $p(150 \leq X \leq 158) = .3413$.

EXAMPLE PROBLEM

6.2

Using the Standard Normal Distribution as a Probability Distribution

Assume that you have the normally distributed population described in example problem 6.1, with $\mu = 80$ and $\sigma = 5$. The problems that follow are like those in example problem 6.1 except that they ask for probabilities rather than proportions of scores. It may be useful to refer to the figures associated with example problem 6.1 to follow the solutions presented.

Problem: What is the probability that a score in this distribution is equal to or greater than 88?

Statistic to Be Used: $z = \dfrac{(\overline{X} - \mu)}{\sigma}$

Solution: The score of 88 must be converted into a z_{obs}. Then Appendix C.1 is used to obtain the proportion of scores equal to or greater than z_{obs}. This proportion represents the probability requested. Substituting numerical values into the formula for z, we obtain

$$z_{obs} = \frac{88 - 80}{5} = \frac{8}{5} = +1.6.$$

Column c of Appendix C.1 indicates that the area of the standard normal distribution equal to or greater than $z = +1.6$ is .0548. Thus, the probability of a score being equal to or greater than 88 is .0548 or, written as a probability statement, $p(X \geq 88) = .0548$.

Problem: What is the probability that a score in this distribution is between 83 and 87?

Solution: Both 83 and 87 must be converted to z_{obs} scores. Then we find the area of the standard normal distribution between the two values of z_{obs} (see Figure 6.6). Substituting numerical values, we obtain

$$z_{obs} \text{ for } 83 = \frac{83 - 80}{5} = \frac{3}{5} = +0.6,$$

$$z_{obs} \text{ for } 87 = \frac{87 - 80}{5} = \frac{7}{5} = +1.4.$$

From column b of Appendix C.1, we see that for $z_{obs} = +0.6$ the proportion of scores between $z = 0$ and $z = +0.6$ is .2257. For $z_{obs} = +1.4$, the proportion of scores between $z = 0$ and $z = +1.4$ is .4192. The area of the distribution between these two values of z provides the proportion of scores between 83 and 87. To obtain this area, we subtract .2257 from .4192. The result is .1935. This proportion represents the probability requested. Thus, the probability of a score falling into the interval from 83 to 87 is .1935. In probability terms, $p(83 \leq X \leq 87) = .1935$.

Problem: What is the probability that a score in this distribution is between 65 and 74?

Solution: Both 65 and 74 must be converted to z_{obs} scores. Then we find the area of the standard normal distribution between the two values of z_{obs} (see Figure 6.7). Substituting numerical values, we obtain

$$z_{obs} \text{ for } 65 = \frac{65 - 80}{5} = \frac{-15}{5} = -3.0,$$

$$z_{obs} \text{ for } 74 = \frac{74 - 80}{5} = \frac{-6}{5} = -1.2.$$

Consulting column b of Appendix C.1 and recalling that, because the standard normal distribution is symmetrical, the same relations hold for negative z scores as for positive z scores, we find that .4987 of the scores lies between $z = 0$ and $z = -3.0$. For $z_{obs} = -1.2$, .3849 of the scores lies between $z = 0$ and $z = -1.2$. Accordingly, we obtain the proportion of scores between $z = -3.0$ and $z = -1.2$ by subtracting .3849 from .4987, which equals .1138. This proportion represents the probability requested; hence, $p(65 \leq X \leq 74) = .1138$.

Testing Your Knowledge 6.3

1. Define: additivity rule, discrete outcome, empirical probability, event, mutually exclusive outcome, probability of an event, theoretical probability, outcome.
2. What is the formula for the probability of occurrence of an event?
3. You have purchased a ticket for a raffle of a bicycle. The ticket states that one bicycle will be raffled off for every 700 tickets sold. Assuming each ticket has an equal chance of being selected, what is the probability that you will win a bicycle?
4. For each of the following values of X, μ, and σ, obtain the value of z. Then use Appendix C.1 to find the probability of a score being equal to or larger than the score given.

	μ	σ	X
a.	73	4.2	81
b.	127	11.6	121
c.	17	1.3	18
d.	50	6.0	39
e.	5	0.4	5.7
f.	256	35.0	212

5. You have conducted a large-scale testing project measuring students on a test of reasoning skills. Assume that the distribution of test scores is normally distributed, with $\mu = 72$ and $\sigma = 8$.

   a. What is the probability of a score in the distribution being equal to or greater than 84?

   b. What is the probability of a score in the distribution falling between 78 and 86?

   c. What is the probability of a score in the distribution falling between 64 and 70?

6. Your high school-age child is equally talented in football, baseball, and soccer and would like to play a professional sport. Your child has found the following information (National Collegiate Athletic Association, 2007): At the high school interscholastic level, there are about 134,000 baseball players, 306,000 football players, and 103,000 men's soccer players. Of these players, approximately 245 football players, 600 baseball players, and 72 soccer players will be drafted by a major league team. Which sport should your child choose and why?

Standard Scores

We have seen that we can take a normally distributed raw score and transform it into a score on the standard normal distribution by using the formula

$$z = \frac{X - \mu}{\sigma}.$$

The z is a standard score that can be used for comparing scores from two different normal distributions. For example, suppose that a person obtained a score of 75 on a test with $\mu = 70$ and $\sigma = 5$ and a score of 110 on a second test with $\mu = 100$ and $\sigma = 10$. Assume that scores on both tests are normally distributed. For the scores of 75 and 110, z_{obs} is $+1$ for each. On both tests, the individual scored one standard deviation above the mean. Accordingly, the person's standing in relation to other scores on the tests is identical for both tests; he or she has obtained a score one standard deviation above the mean.

It would be useful to make a similar transformation on scores from a sample, even if the scores were not normally distributed. We may make such a transformation using the formula

$$z = \frac{X - \overline{X}}{S},$$

where X = score of interest.
  $\overline{X}$ = mean of the sample of scores.
  S = sample standard deviation using the formula

$$S = \sqrt{\frac{\sum(X - \overline{X})^2}{N}} = \sqrt{\frac{SS}{N}}.$$

Notice this formula for the standard deviation divides the SS by N rather than $N - 1$ as does the formula for the estimated population standard deviation, s, presented in

TABLE 6.4	Raw scores and standard scores for five students on a statistics test and a history test.

		Test			
		Statistics		History	
Person	Raw Score	z Score	Raw Score	z Score
Amalia	91	+1.34	93	+1.18
Denise	62	−0.70	79	0.00
Jeff	87	+1.06	73	−0.50
Hans	56	−1.13	90	+0.92
Matt	64	−0.56	60	−1.60
$\overline{X}$	72.0		79.0	
S	14.2		11.9	

Chapter 5. The purpose of S is not to estimate σ; rather, it is used in the formula for z to locate a score in a distribution in relation to the mean of the scores in the distribution. S is used only to describe the standard deviation of a sample of scores. Thus, to distinguish it from the formula for the estimated population standard deviation, we identify it as S rather than s.

The z value obtained from this formula is often called a **standard score**. This formula transforms a score into a number indicating how far away from the mean of the sample the score is in standard deviation units. To illustrate, suppose that we gave a statistics test and a history test to five students and obtained the raw and z scores given in Table 6.4. Standard scores were obtained using the formula given previously. For example, Amalia's raw score on the statistics test was 91. The mean on the test was 72.0 and S was 14.2. Thus, Amalia's z score is found as

$$z_{obs} = \frac{X − \overline{X}}{S} = \frac{91 − 72.0}{14.2} = \frac{91.0}{14.2} = +1.34.$$

By knowing the standard score, we know Amalia's score in relation to the class mean; it is 1.34 standard deviations above the mean.

With standard scores we can easily compare scores from one test to the other, something we cannot do from the raw scores alone. For example, Jeff is 1.06 standard deviation units above the mean on his statistics test, but 0.50 standard deviation units below the mean on his history test. Positive standard scores indicate scores above the sample mean, scores of 0 (such as the history score of Denise) are equal to the sample mean, and negative standard scores are below the sample mean. You should note, however, that because this z is obtained from a sample of scores, it will not possess the same characteristics with respect to the normal distribution as the z obtained by $z = (X − \mu)/\sigma$. Nevertheless, standard scores are often used when reporting test results, for the score provides the person's relative standing with respect to others taking the same test. The standard score conversion does not change the shape of the distribution of scores, however. If the distribution of raw scores was skewed, then the distribution of standard scores will remain skewed.

Summary

▶ The normal distribution is a theoretical relative frequency distribution; no measured scores are exactly normally distributed. It is often useful, however, to assume that some behavioral measures are approximately normally distributed.

▶ A score from a normal distribution can be transformed into a value on the standard normal distribution with $\mu = 0$ and $\sigma = 1$ by the relation

$$z = (X - \mu)/\sigma.$$

▶ The probability of a discrete event is found by

$$p(\text{event}) = \frac{\text{Number of outcomes composing the event}}{\text{Total number of possible outcomes}}.$$

▶ For any probability distribution, the probability of an outcome must be between .00 and 1.00.

▶ The individual probabilities associated with the total number of outcomes in a probability distribution add to 1.00.

▶ If A and B are mutually exclusive outcomes, then $p(A \text{ or } B) = p(A) + p(B)$.

▶ The standard normal distribution is a probability distribution specifying the probabilities associated with scores falling into a certain interval of the distribution. It can be used with normally distributed scores to either obtain the proportion of scores that will fall within specified intervals or to find the probability of scores occurring within specified intervals.

▶ Raw scores from a sample may be transformed into standard scores using the formula

$$z = \frac{(X - \overline{X})}{S}, \text{ where } S = \sqrt{\frac{SS}{N}}.$$

This formula transforms a score into a number indicating how far away from the mean the score is in standard deviation units. It does not change the shape of the distribution of the raw scores.

 ## Key Terms and Symbols

additivity rule (124)
asymptotic distribution (108)
continuous distribution (108)
discrete outcome (123)
empirical probability distribution (125)
event (122)
mutually exclusive outcomes (124)
μ (106)
normal distribution (106)

outcome (122)
parameter (106)
population (106)
probability of occurrence of an event (p) (122)
sample (106)
σ (106)
s (106)
S (128)

standard normal deviate (111)
standard normal distribution (111)
standard score (129)
symmetrical distribution (108)
theoretical probability distribution (124)
unimodal distribution (108)
$\overline{X}$ (106)
z (111)
z_{obs} (111)

 ## Review Questions

1. Intelligence tests often involve measures of digit span, ability to follow instructions, vocabulary, analogy completion, picture completion, logical reasoning, and mathematical calculation. Explain why you would expect intelligence test scores to be approximately normally distributed in the population.

2. Measures of reaction time, the amount of time that it takes to initiate a response after the onset of a stimulus, typically are not normally distributed. Rather, the distribution of obtained scores often looks like a reversed letter *J*, with most scores relatively short

and only a few long scores. Explain why you would expect these scores to be distributed as they are.

3. Over the years, thousands of scores have been collected for the Wechsler Adult Intelligence Scale. Assume that the distribution of these scores is normal, with $\mu = 100$ and $\sigma = 15$.

   a. What proportion of intelligence scores is equal to or greater than 115?

   b. What proportion of intelligence scores is less than 70?

   c. What proportion of intelligence scores is less than 60?

   d. What proportion of scores is between 100 and 120?

   e. What proportion of scores is between 75 and 100?

   f. What interval of scores includes the middle 80 percent of scores on the test?

   g. If you select a person at random, what is the probability that his or her intelligence score will be between 90 and 120?

   h. If you select a person at random, what is the probability that his or her intelligence score will be equal to or less than 80?

   i. If you select a person at random, what is the probability that his or her intelligence score will be equal to or greater than 125?

   j. If you select a person at random, what is the probability that his or her intelligence score will be equal to or greater than 140?

4. You have been summoned, along with 64 other people, to a courthouse as a prospective jury member. To choose members of the jury, names are put in a box and drawn one at a time.

   a. What is the probability that your name will be the first chosen?

   b. If your name is not among the first eight chosen, what is the probability that it will be chosen ninth, assuming that the names of the first eight people chosen are removed from the box?

5. Example problem 3.1 presented a frequency distribution for the number of seconds a subject in an experiment could see a pyramid in the Mach pyramid figure (see Figure 3.1). A portion of this frequency distribution is given below.

Score	rf
11	.08
10	.08
9	.08
8	.08
7	.16
6	.08
5	.12
4	.08
3	.12
2	.08
1	.04

Use this frequency distribution to answer the following questions.

    a. What is the probability a subject in this experiment will see the pyramid for 7 to 9 seconds?

    b. What is the probability a subject in this experiment will see the pyramid for 10 seconds or more?

    c. What is the probability a subject in this experiment will see the pyramid for 4 seconds or less?

6. In Chapter 2, we presented an Implicit View of Intelligence rating scale with scores that may vary from 8 to 48. If we assume that this measure has a mean of 32 and a standard deviation of 8 answer the following questions.

    a. What is the probability of selecting a person at random with an Implicit View of Intelligence score of 40 or more?

    b. What is the probability of selecting a person at random with an Implicit View of Intelligence score of 30 or less?

    c. What is the probability of selecting a person at random with a score between 22 and 42?

7. Assume that the mean weight of American males between 21 and 30 years old is 166 pounds, with a standard deviation of 32 pounds.

    a. What proportion of 21- to 30-year-old males weighs 118 pounds or less?

    b. What proportion of 21- to 30-year-old males weighs 222 pounds or less?

    c. What proportion of 21- to 30-year-old males weighs between 102 and 230 pounds?

    d. If you select a 21- to 30-year-old male at random, what is the probability that his weight will be between 118 and 214 pounds?

    e. If you select a 21- to 30-year-old male at random, what is the probability that his weight will be 142 pounds or more?

    f. If you select a 21- to 30-year-old male at random, what is the probability that his weight will be 182 pounds or more?

8. Suppose that you observed six students on the mean amount of time spent playing video games per week (in hours) and their semester grade point average (GPA) and found the following values:

Student	Video Games	GPA
Alex	6	2.5
Lauren	8	2.0
Yvonne	0	3.9
Laval	15	3.4
Bonnie	3	3.1
Jason	16	1.3

    a. Compute the mean and sample standard deviation for each set of scores and then transform each score into a standard score.

    b. Lauren has a standard score of 0 for time spent playing video games. What does this score tell you about the time she spends playing video games each week?

    c. What information does Yvonne's standard score for GPA tell you about her GPA?

    d. What does a negative standard score for GPA indicate?

    e. What does a positive standard score for video game playing time indicate?

9. You recently had examinations in both English Literature and World History classes. Your grades on the exams and the class mean and standard deviation (S) are as follows:

	English Literature	World History
Your score	88	70
Class mean	83	65
Class S	6	5

In comparison to other members of the class, on which exam did you do better? What is the reason for your answer?

10. The U.S. Census Bureau (2005) reports that for households in the United States, the number of people living in a household is distributed as shown in the following relative frequency distribution.

Household Size Number of People	Relative Frequency
1	.268
2	.327
3	.159
4	.146
5	.064
6	.023
7 or more	.013

a. If you select a household at random, what is the probability there will be exactly four people in a household?

b. If you select a household at random, what is the probability there will be six or more people in the household?

11. The following frequency distribution presents the distribution of the ages of husbands in the United States in 2006 (U.S. Census Bureau, 2006).

Age	Relative Frequency
19 or younger	.094
20–24	.091
25–29	.090
30–34	.085
35–39	.091
40–44	.098
45–49	.098
50–54	.088
55–64	.131
65–74	.075
75–84	.047
85 or older	.012

    a. If you select a married couple at random, what is the probability the husband will be 44 or younger?

    b. If you select a married couple at random, what is the probability the husband will be either 34 or younger or 75 or older?

12. Vanity license plates enable people to creatively communicate information via their license plate, and all 50 of the U.S states permit them. Virginia, where 16.2 percent of the license plates are vanity plates, ranks first in the proportion of vanity plates. Montana ranks fifth, with 100,975 vanity plates for 1,030,169 cars (American Association of Motor Vehicle Administrators, 2007).

    a. If you were driving down I-95 in Virginia, what is the probability that the next Virginia license plate you see would be a vanity plate?

    b. What is the probability of a Montana license plate being a vanity plate?

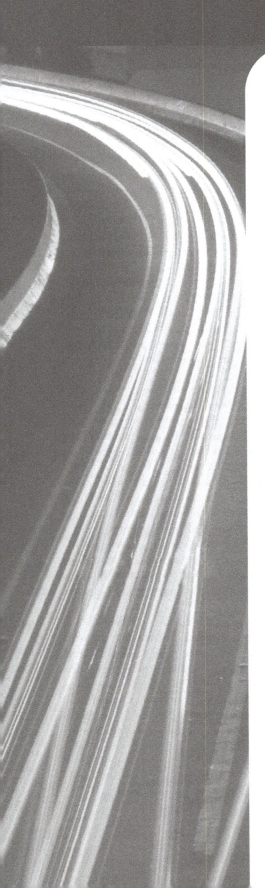

Understanding Data: Using Statistics for Inference and Estimation

I n the age of the Internet, some web sites can offer useful, valid information, and other web sites can provide, well, let's say amusement. One such web site offers to predict your future behavior by reading your facial features. That's right, if your eyes are too close, you are always on time, but if your eyes are farther apart, you are always going to be late! By observing your facial features, this site claims to evaluate your entire personality. Since the time of Aristotle, the Greek philosopher who lived over 2000 years ago, there have been arguments that characteristics of faces, such as the shape of the nose, prominence of the jaw, or the height of the forehead can be important predictors of behavior, a pseudo-science known as *physiognomy*. Psychologists are, of course, very skeptical of such pseudoscientific claims, for there is little or no empirical evidence to support them. Yet, this example raises an interesting problem. There is no question that all of us at times are interested in capturing the entirety of someone's personality or his or her typical behavior in a situation. But because we can never observe all aspects of a person or behavior in all situations, we often try to draw a larger picture from the bits and pieces of knowledge we may have about a person. In the language of statistics, we may "estimate" someone's personality by sampling their behavior in different situations. If we see Cindy is late to lunch, late to class, and late arriving at a prearranged study session, we may estimate that she is likely to be late in other areas of her life. Essentially, we use this limited set of observations from a few situations to make an inference about her typical behaviors in all situations. And, as we all know from experience, sometimes our estimates are accurate and sometimes they are less so, Cindy may be late sometimes, but not always.

This process is analogous to that of behavioral scientists who often want to generalize their results from a sample to the population from which the sample was selected. Essentially, behavioral scientists want to take the bits and pieces of information they obtain from a sample and use this information to draw a larger picture of the population from which the sample was obtained. For example, polling organizations want to predict the outcome of an election. But pollsters cannot possibly evaluate the opinions of all the members of a large voting population. Thus, they measure a sample from a voting population and then generalize to the population. Similarly, it is usually not possible to measure the amount of alcohol consumption, attitudes toward birth control, use of automobile seatbelts, or any other behaviors or opinions among all members of a large population. Estimates of population parameters must be made from the descriptive statistics obtained from a sample of the population. Estimating population parameters from descriptive statistics requires making inferences from sample data. And, just as with our personal estimates of someone's typical behavior, there are varying degrees of accuracy of these scientific inferences.

Inference > A process of reasoning from something known to something unknown.

Inference is a process of reasoning from something known to something unknown. For example, when you take a few "samples" of observations regarding a person's behavior to make an inference about her entire personality, you are reasoning from something known (a set of sample behaviors) to something unknown (the person's personality). **Statistical inference** is estimating unknown population parameters, such as the average amount of alcohol consumed by all college seniors, from known sample statistics, for example, the average amount of alcohol consumed by a group of 25 randomly selected college seniors. In this chapter, we will discuss the characteristics of the sample mean ($\overline{X}$) as an estimate of a population mean (μ). Then we will discuss s^2 and s as estimates of σ^2 and σ, respectively. Finally, we will turn to determining the accuracy of $\overline{X}$ as an estimate of μ.

Statistical inference > Estimating population values from statistics obtained from a sample.

$\overline{X}$ as a Point Estimator of μ

Point estimation ▶ Estimating the value of a parameter as a single point from the value of a statistic.

The sample mean ($\overline{X}$) is often used as a point estimate of a population mean (μ). **Point estimation** is estimating the value of a parameter as a single point from the value of a statistic. Consider the 100 Implicit View of Intelligence scores of Chapter 3's Table 3.3. Suppose these scores were obtained from a randomly selected sample of students at a university. The mean for the sample of scores presented in Table 3.3 is 31.8, and the standard deviation is 6.6. This sample mean of 31.8 may be used as an unbiased and consistent estimator of μ, the mean Implicit View of Intelligence score of the population from which the sample was selected.

Unbiased Estimator

Unbiased estimator ▶ A statistic with a mean value over an infinite number of random samples equal to the parameter it estimates.

An **unbiased estimator** is a statistic for which, if an infinite number of random samples of a certain size is obtained, the mean of the values of the statistic equals the parameter being estimated. The mean, $\overline{X}$, obtained from a sample selected from a population is an unbiased estimator of that population mean, because, if we take all possible random samples of size N from a population, then the mean of the sample means equals μ. On the other hand, if we calculate a sample variance by dividing the sum of squares by N, we have a *biased* estimator of σ^2, for it consistently underestimates σ^2. But as we indicated in Chapter 5, the estimated population variance, s^2, calculated by dividing by $N - 1$, provides an unbiased estimate of σ^2.

Consistent Estimator

Consistent estimator ▶ A statistic for which the probability that the statistic has a value closer to the parameter increases as the sample size increases.

A **consistent estimator** is a statistic for which the probability that the statistic has a value closer to the parameter increases as the sample size increases. Because it is a consistent estimator, a sample mean based on 25 scores has a greater probability of being closer to μ than does a sample mean based on only 5 scores. This characteristic makes intuitive sense for the sample mean. As sample size increases, more scores from the population are included in the calculation of $\overline{X}$, and thus, we expect $\overline{X}$ to better estimate μ. If we were to sample the whole population of interest so that the sample composed the entire population, then $\overline{X}$ would be the same as μ and there would be no error in the estimate.

Accuracy of Estimation

Although $\overline{X}$ is an unbiased and consistent estimator of μ, we should not overlook the fact that an estimate is just an approximate calculation. It is unlikely in any estimate that $\overline{X}$ will be exactly equal to μ. Whether $\overline{X}$ is a good estimate of μ depends on the sampling method, the sample size, and the variability of scores in the population.

Sampling Method

Any sample from a population will provide some idea about characteristics of that population. Indeed, in the absence of any other information, $\overline{X}$ provides the "best guess" about the value of the corresponding μ. But to ensure that $\overline{X}$ is a good estimate of μ, the characteristics of the sample should be similar to those of the population of interest. The method most widely used to select samples representative of a population is random sampling. **Random sampling** is defined as the process of selecting members from a population such that

1. each member of the population has an equal chance of being selected for the sample, and

2. the selection of one member is independent of the selection of any other member of the population.

A random sample is one selected without bias; therefore, the characteristics of the sample should not differ in any systematic or consistent way from the population from which the sample was drawn. But random sampling does not guarantee that a particular sample will be exactly representative of a population. Think back to the fruit salad example in Chapter 5. When you sample from a population, what you get (the fruit in your personal bowl) may not include every aspect of the population (the fruit in the large serving bowl). Even if you don't look at what fruit you are selecting with the serving spoon, you can end up with all melon. If you never looked at the large serving bowl and only saw what was in your bowl, your understanding of the "entire population" based on the sample would be inaccurate as you wouldn't know your spoon missed the kiwi, grapes, and apple pieces. In behavioral research, the same issues are at hand. Because samples are usually much smaller than the population from which they have been selected, we cannot expect the characteristics of the sample to be distributed exactly the same as in the population. As a result, some random samples will be more representative of the population than others, just as some small bowls of fruit salad will be more representative of the large serving bowl than others. Random sampling does ensure, however, that in the long run (i.e., over an infinitely large number of samples) such samples will be representative of the population.

Sample Size

The discussion of consistent estimators indicated that larger samples are more likely to produce a sample mean closer to the value of the population mean than are smaller samples. If you ask 15 students about a professor's typical classroom performance, you are more likely to get a better estimate of that performance than if you ask only 1 student. Thus, for consistent estimators, sample size is related to the accuracy of the estimate obtained.

Variability in Population Measures

Consider the unlikely possibility that the scores for all members of a population are exactly the same. Thus, every score is equal to μ, and σ for the population is zero. Under this condition, it is evident that the $\overline{X}$ obtained from a sample of any size will equal μ. There will be no error in the sample estimate. On the other hand, consider a population that has extensive variation among the scores measured and σ is very large. Although it should occur infrequently, by chance alone the scores in one random sample may consist principally of low values. The resulting $\overline{X}$, then, would differ considerably from μ. Similarly, an inaccurate estimate of μ would be obtained if primarily high scores were randomly sampled from the population. Thus, the accuracy of $\overline{X}$ as a point estimate of μ is related to the amount of variability in the population. The larger the population standard deviation, the less likely a particular sample mean will be an accurate estimate of the population mean. We can use the analogy of sampling from our fruit bowl to illustrate this concept. If the large population salad contains only one type of fruit, then any sample (e.g., your smaller bowl) will perfectly represent the population. But as the variety of fruits in the large bowl increases (i.e., there is more variability in the types of fruit in the bowl), then any sample becomes less likely to contain all the varieties.

Nonrandom Sampling

As the discussion has indicated, the sampling method is crucial in determining how well the sample represents the population. Many polls and surveys, however, use nonrandom sampling methods. In this age of instant communication, it seems that many of us are interested in what others think about an issue, and a whole new industry of immediate polling has arisen to satisfy this urge. Radio stations and television programs offer call-in or text polls on topics of the day or to select the best performer on a reality show. Internet news sites offer similar opportunities. Each of these polls collects information from a sample—those people who respond to the poll. But how useful are these polls for making inferences to the larger population containing the sample? Unfortunately, the answer is that they are not very useful for several reasons.

First, as indicated earlier, the population must be clearly defined. Recall that a population is a complete set of people, animals, objects, or events that share a common characteristic. In order to make inferences to a population from a sample, first we must know what the common characteristic of the population is so that we can ensure that all members of the sample possess this characteristic. Second, the sample must represent the population, and a systematic procedure must be followed for selecting the sample. Neither of these requirements is met when individuals self-select into the sample by deciding they want to call their response to a question in to a radio station or text their preference as to who should go or who should stay to a reality show poll. These polls obviously do not include the responses of those who are not tuning into the program or of those who choose not to respond to the poll. For example, a poll on a major Internet site asked people in the United States to indicate how far they planned to travel on a certain long summer holiday weekend. The poll was made available on the Friday of the weekend. Of the approximately 20,000 people who responded, about 78 percent indicated they had no plans to travel for the weekend. How confident can we be that this number represents travel plans for Americans in general for this weekend? Unfortunately, the sample for this poll is self-selected, representing only those interested enough to respond. Furthermore, because many people were already traveling before the poll was made available, they may have been unable to respond to the poll indicating they had travel plans. Thus, we cannot define the population that this sample represents. No inference to a population is reasonable from this sample. Such polls and surveys are scientifically useless.

Testing Your Knowledge 7.1

1. Define: consistent estimator, point estimation, random sampling, statistical inference, unbiased estimator.

2. Suppose that you could chose between two professors when registering for the General Biology class. You want to find the professor whose teaching style best matches your learning style.

   a. Assume you went to an Internet site offering ratings of professors. What factors might affect who posted ratings to this service? Why might you question the quality of the data from an online professor rating service?

   b. Suppose you were able to randomly select students from among all the students each professor taught in an academic year, asking their opinion on the teaching style of each professor. If they answered you truthfully, how well do you think this sample would help you to select the professor whose teaching style best fits with your learning style? What can you do to maximize your sample offering the best representation?

   c. What are the requirements for obtaining a random sample? If you just asked two of your friends their opinion regarding the best professor, would this be a random sample? Explain your answer.

Estimating the Population Variance and Standard Deviation

Variance

The population variance, σ^2, was defined in Chapter 5 as

$$\sigma^2 = \frac{\Sigma(X - \mu)^2}{N_{\text{population}}}.$$

As you know, however, it is usually impractical to measure all members of a population; thus, σ^2 is typically estimated from a sample. As we discussed in Chapter 5, an **unbiased and consistent estimator of σ^2** is provided by

$$s^2 = \frac{\Sigma(X - \overline{X})^2}{N - 1}.$$

Standard Deviation

The estimated standard deviation, s, is used as an estimator of σ. In contrast to s^2 as an estimator of σ^2, s is not an unbiased estimator of σ. Rather, s slightly underestimates σ. But because the bias in s is small and becomes smaller as sample size increases, s is typically used to estimate σ.

Sampling Distribution of the Mean: Determining the Accuracy of an Estimate

The accuracy of a point estimate of a population mean depends on both sample size and the population standard deviation. Unless the sample includes all the scores in the population or there is no variability of scores in the population, $\overline{X}$ likely will be in error in estimating μ. Although we cannot know for sure just how accurate a point estimate of a population parameter is, we can determine the amount of error to be expected in the estimate by using the concept of a sampling distribution.

Sampling distribution ▶ A theoretical probability distribution of values of a statistic resulting from selecting all possible samples of size N from a population.

Sampling distribution of the mean ▶ The distribution of $\overline{X}$ values when all possible samples of size N are selected from a population.

A **sampling distribution** is a theoretical probability distribution of values of a statistic resulting from selecting all possible samples of size N from a population. For example, the **sampling distribution of the mean** is the distribution of values of $\overline{X}$ obtained when all possible samples of size N are drawn from a population and $\overline{X}$ calculated for each sample. Most sampling distributions are determined theoretically from a mathematical equation, for we can never actually select all possible samples from a typical population. Each statistical test introduced in the following chapters requires a knowledge of the sampling distribution for the statistic used. These sampling distributions are theoretical sampling distributions obtained from mathematical equations.

Although statistical tests use theoretical sampling distributions, we will generate several empirical sampling distributions of the mean to illustrate the concepts involved. An empirical sampling distribution of the mean may be obtained by selecting a number of samples of size N from a population, calculating $\overline{X}$ for each sample, and then plotting a frequency distribution of the means obtained. For this illustration, we generated a population of 100 scores ranging from 8 to 20 with $\mu = 14.0$ and $\sigma = 2.1$. A frequency polygon

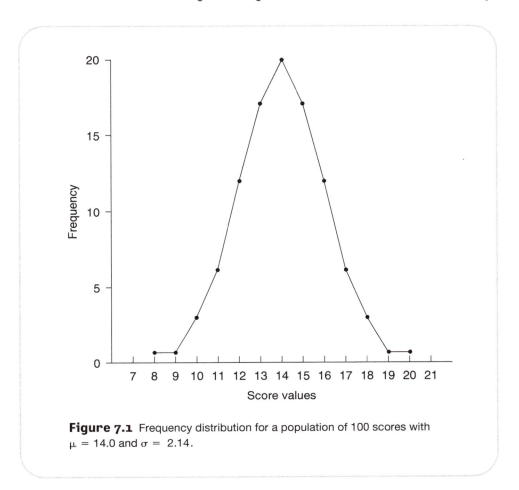

Figure 7.1 Frequency distribution for a population of 100 scores with $\mu = 14.0$ and $\sigma = 2.14$.

of the 100 scores in the population is shown in Figure 7.1. As you can see, the distribution of scores in the population is symmetrical and unimodal.

Empirical sampling distributions of the mean were obtained for three different sample sizes, $N = 2$, $N = 5$, and $N = 10$, by selecting random samples from this population with the aid of a computer. For each sample size, 100 random samples were selected and $\overline{X}$ for each sample was calculated. Each sample mean for a particular sample size was then placed on an ungrouped frequency distribution as shown in Figure 7.2. Each distribution in this figure, (a), (b), and (c), represents an empirical sampling distribution of the mean based on 100 samples of each sample size ($N = 2$, $N = 5$, and $N = 10$, respectively).

Characteristics of the Sampling Distribution of the Mean

The empirical sampling distributions in Figure 7.2 illustrate several characteristics of the theoretical sampling distribution of the mean. Recall that a frequency distribution can be summarized in terms of its shape and measures of central tendency and variability. Because the sampling distribution of the mean is a frequency distribution, it, too, can be described in terms of its shape, mean, and standard deviation.

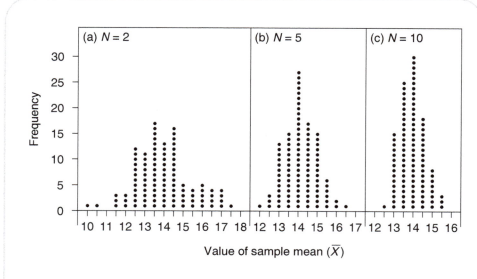

Figure 7.2 Three empirical sampling distributions of the mean for 100 samples drawn from the population of scores presented in Figure 7.1. The sample sizes are (a) $N = 2$, (b) $N = 5$, and (c) $N = 10$.

Shape of a Sampling Distribution of the Mean

The three sampling distributions in Figure 7.2 are relatively symmetrical and unimodal. Any variations from symmetry are simply chance variation in the values of $\overline{X}$ obtained in sampling. Notice that the distribution becomes more peaked and less spread out as the sample size increases (compare $N = 2$ to $N = 10$). A principle known as the **central limit theorem** applies to the shape of the sampling distribution of the mean: *As sample size increases, the sampling distribution of the mean will approach a normal distribution*. This approximation of the normal distribution by the sampling distribution of the mean occurs whether the shape of the distribution of raw scores in the population is symmetrical or skewed.

How large must N be before the sampling distribution of the mean approaches a normal distribution? The answer depends on the shape of the distribution of raw scores in the population. The population from which we sampled is not normally distributed but is unimodal and symmetrical (see Figure 7.1). From such a distribution, the empirical sampling distribution of the mean for sample sizes as small as $N = 5$ or $N = 10$ begins to approach the shape of a normal distribution (see Figures 7.2b and 7.2c). If the distribution of scores in the population is skewed, then the sample size must be larger for the sampling distribution of the mean to approximate a normal distribution. For population distributions that are not heavily skewed, many statisticians consider a sample size of 30 ($N = 30$) to lead to a sampling distribution of the mean that will be approximately normally distributed.

A theoretical sampling distribution of the mean based on the central limit theorem is shown in Figure 7.3. Observe that this distribution is symmetrical, unimodal, and normal. We will use this and other theoretical sampling distributions in developing inferential statistical tests in following chapters. Empirical sampling distributions, such as those presented in Figure 7.2, are typically used only to help understand the concept of a sampling distribution.

Central limit theorem ▶ A mathematical theorem stating that, as sample size increases, the sampling distribution of the mean approaches a normal distribution.

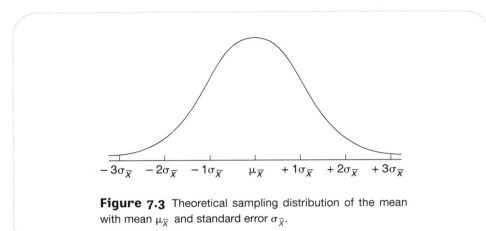

Figure 7.3 Theoretical sampling distribution of the mean with mean $\mu_{\overline{X}}$ and standard error $\sigma_{\overline{X}}$.

Mean of a Sampling Distribution of the Mean

$\mu_{\overline{X}}$ ► Mean of a theoretical sampling distribution of the mean.

$\overline{X}_{\overline{X}}$ ► Mean of an empirical sampling distribution of the mean.

The mean of the sample means (represented by $\mu_{\overline{X}}$) in a theoretical sampling distribution will be equal to μ. In an empirical sampling distribution of the mean, however, the mean of the sample means (represented by $\overline{X}_{\overline{X}}$) will not be exactly equal to the population mean. This point is illustrated by the empirical sampling distributions of Figure 7.2. The means of the sample means in the three sampling distributions are not exactly equal to 14.0, the mean of the parent population. The mean values are $\overline{X}_{\overline{X}} = 13.96$, $\overline{X}_{\overline{X}} = 14.14$, and $\overline{X}_{\overline{X}} = 13.99$ for distributions in parts (a), (b), and (c), respectively.

Sampling Error and the Standard Error of the Mean

Sampling error ► The amount by which a sample mean differs from the population mean.

Sampling Error.   Each sample mean in Figure 7.2 is an estimate of the population mean of 14.0. As you can see, some of the sample means provide more accurate estimates of this μ than do other sample means. **Sampling error** is the amount by which a particular sample mean differs from the population mean (i.e., $\overline{X} - \mu$). If $\overline{X} = \mu$, then $\overline{X} - \mu = 0$, and there is no sampling error in the estimate. Figure 7.2 illustrates that sampling error is related to sample size; the larger the sample size, the smaller the sampling error. The values of the 100 sample means in Figure 7.2a, with each mean based on two scores, are more variable than the sample means in Figures 7.2b and c, which were obtained from either 5 or 10 scores, respectively. Thus, more sampling error is evident in Figure 7.2a than in either Figure 7.2b or c.

Standard error of the mean ($\sigma_{\overline{X}}$) ► The standard deviation of the sampling distribution of the mean found by dividing σ by the square root of the size of the sample.

Standard Error of the Mean.   The variability among the sample means in a sampling distribution of the mean is described by the standard deviation calculated on the values of the sample means. This standard deviation is called the **standard error of the mean**, or simply the *standard error*, to distinguish it from the standard deviation calculated on a population of raw scores. The standard error of the mean, symbolized as $\sigma_{\overline{X}}$, is equal to the standard deviation of the population divided by the square root of the size of the sample. In notation,

$$\text{Standard error of the mean} = \sigma_{\overline{X}} = \frac{\sigma}{\sqrt{N}}$$

where σ = standard deviation of scores in the population
N = size of the sample.

The standard error of the mean, $\sigma_{\overline{X}}$, is a standard deviation, just as σ is a standard deviation. But $\sigma_{\overline{X}}$ is a standard deviation of a distribution of sample means rather than a standard deviation of the raw scores in a population, as is σ.

Look at Figure 7.3, the theoretical sampling distribution of the mean. Notice that we have indicated its mean as $\mu_{\overline{X}}$ and its standard deviation as $\sigma_{\overline{X}}$. In Chapter 6, we discussed the area under the normal distribution and explained how to find the proportion of scores within certain areas of the distribution (see pages 108–111). Because the sampling distribution of the mean is a normal distribution, the same relationships hold for this distribution. In this instance, however, it is not raw scores that are contained in the intervals but sample means. Thus, the following relationships hold between $\mu_{\overline{X}}$, $\sigma_{\overline{X}}$, and the proportion of sample means in certain intervals about $\mu_{\overline{X}}$.

Interval	Proportion of Sample Means in Interval
$\mu_{\overline{X}} - 1\sigma_{\overline{X}}$ to $\mu_{\overline{X}} + 1\sigma_{\overline{X}}$	.6826
$\mu_{\overline{X}} - 2\sigma_{\overline{X}}$ to $\mu_{\overline{X}} + 2\sigma_{\overline{X}}$	.9544
$\mu_{\overline{X}} - 3\sigma_{\overline{X}}$ to $\mu_{\overline{X}} + 3\sigma_{\overline{X}}$	.9974

Notice we have used $\mu_{\overline{X}}$ in these intervals because we are using the sampling distribution of the mean. Because $\mu_{\overline{X}}$ is equal to μ, however, we could write the relationships using μ in place of $\mu_{\overline{X}}$, as in the next example.

To illustrate the use of these relationships, suppose that a population of scores has $\mu = 50$ and $\sigma = 6$, and random samples of $N = 9$ are drawn from this population. The standard error of the mean for this sampling distribution is found by

$$\sigma_{\overline{X}} = \frac{\sigma}{\sqrt{N}} = \frac{6}{\sqrt{9}} = \frac{6}{3} = 2.$$

This value, $\sigma_{\overline{X}} = 2$, is the standard deviation of the sampling distribution of the mean for samples of size $N = 9$ from a population with $\sigma = 6$. Thus, in the theoretical sampling distribution of the mean for samples of $N = 9$ from this population, .6826 of the sample means are in the interval of $\mu - 1\sigma_{\overline{X}}$ (i.e., $50 - 2 = 48$) to $\mu + 1\sigma_{\overline{X}}$ (i.e., $50 + 2 = 52$), or the interval from 48 to 52. The interval of $\mu - 2\sigma_{\overline{X}}$ (i.e., $50 - 4 = 46$) to $\mu + 2\sigma_{\overline{X}}$ (i.e., $50 + 4 = 54$), or the interval from 46 to 54, contains .9544 of the sample means, and .9974 of the values of $\overline{X}$ will be in the interval of $\mu - 3\sigma_{\overline{X}}$ (i.e., $50 - 6 = 44$) to $\mu + 3\sigma_{\overline{X}}$ (i.e., $50 + 6 = 56$), or from 44 to 56. This knowledge will be useful in determining the accuracy of a single value of $\overline{X}$ as an estimate of μ.

Using the Standard Normal Deviate with the Sampling Distribution of the Mean

The sampling distribution of the mean is normally distributed with mean, μ, and standard error, $\sigma_{\overline{X}}$. We may convert a value of $\overline{X}$ from a sampling distribution of the mean to a score on the standard normal distribution by

$$z = \frac{\overline{X} - \mu}{\sigma_{\overline{X}}}.$$

This z score may be used with the sample mean just as it was for an individual score in Chapter 6. Example problem 7.1 illustrates its use.

EXAMPLE PROBLEM

7.1

Using the Sampling Distribution of the Mean

Problem: Suppose that we have a normally distributed population of scores with $\mu = 80$ and $\sigma = 12$. We plan to draw a large number of random samples of size 16 ($N = 16$) from this population and compute the mean for each sample. What proportion of the sample means will be equal to or greater than 82?

Solution: The solution to this problem requires recognizing that the sampling distribution of the mean is normally distributed with $\mu = 80$ and $\sigma_{\overline{X}} = 12/\sqrt{16} = 12/4 = 3.0$. The proportion of sample means in any interval on the theoretical sampling distribution is found by converting the value of the sample mean (i.e., 82) to a value on the standard normal distribution and looking up the appropriate proportion in the standard normal table, Appendix C.1. The sample mean is converted to a z_{obs} value by

$$z_{obs} = \frac{\overline{X} - \mu}{\sigma_{\overline{X}}} = \frac{82 - 80}{3.0} = \frac{2}{3.0} = +0.67.$$

Values of the sample means and the z_{obs} for a sample mean of 82 are shown in Figure 7.4. Column c of Appendix C.1 indicates that the area beyond $z = +0.67$ is .2514 (shown on the axis labeled c in Figure 7.4). Thus, .2514 of the sample means is expected to be equal to or greater than 82. We may write this conclusion in probability terms as

$$p(\overline{X} \geq 82) = .2514.$$

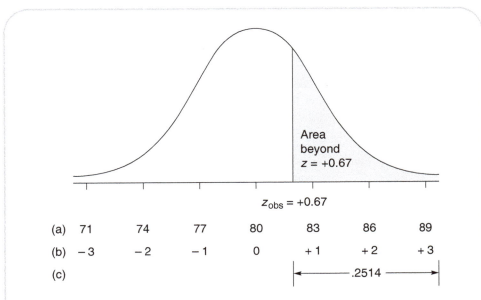

Figure 7.4 Location of a sample mean of 82 on a sampling distribution of the mean with $\mu = 80$ and $\sigma_{\overline{X}} = 3$. The labels on the X axis show (a) values of the sample means, (b) z_{obs} scores corresponding to values of the sample means, and (c) the proportion of sample means equal to or greater than 82.

Estimating the Standard Error of the Mean

The sampling distribution of the mean provides a method of finding the variability expected among sample means. But there is an apparent limit to the use of this knowledge: σ is a population parameter, and any population parameter typically is unknown. How, then, can we determine $\sigma_{\overline{X}}$ if we don't know σ?

The answer to this question lies in estimating σ from the scores of a sample, just as we have estimated μ from $\overline{X}$. In this instance the estimated population standard deviation (s) is used to estimate σ to obtain an estimated standard error of the mean. The **estimated standard error of the mean**, identified as $s_{\overline{X}}$, is based on s and is expressed in notation as

Estimated standard error of the mean (s$_{\overline{X}}$) ▶ The standard error of the mean estimated by using s to estimate σ.

$$\text{Estimated standard error of the mean} = \text{estimated } \sigma_{\overline{X}} = s_{\overline{X}} = \frac{s}{\sqrt{N}},$$

where s is obtained from the scores of a sample and N is the sample size. Thus, $s_{\overline{X}}$ is the estimated standard deviation of the sampling distribution of the mean. In a journal report, this standard error is often identified as SE, rather than $s_{\overline{X}}$.

It is important to understand the distinction between $\sigma_{\overline{X}}$ and $s_{\overline{X}}$. The $\sigma_{\overline{X}}$ is a fixed value that can be determined when σ is known. Because we seldom know σ, however, we typically estimate $\sigma_{\overline{X}}$ by $s_{\overline{X}}$. The $s_{\overline{X}}$, because it is based on the value of s from a sample, will vary from sample to sample. Different random samples from the same population will produce different values of s because of the chance differences in scores that occur from one sample to another. Nevertheless, the scores of the sample provide the only basis for estimating $\sigma_{\overline{X}}$.

Factors Affecting the Value of $s_{\overline{X}}$

The formula for $s_{\overline{X}}$ (i.e., $s/\sqrt{N}$) shows how the variability of sample means in a sampling distribution is related to (1) the variability of scores in the population and (2) the size of the sample. The more variable the scores in the population are, the larger the s of the scores in the sample. And, as s increases, $s_{\overline{X}}$ does also. However, increasing the sample size (N) increases the denominator of the formula for $s_{\overline{X}}$, which contributes to making the standard error smaller. Thus, we can expect to obtain a smaller $s_{\overline{X}}$ with large random samples from populations in which the variability of scores is small. Although an investigator can control sample size, typically little can be done to reduce the variation of scores in a population other than defining a population in a very specific fashion to decrease variability. Thus, to decrease the value of $s_{\overline{X}}$, behavioral scientists often resort to using larger sample sizes.

Use of $s_{\overline{X}}$

The standard error is used to measure the amount of sampling error in the sampling distribution of the mean. Therefore, $s_{\overline{X}}$ may be used to determine how well an obtained sample mean estimates a population mean. The smaller $s_{\overline{X}}$, the more confident we can be that $\overline{X}$ does not differ substantially from the population mean. In Chapter 8, we will use $s_{\overline{X}}$ to make precise statements about the accuracy with which $\overline{X}$ estimates μ. To simplify the discussion in the remainder of this chapter, however, we assume that $\sigma_{\overline{X}}$ is known to us.

You should remember, however, that in practice $\sigma_{\overline{X}}$ will not be known and $s_{\overline{X}}$ must be used in its place as an estimate of $\sigma_{\overline{X}}$.

Review of Types of Distributions

Table 7.1 summarizes the several types of distributions discussed to this point and the symbols used to identify the characteristics of the distributions. Distributions may be composed of either raw scores or of means of samples drawn from a population.

▶ A distribution of raw scores in a population is obtained by measuring all members of a population. If we were able to measure a population, we would be able to calculate μ, σ, and σ^2.

▶ The distribution of raw scores of a sample selected from a population is described by $\overline{X}$, s, and s^2. These statistics may be used to estimate the corresponding parameter of the population from which the sample was selected.

▶ A sampling distribution of the mean is a distribution of means of samples selected from a population. The theoretical sampling distribution of the mean for a given sample size is obtained from a mathematical equation. The mean of a theoretical sampling distribution of the mean is given by $\mu_{\overline{X}}$, which is equal to μ of the population from which the samples were selected. The standard deviation of a sampling distribution of the mean is given by $\sigma_{\overline{X}}$ and the variance by $\sigma^2_{\overline{X}}$. Typically, μ and $\sigma_{\overline{X}}$ are estimated from $\overline{X}$ and $s_{\overline{X}}$ obtained from a sample.

▶ Empirical sampling distributions of the mean are obtained by actually selecting samples from a population and then plotting a frequency distribution of the sample means. The major function of empirical sampling distributions is to assist in understanding the concept of a sampling distribution; they typically are not used in actual research.

TABLE 7.1 Summary of types of distributions and their characteristics

Type of Distribution	Obtained by	Mean	Standard Deviation	Variance
Raw scores				
Population	Measuring all members of the population	μ	σ	σ^2
Sample	Selecting and measuring a sample from a population	$\overline{X}$	s	s^2
Sampling distribution of the mean				
Theoretical	Theoretically from a mathematical equation	$\mu_{\overline{X}}$	$\sigma_{\overline{X}}$	$\sigma^2_{\overline{X}}$
Empirical	Empirically by drawing samples from a population	$\overline{X}_{\overline{X}}$	$s_{\overline{X}}$	$s^2_{\overline{X}}$

Testing Your Knowledge 7.2

1. Define: central limit theorem, estimated standard error of the mean, $\mu_{\bar{X}}$, sampling distribution, sampling distribution of the mean, sampling error, $\sigma_{\bar{X}}$, standard error of the mean.

2. Is the value of s^2 obtained by $s^2 = \Sigma(X - \bar{X})^2/(N - 1)$ an unbiased estimator of σ^2? If it is biased, how is it biased?

3. Is the value of s obtained by $s = \sqrt{\Sigma(X - \bar{X})/(N - 1)}$ an unbiased estimator of σ? If it is biased, how is it biased?

4. Distinguish between an empirical and a theoretical sampling distribution of the mean.

5. State the central limit theorem.

6. Suppose you plan to select 100 random samples of size $N = 25$ from a population of intelligence test scores with $\mu = 100$ and $\sigma = 15$.

    a. What proportion of the sample means do you expect to be between 97 and 103?

    b. What proportion of the sample means do you expect to be greater than 103?

    c. What proportion of the sample means do you expect to be less than 94?

    d. What proportion of the sample means do you expect to be greater than 105?

    e. What proportion of the sample means do you expect to be between 100 and 105?

7. Suppose you have a sample of scores for time on target of a tracking task. In this task, a person must follow a moving target with a mouse on a computer screen. The amount of time the person follows the target during a trial is recorded. The s for the distribution of these scores is 18.0 seconds.

    a. Find the value of $s_{\bar{X}}$ for sample sizes of 4, 9, and 36.

    b. What relationship between the value of $s_{\bar{X}}$ and sample size is illustrated by these samples?

8. Suppose you have three different samples of scores of time on target during a tracking task as described in question 7. The values of s for the three samples are 10, 15, and 20 seconds, respectively. The sample size is $N = 25$.

    a. Find the value of $s_{\bar{X}}$ for each sample.

    b. What relationship between variability of scores and the value of $s_{\bar{X}}$ is illustrated by these samples?

9. You plan to select equal size samples from two different populations of scores, A_1 and A_2. Population A_1 has a σ of 17.0 and population A_2 has a σ of 30.0. Which population, A_1 or A_2, do you expect will lead to a sample with a larger value of $s_{\bar{X}}$? Explain your answer.

Interval Estimation of the Population Mean

The sample mean is an unbiased and consistent estimator of μ. If we were to estimate the mean of a population from which a sample was drawn, the best point estimate of μ would be $\bar{X}$. But, as we have discussed, a point estimate of μ will likely be in error; the value of μ will not be equal to the value estimated by $\bar{X}$. To gain confidence about the accuracy of an estimate, we may estimate not only a point value for μ, but we may also

Confidence interval ▶ A range of score values expected to contain the value of μ with a certain level of confidence.

Confidence limits ▶ The lower and upper scores defining the confidence interval.

construct a **confidence interval** for the estimate by providing a range of values expected to contain μ. For example, rather than estimating the population mean of Implicit View of Intelligence scores as exactly 31.8, a researcher may estimate that an interval from 30.5 to 33.1 contains the value of μ. A level of confidence, or probability value, can be attached to this estimate so that, for example, the scientist can be 95 percent confident that the interval encompasses μ. The lower (e.g., 30.5) and upper (e.g., 33.1) scores of the interval are called **confidence limits**. Let us see how such intervals are constructed and what it means to say that an experimenter is 95 percent confident that the interval includes the value of μ.

Constructing a Confidence Interval

Return to Figure 7.3, the theoretical sampling distribution of the mean. Recall that $\sigma_{\overline{X}}$ is the standard deviation of this sampling distribution and that the distribution is normally distributed. Using this knowledge, we illustrated earlier in this chapter that the interval from $\mu_{\overline{X}} - 1\sigma_{\overline{X}}$ to $\mu_{\overline{X}} + 1\sigma_{\overline{X}}$ contains .6826 of the sample means that could be drawn from this population. Suppose we now asked, if you were to draw one sample and find $\overline{X}$ for that sample, what is the probability that $\overline{X}$ would fall into the interval between $\mu_{\overline{X}} - 1\sigma_{\overline{X}}$ and $\mu_{\overline{X}} + 1\sigma_{\overline{X}}$? The answer is .6826, for .6826 of the sample means has values between $\mu_{\overline{X}} - 1\sigma_{\overline{X}}$ and $\mu_{\overline{X}} + 1\sigma_{\overline{X}}$. Accordingly, if you were to draw a sample, the probability that its mean would be between $\mu_{\overline{X}} - 1\sigma_{\overline{X}}$ and $\mu_{\overline{X}} + 1\sigma_{\overline{X}}$ is .6826. Notice that to answer the question we constructed an interval about $\mu_{\overline{X}}$ (or μ, because $\mu_{\overline{X}}$ is equal to μ) using values of $\sigma_{\overline{X}}$ and then applied known properties of the normal distribution. But in most instances μ is unknown, and we estimate μ with $\overline{X}$. Suppose that we follow the same procedure of constructing an interval around μ, but use $\overline{X}$ to estimate μ. Thus, we obtain an interval of $\overline{X} - 1\sigma_{\overline{X}}$ to $\overline{X} + 1\sigma_{\overline{X}}$. The question we now ask is not whether this interval contains the value of $\overline{X}$, for we already know $\overline{X}$, but does the interval contain μ? We can answer this question with a probability statement also. If the probability that the interval $\mu_{\overline{X}} - 1\sigma_{\overline{X}}$ to $\mu_{\overline{X}} - 1\sigma_{\overline{X}}$ contains $\overline{X}$ is .6826, then it is also true that the probability that the interval $\overline{X} - 1\sigma_{\overline{X}}$ to $\overline{X} + 1\sigma_{\overline{X}}$ contains μ is .6826.

The interval of $\overline{X} - 1\sigma_{\overline{X}}$ to $\overline{X} + 1\sigma_{\overline{X}}$ is a 68 percent (rounding .6826 and then multiplying by 100 to obtain percent) confidence interval. The limits, or extremes, of this interval, $\overline{X} - 1\sigma_{\overline{X}}$ and $\overline{X} + 1\sigma_{\overline{X}}$, are the confidence limits. We can interpret this interval in this way: if we were to repeatedly draw samples and calculate a mean for each sample, and then construct an interval of plus or minus one $\sigma_{\overline{X}}$ about each $\overline{X}$, 68 percent of the intervals would contain the value of μ. Thus, any one of the intervals has a probability of .68 (or a 68 percent chance) of including μ. Notice that because μ is a population parameter and, thus, a specific value, it is either contained or not contained in the interval. Consider a numerical example to illustrate this discussion.

Suppose that we have a population with $\mu = 40$ and $\sigma = 10$, and we draw a sample of size 25 ($N = 25$) from this population and obtain $\overline{X} = 41.5$. Then $\sigma_{\overline{X}} = \sigma/\sqrt{N} = 10/\sqrt{25}$, which equals 2.0. A 68 percent confidence interval for μ is obtained by finding the interval from $\overline{X} - 1\sigma_{\overline{X}}$ to $\overline{X} + 1\sigma_{\overline{X}}$. Substituting values of $\overline{X} = 41.5$ and $\sigma_{\overline{X}} = 2$, the resulting confidence interval is 39.5 (i.e., $\overline{X} - 1\sigma_{\overline{X}} = 41.5 - 2 = 39.5$) to 43.5 (i.e., $\overline{X} + 1\sigma_{\overline{X}} = 41.5 + 2 = 43.5$). We can be 68 percent confident that this interval contains the value of μ. And, in this instance, it does. Suppose, however, that $\overline{X}$ had been 44.0 rather than 41.5. Then the 68 percent confidence interval is 42.0 (i.e., $\overline{X} - 1\sigma_{\overline{X}} = 44 - 2 = 42.0$) to 46.0 (i.e., $\overline{X} + 1\sigma_{\overline{X}} = 44 + 2 = 46.0$). Again, we can be 68 percent confident that this interval contains $\mu = 40$. But in this instance the interval does not contain $\mu = 40$. In practice, of course, we cannot know for sure if the confidence interval contains μ or not, for we do not know the value of μ. If we did know μ, then we would not need to estimate its value. We can only have a certain level of confidence that the interval actually does contain the value of μ.

Confidence intervals used in actual research are typically 95 percent or 99 percent confidence intervals, rather than 68 percent confidence intervals. We find the limits for these intervals by using the properties of the standard normal distribution with $\mu = 0$ and $\sigma = 1$. From Appendix C.1, we find that an interval from $z = -1.96$ to $z = 0$ contains .4750 of the values of z, and an interval of $z = 0$ to $z = +1.96$ also contains .4750 of the values of z. Thus, an interval of $z = -1.96$ to $z = +1.96$ will contain .95 of the values of z (i.e., $.4750 + .4750 = .95$). Accordingly, a **95 percent confidence interval for the population mean** is obtained by

$$\overline{X} - 1.96\sigma_{\overline{X}} \text{ to } \overline{X} + 1.96\sigma_{\overline{X}}.$$

For a **99 percent confidence interval for the population mean**, we find that an interval from $z = -2.58$ to 0 contains .4951 of the values of z, and an interval of $z = 0$ to $z = +2.58$ also contains .4951 of the values of z. Thus, an interval of $z = -2.58$ to $z = +2.58$ will contain .99 of the values of z (i.e., $.4951 + .4951 = .9902$, or .99). Hence, a 99 percent confidence interval for the population mean is obtained by

$$\overline{X} - 2.58\sigma_{\overline{X}} \text{ to } \overline{X} + 2.58\sigma_{\overline{X}}.$$

For the example with $\overline{X} = 41.5$ and $\sigma_{\overline{X}} = 2$, a 95 percent confidence interval equals

$$41.5 - 1.96(2) \text{ to } 41.5 + 1.96(2),$$

which equals

$$41.5 - 3.92 \text{ to } 41.5 + 3.92 \text{ or } 37.6 \text{ to } 45.4.$$

The 99 percent confidence interval equals

$$41.5 - 2.58(2) \text{ to } 41.5 + 2.58(2),$$

which equals

$$41.5 - 5.16 \text{ to } 41.5 + 51.6 \text{ or } 36.3 \text{ to } 46.7.$$

One aspect of this discussion may be puzzling. We have been estimating μ, a population parameter, because we cannot measure the population to obtain the value of this parameter. Yet, in constructing confidence intervals, we have used the value of σ, another parameter, to find $\sigma_{\overline{X}}$. Why should we know the value of σ when we do not know μ? The answer is that we would not; we would, instead, estimate $\sigma_{\overline{X}}$ from $s_{\overline{X}}$. We assumed knowledge of $\sigma_{\overline{X}}$ to simplify the introduction of interval estimation. But in practice, $s_{\overline{X}}$, rather than $\sigma_{\overline{X}}$, is used to determine the confidence limits. When $s_{\overline{X}}$ is used, confidence intervals are slightly larger than those obtained using $\sigma_{\overline{X}}$. The concepts of interval estimation are identical, however, whether $\sigma_{\overline{X}}$ or $s_{\overline{X}}$ is used. We discuss using $s_{\overline{X}}$ in constructing confidence intervals in Chapter 8 and will show how we obtained the confidence interval to the 100 Implicit View of Intelligence scores.

EXAMPLE PROBLEM	Constructing Confidence Intervals When $\sigma_{\overline{X}}$ Is Known

7.2

Problem: We have a sample of 30 scores from a population with $\sigma = 13.5$. The sample mean is 71.0. Find the 95 percent confidence interval for μ.

Solution: We find $\sigma_{\overline{X}}$ and then use Appendix C.1 to find the value of z that defines an interval containing 95 percent of the area on the standard normal distribution.

$$\sigma_{\overline{X}} = \frac{\sigma}{\sqrt{N}} = \frac{13.5}{\sqrt{30}} = \frac{13.5}{5.477} = 2.46.$$

From Appendix C.1, we find that an interval on the standard normal distribution from $z = -1.96$ to $z = +1.96$ contains 95 percent of the area of the distribution. Thus, the 95 percent confidence interval for μ is given by

$$\overline{X} - 1.96\sigma_{\overline{X}} \text{ to } \overline{X} + 1.96\sigma_{\overline{X}}.$$

Substituting numerical values for $\overline{X}$ and $\sigma_{\overline{X}}$ provides an interval

$$71.0 - 1.96(2.46) \text{ to } 71.0 + 1.96(2.46),$$

which equals 66.2 to 75.8. The 95 percent confidence interval for μ is from 66.2 to 75.8.

Testing Your Knowledge 7.3

1. Define: confidence interval, confidence limits, interval estimation.
2. You have drawn a sample of 25 scores from a population with $\sigma = 10.0$. The value of $\overline{X}$ is 73.0.
   a. Provide a point estimate of μ.
   b. Construct a 95 percent confidence interval for μ.
   c. Construct a 99 percent confidence interval for μ.

   Assume for questions 2d, 2e, and 2f that the sample size was 100 ($N = 100$) rather than 25.

   d. Provide a point estimate of μ.
   e. Construct a 95 percent confidence interval for μ.
   f. Construct a 99 percent confidence interval for μ.
   g. The confidence intervals based on $N = 100$ are smaller than those based on $N = 25$. Explain why this difference occurs.

Summary

▶ Statistical inference is a process of drawing conclusions about unknown population values from sample statistics.

▶ $\overline{X}$ is an unbiased and consistent estimator of μ.

▶ To provide accurate estimation, a sample should be representative of the population from which it is selected. Random sampling is often used to obtain a representative sample.

▶ Random sampling requires that each member of the population has an equal chance of being selected for the sample and the selection of one member is independent of the selection of any other member of the population.

▶ s^2 is an unbiased and consistent estimator of σ^2.

▶ s is used to estimate σ, although it slightly underestimates σ.

▶ The sampling distribution of the mean is the theoretical distribution of sample means for a given size sample.

▶ The standard error of the mean is the standard deviation of the sampling distribution of the mean and provides a measure of sampling error.

▶ $\sigma_{\overline{X}}$ is found by $\sigma/\sqrt{N}$. In most cases it is estimated by $s_{\overline{X}} = s/\sqrt{N}$.

▶ The sampling distribution of the mean approaches a normal distribution as sample size increases. Thus, $\sigma_{\overline{X}}$ can be used to find confidence intervals for estimates of μ from $\overline{X}$.

▶ A confidence interval is a range of score values expected to contain the value of μ with a certain level of confidence. The lower and upper scores defining the confidence interval are called the confidence limits.

 ## Key Terms and Symbols

central limit theorem (142)
confidence interval (149)
confidence limits (149)
consistent estimator (137)
estimated standard error of the mean
   $s_{\overline{X}}$ (146)
inference (136)
$\mu_{\overline{X}}$ (143)
95 percent confidence interval for the
  population mean (150)

99 percent confidence interval for the
   population mean (150)
point estimation (137)
random sampling (138)
sampling distribution (140)
sampling distribution of the
  mean (140)
sampling error (143)
σ^2 (136)

s (136)
s^2 (136)
standard error of the mean
  $(\sigma_{\overline{X}})$ (143)
statistical inference (136)
unbiased estimator (137)
$\overline{X}$ (136)
$\overline{X}_{\overline{X}}$ (143)

 ## Chapter Supplement

Review of Important Symbols and Formulas

Chapters 4 through 7 have introduced a number of important statistical symbols and formulas. To help your study and understanding of these materials, they are summarized in the following table.

Symbol	Formula	Definition
N		The number of scores in a sample, or the sample size.
$N_{\text{population}}$		The number of scores in a population, or the population size.
X		An individual score in either a sample or a population.
$\overline{X}$	$\dfrac{\sum X}{N}$	The sample mean. X refers to the individual scores in the sample.
μ	$\dfrac{\sum X}{N_{\text{population}}}$	The population mean. X refers to the individual scores in the population.
s^2	$\dfrac{\sum(X - \overline{X})^2}{N - 1}$	The estimated population variance. This variance is an unbiased estimate of the population variance.
s	$\sqrt{\dfrac{\sum(X - \overline{X})^2}{N - 1}}$	The estimated population standard deviation. This standard deviation is the formula most frequently used to calculate the standard deviation. Unless indicated otherwise, it is the standard deviation used in this text.
SS	$\sum(X - \overline{X})^2$	The sum of squares.
σ^2	$\dfrac{\sum(X - \mu)^2}{N_{\text{population}}}$	The population variance. X refers to individual scores in the population.
σ	$\sqrt{\dfrac{\sum(X - \mu)^2}{N_{\text{population}}}}$	The population standard deviation. X refers to individual scores in the population.
$\mu_{\overline{X}}$		The mean of the theoretical sampling distribution of the mean. This mean is equal to the population mean, μ.
$\overline{X}_{\overline{X}}$		The mean of an empirical sampling distribution of the mean.
$\sigma_{\overline{X}}$	$\dfrac{\sigma}{\sqrt{N}}$	The standard error of the mean for a sample of size N. The standard error of the mean is the standard deviation of the sampling distribution of the mean.
$s_{\overline{X}}$	$\dfrac{s}{\sqrt{N}}$	The estimated standard error of the mean for a sample of size N.
z	$\dfrac{X - \mu}{\sigma}$	The standard normal deviate. This formula converts a normally distributed raw score X to a z score in the standard normal distribution. The value of z_{obs} obtained with this formula can be used with the standard normal distribution of Appendix C.1.
z	$\dfrac{X - \overline{X}}{S}$	A standard score where $S = \sqrt{SS/N}$. This formula converts a raw score into a z score that describes how far above or below $\overline{X}$ the raw score is. The z scores obtained using this formula *cannot* be used with the standard normal distribution of Appendix C.1.
z	$\dfrac{\overline{X} - \mu}{\sigma_{\overline{X}}}$	The z statistic. This formula converts a sample mean to a z score in the standard normal distribution. The value of z_{obs} obtained with this formula can be used with the standard normal distribution of Appendix C.1.

Review Questions

1. Match the statistic with the parameter it estimates.

	Statistic	Parameter
a.	s	μ
b.	$\overline{X}$	$\sigma_{\overline{X}}$
c.	s^2	σ
d.	$s_{\overline{X}}$	σ^2

2. You are learning a new statistic and are told it is an unbiased and consistent estimator. What does this information tell you about the statistic as an estimator of a population parameter?

3. You select two samples from a population with mean μ. Sample 1 is of size $N = 10$. Sample 2 is of size $N = 24$. Which sample mean do you expect to be closer to the value of μ? Why?

4. Questions a to c below assume you have a population of 100 scores with a mean of 50.0 and a standard deviation of 5.0. Assume also that you have a theoretical sampling distribution of the mean for this population. For each of these distributions, answer the following questions to complete the table below.

   a. Define each of these distributions and explain how they would be obtained.

   b. Indicate the numerical value of the mean for each distribution and the appropriate symbol for this mean.

   c. Indicate the numerical value of the standard deviation of each distribution and the appropriate symbol for this standard deviation.

	Type of Distribution	
	Population	Sampling Distribution of the Mean
a. Definition		
b. Mean		
c. Standard deviation		

5. A behavioral scientist is interested in determining whether better looking faculty members receive higher course evaluations. To do so, she decides to go to an Internet rating site where students can evaluate professors based on both their attractiveness and quality of their teaching. Although this data would be easy to collect, what are some limitations to collecting data in this fashion? Explain your answer.

6. A problem of concern to many scientists in the twenty-first century is the issue of global warming and the potential contribution of human behaviors to this phenomenon. How concerned, however, is the average person? One well-known Internet polling site asked visitors to respond to a question about their concern with global warming. Of the approximately 25,000 responses to the question, about 72 percent of the respondents indicated that they, too, were concerned about the potential effects of global warming. The remaining respondents indicated they were not concerned about

the issue. Each day at least several hundred thousand people visit this site. What conclusions can you reach from this poll about people's concern with the problem of global warming? Explain your answer.

7. To estimate the number of cigarettes smoked per day by smokers in a high school population, you randomly sample 16 students from among those who identify themselves as smokers. You find that the sample mean for this group is 9.0 cigarettes per day.

   a. Provide a point estimate of the population mean.

   b. Suppose that $\sigma = 3.1$ cigarettes per day. Find the 95 percent confidence interval of the mean.

8. Suppose that the mean number of hours of sleep for a population of college students is 7.1 hours, with $\sigma = 1.2$ hours. You randomly sample 16 college students and determine the mean hours of sleep for this sample.

   a. What is the standard error of the mean for samples of size $N = 16$?

   b. What is the probability that the mean of your sample will be equal to or greater than 8.0 hours?

   c. What is the probability that the mean of your sample will be equal to or less than 6.8 hours?

   d. What is the probability that the mean of your sample will be between 6.5 to 7.7 hours?

9. What is the difference between s and $s_{\bar{X}}$?

10. Stephenson, Hoyle, Palmgreen, and Slater (2003) developed a four-item scale to measure sensation seeking. People who are high in sensation seeking appear to be easily bored and have a high need to participate in new and sometimes risky activities. Scores on the scale can range from 0 to 20, with higher scores indicating a higher need for sensation seeking. Suppose that this measure was given to all students at your college and the population mean was 10.0, with $\sigma = 2.5$. Assume now that you have measured five samples (samples A to E) of students from your college on this scale. Each of your samples was of a different size, as indicated next.

Sample	N
A	4
B	9
C	16
D	25
E	100

For each sample size:

a. Calculate $\sigma_{\bar{X}}$.

b. Find the probability that your sample mean will be equal to or greater than 11.0.

c. What relationship between $\sigma_{\bar{X}}$ and N is illustrated in this example?

d. For each sample size, find the probability that your sample mean will be between 10 and 12.

knowledge

A Look at a Problem   Binge drinking is defined as consuming five or more alcoholic beverages in a row for men or four or more alcoholic beverages in a row for women. Binge drinking leads to many serious problems from car crashes to risking sexually transmitted diseases and may even result in death from alcohol overdose. The culture on many college campuses seems to promote binge drinking, thus it is a topic of numerous research studies as behavioral scientists attempt to understand this risky behavior. One avenue of interest is the effect of participating in organized athletic programs on binge drinking. Some believe that participating in athletic programs may decrease binge drinking because athletes may have less free time. Athletes may also fear that alcohol may damage their athletic performance. Others, however, believe that athletic participation may increase binge drinking as encouraged by one's fellow athletes. To more fully investigate this problem, Turrisi, Mastroleo, Mallett, Larimer, and Kilmer (2007) compared binge drinking of college athletes (defined by active participation in a varsity or club sport at the collegiate level) and non-athletes at a moderate-sized university. Turrisi et al. found that in response to the question "In the last two weeks, how many times did you have five or more drinks in a row on a single occasion (e.g., in the same evening)?" (p. 455), athletes reported a mean of 1.7 binge-drinking incidents, with a standard deviation of 2.4 incidents. Non-athletes reported a mean of 1.0 binge-drinking incidents, with a standard deviation of 1.9 incidents.

1. How did Turrisi et al. operationally define binge drinking in this study? How did they operationally define a college athlete in this study? Why are operational definitions so important to behavioral science research?

2. For the athletes, find the range of binge-drinking incidents encompassed by two standard deviations around the mean (i.e., $\overline{X} \pm 2s$).

   a. What do you notice is unusual about this range of incidents?

   b. What does this range of incidents tell you about the shape of the distribution of reports of binge drinking for athletes? Do you think the distribution of incidents is approximately normally distributed, or do you think it is skewed? What is the reason for your judgment?

   c. Based on the range of incidents that you found, is it likely that some athletes reported no instances of binge drinking in the two-week period?

PART B

Your Turn: Selecting Your Research Tools   Let's say you have been assigned to a task force on your college campus to identify which of two proposed programs (A or B) will most effectively decrease binge drinking. In addition to the proposed programs aimed at decreasing binge drinking, you also use a control group of students who have not participated in a program aimed at decreasing binge drinking. After the programs have been implemented, you measure the number of binge-drinking episodes over a two-week period for each student who participated in the program.

1. What statistic would you use to represent the typical amount of binge drinking in each program condition? Why would you use this statistic?

2. What information would you need to obtain from each subject to calculate this statistic?

3. By simply looking at your measures of central tendency, would you be able to know if the programs had an effect on binge drinking? Explain your answer. (*Hint:* Remember the problem of sampling error in any measure obtained from a sample.)

PART C

Using Your Statistical Tools   Not all college students drink alcohol, and of those who do, many never consume enough alcohol in a single sitting to constitute binge drinking. To understand the current state of binge drinking on your campus, you randomly selected 100 male students and ask them to report the largest number of consecutive alcoholic drinks they had consumed in a single sitting during the past two weeks. You found the following results:

Consecutive Alcoholic Drinks	Number of Students
6 or more	3
5	7
4	11
3	15
2	14
1	11
0	39

1. From these results, what is the probability that a student would have consumed the specified number of consecutive alcoholic drinks in the past two weeks?

   a. 0 drinks

   b. 3 drinks

   c. 0 to 2 drinks

   d. 5 or more drinks

2. From this distribution, what is the most frequent number of consecutive drinks reported? What is the name of this statistic?

3. What number of consecutive drinks divides the distributions in half such that 50% of the students had more consecutive drinks than this number in a two-week period? What is the name of this statistic?

4. Which statistic, the one you identified in question 2 or the one you identified in question 3, do you think provides the most representative number of consecutive drinks by students in a two-week period? Explain the reason for your answer.

Your college had previously completed a survey of every male student on their incidents of binge drinking and found that the population standard deviation for the number of incidents of binge drinking at your college was 1.5. Having followed through with the proposed study described in section B, you randomly assigned 75 males to one of three programs, resulting in 25 students in each of the three conditions. You found the following mean incidents of binge drinking in a two-week period:

	Mean
Program A	0.6
Program B	1.2
Program C (control)	2.0

5. Calculate a 95 percent confidence interval for the population mean for each condition.

6. Compare the confidence intervals for programs A and B. Do these intervals overlap? That is, is it probable that each sample mean estimates a population mean of 0.9, for example? What do you think this information tells you about the difference between the program A and B sample means?

7. Compare the confidence intervals for programs A and C. Do these intervals overlap? What do you think this information tells you about the difference of the program A and C sample means?

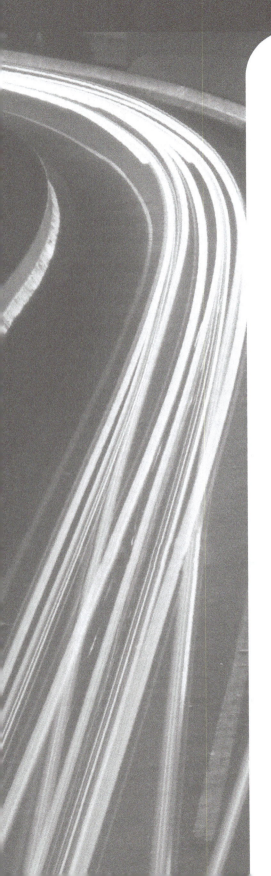

Is There Really a Difference? Introduction to Statistical Hypothesis Testing

A re you a big spender? As a college student, perhaps not. Nevertheless, today's college students are an important economic force in their college communities. They are viewed by marketers as sophisticated consumers who are often trendsetters in the marketplace with a considerable amount of discretionary income to spend on purchases such as clothing, electronics, and entertainment. Although it would be impossible to assess the discretionary monthly income for all college students in the country, several surveys of students have estimated the typical college student has about $250 per month of discretionary income, with a standard deviation of about $50. Given all the shiny new electronic gadgets you see in your dorm, you are curious whether this population mean is characteristic of the discretionary income of students at your college. You suspect that the mean for your college may differ from this population mean. To test this hypothesis, you obtain a sample of 25 students sampled randomly and independently from the population of students at your college. The mean discretionary income for this sample of 25 students is $280. Obviously, this $\overline{X}$ of $280 is not the same as the population mean of $\mu =$ $250. Recall from the discussion of sampling error in Chapter 7, however, that a sample mean will usually differ from the mean of the population from which it was selected. Thus, what does this difference between $\overline{X}$ and μ tell you about the population from which the sample was selected? There are two possibilities. The first is that the population from which the sample was drawn actually has a mean discretionary income of $250, and your sample mean of $280 differs from this μ only because of sampling error. By chance, you selected a sample with an $\overline{X}$ greater than $250. The second possibility is that this $\overline{X}$ represents a population with a μ other than $250. The population of students at your college has a mean discretionary income different from $250. Which of these two possibilities should you select as representing the situation existing at your college?

We have posed a problem that requires statistical hypothesis testing to arrive at a choice of which of the two possible situations described is more probable. In statistical terms, this problem requires using a statistical hypothesis test to decide whether the sample mean of $280 differs significantly from a population mean of $250. Figure 8.1 illustrates this problem. We will use this example to introduce the use of statistics for hypothesis testing to answer questions such as the one we just posed.

Statistical Hypothesis Testing

Parametric and Nonparametric Tests

Parametric Tests

Parametric test ▷ A statistical test involving hypotheses that state a relationship about a population parameter.

There are two types of statistical hypothesis tests that are typically used: parametric and nonparametric. A **parametric test** involves a hypothesis that makes a statement about a population parameter such as μ or σ. Thus, parametric tests typically require measurements at the interval or ratio level. Parametric tests also often assume certain conditions are true for the scores in the population from which a sample is drawn. As we introduce specific parametric tests, we also identify the assumptions of these tests and what happens if those assumptions are not met. In this chapter, we introduce statistical hypothesis testing using two different parametric tests, the one-sample z test and the one-sample t test. Other parametric tests are introduced in Chapters 9 through 12.

Nonparametric Tests

Nonparametric test ▷ A statistical test involving hypotheses that do not state a relationship about a population parameter.

A **nonparametric test** involves a hypothesis that does not make a statement about a population parameter such as μ. Typically, nonparametric tests make no assumptions about the

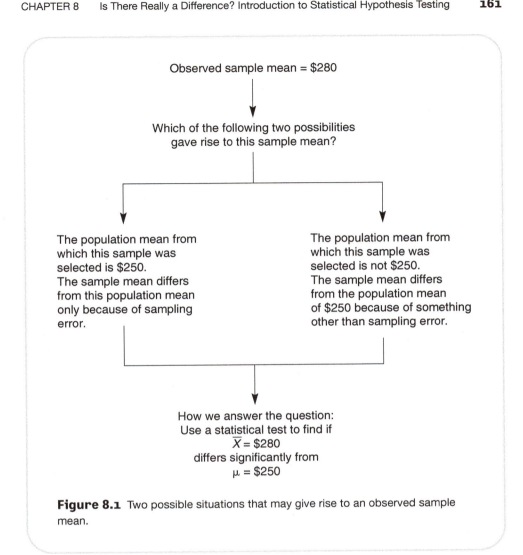

Figure 8.1 Two possible situations that may give rise to an observed sample mean.

distribution of scores in the population from which the sample is drawn. For this reason, they are also referred to as *distribution-free tests*. Nonparametric tests are often used when the assumptions necessary for parametric tests are not met by the data. For many, but not all parametric statistical tests, there are alternative nonparametric tests for analyzing the same data. Nonparametric tests are also useful for nominal or ordinal level data, as neither type of measurement can be used in parametric tests. Several nonparametric tests are presented in Chapter 15. The fundamental concepts of statistical hypothesis testing, though, are much the same for both parametric and nonparametric tests.

Statistical Hypotheses

Statistical hypothesis ▷
A statement about a population
parameter (for a parametric test).

Statistical hypothesis testing, parametric and nonparametric, begins with stating a statistical hypothesis. For a parametric test, a **statistical hypothesis** is a statement about a population parameter. This statement may or may not be true; it is made simply to establish a testable condition and is based on the research hypothesis that is being tested. For our example problem, we may hypothesize that the mean discretionary income for the population from which we obtained the sample of 25 students is $250. In actuality, the population mean may or may not be $250; we simply are proposing that it is $250 and that we will test this hypothesis. Statistical tests require that two hypotheses be formulated, the null and the alternative hypothesis.

Null Hypothesis

The **null hypothesis** is a statement of a condition that we tentatively hold to be true about a population, and it is the hypothesis that is tested by a statistical test. Null hypotheses usually are written in symbolic or notational form using H_0 to indicate that a hypothesis, such as $\mu = \$250$, is being offered. In statistical notation, the expression of this null hypothesis is H_0: $\mu = \$250$. The subscripted zero is often pronounced "naught"; thus, we say, "H naught: mu equals 250 dollars." The word *null* implies there is no difference. Its use becomes clearer in Chapter 9 in which we propose a null hypothesis of no difference between two population means.

Null hypothesis ▷ A statement of a condition that a scientist tentatively holds to be true about a population; it is the hypothesis that is tested by a statistical test.

Alternative Hypothesis

The **alternative hypothesis** is a statement of what must be true if the null hypothesis is false. In the example, if H_0: $\mu = \$250$ is not true, then the alternative must be that μ does not equal $250. This alternative hypothesis is identified as H_1 and written as H_1: $\mu \neq \$250$, where $\neq$ is the symbol for "does not equal." Hence, H_1: $\mu \neq \$250$ is read as "H one: mu does not equal 250 dollars."

Alternative hypothesis ▷ A statement of what must be true if the null hypothesis is false.

Properties of Statistical Hypotheses

Every statistical test requires null and alternative hypotheses. These hypotheses must be expressed so that they have the following characteristics:

- They are mutually exclusive. *Mutually exclusive* means both hypotheses cannot be true at the same time. For example, it is impossible for H_0: $\mu = \$250$ and H_1: $\mu \neq \$250$ to be true simultaneously for the same population.

- They include all possible values of the parameter involved in the hypothesis. The hypotheses H_0: $\mu = \$250$ and H_1: $\mu \neq \$250$ meet this requirement; between them they include all possible values of μ for the population of interest.

Because of these characteristics, one of the two hypotheses must represent the true condition in the population. For the example, the population mean of discretionary income is either $250 and H_0 is true, or it is not $250, and the alternative hypothesis, H_1 is true.

In summary, for the example problem the statistical hypotheses are

H_0: $\mu = \$250$ (null hypothesis), and
H_1: $\mu \neq \$250$ (alternative hypothesis).

Function of the Statistical Hypotheses

The function of the null hypothesis in a statistical test is to establish a condition under which the sampling distribution of a statistic may be obtained. In Chapter 7, we defined a sampling distribution of the mean as the distribution of $\overline{X}$ values when all possible samples of size N were selected from a population and $\overline{X}$ calculated for each sample. For example, assuming H_0: $\mu = \$250$ is true and $\sigma = \$50$ for the population, we may obtain the sampling distribution of $\overline{X}$ for samples of size 25 from this population. This

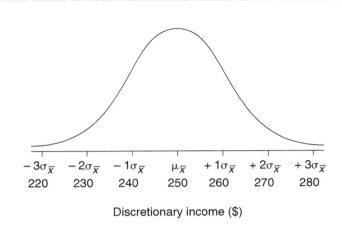

Figure 8.2 Theoretical sampling distribution of the mean for samples of $N = 25$ from a population with $\mu_{\bar{x}} = 250$ and $\sigma_{\bar{x}} = 10$.

sampling distribution, shown in Figure 8.2, is normally distributed with $\mu_{\bar{X}} = \$250$ and a standard error equal to $\sigma_{\bar{X}}$ where

$$\sigma_{\bar{X}} = \frac{\sigma}{\sqrt{N}} = \frac{50}{\sqrt{25}} = \frac{50}{5} = 10.$$

In this distribution a sample mean of \$280 falls at three standard errors of the mean away from $\mu_{\bar{X}}$. Accordingly, under the condition established by H_0: $\mu = \$250$, a sample mean equal to \$280 is a very infrequent occurrence if samples of size 25 are drawn from this population. Hence, we might be inclined to reject the null hypothesis, H_0: $\mu = \$250$, if we obtained a sample mean of \$280. This is a statistically rare event if H_0: $\mu = \$250$ is true. But, before we can definitely make a decision on whether to treat H_0 as true or not, we must

▶ define what we mean by a statistically rare event, a step that requires choosing a significance level, and

▶ identify the probability of obtaining a value of $\overline{X}$ as large or larger than \$280 if H_0: $\mu = \$250$ is true, a step that requires using a test statistic.

A Test Statistic: *z*

Test statistic ▶ A number calculated from the scores of the sample that allows testing a statistical null hypothesis.

A **test statistic** is a number calculated from the scores of the sample that allows us to test a null hypothesis. For the example given in the chapter introduction, we want a test to find the probability of occurrence of a sample mean as large or larger than \$280 if H_0: $\mu = \$250$ is true. Because the sampling distribution of the mean illustrated in Figure 8.2

is normally distributed with $\mu_{\overline{X}} = \$250$ and $\sigma_{\overline{X}} = 10$, we can transform any value of $\overline{X}$ into a value on the standard normal distribution by using the **z statistic**

$$z = \frac{\overline{X} - \mu}{\sigma_{\overline{X}}}$$

where $\overline{X}$ = sample mean.
          μ = hypothesized population mean.
          $\sigma_{\overline{X}}$ = standard error of the mean.

The value of z locates the sample mean on the standard normal distribution. Notice that this formula is identical to that given for z in Chapter 7.

The value of z_{obs} with $\overline{X}$ of \$280, the value of μ hypothesized to be \$250, and $\sigma_{\overline{X}} = 10$ is

$$z_{obs} = \frac{\overline{X} - \mu}{\sigma_{\overline{X}}} = \frac{280 - 250}{10} = \frac{30}{10} = +3.00.$$

The z statistic is identified as z_{obs} because it is observed from the value of $\overline{X}$ of the sample. Whenever you see a subscripted *obs* with a statistic in this or future chapters, it means the value being given is the calculated value of the statistic from the sample data. From the sampling distribution of the z statistic given in Appendix C.1, we find that the probability of z being as large as or larger than $+3.00$ is .0013 (see column c of Appendix C.1 for $z = 3.00$). Consequently, the probability of obtaining $\overline{X} = \$280$ or larger from a sample of size 25 is equal to .0013 if $H_0: \mu = \$250$ is true. In other words, if we were to randomly select 10,000 samples of $N = 25$ from a population with $\mu = \$250$ and $\sigma = \$50$, we would expect only 13 of the 10,000 sample means to be as large as or larger than \$280. Thus, if $H_0: \mu = \$250$ is true, obtaining a sample with $\overline{X}$ equal to \$280 would be a statistically rare event. If we had obtained this $\overline{X}$, we certainly would reject the hypothesis that it was drawn from a population with a mean discretionary income of \$250, and we would accept the alternative hypothesis that $\mu \neq \$250$.

The logic of this decision is that if the population mean is \$250, then obtaining a sample with a mean of \$280 would occur only 13 times out of every 10,000 samples selected. Although obtaining $\overline{X} = \$280$ is a possible event if $\mu = \$250$, it is not a very probable event. It would be a more probable event if the population mean were something other than \$250. Thus, we reject H_0 and accept H_1. This decision may be in error; it is possible to obtain $\overline{X} = \$280$ if $\mu = \$250$, but it is not very probable.

Suppose, however, that we had obtained a sample mean of \$258, instead of \$280. Here the value of z is

$$z_{obs} = \frac{258 - 250}{10} = \frac{8}{10} = +0.80.$$

From column c of Appendix C.1, we find that the probability of obtaining a value of $z_{obs} = +0.80$ or larger is equal to .2119. Thus, if H_0 were true and we drew 10,000 samples of $N = 25$, 2119 of them would have values of $\overline{X}$ equal to or larger than \$258. Is a sample mean of \$258 a statistically rare event if $H_0: \mu = \$250$ is true? What decision would you make about the null hypothesis in this instance? Would you reject H_0: $\mu = \$250$ and accept H_1: $\mu \neq \$250$? Or, would you not reject H_0 and, therefore, not accept H_1? To answer these questions, we must define what value of z_{obs} will be considered a statistically rare outcome if H_0 is true. The definition of statistical rareness is given by the significance level selected.

Significance Levels: Statistical Rareness

Significance level ▷ A probability value that provides the criterion for rejecting a null hypothesis in a statistical test.

Alpha or α ▷ The value of the significance level stated as a probability.

The **significance level** is a probability value that provides the criterion for rejecting a null hypothesis in a statistical test. Significance levels are given as values of **alpha** or α, the first letter of the Greek alphabet. Typically, behavioral scientists use alpha levels of either .05 or .01. Thus, if $\alpha = .05$, values of z_{obs} occurring only 5 or fewer times in 100 occasions if H_0 is true are sufficiently rare that we are willing to reject H_0 and decide that H_1 is true. Thus, the value of α selected defines a statistically rare outcome if H_0 is true.

Using the Test Statistic and the Significance Level to Decide About the Statistical Hypotheses

After choosing a test statistic and a significance level, we are ready to decide about the statistical hypotheses. Three steps are involved:

1. Locating a rejection region or regions in the sampling distribution of the test statistic.
2. Calculating the value of the test statistic on the sample data.
3. Deciding about the statistical hypotheses by observing whether the test statistic falls into a rejection region.

Locating Rejection Regions

Rejection region ▷ Values on the sampling distribution of the test statistic that have a probability equal to or less than α if H_0 is true. If the test statistic falls into the rejection region, H_0 is rejected.

The **rejection region** represents values on the sampling distribution of the test statistic that have a probability equal to or less than α if H_0 is true. For the example, the rejection region identifies the values of z that meet the criterion for rejecting H_0.

The sampling distribution of the z statistic with rejection regions located in each tail of the distribution is shown in Figure 8.3. Statistically rare values of z occur at either tail, or end, of the distribution. For example, z_{obs} values of either $+3.00$ or -3.00 are equally improbable values of z_{obs} if H_0 is true. Either large positive or negative values of z for the example problem would cast doubt on the truth of H_0: $\mu = \$250$. Thus, rejection regions for the z statistic will be in either tail of the sampling distribution. A statistical test with rejection regions in both tails of the sampling distribution of the test statistic is identified as a **two-tailed**, or **nondirectional**, **test**. A value of a z_{obs} statistic falling into either rejection region is improbable or rare if H_0 is true, but more likely to occur if H_1 is true. Therefore, if a value of z_{obs} falls into either rejection region, H_0 is rejected and H_1 accepted.

Two-tailed test ▷ A statistical test using rejection regions in both tails of the sampling distribution of the test statistic.

One-tailed test ▷ A statistical test using a rejection region in only one tail of the sampling distribution of the test statistic.

On occasion, we may have reason to place the rejection region in only one tail of the sampling distribution of z. In this instance, a **one-tailed**, or **directional**, **test** is used. The benefit of a one-tailed test is that a smaller value of z statistic may fall into the rejection region. We discuss one-tailed tests more fully later in this chapter. For the current example, we use a two-tailed test.

Critical value ▷ The specific numerical values that define the boundaries of the rejection region.

Critical Values.   **Critical values** are the specific numerical values that define the boundaries of the rejection region. Critical values for z are found in column c of Appendix C.1. The first step in finding a critical value is to choose a significance level, such as $\alpha = .05$.

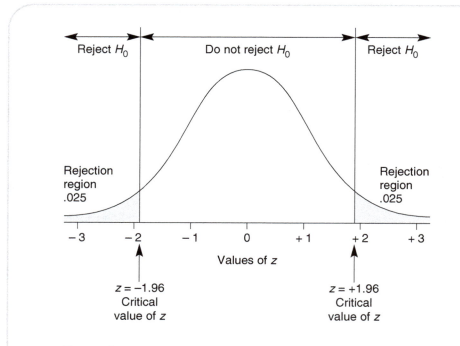

Figure 8.3 Sampling distribution of the z statistic illustrating rejection regions for a two-tailed test and $\alpha = .05$. A value of z_{obs} that falls into either rejection region leads to rejecting H_0.

For a two-tailed test, rejection regions are located in each tail of the sampling distribution of z. Accordingly, we want the area in each tail of the distribution to equal one-half of α, or .05/2, which equals .025. What values of z meet the requirement that .025 of the area of the sampling distribution of z lies beyond their values in each tail? Consulting Appendix C.1, we read down column c until we find the area beyond z equal to .025. When we find this area, we read the corresponding value of z in column a. This value of z is 1.96. Thus, for $\alpha = .05$, the two-tailed critical values are $z = -1.96$ and $z = +1.96$. These critical values of z (symbolized as $z_{\textbf{crit}}$) locate the rejection regions in the sampling distribution of z, as shown in Figure 8.3. Whenever you see a subscripted *crit* with a statistic in this or future chapters, it means the value being given is the critical value obtained from the sampling distribution of the statistic.

Decisions About the Statistical Hypotheses

We decide to reject or not reject H_0 by comparing the value of z_{obs} to z_{crit}. A value of z_{obs} equal to or less than $z_{crit} = -1.96$ or equal to or greater than $z_{crit} = +1.96$ falls into a rejection region. Values of z_{obs} that fall into a rejection region are statistically rare if H_0 is true, but are more common occurrences if H_1 is true. Thus, a z_{obs} falling into a rejection region leads us to *reject H_0*. If we reject H_0, then we must *accept H_1*. If, however, z does not fall into a rejection region, then we *fail to reject H_0*. And if we fail to reject H_0, then we *do not accept H_1*.

Notice that we use the value of z_{obs} to make a decision about H_0; we either reject H_0 or we fail to reject H_0. The decision about H_0 then dictates the decision to be made about H_1. If we reject H_0, then we must accept H_1. On the other hand, if we fail to reject H_0, we cannot accept H_1.

For the example of discretionary income of students at your college, $z_{obs} = +3.00$ is larger than $z_{crit} = +1.96$; thus, it falls into the upper rejection region. Accordingly, we reject H_0: $\mu = \$250$ and accept H_1: $\mu \neq \$250$. We reject the null hypothesis that the sample was selected from a population with a mean of $250 discretionary income per month. Because the sample mean, $\overline{X} = \$280$, is greater than the hypothesized population mean of $250, the decision to reject H_0 and accept H_1 leads us to conclude that the mean discretionary income of the population of students from which we sampled is greater than $250. The best point estimate we have of this population mean is the sample mean, $\overline{X} = \$280$.

To summarize decision making about the statistical hypotheses,

▶ if the z_{obs} statistic *falls into a rejection region*, then H_0 is rejected and H_1 is accepted; and

▶ if the z_{obs} statistic *does not fall into a rejection region*, then H_0 is not rejected and H_1 is not accepted.

Statistically Significant Difference

Statistically significant difference
▶ The observed value of the test statistic falls into a rejection region and H_0 is rejected.

A **statistically significant difference** occurs when the observed value of the test statistic falls into a rejection region and H_0 is rejected. For the z statistic, a statistically significant difference indicates that we have decided that the sample mean comes from a population with a mean different from the hypothesized population mean.

Statistically significant differences are typically reported in the form $z_{obs} = +3.00$, $p \leq .05$. Often the subscripted *obs* is not used. The symbol $\leq$ implies less than or equal to; thus, $p \leq .05$ is read as "p less than or equal to .05." The less-than symbol ($<$) is frequently used in place of the $\leq$ symbol, so the z_{obs} is reported as $z = +3.00$, $p < .05$. In either case, this report indicates that H_0 was rejected at the .05 significance level because the probability (p) of z_{obs} when H_0 is true is equal to or less than .05. The decisions and conclusions reached from a significant difference with the z test are summarized in the left column of Table 8.1.

TABLE 8.1

Summary of decisions and conclusions in statistical hypothesis testing using the z test for testing a sample mean against a population mean. A .05 significance level is used.

If z_{obs} falls into the rejection region for $\alpha = .05$, then:	If z_{obs} does not fall into the rejection region for $\alpha = .05$, then:
▶ Probability of z_{obs} is less than or equal to .05 or $p \leq .05$.	▶ Probability of z_{obs} is greater than .05 or $p > .05$.
▶ H_0 is rejected.	▶ H_0 is not rejected.
▶ H_1 is accepted.	▶ H_1 is not accepted.
▶ We found a statistically significant difference at the .05 level.	▶ We failed to find a statistically significant difference at the .05 level.
▶ The sample mean is considered to be from a different population.	▶ There is no evidence that the sample is from a different population.
▶ Something in addition to sampling error alone is responsible for differences difference between $\overline{X}$ and μ.	▶ Sampling error alone is the most plausible explanation of the difference between $\overline{X}$ and μ.

Nonsignificant difference ▶ The observed value of the test statistic does not fall into a rejection region and the null hypothesis is not rejected.

Nonsignificant Difference

A difference between a sample mean and a population mean is a **nonsignificant difference** if the observed value of the test statistic does not fall into a rejection region. The null hypothesis is not rejected, and the observed difference between $\overline{X}$ and the hypothesized μ is treated as due only to sampling error. A nonsignificant difference is indicated by $p > .05$ following the numerical value of z_{obs}. The decisions and conclusions reached from a nonsignificant difference with the z test are summarized in the right column of Table 8.1.

Summary of the Steps of Statistical Hypothesis Testing

All statistical tests require the following:

▶ Selecting a test statistic, such as z.

▶ Formulating two statistical hypotheses, H_0 and H_1.

▶ Obtaining the sampling distribution of the test statistic assuming that H_0 is true.

▶ Selecting a significance level.

▶ Finding a critical value or values of the test statistic.

▶ Locating a rejection region or regions in the sampling distribution of the test statistic.

▶ Formulating decision rules regarding the statistical hypotheses.

▶ Calculating the value of the test statistic on the sample data.

▶ Deciding to reject or not reject H_0 based on whether the observed value of the test statistic does or does not fall into a rejection region.

▶ Deciding to accept or not accept H_1 based on the decision for H_0.

▶ Relating the decisions about the statistical hypotheses to the research hypothesis.

This introduction to statistical hypothesis testing may seem complicated to you, but it soon becomes routine because the same steps are followed for each of the statistical tests presented in this text.

Testing Your Knowledge 8.1

1. Define: alpha level, α, alternative hypothesis, critical value, H_0, H_1, nonparametric test, nonsignificant difference, null hypothesis, one-tailed test, parametric test, rejection region, significance level, statistical hypothesis, statistically significant difference, test statistic, two-tailed test, z_{crit}, z_{obs}, z statistic.

2. Identify the two properties of statistical hypotheses.

3. The z score discussed in Chapter 6 (pages 111–120) and the z statistic discussed in this chapter are very similar; however, there are some critical differences as well. First, write the formula for each z, then compare the information a z score provides compared to that given by a z statistic.

4. Write H_0 and H_1 in notation for each of the following statements.

   a. The μ for scores on the Wechsler Adult Intelligence Test is 100.

   b. For a population of 25- to 54-year-old women, the mean amount of television watched each day is 4.4 hours.

   c. The mean reaction time of 19-year-old males to a simple stimulus is 423.0 milliseconds.

5. For each of the following, μ represents a population mean, $\sigma_{\overline{X}}$ the standard error of the mean for the population, and $\overline{X}$ a mean of a sample drawn from the population. For each set of values, formulate H_0 and H_1 and find the value of z_{obs}. Then, using Appendix C.1, determine whether the z_{obs} falls into a two-tailed rejection region at the .05 significance level and indicate your decision for H_0 and H_1.

	μ	$\sigma_{\overline{X}}$	$\overline{X}$
a.	50	4.7	40
b.	100	25.0	70
c.	143	0.4	143.9
d.	87	2.9	92

6. Complete the following problem using a .05 significance level and a two-tailed test. The population mean for a reading comprehension test is 100 and $\sigma = 15$. You are the principal of an elementary school in a rural county. For the 121 students in your school, $\overline{X}$ on this scale is 103.4. Does the mean of the students in your school differ significantly from the population mean? In your answer, indicate:

   a. The statistic to be used
   b. The statistical hypotheses
   c. The significance level
   d. z_{crit}
   e. The location of the rejection regions
   f. z_{obs}
   g. Your decision about H_0 and H_1
   h. Your conclusion regarding the mean of your students in relation to a population mean of 100

The One-Sample *t* Test

Imagine you were to ask a commuter student on your campus what is the biggest problem they face each day? We suspect she or he will answer with one word, *parking*. Suppose that a year ago, prior to making some changes in parking on your campus, a survey of all commuter students found a population mean for the amount of time it took to find a parking space on campus of 15.0 minutes. The population standard deviation, however, was not calculated for the survey, so it is unknown to you. There are more commuter students on campus this year, thus you expect this population mean no longer characterizes the parking situation on your campus today. Consequently you randomly sample 30 commuter students from your campus and ask them to time how long it takes them to find a parking space once they arrive on campus. You obtain a sample mean of 18.0 minutes ($\overline{X} = 18.0$ minutes), with a standard deviation of 7.0 minutes ($s = 7.0$ minutes). Does this sample mean differ significantly from the population mean of 15.0 minutes that existed a year ago? Because you do not know $\sigma_{\overline{X}}$, however, you will need to estimate it from $s_{\overline{X}}$. When we estimate $\sigma_{\overline{X}}$ from $s_{\overline{X}}$, we cannot use the z statistic. Rather, we use a different statistic, the *t*, defined as

$$t = \frac{\overline{X} - \mu}{s_{\overline{X}}}$$

or, substituting $s/\sqrt{N}$ for $s_{\overline{X}}$,

$$t = \frac{\overline{X} - \mu}{s/\sqrt{N}}$$

where
$\overline{X}$ = sample mean.
μ = hypothesized population mean.
$s_{\overline{X}}$ = estimated standard error of the mean obtained from the estimated population standard deviation s.
N = sample size.

The z statistic is used for hypothesis testing when you know $\sigma_{\overline{X}}$, whereas the t statistic is used to test the difference between a sample mean and a hypothesized population mean for statistical significance when $\sigma_{\overline{X}}$ is estimated by $s_{\overline{X}}$. Because only one sample mean is involved, the statistic is called the **one-sample *t*** to distinguish it from a t test involving two sample means that is introduced in Chapter 9.

One-sample *t* test ▶ A *t* test used to test the difference between a sample mean and a hypothesized population mean for statistical significance when $\sigma_{\overline{X}}$ is estimated by $s_{\overline{X}}$.

The t statistic was developed by the British mathematician William Sealy Gosset shortly after the turn of the twentieth century. Gosset published his work under the pseudonym of "Student." Consequently, the t statistic is often identified as "Student's t."

Sampling Distribution of *t*

Sampling distribution of *t* ▶ The distribution of *t* values for all possible sample sizes.

To use the t statistic, we must know its sampling distribution. The **sampling distribution of the *t*** differs slightly from the sampling distribution of the z. The z statistic, because it uses the population parameter $\sigma_{\overline{X}}$, has only one sampling distribution, the distribution presented in Appendix C.1. The t statistic, however, uses s, the **estimated population standard deviation**, defined as

$$s = \sqrt{\frac{\sum(X - \overline{X})^2}{N - 1}}.$$

The calculation of s involves the sample size N; therefore, the sampling distribution of t varies with the sample size or, more specifically, the *degrees of freedom* of the sample.

Degrees of Freedom

Degrees of freedom ▶ The number of scores free to vary when calculating a statistic.

Degrees of freedom (abbreviated ***df***) are determined by the number of scores free to vary when calculating a statistic. Several examples will be helpful in understanding what is meant by "scores free to vary" when computing a statistic. Suppose that you are asked to choose three scores between 0 and 100 on a test. You may choose any three scores, say 75, 62, and 97. For this request there are no limitations on the scores that you may choose; each score is free to vary. Accordingly, there are N or 3 df for this set of scores. Consider a second request, however, where you are asked to choose three scores, but the sum of the three scores must be 254. Suppose you choose 81 and 78 as your first two scores; they can have any value you want. These two scores are free to vary. Is the third score also free to vary? It is not. Because the three scores must total 254, the third score must be 95; no other score provides a total of 254. Consequently, if you are told that the total of the scores is 254, two scores are free to vary, but the value of the third score is *fixed* by the value of the two scores free to vary and the total of the three scores. Accordingly, if you know the total of the three scores, then there are $N - 1 = 3 - 1 = 2$ degrees of freedom for the three scores.

Applying this reasoning to the calculation of the sample mean, $\overline{X}$ has N *df*. All scores in a set of scores are free to vary when calculating $\overline{X}$. To illustrate, suppose you are asked to calculate the sample mean of a set of five scores, four of which are 7, 10, 3, and 6. Given only this information, you cannot find the mean. The fifth score may assume any value, and you cannot know the value of the fifth score from knowledge of the four scores. Thus, all N scores (where $N = 5$ for this example) are free to vary when calculating the sample mean. The degrees of freedom for s, however, are $N - 1$. To illustrate, suppose that you are asked to calculate s on a sample of five scores using the formula

$$s = \sqrt{\frac{\sum (X - \overline{X})^2}{N - 1}}.$$

Notice that to calculate s you must know $\overline{X}$. Assume that four of the five scores have values of 13, 15, 13, and 12 and that the mean of the five scores is 13.4. We know also that $\sum (X - \overline{X}) = 0$. If we subtract $\overline{X}$ from each of the four known scores, we obtain

$$X - \overline{X}$$
$$13 - 13.4 = -0.4$$
$$15 - 13.4 = +1.6$$
$$13 - 13.4 = -0.4$$
$$12 - 13.4 = \underline{-1.4}$$
$$\text{Sum} \quad = -0.6$$

The sum of these four $X - \overline{X}$ differences is -0.6. When the fifth score is included in the set, this sum must be zero. Thus, the fifth score must result in an $X_5 - \overline{X}$ value of $+0.6$, for $+0.6$ added to -0.6 will equal zero. If $X_5 - 13.4 = +0.6$, then X_5 must equal 14. Accordingly, if $\overline{X}$ is known for the set of five scores, the values of only four of the five scores are free to vary. The value of the fifth score is not free to vary; its value is fixed by the restriction that the value of the mean imposes. Because $\overline{X}$ must be known to calculate s, all scores but one are free to vary in calculating s. Thus, when calculating either s or s^2, a set of N scores possesses $N - 1$ *df*.

We can apply this knowledge of degrees of freedom to the formula for s to write it more briefly. Because $\sum (X - \overline{X})^2$ is also called a *sum of squares (SS)*, and $N - 1$ represents the degrees of freedom when obtaining an *SS*, the estimated population standard deviation can be expressed as the square root of a sum of squares divided by the degrees of freedom, or

$$\textbf{Estimated population standard deviation} = s = \sqrt{\frac{SS}{df}}.$$

We will find this expression of s useful in later chapters.

Degrees of Freedom for the One-Sample *t* Test

We now apply our knowledge of *df* to the *t* test. The estimated standard error of the mean, $s_{\overline{X}}$, is given by $s/\sqrt{N}$. Because *s* has $N - 1$ *df*, $s_{\overline{X}}$, too, has $N - 1$ *df*. Hence, the degrees of freedom for the sampling distribution of the one-sample *t* statistic are $N - 1$ also.

Sampling Distribution of the *t*

There is a different theoretical sampling distribution of *t* for each number of *df*. Because potentially any number of scores can be obtained in a sample, there is an unlimited number of *df* ranging from 1 to infinity for the *t* statistic. For example, Figure 8.4 (on page 174) illustrates the sampling distribution of *t* for 29 *df*. Although the shape of the *t* distribution changes with its degrees of freedom, it is similar to the normal distribution in several respects. Each *t* distribution is symmetrical, unimodal, and has a mean equal to zero. Consider why these properties arise. When a null hypothesis, such as H_0: μ = some hypothesized value of the population mean, is true, the expected value of *t* will be zero, because the average $\overline{X} - \mu$ value in a sampling distribution from such a population will be zero. But, even when H_0 is true, values of $\overline{X} - \mu$ will vary around a mean of zero because of sampling error. Furthermore, we expect that $\overline{X}$ will be larger than μ about as often as it will be smaller than μ. In the long run, the $\overline{X} - \mu$ values will be positive and negative equally often when the null hypothesis is true. Consequently, the expected *t* values will be symmetrical around a mean of zero. For an infinite number of degrees of freedom (a theoretical but not actual possibility), the sampling distribution of *t* is the same as the normal. All other *t* distributions are more spread out than a normal distribution.

Why Are Degrees of Freedom Used Rather Than *N*?

If the *df* for the one-sample *t* test are given by $N - 1$, why not present the sampling distribution of *t* in terms of *N* rather than *df*? For the one-sample *t* statistic, we have gained no advantage by using *df* rather than *N*, for the *df* are always one less than *N*. The advantage of using *df* becomes apparent in Chapter 9, however, when we introduce another *t* statistic used for comparing two sample means. For this *t*, the *df* are $N - 2$ rather than $N - 1$. For equal *df*, however, both *t* tests possess the same sampling distribution. We will encounter similar instances with other statistics in later chapters.

Testing Your Knowledge 8.2

1. Write the formula for the one-sample *t* statistic.

2. Why is the *t* statistic sometimes called Student's *t*?

3. You are given seven scores: 73, 42, 51, 68, 49, 62, and 57. How many *df* does this set of scores possess for calculating (a) $\overline{X}$, (b) *s*, and (c) s^2?

4. You plan to compute the one-sample *t* statistic on samples of the following sizes. For each sample, find the *df*. (a) $N = 10$, (b) $N = 16$, (c) $N = 7$, (d) $N = 54$, (e) $N = 120$, (f) $N = 30$.

5. You have two theoretical sampling distributions of *t*, one with 13 *df* and one with 27 *df*. Which distribution will be wider and flatter?

6. Under what conditions will the sampling distribution of the *t* statistic be identical to the sampling distribution of *z*?

Statistical Hypothesis Testing with the One-Sample *t*

The one-sample *t* allows us to determine whether an $\overline{X}$ differs from an hypothesized μ by more than expected from sampling error alone when σ is estimated by *s*. The procedure for statistical hypothesis testing with the *t* is identical to that for the *z* statistic. The necessary steps include the following:

▶ Formulating H_0 and H_1.

▶ Obtaining the sampling distribution of the *t* statistic, assuming that H_0 is true.

▶ Selecting a significance level.

▶ Finding a critical value or values of *t*.

▶ Locating a rejection region or regions in the sampling distribution of *t*.

▶ Formulating decision rules regarding the statistical hypotheses.

▶ Calculating the value of *t* on the sample data.

▶ Making decisions about H_0 and H_1 from the value of *t*.

▶ Relating the results of the statistical decision to the research hypothesis.

To illustrate these steps, let's return to our example problem of the time it takes to find parking on your campus. Recall that a year ago the population mean for the time to find a parking space was 15.0 minutes. Your research hypothesis was that this μ no longer holds because of the greater number of commuter students. From your sample of 30 students you obtained $\overline{X} = 18.0$ minutes with $s = 7.0$ minutes. Does this sample mean of 18.0 minutes differ significantly from the population mean of 15.0 minutes? Because $\sigma_{\overline{X}}$ is not known, and thus must be estimated from $s_{\overline{X}}$, the one-sample *t* test will be used to answer this question.

Formulating Statistical Hypotheses

The statistical hypotheses for the one-sample *t* statistic are identical to those of the *z* statistic. The *null hypothesis*, H_0, is stated as an hypothesized value of a population mean. The *alternative hypothesis*, H_1, is a statement that the population mean is not that hypothesized in H_0. For the example, the *statistical hypotheses expressed in notation* are

$$H_0: \mu = 15.0 \text{ minutes,}$$
$$H_1: \mu \neq 15.0 \text{ minutes.}$$

Obtaining the Sampling Distribution of the *t* Statistic

The sampling distribution of *t* depends on the degrees of freedom for the *t* calculated on the sample scores. The *df* for the one-sample *t* are given by $N - 1$. For a mean based on 30 scores, the *df* for $t = 30 - 1$, or 29. After selecting a significance level and locating rejection regions, we will use these degrees of freedom with a table of the sampling distribution of *t* to find t_{crit}.

Selecting a Significance Level

The significance level is a probability value that provides the criterion for rejecting H_0. Either the .05 or .01 significance level is typically used in statistical hypothesis testing. For the example, we use $\alpha = .05$.

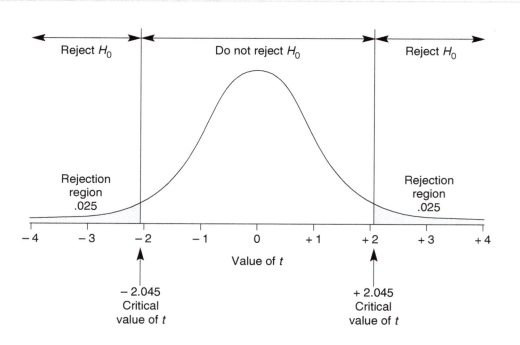

Figure 8.4 Two-tailed rejection regions for the t distribution for 29 *df* and $\alpha = .05$. A value of t_{obs} falling into either rejection region leads to rejection of H_0 and acceptance of H_1.

Locating Rejection Regions for *t*: Two-Tailed Test

A rejection region consists of values in the sampling distribution of t that occur with a probability equal to or less than α when H_0 is true. Thus, the rejection region defines values of t that meet the criterion for rejecting H_0.

In a *two-tailed* or *nondirectional test*, rejection regions for the t test are located in either tail of the theoretical sampling distribution, as illustrated in Figure 8.4. When H_0 is true, most values of $\overline{X}$ will differ only slightly from μ, and thus, most values of t will be clustered around zero in the middle of the distribution. Because of sampling error, however, some values of t will be at either end of the distribution even when H_0 is true. These values are obtained when the numerator of the t (i.e., the difference $\overline{X} - \mu$) is large compared to the denominator (i.e., $s_{\overline{X}}$). But these large values of t are rare occurrences if the null hypothesis is true.

On the other hand, if H1 is true and $\overline{X}$ represents a sample from a population with a mean other than μ, then large values of $\overline{X} - \mu$ and, thus, of t are expected to occur more frequently. Therefore, a rejection region is located in each tail of the theoretical sampling distribution of t, and the total α is divided between the tails. If $\alpha = .05$, then each rejection region includes a probability of $\alpha/2$, or .025. If the value of t calculated on the scores of the sample (identified as tobs) falls into either rejection region, then the null hypothesis is rejected and the alternative hypothesis accepted. By locating a rejection region in each tail of the t distribution, the experimenter covers both possibilities implied by the alternative hypothesis; that is, $\overline{X}$ is greater than μ or $\overline{X}$ is less than μ. The total probability of an outcome in either of the two rejection regions is .05 if H0 is true.

The two rejection regions for the sampling distribution of t based on 29 df are illustrated in Figure 8.4. For 29 df, if H_0 is true, then the probability that a t will be equal to or less than -2.045 is .025, and the probability that it will be equal to or larger than $+2.045$ is also .025. Any t_{obs} equal to or less than -2.045 or equal to or larger than $+2.045$ falls into a rejection region. This outcome will occur only 5 percent of the time when the null hypothesis is true. The values of -2.045 and $+2.045$ were obtained from a table of critical values of the sampling distribution of t. The use of this table is explained next.

Using the Table of Critical *t* Values

For a particular significance level, the critical t values (identified as **t_{crit}**) needed for locating the rejection regions depend on the df of t_{obs}. Figures of the sampling distribution of t are useful in visualizing how the shape of the t distribution varies with the degrees of freedom, but it is difficult to find exact values of t_{crit} from them. Accordingly, values of t_{crit} for the .05 and .01 significance levels have been calculated and are presented in tables.

Table 8.2 presents the two-tailed values of t_{crit} for $\alpha = 0.5$ and .01. Table 8.2 is part of Appendix C.2. The first column lists degrees of freedom for t distributions. The values in any row of the $\alpha = .05$ or .01 columns are the two-tailed values of t_{crit} for the corresponding degrees of freedom for that significance level. For the example with $\alpha = .05$, the two-tailed t_{crit} value for a t_{obs} with 29 degrees of freedom is 2.045. Notice that this value is not preceded by a plus or minus sign. Rather, it is presented as an absolute value of t. For locating rejection regions, however, this value should be treated as both -2.045 and $+2.045$. Similarly, for $\alpha = .01$, the two-tailed t_{crit} value for 29 degrees of freedom is 2.756. Notice that a significance level of .01 imposes a more stringent criterion for rejecting H_0 than does $\alpha = .05$. Any observed $\overline{X} - \mu$ difference will have to be larger to reject H_0 when a .01 significance level is adopted instead of .05.

For more than 30 degrees of freedom, only selected critical values are included in the table. When the df for t_{obs} exceed 30, we recommend that the t_{crit} value used be based on the df in the table closest to but fewer than the degrees of freedom associated with the t_{obs}. For example, if $df = 35$, Table 8.2 shows t_{crit} values for 30 and 40 df but none between. Accordingly, for 35 df we use 30 df to determine the t_{crit} (which is 2.042 for $\alpha = .05$) instead of 40 df. This procedure makes the actual significance level used slightly smaller than .05. If 40 df were used to find the t_{crit} instead, then the significance level would be slightly greater than .05. If t_{obs} falls into the rejection region for 30 df, then it will also fall in the rejection region for 40 df. Should t_{obs} (e.g., $t_{obs} = 2.033$) fall between the tabled values for the next lower df (e.g., $t_{crit} = 2.045$ for 30 df) and the next higher df (e.g., $t_{crit} = 2.021$ for 40 df), then a more accurate value of t_{crit} can be interpolated from the tabled values.

Locating a Rejection Region for *t*: One-Tailed Test

In a two-tailed test, H_0 is rejected if t_{obs} falls into a rejection region in either tail of the t distribution. However, when a research hypothesis predicts a directional relationship among the means (e.g., if we had predicted that the parking changes would improve parking compared to the past and thus that $\overline{X}$ would be less than μ) and there is no interest in an outcome opposite that predicted (e.g., if $\overline{X}$ greater than μ occurs), then some researchers use a one-tailed test. In a *one-tailed* or *directional test*, a rejection region encompassing the entire value of a is located in the tail of the t distribution, corresponding to the direction of the outcome predicted by the research hypothesis. Values of t_{crit} for a one-tailed test at the .01 and .05 significance levels are also presented in

TABLE	
8.2	Critical values of the *t* distribution for $\alpha = .05$ and $\alpha = .01$. The values provided are for a two-tailed test.

Source: Reprinted from Table 12. Percentage points of the *t*-distribution. E. S Pearson and H. O. Hartley, *Biometrika Tables for Statisticians*, Volume 1, Copyright 1976, Cambridge University Press. Reprinted by permission of the Biometrika Trustees.

df	$\alpha = .05$	$\alpha = .01$
1	12.706	63.657
2	4.303	9.925
3	3.182	5.841
4	2.776	4.604
5	2.571	4.032
6	2.447	3.707
7	2.365	3.499
8	2.306	3.355
9	2.262	3.250
10	2.228	3.169
11	2.201	3.106
12	2.179	3.055
13	2.160	3.012
14	2.145	2.977
15	2.131	2.947
16	2.120	2.921
17	2.110	2.898
18	2.101	2.878
19	2.093	2.861
20	2.086	2.845
21	2.080	2.831
22	2.074	2.819
23	2.069	2.807
24	2.064	2.797
25	2.060	2.787
26	2.056	2.779
27	2.052	2.771
28	2.048	2.763
29	2.045	2.756
30	2.042	2.750
40	2.021	2.704
60	2.000	2.660
120	1.980	2.617
∞	1.960	2.576

Appendix C.2. For 29 *df*, the one-tailed t_{crit} at the .05 significance level is 1.699. A one-tailed rejection region with $t_{crit} = -1.699$ in the left tail of a *t* distribution is illustrated in Figure 8.5. This rejection region would be appropriate for the example if we had stated the following statistical hypotheses:

$$H_0: \mu \geq 15.0,$$
$$H_1: \mu < 15.0.$$

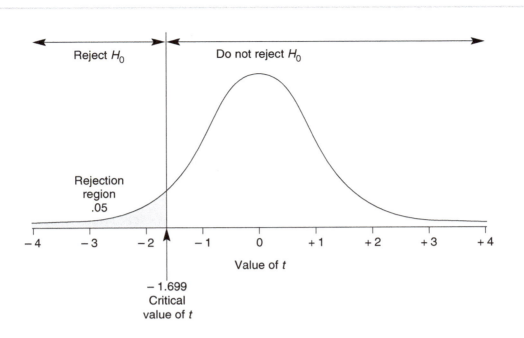

Figure 8.5 One-tailed rejection region for the t distribution for 29 df and $\alpha = .05$. A value of t_{obs} falling into the rejection region leads to rejection of H_0 and acceptance of H_1.

When Should a One-Tailed Test Be Used?

The advantage of a one-tailed rejection region is that t_{crit} moves closer to zero because the entire rejection region lies in only one tail of the distribution. Thus, it is easier to reject H_0 because a smaller difference between $\overline{X}$ and μ will result in a t_{obs} falling into the rejection region. This advantage is accompanied by a limitation, however. The decision to adopt a one-tailed or two-tailed rejection region must be made at the time the research is being planned and before the data are collected and analyzed. If a one-tailed rejection region is adopted, then the experimenter cannot reject H_0 from an obtained difference in means opposite in direction to that hypothesized, because no rejection region for such an outcome has been located. We discuss one- and two-tailed tests more fully in Chapter 9. In practice, two-tailed tests are most commonly used; however, we illustrate the use of a one-tailed test in example problem 8.1.

Calculating t_{obs}

Calculating t_{obs} requires substituting values of $\overline{X}$, μ, and $s_{\overline{X}}$ into the formula for t. For the example of 30 college students attempting to find a parking place, $\overline{X} = 18.0$ minutes, $s = 7.0$ minutes, $\mu = 15.0$ minutes, and $N = 30$. The value of $s_{\overline{X}}$ is obtained from $s/\sqrt{N}$; thus,

$$s_{\overline{X}} = \frac{7.0}{\sqrt{30}} = \frac{7.0}{5.48} = 1.28.$$

As a result,

$$t_{obs} = \frac{\overline{X} - \mu}{s_{\overline{X}}}$$

$$= \frac{18.0 - 15.0}{1.28}$$

$$= +2.344$$

with $N - 1 = 29$ *df*.

Decisions About the Statistical Hypotheses

The decision rules for statistical hypotheses are the same for all statistical tests. Accordingly, for the one-sample t test the following is true:

▶ if t_{obs} falls into a rejection region, then H_0 is rejected and H_1 is accepted; but

▶ if t_{obs} does not fall into a rejection region, then H_0 is not rejected, and H_1 is not accepted.

The two-tailed value of t_{crit} for 29 *df* and $\alpha = .05$ is 2.045. Consequently, as illustrated in Figure 8.4, a t_{obs} equal to or less than -2.045 or equal to or larger than $+2.045$ falls into a rejection region. The t_{obs} of $+2.344$ is more extreme than $t_{crit} = +2.045$ and, therefore, falls into the rejection region in the right tail of the distribution. We reject H_0: $\mu = 15.0$ minutes and accept H_1: $\mu \neq 15.0$ minutes. The difference between the sample mean and the population mean is statistically significant at the .05 level. We conclude that the sample mean of 18.0 minutes is from a population with a μ greater than 15.0 minutes. The mean amount of time students take to find a parking spot is longer than the previous population mean of 15.0 minutes. Your research hypothesis that the μ for the length of time to find a parking space is not 15 minutes is supported.

If t_{obs} had fallen between the two critical values of -2.045 and $+2.045$ (e.g., if $\overline{X}$ had been 16.0 minutes and, thus, $t_{obs} = +0.781$), then we would fail to reject H_0 and not accept H_1. The observed difference between the sample mean and hypothesized population mean would be nonsignificant. In this instance, there would be no evidence that H_0 is not true.

The decisions about the statistical hypotheses and the conclusions reached from either a statistically significant or a nonsignificant one-sample t test are summarized in Table 8.3.

Assumptions of the One-Sample t Test

The one-sample t test makes the following assumptions of the scores in the sample:

▶ Each subject in the experiment is randomly and independently selected from the population.

▶ The scores in the population sampled are normally distributed.

In practice, these assumptions may not be met fully by the scores in a sample, yet researchers often proceed to use the t test on the data. We discuss the consequences of this action more fully in Chapter 9.

TABLE 8.3	Summary of decisions and conclusions in statistical hypothesis testing using the one-sample t test for testing a sample mean against a population mean. A .05 significance level is used.

If t_{obs} falls into a rejection region for $\alpha = .05$, then:	If t_{obs} does not fall into a rejection region for $\alpha = .05$, then:
▶ Probability of t_{obs} is less than or equal to .05, or $p \leq .05$.	▶ Probability of t_{obs} is greater than .05, or $p > .05$.
▶ H_0 is rejected.	▶ H_0 is not rejected.
▶ H_1 is accepted.	▶ H_1 is not accepted.
▶ We found a statistically significant difference at the .05 level.	▶ We failed to find a statistically significant difference at the .05 level.
▶ The sample mean is considered to be from a different population.	▶ There is no evidence that the sample is from a different population.
▶ Something other than sampling error alone is responsible for the difference between $\overline{X}$ and μ.	▶ Sampling error alone is the most plausible explanation of the difference between $\overline{X}$ and μ.

EXAMPLE PROBLEM 8.1

Using the One-Sample t Test

Problem: The social sciences faculty at a small university noticed that many students in the social sciences performed poorly on their Graduate Record Examinations (GREs). To assist their students in preparing for these important exams, the faculty designed a program to improve test-taking skills. They randomly selected 36 students from the population of students planning to take the GREs and gave them a series of study sessions. Educational Testing Service reported that the mean score for the verbal portion of the GRE test for students applying for graduate school in the social sciences was 486 (2006). If the 36 students participating in the study sessions obtained a sample mean of 498 and a standard deviation of 101 on the verbal portion of the GRE, does this $\overline{X}$ differ significantly from a μ of 486 at the .05 level? Because the faculty members are not interested in any program that might worsen student's performance on the GREs, they are interested in testing only for a difference reflecting improvement on the GREs. Accordingly, we will use a one-tailed test.

Statistic to Be Used: Because σ is being estimated by s, the one-sample t test is appropriate.

Assumptions for Use

1. The individuals measured are randomly and independently drawn from a population of college students planning to take the GREs.
2. GRE verbal scores are normally distributed in the population sampled.

Statistical Hypotheses: $H_0: \mu \leq 486; H_1: \mu > 486$.

Significance Level: $\alpha = .05$.

df for t: $N - 1 = 36 - 1 = 35$.

Critical Value of t: $t_{crit} = +1.697$. A critical value of t with 35 df is not presented in Appendix C.2. We used t_{crit} for the next-lower df table, 30 df. This value is from the one-tailed test column of Appendix C.2.

Rejection Regions: Values of t_{obs} equal to or greater than $+1.697$.

Calculation:

$$s_{\overline{X}} = \frac{101}{\sqrt{36}} = \frac{101}{6} = 16.833.$$

Thus,

$$
\begin{aligned}
t_{obs} &= \frac{\overline{X} - \mu}{s_{\overline{X}}} \\
&= \frac{498 - 486}{16.833} \\
&= \frac{12}{16.833} = +0.713.
\end{aligned}
$$

Decision: t_{obs} is not more extreme than $t_{crit} = +1.697$ and does not fall into a rejection region. Thus, we will not reject H_0 and, as such, will not accept H_1.

Conclusion: There is no evidence to indicate that the program improved GRE scores. The difference between the sample mean and the population mean for the verbal scores is attributed to sampling error. ▬▬▬

Reporting the Results of the One-Sample *t* Test

The *Publication Manual of the American Psychological Association* (American Psychological Association, 2001; pp. 20–26) requires a report of an inferential statistical test to give the symbol for the statistical test, the *df* for the test, the observed value of the statistic, the alpha level used, and the probability of obtaining the observed value of the statistic or an even more extreme value assuming that the null hypothesis is true. Relevant descriptive statistics, such as the sample mean and standard deviation, are also required. We illustrate this style with the results of our example problem of parking on a college campus.

The mean amount of time undergraduate students spent seeking a parking spot on their college campus was 18.0 minutes ($SD = 7.0$ minutes). With an alpha level of .05, a two-tailed one-sample t test indicated that the sample mean differed significantly from a hypothesized population mean of 15 minutes; $t(24) = +2.344, p < .05$.

The report uses the following:

$\alpha = .05$ Indicates the significance level selected for the test.

$t(24)$ Identifies the test statistic as the t. This t identifies t_{obs}, although the subscript *obs* is not included. Because the t is identified as the one-sample t, we know that the test is a comparison of a sample mean against a hypothesized population mean. The degrees of freedom for t are shown in parentheses. Thus, we know that 25 scores were used in the calculation of t (because $df = N - 1$: thus, $24 = 25 - 1$).

$= +2.344$ The value of t_{obs} (not the t_{crit} value found in Appendix C.2). The value of t_{obs} should be given to at least two decimal places.

$p < .05.$ Indicates the following:

    a. The p and less than sign ($p <$) indicate that the probability of t_{obs} if H_0 is true is less than (or equal to) .05. This value is the probability of t or an even more extreme value of t_{obs} if H_0 is true. Sometimes the exact probability of t_{obs} is given, such as $p = .003$, rather than indicating it is simply $p < .05$. The value of $p = .003$, called a *significance probability*, provides the exact probability of obtaining a value of t as large as or larger than the value reported if the null hypothesis is true.

    b. $H_0: \mu = 15.0$ minutes was rejected.

    c. $H_0: \mu \neq 15.0$ minutes was accepted.

    d. The difference between the sample mean and the hypothesized μ is statistically significant.

    e. The sample mean is treated as being from a population with a mean greater than the hypothesized $\mu = 15.0$ minutes.

    f. If $p > .05$ had been reported, then the greater than sign ($>$) would indicate that H_0 was not rejected and $\overline{X}$ did not differ significantly from the hypothesized μ at the .05 significance level.

Testing Your Knowledge 8.3

1. Write H_0 and H_1 for the one-sample t test for each of the following statements.

    a. The population mean for time sleeping per night is 493 minutes.

    b. The population mean on an inventory of depression proneness is 36.1.

    c. The population mean on a standardized intelligence test is 100.

2. Using Appendix C.2, find the values of t_{crit} for the *df* and value of α indicated. Use a two-tailed test.

	df	α
a.	6	.05
b.	17	.01
c.	23	.05
d.	32	.05
e.	39	.05
f.	75	.01
g.	103	.05
h.	256	.05

3. Indicate whether each of the following t_{obs} does or does not fall into a rejection region. Then indicate your decision for H_0 and H_1. Remember that you *fail to reject* or *reject* H_0 and you *do not accept* or *accept* H_1. Use $\alpha = .05$ and a two-tailed test. The *df* for each t_{obs} are given in parentheses.

    a. $t_{obs}(19) = +3.014$

    b. $t_{obs}(19) = -1.989$

   c. $t_{obs}(16) = -2.179$

   d. $t_{obs}(16) = +2.040$

   e. $t_{obs}(30) = -3.961$

   f. $t_{obs}(30) = +2.743$

   g. $t_{obs}(6) = -2.364$

   h. $t_{obs}(6) = +2.447$

   i. $t_{obs}(9) = -2.262$

   j. $t_{obs}(37) = +2.938$

   k. $t_{obs}(42) = -2.410$

4. Identify the assumptions underlying the use of the one-sample t test.

5. Complete the following problem and answer the questions asked. Use a two-tailed test and .05 significance level. You are interested in how well people can estimate the passage of time without the use of a watch or clock. Accordingly, you ask 11 people to tell you when they think a 7-minute interval has passed without using a watch or clock. The mean of the 11 estimates was 5.8 minutes with $s = 0.8$ minutes. Is your sample mean significantly different from a population mean of 7 minutes? In your answer, indicate the following:

   a. The statistic to be used

   b. The assumptions for its use

   c. The statistical hypotheses

   d. The significance level

   e. The critical value of the test statistic

   f. The rejection regions

   g. The value of t_{obs}

   h. Your decisions about the statistical hypotheses

   i. Your conclusion regarding the sample mean

6. This exercise presents reports of the use of the t test adapted from results of published studies. For each report, answer the following questions:

   a. What is the value of the sample mean?

   b. What is the value of the estimated population standard deviation?

   c. What t test was used in this study?

   d. What are H_0 and H_1 for this t test?

   e. How many scores were obtained in this study?

   f. What is the value of t_{obs} for this study?

   g. What are the df for this t_{obs}?

   h. What is t_{crit} for $\alpha = .05$ and a two-tailed rejection region?

   i. Do you reject or fail to reject H_0?

   j. Do you accept or not accept H_1?

   k. Do you conclude that the sample mean differs significantly from the hypothesized population mean?

Report 1: The mean weight of the male runners was 70.4 kilograms ($SD = 7.6$ kg). For a two-tailed test, a one-sample t test indicated that the sample mean did not differ significantly from a population mean of 75 kg for 25-year-old males; $t(5) = -1.48, p > .05$.

Report 2: The mean hospital stay for males age 65 and over with nonterminal diseases was 10.4 days ($SD = 2.3$ days). For a two-tailed test, a one-sample t test revealed that the sample mean differed significantly from a population mean of 8.7 days; $t(24) = +3.70, p < .01$.

Important Considerations in Statistical Hypothesis Testing

Why We Don't Accept the Null Hypothesis

If a test statistic does not fall into a rejection region, then we do not reject the null hypothesis. This decision is often stated as "we fail to reject the null hypothesis." You may wonder why we use this awkward phrasing; typically, if we do not reject something, then we accept it. Why don't we simply accept the null hypothesis if the test statistic does not fall into a rejection region? To answer this question, let us look to an example. After reading an article on the benefits of student motivation and classroom climate for professors who participate on Facebook, a professor attempting to increase his course evaluations placed a personal page on Facebook, including information and photographs about his teaching, research, and personal activities (Ellison, Steinfield, & Lampe, 2007). The professor had figured out that his mean performance on his previous course evaluations was 3.7 out of a 5-point scale, with a standard deviation of 0.9. Because this mean represents all the evaluations of this professor, we can think of it as a population mean (μ) for the professor's course evaluations and the standard deviation as a population standard deviation (σ) for these evaluations. He would like to find out if participation on Facebook helped improve his course evaluations from the 169 students he taught in the semester after he created his Facebook page. The sample mean for the 169 evaluations in that semester was 3.8. Does this sample mean differ significantly from the population mean of 3.7? To answer this question we use the one-sample z test

$$z = \frac{\overline{X} - \mu}{\sigma_{\overline{X}}}.$$

For this z, $\mu = 3.7$, $\sigma = 0.9$, $\overline{X} = 3.8$, and $N = 169$, thus

$$z_{\text{obs}} = \frac{3.8 - 3.7}{0.9/\sqrt{169}}$$

$$= \frac{0.1}{0.07} = +1.43.$$

This z_{obs} does not fall into the rejection region defined by $z_{\text{crit}} =$ plus or minus 1.96 for $\alpha = .05$ and is, thus, nonsignificant. Consequently, we fail to reject $H_0: \mu = 3.7$. But does this decision imply that the mean of the course evaluations for the professor must be exactly 3.7? Obviously, the answer is no; a sample mean of 3.8 on a course evaluation does not imply that the mean of the population from which the sample was drawn must be 3.7. On the other hand, $\overline{X} = 3.8$ also does not provide any evidence that μ may not be 3.7. That is, an $\overline{X}$ of 3.8 does not provide evidence that we should reject H_0: $\mu = 3.7$, but neither does it provide evidence that μ is exactly 3.7. It indicates only that we should not reject H_0.

Suppose, however, that $\overline{X}$ had been 3.9 so that $z_{obs} = +2.86$. This z_{obs} is statistically significant at the .05 level and leads to rejecting H_0: $\mu = 3.7$ and accepting H_1: $\mu \neq 3.7$. It is appropriate to accept H_1 because H_1 states that μ is some value other than 3.7, and $\overline{X} = 3.9$ indicates that the population μ for course evaluations after creating the Facebook page indeed is some value other than 3.7, as $z_{obs} = +2.86$ fell in the rejection region.

The correct decisions about the statistical hypotheses are thus as follows:

▶ If the test statistic falls into a rejection region, then *reject H_0* and *accept H_1*.

▶ If the test statistic does not fall into a rejection region, then *fail to reject H_0* and *do not accept H_1*.

Some behavioral scientists feel uncomfortable with the statement "accepting H_1" because the evidence for believing that H_1 is true is gained only by rejecting H_0. Thus, they prefer to use terminology such as "H_0 is rejected in favor of H_1" or "H_0 is rejected lending support to H_1." However, given the properties of statistical hypotheses, they are mutually exclusive and they include all possible values of the parameter involved, then rejecting H_0 implies that H_1 is accepted. Thus, we will use the terminology of accepting H_1 when H_0 is rejected. But you should realize that some researchers prefer a more tentative statement, such as "H_1 is supported when H_0 is rejected."

Type I and Type II Errors in Statistical Tests

Type I error ▶ The error in statistical decision making that occurs if the null hypothesis is rejected when actually it is true of the population.

Type II error ▶ The error in statistical decision making that occurs if H_0 is not rejected when it is false and the alternative hypothesis (H_1) is true.

A statistical test allows a researcher to either (1) reject H_0 or (2) fail to reject H_0. The decision may be correct or incorrect depending on whether the null hypothesis is, in fact, true of the population. A **Type I error** occurs if the null hypothesis is rejected when actually it is true. A **Type II error** occurs if we fail to reject H_0 when it is false and H_1 is true. Table 8.4 illustrates these possible errors and correct decisions that may occur with a statistical test.

TABLE 8.4

Errors and correct decisions in statistical decision making and the probability associated with each outcome

| | | Decision by the Experimenter | |
		Fails to Reject H_0	Rejects H_0, Accepts H_1
True situation in the population	H_0 true	Correct decision: $p = 1 - \alpha$	Type I error: $p = \alpha$
	H_1 true	Type II error: $p = \beta$	Correct decision: $p = 1 - \beta$

Beta (β) ▶ The probability of a Type II error.

Power ▶ The probability of rejecting H_0 when H_0 is false and H_1 is true. The power of a statistical test is given by $1 - β$.

Type I and Type II errors occur because statistical decision making is probabilistic. If H_0 is true, the probability of a Type I error is given by $α$. Thus, the probability of making a correct decision and not rejecting H_0 when it is true is provided by $1 - α$. The probability of a Type II error is given by $β$ (the lowercase Greek letter **beta**). Hence, the probability of correctly accepting H_1 when H_1 is true is provided by $1 - β$. The value $1 - β$ is the power of a statistical test. Therefore, the *power of a statistical test*, or simply, **power**, is the probability of rejecting H_0 when H_0 is false and H_1 is true. The value of $β$ depends on a number of factors, and we discuss these factors in Chapter 9. Each of these probabilities is identified in Table 8.4.

A Type I error can occur only when H_0 is true; hence, the probability of making a Type I error depends directly on the significance level selected. Recall that the significance level indicates the probability of obtaining a value of the test statistic (e.g., either z or t) that leads to rejection of H_0 when H_0 is actually true. Accordingly, when alpha is selected for a statistical test, the risk of making a Type I error is established. With $α = .05$, for example, the probability of wrongly rejecting a true H_0 is .05. Similarly, if $α = .01$, then there is only a 1 in 100 chance of making a Type I error by incorrectly rejecting H_0 when it is true. Scientists typically adopt a conservative stance to assure a low probability of making a Type I error in their research. Consequently, the value of $α$ is typically selected to be a small value, such as $α = .05$ or $α = .01$.

Statistical and Scientific Significance

Using the word *significant* to characterize the rejection of H_0 in a statistical hypothesis test reflects an unfortunate choice of words by statisticians. The typical connotation to something significant is that it is important. But it is inappropriate to apply this meaning to a statistically significant difference. In statistical testing, significance indicates only that H_0 has been rejected. If H_0 is rejected, the statistical test neither gives a reason for this result nor indicates if the difference is scientifically important. This responsibility rests with the researcher, who must examine carefully the conditions of the study and the nature of the data obtained.

Observed values of the test statistic that do not fall into the rejection region are referred to as *nonsignificant* and not as insignificant. *Insignificant* implies that something is lacking importance or is inconsequential. Yet, a nonsignificant difference may be scientifically important. For example, suppose that a program is introduced in an after-school childcare center to reduce the amount of television that the children watch. If, in comparing $\overline{X}$ to $μ$, a nonsignificant difference is found, the implication is that the program was ineffective in changing the children's watching of television, and this may be an important result for the researcher.

Using the *t* Statistic to Construct Confidence Intervals for the Population Mean

Confidence intervals for the population mean were defined in Chapter 7 as intervals in which we have a certain degree of confidence that the interval contains the population mean. In that chapter we constructed these intervals using $\overline{X}$, z, and $σ_{\overline{X}}$. For example, if $σ_{\overline{X}}$ is known, a 95 percent confidence interval for the population mean is given by the interval from

$$\overline{X} - 1.96σ_{\overline{X}} \text{ to } \overline{X} + 1.96σ_{\overline{X}}.$$

Most often $\sigma_{\overline{X}}$ is unknown, however, and its value is estimated from $s_{\overline{X}}$. When $s_{\overline{X}}$ is used to estimate $\sigma_{\overline{X}}$, a confidence interval is constructed using the t statistic rather than z. Using t and $s_{\overline{X}}$, the **95 percent confidence interval for the population mean** is given by the interval from

$$\overline{X} - (t_{.05})(s_{\overline{X}}) \text{ to } \overline{X} + (t_{.05})(s_{\overline{X}}),$$

where $\overline{X}$ = observed sample mean.
          $s_{\overline{X}}$ = estimated standard error of the mean obtained from $s/\sqrt{N}$.
          $t_{.05}$ = two-tailed value of t_{crit} at the .05 significance level with $N - 1$ degrees of freedom.

Similarly, a **99 percent confidence interval for the population mean** is given by

$$\overline{X} - (t_{.01})(s_{\overline{X}}) \text{ to } \overline{X} + (t_{.01})(s_{\overline{X}}).$$

To illustrate, we find the 95 percent confidence interval for the 30 college students finding a parking space with $\overline{X} = 18.0$ minutes and $s = 7.0$ minutes. Because $N = 30$, there are 29 df for this sample, and the two-tailed value of $t_{crit}(29)$ at the .05 level is 2.045. The standard error of the mean, $s_{\overline{X}}$, equals $7.0/\sqrt{30} = 7.0/5.48$ or 1.28 minutes. Thus, the 95 percent confidence interval for μ is

$$18.0 - (2.045)(1.28) \text{ to } 18.0 + (2.045)(1.28),$$

or, carrying out the mathematical operations indicated,

$$18.0 - 2.6 \text{ to } 18.0 + 2.6 \text{ minutes,}$$

which equals 15.4 to 20.6 minutes. This interval has a .95 probability of including the value of μ.

As another example, we find the 95 percent confidence interval for the population mean of the sample of 100 Implicit View of Intelligence scores given in Table 3.3. The sample mean for these scores is 31.8 and the standard deviation is 6.6. The standard error of the mean for these scores, $s_{\overline{X}}$, equals $6.6/\sqrt{100} = 6.6/10 = 0.66$. There are 100 scores, thus there are $100 - 1$ or 99 df for this sample. Ninety-nine degrees of freedom are not tabled in Appendix C.2, the next lower df are 60, with a t_{crit} at the .05 level equal to 2.000. Thus, the 95 percent confidence interval for μ is

$$31.8 - (2.000)(0.66) \text{ to } 31.8 + (2.000)(0.66),$$

or, carrying out the mathematical operations indicated,

$$31.8 - 1.3 \text{ to } 31.8 + 1.3 \text{ or,}$$
$$30.5 \text{ to } 33.1.$$

We can be 95 percent confident that the population mean for the Implicit View of Intelligence scores falls between 30.5 to 33.1.

Similarly, we can find the 99 percent confidence interval by using t_{crit} at the .01 level. For 60 df, t_{crit} from Appendix C.2 is 2.660. Thus, the 99 percent confidence interval for μ is

$$31.8 - (2.660)(0.66) \text{ to } 31.8 + (2.660)(0.66),$$

or, carrying out the mathematical operations indicated,

$$31.8 - 1.8 \text{ to } 31.8 + 1.8$$

or,

$$30.0 \text{ to } 33.6.$$

Notice that the 99 percent confidence interval is larger than the 95 percent confidence interval. The 99 percent confidence interval provides us with greater confidence that we have created an interval containing μ than does the 95 percent confidence interval. This greater confidence, however, comes at the expense of a larger interval. Although confidence intervals have not been widely reported in research studies, researchers are being encouraged to include them in reports of their work (American Psychological Association, 2001). In the event that confidence intervals are not presented, you can still calculate them for yourself as long as the mean and standard error are presented or the mean and the standard deviation and number of subjects are presented.

Testing Your Knowledge 8.4

1. Explain why a researcher does not accept H_0 if t_{obs} does not fall into a rejection region.
2. Answer the following.
   a. What is a Type I error?
   b. What is the probability of making a Type I error if H_0 is true?
   c. What is the probability of making a Type I error if H_0 is false?
   d. What is a Type II error?
   e. Is it possible for an experimenter to make both Type I and Type II errors in the same statistical test? Explain your answer.
3. Distinguish between statistical significance and scientific significance.
4. An experimenter observed the amount of time that adolescents spent playing video games on their computers. The mean playing time per day for a sample of 23 males was 97 minutes, with a standard deviation of 39 minutes. Construct a 95 percent confidence interval for the population mean for the amount of time male adolescents spent playing video games.

 ## Summary

▶ Statistical tests may be either parametric or nonparametric.

▶ Statistical hypothesis testing involves the following steps:

  ▷ Selecting a test statistic (e.g., either z or t).

  ▷ Formulating H_0 and H_1. H_0 is used to find the sampling distribution of the test statistic.

  ▷ Selecting a significance level. The significance level, specified by the value of α, is a probability value that provides the criterion for rejecting H_0 as being true.

  ▷ Finding a critical value or values of the test statistic from value tables. Critical values of the test statistic determine the boundaries of the rejection region or regions.

▶ Locating a rejection region or regions. The rejection region represents values on the sampling distribution of the test statistic that have a probability equal to or less than α if H_0 is true.

▶ Formulating decision rules regarding the statistical hypotheses. These rules are as follows:

   ▶ If the test statistic falls into a rejection region, then *reject H_0* and *accept H_1*. The difference between a sample mean and a hypothesized population mean is statistically significant.

   ▶ If the test statistic does not fall into a rejection region, then *fail to reject H_0* and *do not accept H_1*. The difference between a sample mean and a hypothesized population mean is nonsignificant.

▶ Calculating the observed value of the test statistic from the sample scores.

▶ Making decisions about H_0 and H_1 based on whether the observed value of the test statistic does or does not fall into the rejection region.

▶ Relating the results of the statistical decisions to the research hypothesis.

▶ The z statistic, given by $z = (\overline{X} - \mu)/\sigma_{\overline{X}}$, is used to test a sample mean against a hypothesized population mean when σ is known.

▶ The t statistic, given by $t = (\overline{X} - \mu)/s_{\overline{X}}$, is used to test a sample mean against a hypothesized population mean when $\sigma_{\overline{X}}$ is estimated from $s_{\overline{X}}$.

▶ The sampling distribution of the t statistic depends on the *df* of the t, where the $df = N - 1$.

▶ Statistical decision making is inherently probabilistic. A Type I error occurs if a true H_0 is rejected. A Type II error occurs if a false H_0 is not rejected.

▶ The probability of a Type I error is given by α; the probability of a Type II error is given by β.

▶ The power of a statistical test is the probability of rejecting H_0 when H_0 is false and H_1 is true.

▶ The t distribution may be used with $s_{\overline{X}}$ to find confidence intervals for the population mean.

Key Terms and Symbols

alpha (α) (165)
alternative hypothesis (H_1) (162)
beta (β) (185)
critical value (165)
confidence interval (185)
degrees of freedom (*df*) (170)
nonparametric tests (160)
nonsignificant difference (168)
null hypothesis (H_0) (162)
one-sample t test (170)

one-tailed test (165)
parametric tests (160)
power (185)
rejection region (165)
sampling distribution of t (170)
significance level (165)
statistical hypothesis (161)
statistically significant difference (167)
t_{crit} (175)
t_{obs} (174)

test statistic (163)
two-tailed test (165)
t statistic (170)
Type I error (184)
Type II error (184)
z statistic (164)
z_{crit} (166)
z_{obs} (164)

Review Questions

1. What are the requirements that any set of statistical hypotheses must meet?
2. What function does the null hypothesis serve in a statistical test?
3. What is a significance level?
4. What is the critical value of a test statistic?
5. What decision is made regarding H_0 and H_1 if
   a. the observed value of a test statistic falls into a rejection region?
   b. the observed value of a test statistic does not fall into a rejection region?

6. You have been asked to test whether a sample mean of 73 differs significantly from a hypothesized population mean of 75. What will determine whether you use the z test or the one-sample t test?

7. What decision do you make about the value of a sample mean with respect to a hypothesized population mean if

   a. z_{obs} falls into a rejection region?

   b. z_{obs} does not fall into a rejection region?

8. For each of the following values of z_{obs}, determine whether the z_{obs} falls into a two-tailed rejection region at the .01 significance level. Then indicate your decision for H_0 and H_1. Remember that you either (1) *fail to reject* or *reject* H_0, and (2) *do not accept* or *accept* H_1. (a) $z_{obs} = +3.71$, (b) $z_{obs} = -2.60$, (c) $z_{obs} = +1.74$, (d) $z_{obs} = -3.05$, (e) $z_{obs} = -1.96$, (f) $z_{obs} = +2.58$.

9. The population mean for a group intelligence scale is 100 and $\sigma = 16$. A school counselor tests seventeen 10-year-olds on this scale and obtains $\overline{X} = 94.1$. Conduct a statistical test on these data to determine if the difference between the population mean and the sample mean is statistically significant. Use a .05 significance level and a two-tailed test.

10. Based on the outcome of a z test, there is a statistically significant difference between a sample mean and a population mean. Explain what is meant by statistical significance in this case.

11. What decision do you make about the value of a sample mean with respect to a population mean if

    a. t_{obs} falls into a rejection region?

    b. t_{obs} does not fall into a rejection region?

12. Indicate whether each of the following t_{obs} does or does not fall into a rejection region. Assume that $\alpha = .01$ and use a two-tailed test. The df for each t_{obs} are given in parentheses.

    a. $t_{obs}(18) = +3.713$

    b. $t_{obs}(7) = -3.015$

    c. $t_{obs}(35) = +2.794$

    d. $t_{obs}(44) = -3.058$

    e. $t_{obs}(74) = -1.960$

    f. $t_{obs}(15) = -2.368$

13. Mothers with young children often complain that they do not get enough sleep. Suppose that you obtained a measure of the typical amount of sleep of nine mothers of children under one year of age and found the following durations of sleep (in hours): 6.4, 7.5, 6.9, 7.3, 7.6, 7.1, 6.5, 7.7, and 7.8.

    a. Does the mean amount of sleep for these mothers differ significantly from a population mean of 7.7 hours sleep per night? Use a two-tailed test and a .05 significance level.

    b. Describe your results following the example illustrated in the Reporting the Results of the One-Sample t Test section of this chapter.

    c. Could your decision about the statistical hypotheses represent the occurrence of a Type I error?

    d. Could your decision about the statistical hypotheses represent the occurrence of a Type II error?

    e. Compute the 95 percent confidence interval for the population mean of these scores. Is the population mean of 7.7 hours per night included in this interval?

14. A medical researcher attempted to learn if a poorly understood disease is accompanied by an increase in body temperature. She measured the body temperature of 12 people diagnosed as having the disease and obtained the following temperatures (in °F): 99.3, 99.1, 100.4, 98.4, 98.2, 98.9, 99.7, 100.1, 100.7, 99.0, 98.8, and 99.2.

    a. Does the mean body temperature of these individuals differ from a population mean of 98.6°F? Use a two-tailed test and a .05 significance level.

    b. Could your decision regarding the statistical hypothesis represent a Type II error? Explain your answer.

15. For each of the following statements, indicate whether the decision is correct or in error. If an error is made, indicate whether it is a Type I or Type II error.

    a. H_0 is true of the population, but on the basis of z_{obs} an experimenter rejects H_0.

    b. H_1 is true of the population, but on the basis of z_{obs} an experimenter fails to reject H_0.

    c. H_0 is true of the population, and on the basis of z_{obs} the experimenter fails to reject H_0.

    d. H_1 is true of the population, and on the basis of z_{obs} the experimenter rejects H_0.

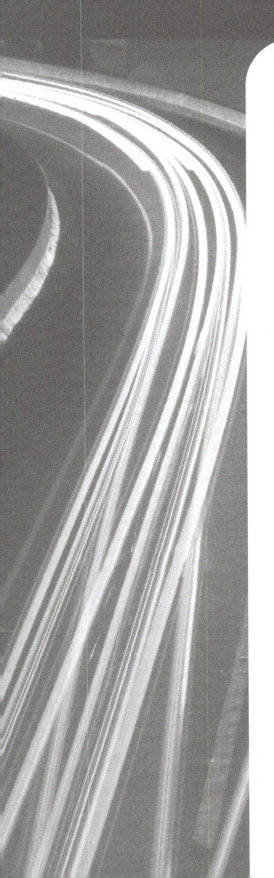

The Basics of Experimentation and Testing for a Difference Between Means

One of the most exciting aspects of psychology is our search for the understanding of human behavior and mental processes. This task is so complex that it is unlikely we will run out of questions to ask and answer. In Chapter 8, we introduced the use of statistical hypothesis testing to answer questions comparing the mean from a sample of subjects to a population mean. Many times, however, our questions can be better answered by comparing the means of two samples of subjects rather than comparing a sample mean to a population mean. In this chapter, we introduce statistical hypothesis testing to compare two sample means to determine if they differ by more than sampling error alone.

A primary use of this type of statistical hypothesis testing is to analyze the results of experimental research, thus this chapter will more fully develop concepts of experimentation that were introduced in Chapters 1 and 2. The initial discussion will be limited to between-subjects designs with different subjects in each of the conditions. Later in the chapter, we discuss within-subjects designs for comparing a single group of subjects in two different conditions.

A Review of the Research Process

Research hypothesis ▶ A statement of an expected or predicted relationship between two or more variables. In an experiment, a research hypothesis is a predicted relationship between an independent variable and a dependent variable.

Experiment ▶ A controlled situation in which one or more independent variables are manipulated to observe the effects on the dependent variable.

All scientific research begins with asking a question that can be empirically answered. Usually, a scientist will offer a tentative answer to the question in the form of a research hypothesis. A **research hypothesis** is a statement of an expected or predicted relationship between two or more variables. In an **experiment**, a research hypothesis is a prediction that a change in an independent variable will cause a change in the dependent variable. Recall that the independent variable is a variable that the experimenter plans to manipulate to find its effect on the dependent variable. The dependent variable is typically some measured behavior or a measure of a mental process of a person. The form of the research hypothesis indicates to the scientist the type of research design to be used. If the research hypothesis predicts that the manipulation of an independent variable will cause a change in the dependent variable and it is possible to manipulate the independent variable, then an experiment is often the appropriate form of research design to empirically test this research hypothesis.

A simple experiment begins by creating two equivalent groups of subjects. Each group is treated identically except for being given different levels of the independent variable. After the independent variable is manipulated, the dependent variable is measured. These scores are then analyzed to find if the independent variable had an effect on the dependent variable. Consider an example of this process.

We live in a colorful environment. Lush green grass invites us to play. Red or yellow signs often signal danger ahead. A bright blue sky cheers us up, but a gray one may make us glum. There is no question that color influences our behavior and thought processes, but exactly how and why does color do this? Elliot, Maier, Moller, Friedman, and Meinhardt (2007) propose that color may influence us through learned associations. For example, they suggest that the color red is often associated with danger and failure. Businesses that are losing money are typically said to be "in the red," instructors often grade papers with a red pen, warning and stop signs are frequently red, and crooks are sometimes caught "red-handed." Given these associations, they hypothesized that the color red may impair performance on a task measuring achievement. This research hypothesis predicts that an independent variable, a specific color, will affect a dependent variable, some measure of a person's achievement. To test this hypothesis, Elliot et al. conducted a between-subjects experiment.

The experiment involved creating two equivalent groups of subjects. As a measure of achievement, subjects in each group were asked to solve anagrams. An anagram is a scrambled word. For example, *esuho* is an anagram for the word *house*. One group, the *control group*, was given the anagrams with the identification number assigned to each subject written in large numbers with green ink on each anagram to be solved. The other group, the *experimental group*, was given the anagrams with the identification number assigned each subject written in large numbers with red ink on each anagram to be solved. Thus, the independent variable was the color in which the subject's number was written, either red or green, and the dependent variable was the number of anagrams solved in a five-minute time period. Suppose you decided to perform a similar study and randomly assigned a total of 24 college students to one of two groups, a control group and an experimental group. Each group contained 12 people. The students in the control group were given the anagrams with a large green cover sheet, whereas the students in the experimental group were given the anagrams with a large red cover sheet. Other than different color cover sheets for the anagrams, all other conditions were identical for the two groups. The mean number of anagrams correctly solved for subjects in the control group who received the green cover sheet was 7.8 with $s = 1.1$ anagrams. For subjects in the experimental group who received the red cover sheet, the mean was 6.6 anagrams correctly solved with $s = 1.3$ anagrams. Is this difference one that could be simply due to a chance difference from sampling error? To evaluate this possibility, we must statistically analyze these means using the t test for independent groups. Using this statistical test, we can determine if subjects in the experimental group solved fewer anagrams than subjects in the control group than would be expected from chance differences alone.

Conducting an experiment requires a number of steps prior to the statistical analysis of the data. These steps are similar in all experiments and include asking a scientific question, formulating a research hypothesis, selecting a research design, selecting subjects, creating equivalent groups of subjects, controlling extraneous variables, manipulating the independent variable, and measuring the dependent variable. It is important to note that the order in which an experiment is designed matters. The scientific question determines the research hypothesis, which determines the research design and the population from which the sample will be drawn. The research hypothesis also determines how we are going to operationally define our independent and dependent variables.

Asking a Scientific Question and Formulating the Research Hypothesis

Recall that a scientific question is one that allows an answer to be found by the collection of empirical data. Our example is based on a scientific question: "What is the effect of the color red on achievement performance?" Clearly, this question permits systematic observation to provide an answer. The research hypothesis of our example offers a tentative answer to this question; it states that the color red will impair a person's performance on the solution of anagrams in comparison to the color green.

Selecting a Research Design

The research design is the plan used to guide the collection of data. Testing the research hypothesis of the example requires comparing one group of people who received anagrams with a red cover to another group who received anagrams with a green cover. In Chapter 1, we identified this design as a **between-subjects design**. The simplest between-subjects design is one in which only two groups are created, as in the example experiment. This design requires selecting subjects and then assigning those subjects to create equivalent groups.

Between-subjects design ▷ An experiment in which two or more groups of different subjects are created.

Selecting Subjects

Random Sampling

An experiment is conducted on a sample of subjects selected from a population. To generalize the results of the experiment beyond the sample used, it is recommended that **random sampling** be used to select subjects. But, because of the difficulty of obtaining true random samples, random sampling is rarely achieved in actual experimentation. Often, convenience sampling is used.

Random sampling ▷ A sampling method in which individuals are selected so that each member of the population has an equal chance of being selected for the sample, and the selection of one member is independent of any other member of the population.

Convenience Sampling

Convenience sampling obtains subjects from among people who are accessible or convenient to the researcher. Convenience sampling clearly is not adequate if we are trying to accurately estimate a population mean, such as estimating the outcome of an election from a poll. But, the purpose of an experiment is not to estimate a specific value of a population mean; rather, it is to determine if two or more groups differ because of the effect of an independent variable. If the independent variable has an effect, it should occur with any subjects, whether they are randomly selected or not. Thus, as long as subjects are selected independently of each other, and provided the groups created are equivalent through random assignment, convenience sampling typically does not limit the interpretation or importance of an experiment.

Convenience sampling ▷ Obtaining subjects from among people who are accessible or convenient to the researcher.

Creating Equivalent Groups

Equivalent groups are groups in which the subjects are not expected to differ in any systematic or consistent way prior to receiving the independent variable. Equivalent groups do not imply that subjects in each group will be exactly alike prior to administration of the independent variable; rather, it implies that an unbiased procedure was used to assign

Equivalent groups ▷ Groups of subjects that are not expected to differ in any consistent or systematic way prior to receiving the independent variable of the experiment.

individuals to levels of the independent variable. Any differences that may then exist between the groups prior to manipulation of the independent variable will be only chance differences. As we explain later, a *t* test allows us to assess the probability of occurrence of such chance differences.

Random Assignment

The typical method of creating equivalent groups is to randomly assign subjects to treatment conditions. **Random assignment** means that any individual selected for the experiment has an equal chance of being assigned to any one of the treatment groups. Specifically, random assignment satisfies two criteria:

1. The probability of assignment to any of the groups is equal for every individual.
2. The assignment of one person to a group does not affect the assignment of any other individual to that same group.

Random assignment ensures that the effects of variables such as motivation, gender, anxiety, intelligence, and age are distributed without bias among the groups. After random assignment, the groups should not differ in any systematic way before the treatments are given. Any difference that is present between the groups is merely one of sampling error, which can be statistically analyzed.

Manipulating the Independent Variable

The **independent variable** is the variable that is manipulated and administered to subjects in the different groups in order to determine its effect on the dependent variable. An independent variable must take on at least two different levels. A **level of an independent variable** is one value of the independent variable. A level of an independent variable is also often referred to as a *treatment* or *treatment condition*. Although an independent variable may take on many levels or treatment conditions, in this chapter we discuss experiments with only two levels, which we will identify as 1 and 2. We indicate the number of subjects in each level or treatment condition by n_1 and n_2. The subscripts 1 and 2 refer to the level of the independent variable. Notice that up to now, because we have had only one set of scores to deal with, we have used N to indicate the number of subjects in a group. Now, however, we have two groups and use n to indicate the number of subjects in a group. The total number of subjects in the experiment will then be indicated by N where $N = n_1 + n_2$.

In a between-subjects design, each level of the independent variable is administered to one of the groups of subjects that has been formed. In the example experiment, the independent variable is the color of the cover on the anagram task, and there are two levels: level 1, control, the green cover, and level 2, experimental, the red cover. Thus, one group (of size $n_1 = 12$) was given the anagrams with the green cover, and the other group (of size $n_2 = 12$) was given the anagrams with the red cover.

An independent variable often is identified as a **factor**. Factors are frequently identified using letters such as A and B. So, a study with two independent variables will have factor A and factor B. In this chapter, however, we are discussing experiments with only one independent variable, thus we will not identify it as factor A. This design, however, is often called a **one-factor between-subjects design**, for one independent variable is manipulated and the comparison needed to decide if the independent variable has an effect is between the two different groups of subjects.

Random assignment ▶ A method of assigning subjects to treatment groups so that any individual selected for the experiment has an equal probability of assignment to any of the groups, and the assignment of one person to a group does not affect the assignment of any other individual to that same group.

Independent variable ▶ A variable manipulated in an experiment to determine its effect on the dependent variable.

Level of an independent variable ▶ One value of the independent variable. To be a variable, an independent variable must take on at least two different levels.

Factor ▶ An alternate name for independent variable.

One-factor between-subjects design ▶ A research design in which one independent variable is manipulated and two or more groups are created.

Controlling Extraneous Variables

Extraneous variables ▶ Any variables, other than the independent variable, that can affect the dependent variable in an experiment.

To ensure that any difference created between the groups is due only to the independent variable, extraneous variables must be controlled. **Extraneous variables** are any variables, other than the independent variable, that can affect the dependent variable. They may arise from characteristics of people, such as age, gender, educational background, anxiety level, sensitivity to drugs, or motivation; changes from one person to another in the physical environment in which the experiment is conducted; or variations from one person to another in the experimental procedure. To be sure that any difference found between the control and experimental groups is due only to the independent variable manipulated, extraneous variables must not vary in any systematic or consistent way with the independent variable. In a **confounded experiment**, an extraneous variable is allowed to vary consistently with the independent variable. When confounding occurs, the effect of the independent variable cannot be separated from the possible effect of the confounded extraneous variable. As such, a **confound** is an extraneous variable that varies along with the independent variable and prevents the researcher from determining the effects of the independent variable.

Confounded experiment ▶ An experiment in which an extraneous variable is allowed to vary consistently with the independent variable.

Confound ▶ An extraneous variable that is covarying with the independent variable, potentially masking the true effects of the independent variable on the dependent variable.

Placebo control ▶ A simulated treatment condition.

It is important in an experiment that each of the two groups be treated identically, except for the administration of the independent variable. To ensure this identical treatment of subjects, sometimes researchers use a placebo control group. One situation where placebo control groups are used is in studying the effectiveness of a drug. In research using drugs, a **placebo control** is a simulated treatment condition in which subjects are given a pill or substance that has no active ingredients. Thus, both the placebo control and the experimental group are given a pill. If only the experimental group had been given a pill, then the experiment would have been confounded. People may behave differently simply because they expect a drug to affect them. Thus, when given a drug, behaviors may change for two reasons: (1) the effect of the drug itself and (2) the expectation that the drug will have an effect. By giving the placebo control group a pill with no active ingredients, researchers can control for these expectations, for both groups have the same expectations about the effect of the drug. Avoiding confounding is vital to conducting a meaningful experiment.

Measuring the Dependent Variable

Dependent variable ▶ The variable in an experiment that depends on the independent variable.

The **dependent variable** is the variable that we expect to be affected by the independent variable. Thus, after the independent variable is manipulated, the dependent variable must be measured to obtain a *score* for each subject. As we have seen in Chapters 2 to 5, the scores are summarized with a measure of central tendency and variability.

The research hypothesis for our example experiment predicted that the color red would affect a subject's performance on the anagram solution task. The dependent variable was the performance on the anagram solution task measured by how many anagrams a subject correctly solved in a five-minute period. This performance was summarized by presenting the mean and standard deviation of each group. Because we now have two means and two standard deviations, we will use subscripting to identify them. Thus, $\overline{X}_1$ is the mean of the first group, and s_1 is the estimated population standard deviation of the first group. Similarly, $\overline{X}_2$ is the mean of the second group, and s_2 is the estimated population standard deviation of the second group. For the example, $\overline{X}_1 = 7.8$ and $s_1 = 1.1$ for the control group, and $\overline{X}_2 = 6.6$ and $s_2 = 1.3$ for the experimental group. The difference between the means can now be analyzed for statistical significance with a *t* test for independent groups, which we develop next in this chapter.

Figure 9.1 illustrates the various steps of designing and conducting an experiment using the example experiment. Review the steps using this figure.

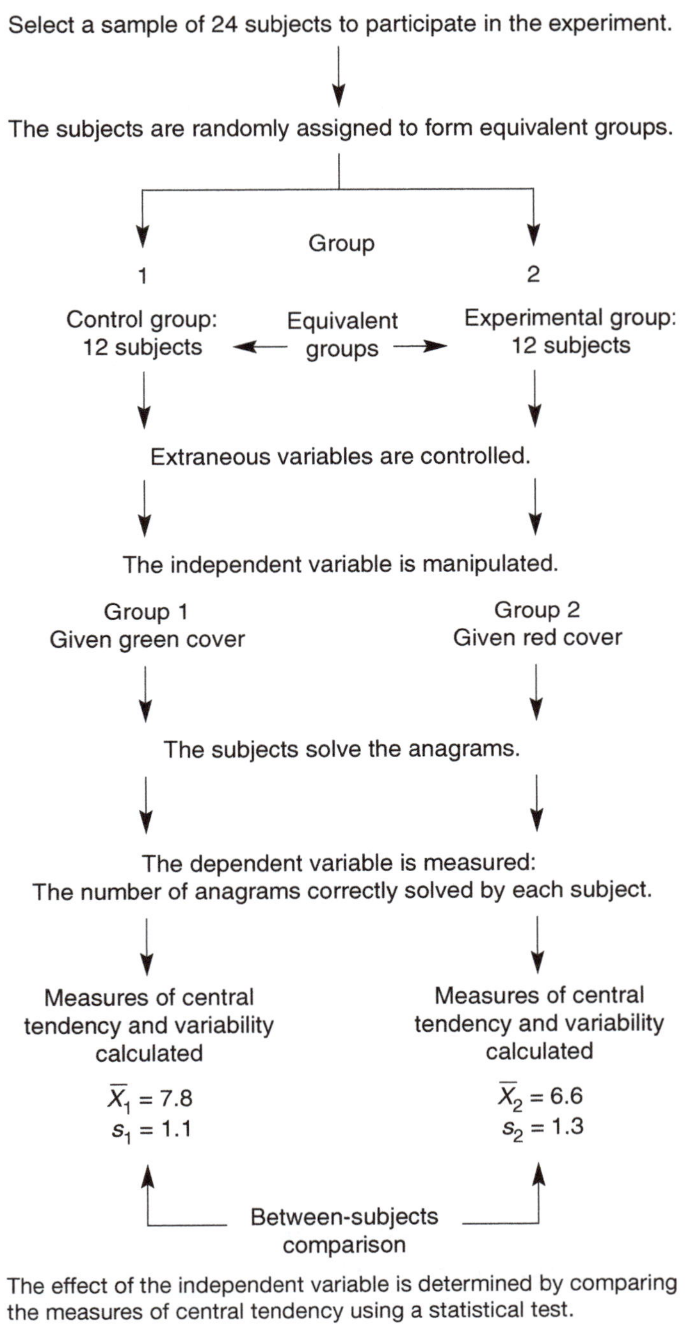

Select a sample of 24 subjects to participate in the experiment.

The subjects are randomly assigned to form equivalent groups.

Group

1   2

Control group: Equivalent   Experimental group:
12 subjects   ⟵   groups   ⟶   12 subjects

Extraneous variables are controlled.

The independent variable is manipulated.

Group 1   Group 2
Given green cover   Given red cover

The subjects solve the anagrams.

The dependent variable is measured:
The number of anagrams correctly solved by each subject.

Measures of central   Measures of central
tendency and variability   tendency and variability
calculated   calculated

$\overline{X}_1 = 7.8$ $\overline{X}_2 = 6.6$
$s_1 = 1.1$ $s_2 = 1.3$

Between-subjects
comparison

The effect of the independent variable is determined by comparing
the measures of central tendency using a statistical test.

Figure 9.1 Aspects of designing and conducting an experiment using a
between-subjects design. The figure illustrates the example experiment
to determine the effect of color on anagram solution.

Testing Your Knowledge 9.1

1. Define: between-subjects design, confound, confounding, control group, convenience sampling, dependent variable, equivalent groups, experiment, extraneous variable, factor, independent variable, level of an independent variable, one-factor between-subjects design, placebo control, random assignment, random sampling, research hypothesis.

2. What is the purpose of creating equivalent groups? What method is used for creating equivalent groups?

3. What is the difference between random selection of subjects and random assignment of subjects to treatment groups?

4. When does confounding occur in an experiment?

5. What difficulty does a confounded experiment pose for reaching a conclusion about the effect of an independent variable on the dependent variable?

6. An experimenter is investigating the effects of noise on the performance of a tracking task. The task is to use a mouse to keep a cursor on a computer screen on a randomly moving target dot. The dependent variable is the amount of time a person is able to keep the cursor on the dot. The experimenter hypothesized that subjects performing the task when no environmental noise is present will keep the cursor on the target for a greater amount of time than subjects who perform the task while listening to a loud noise. Each action by the experimenter that is described next confounds this experiment by letting an extraneous variable vary systematically with the independent variable of noise condition. For each action, identify the extraneous variable confounding the experiment and then explain why the experiment is confounded.

   a. The experimenter assigns ten 20-year-old males to the no-noise condition and ten 60-year-old males to the noise condition.

   b. The experimenter urges the subjects in the no-noise condition to try very hard, but does not encourage the subjects in the noise condition.

   c. The experimenter assigns males to the no-noise condition and females to the noise condition.

   d. The experimenter assigns physical education majors to the no-noise condition and social science majors to the noise condition.

   e. Subjects in the no-noise condition do the experiment between 9:00 and 10:00 A.M., and subjects in the noise condition do the experiment between 4:00 and 5:00 P.M.

Did the Treatment Have an Effect? The Need for Statistical Testing

The Implications of Sampling Error for an Experiment

The steps of conducting an experiment are straightforward, yet a problem arises. Any decision about the effect of an independent variable must be made by comparing the sample means with each other. In principle, if the sample means are equal to each other, then the treatment had no effect. On the other hand, if the sample means are not equal to each other, then it seems there is evidence that the treatment had an effect. But, because of sampling error, this decision is not made quite so simply. In Chapter 7, we defined *sampling error* as the amount a sample mean differs from the population mean (i.e., $\overline{X} - \mu$). If you were to draw two samples of subjects from the same population, measure a behavior, and calculate $\overline{X}$ for each sample, because of sampling error it would be unlikely that the two sample means would be equal to each other or to the population mean. This fact was illustrated by the empirical sampling distributions of the mean presented in Figure 7.2.

What are the implications of sampling error for reaching a decision about the effect of an independent variable in an experiment? Simply that chance differences between the means of different groups drawn from the same population are expected in any experiment, whether or not the independent variable has an effect on the dependent variable. Even if the independent variable has no effect whatsoever, the mean scores of the two treatment groups will differ from each other simply because of sampling error. How, then, does a behavioral scientist answer the following question:

> How large a difference between the sample means is enough to decide that something other than sampling error is at work in the experiment?

The answer is provided by a statistical hypothesis test of the difference between two means.

An Overview of Statistical Hypothesis Testing for the Difference Between Two Means

The approach used in statistical hypothesis testing is to assume that $\overline{X}_1$ represents a sample drawn from a population with μ_1 and $\overline{X}_2$ represents a sample drawn from a population with μ_2. Then, assuming that the two population means will be equal (i.e., that $\mu_1 = \mu_2$) if the independent variable has no effect, we can find the expected sampling error between the means. The difference between the sample means observed in the experiment is then compared to the differences expected from sampling error alone. If the observed difference between the sample means is large enough so that it is unlikely to occur from sampling error alone, then we decide that the difference is due, not to sampling error, but to the effect of the independent variable.

We have introduced a very important point in statistical hypothesis testing: To decide whether the means of two different groups differ by more than chance, we must first find the extent of **chance differences** between the means, differences expected from sampling error alone. If the observed difference between the sample means is among the commonly occurring chance differences, then we treat the observed difference as a chance difference. We then decide that the independent variable did not affect the dependent variable. On the other hand, if the observed difference between the means is sufficiently large that it rarely occurs by chance, then we decide that the sample means do not differ by chance alone; rather, if the experiment is well designed and not confounded, then we treat the difference as due to the independent variable.

There are many different statistical tests for use with different types of data and research designs; however, basic concepts of hypothesis testing are applicable to all statistical tests. We next introduce the *t* test for two independent groups. This *t* test allows us to statistically test the difference between two sample means when each mean is obtained from a different group of subjects.

The *t* Test for Two Independent Groups

The ***t* test for two independent groups** is defined as

$$t_{\text{ind}} = \frac{(\overline{X}_1 - \overline{X}_2) - (\mu_1 - \mu_2)}{s_{\overline{X}_1 - \overline{X}_2}}.$$

The subscripted *ind* is used to indicate that this *t* is used to test for differences between two independent groups of subjects. When we are presenting the formula symbolically, as above, we will use the *ind* subscript. When values are substituted into the formula to create a numerical value of *t*, we will continue our use of the *obs* subscript to indicate the value is a value of *t* observed from the data.

The numerator of t_{ind} indicates how much an obtained difference between two sample means (i.e., $\overline{X}_1 - \overline{X}_2$) differs from that between the two population means (i.e., $\mu_1 - \mu_2$) the sample means are assumed to represent. In most instances, the population means are hypothesized to be equal; thus, the difference between them (i.e., $\mu_1 - \mu_2$) is zero, and the numerator of the t_{ind} simplifies to $\overline{X}_1 - \overline{X}_2$. The denominator (i.e., $s_{\overline{X}_1 - \overline{X}_2}$) is a measure of error variation called the *standard error of the difference between means*. The standard error of the difference between means is the standard deviation of a sampling distribution of differences between means. To understand this measure of error variation, we must develop the concept of a sampling distribution of differences between two means.

Sampling Distribution of Differences Between Means

Consider an experiment in which two levels (1 and 2) of an independent variable are manipulated. Suppose that the independent variable has no effect on the dependent variable. Because the independent variable has no effect, we can simulate this instance by sampling scores from two populations, 1 and 2, with equal means (i.e., $\mu_1 = \mu_2$). Imagine that we conduct this experiment by drawing two samples of size 5 each (i.e., $n_1 = 5$, $n_2 = 5$), one sample from each population, 1 and 2, respectively. This sample size is arbitrary; any sample size would serve to illustrate the point. We calculate the mean for each sample and then subtract $\overline{X}_2$ from $\overline{X}_1$. Suppose that we replicated the hypothetical experiment 100 times and found 100 $\overline{X}_1 - \overline{X}_2$ differences. Plotting a frequency distribution of $\overline{X}_1 - \overline{X}_2$ values results in an **empirical sampling distribution of differences between means**. The sampling distribution of 100 such differences between means is portrayed in Figure 9.2. This distribution is an empirical sampling distribution of differences between means because we obtained and calculated the values of 100 differences between $\overline{X}_1$ and $\overline{X}_2$. In practice, however, a researcher would not calculate and construct such an empirical sampling distribution. Rather, he or she would use the theoretical sampling distribution of the difference between means as presented in Figure 9.3. A **theoretical sampling distribution of the difference between means** is the distribution of $\overline{X}_1 - \overline{X}_2$ differences when all possible pairs of samples of size *n* are selected from a population and $\overline{X}_1 - \overline{X}_2$ found for each pair of samples. Recall from Chapter 7 that the theoretical sampling distribution of the mean possesses important characteristics concerning its shape, mean, and standard error. A theoretical sampling distribution of the difference between means shares these characteristics.

Sampling distribution of the difference between means ▶ The distribution of $\overline{X}_1 - \overline{X}_2$ differences when all possible pairs of samples of size *n* are selected from a population and $\overline{X}_1 - \overline{X}_2$ found for each pair of samples.

Shape of a Sampling Distribution of Differences Between Means

Observe that the empirical sampling distribution in Figure 9.2 is relatively symmetrical and unimodal. Because of the central limit theorem, as sample size increases, a sampling distribution of the difference between means approaches a normal distribution regardless

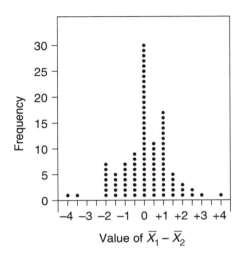

Figure 9.2 Empirical sampling distribution of the difference between means $(\bar{X}_1 - \bar{X}_2)$ for 100 samples drawn from two populations with identical means $(\mu_1 = \mu_2)$.

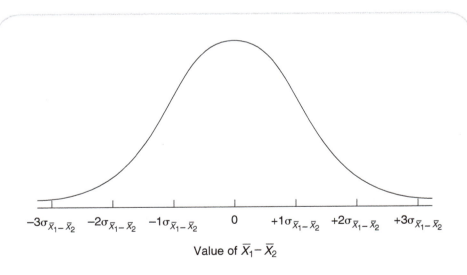

Figure 9.3 Theoretical sampling distribution of the difference between two means when $\mu_1 = \mu_2$.

of the shape of the distributions of the underlying population of scores. This characteristic is present in the theoretical distribution illustrated in Figure 9.3.

Mean of a Sampling Distribution of Differences Between Means

The mean of the distribution of an unlimited set of $\overline{X}_1 - \overline{X}_2$ differences, $\overline{X}_{\overline{X}_1-\overline{X}_2}$, will be equal to the difference in population means $\mu_1 - \mu_2$. Therefore, when $\mu_1 = \mu_2$ and, thus, $\mu_1 - \mu_2 = 0$, the mean of the obtained $\overline{X}_1 - \overline{X}_2$ values will, in the long run, equal zero, and the obtained differences in sample means will be clustered around the difference of zero between the population means. This characteristic is demonstrated in the empirical distribution shown in Figure 9.2. The mean $\overline{X}_1 - \overline{X}_2$ difference of this distribution is $+0.07$. Even with only 100 sets of samples, the mean of the $\overline{X}_1 - \overline{X}_2$ difference is very close to the population difference of zero. For the theoretical distribution shown in Figure 9.3, the mean $\overline{X}_1 - \overline{X}_2$ difference is zero.

Standard Error of a Sampling Distribution of Differences Between Means

The standard deviation of a theoretical sampling distribution of $\overline{X}_1 - \overline{X}_2$ values is called the **standard error of the difference between means**, or simply the **standard error of the difference**. It is symbolized as $\sigma_{\overline{X}_1-\overline{X}_2}$ as shown in Figure 9.3 and defined as

Standard error of the difference between means ▶ The standard deviation of a theoretical sampling distribution of $\overline{X}_1 - \overline{X}_2$ values.

$$\sigma_{\overline{X}_1-\overline{X}_2} = \sqrt{\frac{\sigma_1^2}{n_1} + \frac{\sigma_2^2}{n_2}}.$$

Notice that the standard error is found by combining the standard error of the sampling distribution of the mean for each population. Thus, its value will vary with the standard error of the mean for each distribution. In practice, however, σ^2 is not known, and the value of $\sigma_{\overline{X}_1-\overline{X}_2}$ is estimated from the estimated population variances, s_1^2 and s_2^2. To obtain the estimated standard error of the difference between means, a pooled or combined variance estimate, indicated by s_{pooled}^2, is first obtained from the two estimated population variances s_1^2 and s_2^2 using the following equation:

$$s_{pooled}^2 = \frac{(n_1 - 1)s_1^2 + (n_2 - 1)s_2^2}{n_1 + n_2 - 2}.$$

This equation indicates that to obtain s_{pooled}^2 we multiply each estimated population variance by its degrees of freedom (i.e., $n - 1$), add the resulting values, and then divide the sum by the total of the degrees of freedom of the two groups. The next step in obtaining the estimated standard error of the difference between means is to recall from Chapter 7 that the estimated standard error of the mean, $s_{\overline{X}}$, was given by $s/\sqrt{N}$. Notice that this formula could be written as $s_{\overline{X}} = \sqrt{(s^2)(1/N)}$. The **estimated standard error of the difference between means,** identified as $s_{\overline{X}_1-\overline{X}_2}$, is found similarly by

Estimated standard error of the difference between means ▶ The standard error of the difference between means obtained by using s^2 to estimate σ^2.

$$s_{\overline{X}_1-\overline{X}_2} = \sqrt{s_{pooled}^2 \left[\frac{1}{n_1} + \frac{1}{n_2}\right]}.$$

Substituting the formula for s_{pooled}^2, we obtain

$$\begin{array}{c} \textbf{Estimated standard} \\ \textbf{error of the difference} \\ \textbf{between means} \end{array} = s_{\overline{X}_1-\overline{X}_2} = \sqrt{\left[\frac{(n_1 - 1)s_1^2 + (n_2 - 1)s_2^2}{n_1 + n_2 - 2}\right]\left[\frac{1}{n_1} + \frac{1}{n_2}\right]}.$$

The estimated standard error of the difference is the denominator of the t_{ind} statistic. Thus, the value of t_{ind} indicates how many estimated standard errors away from the mean of the sampling distribution of the difference between $\overline{X}_1$ and $\overline{X}_2$ an observed $\overline{X}_1 - \overline{X}_2$ difference lies. For example, suppose that an obtained $\overline{X}_1 - \overline{X}_2 = 3$ and $s_{\overline{X}_1 - \overline{X}_2} = 3$. The value of t then equals $3/3$ or 1, indicating that the observed $\overline{X}_1 - \overline{X}_2$ difference is one standard error away from the mean of the sampling distribution of $\overline{X}_1 - \overline{X}_2$. If an obtained $\overline{X}_1 - \overline{X}_2 = 6$ and $s_{\overline{X}_1 - \overline{X}_2} = 3$, then t equals $6/3$ or 2, indicating that the observed $\overline{X}_1 - \overline{X}_2$ difference is two standard errors away from the mean of the sampling distribution of the difference between $\overline{X}_1$ and $\overline{X}_2$. Notice that, if an independent variable has no effect and sampling error alone is operating in an experiment, we expect the value of t to

Testing Your Knowledge 9.2

1. Define: empirical sampling distribution of the difference between means, standard error of the difference between means, theoretical sampling distribution of the difference between means.

2. Explain why you cannot simply look at the difference between the mean scores of two groups given different treatments and decide if the difference between the means is due to the independent variable.

3. Calculate $s_{\overline{X}_1 - \overline{X}_2}$ for each of the following sets of scores.

a.	Group		b.	Group	
X_1		X_2	X_1		X_2
104		99	77		82
111		107	84		86
120		105	68		78
113		110	71		74
108		115	82		69
					79
					80

c.	Group		d.	Group	
X_1		X_2	X_1		X_2
71		85	32		38
82		80	37		42
63		73	28		29
74		76	41		36
68		70	35		30
76		67	33		37
					36
					39
					34

be close to zero, whereas if an independent variable has an effect and causes $\overline{X}_1$ and $\overline{X}_2$ to differ, then the value of t should become larger.

Statistical Testing with t_{ind}

In using t_{ind} to test for a significant difference between two means, the steps for statistical hypothesis testing outlined in Chapter 8 are followed:

▶ A null hypothesis, H_0, and an alternative hypothesis, H_1, are formulated.

▶ The sampling distribution of t assuming H_0 is true is obtained. This distribution is given in Appendix C.2.

▶ A significance level is selected.

▶ A critical value of t, identified as t_{crit}, is found from the sampling distribution of t given in Appendix C.2.

▶ Rejection regions are located in the theoretical sampling distribution of the t statistic.

▶ The t statistic, identified as t_{obs}, is calculated from the sample data.

▶ A decision to reject or not reject H_0 is made on the basis of whether t_{obs} falls into a rejection region.

▶ The results of the statistical decisions are related to the research hypothesis.

Statistical Hypotheses

For a parametric test, a statistical hypothesis is a statement about population parameters. The parameters corresponding to a statistical test of $\overline{X}_1$ and $\overline{X}_2$ are the population means, μ_1 and μ_2, respectively. For t_{ind}, the statistical hypotheses are

$$H_0: \mu_1 = \mu_2 \quad \text{(null hypothesis),}$$

$$H_1: \mu_1 \neq \mu_2 \quad \text{(alternative hypothesis).}$$

For two populations of scores, one or the other of these hypotheses must be true.

Null Hypothesis. The null hypothesis does not specify numerical values for population parameters, which, of course, are unknown. It states only that the population means are equal. Essentially, $H_0: \mu_1 = \mu_2$ corresponds to the situation that exists if the independent variable has no effect on the dependent variable. If the independent variable has no effect, then all the subjects in the experiment are representative of the same population and any obtained difference between the two sample means is due only to sampling error. Thus, H_0 establishes a situation under which the theoretical sampling distribution of the t statistic may be found. By knowing the sampling distribution of t, we can determine how likely or unlikely any value of t_{obs} is if sampling error alone is responsible for the difference between the sample means.

Alternative Hypothesis. The alternative hypothesis represents the situation if $\overline{X}_1$ and $\overline{X}_2$ differ because the subjects in each group are from populations with different means. This situation occurs if the independent variable has an effect. And, if the independent variable has an effect and H_1 is true, then we expect $\overline{X}_1$ and $\overline{X}_2$ to differ by an amount greater than that expected from sampling error alone. Hence, if H_1 is true, the value of t_{obs} should typically be larger than the value of t_{obs} if H_0 is true.

Support for the research hypothesis of the experiment occurs by rejecting H_0 and accepting H_1. The decision to reject H_0 and accept H_1 signifies that the observed difference in sample means is treated as resulting from the effect of the independent variable and not the result of sampling error. As an example of this reasoning, the research hypothesis for our example experiment predicted that the color red would affect people's performance on the solution of anagrams in comparison to the color green. This hypothesis is supported only if the mean number of anagrams solved for the two treatment groups represent populations with different means, the situation stated in the alternative hypothesis. Thus, rejecting H_0 and accepting H_1 provide support for the research hypothesis.

Selecting a Significance Level

The significance level is a probability value that provides the criterion for rejecting a null hypothesis in a statistical test. As you know, behavioral scientists typically choose an alpha of either .05 or .01. By doing so, they have decided that values of t occurring only 5 or fewer times in 100 occasions or only 1 or fewer times in 100 occasions if H_0 is true are statistically rare. We choose $\alpha = .05$ for the example.

Locating Rejection Regions and Finding Critical Values of t: Two-Tailed Tests

A rejection region represents values of t in the sampling distribution of t that have a probability equal to or less than α if H_0 is true. Hence, a rejection region defines values of t_{obs} that meet the criterion for rejecting H_0.

As discussed in Chapter 8, in a **two-tailed** or **nondirectional test**, rejection regions for t are located in either tail of the theoretical sampling distribution as illustrated in Figure 9.4. When H_0 is true, most values of t_{obs} will be clustered around 0, for most values

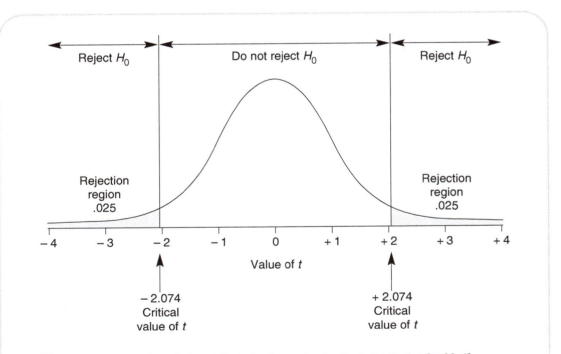

Figure 9.4 Illustration of a two-tailed rejection region for the t distribution for 22 *df* and $\alpha = .05$.

of $\overline{X}_1 - \overline{X}_2$ will differ only slightly from zero. But some values of t_{obs} will fall in either end of the distribution even when H_0 is true. These relatively large values of t_{obs} occur when the numerator of the t (i.e., $\overline{X}_1 - \overline{X}_2$) is large compared to the denominator (i.e., the standard error of the difference). These large values of t_{obs} are rare occurrences, however, if H_0: $\mu_1 = \mu_2$ is true.

On the other hand, if H_1 is true and $\mu_1 \neq \mu_2$, then large positive or negative values of $\overline{X}_1 - \overline{X}_2$ and thus of t_{obs}, are expected to occur more frequently. Hence, the rejection regions for the t are located in each tail of the theoretical sampling distribution of t. The total probability specified by α is divided between both tails of the t distribution. If t_{obs} falls into either rejection region, then H_0 is rejected and H_1 accepted. As with the one-sample t test, the two-tailed critical values given in Appendix C.2 define the exact location of the rejection regions. To use this table, we must know the degrees of freedom for t_{obs}.

Degrees of Freedom for t_{ind}. Degrees of freedom represent the number of scores that are free to vary when calculating a statistic. In Chapter 8, we demonstrated that s^2 has $N - 1$ df, where N represents the number of scores on which the variance is calculated. For the t_{ind} statistic, $s_{\overline{X}_1 - \overline{X}_2}$ is found by calculating the variances from each group, s_1^2 and s_2^2. Accordingly, the df for t_{ind} are based on the combined df of s_1^2 and s_2^2. When n_1 and n_2 represent the number of scores in groups 1 and 2, respectively, s_1^2 has $n_1 - 1$ df and s_2^2 has $n_2 - 1$ df. Hence, the combined df for t_{ind} are $(n_1 - 1)$ plus $(n_2 - 1)$. If N is used to represent the total number of scores in the two groups (i.e., $N = n_1 + n_2$), then the df for t_{ind} are $N - 2$. Accordingly, for an experiment with 12 scores in each group (i.e., $n_1 = 12$, $n_2 = 12$, thus $N = 24$), the df for t_{ind} are $24 - 2 = 22$. From Appendix C.2, the two-tailed t_{crit} for 22 df and $\alpha = .05$ is 2.074. This value of t_{crit} is shown in Figure 9.4, locating the rejection region in each tail of the t distribution.

Locating a Rejection Region: One-Tailed Tests

When a research hypothesis predicts a directional relationship between the means (e.g., that $\overline{X}_1$ should be greater than $\overline{X}_2$) and there is no interest in an outcome opposite the one predicted (e.g., if $\overline{X}_1$ less than $\overline{X}_2$ occurs), then researchers may use a one-tailed or directional test. In a **one-tailed** or **directional test**, a rejection region including the total value of α is located in the tail of the t distribution corresponding to the direction of the outcome predicted by the research hypothesis. Values of t_{crit} for a one-tailed test at the .01 and .05 significance levels are also presented in Appendix C.2. For 22 df, the one-tailed t_{crit} at the .05 significance level is 1.717. A one-tailed rejection region with $t_{crit} = +1.717$ in the right tail of a t distribution is illustrated in Figure 9.5. The null and alternative hypotheses for the use of this rejection region are

$$H_0: \mu_1 \leq \mu_2,$$
$$H_1: \mu_1 > \mu_2.$$

There is controversy about the use of one-tailed tests, however. The sampling distribution of t presented in Appendix C.2 is developed assuming H_0: $\mu_1 = \mu_2$, is true. This sampling distribution is symmetric about 0, and positive and negative differences from 0 are expected to occur equally. For a one-tailed test, however, the statistical hypotheses are either

$$H_0: \mu_1 \leq \mu_2, \text{ and } H_1: \mu_1 > \mu_2$$

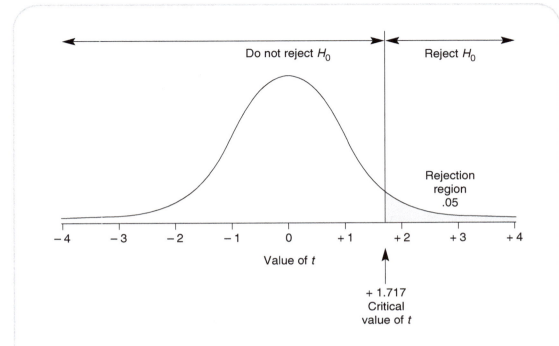

Figure 9.5 Illustration of a one-tailed rejection region for the t distribution for 22 df and $\alpha = .05$.

or

$$H_0: \mu_1 \geq \mu_2, \text{ and } H_1: \mu_1 < \mu_2.$$

But we cannot develop a sampling distribution for t under either of these null hypotheses because there are an infinite number of ways $H_0: \mu_1 \leq \mu_2$ or $H_0: \mu_1 \geq \mu_2$ could be true. Thus, the sampling distribution for $H_0: \mu_1 = \mu_2$ is used to determine critical values of t for one-tailed as well as two-tailed tests. For this and other reasons, some behavioral scientists recommend against using one-tailed t tests (Gaito, 1977). Consequently, two-tailed tests are used for all examples in this chapter.

Calculating t_{ind}
The definitional formula for t_{ind} is

$$t_{ind} = \frac{(\overline{X}_1 - \overline{X}_2) - (\mu_1 - \mu_2)}{s_{\overline{X}_1 - \overline{X}_2}}.$$

The null hypothesis for t_{ind}, $H_0: \mu_1 = \mu_2$, is equivalent to $H_0: \mu_1 - \mu_2 = 0$. Thus, the difference of $\mu_1 - \mu_2$ is hypothesized to be zero, and $\mu_1 - \mu_2$ drops from the formula, so

$$t_{\text{ind}} = \frac{\overline{X}_1 - \overline{X}_2}{s_{\overline{X}_1 - \overline{X}_2}},$$

where $s_{\overline{X}_1 - \overline{X}_2}$ is given by

$$s_{\overline{X}_1 - \overline{X}_2} = \sqrt{\left[\frac{(n_1 - 1)s_1^2 + (n_2 - 1)s_2^2}{n_1 + n_2 - 2}\right]\left[\frac{1}{n_1} + \frac{1}{n_2}\right]}.$$

Consequently, for computational purposes,

$$t_{\text{ind}} = \frac{\overline{X}_1 - \overline{X}_2}{\sqrt{\left[\frac{(n_1 - 1)s_1^2 + (n_2 - 1)s_2^2}{n_1 + n_2 - 2}\right]\left[\frac{1}{n_1} + \frac{1}{n_2}\right]}}.$$

To use this formula, we need know only the sample mean ($\overline{X}$), number of subjects (n), and estimated population variance (s^2) for each group. Use of this formula is illustrated in example problem 9.1.

Decisions About the Statistical Hypotheses

Statistically Significant Difference. If t_{obs} falls into a rejection region, then H_0: $\mu_1 = \mu_2$ is rejected. Rejection of H_0 implies acceptance of H_1: $\mu_1 \neq \mu_2$. The difference between the sample means is *statistically significant*. We conclude that the two sample means involved in t_{obs} are not estimates of the same population mean, and the difference between them is due to something other than sampling error alone. If the experiment has been carefully designed and conducted, then the difference between the sample means is due to the independent variable manipulated. These decisions and conclusions are summarized in the left column of Table 9.1.

Nonsignificant Difference. If t_{obs} does not fall into a rejection region, then we fail to reject H_0. Failing to reject H_0 implies not accepting H_1. The difference between the sample means is *nonsignificant*. The two sample means are considered to be from populations with identical means, and they differ only because of sampling error. The implication for the experiment is that the independent variable had no effect, and the difference between the sample means is a chance occurrence. These decisions and conclusions are summarized in the right column of Table 9.1.

Relating Decisions About the Statistical Hypotheses to the Research Hypothesis

The essential purpose of running a statistical test is to make a decision about the research hypothesis of the study. If a statistically significant difference occurs and H_0 is rejected, then the sample means must be examined to determine if the difference between them is in the direction predicted by the research hypothesis. We will discuss this more fully after we present several examples.

Assumptions for Use of t_{ind}

The use of t_{ind} rests on the following assumptions:

1. Each subject in the experiment is randomly selected from a population, and each subject is independent of every other subject.

2. The scores on the dependent variable in the populations sampled are normally distributed.

3. The variances of scores in the populations are equal; that is, $\sigma_1^2 = \sigma_2^2$.

TABLE **9.1**	Summary of decisions and conclusions in statistical hypothesis testing using the *t* test for two independent groups. A .05 significance level is used.

If t_{obs} falls into the rejection region for $\alpha = .05$, then:	If t_{obs} does not fall into the rejection region for $\alpha = .05$, then:

▶ Probability of t_{obs} is less than or equal to .05 or $p \leq .05$.
 	
▶ H_0 is rejected.
 	
▶ H_1 is accepted.
 	
▶ We found a statistically significant difference at the .05 level.
 	
   ▷ The sample means are from two different populations.
 	
   ▷ Something, in addition to sampling error, is responsible for differences between the sample means.
 	
   ▷ In a carefully designed experiment, changes in the independent variable are causing changes in the dependent variable.
	▶ Probability of t_{obs} is greater than .05 or $p > .05$.
	
	▶ H_0 is not rejected.
	
	▶ H_1 is not accepted.
	
	▶ We failed to find a statistically significant difference at the .05 level.
	
	   ▷ Sampling error alone is the most plausible explanation for the differences between the sample means.
	
	   ▷ There is no evidence that the independent variable had an effect.

In Chapter 8, we indicated that the assumptions of the *t* test are often not fully met in actual research; they are violated. Yet, researchers may proceed to use the *t* test on the data. What are the consequences of such violations?

The requirement of the first assumption is that each subject in a group be independent of every other subject in the group. That is, knowing one subject's score in a group will give you no information about any other subject's score in the group. This assumption requires that each subject be given only one level of the independent variable and contribute only one score in the experiment. This requirement of independence of scores cannot be violated for t_{ind}. If a subject is given both levels of the independent variable and contributes two scores for analysis, then you must use the *t* test for related scores, which is presented later in this chapter.

The assumption of independence also indicates that subjects are to be selected randomly, but, the statistic can still be used if subjects are obtained by convenience sampling rather than random sampling, as long as they are selected independently of each other. The major impact of convenience sampling is to limit the extent to which the results can be generalized to a population. For example, if your sample consists only of female college students, your ability to generalize the findings to adult males who have never attended college could be weakened.

Violations of the second (the normal distribution of scores) and the third (the equality of variances, often called the *homogeneity of variances*) assumptions can increase the probability of making a Type I error from that specified by the value of α. But the *t* test is thought to be *robust* against violations of these assumptions. **Robustness** means that violation of the assumptions has little effect on the probability of making a Type I error. Research by Bradley (1980, 1984) has challenged this robustness notion, however. Bradley argues that there is no one set of conditions under which these assumptions may

Robustness ▶ A term used to indicate that violating the assumptions of a statistical test has little effect on the probability of a Type I error.

be violated and robustness of the *t* test assured. But violations of the normality and equality of variances assumptions are more likely to have minimal effects on the probability of making a Type I error when the following conditions are met:

▶ The number of subjects in each group is the same.

▶ The two distributions of scores have about the same shape, and the distributions are neither very peaked nor very flat.

▶ The significance level is set at .05 rather than .01.

▶ A two-tailed test is used even with a directional research hypothesis.

<table>
<tr><td>EXAMPLE PROBLEM

9.1</td><td>### Using t_{ind} to Find the Effect of the Color of a Cover on Anagram Solutions</td></tr>
</table>

Problem: We use our example of the effect of color on anagram solution to illustrate calculating t_{ind} when $\overline{X}$ and s are given. Our experiment had two treatment groups of 12 people each. The mean number of correct anagram solutions for the control group (1) which received the green test cover was 7.8, with $s_1 = 1.1$. For the experimental group (2), which received the red cover, the mean number of correct anagram solutions was 6.6, with $s_2 = 1.3$. Do these means differ significantly at the .05 level? Use a two-tailed test.

Statistic to Be Used:

$$t_{ind} = \frac{\overline{X}_1 - \overline{X}_2}{\sqrt{\left[\frac{(n_1 - 1)s_1^2 + (n_2 - 1)s_2^2}{n_1 + n_2 - 2}\right]\left[\frac{1}{n_1} + \frac{1}{n_2}\right]}}.$$

Assumptions

1. The subjects were sampled randomly and each subject is independent of every other subject.

2. Performance on the anagram solution task is normally distributed in the population.

3. The variances for the number of correct anagram solutions are equal in the populations for the two treatment groups.

Statistical Hypotheses: $H_0: \mu_1 = \mu_2,$
$H_1: \mu_1 \neq \mu_2.$

Significance Level: $\alpha = .05.$

***df* for *t*:** $(n_1 - 1) + (n_2 - 1) = (12 - 1) + (12 - 1) = 22,$
or $N - 2 = 24 - 2 = 22.$

Critical Value of *t*: $t_{crit} = 2.074$ from Appendix C.2.

Rejection Regions: Values of t_{obs} equal to or less than -2.074 or equal to or greater than $+2.074$.

Calculation:

$$t_{obs} = \frac{7.8 - 6.6}{\sqrt{\left[\frac{(12-1)(1.1)^2 + (12-1)(1.3)^2}{12+12-2}\right]\left[\frac{1}{12} + \frac{1}{12}\right]}}$$

$$= \frac{+1.2}{\sqrt{\left[\frac{31.90}{22}\right]\left[\frac{1}{12} + \frac{1}{12}\right]}}$$

$$= \frac{+1.2}{0.492} = +2.439.$$

Decision: t_{obs} falls into the rejection region of equal to or greater than $t_{crit} = +2.074$. We reject H_0 and accept H_1.

Conclusion: The two sample means of 7.8 and 6.6 differ significantly at the .05 level. Because the treatment groups were equivalent before the treatment was administered, the difference between the number of anagrams solved is treated as due to the effect of the independent variable of the color of the cover. The students who are given anagrams with a red cover do not solve as many anagrams as students who are given anagrams with a green cover. The results are in agreement with the research hypothesis.   ▬▬▬

EXAMPLE PROBLEM

9.2

Using t_{ind} with Raw Scores

Problem: Behavioral scientists have proposed that people often evaluate their initials more favorably than other letters of the alphabet. In this context, Nelson and Simmons (2007) hypothesized that students who have initials containing a C or D may find the academic grade of C or D less aversive than students who have initials containing an A or B. Suppose you investigated this hypothesis by randomly selecting undergraduate college seniors whose first or last name began with the letters A or B, or C or D, and compared their grade point averages (GPA). Students whose initials contain an A or a B were placed into one group, and students whose initials contain a C or a D were placed into another group. Notice in this study the independent variable of the person's initials is not an independent variable you can actively manipulate; that is, you cannot assign a person their initials. Instead, you must select people containing the correct initials for each group. This procedure creates a *quasi-experiment* that uses a subject variable, the person's initials, as the independent variable. Recall from Chapter 2 that although quasi-experiments are widely used in the behavioral sciences, it is more difficult to reach causal relations between the independent and dependent variable from a quasi-experiment than it is in a true experiment with an independent variable that can be actively manipulated. Nevertheless, in a one-factor between-subjects design we can use the same statistical analysis with either a manipulated independent variable or a subject variable.

After the students were selected and categorized by initials, you then obtained each of their grade point averages. The following GPAs were obtained for 14 students in each group.

Letters of Initials	
A or B (X_1)	C or D (X_2)
3.2	3.3
3.4	2.9
3.5	2.7
3.4	3.2
3.4	3.0
2.7	2.6
2.8	3.4
3.1	2.2
2.5	2.9
2.9	3.3
3.3	3.5
3.7	2.9
3.4	2.8
3.5	3.3

Do these GPAs differ significantly at the .05 level? Use a two-tailed test.

Statistic to Be Used: t_{ind}.

Assumptions

1. The students whose names began with an A or B, or C or D, were sampled randomly from among students with those initials, and each student is independent of every other student.

2. GPA is normally distributed in the populations sampled.

3. The variances for GPAs are equal in the populations for the two groups.

Statistical Hypotheses: $H_0: \mu_1 = \mu_2,$
$$H_1: \mu_1 \neq \mu_2.$$

Significance Level: $\alpha = .05$.

df for t: $(n_1 - 1) + (n_2 - 1) = (14 - 1) + (14 - 1) = 26,$
or $N - 2 = 28 - 2 = 26$.

Critical Value of t: $t_{crit} = 2.056$ from Appendix C.2.

Rejection Regions: Values of t_{obs} equal to or less than -2.056 or equal to or greater than $+2.056$.

Calculation: The first step in the calculation is to find the mean and standard deviation for each group. Students whose first or last name began with an A or a B had a mean GPA of 3.2 with $s = 0.35$. Students whose first or last name began with a C or D had a mean GPA of 3.0, with $s = 0.36$. Substituting these values into the formula for t_{obs}, we obtain

$$t_{obs} = \frac{3.2 - 3.0}{\sqrt{\left[\frac{(14-1)(0.35)^2 + (14-1)(0.36)^2}{14 + 14 - 2}\right]\left[\frac{1}{14} + \frac{1}{14}\right]}}$$

$$= \frac{+0.2}{\sqrt{\left[\frac{3.28}{26}\right]\left[\frac{2}{14}\right]}}$$

$$= \frac{+0.2}{0.134} = +1.493.$$

Decision: t_{obs} does not fall into the rejection region of equal to or greater than $t_{crit} = +2.056$. We fail to reject H_0.

Conclusion: The two sample means of 3.2 and 3.0 do not differ significantly. There is no evidence that GPA is related to the person's initials in this study, and the research hypothesis is not supported. The difference between the sample means is due to sampling error.

Testing Your Knowledge 9.3

1. Define: directional test, nondirectional test, one-tailed rejection region, rejection region, robustness, t_{crit}, t_{ind}, t_{obs}, two-tailed rejection region.
2. Identify the steps in statistical testing with t_{ind}.
3. Write the statistical hypotheses for t_{ind} for a two-tailed test.
4. To what situation in an experiment does H_0 correspond?
5. To what situation in an experiment does H_1 correspond?
6. Assume that you have two groups of size n_1 and n_2, respectively. Complete the following exercise for each set of samples given in the table by (a) finding the df for the t test on the two samples, (b) finding t_{crit} for a two-tailed test for $\alpha = .05$ (if the exact df are not in the table, then use the next lower value), (c) indicating whether the t_{obs} falls into a rejection region, and (d) indicating your decisions with respect to the statistical hypotheses.

Sample Set	n_1	n_2	t_{obs}
1	10	10	2.341
2	8	12	1.763
3	15	15	2.120
4	16	14	3.479
5	35	35	2.912
6	19	16	2.007
7	65	64	2.002
8	75	75	2.193

7. Identify the assumptions underlying the use of t_{ind}.
8. a. The t test is said to be robust. What is meant by this term?
   b. Under what conditions is the t test likely to be robust?

9. For problems 1 and 2 presented below, answer the following questions. Use a two-tailed test and a .05 significance level for each problem.

   a. State the statistical hypotheses for t_{ind} for these scores.

   b. What are the *df* for this *t*?

   c. What is the value of t_{crit}?

   d. What are the rejection regions for t_{obs}?

   e. What is the value of t_{obs}?

   f. Does t_{obs} fall into a rejection region?

   g. What decisions do you make about the statistical hypotheses? Do you reject or fail to reject H_0? Accept or not accept H_1?

   h. Do you conclude that the sample means are from the same or different populations?

   i. Is the difference between the means statistically significant?

   j. Did the groups differ significantly in their estimates of the time they spent waiting? If so, what is the direction of the difference?

Problem 1: Does time seem to pass more slowly when you are expecting a delay before an event occurs? Suppose that to answer this question you randomly assigned a total of 36 subjects to either a control group or an experimental group with $n_1 = n_2$. In both groups you told the subjects that the experiment would take only a few minutes and that they were going to fill out a questionnaire on anxiety. Subjects in the control group were told that the assistant would arrive with the questionnaires in a few minutes. Subjects in the experimental group were told that the assistant was late and that there would be a short delay. For both groups, however, the assistant arrived in exactly five minutes. When the assistant arrived, the subjects were asked to estimate how long they had waited. Suppose that you obtained the following mean time estimates and standard deviations (in minutes) for your groups:

	Group	
	Control	Experimental
$\overline{X}$	6.9	8.9
s	1.6	1.7

Problem 2: Suppose that you are interested in answering the same question as in problem 1: Does time seem to pass more slowly when you are expecting a delay before an event occurs? Again, you randomly assign subjects to one of two groups. Rather than an equal number in each group, however, you assign 13 subjects to the control group and 17 to the experimental group. In all other respects the experiment is identical to that described in problem 1. Suppose that you obtained the following mean estimates and standard deviations (in minutes) for your groups:

	Group	
	Control	Experimental
$\overline{X}$	6.6	7.8
s	1.8	1.9

Power and t_{ind}

Power ▶ The probability of rejecting H_0 when H_0 is false and H_1 is true.

The **power** of a statistical test was defined in Chapter 8 as the probability of rejecting H_0 when H_0 is false. Because rejecting H_0 means that the experimenter accepts H_1 and decides that the independent variable had an effect in his or her experiment, the *power of a statistical test* is the probability that an effect of an independent variable will be detected in an experiment when such an effect is present. An experimenter always wants to maximize the power of a statistical test so that he or she can detect an effect of an independent variable if it is present.

The null hypothesis is rejected when t_{obs} falls into a rejection region, and the larger t_{obs} is, the more likely it will fall into a rejection region. There are several actions we can take to increase the value of t_{obs} and, thus, the power of t_{ind}. We can understand these actions by examining the formula for t_{ind},

$$t_{ind} = \frac{\overline{X}_1 - \overline{X}_2}{s_{\overline{X}_1 - \overline{X}_2}}.$$

With this formula there are two ways to increase the value of t_{obs}: (1) increase the difference between $\overline{X}_1$ and $\overline{X}_2$ and (2) decrease the value of $s_{\overline{X}_1 - \overline{X}_2}$.

The first approach is to maximize the effect of the independent variable. That is, we want to manipulate the independent variable in such a way that it makes $\overline{X}_1$ and $\overline{X}_2$ differ as much as possible. For this reason, behavioral scientists often use widely differing levels of the independent variable. For example, in the example study about the effects of color of the cover page on the solution of anagrams, the control color of green was selected because it is considered to be the chromatic opposite of red. By selecting colors that are as far from each other as possible on the color wheel (instead of red and pink, for example) you are maximizing the possible effect of the independent variable.

To decrease the value of $s_{\overline{X}_1 - \overline{X}_2}$, we may do two things: increase the sample size and decrease the amount of variability in the scores of the samples. To illustrate the relationship of $s_{\overline{X}_1 - \overline{X}_2}$ to sample size, suppose that both s_1^2 and $s_2^2 = 36$. Consider also that these values of s^2 came from one of three sample sizes: $n_1 = n_2 = 3$, $n_1 = n_2 = 6$, or $n_1 = n_2 = 9$. Then, substituting the differing values of n into the formula for $s_{\overline{X}_1 - \overline{X}_2}$:

▶ For $n_1 = n_2 = 3$, $s_{\overline{X}_1 - \overline{X}_2} = 4.9$.
▶ For $n_1 = n_2 = 6$, $s_{\overline{X}_1 - \overline{X}_2} = 3.5$.
▶ For $n_1 = n_2 = 9$, $s_{\overline{X}_1 - \overline{X}_2} = 2.8$.

Here we see that, as the sample size increases, the standard error of the difference decreases. Thus, for a given difference between $\overline{X}_1$ and $\overline{X}_2$, the value of t_{obs} increases as sample size becomes larger and $s_{\overline{X}_1 - \overline{X}_2}$ decreases in size. And, as t_{obs} increases, it becomes more likely that t_{obs} will fall into a rejection region and H_0 will be rejected and H_1 accepted.

In general, any treatment effect, no matter how small, may be detected if the sample size is large enough. Thus, a researcher can minimize the probability of making a Type II error by maximizing sample size. But reality must intrude here, for increasing the size of a sample is often costly and time consuming. Moreover, if it takes a sample of 1000 people in each group to detect the effect of an independent variable, then we may expect this independent variable to have a very minimal effect on behavior.

A second step in decreasing $s_{\overline{X}_1 - \overline{X}_2}$ is to reduce the variability among the scores in each group. If the scores vary less within the groups, then s^2 will decrease for each group and consequently $s_{\overline{X}_1 - \overline{X}_2}$ will also decrease. This decrease in $s_{\overline{X}_1 - \overline{X}_2}$ will lead to an increase in t_{obs} and, thus, an increase in the probability that t_{obs} will fall into a rejection region. Because of this relationship, experimenters typically carefully control the conditions under which research is conducted to minimize the variability of the scores within each group in an experiment.

Effect Size Measures

Effect size ▷ The size of the effect of an independent variable.

A statistically significant difference indicates that an independent variable has an effect on the dependent variable of the experiment, but it does not indicate the size of that effect. Thus, **effect size** measures have been developed for measuring the size of the effect of the independent variable after an experiment has been completed. One such measure is **eta squared**, represented by η^2, where η is the lowercase Greek letter *eta*. Eta squared is calculated from the t_{obs} value and degrees of freedom for t by

$$\eta^2 = \frac{t_{obs}^2}{t_{obs}^2 + df}.$$

To illustrate, in example problem 9.1, t_{obs} for the difference between the number of anagrams solved based on whether a person received a green or a red test cover, with 22 *df* was +2.439. Eta squared for this t_{obs} equals

$$\eta^2 = \frac{t_{obs}^2}{t_{obs}^2 + df} = \frac{(+2.439)^2}{(+2.439)^2 + 22} = \frac{5.949}{27.949} = .21, \text{ rounded to two decimal places.}$$

Eta squared is a measure of how much knowing the level of an independent variable that a subject received reduces the error in predicting the subject's score in the sample tested. The value of η^2 may range between .00 to 1.00. An η^2 of .00 indicates that knowing the level of an independent variable that a person received does not reduce the error variance of the dependent variable. There is no relation between the level of the independent variable and the score on the dependent variable. On the other hand, η^2 of 1.00 indicates that knowing the level of the independent variable that a person received allows perfect prediction of the subject's score. There will be no error in using the treatment group mean to predict a person's score. In practice, an η^2 of about .10 to .15 often is treated as indicating a strong treatment effect.

The *Publication Manual of the American Psychological Association* (American Psychological Association, 2001) suggests that effect size measures, such as eta squared, be included in a journal report of a statistical test. A sample report is illustrated later in this chapter. One caution is in order here, however. Authors may report a value of eta squared when a value of t is nonsignificant. In such an instance, the t test indicates there is no relationship between the independent and dependent variables; consequently, the value of eta squared reflects only a chance association of the independent and dependent variables and should not be interpreted as revealing an effect of the independent variable.

EXAMPLE PROBLEM

9.3

Calculating η^2 in an Experiment

Problem: Women in our society are surrounded daily by images of idealized beauty in magazines, television, and the Internet. What effect might these images have on eating patterns of women? Gurari, Hetts, and Strube (2006) hypothesized that women who were asked to rate advertisements featuring idealized images of female beauty would eat less junk food after seeing those advertisements than women who were asked to rate advertisements that did not have female models. They found that women in the experimental group exposed to advertisements with female models ate less candy and other junk food ($\overline{X} = 5.55$ grams) than women shown control advertisements without female models ($\overline{X} = 12.57$ grams). These means differed significantly in the direction predicted by their hypothesis, $t_{obs}(48) = 2.16$. What is the value of η^2 for the independent variable of type of advertisement on a women's consumption of junk food?

Solution: The strength of effect is given by η^2, where

$$\eta^2 = \frac{t_{obs}^2}{t_{obs}^2 + df}.$$

Substituting numerical values for t_{obs} and df,

$$\eta^2 = \frac{(2.16)^2}{(2.16)^2 + 48} = \frac{4.666}{4.666 + 48} = \frac{4.666}{52.666} = .089.$$

Conclusion: The value of η^2 indicates that knowing the advertisement condition a woman was assigned to results in a 9 percent reduction of the total variance in the study.   ▬▬

Using the *t* Statistic to Construct Confidence Intervals for the Difference Between Two Independent Population Means

A confidence interval for a population mean was defined as an interval in which we have a certain degree of confidence that the interval contains the population mean. In this chapter, we have been interested in the difference between two population means. Here we want a *confidence interval for the difference between two independent population means*, $\mu_1 - \mu_2$. The approach is similar to that used in Chapter 8, except that $\overline{X}_1 - \overline{X}_2$ is used in place of $\overline{X}$ and $s_{\overline{X}_1 - \overline{X}_2}$ is used in place of $s_{\overline{X}}$. Accordingly, the **95 percent confidence interval for the difference between two independent population means** is given by the interval from

$$(\overline{X}_1 - \overline{X}_2) - t_{.05}(s_{\overline{X}_1 - \overline{X}_2}) \text{ to } (\overline{X}_1 - \overline{X}_2) + t_{.05}(s_{\overline{X}_1 - \overline{X}_2})$$

where $\overline{X}_1 - \overline{X}_2$ = difference between the two observed sample means.
$s_{\overline{X}_1 - \overline{X}_2}$ = estimated standard error of the difference between means.
$t_{.05}$ = two-tailed value of t_{crit} at the .05 significance level with $N - 2$ degrees of freedom.

The interval given by this formula has a .95 probability of including the value of $\mu_1 - \mu_2$.
    Similarly, a **99 percent confidence interval for the difference between two independent population means** is given by the interval from

$$(\overline{X}_1 - \overline{X}_2) - t_{.01}(s_{\overline{X}_1 - \overline{X}_2}) \text{ to } (\overline{X}_1 - \overline{X}_2) + t_{.01}(s_{\overline{X}_1 - \overline{X}_2}),$$

where $t_{.01}$ is the two-tailed value of t_{crit} at the .01 significance level with $N - 2$ degrees of freedom.

To illustrate the use of these formulas, we find the 95 percent confidence interval for example problem 9.1 on the effect of a color of a cover page on the number of correct anagram solutions. Here $\overline{X}_1 = 7.8$ correct solutions, $\overline{X}_2 = 6.6$ correct solutions, and $s_{\overline{X}_1 - \overline{X}_2} = 0.492$. There are 22 degrees of freedom for this example (see example problem 9.1); thus, the two-tailed value of t_{crit} at the .05 level is 2.074. The 95 percent confidence interval for $\mu_1 - \mu_2$ is

$$(7.8 - 6.6) - (2.074)(0.492) \text{ to } (7.8 - 6.6) + (2.074)(0.492),$$

or, carrying out the mathematical operations indicated,

$$1.2 - 1.0 \text{ to } 1.2 + 1.0,$$

which equals

$$0.2 \text{ to } 2.2 \text{ solutions.}$$

The interval of 0.2 to 2.2 correct solutions has a .95 probability of including the value of $\mu_1 - \mu_2$. We can be 95 percent confident that the difference between the population means of the number of correct anagram solutions when given a green versus a red test cover is between 0.2 to 2.2 anagrams. Notice that this confidence interval does not include a value of zero solutions, the value that is implied in the null hypothesis, $H_0: \mu_1 = \mu_2$. The t_{obs} for this example was statistically significant at the .05 level, thus $H_0: \mu_1 = \mu_2$ was rejected and $H_1: \mu_1 \neq \mu_2$ was accepted. We rejected the hypothesis of a zero difference between the population means in favor of an hypothesis of a real difference between the means. The confidence interval of 0.2 to 2.2 solutions indicates that we can be 95 percent confident that the difference between the population means of the number of correct anagram solutions is between 0.2 to 2.2.

For another example of the use and interpretation of confidence intervals, consider example problem 9.2, which compared the grade point averages of students whose initials began with an A or B to students whose initials began with a C or D. The t_{obs} for this example was not statistically significant at the .05 level, thus $H_0: \mu_1 = \mu_2$ was not rejected and $H_1: \mu_1 \neq \mu_2$ was not accepted. This decision implies that there is no evidence to reject the hypothesis that the difference between the population means is zero. The 95 percent confidence interval for the difference between these population means is

$$(\overline{X}_1 - \overline{X}_2) - t_{.05}(s_{\overline{X}_1 - \overline{X}_2}) \text{ to } (\overline{X}_1 - \overline{X}_2) + t_{.05}(s_{\overline{X}_1 - \overline{X}_2}),$$

where $\overline{X}_1 = 3.2$, $\overline{X}_2 = 3.0$, $s_{\overline{X}_1 - \overline{X}_2} = 0.134$, and $t_{.05} = 2.056$. Substituting these numerical values, we obtain,

$$(3.2 - 3.0) - 2.056(0.134) \text{ to } (3.2 - 3.0) + 2.056(0.134),$$

or, -0.1 to $+.5$. Notice that this interval does include the difference of zero between the population means, a value that would occur if the null hypothesis is true. Thus, the t test and the confidence intervals provide a consistent result that the sample means differ only by chance.

What Does a *t* Test Actually Test?

The *t* test provides information needed for deciding whether a research hypothesis is or is not supported by the data of the experiment. It is important to recognize, however, that a research hypothesis is not tested directly by the *t* test. The *t* test is simply a procedure for testing the statistical hypothesis, H_0: $\mu_1 = \mu_2$. Regardless of the independent and dependent variables stated in the research hypothesis, the null and alternative hypotheses for a two-tailed *t* test are always H_0: $\mu_1 = \mu_2$ and H_1: $\mu_1 \neq \mu_2$, respectively. A research hypothesis for an experiment, however, is a statement predicting a relationship between an independent variable and a dependent variable. For example, the statement "it is expected that the number of anagram solutions for students given a red cover will be less than the number of solutions of students given a green cover" is a research hypothesis.

A statistically significant t_{obs} with a nondirectional alternative hypothesis (i.e., H_1: $\mu_1 \neq \mu_2$) does not necessarily provide support for the research hypothesis. As an illustration, consider that support for the stated research hypothesis occurs if $\overline{X}_2$ for the number of anagram solutions for people in the experimental group who received a red-covered test is significantly lower than $\overline{X}_1$ for the control group who received a green-covered test. But an $\overline{X}_2$ significantly greater than $\overline{X}_1$ does not agree with this research hypothesis. Consequently, after obtaining a statistically significant t_{obs}, we must always examine the direction of the difference between the sample means to find if it agrees or disagrees with the research hypothesis.

Statistical and Scientific Significance Revisited

In Chapter 8, we pointed out that in statistical hypothesis testing the word *significant* means only that a null hypothesis has been rejected. But a statistically significant difference between the means in an experiment is not necessarily scientifically important. The scientific importance of an experiment is determined before the data are subjected to statistical analysis. In a well-conceived and well-designed experiment, either a statistically significant or nonsignificant difference may be important scientifically. Indeed, if a particular relationship is predicted between the independent variable and the dependent variable, a failure to find that relationship empirically may have scientific importance. In a poorly designed experiment, however, in which the independent variable is confounded with an extraneous variable, even a statistically significant difference between two sample means cannot be interpreted meaningfully.

The Controversy over Statistical Hypothesis Testing

In Chapter 1, we indicated that statistical analysis of data would not be needed if there were no variability among members of a population. But such variability is a fact of life and, thus, provides the need for statistical analysis of data. Statistical hypothesis testing was developed to help scientists make decisions in the context of the variability always found in data. Although statistical hypothesis testing may seem conceptually complex to you right now, with practice and more experience, its application to data will become routine and be easily accomplished. It would seem to be a process totally devoid of controversy, but such is not the case. On the contrary, there has been a lively discussion with both critics and defenders of its use (e.g., Abelson, 1997; Cohen, 1994; Cortina and Dunlap, 1997; Frick, 1996; Hagen, 1997; Harris, 1997; Hunter, 1997; Wainer, 1999). There are varied criticisms of statistical hypothesis testing, some of which are more complex than can be given justice to in an introductory-level text. Essentially, however, many of the critiques focus about the following points:

▶ Statistical hypothesis testing tests a null hypothesis stating that H_0: $\mu_1 = \mu_2$. But it is very unlikely that such a null hypothesis will ever be exactly true.

▶ Statistical hypothesis testing imposes a dichotomous decision of either rejecting or failing to reject H_0 based on an arbitrary set value of α, usually .05.

▶ The probability of a Type II error cannot be precisely identified for any study. Thus, when an experimenter fails to reject H_0, she or he may be making a Type II error. Although behavioral scientists have generally thought Type II errors to be less important than Type I errors, this may not necessarily be true of all research problems.

▶ Statistical hypothesis testing encourages researchers to not carefully examine their data and to use computerized statistical tests they may not fully understand.

There are no simple or noncontroversial responses to these criticisms. Abelson (1997) points out that data analysis is an uncertain process that involves human judgment. All decision making regarding the outcomes of research in the behavioral sciences takes place against a background of error variation due to both measurement and sampling error, and when judging whether two means differ sufficiently to indicate the effect of a treatment, humans are not very good at taking error variation into account without using a statistical test. Two example problems in the next chapter, example problems 10.2 and 10.3, illustrate this issue. In example problem 10.2, the differences among the means in Table 10.13 look relatively large, and a quick visual judgment might lead to an erroneous decision that the independent variable had an effect. But the large amount of error variation in this experiment indicates that the most appropriate interpretation of the differences among the means is that they are due to sampling error and not the effect of the independent variable. In contrast, a visual interpretation of the means in Table 10.14 for example problem 10.3 reveals that the means do not appear to differ by much and, thus, may lead us to believe the independent variable was ineffective. But this simple inspection overlooks the small amount of error variation in these scores. The statistical test, however, takes this error variation into account and indicates to us that the difference between the means of the two groups is best accounted for by the effect of the independent variable; it is not a chance difference. Study these problems carefully when you encounter them in the next chapter.

In response to concerns raised by critics of hypothesis testing, the American Psychological Association appointed a Task Force on Statistical Inference to make recommendations regarding the use of statistical analysis in research. This task force made several recommendations relevant to introductory statistical analysis (Wilkinson & the Task Force on Statistical Inference, 1999):

▶ Researchers should thoroughly describe their data, including sample sizes and measures of central tendency and variability.

▶ Confidence intervals should routinely be provided along with effect size measures such as η^2.

▶ Researchers should be aware of what computerized data analysis programs do with the data. Using two different data analysis programs to verify results is suggested.

Along with these recommendations, we refer you back to the discussion of power earlier in this chapter. That discussion provided several recommendations for increasing the power of a research study and, thus, reducing the possibility of a Type II error.

There is no doubt that questions and criticisms of statistical hypothesis testing will continue to arise in the future. It is also likely that statistical hypothesis testing, perhaps in a modified form, will continue to be used in behavioral science research, for even its severest critics indicate there is no ready replacement for it (Cohen, 1994).

Reporting the Results of a *t* Test

Following the guidelines of the *Publication Manual of the American Psychological Association* (American Psychological Association (2001) and the Task Force on Statistical Inference (Wilkinson & the Task Force on Statistical Inference, 1999), the results of example problem 9.1 might be described in a published scientific report as follows:

> With an alpha level of .05 and a two-tailed test, the mean number of correctly solved anagrams by students who received a test booklet with a green cover ($M = 7.8$, $SD = 1.1$) was significantly greater than the mean number of correctly solved anagrams by students who received a red cover ($M = 6.6$, $SD = 1.3$), $t(22) = 2.439$, $p < .05$, $\eta^2 = .21$. The 95 percent confidence interval for the difference between the two population means is 0.2 to 2.2 correct solutions.

In this presentation,

$\alpha = .05$ Indicates the significance level selected for the test.

$t(22)$ Identifies the test statistic as the *t*. This *t* is t_{obs}; the subscript *obs* is not used. Because two groups were identified in the description, you know the *t* test is the t_{ind}. The degrees of freedom for t_{obs} are shown in parentheses; thus, scores were analyzed from 24 different subjects (because $df = N - 2$).

$= 2.439$ the value of t_{obs} (not the t_{crit} value found in Appendix C.2).

$p < .05$ Indicates the following:

    a. The probability of t_{obs} if H_0 is true is less than (or equal to) .05. This value is the probability of t_{obs} or an even more extreme value of t_{obs} if H_0 is true; it may not be the same as the value of α selected.

    b. H_0: $\mu_1 = \mu_2$ was rejected.
       H_1: $\mu_1 \neq \mu_2$ was accepted.

    c. The difference between the sample means is statistically significant.

    d. Something other than sampling error is responsible for the observed difference in the means. Because this was a controlled experiment, we infer that the difference was due to the color of the cover given the subjects.

    e. If $p > .05$ had been reported, then the greater than ($>$) sign would indicate that H_0 was not rejected and the two sample means did not differ significantly at the .05 significance level. In this instance, we would conclude that the color of the cover has no effect on the number of anagrams solved.

$\eta^2 = .21$ Proportion of variance due to the independent variable.

95 percent confidence interval 0.2 to 2.2 solutions   This confidence interval is for the difference between the two population means. Alternatively, 95 percent confidence intervals for each of the means might have been presented. Often, authors will present the standard error of the mean ($s_{\bar{X}}$, identified as *SE*) in place of a confidence interval.

Testing Your Knowledge 9.4

1. Define: effect size, η^2, power.

2. Two sets of two samples each are obtained. For set 1, $s_1 = 6.3$ and $s_2 = 7.6$. For set 2, $s_1 = 11.7$ and $s_2 = 10.3$.

   a. Which set of scores has greater error variation?

   b. If H_1 is true, which set of scores will more likely lead to a Type II error in a statistical test?

   c. Which set of scores will lead to a more powerful statistical test?

3. Which of the following two sample sizes would be expected to lead to a smaller value of $s_{\bar{X}_1 - \bar{X}_2}$ in a t test: $n_1 = n_2 = 12$ or $n_1 = n_2 = 20$? Why? Which sample size would lead to a more powerful statistical test?

4. Find η^2 for each of the following values of t_{obs}. The df for each t are presented in parentheses. Each t_{obs} is statistically significant at the .05 level with a two-tailed test.

   a. $t(8) = 2.413$

   b. $t(14) = 2.284$

   c. $t(20) = 2.174$

   d. $t(29) = 2.939$

   e. $t(60) = 2.306$

5. Distinguish between a research hypothesis and a statistical hypothesis.

6. Does a statistically significant difference necessarily mean that a scientifically important result has been found? Explain your answer.

7. The following reports of the use of t_{ind} have been adapted from results of published studies. Answer the following questions for each report:

   a. How many levels of the independent variable were used in this experiment?

   b. How many subjects were in this experiment?

   c. What is the value of the sample mean for each treatment condition?

   d. What is the value of the estimated population standard deviation for each treatment condition?

   e. What is the value of t_{crit} at the .05 significance level for a two-tailed rejection region?

   f. What is the value of t_{obs}?

   g. Do you reject or fail to reject H_0?

   h. Do you accept or not accept H_1?

   i. Is the difference between the means statistically significant or nonsignificant?

   j. To what do you attribute the observed difference in the sample means?

   Report 1: With alpha equal to .05 and a two-tailed test, a t test indicated that subjects correctly detected a larger percentage of targets while listening to the familiar poem ($M = 79.7$, $SD = 8.6$) than while listening to the unfamiliar poem ($M = 73.0$, $SD = 5.9$), $t(60) = 3.60, p < .05$.

   Report 2: With alpha equal to .05 and a two-tailed test, a t test revealed no difference in the number of words recalled after a retention interval of 5 minutes ($M = 22.8$, $SD = 5.2$) and a retention interval of 0.5 minutes ($M = 24.3$, $SD = 5.1$), $t(28) = -0.82, p > .05$.

Within-Subjects Designs and the *t* Test for Related Scores

Within-subjects design ▶ A research design in which one group of subjects is exposed to and measured under each level of an independent variable. In a within-subjects design, each person receives each treatment condition.

Our interest to this point has been with the analysis of between-subjects designs in which each level of the independent variable is given to a different group of subjects. A second type of research design is the **within-subjects design** in which a single group of subjects is exposed to and measured under each level of an independent variable. Thus, in a within-subjects design, each subject receives each treatment condition.

Consider the following example of a one-factor within-subjects design with two levels of the independent variable. There are many strategies people use for assuring accuracy in basic arithmetic tasks, including counting on one's fingers or pointing to numbers when working with them. Although such gestures are often used, there is little research on their effectiveness. Thus, Carlson, Avraamides, Cary, and Strasberg (2007) conducted several studies to examine the role that hand gestures, such as pointing to items to be counted, have in simple arithmetic tasks. In one study, they wanted to test whether requiring subjects to point when counting a set of asterisks would help or hinder accuracy with the task. They used a within-subjects design in which college students participated in two treatment conditions. In one condition (1), the students did not point to asterisks appearing on a computer screen as they counted them; in the other condition (2), they pointed to the asterisks as they counted them. Carlson et al. found that students counted correctly more often when pointing than when not pointing. Suppose you conducted a similar study with 10 college students as subjects. Each student was asked to count the number of asterisks appearing on a computer screen under two different conditions. In condition 1, the students were asked to not point to the asterisks as they counted, in condition 2, they were asked to point to each asterisk as they counted. Because the students were tested in each treatment condition, a within-subjects design was used. Suppose you found the number of trials out of 10 on which students made errors, as presented in Table 9.2. Do the mean number of trials with errors differ significantly in the two conditions? Notice that a *t* test for independent groups cannot be used to answer the question because each student contributed scores to each of the two conditions. Instead, we use a *t* test for related scores to compare the means.

The *t* Test for Related Scores

In a within-subjects design, the same subjects are measured under each treatment condition; thus, the scores in each treatment condition are related. The factors that affect a person's

TABLE 9.2	Number of counting errors of 10 subjects in a no-pointing (1) and a pointing condition (2)	
	Pointing Condition	
Subject	**No Pointing (X_1)**	**Pointing (X_2)**
Anne	3	1
Jose	2	2
Trevor	1	1
Maria	2	1
Danielle	5	4
Jakeem	3	2
Elle	2	3
Ethan	5	4
Jenna	4	1
Gabbi	3	1

score in one condition will affect that person's score in the other condition. Thus, as we have stated, the t_{ind} is not appropriate for a within-subjects design; rather, a **t test for related scores**, defined as

$$t_{\text{rel}} = \frac{\overline{X}_1 - \overline{X}_2}{s_{\overline{D}}},$$

is used, where $s_{\overline{D}}$ is the standard error of the difference between the two related means. The formula for $s_{\overline{D}}$ is

$$s_{\overline{D}} = \sqrt{\frac{s_D^2}{N_{\text{pairs}}}}$$

where D = the difference between the two scores of a subject.
s_D^2 = variance for the difference D.
N_{pairs} = the number of pairs of scores, or equivalently, the number of subjects.

Substituting the formula for $s_{\overline{D}}$, the formula for t_{rel} becomes

$$t_{\text{rel}} = \frac{\overline{X}_1 - \overline{X}_2}{\sqrt{\dfrac{s_D^2}{N_{\text{pairs}}}}}.$$

Notice that for the standard error of this t test, $s_{\overline{D}}$, we use the standard error of the difference between two related means, $\overline{X}_1$ and $\overline{X}_2$. We find $s_{\overline{D}}$ by obtaining the variance of the differences between each subject's score for each of the two treatment conditions, s_D^2. We then use s_D^2 to calculate the standard error of the difference, $s_{\overline{D}}$.

The df for t_{rel} are equal to $N_{\text{pairs}} - 1$, which represents the number of pairs of scores that are free to vary. Notice that we have returned to the upper-case N to indicate the number of subjects, but this time with the subscript of pairs, N_{pairs}. We use this subscript to remind us that we are discussing a within-subject design, and we are using the same subjects in each condition.

The application of this formula to the scores in Table 9.2 is illustrated in Table 9.3. The steps in this calculation are as follows:

1. Find $\overline{X}_1$ and $\overline{X}_2$. For the example, these values are 3.0 and 2.0 errors for the no-pointing and pointing conditions, respectively. The values for s_1 and s_2 are also shown in the table. These values are not needed for the calculation of t_{rel}, but they are necessary for reporting the results following the guidelines of the *Publication Manual of the American Psychological Association* (American Psychological Association, 2001).

2. D represents the difference between a subject's performance for both levels of the independent variable. Find this value of D for each subject by subtracting the subject's score in condition 2 from her or his score in condition 1. Maintain the algebraic sign of the difference for each subject. For example, Anne made three errors in the no-pointing condition and one error in the pointing condition. Thus, her D score is $3 - 1$ or $+2$. This step is shown in the column headed by $D = X_1 - X_2$ in Table 9.3.

3. Find the value of $\overline{D}$. For Table 9.3, the sum of the D values is $+10$. Thus, $\overline{D} = +10/10 = +1.0$.

4. The variance of the D values is found by obtaining the SS_D and then dividing SS_D by its df, $N_{\text{pairs}} - 1$. We find SS_D by first finding the difference of each person's D score

from $\overline{D}$ or $D - \overline{D}$. This step is illustrated in the column headed by $D - \overline{D}$. For example, the D for Anne's two scores is $+2$. Thus, for Anne, $D - \overline{D} = +2 - (+1) = +1$. Again, we maintain the algebraic sign of each $D - \overline{D}$ difference. The next step in obtaining SS_D is to square each of the $D - \overline{D}$ differences. This step is illustrated in the column headed by $(D - \overline{D})^2$ in the table. The sum of the $(D - \overline{D})^2$ then provides SS_D. For our example, the SS_D is 12.

5. Determine N_{pairs}. For the example, $N_{pairs} = 10$.
6. Find the variance for D, or $s_D^2 = SS_D/(N_{pairs} - 1)$. For our example, $s_D^2 = 12/9 = 1.33$.

7. Use s_D^2 to find $s_{\overline{D}} = \sqrt{\dfrac{s_D^2}{N_{pairs}}} = \sqrt{1.33/10} = 0.365$.

8. Substitute the numerical values into the equation for t_{rel}.
9. Find the df, where $df = N_{pairs} - 1$, which equals $10 - 1 = 9$.

The t_{obs} for the scores of Table 9.2 is $+2.740$. The remaining steps for using this t_{obs} are identical to those for the t_{ind}. A value of α is selected, the value of t_{crit} found from Appendix C.2, and rejection regions are located on the sampling distribution of t. If the value of t_{obs} falls into a rejection region, then

$$H_0: \mu_1 = \mu_2 \text{ is rejected, and}$$
$$H_1: \mu_1 \neq \mu_2 \text{ is accepted.}$$

TABLE						
9·3		Computation of t_{rel} on the scores of Table 9.2				

	Pointing Condition				
	No Pointing	**Pointing**			
Subject	**(X_1)**	**(X_2)**	**$D = X_1 - X_2$**	**$D - \overline{D}$**	**$(D - \overline{D})^2$**
Anne	3	1	$+2$	$+1$	1
Jose	2	2	0	-1	1
Trevor	1	1	0	-1	1
Maria	2	1	$+1$	0	0
Danielle	5	4	$+1$	0	0
Jakeem	3	2	$+1$	0	0
Elle	2	3	-1	-2	4
Ethan	5	4	$+1$	0	0
Jenna	4	1	$+3$	$+2$	4
Gabbi	3	1	$+2$	$+1$	1
	$\overline{X} = 3.0$	$\overline{X} = 2.0$	$\Sigma D = +10$	$\Sigma D - \overline{D} = 0$	$\Sigma(D - \overline{D})^2 = SS_D = 12$
	$s_1 = 1.3$	$s_2 = 1.3$	$\overline{D} = +1.0$		

$$t_{obs} = \frac{\overline{X}_1 - \overline{X}_2}{\sqrt{\dfrac{s_D^2}{N_{pairs}}}} = \frac{3.0 - 2.0}{\sqrt{\dfrac{1.33}{10}}} = \frac{+1.0}{\sqrt{0.133}}$$

$$t_{obs} = \frac{+1.0}{0.365} = +2.740 \text{ with 9 } df.$$

For 9 *df* and a .05 significance level, t_{crit} for a two-tailed rejection region is 2.262. The rejection region comprises values of t_{obs} less than or equal to -2.262 or equal to or greater than $+2.262$. The t_{obs} of $+2.740$ is greater than $+2.262$; hence, it falls into a rejection region; H_0 is rejected and H_1 accepted. The difference between the sample means is statistically significant at the .05 level. Subjects make fewer counting errors when they use a pointing gesture then when they do not.

Eta squared is found for this t_{rel} by

$$\eta^2 = \frac{t_{obs}^2}{t_{obs}^2 + df}.$$

Substituting numerical values for t_{obs} and *df*,

$$\eta^2 = \frac{(+2.740)^2}{(+2.740)^2 + 9} = .45.$$

This eta squared indicates that 45 percent of the variance in errors while counting asterisks can be attributed to whether a person pointed or did not point when counting.

Constructing Confidence Intervals for the Difference Between Two Related Population Means

The **95 percent confidence interval for the difference between two related population means** is given by the interval from

$$(\overline{X}_1 - \overline{X}_2) - t_{.05}(s_{\overline{D}}) \text{ to } (\overline{X}_1 - \overline{X}_2) + t_{.05}(s_{\overline{D}})$$

where $\overline{X}_1 - \overline{X}_2 =$ the difference between the two sample means.

$s_{\overline{D}} =$ the standard error of the mean for the difference between each $\overline{X}_1$ and $\overline{X}_2$ score.

$t_{.05} =$ the two-tailed value of t_{crit} at the .05 significance level with $N - 1$ degrees of freedom.

The interval given by this formula has a .95 probability of including the value of $\mu_1 - \mu_2$.

For the example problem, $\overline{X}_1 = 3.0$, $\overline{X}_2 = 2.0$, $N_{pairs} = 10$, $s_{\overline{D}} = 0.365$ and $t_{.05}$ for 9 degrees of freedom equals 2.262. Substituting numerical values, the 95 percent confidence interval for the difference between μ_1 and μ_2 is

$$(3.0 - 2.0) - (2.262)(0.365) \text{ to } (3.0 - 2.0) + (2.262)(0.365),$$

which equals an interval of 0.17 to 1.83 errors. The 95 percent confidence interval for the difference between the population means pointing when counting or not is 0.17 to 1.83 errors.

Testing Your Knowledge 9.5

1. Explain the difference between a between-subjects research design and a within-subjects research design.

2. More and more, people seem to be considering their cars as an extension of their office, and many traffic safety experts are concerned that the increasing distractions

are leading to more accidents. Suppose in an attempt to provide empirical evidence on this problem, you asked 11 people to drive a simulated trip under two conditions, a control condition with no distractions present and an experimental condition with the subject driving the trip while carrying on a conversation on a mobile telephone. The subjects' reaction time to a simulated event requiring braking was measured, and you obtained the following reaction times (in milliseconds):

	Condition	
Subject	Control (X_1)	Experimental (X_2)
1	426	448
2	501	552
3	525	506
4	478	507
5	537	574
6	452	491
7	394	438
8	443	477
9	491	523
10	382	413
11	572	541

Find the mean and standard deviation for each condition; then calculate t_{rel} on the scores and answer the following questions.

a. What type of research design, between-subjects or within-subjects, was used in this study?

b. State the statistical hypotheses for t_{rel} for these scores.

c. What are the *df* for this *t*?

d. What is the value of t_{crit}?

e. What are the rejection regions for t_{obs}?

f. What is the value of t_{obs}?

g. Does t_{obs} fall into a rejection region?

h. What decisions do you make about the statistical hypotheses? Do you reject or fail to reject H_0? Accept or not accept H_1?

i. Is the difference between the means statistically significant?

j. Do you conclude that the sample means are from the same or different populations?

k. Did the conditions differ significantly in their reaction times? If so, what is the direction of the difference?

l. What is the value of η^2 for this study?

m. What is the 95 percent confidence interval for the difference between the population means?

Summary

- An experiment requires:
  - Asking a scientific question and formulating a research hypothesis
  - Selecting subjects
  - Creating equivalent groups by random assignment
  - Controlling extraneous variables
  - Manipulating an independent variable
  - Measuring the dependent variable
- The t_{ind} may be used to determine if two sample means from an experiment differ significantly.
- The formula for t_{ind} is

$$t_{ind} = \frac{\overline{X}_1 - \overline{X}_2}{s_{\overline{X}_1 - \overline{X}_2}}$$

where $s_{\overline{X}_1 - \overline{X}_2}$ is the standard error of the difference between means.
- Statistical hypothesis testing with t_{ind} follows the steps common to all statistical testing.
- The power of a statistical test is the probability of rejecting H_0 when H_0 is false.
- Factors affecting power of the t test include the magnitude of the effect induced by the independent variable, the amount of variability in the measure of the dependent variable, and sample size.

- Eta squared (η^2) is a measure of effect size in the sample measured and is calculated from t_{obs}.
- Eta squared indicates the proportion of the total variation in the dependent variable accounted for by the independent variable.
- The 95 percent confidence interval for the difference between two independent population means is given by the interval from

$$(\overline{X}_1 - \overline{X}_2) - t_{.05}(s_{\overline{X}_1 - \overline{X}_2}) \text{ to } (\overline{X}_1 - \overline{X}_2) + t_{.05}(s_{\overline{X}_1 - \overline{X}_2}).$$

- In a within-subjects design, a single group of subjects is exposed to all levels of each independent variable.
- The t_{rel} may be used when there are two levels of an independent variable in a one-factor within-subjects design.
- The formula for t_{rel} is

$$t_{rel} = \frac{\overline{X}_1 - \overline{X}_2}{s_{\overline{D}}}$$

where $s_{\overline{D}}$ is the standard error of the difference between each $\overline{X}_1$ and $\overline{X}_2$ score.
- The 95 percent confidence interval for the difference between two related population means is given by the interval from

$$(\overline{X}_1 - \overline{X}_2) - t_{.05}(s_{\overline{D}}) \text{ to } (\overline{X}_1 - \overline{X}_2) + t_{.05}(s_{\overline{D}}).$$

Key Terms and Symbols

between-subjects design (194)
chance difference (199)
confidence interval for the difference between two population means (217)
confound (196)
confounded experiment (196)
convenience sampling (194)
D (224)
dependent variable (196)
directional test (206)
effect size (216)
equivalent groups (194)
estimated standard error of the difference between means ($s_{\overline{X}_1 - \overline{X}_2}$) (202)

eta squared (η^2) (216)
experiment (192)
extraneous variable (196)
factor (195)
independent variable (195)
level of an independent variable (195)
95 percent confidence interval for the difference between two independent population means (217)
99 percent confidence interval for the difference between two independent population means (217)
nondirectional test (205)
one-factor between-subjects design (195)

one-tailed test (206)
placebo control (196)
power (215)
random assignment (195)
random sampling (194)
research hypothesis (192)
robustness (209)
s_D (224)
$s_{\overline{D}}$ (224)
s^2_{pooled} (202)
sampling distribution of the difference between means (200)
standard error of the difference between means (202)

standard error of the difference between related means (224)

t_{crit} (204)

t test for related scores (t_{rel}) (224)

t test for two independent groups (t_{ind}) (200)

t_{obs} (204)

two-tailed test (205)

within-subjects design (223)

 ## Review Questions

1. Suppose that you were interested in finding if noise has any effect on blood pressure. You randomly assigned 22 individuals to either a control or an experimental group ($n_1 = n_2$). Subjects in the quiet group (1) relaxed in comfortable chairs in a quiet room for 30 minutes. At the end of the 30 minutes you measured their systolic blood pressure (i.e., the blood pressure during the contraction of the heart). Subjects in the noise group (2) also sat in the chairs for 30 minutes. During the 30-minute wait, however, they listened to a recording of rush hour traffic noise from a large city. After listening to the noise for 30 minutes, the systolic blood pressure of these subjects was also recorded. Suppose that you obtained the following blood pressures in millimeters of mercury.

Group	
Quiet (X_1)	Noise (X_2)
106	141
117	136
124	124
129	139
115	121
131	119
121	147
115	128
128	115
136	134
127	140

a. What type of research design, between-subjects or within-subjects, was used in this study?

b. Find the mean and standard deviation for each group. Then use a t test to answer the following question: Does noise affect systolic blood pressure? Use a two-tailed test and a .05 significance level.

c. What is the value of η^2 for this experiment? What proportion of the variance in the dependent variable can be accounted for by knowing the level of the independent variable?

d. Find the 95 percent confidence interval for the difference between the two population means.

e. Describe your results following the example illustrated in the Reporting the Results of a t Test section of this chapter.

2. Suppose that you obtained the blood pressures given next for question 1. Does noise affect systolic blood pressure? Use a .05 significance level and a two-tailed test.

Group	
Quiet (X_1)	Noise (X_2)
110	116
114	111
106	120
117	119
108	123
116	108
120	122
111	115
115	117
109	101
118	116

3. Text messaging is an increasingly popular form of communication. But, as with all written communication, a question arises about how emotional content is perceived in these messages. One group of students hypothesized that when reading a text message thought to be from a female, both males and females would read more emotion into the message than if they thought the text message was from a male. To test this hypothesis, they selected eight students who read 12 text messages, six that they believed came from males and six they believed came from females. The subjects were asked to rate how emotional each message was using a scale from 1 (not at all emotional) to 7 (extremely emotional). The messages were designed and tested to be low in amounts of emotion. Immediately before the message appeared on the screen, the students were told whether the message was from a male or a female. The students were then asked to rate the amount of emotion they believed was present in the message. The ratings of each subject for the male and female messages are given next.

Subject	Message From	
	Female (X_1)	Male (X_2)
1	14	11
2	12	13
3	18	17
4	19	18
5	18	14
6	16	10
7	16	12
8	15	13

a. What type of research design, between-subjects or within-subjects, was used in this study?

b. Find the mean and standard deviation for each group. Then use a t test to answer the following question: Do students who are reading text messages interpret text messages from females as containing more emotion than text messages from males? Use a two-tailed test and a .05 significance level.

c. What is the value of η^2 for this study? What proportion of the variance in the dependent variable can be accounted for by knowing the level of the independent variable?

d. Find the 95 percent confidence interval for the difference between the two population means.

e. Describe your results following the example illustrated in the Reporting the Results of a *t* Test section of this chapter.

4. It has long been known that learning large amounts of new information over a period of time (i.e., distributed learning) often results in better retention of that material than learning the material all at one time (i.e., massed learning). To demonstrate this phenomenon to his students, Balch (2006) conducted a study where students were asked to use massed learning or distributed learning to learn a list of words. Suppose the following study was done. Twenty-four students were selected for a study where they were asked to learn a list of words. The students were randomly assigned to two groups of 12 students each, a distributed learning group and a massed learning group. Each group heard the same list of words twice, however, the massed learning group heard each word back-to-back, whereas the distributed learning group heard each word twice, but in a random order. Following a delay, the students' memory for the list of words was tested. The number of words recalled for each group is listed below.

Learning Condition	
Distributed (X_1)	Massed (X_2)
7	6
8	5
6	6
7	2
5	7
7	4
8	7
7	4
5	6
7	7
8	6
9	6

a. What type of research design, between-subjects or within-subjects, was used in this study?

b. Find the mean and standard deviation for each treatment condition. Then use a *t* test to answer the question: Does distributed learning lead to better retention of a list of words than massed learning? Use a two-tailed test and a .05 significance level.

c. What is the value of η^2 for this study? What proportion of the variance in the dependent variable can be accounted for by knowing the level of the independent variable?

d. Find the 95 percent confidence interval for the difference between the two population means.

e. Describe your results following the example illustrated in the Reporting the Results of a *t* Test section of this chapter.

5. It often seems that when people are upset or under stress, they are more likely to make errors in pronunciation. To empirically test this observation, a group of students hypothesized that discussing a stressful topic would decrease the likelihood of someone clearly enunciating their words. To test this hypothesis, they first recorded students talking about a non-stressful topic, then they recorded the same students talking about a stressful topic. They then identified the number of words that were not fully enunciated for the first 100 words each subject uttered in each condition. The results from the 11 students participating in this study are presented below.

Student	Type of Topic	
	Non stressful (X_1)	Stressful (X_2)
1	1	2
2	2	2
3	0	3
4	5	6
5	3	2
6	2	3
7	1	3
8	4	5
9	6	7
10	7	7
11	2	4

a. What type of research design, between-subjects or within-subjects, was used in this study?

b. Find the mean and standard deviation for each treatment condition. Then, use a t test to answer this question: Does discussing a stressful topic increase the number of errors a person makes when pronouncing words? Use a two-tailed test and a .05 significance level.

c. What is the value of η^2 for this study? What proportion of the variance in the dependent variable can be accounted for by knowing the level of the independent variable?

d. Find the 95 percent confidence interval for the difference between the two population means.

e. Describe your results following the example illustrated in the Reporting the Results of a t Test section of this chapter.

6. Example problem 9.3 introduced the research of Gurari et al. (2006) regarding the effect on women of images of idealized beauty in magazines, television, and the Internet. Several students wanted to investigate this question by comparing the effects on a person's self-image of viewing photographs of "regular" people versus photographs of idealized feminine beauty. After viewing the photographs of either regular or "media

image" people, students were provided with a 10-question self-image measure and asked to respond to each question with a 0 to 3 response. The higher the score reported by the student, the higher the student's self-image. The 34 subjects in the control group who saw standard photographs had a mean self-image rating of 18.7 with $s_1 = 5.5$, whereas the 37 subjects who saw the media type images had a mean self-image rating of 18.0 with $s_2 = 5.4$.

a. What type of research design, between-subjects or within-subjects, was used in this study?

b. Use a t test to answer this question: Do the self images differ significantly? Use a two-tailed test and a .05 significance level.

c. Why would you not calculate a value of η^2 for this study?

d. Find the 95 percent confidence interval for the difference between the two population means.

e. Describe your results following the example illustrated in the Reporting the Results of a t Test section of this chapter.

7. Many students experience test anxiety that severely interferes with their academic performance. Suppose a college counselor hypothesized that listening to relaxing music before an examination would reduce this anxiety. To test this hypothesis, the therapist selected 34 students with severe test anxiety from a large introductory course. The students were randomly assigned to either a control or an experimental group, with an equal number of subjects in each group. Subjects in the control group spent the hour before the next exam in the course sitting in a quiet lounge where they read magazines. Subjects in the experimental group spent the hour listening to relaxing music. The mean exam grade for the control group was 73.2 ($s_1 = 8.4$) and the mean grade for the experimental group was 75.6 ($s_2 = 8.7$).

a. What type of research design, between-subjects or within-subjects, was used in this study?

b. Use a t test to answer this question: Did the groups differ significantly on the mean test grades? Use a two-tailed test and a .05 significance level.

c. Why would you not calculate a value of η^2 for this study?

d. Describe your results following the example illustrated in the Reporting the Results of a t Test section of this chapter.

8. Motivational speakers want to be perceived as trustworthy. One hypothesis is that speakers who exhibit immediacy behaviors such as making eye contact, smiling, and leaning forward will be perceived as more trustworthy than those who do not engage in these behaviors. To test this research hypothesis, suppose a psychologist created two equivalent groups of 13 subjects each and each group listened to a speaker giving a short motivational speech. For people in a non-immediacy group (1), the speaker did not engage in any immediacy behaviors while giving the speech. For the immediacy group (2), however, the speaker made eye contact, smiled, and leaned forward toward the audience while giving the speech. After the speech was given, subjects in both groups rated the speaker on a scale of trustworthiness ranging from 1 (not at all trustworthy) to 9 (highly trustworthy). Suppose the following ratings were obtained.

Immediacy Condition	
No Immediacy Behaviors (X_1)	Immediacy Behaviors (X_2)
4	7
5	6
3	9
4	8
6	8
7	7
7	6
4	4
3	5
5	8
6	7
3	6
5	8

a. What type of research design, between-subjects or within-subjects, was used in this study?

b. Find the mean and standard deviation for each treatment condition. Then, use a *t* test to answer the question: Is rated trustworthiness affected by the immediacy behaviors of the speaker? Use a two-tailed test and a .05 significance level.

c. What is the value of η^2 for this study? What proportion of the variance in the dependent variable can be accounted for by knowing the level of the independent variable?

d. Find the 95 percent confidence interval for the difference between the two population means.

e. Describe your results following the example illustrated in the Reporting the Results of a *t* Test section of this chapter.

knowledge

A Look at a Problem Many problems investigated by behavioral scientists require more than one study to find an answer. This example illustrates such a problem. As you answer the questions below, remember, there are often several different ways to investigate a problem.

Professors and students alike both agree on two points regarding textbooks: they are expensive, and they are necessary for success in college. A dean of students at a small liberal arts college was concerned that first-year students at her college were not budgeting enough money for college textbooks. She believed that incoming students were considerably underestimating what they would spend on textbooks for their first semester. Since the college held a new student orientation in June prior to students coming to campus in fall, she decided to see if she was correct in this belief that incoming first-year students were underestimating the true cost of textbooks. Then, if she was correct in her belief, she wanted to determine if an instructional activity would change these estimates.

1. The scenario we have presented includes two research hypotheses expressed by the dean of students. What are these hypotheses?

2. How many studies will the dean of students have to complete in order to test these hypotheses?

3. The dean expressed a belief that incoming students underestimate the actual cost of textbooks for their first semester. What information would the dean need to collect to empirically test this belief?

PART B

Your Turn: Selecting Your Research Tools The dean, recognizing that she needed help with this project, asked you to assist her. Consider the first question, that of whether incoming first-year students underestimate the cost of their textbooks. The dean asked you to obtain estimates of textbook costs for the first semester from incoming students. Because time was limited, however, you could get estimates from only a portion of the 451 incoming new students. Answer the following questions for this task assigned you.

1. Which of the research methods presented in Chapter 1 would you use to obtain the estimates? Why?

2. Given that you could select only some of the incoming students to give you estimates, would the estimates you obtain be based on a sample or a population?

3. How would you select the students to give you the estimates? What sample size would you use?

4. How would you have the students selected give you estimates?
   a. What level of measurement would these estimates represent?
   b. Would these estimates be qualitative or quantitative data?
   c. Would these estimates be discrete or continuous data?

5. What statistic would you expect to provide the most representative measure of central tendency for these estimates? What statistic would you use to present a measure of variability for these estimates?

6. While investigating the cost of textbooks, the dean had obtained the actual amount spent on textbooks for the first semester of the previous year from each of the 432 incoming students of that year. Do these values represent a sample or a population?

7. If you want to compare the estimates you obtained from the new incoming students to the values of the students from the previous year, what statistical test would you use? Explain why you would use this test.

Consider now the second question posed by the dean: would an instructional activity change the estimates given by incoming students? Suppose the dean gave a presentation regarding the cost of textbooks to the incoming students who had given you estimates. During this presentation, she held up books from typical first-year classes, such as Introduction to Biology, Math 1, or General Psychology, telling the price of each book. In addition, she informed the students what the typical student spent last year on textbooks in the first semester. Included in this presentation were testimonials from students entering their second year regarding why they wish they had spent their money more wisely during their first year in college and why they find textbooks helpful for their academic success. After this presentation, the dean asked the same incoming students who had given you estimates to complete the same survey again stating how much they now expect to spend on textbooks.

8. What type of a research design is the dean using here? Remember, the students were measured twice, before and after the presentation.

9. What is the independent variable for this research design?

10. What is the dependent variable for this research design?

11. If the dean asks you to compare the two estimates of this group of students, what statistical test will you choose? Why would you choose this test?

PART C

Using Your Statistical Tools

1. For the 432 students of the previous year, the dean found the following values for the amount spent on texts for the first semester:

$$\Sigma X = \$196,560.00$$
$$SS = 10,423,641.00$$

Calculate the mean and standard deviation for these estimates. Do these values represent statistics or parameters? Explain your answer.

2. In your survey, you selected 100 incoming first-year students from the total 451 incoming students to give you their estimates and obtained the following values. The subscripted 1 indicates this was the first estimate given by these students.

$$n_1 = 100$$
$$\Sigma X_1 = \$34,155.00$$
$$SS_1 = 1,250,050.00$$

Calculate the mean and standard deviation for these estimates. Do the values you have calculated represent statistics or parameters? Explain your answer.

3. Setting alpha at .05 and using a two-tailed test, compare the mean estimate of the 100 incoming first-year students with the mean of the 432 previous-year students. Remember, the 432 students compose the entire class of incoming students from the previous year. Explain why you chose the test you did. Does the outcome of this test support the dean's belief that first-year students underestimate how much textbooks will cost in their first semester are failing to budget enough money for textbooks?

Recall that the same 100 students that you obtained estimates from were asked to give estimates again after they had heard the dean's presentation on the cost of textbooks. The following values were obtained for these estimates. The subscripted 2 indicates this was the second estimate given by these students.

$$n_2 = 100$$
$$\Sigma X_2 = \$40,815.00$$
$$SS_2 = 1,580,578.00$$
$$SS_D = 1,890,045.00$$

4. Calculate the mean and standard deviation for these estimates.

5. Compare the two estimates to determine if they differ significantly. Explain which statistical test you will use.

6. Does the outcome of the statistical test provide any support for the hypothesis that the presentation on the cost of textbooks changed the students' estimates? Write a brief summary of your results following the guidelines of the *Publication Manual of the American Psychological Association* (American Psychological Association, 2001). Include a measure of effect size in your description.

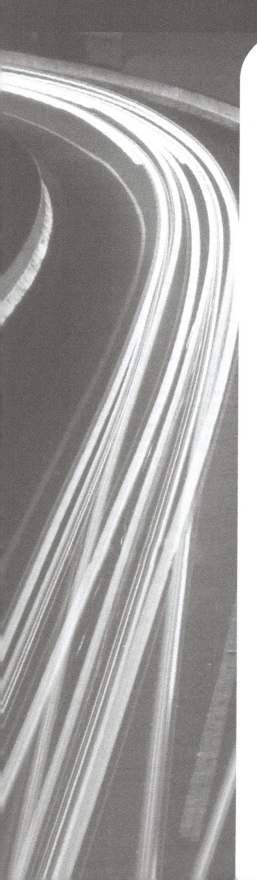

One-Factor Between-Subjects Analysis of Variance

T he *t* test introduced many of the important concepts of statistical hypothesis testing in behavioral science research. But the *t* test possesses a major limitation; it can be used to compare the means from only two groups at a time. Many behavioral science experiments, however, are multilevel designs. A **one-factor multilevel design** (also called a *one-way multilevel design*) is an experiment with one independent variable and three or more levels of that independent variable. For these designs, a statistical technique known as **analysis of variance** (abbreviated **ANOVA**) is used as a statistical hypothesis test. Analysis of variance is the most widely used statistical test in psychological research. It can be used for both between-subjects and within-subjects designs and for designs in which two or more independent variables are varied. For a design with one independent variable with only two levels, analysis of variance may be used in place of the *t* test. This chapter presents the analysis of variance for the one-factor between-subjects multilevel design, the design in which one independent variable is manipulated and each level of the independent variable is given to a different group of subjects. Its uses in other designs are presented in Chapters 11 and 12. Let us consider an example of an experiment requiring analysis of variance.

One-factor multilevel design ▷
An experiment with one independent variable and three or more levels of that independent variable.

Analysis of variance (ANOVA) ▷
A statistical test used to analyze multilevel designs.

An Example One-Factor Multilevel Design

As the end of another semester rapidly approaches, thoughts of sleep-deprived nights spent studying for final exams arise for many students. For generations, students have attempted to prepare for final exams by foregoing sleep for studying, yet several studies have demonstrated that sleep deprivation can decrease intellectual performance. One such study (Wertz, Wright, Ronda, & Czeisler, 2006) investigated how people perform on a series of addition tests over a 26-hour time period without sleep. In general, people who just woke up did poorly, as did people who were up for more than 24 hours. So, waiting to study until the night before an exam and foregoing sleep to study for a test that requires calculations may not be a good idea. However, many tests require remembering verbal materials rather than performing mathematical calculations. Moreover, seldom is anyone asked to complete an exam within a few minutes after waking. Suppose, then, that we wanted to investigate the effect of sleep deprivation upon memory more fully and designed the following experiment.

To determine the effect of sleep deprivation on recalling a list of words, we manipulated the independent variable of length of time since waking from a standard night's sleep (factor *A*) over three levels: 2 hours (A_1), 24 hours (A_2), and 36 hours (A_3) on the performance of a memory task. Because the analysis of variance allows us to use more than one independent variable, we will now start to identify independent variables as *factors*, such as factor *A* or factor *B*, if there is a second independent variable, with the levels of factor *A* identified as A_1, A_2, A_3, for as many levels of the independent variable as are used. We randomly assigned a total of 15 subjects to one of the three levels of length of time awake (2, 24, or 36 hours) when performing the task to form three equivalent groups of 5 subjects each. After the appropriate length of time awake, the subjects in each group were given a list of 20 unrelated but common words to remember. After viewing each of the 20 words for four seconds, each subject was asked to orally recall as many of the words as possible. The number of words recalled by each subject, the mean and standard deviation for each group, and the grand mean for the scores are presented in Table 10.1. The **grand mean**, identified as $\overline{X}_G$, is the mean of all 15 scores in the experiment. Is the number of words recalled affected by how long a subject has been awake before learning the list? To answer this question, we use the one-factor between-subjects analysis of variance.

Grand mean ▷ The mean of all scores in an experiment.

TABLE 10.1	Hypothetical scores for number of words recalled as a function of the length of time awake. The mean ($\overline{X}_A$) and standard deviation (s_A) are provided for each condition. $\overline{X}_G$ is the grand mean of the 15 scores.

	Length of Time Awake (Factor A)			
	2 hours (A_1)	24 hours (A_2)	36 hours (A_3)	
	19	14	15	
	13	13	10	
	16	16	11	
	17	12	12	
	20	10	12	
$\overline{X}_A$	17.0	13.0	12.0	$\overline{X}_G = 14.0$
s_A	2.7	2.2	1.9	

Between-Groups and Within-Groups Variation

Mean square ▶ The name used for a variance in the analysis of variance.

The analysis of variance for a one-factor between-subjects design breaks down the total variation in the scores of an experiment into two parts, often called *sources*: (1) a variance that varies with both the systematic effect of an independent variable and sampling error among the group means and (2) a variance that varies only with the within-groups error variation. Recall that a variance is essentially the average or mean of a sum of squares. As such, in the analysis of variance, a variance is called a *mean square*. **Mean square** (abbreviated *MS*) is another term for a variance, and it is the name used in analysis of variance.

Figure 10.1 helps to conceptualize these variances. Panel (a) of this figure presents a frequency distribution of all 15 scores from Table 10.1. The total variation of these scores is the variance of the scores around the grand mean of 14.0. Panels (b), (c), and (d) present frequency distributions of the scores within each group for the 2 hours awake, 24 hours awake, and 36 hours awake groups, respectively. Notice that although the subjects within each group received the same treatment condition, the scores within a group vary about the group mean. The within-groups variation is given by the variance of the scores around their respective group means. In analysis of variance, this variation is called **within-groups error variance**, or simply *error variance*, and is measured by MS_{Error}. The term *error* is used to indicate that scores within a group are not all identical, even though all subjects within a group received the same treatment. Because all of the subjects within a group were treated the same, it is believed that the only reason their scores would differ is due to individual differences in each subject. That is, any variability occurring within a group is believed to be caused simply by sampling error.

Within-groups error variance ▶ The variance of the scores in a group calculated about the group mean.

The variability between groups is reflected in the differences of the group means (i.e., $\overline{X}_{A_1}$, $\overline{X}_{A_2}$, and $\overline{X}_{A_3}$) from the grand mean, $\overline{X}_G$. This variation in group means is called **between-groups variance** and is measured by MS_A.

Between-groups variance ▶ The variance calculated using the variation of the group means about the grand mean.

The group means in an experiment may differ from each other for two reasons: (1) the effect of an independent variable and (2) sampling error. Thus, MS_A reflects systematic

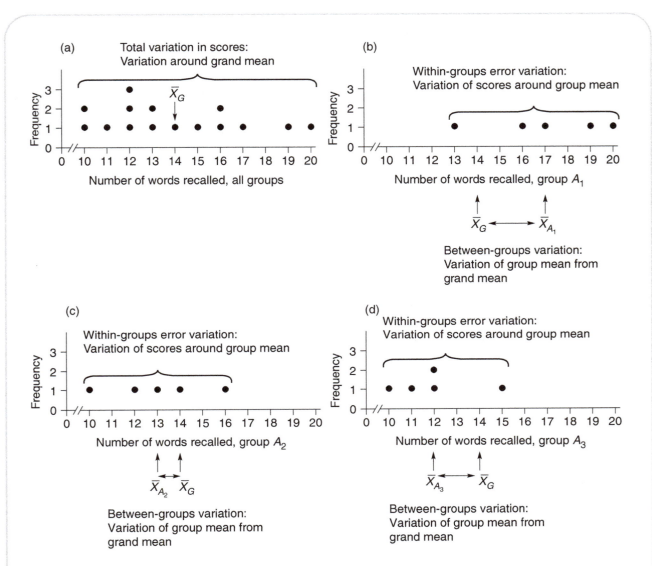

Figure 10.1 (a) A frequency distribution of all 15 scores from Table 10.1. (b) A frequency distribution of the 2 hours awake group (A_1) scores. (c) A frequency distribution of the 24 hours awake group (A_2) scores. (d) A frequency distribution of the 36 hours awake group (A_3) scores.

variation among the means of the treatment groups due to the effect of the independent variable and variation due to sampling error. In the example experiment, the group means $\overline{X}_{A_1}$, $\overline{X}_{A_2}$, and $\overline{X}_{A_3}$ will differ from each other if the length of time since waking affects recall, but they will differ also simply due to sampling error.

The sorting of the total variation into between-groups variance and within-groups error variance results in a test statistic called F, named after Sir Ronald A. Fisher (1890–1962), a British statistician who developed the concepts of analysis of variance. The F statistic is a ratio of MS_A to MS_{Error} and is expressed as

$$F = \frac{MS_A}{MS_{Error}}.$$

The numerator of the F statistic, MS_A, measures the effect of the independent variable as well as sampling error among the group means. The denominator, MS_{Error}, measures only error variation of scores within treatment conditions. If the independent variable has no effect, then the variation among the treatment group means will be due only to sampling error. Consequently, MS_A and MS_{Error} will be about the same, and F will be about 1.00. But if the independent variable has an effect, it will increase the differences among sample means beyond the differences expected from sampling error alone. In this instance, the between-groups variance of the numerator, MS_A, will be greater than the within-groups variance of the denominator, MS_{Error}, and the F ratio will be larger than 1.00. Thus, F increases in value as a treatment has an effect. Accordingly, the F statistic provides the basis for a statistical hypothesis test.

Obtaining the *F* Statistic

In the following section we derive the variances that enter into F in order to provide a conceptual understanding of ANOVA. If you were to perform an analysis of variance on an actual set of data, you would use a computer data analysis program, such as SPSS or Minitab.

The F statistic requires two measures of the variability of scores, MS_A and MS_{Error}. In Chapter 5, we defined a variance, or a MS, as $SS/(n-1)$, where SS stands for sum of squares. The denominator, $n-1$, corresponds to the degrees of freedom (df) involved in obtaining the variance estimate. Thus, the general formula for a variance providing an unbiased estimate of the population variance is

$$MS = SS/df.$$

To obtain MS_A and MS_{Error}, we find SS_A and SS_{Error}, respectively, from the scores and then divide each sum of squares by its df. The first step, obtaining the sums of squares, begins by partitioning a score.

Partitioning a Score

The analysis of variance sorts the total variation of the scores in an experiment into between-groups and within-groups variances by assuming a simple model for a subject's score. Although the example problem uses only three levels of an independent variable, the model introduced here applies to the analysis of variance for any number of levels of a one-factor between-subjects design.

The scores in Table 10.1 are represented symbolically in Table 10.2. The symbols are similar to those used to this point. The independent variable is identified as **factor *A***, with three levels, A_1, A_2, and A_3. The letter ***a*** represents the number of levels of factor A. For Tables 10.1 and 10.2, $a = 3$. A score is represented by X_{ij}, where the subscript i represents a number identifying the subject within a group and the subscript j represents the number of the group, A_1, A_2, or A_3. For example, X_{52} is the fifth subject in group A_2. In Table 10.1, this score is 10, or $X_{52} = 10$. When it is not necessary to identify a specific subject, we drop the

a ▶ The number of levels of factor A.

TABLE 10.2	Notational representation of scores from the hypothetical experiment in Table 10.1 with three levels of an independent variable, factor A. The means for each level of factor A are represented by $\overline{X}_A$ and the grand mean by $\overline{X}_G$.

	Factor A	
A_1	A_2	A_3
X_{11}	X_{12}	X_{13}
X_{21}	X_{22}	X_{23}
X_{31}	X_{32}	X_{33}
X_{41}	X_{42}	X_{43}
X_{51}	X_{52}	X_{53}
$\overline{X}_{A_1}$	$\overline{X}_{A_2}$	$\overline{X}_{A_3}$ $\quad\quad \overline{X}_G$

n_A ▶ Number of scores in a level of a one-factor design.

ij subscripts and simply use X. The sample means for each level of the independent variable are indicated by $\overline{X}_{A_1}, \overline{X}_{A_2}$, and $\overline{X}_{A_3}$ or, generally, by $\overline{X}_A$. The grand mean is labeled $\overline{X}_G$. The number of scores in a level of the independent variable is $\overline{X}_{A_1}, \overline{X}_{A_2}$, and $\overline{X}_{A_3}$, represented by n_A, and the total number of scores in the experiment is represented by N. For Table 10.1, $n_{A_1} = 5, n_{A_2} = 5, n_{A_3} = 5, N = 15, \overline{X}_{A_1} = 17.0, \overline{X}_{A_2} = 13.0, \overline{X}_{A_3} = 12.0$, and $\overline{X}_G = 14.0$. Although analysis of variance does not require an equal number of scores in each treatment condition, having equal numbers simplifies the computations needed. All the examples in the chapter use an equal number of scores in each treatment condition.

The analysis of variance takes the total variation of a score, that is, the total amount by which a score (i.e., X_{ij}) differs from the grand mean of the scores (i.e., $\overline{X}_G$), and partitions, or separates, this total difference into two parts. One part, which becomes the between-groups variance (i.e., MS_A), varies with an effect of the independent variable and sampling error. The other part, which measures the error of individual scores about their group mean, becomes the within-groups error variance (i.e., MS_{Error}). This model for representing a score can be expressed as

$$\text{Total variation in a score} = \text{Variation due to factor } A \text{ plus sampling error} + \text{Variation due to within-groups error} \quad (10.1)$$

In terms of scores, this equation can be written as

$$X - \overline{X}_G = (\overline{X}_A - \overline{X}_G) + (X - \overline{X}_A)$$

Difference of a score from the grand mean = Difference of the treatment group mean from the grand mean + Difference of the score from its treatment group mean   (10.2)

We examine each part of equation 10.2.

Total Variation

The difference of a score from the grand mean (i.e., $X - \overline{X}_G$) is the total variation of that score. As equation 10.2 indicates, a part of this variation is due to the effect of the independent variable and a part of it is due to error variation.

Variation Due to the Effect of the Independent Variable and Sampling Error

The difference between a group mean and the grand mean (i.e., $\overline{X}_A - \overline{X}_G$) varies with the effect of an independent variable and with sampling error. Accordingly, it enters into the computation of MS_A.

Effect of the Independent Variable. The analysis of variance uses the difference between each group mean and the grand mean to measure the effect of the independent variable. These differences will increase with an effect of the independent variable. A numerical illustration helps to clarify this important point.

Table 10.3 presents three possible outcomes of an experiment involving only three scores in each of two treatment groups. In panel (a) of this table, no treatment effect is present. Each group mean is equal to the grand mean. Furthermore, each of the two $\overline{X}_A - \overline{X}_G$ differences is equal to zero. A treatment effect of +2 is added to the scores of A_2 in panel (b); thus, neither group mean is equal to the grand mean. This treatment effect of +2 is represented by a value of -1 for the $\overline{X}_{A_1} - \overline{X}_G$ difference and a value of $+1$ for the $\overline{X}_{A_2} - \overline{X}_G$ difference. Panel (c) presents a treatment effect of +6 added to the scores of A_2. In the analysis of variance, this effect is broken into a -3 for the $\overline{X}_{A_1} - \overline{X}_G$ difference

TABLE
10.3

Demonstration that $\overline{X}_A - \overline{X}_G$ responds to the effect of an independent variable in an experiment. Treatment means are represented by $\overline{X}_A$ and the grand mean for each set of scores by $\overline{X}_G$. The difference between each treatment group mean and the grand mean is shown at the bottom of each set of scores.

Panel (a) scores: No treatment effect is present.
Panel (b) scores: A treatment effect of +2 is present.
Panel (c) scores: A treatment effect of +6 is present.

	(a)		(b)		(c)	
	A_1	A_2	A_1	A_2	A_1	A_2
	11	12	11	14	11	18
	12	13	12	15	12	19
	$\underline{13}$	$\underline{11}$	$\underline{13}$	$\underline{13}$	$\underline{13}$	$\underline{17}$
$\overline{X}_A$	12	12	12	14	12	18
$\overline{X}_G$	12		13		15	
	$\overline{X}_{A_1} - \overline{X}_G = 0$		$\overline{X}_{A_1} - \overline{X}_G = -1$		$\overline{X}_{A_1} - \overline{X}_G = -3$	
	$\overline{X}_{A_2} - \overline{X}_G = 0$		$\overline{X}_{A_2} - \overline{X}_G = +1$		$\overline{X}_{A_2} - \overline{X}_G = +3$	

and a value of $+3$ for the $\overline{X}_{A_2} - \overline{X}_G$ difference. Notice from this illustration that, if a treatment has an effect and causes the group means to differ from each other, the effect will be reflected in the value of the $\overline{X}_A - \overline{X}_G$ differences that can be calculated in an experiment.

Sampling Error.   In addition to any treatment effect, the group means also differ from each other because of sampling error. Even if the independent variable has no effect, we expect a group mean to differ somewhat from the grand mean simply because of sampling error. Thus, any effect of the independent variable in an experiment occurs against a background of sampling error.

Variation Due to Within-Groups Error
The difference of an individual score from its treatment group mean (i.e., $X - \overline{X}_A$) enters into the computation of MS_{Error}. It varies only with within-groups error variation in the experiment. In fact, this difference was used in Chapter 5 as the numerator of the standard deviation and variance, measures of error variation among scores within a group. The numerical value of this difference does not vary with an effect of an independent variable. Because any effect of the independent variable is assumed to equally increase or decrease the scores of all subjects receiving a particular treatment, the treatment group mean will change by an equal amount. Thus, $X - \overline{X}_A$ will remain constant regardless of the effect of an independent variable. For example, for the second subject in A_2 of Table 10.3 [i.e., the score represented by $X_{22} = 13$ in panel (a)], the $X - \overline{X}_A$ difference remains a $+1$ over all panels of the table regardless of the absence or presence of a treatment effect. Thus, the values of $X - \overline{X}_A$ reflect only error variation among the scores within a treatment condition.

Obtaining Mean Squares from Partitioned Scores

Partitioning or breaking a score into parts that measure between-groups and within-groups variation establishes the basis for obtaining the MS_A and MS_{Error} needed for the F statistic. Recall from Chapter 5 that the estimated population variance is given by

$$s^2 = \frac{\sum(X - \overline{X})^2}{N - 1}.$$

Notice that each term in equation 10.2 resembles the numerator of a variance. By using MS in place of s^2, *sum of squares* (*SS*) to represent $\sum(X - \overline{X})^2$, and *df* to represent $N - 1$, this variance may be expressed as

$$MS = \frac{SS}{df}.$$

This formula for the variance suggests that if each difference represented in equation 10.2 were squared for each subject and then summed over all scores in an experiment, the result would be a sum of squared differences, or *SS*, the numerator of a mean square. From equation 10.2, three *SS* terms can be obtained. The term $X - \overline{X}_G$ leads to $\mathbf{SS_{Total}}$, which represents the total difference of scores from the grand mean. The $\overline{X}_A - \overline{X}_G$ difference leads to SS_A, which is a measure of between-group variation due to an effect of the independent variable and sampling error. Finally, $X - \overline{X}_A$ leads to SS_{Error}, which is a measure of within-group error variation in the experiment.

Obtaining the Three Sums of Squares

We illustrate how equation 10.2 may be used to find these sums of squares by partitioning the score of subject 1 of group A_1 (i.e., X_{11}) of Table 10.1, which is 19. For this score, equation 10.2 becomes

$$X_{11} - \overline{X}_G = (\overline{X}_{A_1} - \overline{X}_G) + (X_{11} - \overline{X}_{A_1}).$$

Substituting the appropriate numerical values for $X_{11}, \overline{X}_{A_1}$, and $\overline{X}_G$ leads to

$$19.0 - 14.0 = (17.0 - 14.0) + (19.0 - 17.0),$$
$$(+5.0) \quad = \quad (+3.0) \quad + \quad (+2.0).$$

The partitioning shows that the score differs from the grand mean (i.e., $X_{11} - \overline{X}_G = +5.0$) as much as it does because of the treatment condition that the subject is in (reflected in $\overline{X}_{A_1} - \overline{X}_G = +3.0$) and because of the unsystematic influences of error or chance factors (reflected in $X_{11} - \overline{X}_{A_1} = +2.0$).

To obtain the SS, each subject's score is similarly partitioned as shown in Table 10.4 for the 15 scores of Table 10.1. Table 10.4 may appear intimidating, but the computations in the table require only addition, subtraction, and multiplication and proceed in a step-by-step fashion. Follow each step carefully.

TABLE

10.4

Obtaining sums of squares for a one-factor between-subjects analysis of variance. The scores used are those in Table 10.1.

Step 1: Partition scores for the 15 subjects using the following equation.

		$(X - \overline{X}_G)$	=	$(\overline{X}_A - \overline{X}_G)$	+	$(X - \overline{X}_A)$
Scores in A_1	X_{11}	$19 - 14$	=	$(17 - 14)$	+	$(19 - 17)$
	X_{21}	$13 - 14$	=	$(17 - 14)$	+	$(13 - 17)$
	X_{31}	$16 - 14$	=	$(17 - 14)$	+	$(16 - 17)$
	X_{41}	$17 - 14$	=	$(17 - 14)$	+	$(17 - 17)$
	X_{51}	$20 - 14$	=	$(17 - 14)$	+	$(20 - 17)$
Scores in A_2	X_{12}	$14 - 14$	=	$(13 - 14)$	+	$(14 - 13)$
	X_{22}	$13 - 14$	=	$(13 - 14)$	+	$(13 - 13)$
	X_{32}	$16 - 14$	=	$(13 - 14)$	+	$(16 - 13)$
	X_{42}	$12 - 14$	=	$(13 - 14)$	+	$(12 - 13)$
	X_{52}	$10 - 14$	=	$(13 - 14)$	+	$(10 - 13)$
Scores in A_3	X_{13}	$15 - 14$	=	$(12 - 14)$	+	$(15 - 12)$
	X_{23}	$10 - 14$	=	$(12 - 14)$	+	$(10 - 12)$
	X_{33}	$11 - 14$	=	$(12 - 14)$	+	$(11 - 12)$
	X_{43}	$12 - 14$	=	$(12 - 14)$	+	$(12 - 12)$
	X_{53}	$12 - 14$	=	$(12 - 14)$	+	$(12 - 12)$

TABLE
10.4

(Continued)

Step 2: Perform the subtractions in step 1 to obtain numerical differences for each subject.

		$(X - \overline{X}_G)$	=	$(\overline{X}_A - \overline{X}_G)$	+	$(X - \overline{X}_A)$
Scores in A_1	X_{11}	+5	=	+3	+	+2
	X_{21}	−1	=	+3	+	−4
	X_{31}	+2	=	+3	+	−1
	X_{41}	+3	=	+3	+	0
	X_{51}	+6	=	+3	+	+3
Scores in A_2	X_{12}	0	=	−1	+	+1
	X_{22}	−1	=	−1	+	0
	X_{32}	+2	=	−1	+	+3
	X_{42}	−2	=	−1	+	−1
	X_{52}	−4	=	−1	+	−3
Scores in A_3	X_{13}	+1	=	−2	+	+3
	X_{23}	−4	=	−2	+	−2
	X_{33}	−3	=	−2	+	−1
	X_{43}	−2	=	−2	+	0
	X_{53}	−2	=	−2	+	0

Step 3: Square each difference.

		$(X - \overline{X}_G)^2$	$(\overline{X}_A - \overline{X}_G)^2$	$(X - \overline{X}_A)^2$
Scores in A_1	X_{11}	25	9	4
	X_{21}	1	9	16
	X_{31}	4	9	1
	X_{41}	9	9	0
	X_{51}	36	9	9
Scores in A_2	X_{12}	0	1	1
	X_{22}	1	1	0
	X_{32}	4	1	9
	X_{42}	4	1	1
	X_{52}	16	1	9
Scores in A_3	X_{13}	1	4	9
	X_{23}	16	4	4
	X_{33}	9	4	1
	X_{43}	4	4	0
	X_{53}	4	4	0

Step 4: Sum the squared differences for each partition over all scores.

$$\sum_{j=1}^{a=3} \sum_{i=1}^{n_A=5} (X - \overline{X}_G)^2 = \sum_{j=1}^{a=3} \sum_{i=1}^{n_A=5} (\overline{X}_A - \overline{X}_G)^2 + \sum_{j=1}^{a=3} \sum_{i=1}^{n_A=5} (X - \overline{X}_A)^2$$

134.00	=	70.00	+	64.00
SS_{Total}	=	SS_A	+	SS_{Error}

Step 1   The scores of all 15 subjects in the experiment are partitioned following equation 10.2.

Step 2   The numerical differences are found for each score.

Step 3   Each of the positive and negative differences found in step 2 is squared.

Step 4   The values of the squared differences are summed over the 15 values in each of the columns. The result is three sums of squares:

$$SS_{Total} = 134.00.$$
$$SS_A = 70.00,$$
$$SS_{Error} = 64.00.$$

As shown in step 4, the SS_{Total} is represented mathematically by

$$SS_{Total} = \sum_{j=1}^{a=3} \sum_{i=1}^{n_A=5} (X - \overline{X}_G)^2.$$

The double summation sign indicates that the squared differences [i.e., $(X - \overline{X}_G)^2$] are to be summed over all subjects in each treatment group (from the first subject, $i = 1$, to the last subject, n_A, in a particular group) and over all groups (from the first level of the independent variable, $j = 1$, to the last level, a). In the example there are five scores in each group ($n_A = 5$) and three groups ($a = 3$); thus, the summation limits are from $i = 1$ to $n_A = 5$ and from $j = 1$ to $a = 3$, or

$$\sum_{j=1}^{3} \sum_{i=1}^{5}.$$

Because we always sum over all scores in a group and over all groups, the double summation sign without the limits is typically used.

Similarly, to obtain SS_A, the squared differences of the treatment group mean from the grand mean are summed over all scores in the experiment; accordingly,

$$\boldsymbol{SS_A} = \sum \sum (\overline{X}_A - \overline{X}_G)^2.$$

Finally, SS_{Error} is obtained by summing each squared difference of a subject's score from the mean of his or her treatment group, or

$$\boldsymbol{SS_{Error}} = \sum \sum (X - \overline{X}_A)^2.$$

An important relationship exists among the sum of squares terms and is shown at the bottom of Table 10.4. The SS_{Total} is equal to the sum of SS_A and SS_{Error}, or

$$\boldsymbol{SS_{Total} = SS_A + SS_{Error}.} \tag{10.3}$$

Thus, the total variation in scores of an experiment, $\boldsymbol{SS_{Total}}$, is the result of systematic variation that occurs between groups receiving different treatments, $\boldsymbol{SS_A}$ (sometimes identified as $\boldsymbol{SS_{Between\text{-}groups}}$ or $\boldsymbol{SS_{Treatments}}$), and error variation that occurs within groups, $\boldsymbol{SS_{Error}}$ (sometimes expressed as $\boldsymbol{SS_{Within\text{-}groups}}$).

Finding Degrees of Freedom

The final step in obtaining MS_A and MS_{Error} is to divide each SS by its df. Recall that *degrees of freedom* refers to the number of scores free to vary in the computation of a statistic. The df for each sum of squares of equation 10.3 are easily determined from this definition.

Total Degrees of Freedom.   To find SS_{Total}, the grand mean, $\overline{X}_G$, must be known. Because the total sum of squares is based on the difference of every score in the experiment from the grand mean (i.e., $X - \overline{X}_G$), then one less than the total number of scores are free to vary. To illustrate, the grand mean for the 15 scores in Table 10.1 is 14.0. To obtain SS_{Total}, 14.0 is subtracted from each of the 15 scores. The sum of these 15 differences must equal 0. Thus, any 14 of the 15 scores are free to vary, but the fifteenth score becomes fixed if $\overline{X}_G$ is known. Accordingly, there are 14 df associated with the SS_{Total}. In general, the **total degrees of freedom**, or df_{Total}, are equal to one less than the total number of scores analyzed. In notation,

$$\text{Total degrees of freedom} = df_{\text{Total}} = N - 1,$$

where N is the total number of scores in the experiment.

Degrees of Freedom for SS$_A$.   The SS_A is computed from the differences of the means of the treatment groups (e.g., $\overline{X}_{A_1}$, $\overline{X}_{A_2}$, and $\overline{X}_{A_3}$ for the example) from $\overline{X}_G$. For a research design with three levels of the independent variable and an equal number of scores in each condition, if $\overline{X}_G$ is known, then only two treatment means are free to vary. For example, if we know that $\overline{X}_G = 14.0$, $\overline{X}_{A_1} = 17.0$, and $\overline{X}_{A_3} = 12.0$, as in Table 10.1, then $\overline{X}_{A_2}$ is also known; it must equal 13.0. Any other value of $\overline{X}_{A_2}$ would not be consistent with $\overline{X}_G$ equal to 14.0. Accordingly, there are 2 df for SS_A in the example.

In general, the **df for SS$_A$**, or **df_A**, are equal to one less than the number of levels of the independent variable. In notation,

$$df \text{ for } SS_A = df_A = a - 1,$$

where a is the number of levels of the independent variable A.

Degrees of Freedom for SS$_{\text{Error}}$.   The SS_{Error} is based on subtracting the mean of each treatment group, $\overline{X}_A$, from each score within that treatment group for each group in the experiment. Thus, for each level of the independent variable, after $\overline{X}_A$ is determined, only $n_A - 1$ scores are free to vary within that level. In Table 10.1, if $\overline{X}_A$ is known, only four of the five scores are free to vary within each treatment condition A_1, A_2, and A_3. Because there are three levels of the independent variable and four scores free to vary within each level, there are 12 df for SS_{Error} (4 df for A_1 plus 4 df for A_2 plus 4 df for A_3 equals 12).

In general, where a is the number of levels of the independent variable and there are n_A scores within each level of the independent variable, the **df for SS$_{\text{Error}}$** or **df_{Error}** $= a(n_A - 1)$. Because $(a)(n)$ equals the total number of scores (N), the df_{Error} may also be expressed as N minus a, or

$$df \text{ for } SS_{\text{Error}} = df_{\text{Error}} = N - a.$$

Additivity of Degrees of Freedom.   The degrees of freedom are additive in the same manner as the corresponding sums of squares values. Thus,

$$df_{\text{Total}} = df_A + df_{\text{Error}}. \tag{10.4}$$

This relationship holds in the example, for $df_{\text{Total}} = 14$, $df_A = 2$, and $df_{\text{Error}} = 12$.

Finding Mean Squares from *SS* and *df*

The F statistic is a ratio of two mean squares, MS_A and MS_{Error}. The two required MS values are derived from the SS obtained in equation 10.3 and the df value associated with each SS. Specifically, these mean squares are

$$MS_A = \frac{SS_A}{df_A}$$

and

$$MS_{Error} = \frac{SS_{Error}}{df_{Error}}.$$

Although it is possible to obtain the MS_{Total} by dividing the SS_{Total} by the df_{Total}, this value provides no useful information in an analysis of variance and typically it is not calculated. For the scores in Table 10.1, we have found $SS_A = 70.00$ and $SS_{Error} = 64.00$ (see Table 10.4), $df_A = 2$ and $df_{Error} = 12$. Consequently,

$$MS_A = \frac{SS_A}{df_A} = \frac{70.00}{2} = 35.000$$

and

$$MS_{Error} = \frac{SS_{Error}}{df_{Error}} = \frac{64.00}{12} = 5.333.$$

MS_A and MS_{Error} are involved in further computations to obtain F, thus we are carrying the values to three decimal places here.

Computing the *F* Statistic

At the beginning of this chapter the F statistic was defined as

$$F = \frac{MS_A}{MS_{Error}}.$$

For the scores of Table 10.1 $MS_A = 35.000$ and $MS_{Error} = 5.333$. Thus,

$$F_{obs} = \frac{35.000}{5.333} = 6.563 = 6.56 \quad \text{rounded to two decimal places,}$$

where $\boldsymbol{F_{obs}}$ indicates the value of F observed from the scores analyzed. Notice that because MS_A and MS_{Error} are based on sum of squares values, which must always be positive, F, too, must always be positive. A negative value of F indicates a mistake in calculations. Values of F are typically rounded to two decimal places.

The numerical values of an analysis of variance are frequently summarized in a table identifying the sources of variation; SS, df, and MS values; and the value of F_{obs}. Table 10.5 illustrates how such a summary table is organized using the numerical values obtained from the data of Table 10.1. The value of F is carried to two decimal places in a summary

TABLE					
10.5	Numerical summary of the analysis of variance on the scores in Table 10.1				
	Source	**SS**	**df**	**MS**	**F**[a]
	Length of time awake (A)	70.00	2	35.000	6.56*
	Error	64.00	12	5.333	
	Total	134.00	14		

*$p < .05$.

[a]Statistically significant values of F are indicated by a probability level footnote on a summary table (i.e., *$p < .05$.).

TABLE					
10.6	Summary of definitional formulas for a one-factor between-subjects analysis of variance				
	Source	**SS**	**df**[a]	**MS**	**F**
	Factor A	$\sum\sum(\overline{X}_A - \overline{X}_G)^2$	$a - 1$	SS_A/df_A	MS_A/MS_{Error}
	Error	$\sum\sum(X - \overline{X}_A)^2$	$N - a$	SS_{Error}/df_{Error}	
	Total	$\sum\sum(X - \overline{X}_G)^2$	$N - 1$	Not calculated	

[a]a = number of levels of factor A, N = total number of scores.

table, and values of the SS and MS are carried to two or more decimal places as needed to minimize rounding error. Table 10.6 summarizes the definitional formulas for the SS, df, and MS.

It has taken considerable discussion to derive the F statistic and calculate its value. However, in actual practice, its value is most often found using a computer data analysis program or from computational formulas. Our goal in this section was not ease of computation but to demonstrate how the F statistic arises from a set of scores. We discuss how to interpret and use this information next.

Testing Your Knowledge 10.1

1. Define: a, between-groups variance, df_A, df_{Error}, df_{Total}, F, F_{obs}, factor A, MS_A, MS_{Error}, N, n_A, one-factor multilevel designs, SS_A, SS_{Error}, SS_{Total}, within-groups variance, $X - \overline{X}_G$, $\overline{X}_A - X_G$, $X - \overline{X}_A$.

2. What is the limitation of a t test for analyzing the data of an experiment?

3. What is the test statistic used in analysis of variance?

4. Write the general equation for the F statistic.

5. Into what two sources does a one-factor between-subjects analysis of variance partition or break down the total variation of the scores in an experiment?

6. An experimenter used a one-factor between-subjects experiment with four levels of factor A: A_1, A_2, A_3, and A_4. There were 11 different subjects in each level. What are the values of a, n_A, and N?

7. Write the general equation for partitioning scores obtained in a one-factor between-subjects experiment.

8. Explain why the value of $\overline{X}_A - \overline{X}_G$ varies with the effect of an independent variable in an experiment.

9. Explain why the value of $X - \overline{X}_A$ varies with error variation in an experiment.

10. Complete the following equations for a one-factor between-subjects analysis of variance.

   a. $\sum\sum(X - \overline{X}_G)^2 =$

   b. $SS_{Total} =$

   c. $df_A =$

   d. $df_{Error} =$

   e. $MS_A =$

   f. $MS_{Error} =$

   g. $F =$

11. What is the value of SS_{Total} if $SS_A = 50.00$ and $SS_{Error} = 100.00$?

12. What is the value of SS_A if $SS_{Total} = 75.00$ and $SS_{Error} = 50.00$?

13. What is the value of df_{Total} if $df_A = 4$ and $df_{Error} = 75$?

14. What is the value of MS_A if $SS_A = 100.00$ and $df_A = 4$?

15. What is the value of MS_{Error} if $SS_{Error} = 760.00$ and $df_{Error} = 76$?

16. A behavioral scientist used a one-factor between-subjects design with four levels of factor A. There were 11 subjects in each level. What are the values of df_A, df_{Error}, and df_{Total}?

17. You conducted an experiment with two levels of an independent variable and three subjects in each group and obtained the following scores:

Factor A	
A_1	A_2
30	34
32	36
28	32

Partition these scores following the approach illustrated in Table 10.4. Find the SS_{Total}, SS_A, and SS_{Error} and the df for each SS. Then complete a numerical summary table for the analysis.

18. You conducted an experiment with three levels of an independent variable and three subjects in each group and obtained the following scores:

Factor A		
A_1	A_2	A_3
30	34	37
32	36	35
28	32	33

Partition these scores following the approach illustrated in Table 10.4. Find the SS_{Total}, SS_A, and SS_{Error} and the df for each SS. Then complete a numerical summary table for the analysis.

19. The following two tables are incomplete summary tables for a one-factor between-subjects analysis of variance. Assume an equal number of scores in each level of the independent variable. Fill in the missing values in each table by using the relationships among SS and df given in equations 10.3 and 10.4, respectively, and the formulas in Table 10.6. Then answer these questions for each table.

   a. How many levels of the independent variable were used?

   b. How many subjects were measured in each treatment group?

   c. How many subjects participated in the study?

Table 1				
Source	SS	df	MS	F
Factor A	50.00	1	—	—
Error	260.00	26	—	
Total	—	—		

Table 2				
Source	SS	df	MS	F
Factor A	—	3	6.00	—
Error	—	76	—	
Total	170.00	79		

Statistical Hypothesis Testing with F

The value of F_{obs} allows us to decide if the treatment means differ significantly. To understand how this decision is made, it is necessary to review briefly the factors influencing MS_A and MS_{Error} and the relationship of MS_A to MS_{Error}.

Factors Affecting the Value of MS_A and MS_{Error}

MS_A
The value of MS_A is given by

$$MS_A = \frac{SS_A}{df_A},$$

where

$$SS_A = \sum\sum(\overline{X}_A - \overline{X}_G)^2.$$

As we indicated in the discussion of partitioning a score, two sources of variation affect the extent of the difference between a group mean and a grand mean and, thus, the value of SS_A in any experiment: (1) the effect of the independent variable and (2) sampling error. Hence, MS_A, too, varies with the effect of the independent variable and sampling

TABLE	Factors affecting MS_A and MS_{Error} in an experiment	
10.7		

Mean Square	Affected By:
MS_A	The effect of the independent variable Sampling error
MS_{Error}	Within-groups error variation

error. Because MS_A increases with an effect of an independent variable, it is used as a measure of the systematic variance created by the independent variable.

MS_{Error}

The MS_{Error} is obtained by

$$\frac{\sum\sum(X - \overline{X}_A)^2}{df_{Error}}$$

and measures only the within-groups error variation in an experiment. It is not affected by an independent variable. As we indicated earlier, this result occurs because any systematic changes in scores due to a treatment effect will also be accompanied by a corresponding increase or decrease in the treatment group mean. Thus, the difference between a subject's score and the group mean, $(X - \overline{X}_A)$, will not change with a treatment effect. Hence, MS_{Error} measures only within-groups error variation in the scores of an experiment. The factors affecting each mean square are summarized in Table 10.7.

The Relationship of MS_A and MS_{Error}

Unbiased Estimates.   Both MS_A and MS_{Error} are unbiased estimates of the population variance of scores, σ^2. They are unbiased because to obtain each MS the sum of squares is divided by degrees of freedom rather than by the actual number of scores involved in the computation of the variance. As unbiased estimates, neither MS should be systematically smaller nor larger than σ^2 when error variation alone is responsible for the variability in scores on which the estimate is based.

Independent Estimates. MS_A and MS_{Error} are also independent estimates of the population variance. *Independent estimates* mean that either mean square may change in value without affecting the value of the other, a point demonstrated in the discussion of the factors affecting SS values. These characteristics of MS_A and MS_{Error} lead to the following expectations of the value of F_{obs}.

▶ **Expected value of F when an independent variable has no effect:** If an independent variable has no effect, then only error variation occurs in an experiment. In this circumstance, we expect MS_A and MS_{Error} to estimate only error variation and, thus, to be about equal. Accordingly, the value of F_{obs} should be equal to about 1.00.

▶ **Expected value of F when an independent variable has an effect:** When an independent variable does produce an effect, then MS_A responds to the systematic variation contributed by the independent variable in addition to the existing sampling error. Consequently, MS_A will be larger than MS_{Error} and F_{obs} will be greater than 1.00. This relationship allows using F in a statistical hypothesis test.

Statistical Decision Making from the *F* Statistic

Statistical testing with the *F* statistic follows the familiar steps:

▶ A null hypothesis, H_0, and an alternative hypothesis, H_1, are formulated.

▶ The sampling distribution of F, assuming that H_0 is true, is obtained. This distribution is given in Appendix C.3.

▶ A significance level is selected.

▶ A critical value of F, identified as F_{crit}, is found from the sampling distribution of F given in Appendix C.3.

▶ A rejection region is located in the sampling distribution of F.

▶ The F ratio, identified as F_{obs}, is calculated from the sample data.

▶ A decision to reject or not reject H_0 is made on the basis of whether or not F_{obs} falls into the rejection region.

▶ The statistical decisions are related to the research hypothesis.

Statistical Hypotheses

Null Hypothesis. For an experiment with three levels of an independent variable, the null hypothesis tested in an analysis of variance is that the populations from which the three samples were selected have the same means and is written

$$H_0: \mu_{A_1} = \mu_{A_2} = \mu_{A_3}.$$

This null hypothesis represents the situation that exists if the independent variable has no effect. If H_0 is true for an experiment, then any observed difference among the group means is due only to sampling error.

The number of population means identified in the null hypothesis always corresponds to the number of levels of the independent variable. If an experiment involves five levels of an independent variable, then H_0 is written

$$H_0: \mu_{A_1} = \mu_{A_2} = \mu_{A_3} = \mu_{A_4} = \mu_{A_5}.$$

Alternative Hypothesis. The alternative hypothesis, H_1, is

$$H_1: \text{The } \mu_A\text{'s are not all equal,}$$

regardless of the number of population means involved in the null hypothesis. The alternative hypothesis states a situation that exists if the independent variable has an effect.

The Sampling Distribution of *F*

The decision to reject or not reject H_0 depends on how rare or unlikely a value of F_{obs} would be if H_0 were true. The sampling distribution of a statistic provides the probability of values of the statistic when H_0 is true. Thus, the probability of obtaining a certain value of F_{obs} if H_0 is true is determined from the sampling distribution of the F statistic. There is not just one sampling distribution of F, however, for the sampling distribution of F depends on the number of levels of the independent variable and the number of scores in each treatment group. Specifically, the sampling distribution of F varies with the degrees of freedom for the numerator (i.e., df_A) and the denominator (i.e., df_{Error}) of the F statistic.

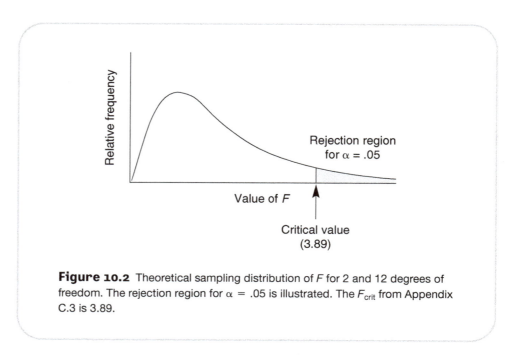

Figure 10.2 Theoretical sampling distribution of F for 2 and 12 degrees of freedom. The rejection region for $\alpha = .05$ is illustrated. The F_{crit} from Appendix C.3 is 3.89.

As an illustration, the sampling distribution of F for the example experiment with 2 *df* for the numerator (i.e., 2 *df* for df_A) and 12 degrees of freedom for the denominator (i.e., 12 *df* for df_{Error}) is illustrated in Figure 10.2. This distribution is positively skewed and its lowest value is zero; the value of F obtained if the sample means are equal to each other and the resulting MS_A value is zero. The most probable value of F is about 1.00, for if H_0 is true, then MS_A should be about the same as MS_{Error}. There is no upper limit to the values that F may attain; F may take on any value between 0 and positive infinity. Because the probability of obtaining a value of F between 0 and positive infinity is 1.00, the area under the distribution is equal to 1.00.

Selecting a Significance Level
The significance level is a probability value that provides the criterion for rejecting H_0. As we have discussed, the significance level usually adopted in behavioral science research is either $\alpha = .05$ or $\alpha = .01$. We illustrate locating a rejection region for a .05 significance level in Figure 10.2.

Locating the Rejection Region for F
The rejection region represents values of F that have a probability equal to or less than α if H_0 is true. Thus, the rejection region identifies values of F_{obs} that meet the criterion for rejecting H_0. The rejection region for F_{obs} is always in the right tail of the sampling distribution for F, as shown in Figure 10.2. We can see why the rejection region is located here by recalling how the value of F_{obs} varies with the effect of an independent variable.

If an independent variable has no effect and, therefore, H_0 is true, then it is expected that MS_A and MS_{Error} will be nearly equal; consequently, F_{obs} should be about 1.00. If the independent variable does have an effect and, therefore, H_0 is not true, then MS_A will be larger than MS_{Error}, and F_{obs} will become greater than 1.00. In order to reject the null hypothesis, then, F_{obs} must be sufficiently larger than 1.00 so that the probability of such a

TABLE **10.8**	Values of F_{crit} for $\alpha = .05$				
Degrees of Freedom for Denominator	Degrees of Freedom for Numerator				
	1	2	3	4	5
1	161.4	199.5	215.7	224.6	230.2
2	18.51	19.00	19.16	19.25	19.30
3	10.13	9.55	9.28	9.12	9.01
4	7.71	6.94	6.59	6.39	6.26
5	6.61	5.79	5.41	5.19	5.05
6	5.99	5.14	4.76	4.53	4.39
7	5.59	4.74	4.35	4.12	3.97
8	5.32	4.46	4.07	3.84	3.69
9	5.12	4.26	3.86	3.63	3.48
10	4.96	4.10	3.71	3.48	3.33
11	4.84	3.98	3.59	3.36	3.20
12	4.75	**3.89**	3.49	3.26	3.11

Note: This table is only a portion of the complete table presented in Appendix C.3.

value of F_{obs} occurring if H_0 were true is equal to or less than the alpha level selected. Therefore, the rejection region for F always lies among the larger values of F in the right tail of the distribution.

Critical values of F (identified as F_{crit}) identifying the lower limit of the rejection region for $\alpha = .05$ and .01 are presented in Appendix C.3. A portion of Appendix C.3a for the .05 significance level is presented in Table 10.8. This table is arranged so that the degrees of freedom for the numerator (i.e., df_A) of the F ratio appear in a row across the top of the table. The degrees of freedom for the denominator (i.e., df_{Error}) appear in the column on the left side of the table.

To locate the value of F_{crit} for the example with 2 degrees of freedom for the numerator and 12 degrees of freedom for the denominator, we find the column for 2 df and then locate the row for 12 df. This column and row intersect at the value of 3.89 (boldfaced in Table 10.8). This value is F_{crit} and locates the rejection region for F_{obs} with 2 and 12 df, as illustrated in Figure 10.2. Any value of F_{obs} with 2 and 12 df and equal to or larger than 3.89 lies in the rejection region. Values of F equal to or greater than 3.89 occur only five or fewer times in every 100 experiments if H_0 is true.

Decisions About the Statistical Hypotheses
The value of F_{obs} provides the basis for making decisions about the statistical hypotheses. If F_{obs} falls into the rejection region, then H_0 is rejected and H_1 accepted. There is a *statistically significant difference* among the sample means. If F_{obs} does not fall into the rejection region, then we fail to reject H_0 and do not accept H_1. The differences among the sample means are *nonsignificant*.

Statistically Significant Difference.   To illustrate a statistically significant difference, we use the example experiment which studied the effect length of time awake has on remembering a list of words. In this experiment we manipulated the amount of time a student was awake, 2 hours, 24 hours, or 36 hours before learning and recalling a list of words. The mean number of words recalled as a function of how long a subject was awake is listed below.

Length of Time Awake (A)		
2 hours (A_1)	24 hours (A_2)	36 hours (A_3)
$\overline{X}_A$ 17.0	13.0	12.0

The analysis of variance on the scores of Table 10.1 resulted in $F_{obs}(2, 12) = 6.56$ (see Table 10.5). For 2, 12 df, F_{crit} at the .05 level is 3.89. F_{obs} is larger than F_{crit} and, thus, falls into the rejection region. Accordingly, we reject the null hypothesis

$$H_0: \mu_{A_1} = \mu_{A_2} = \mu_{A_3},$$

and accept the alternative

$$H_1: \text{The } \mu_A\text{'s are not all equal.}$$

We conclude that the three sample means are not all from the same population. The independent variable of length of time awake did affect the number of words recalled. Notice, however, that there are many ways for "H_1: The μ_A's are not all equal" to be true. The null hypothesis will be true, for example, if μ_{A_1} is greater than either μ_{A_2} or μ_{A_3}, and μ_{A_2} and μ_{A_3} are equal, or if μ_{A_1} is greater than μ_{A_2}, and μ_{A_2} is greater than μ_{A_3}. Which relationship holds for the pattern of means in the example? The analysis of variance alone does not answer this question with certainty, for rejection of H_0 when there are three or more treatment groups in an experiment simply lets us conclude that there is at least one statistically significant difference among the means. A follow-up with a multiple comparison test is necessary to find the specific significant differences between the means. We discuss this test in a later section of this chapter. The decision-making procedures and corresponding conclusions for a statistically significant difference are summarized in the left column of Table 10.9.

Nonsignificant Difference. If we fail to reject H_0 and do not accept H_1, then we have no evidence that the null hypothesis is not true. The implication for the experiment is that there is no evidence that the independent variable had an effect. Any observed numerical differences among the means are attributed to sampling error. These decisions and conclusions are summarized in the right column of Table 10.9.

Assumptions of One-Factor Between-Subjects Analysis of Variance

Similar to the t test, the between-subjects analysis of variance is based on three assumptions about the scores obtained in an experiment:

1. Each subject in the experiment is randomly selected from a population, and each subject is independent of every other subject.
2. The scores on the dependent variable in the populations sampled are normally distributed.
3. The variances of scores in the populations are equal.

TABLE **10.9**	Summary of decisions and conclusions in statistical hypothesis testing using the analysis of variance for a one-factor between-subjects design. A .05 significance level is used.

If F_{obs} falls into the rejection region for $\alpha = .05$, then:	If F_{obs} does not fall into the rejection region for $\alpha = .05$, then:
▶ Probability of F_{obs} is less than or equal to .05 or $p \le .05$.	▶ Probability of F_{obs} is greater than .05 or $p > .05$.
▶ H_0 is rejected.	▶ H_0 is not rejected.
▶ H_1 is accepted.	▶ H_1 is not accepted.
▶ We found a statistically significant difference at the .05 level.	▶ We failed to find a statistically significant difference at the .05 level.
▷ The sample means are not all from the same population.	▷ Sampling error alone is the most plausible explanation for the differences among the sample means.
▷ At least one difference between the treatment means exists.	▷ There is no evidence that the independent variable had an effect.
▷ Something, in addition to sampling error, is responsible for differences among the sample means.	
▷ In a carefully designed experiment, changes in the independent variable are causing changes in the dependent variable.	
▶ Multiple comparison tests are needed if the independent variable has three or more levels.	▶ No multiple comparison tests are needed.

These assumptions are important because the sampling distribution of F and, therefore, the values of F_{crit} given in Appendix C.3 are generated from populations that meet these assumptions. In order for the between-subjects analysis of variance to be used, each score in the experiment must be independent of every other score. That is, every subject may be given only one level of the independent variable and contribute only one score in the experiment. If a within-subjects design is used, where a subject is given more than one level of the independent variable, and two or more scores are analyzed for a subject, then the within-subjects analysis of variance must be used. This analysis of variance is discussed in Chapter 12.

The second and third assumptions may not be met by some experiments. Violations of the second (the normal distribution of scores) and the third (the equality of variances) assumption can change the probability of obtaining a particular value of F_{obs} and, thus, affect the probability of making a Type I error. Violations of these assumptions are more likely to have minimal effects on the probability of making a Type I error when the following conditions are met:

▶ The number of scores in each group is the same.
▶ The shape of the distributions of the scores for each group is about the same, and the distributions are neither very peaked nor very flat.
▶ The significance level is set at .05 rather than .01.

Testing Your Knowledge 10.2

1. Define: F_{crit}, rejection region.

2. What factors affect the value of MS_A in an experiment?

3. Explain why MS_A increases in value if an independent variable has an effect in an experiment.

4. What factors affect the value of MS_{Error} in an experiment?

5. Explain why the value of MS_{Error} does not change if an independent variable has an effect in an experiment.

6. What value of F_{obs} is expected if an independent variable has no effect in an experiment?

7. What is expected to happen to the value of F_{obs} if an independent variable has an effect in an experiment?

8. Write the statistical hypotheses for the F test for:

   a. Two independent groups.

   b. Four independent groups.

   c. Six independent groups.

9. To what situation in an experiment does H_0 of an analysis of variance correspond?

10. To what situation in an experiment does H_1 of an analysis of variance correspond?

11. What is the lower limit for the value of F if H_0 is true?

12. What is the upper limit for the value of F if H_0 is true?

13. This exercise provides values for df_A, df_{Error}, and F_{obs} for several hypothetical one-factor between-subjects experiments. For each set of values, obtain the value of F_{crit} for a .05 significance level from Appendix C.3a. Then indicate whether F_{obs} falls into the rejection region and what decision you make with respect to H_0 and H_1. If the exact df are not in the table for df_{Error}, then use the next lower value in the table.

Experiment	df_A	df_{Error}	F_{obs}
1	1	10	5.12
2	2	24	3.29
3	1	24	4.26
4	2	90	3.24
5	2	12	3.94
6	2	15	3.60
7	4	45	1.93
8	3	20	1.46
9	6	63	2.30
10	4	95	2.13

14. Identify the assumptions underlying the use of the one-factor between-subjects analysis of variance.

15. Under what conditions will violation of normality of the distribution of scores in the population have the least effect on Type I errors for a one-factor between-subjects analysis of variance?

Interpreting a Statistically Significant *F* in a Multilevel Design

Multiple Comparison Tests

The final step in statistical testing with the analysis of variance is to relate the decisions about H_0 and H_1 to the research hypothesis. Experiments requiring the analysis of variance, however, usually have three or more levels of the independent variable, and earlier we indicated that rejecting H_0 when there are three or more levels of an independent variable leads us to conclude that there is at least one statistically significant difference among the means. But the analysis of variance alone does not identify specifically which means differ significantly from which other means. To decide which pairs of means differ significantly, we use multiple comparison tests. **Multiple comparison tests** are statistical tests used to make pairwise comparisons to find which means differ significantly from one another in a one-factor multilevel design.

▶ **Multiple comparison tests**
Statistical tests used to make pairwise comparisons to find which means differ significantly from one another in a one-factor multilevel design.

Given the three sample means from the experiment on the effect of type of length of time awake on recall of words, we can make three two-mean comparisons:

$$\overline{X}_{A_1} \quad \text{compared to} \quad \overline{X}_{A_2},$$
$$\overline{X}_{A_1} \quad \text{compared to} \quad \overline{X}_{A_3},$$
$$\overline{X}_{A_2} \quad \text{compared to} \quad \overline{X}_{A_3}.$$

Because these comparisons each involve two means, they are called **pairwise comparisons**. By performing statistical tests on these three pairwise comparisons, we can find which pairs of means differ significantly.

▶ **Pairwise comparisons**
Statistical comparisons involving two means.

One way of making pairwise comparisons would be to use t_{ind} to conduct three t tests, one for each comparison. From the outcome of these three tests, we could determine which means differ significantly from each other. The issue is not so easily resolved, however, because of the probability of a Type I error occurring in the comparisons to be made. Recall that a Type I error occurs when H_0 is actually true but is rejected in the statistical hypothesis test. To keep the probability of making a Type I error low, researchers usually set the significance level at .05 or .01. For the overall analysis of variance on the example problem (reported in Table 10.5), the probability of a Type I error is equal to the value of α, or .05. But when conducting multiple comparisons, an investigator runs many more statistical tests, the exact number depending on the number of comparisons to be made. Consider, for example, conducting a t_{ind} on each of the three pairwise comparisons in the example experiment. For each t test, the probability of a Type I error is equal to α. Hence, the probability of making at least one Type I error among the three comparisons is about .14, an unacceptably high value. The **error rate in an experiment** is the probability of making at least one Type I error in the comparisons conducted. The error rate in an experiment increases very rapidly with a growing number of comparisons. For example, consider using the t test for five pairwise comparisons with $\alpha = .05$ for each comparison. If H_0 is true, then the probability of at least one Type I error in the five comparisons is equal to about .23. This error rate is obviously too high for most researchers. To control this error rate, alternatives to the t test have been developed for making multiple comparisons. We present one specific test for making one type of multiple comparisons, *post hoc comparisons*.

▶ **Error rate in an experiment**
The probability of making at least one Type I error in the statistical comparisons conducted in an experiment.

Post hoc comparisons make all possible pairwise comparisons after a statistically significant F_{obs} has occurred for the overall analysis of variance. The term *post hoc* is Latin for "after this" or "after the fact." Its use here means a comparison made after F_{obs} is statistically significant. If F_{obs} of the overall analysis of variance is nonsignificant and

▶ **Post hoc comparisons**
Statistical tests that make all possible pairwise comparisons after a statistically significant F_{obs} has occurred for the overall analysis of variance.

H_0 is not rejected, no further data analysis is needed and post hoc comparisons are not carried out. The next section presents the Tukey HSD test for post hoc comparisons.

The Tukey HSD Test for Post Hoc Comparisons

The **Tukey HSD test** (HSD is an acronym for *honestly significant difference*), named after statistician John W. Tukey (1915–2000), provides a **critical difference** (abbreviated *CD*) that specifies the minimum difference between two treatment means that is statistically significant at the α level chosen. The absolute value of an observed difference in a pairwise comparison of means is compared with the Tukey *CD*. If the absolute value of the observed difference between the means is equal to or larger than the *CD*, then the sample means differ significantly and are treated as representing different populations.

The *CD* for the Tukey HSD test is found from

$$CD = q\sqrt{\frac{MS_{\text{Error}}}{n_A}},$$

where $q =$ the *studentized range statistic*, a numerical value that depends on (1) the level of α selected, (2) the number of levels of the independent variable, and (3) the *df* for MS_{Error} in the analysis of variance. Values of q are given in Appendix C.4 for $\alpha = .01$ and $\alpha = .05$ for up to 10 levels of an independent variable.

$MS_{\text{Error}} =$ the error term from the overall analysis of variance.

$n_A =$ the number of scores in each treatment condition. The values of n_A for each treatment condition must be equal to use this formula.

Obtaining the Tukey *CD*

We illustrate calculating the Tukey HSD *CD* with the example scores given in Table 10.1 and the analysis of variance of those scores summarized in Table 10.5. The F_{obs}, 6.56, is statistically significant at the .05 level; thus, we reject H_0: $\mu_{A_1} = \mu_{A_2} = \mu_{A_3}$ and accept H_1: The μ_A's are not all equal. The overall analysis of variance indicates that there is at least one significant difference among the three means being compared. To find specifically which means differ from each other, we will calculate the Tukey HSD *CD*.

From the analysis of variance summarized in Table 10.5, $MS_{\text{Error}} = 5.333$. The number of scores in each treatment group is 5; thus, $n_A = 5$. The value of q is obtained from Appendix C.4. This table requires knowing (1) the number of levels of the independent variable a (in the example $a = 3$) and (2) the df_{Error} from the analysis of variance (in this case, 12). At the .05 level, for $a = 3$ and 12 df_{Error}, $q = 3.77$. Substituting these values into the formula for the *CD* leads to

$$CD = q\sqrt{\frac{MS_{\text{Error}}}{n_A}} = 3.77\sqrt{\frac{5.333}{5}}$$

$$= 3.9 \quad \text{rounded to one decimal place.}$$

Interpreting the Tukey *CD*

The *CD* for the Tukey test for the example is 3.9. A difference between two treatment means in Table 10.1 equal to or larger in absolute value (i.e., the value of the difference ignoring the $+$ or $-$ sign) to 3.9 words recalled is statistically significant at the .05 level.

TABLE

10.10   Application of the Tukey HSD *CD* to the pairwise comparisons of the example experiment. The value of the *CD* = 3.9.

Comparison	Absolute Value of Comparison	Statistical Hypotheses	Decision
$\overline{X}_{A_1}$ vs. $\overline{X}_{A_2}$ (17.0 − 13.0)	4.0	H_0: $\mu_{A_1} = \mu_{A_2}$ H_1: $\mu_{A_1} \neq \mu_{A_2}$	Reject Accept
$\overline{X}_{A_1}$ vs. $\overline{X}_{A_3}$ (17.0 − 12.0)	5.0	H_0: $\mu_{A_1} = \mu_{A_3}$ H_1: $\mu_{A_1} \neq \mu_{A_3}$	Reject Accept
$\overline{X}_{A_2}$ vs. $\overline{X}_{A_3}$ (13.0 − 12.0)	1.0	H_0: $\mu_{A_2} = \mu_{A_3}$ H_1: $\mu_{A_2} \neq \mu_{A_3}$	Fail to reject Do not accept

Note: A_1 = 2 hours awake, A_2 = 24 hours awake, A_3 = 36 hours awake.

The three pairwise comparisons, the absolute values of each comparison, the statistical hypothesis, and the decision for each hypothesis are shown in Table 10.10.

Notice that two pairwise comparisons are larger than 3.9 in absolute value: $\overline{X}_{A_1}$ versus $\overline{X}_{A_2}$ (17.0 − 13.0 = 4.0) and $\overline{X}_{A_1}$ versus $\overline{X}_{A_3}$ (17.0 − 12.0 = 5.0). Each of these comparisons reveals a statistically significant difference between the means compared. The absolute value of the comparison of $\overline{X}_{A_2}$ versus $\overline{X}_{A_3}$ (13.0 − 12.0 = 1.0) is less than 3.9. Thus, the difference in recall of words between being awake for 24 hours and 36 hours is nonsignificant. Hence, the Tukey test leads to the conclusion that taking a memory test two hours after waking ($\overline{X}_{A_1}$) leads to significantly greater recall of words than after being awake for either 24 hours ($\overline{X}_{A_2}$) or 36 hours ($\overline{X}_{A_3}$), but recall does not differ significantly after being awake 24 hours ($\overline{X}_{A_2}$) or 36 hours ($\overline{X}_{A_3}$).

This result provides support for the hypothesis that students will perform better on a memory task after being awake for 2 hours in comparison to being awake either 24 or 36 hours. The result, however, provides no evidence to support that being awake for 24 hours will lead to greater recall than being awake for 36 hours.

Two Instances When a Post Hoc Test Is Not Needed

There are two instances when a post hoc test is not needed. The first is when F_{obs} for the analysis of variance is nonsignificant. A nonsignificant F_{obs} indicates there are no significant differences between any of the means in the analysis; thus, no follow-up test is needed.

The second instance is when there are only two levels of the independent variable. If F_{obs} is significant for this analysis, then H_0: $\mu_{A_1} = \mu_{A_2}$ is rejected and H_1: The μ_A's are not equal is accepted. Obviously, the only means that can differ significantly in this instance are $\overline{X}_{A_1}$ and $\overline{X}_{A_2}$. Thus, no further test is needed on these means.

Effect Size

Similar to the *t* test, the analysis of variance indicates whether an independent variable has an effect on the dependent variable of an experiment, but it does not indicate the size of that effect. Again, η^2 may be used as a measure of effect size when a statistically significant value of F_{obs} occurs.

Calculating Eta Squared for the Analysis of Variance

For a one-factor between-subjects analysis of variance, η^2 may be obtained from two alternative formulas. If sums of squares values are known, η^2 is given by

$$\eta^2 = \frac{SS_A}{SS_{Total}}.$$

When only F_{obs} and df are known for an analysis of variance, η^2 can be obtained by

$$\eta^2 = \frac{(df_A)(F_{obs})}{(df_A)(F_{obs}) + df_{Error}}.$$

Example of Calculating η^2 for the One-Factor Between-Subjects Analysis of Variance

An η^2 may be calculated for the example problem either from the SS values or the F_{obs} and df values of the analysis of variance summarized in Table 10.5.

η^2 **from SS Values**

$$\eta^2 = \frac{SS_A}{SS_{Total}} = \frac{70.00}{134.00} = .52.$$

η^2 **from F_{obs} and df Values**

$$\eta^2 = \frac{(df_A)(F_{obs})}{(df_A)(F_{obs}) + df_{Error}} = \frac{(2)(6.56)}{(2)(6.56) + 12} = .52.$$

This η^2 indicates that a 52 percent reduction in the total variance of the scores occurs when the means of the levels of the independent variable are used to predict scores in comparison to using the grand mean as the predicted score. This independent variable accounts for a large proportion of the variance in the recall of words.

The Relationship Between t_{ind} and F

The t_{ind} and the one-factor between-subjects analysis of variance lead to the same statistical decisions when analyzing data from an experiment with two levels of the independent variable. If we reject H_0 with a two-tailed t_{ind} at the .05 level, then we would also reject H_0 with an analysis of variance on the same data. The reason is that $t^2 = F$ or $t = \sqrt{F}$. This relation also holds for the tabled critical values of t and F for the analysis of two sample means when the same significance level is adopted. For example, for $\alpha = .05$, F_{crit} for 1, 8 df is 5.32. The value of t_{crit} for 8 df and $\alpha = .05$ in a two-tailed test is 2.306, which is the square root of 5.32. Thus, $(2.306)^2 = 5.32$ and $t^2 = F$. Because of this relationship between t and F, either test may be used for comparing two independent sample means; the tests provide identical outcomes and one is not preferred over the other. The advantage of analysis of variance appears only when three or more treatment conditions are being compared.

EXAMPLE PROBLEM

10.1

Using the One-Factor Between-Subjects Analysis of Variance with the Tukey HSD Test

Problem: As you were looking at some classic research studies in psychology, you came across a study on mood-state-dependent memory. Mood-state-dependent memory refers to the finding that recall of material is improved when one is in the same mood state at the time of recall as at the time of learning (Bower, 1981). Suppose that to study mood-state-dependent memory, you create five equivalent groups of 10 people each. For each group, you generate a mood state by having subjects read a series of statements designed to induce either a happy, sad, or neutral mood state. After the mood state is induced, the subjects learn a list of 15 common nouns. Twenty-four hours later, the subjects return, and you again induce a mood state and have the subjects recall the previously learned list of nouns. At this recall session, the mood state may be the same or different from the mood state induced at learning. The mood states induced at learning and recall for the five groups are as follows:

	Mood-State Group				
	A_1	A_2	A_3	A_4	A_5
Mood induced at learning	Happy	Sad	Neutral	Happy	Sad
Mood induced at recall	Happy	Sad	Neutral	Sad	Happy

Mood-state-dependent memory predicts that the groups having congruent learning and recall states (i.e., groups A_1, A_2, and A_3) should have greater recall of the list of nouns than groups having different learning and recall mood states (i.e., groups A_4 and A_5). Suppose that you obtained the numbers of items recalled for each group, as shown in Table 10.11. Which group means differ significantly from each other at the .05 level?

TABLE

10.11

Number of nouns correctly recalled as a function of mood-state group

	Mood-State Group				
	A_1	A_2	A_3	A_4	A_5
	8	14	9	5	6
	12	13	12	9	9
	12	6	7	6	8
	7	9	7	8	8
	10	12	11	4	5
	9	10	6	6	4
	13	8	10	10	5
	8	7	8	3	7
	14	11	13	7	7
	11	9	10	3	3
$\overline{X}_A$	10.4	9.9	9.3	6.1	6.2
s_A	2.4	2.6	2.3	2.4	1.9

Solution: The design is a one-factor between-subjects design with five levels of the independent variable, mood-state group. The first step in data analysis is to calculate a one-factor between-subjects analysis of variance on the scores. If F_{obs} is statistically significant, we will use the Tukey HSD test to find the statistically significant pairwise differences between the treatment means.

Statistic to Be Used: $F = MS_A/MS_{Error}$.

Assumptions for Use

1. The subjects were sampled randomly and independently from a population.
2. Item recall is normally distributed in the population.
3. The variances for item recall are equal in the populations sampled.

Statistical Hypotheses: $H_0: \mu_{A_1} = \mu_{A_2} = \mu_{A_3} = \mu_{A_4} = \mu_{A_5}$.

H_1: The μ_A's are not all equal.

Significance Level: $\alpha = .05$.

df:

$$df_A = a - 1 = 5 - 1 = 4$$
$$df_{Error} = N - a = 50 - 5 = 45$$
$$df_{Total} = N - 1 = 50 - 1 = 49$$

Critical Value of F: $F_{crit}(4, 45) = 2.61$. A value of 45 df for the denominator is not presented in Appendix C.3a. We used the critical value for the next lower df in the table for df_{Error}, 40.

Rejection Region: Values of F_{obs} equal to or greater than 2.61.

Calculation: The software program SPSS was used to obtain the following analysis of variance summary table.

Source	SS	df	MS	F
Mood-state group (A)	171.880	4	42.970	7.86*
Error	245.900	45	5.464	
Total	417.780	49		

*$p < 05$.

Decision: $F_{obs} = 7.86$ falls into the rejection region. We reject $H_0: \mu_{A_1} = \mu_{A_2} = \mu_{A_3} = \mu_{A_4} = \mu_{A_5}$ and accept H_1: The μ_A's are not all equal. Rejection of H_0 indicates that there is at least one statistically significant difference between the sample means. To find the statistically significant pairwise differences, we use the Tukey HSD test.

Tukey Test: The numerical values needed for this test are found as follows:

▶ q is obtained from Appendix C.4. There are five levels of the independent variable and 45 df for MS_{Error} from the analysis of variance summary table. Because 45 df is not given in Appendix C.4, we use 40 df, the next lower df in the table from the 45 df for MS_{Error}. Thus, $q = 4.04$ for a .05 significance level.

▶ MS_{Error}, obtained from the analysis of variance, is 5.464.

▶ n_A, the number of scores in each of the means to be compared, is 10.

Substituting these numerical values into the formula,

$$CD = q\sqrt{\frac{MS_{\text{Error}}}{n_A}} = 4.04\sqrt{\frac{5.464}{10}}$$

$$= 3.0 \text{ words, rounded to one decimal place.}$$

A difference between two means equal to or larger in absolute value than 3.0 words is statistically significant at the .05 level. The pairwise comparisons and their absolute values, the statistical hypotheses tested, and the decisions reached on the statistical hypotheses for each comparison are given in Table 10.12.

The absolute values of the comparisons of $\overline{X}_{A_1}$ versus $\overline{X}_{A_4}$ and $\overline{X}_{A_5}$, $\overline{X}_{A_2}$ versus $\overline{X}_{A_4}$ and $\overline{X}_{A_5}$, and $\overline{X}_{A_3}$ versus $\overline{X}_{A_4}$ and $\overline{X}_{A_5}$ exceed the CD of 3.0 words. Each of these differences is statistically significant. The absolute values of the remaining comparisons, $\overline{X}_{A_1}$

TABLE 10.12

Application of the Tukey HSD CD to the pairwise comparisons of the five mood-state groups. The value of the $CD = 3.0$.

Comparison	Absolute Value of Comparison	Statistical Hypotheses	Decision
$\overline{X}_{A_1}$ vs. $\overline{X}_{A_2}$ (10.4 − 9.9)	0.5	$H_0: \mu_{A_1} = \mu_{A_2}$ $H_1: \mu_{A_1} \neq \mu_{A_2}$	Fail to reject Do not accept
$\overline{X}_{A_1}$ vs. $\overline{X}_{A_3}$ (10.4 − 9.3)	1.1	$H_0: \mu_{A_1} = \mu_{A_3}$ $H_1: \mu_{A_1} \neq \mu_{A_3}$	Fail to reject Do not accept
$\overline{X}_{A_1}$ vs. $\overline{X}_{A_4}$ (10.4 − 6.1)	4.3	$H_0: \mu_{A_1} = \mu_{A_4}$ $H_1: \mu_{A_1} \neq \mu_{A_4}$	Reject Accept
$\overline{X}_{A_1}$ vs. $\overline{X}_{A_5}$ (10.4 − 6.2)	4.2	$H_0: \mu_{A_1} = \mu_{A_5}$ $H_1: \mu_{A_1} \neq \mu_{A_5}$	Reject Accept
$\overline{X}_{A_2}$ vs. $\overline{X}_{A_3}$ (9.9 − 9.3)	0.6	$H_0: \mu_{A_2} = \mu_{A_3}$ $H_1: \mu_{A_2} \neq \mu_{A_3}$	Fail to reject Do not accept
$\overline{X}_{A_2}$ vs. $\overline{X}_{A_4}$ (9.9 − 6.1)	3.8	$H_0: \mu_{A_2} = \mu_{A_4}$ $H_1: \mu_{A_2} \neq \mu_{A_4}$	Reject Accept
$\overline{X}_{A_2}$ vs. $\overline{X}_{A_5}$ (9.9 − 6.2)	3.7	$H_0: \mu_{A_2} = \mu_{A_5}$ $H_1: \mu_{A_2} \neq \mu_{A_5}$	Reject Accept
$\overline{X}_{A_3}$ vs. $\overline{X}_{A_4}$ (9.3 − 6.1)	3.2	$H_0: \mu_{A_3} = \mu_{A_4}$ $H_1: \mu_{A_3} \neq \mu_{A_4}$	Reject Accept
$\overline{X}_{A_3}$ vs. $\overline{X}_{A_5}$ (9.3 − 6.2)	3.1	$H_0: \mu_{A_3} = \mu_{A_5}$ $H_1: \mu_{A_3} \neq \mu_{A_5}$	Reject Accept
$\overline{X}_{A_4}$ vs. $\overline{X}_{A_5}$ (6.1 − 6.2)	0.1	$H_0: \mu_{A_4} = \mu_{A_5}$ $H_1: \mu_{A_4} \neq \mu_{A_5}$	Fail to reject Do not accept

A_1 = happy/happy group, A_2 = sad/sad group, A_3 = neutral/neutral group, A_4 = happy/sad group, and A_5 = sad/happy group.

versus $\overline{X}_{A_2}$, $\overline{X}_{A_1}$ versus $\overline{X}_{A_3}$, $\overline{X}_{A_2}$ versus $\overline{X}_{A_3}$, and $\overline{X}_{A_4}$ versus $\overline{X}_{A_5}$ are less than the *CD*. These comparisons are nonsignificant, and the observed differences between these sample means are best explained by sampling error.

Effect Size: $\eta^2 = 171.880/417.780 = .41.$

Conclusion: The Tukey test leads to the conclusion that mood-state groups that had congruent learning and recall conditions (i.e., the happy/happy, sad/sad, and neutral/neutral groups) did not differ significantly from each other in recall. Each of these groups, however, recalled significantly more words than did either of the noncongruent mood state groups (i.e., the happy/sad and sad/happy groups). In addition, the happy/sad and sad/happy groups did not differ significantly from each other. Accordingly, the inferred relationship among the population means is

$$(\mu_{A_1} = \mu_{A_2} = \mu_{A_3}) > (\mu_{A_4} = \mu_{A_5}).$$

The η^2 indicates that knowledge of mood-state group reduces the total variance in prediction by 41 percent.

EXAMPLE PROBLEM

10.2

Using the One-Factor Between-Subjects Analysis of Variance: A Nonsignificant F_{obs}

Problem: A statistics professor is looking for the best way to encourage her students to work statistics problems neatly. She knows that solving statistics problems neatly will result in students making fewer careless errors, and if a mistake is made, it is easier to find the error. Many professors attempt to get students to accomplish this behavior through specific instructions to work neatly. What if a professor tried a more indirect, or implicit, approach of simply giving praise or criticism of the neatness of the work? Would this approach improve neatness as well as a direct approach?

To test this hypothesis, students were randomly assigned to one of three instructional conditions: a control condition (A_1), where the instructor said nothing about neatness and did not give any feedback about neatness to students; an explicit instructions condition (A_2), where the professor specifically discussed doing work neatly but did not give any feedback about neatness to students; and an implicit instructions condition (A_3), where the professor did not say anything about neatness but gave praise or criticism about the neatness of the work. Every other aspect of her teaching was the same. Students in each group were taught how to use a new statistical test and then were asked to complete several homework problems using the statistic. A second instructor, who did not know the hypothesis of this study, rated the neatness of the homework using a 0 to 50-point rating scale. The results are listed in Table 10.13. Does the instructional condition improve neatness in students' statistical homework?

Solution: The design used is a one-factor between-subjects design with three levels of the independent variable, which is the instructional condition. The one-factor between-subjects analysis of variance is the appropriate statistical test for these data. We use a .05 significance level.

Statistic to Be Used: $F = MS_A/MS_{Error}.$

TABLE
10.13

Neatness score as a function of type of instructions

	Type of Instructions (A)		
	Control (A_1)	Explicit (A_2)	Implicit (A_3)
	18	17	31
	2	19	27
	11	26	16
	3	4	24
	26	18	41
	18	23	17
	9	31	12
	24	35	32
	17	11	16
	21	8	19
	14	29	35
	19	25	26
	33	38	17
$\overline{X}_A$	16.5	21.8	24.1
s_A	8.8	10.3	8.8

Assumptions for Use

1. The subjects were sampled randomly and independently from a population.

2. The neatness with which students complete statistical homework is normally distributed in the population.

3. The variances for neatness scores are equal in the populations sampled.

Statistical Hypotheses: H_0: $\mu_{A_1} = \mu_{A_2} = \mu_{A_3}$.

H_1: The μ_A's are not all equal.

Significance Level: $\alpha = .05$.

df:

$$df_A = a - 1 = 3 - 1 = 2$$
$$df_{Error} = N - a = 39 - 3 = 36$$
$$df_{Total} = N - 1 = 39 - 1 = 38$$

Critical Value of F: $F_{crit}(2, 36) = 3.32$. The value of F_{crit} for 2, 36 df is not included in the table in Appendix C.3a; hence, we used F_{crit} for 2, 30 df.

Rejection Region: Values of F_{obs} equal to or greater than 3.32.

Calculation: The analysis of variance was calculated using the SPSS software program. A summary of this analysis is as follows:

Source	SS	df	MS	F
Instructional condition (A)	389.898	2	194.949	2.24
Error	3137.846	36	87.162	
Total	3527.744	38		

Decision: $F_{obs} = 2.24$ is less than $F_{crit} = 3.32$ and does not fall into the rejection region; thus, we fail to reject H_0 and do not accept H_1.

Conclusion: The observed differences among the means are nonsignificant; the sample means of 16.5, 21.8, and 24.1 are treated as samples from the same population. There is no evidence that there is an effect of the independent variable of instructional condition on the neatness of the students' homework. The observed differences among the sample means are treated as due only to sampling error. Because the F_{obs} was nonsignificant, there is no need for multiple comparison tests or an effect size measure.

The results of this example illustrate the need for statistical hypothesis testing to determine whether group means differ by more than chance alone. From a visual examination of the means, it appears that they differ by quite a large amount. But there are also large differences among scores within the groups, leading to a considerable amount of error variation as reflected in the relatively large values of the standard deviations for the groups. When there is a large amount of error variation, then we may expect relatively large differences between group means due simply to sampling error, as is the case in this example.

EXAMPLE PROBLEM

10.3

Using the One-Factor Between-Subjects Analysis of Variance with Two Levels of an Independent Variable

Problem: Review question 4 of Chapter 9 (see page 231) introduced the hypothesis that distributed practice in learning words results in better recall of those words than massed practice for learning a list of words. Would a similar effect occur if students were taught a new statistical test and asked to use massed or distributed practice to learn that test? To answer this question, a psychologist created two equivalent groups of 10 students each, a distributed learning group (A_1) and a massed learning group (A_2). Students in both groups were then asked to learn a new statistical test. Each group was given the same instructional material about the test and the same number of homework problems on the material. Students in the massed learning condition were told to study all the instructional material and complete all homework problems within 24 hours of the start of the study. Students in the distributed learning condition were told to complete two problems a day over a one-week period. One week after being given the instructional material, students in both groups were given a 10-question exam on the material that they had studied. Suppose the exam scores for each group in Table 10.14 were obtained. Does the learning condition affect the number of exam questions correctly answered?

Solution: To find if the means differ significantly, we use the one-factor between-subjects analysis of variance. (Because only two groups are involved, a t_{ind} is also an appropriate statistical test.) We use a .05 significance level.

Statistic to Be Used: $F = MS_A/MS_{Error}$.

Assumptions for Use
1. The subjects were sampled randomly and independently from a population.
2. The performance on the exam questions is normally distributed in the population.
3. The variances for the number of exam questions correctly answered are equal in the populations sampled.

TABLE 10.14	Number of exam questions correct as a function of learning condition

	Learning Condition (A)	
	Distributed (A_1)	Massed (A_2)
	6	5
	7	4
	8	2
	5	6
	7	4
	8	7
	5	4
	6	6
	8	7
	5	5
$\overline{X}_A$	6.5	5.0
s_A	1.3	1.6

Statistical Hypotheses: $H_0: \mu_{A_1} = \mu_{A_2}.$
$H_1:$ The μ_A's are not equal.

Significance Level: $\alpha = .05.$

df:

$$df_A = a - 1 = 2 - 1 = 1$$
$$df_{Error} = N - a = 20 - 2 = 18$$
$$df_{Total} = N - 1 = 20 - 1 = 19$$

Critical Value of F: $F_{crit}(1, 18) = 4.41.$

Rejection Region: Values of F_{obs} equal to or greater than 4.41.

Calculation: A summary of the analysis of variance using SPSS is as follows:

Source	SS	df	MS	F
Learning condition (A)	11.250	1	11.250	5.55*
Error	36.500	18	2.028	
Total	47.750	19		

*$p < .05.$

Decision: F_{obs} falls into the rejection region; thus, we reject H_0 and accept H_1.

Effect Size: $\eta^2 = 11.250/47.750 = .24.$

Conclusion: The means of 6.5 problems correct and 5.0 problems correct differ significantly at the .05 level; the mean of 6.5 is significantly larger than the mean of 5.0. Because the two groups were equivalent before the independent variable was administered and extraneous variables were controlled, the observed difference between the groups is treated as due to the effect of the learning condition. Students performed better on the test with distributed practice rather than with massed practice. The Tukey HSD test is not needed because only two means are being compared. The $\eta^2 = .24$ indicates the independent variable accounts for 24 percent of the variance in the dependent variable. If a t_{ind} had been used in place of the analysis of variance, $t_{obs}(18) = 2.355$. This value of t_{obs} is equal to the square root of $F_{obs}(1, 18) = 5.547$. This t is statistically significant at the .05 level and leads to the same conclusion as the analysis of variance. This result, too, illustrates the importance of statistical hypothesis testing in data analysis. At first glance, the group means reveal what appears to be a relatively small difference between them. But notice that there is also relatively little variability among subjects within the groups. With little within-groups error variation, even small differences between groups may be statistically significant.

Computerized Data Analysis

We have developed both the t test and the analysis of variance using definitional formulas to provide a conceptual understanding of the statistic. Actual computation of statistical analysis is most often done with computer software such as SPSS or Minitab. There are numerous software programs available for this purpose, and we do not present specific programs in this text. Most programs, however, provide a complete set of descriptive statistics, including treatment means, standard deviations and standard errors for those means, confidence intervals for each mean, a summary table of the analysis of variance, post hoc comparisons, and a graph of the treatment means. Typically, the output of these programs is similar to what we have used in this text, with the exception of reporting the significance or probability values for F_{obs} or t_{obs}. In the text, we have always compared F_{obs} to F_{crit} or t_{obs} to t_{crit} in order to determine if the observed or calculated value of the statistic falls into the rejection region. Statistics software programs, however, usually report the observed value of the statistic along with the exact probability of its occurrence if the null hypothesis is true. For example, most data analysis programs would report the value of F_{obs} obtained for our example problem (shown in Table 10.5) as $F = 6.56$, $p = .012$. The value of $p = .012$, sometimes called a *significance probability*, provides the exact probability of obtaining a value of F_{obs} as large as or larger than the value reported if the null hypothesis is true. Thus, for our example, if H_0: $\mu_{A_1} = \mu_{A_2} = \mu_{A_3}$ is true, then the probability of obtaining a value of F_{obs} equal to or larger than 6.56 is .012. Because $p = .012$ is less than $\alpha = .05$, it indicates that $F = 6.56$ falls into the rejection region and F_{obs} is statistically significant. The null hypothesis, H_0: $\mu_{A_1} = \mu_{A_2} = \mu_{A_3}$, is rejected and the alternative hypothesis, H_1: The μ_A's are not all equal, is accepted. If, however, the exact probability of F_{obs} had been something such as $p = .23$, then this value of p is greater than $\alpha = .05$, and the value of F_{obs} would not fall into the rejection region and H_0 would not be rejected. Both approaches to reporting the probability level of an observed statistic, $F = 6.56$, $p < .05$ and $F = 6.56$, $p = .012$, are used and acceptable in journal reports.

It is also likely that any analysis of variance summary tables that are given will identify the sources of variation using generic terminology rather than the specific name of the independent variable as we have done in the text. For example, in Table 10.5, we have identified the sources of variation as length of time awake (A) and error. In a computerized output, unless you are asked to provide a specific name for the independent variable, the analysis of variance summary table will likely identify the source of variation due to the independent variable as "between groups" variation and variation due to error as "within groups" variation.

Reporting the Results of the Analysis of Variance

The *Publication Manual of the American Psychological Association* (American Psychological Association, 2001) requires the report of the results of an analysis of variance to present group means, standard deviations, the value of alpha selected, the observed value of F and its degrees of freedom, the MS_{Error}, and the probability of the observed value of F if H_0 is true. We illustrate this style using the results from the example of the effect length of time awake has on word recall. The analysis of variance for this problem is summarized in Table 10.5. Although we have been using summary tables for analysis of variance, such tables may not be included in journal articles because of their expense to print. If a summary table is not included, the analysis of variance is summarized in text, as illustrated here.

> The mean number of words correctly recalled was 17.0 after waking from sleep 2 hours earlier ($SD = 2.7$), 13.0 after being awake for 24 hours ($SD = 2.2$), and 12.0 for being awake for 36 hours ($SD = 1.9$). With alpha equal to .05, a one-factor between-subjects analysis of variance indicated a significant effect for the length of time awake: $F(2, 12) = 6.56$, $MSE = 5.333$, $p < .05$. Post hoc comparisons using the Tukey HSD test ($CD = 3.9$, $\alpha = .05$) indicated significantly more words recalled for people who were awake for 2 hours compared with either the 24-hour or 36-hour length of time awake conditions. There was no significant difference in the number of words recalled for people who were without sleep for 24 or 36 hours prior to testing. Eta squared for the scores was .52.

In this presentation:

$\alpha = .05$ Indicates the significance level selected for the test.

$F(2, 12)$ Identifies the test statistic as the F; hence, an analysis of variance was used to analyze the data. This F is F_{obs}; the subscript *obs* is not used. The *df* for the numerator (i.e., 2) and the denominator (i.e., 12) of F_{obs} are shown in parentheses. From these *df* you can determine the number of groups involved and the number of subjects used in the experiment as follows: The *df* for the numerator equal $a - 1$. In this report, $df_A = 2$; thus $a = 3$. The *df* for the denominator equal df_{Error}, which equal $N - a$. In the example, $df_{Error} = 12$ and $a = 3$; therefore, $12 = N - 3$ and the total number of subjects in the experiment equals 15.

$= 6.56$ Gives the value of F_{obs} (not the F_{crit} value found in Appendix C.3). If F_{obs} is less than 1.00, it may be reported simply as $F < 1.00$.

$p < .05$ Indicates that
    a. The probability of F_{obs} if H_0 is true is less than or equal to .05. This value is the probability of F_{obs} or an even more extreme value of F_{obs} if H_0 is true; it may not be the same as the value of α selected.
    b. H_0: $\mu_{A_1} = \mu_{A_2} = \mu_{A_3}$ was rejected.
        H_1: The μ_A's are not all equal was accepted.
    c. At least one difference between group means is statistically significant.
    d. Something other than sampling error is responsible for the observed difference in sample means.
    e. If $p > .05$ had been reported, then the greater than sign would indicate that H_0 was not rejected and the sample means did not differ significantly at the .05 significance level. In this instance we would conclude that the length of time awake did not affect the recall of words.

$MSE =$ 5.333   Gives the value of MS_{Error} for the F_{obs}. This value is a measure of the within-group error variation in the scores.

$CD = 3.9$ Gives the critical difference for pairwise comparisons using the Tukey HSD test. The statistically significant pairwise comparisons are then described.

Eta squared $= .52$ Presents the value of η^2 indicating that 52 percent of the variance in the recall scores of this experiment is accounted for by the independent variable of length of time awake. Sometimes a similar effect size measure, ω^2 (omega squared), is given. The value of ω^2 will be slightly less than η^2.

Testing Your Knowledge 10.3

1. In Example 9.3 we looked at the effects of idealized female images in advertisements and the impact such images have on the amount of junk food a person consumes (Gurari, Hetts, & Strube, 2006). Recall that subjects in the control group were shown advertisements that did not include images of the "ideal" body, whereas the experimental group subjects saw advertisements with idealized images of female beauty. Subjects were then asked to wait in a room where junk food and healthy food was present. The researchers measured the amount of junk food in grams each person consumed. Suppose that you replicated this experiment with a total of 22 female subjects and obtained the following grams of junk food eaten by each subject:

Group	
Control	Idealized Image
8	6
9	7
11	9
10	7
9	6
8	8
7	5
6	9
10	6
10	8
9	7

Find the mean and standard deviation for each group, then calculate an analysis of variance on these scores and answer the following questions.

a. State the statistical hypotheses for the F test for these scores.

b. What is the value of F_{obs}?

c. What are the df for F_{obs}?

d. What is F_{crit} at the .05 level?

e. What is the rejection region for F_{obs}?

f. Does F_{obs} fall into the rejection region?

g. What decisions do you make about the statistical hypotheses? Do you reject or fail to reject H_0? Accept or not accept H_1?

h. Do you conclude that the group means are from the same or different populations?

i. Is the difference between the means statistically significant?

j. Did the groups differ in how much junk food they consumed? If so, what is the direction of the difference?

k. Are multiple comparison tests needed in this experiment? Give the reason for your answer.

l. What is η^2 for this experiment?

m. How much of the variance is accounted for by the independent variable in this experiment?

2. Sadeh, Raviv, and Gruber (2000) investigated sleeping patterns in second-, fourth-, and sixth-grade children. Suppose you also investigated this problem and found the following sleep periods in minutes for groups of second-, fourth-, and sixth-grade girls. There were 14 students in each group. Sleep period is defined as the amount of time from the onset of sleep to awakening in the morning.

Grade		
2nd	4th	6th
580	497	525
525	515	506
562	543	475
590	478	493
575	567	537
603	532	532
594	517	480
521	510	501
536	534	472
612	556	463
514	511	521
544	523	517
573	572	477
592	574	515

Find the mean and standard deviation for each group and then calculate an analysis of variance on these scores and answer the following questions.

a. State the statistical hypotheses for the F test for these scores.

b. What is the value of F_{obs}?

c. What are the df for F_{obs}?

d. What is F_{crit} at the .05 level?

e. What is the rejection region for F_{obs}?

f. Does F_{obs} fall into the rejection region?

   g. What decisions do you make about the statistical hypotheses? Do you reject or fail to reject H_0? Accept or not accept H_1?

   h. What can you conclude from the overall analysis of variance on these scores?

   i. Are multiple comparison tests needed in this experiment? Give the reason for your answer.

   j. What is the value of the Tukey CD?

   k. Which pairwise differences are statistically significant?

   l. Describe how the groups differ in sleep periods.

   m. What is η^2 for this experiment?

   n. How much of the variance is accounted for by the independent variable in this experiment?

3. The following problems present brief reports of one-factor between-subjects analysis of variance. Answer the following questions for each report.

   a. How many levels of the independent variable were used in this experiment?

   b. How many subjects were used in this experiment?

   c. What is the value of F_{obs}?

   d. What is the value of F_{crit} at the .05 significance level?

   e. Do you reject or fail to reject H_0?

   f. Do you accept or not accept H_1?

   g. Is there at least one statistically significant difference between the means?

   h. Which means, if any, differ significantly?

Problem 1: The mean number of tones detected while listening to a familiar poetry passage was 79.9 compared to a mean of 73.0 when listening to an unfamiliar poetry passage. With alpha equal to .05, a one-factor between-subjects analysis of variance indicated that the means differed significantly, $F(1, 60) = 14.15$, $MSE = 5.740$, $p < .01$.

Problem 2: With alpha equal to .05, no difference was found in the number of words recalled as a function of retention interval, $F(3, 36) = 1.13$, $MSE = 14.342$, $p > .05$.

Problem 3: The mean number of typing errors was 18.5 for the group listening to classical music, 29.9 for the group listening to hard-rock music, and 17.5 for the no-music control group. With alpha equal to .05, a one-factor between-subjects analysis of variance indicated a significant effect for the type of music, $F(2, 36) = 33.94$, $MSE = 18.261$, $p < .001$. Post hoc comparisons using the Tukey HSD test ($CD = 4.1$, $\alpha = .05$) indicated significantly more typing errors for the hard-rock music condition than for either the no-music control or the classical-music condition. The no-music and classical-music conditions did not differ significantly.

Summary

▶ A one-factor multilevel design is an experiment with one independent variable and three or more levels of that independent variable.

▶ The one-factor between-subjects analysis of variance is used to analyze scores from a one-factor multilevel design.

▶ The F statistic is given by $F = MS_A/MS_{Error}$.

▶ A MS is a variance and is found by SS/df.

▶ MS_A varies with the effect of the independent variable and sampling error.

▶ MS_{Error} varies with the within-groups error variation.

▶ If the independent variable has no effect, then MS_A and MS_{Error} estimate only error variation in the scores and F should be about equal to 1.00.

▶ When an independent variable has an effect, MS_A increases in value, but MS_{Error} is not affected. The value of F becomes larger than 1.00.

▶ Using the F statistic in a statistical test follows the usual steps of formulating statistical hypotheses, setting a significance level, locating a rejection region, calculating F_{obs}, and making decisions concerning the statistical hypotheses.

▶ A statistically significant F_{obs} when three or more levels of an independent variable are manipulated requires a multiple comparison test to follow up the analysis of variance.

▶ Multiple comparison tests are used to find which means differ significantly from one another in a one-factor multilevel design after a statistically significant F_{obs} has occurred for the overall analysis of variance. A comparison of two means is a pairwise comparison.

▶ The Tukey test is used for all possible pairwise post hoc comparisons for a set of means. The Tukey test holds the probability of a Type I error equal to or less than α for all possible pairwise comparisons.

▶ η^2 may be used as a measure of effect size.

Key Terms and Symbols

Review Questions

1. Music seems to be everywhere in modern society, and psychologists have investigated its effects on a variety of performances. For example, suppose an experimenter created three equivalent groups of eight people each and asked each person to perform a proofreading task on a short research paper. Subjects in group A_1 performed the task with no music playing in the background, subjects in group A_2 performed the task with a selection of oldies playing in the background, and subjects in group A_3 performed the task while listening to hard rock. The dependent variable was the

number of errors detected out of a possible 50. Suppose the following scores were obtained:

Treatment Group		
No Music (A_1)	Oldies (A_2)	Hard Rock (A_3)
40	34	26
41	39	24
39	38	19
36	40	23
35	34	18
32	35	21
31	29	23
34	36	29

a. Identify the type of research design used in this study.

b. Find the mean and standard deviation for each group. Then, analyze the scores with a one-factor between-subjects analysis to answer the question: Did the music condition affect the number of errors detected by a subject? Use a .05 significance level. If needed, use the Tukey HSD test for multiple comparisons.

c. What is the value of η^2 for this experiment? What proportion of the variance in the dependent variable can be accounted for by knowing the level of the independent variable?

d. Describe the results of this experiment following the style illustrated in the Reporting the Results of the Analysis of Variance section of this chapter.

2. Suppose you had been asked to perform boring tasks for an hour and then requested to tell someone the tasks were enjoyable and interesting, and did so. How would you feel about this? It is likely you would experience cognitive dissonance or disagreement between your belief about the task and your behavior; that is, you believe that the tasks were boring, but your behavior by saying they were enjoyable and interesting was inconsistent with this belief. Festinger and Carlsmith (1959) performed a now classic experiment exploring this problem. Subjects in the experiment were given a tray containing 12 spools and asked to empty the tray onto the table and then refill the tray with the spools, repeating this task for 30 minutes. The subjects were then given a board with square pegs and asked to turn each peg one-quarter of the way for another 30 minutes. Following these tasks, subjects were randomly assigned to one of three conditions. Subjects in the control group (A_1) were simply asked to rate how enjoyable they found the task on a scale from -5 to $+5$ (-5 extremely dull and boring, 0 neutral, $+5$ extremely interesting and enjoyable). Subjects in the other two groups, however, were asked to tell the next person in the experiment that the tasks they were about to do were interesting and enjoyable. The subjects were given either $1 (group A_2) or $20 (group A_3) for their time. (Remember, this study took place in the 1950s where $1 would have the purchasing power of about $7 today and $20 would have the purchasing power of about $140 today.) After the subjects in the $1 and $20 groups spoke to the next subject, they completed the -5 to $+5$ rating scale on the enjoyableness of the tasks they had performed. Festinger and Carlsmith anticipated the subjects in the $1 condition would have the greatest dissonance between their belief and behavior—"the tasks were boring, yet I told someone they were fun but got paid only a small amount to do so." To resolve this dissonance, Festinger and Carlsmith believed

the subjects in this group would change their belief about the tasks and rate the tasks more favorably than either the control or $20 subjects. Suppose the following scores on the -5 to $+5$ scale were obtained for eight people in each treatment condition.

Payment Condition		
None (A_1)	$1 (A_2)	$20 (A_3)
0	1	-1
-1	3	0
-1	1	1
0	0	2
-2	2	-2
1	3	1
0	1	0
-1	1	-1

a. Identify the type of research design used in this study.

b. Find the mean and standard deviation for each group. Then, analyze the scores with a one-factor between-subjects analysis of variance to answer the following question: Did paying the subjects affect the ratings on the enjoyableness of the task? Use a .05 significance level. If needed, use the Tukey HSD test for multiple comparisons. Is the outcome of the experiment in agreement with the research hypothesis we expressed in the question?

c. What is the value of η^2 for this experiment? What proportion of the variance in the dependent variable can be accounted for by knowing the level of the independent variable?

d. Describe the results of this experiment following the style illustrated in the Reporting the Results of the Analysis of Variance section of this chapter.

3. Problem 1 of the Chapter 9 Review Questions dealt with the physiological effects of noise. In the experiment described, subjects either sat in a quiet room for 30 minutes or listened to a recording of traffic noise for 30 minutes. At the end of 30 minutes, their systolic blood pressures were measured and the following scores obtained (in millimeters of mercury).

Group	
Quiet (A_1)	Noise (A_2)
106	141
117	136
124	124
129	139
115	121
131	119
121	147
115	128
128	115
136	134
127	140

a. Find the mean and standard deviation for each group. Then, analyze the scores with a one-factor between-subjects analysis to answer the following question: Does noise affect systolic blood pressure? Use a .05 significance level.

b. Compare the value of F_{obs} to the value of t_{obs} for problem 1 of the Chapter 9 Review Questions. Do you find the expected relationship between t and F?

4. An experimenter used a one-factor between-subjects design with six levels of the independent variable, A_1, A_2, A_3, A_4, A_5, and A_6, and seven subjects in each level.

a. What are the values of a, n_A, and N for this experiment?

b. What are the values of df_A, df_{Error}, and df_{Total} for the analysis of variance for this experiment?

5. The following tables are incomplete summary tables for an analysis of variance. Assume an equal number of scores in each level of the independent variable. By using the relationships among SS, df, and MS, provide the missing values in each table. Then, answer the following questions for each table.

a. How many levels of the independent variable were manipulated?

b. How many subjects were tested in each treatment condition?

c. What was the total number of subjects in the experiment?

d. Is the value of F_{obs} statistically significant at the .05 level?

e. What decision do you make for H_0 and H_1 for each analysis?

Table 1				
Source	SS	df	MS	F
Factor A	50.0	2	—	—
Error	270.0	27	—	
Total	—	—		

Table 2				
Source	SS	df	MS	F
Factor A	60.0	—	12.0	—
Error	—	72	—	
Total	276.0	77		

Table 3				
Source	SS	df	MS	F
Factor A	—	—	—	3.00
Error	320.0	—	5.0	
Total	365.0	67		

6. Does rejection of H_0 and acceptance of H_1 in an analysis of variance necessarily provide support for a research hypothesis? Explain your answer.

7. You conducted a t_{ind} on two groups and t_{obs} (18) = 2.000. If you had analyzed the scores with an analysis of variance, what value of F_{obs} would you have found? Indicate the df for F_{obs}.

8. You conducted an analysis of variance on two independent groups and F_{obs} (1, 22) = 9.00. If you had analyzed the scores with a t_{ind}, what value of t_{obs} would you have found? Indicate the df for t_{obs}.

9. Explain why a statistical test cannot identify the reason for two groups differing significantly.

10. A psychologist was interested in comparing four treatments for a smoking-cessation program. She created four groups of 17 smokers each by random assignment and gave each group a different treatment. The dependent variable measured was the mean time between smoking cigarettes after five weeks of treatment. The treatment groups and the mean time between cigarettes (in minutes) are given in Table 1, and an analysis of variance for these data is presented in Table 2.

TABLE 1

Treatment conditions and mean times between smoking cigarettes (in minutes)

Treatment Condition		Mean Time
A_1	Control group; no treatment given	24.0
A_2	Behavior modification	38.0
A_3	Cigarettes anonymous club	34.0
A_4	Smoke-Stop gum	28.0

TABLE 2

Analysis of variance summary table for mean time between smoking cigarettes in Table 1

Source	SS	df	MS	F
Treatment condition	1972.00	3	657.333	21.64*
Error	1944.00	64	30.375	
Total	3916.00	67		

*$p < .01$.

A Tukey HSD gave a $CD = 5.0$ minutes at the .05 significance level.

a. What is the effect of the treatment conditions on the amount of time between smoking cigarettes?

b. Describe the results of this experiment following the style illustrated in the Reporting the Results of the Analysis of Variance section of this chapter.

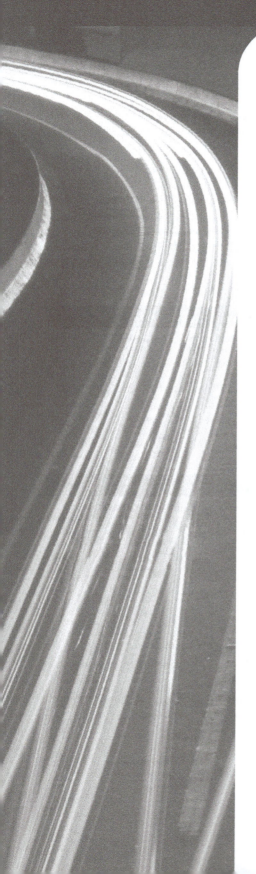

Two-Factor Between-Subjects Analysis of Variance

College is a time for academic growth as well as a time when people form life-long relationships, some of which may be romantic in nature. Romantic relationships typically involve feelings of emotional intimacy between the partners. What helps to develop these feelings of emotional intimacy? One factor is the disclosure of personal information and emotions between romantic partners (Mitchell et al., 2008). As people develop and maintain emotionally intimate relationships, they often spend time listening and disclosing personal information to their partners.

It is easy to imagine, however, that there may be gender differences between men and women in how disclosure of personal information leads to greater emotional intimacy in a relationship. For example, Mitchell et al. (2008) found that women felt greater emotional intimacy when their partners were disclosing personal situations, yet men felt greater emotional intimacy when they were disclosing their own personal situations. Notice in this study there are two independent variables that affect the dependent variable of emotional intimacy: (1) the disclosure condition, either partner disclosure or self disclosure, and (2) the gender of the person, a subject variable. One-factor designs do not permit the study of more than one independent variable at a time; thus, to study the effect of two or more independent variables on a dependent variable, factorial designs are used.

Factorial design ▶ A research design in which two or more independent variables are varied simultaneously.

Factorial designs are research designs in which two or more independent variables are simultaneously varied. In the simplest factorial design, two independent variables are varied and each independent variable assumes two levels. This design often is called a 2×2 ("two-by-two") design. The first 2 of the 2×2 indicates that there are two levels of the first independent variable (identified as **factor A**), and the second 2 indicates the number of levels of the second independent variable (identified as **factor B**). A $2 \times 2 \times 2$ design is a three-factor design with factors A, B, and C, and each independent variable varies over two levels. There are many possible factorial designs, such as a 2×4 design (two levels of factor A, four levels of factor B), a $3 \times 3 \times 2$ design (three levels of factors A and B, two levels of factor C), and a $2 \times 2 \times 2 \times 2$ design (four factors, A, B, C, and D, with two levels of each). Factorial designs may also be totally between subjects, totally within subjects, or a combination of the two, resulting in a mixed design. In this text we discuss only the two-factor (also called a *two-way*) between-subjects design.

The 2×2 between-subjects design is convenient for introducing the statistical data analysis of factorial designs. Table 11.1 illustrates two independent variables or factors identified as A and B, each taking on two levels: factor A with levels A_1 and A_2 and factor B

TABLE 11.1

Plan of a 2×2 between-subjects design. The combination of a level of factor A with a level of factor B forms a treatment condition or cell.

| | | Factor A | |
		A_1	A_2
Factor B	B_1	A_1B_1 treatment condition (A_1B_1 cell)	A_2B_1 treatment condition (A_2B_1 cell)
	B_2	A_1B_2 treatment condition (A_1B_2 cell)	A_2B_2 treatment condition (A_2B_2 cell)

Cell or treatment condition ▷
A combination formed from one level of each independent variable in a factorial design.

with levels B_1 and B_2. Generally, there are a levels of factor A and b levels of factor B. In the example, $a = 2$ and $b = 2$, the combination of the two independent variables creates four treatment conditions, called *cells*, in the table. Each **cell** or **treatment condition** represents a combination formed from one level of each independent variable, for example, the A_1B_1, A_1B_2, A_2B_1 and A_2B_2, cells. An equal number of subjects typically is randomly assigned to each of the treatment conditions. Thus, if 20 subjects are used in a 2×2 between-subjects design, five people are assigned to each treatment condition or cell. Each person experiences only one treatment condition.

An Example 2 × 2 Between-Subjects Design

There are many variables that can affect how well a person does on a mathematics achievement test. Certainly, aptitude, experience, and effort are critical for performance on a math test. Yet, some research has found that the attitudes and stereotypes people possess can also impact performance on tests of mathematical achievement. A stereotype is a generalization, often oversimplified, about the characteristics of a group. Recently, behavioral scientists have studied the concept of stereotype threat. Stereotype threat theory hypothesizes that people may fear their behavior will be in accord with the stereotype of a group with which they identify. This type of thinking may actually diminish people's ability to perform well on certain tasks. For example, one common stereotype is that females do not do as well on mathematics tasks as males. In this instance, stereotype threat theory hypothesizes that if a female has been exposed to the stereotype that women do poorly in mathematics, then when in a stereotype threat situation, it may lead her to worry that her performance on a mathematics achievement test will confirm this stereotype, thus reducing her performance on the test. Keller (2007), however, hypothesized that the effect of a stereotype threat on performing a mathematics achievement task will depend upon how much a person identifies with mathematics. That is, a female who believes it is important to be good at math and thus identifies with mathematics will be affected more by the stereotype threat than a female who does not care about her math performance. This hypothesis thus predicts that when a female identifies strongly with mathematics, exposure to a stereotype threat that females do not do as well as males on math tasks will decrease her math performance when compared to a female who does not experience this stereotype threat. For females low in mathematics identification, however, the presence or absence of this stereotype threat should have no effect. Notice that these hypotheses identify two independent variables: a person's identification with mathematics (called *math identification*) and presence or absence of stereotype threat. The dependent variable is the female's math performance.

We will use a 2×2 between-subjects design to empirically test these hypotheses. The first independent variable, factor A, is level of math identification, how much a person indicates that good math performance is important to her, with two levels: A_1, low math identification, and A_2, high math identification. This independent variable is a subject variable, subjects are either high or low in math identification (see page 21 for a discussion of subject variables). The second independent variable, factor B, is stereotype threat, with two levels: the threat present condition, B_1, occurs when subjects are placed in a situation that elicits stereotype threat, and the no threat present condition, B_2, when subjects are not exposed to a stereotype threat situation. Assume the experimental procedure was as follows. Female students were administered a short questionnaire that assessed how strongly they identified with mathematics and then divided into two groups based on their responses: low math identification (level A_1), for whom good math performance was not important, or high math identification (level A_2), for whom good math performance was important. Stereotype threat was manipulated by informing the subjects how males and females typically perform on the mathematics achievement test they were preparing to take. In the threat present condition (level B_1), a stereotype threat was induced by telling the subjects that males typically outperform females on mathematics achievement tests. In the no threat present condition (level B_2), the subjects were told that males and females do equally well on the mathematics achievement test. Half of the females with low math identification (level A_1) were randomly assigned to the stereotype threat present condition (level B_1), and the other half were randomly assigned to the no threat present condition (level B_2). Likewise, half of the females with high math identification (level A_2) were randomly assigned to the stereotype threat present condition (level B_1), the other half were randomly assigned to the no threat present condition (level B_2). The dependent variable was the subject's performance on a mathematics achievement test.

Stereotype threat theory leads to several research hypotheses about the outcome of this study. First, for low math identification females, the presence of a stereotype threat should have no effect because good math performance is not important to them. Second, for high math identification females, the presence of a stereotype threat should lead to poorer performance than no threat because good math performance is important to them. Third, for the threat present condition, performance between high and low math identification subjects may not differ because the threat present condition will lower the high math identification subjects' scores. And, fourth, for the no threat present condition, it is expected that the high math identification subjects, for whom good math performance is important, will obtain higher scores than the low math identification subjects for whom good math performance is not important. The scores obtained on the test are given in Table 11.2. Do the data given in this table support these hypotheses?

TABLE	
11.2	Hypothetical mathematics achievement test performance scores as a function of stereotype threat condition and level of math identification for 20 female subjects in the example 2 × 2 between-subjects experiment.

		Level of Math Identification (Factor A)	
		Low (A_1)	**High (A_2)**
	Threat Present (B_1)	97	70
		90	87
		80	81
		107	95
		80	90
Stereotype Threat Condition (Factor B)	**No Threat Present (B_2)**	68	114
		87	96
		92	127
		80	110
		84	115

Information Obtained from a Factorial Design

The scores in Table 11.2 are represented in notation in Table 11.3. A score for a subject is represented by X_{ijk}, where the subscripts provide the following information:

i = number identifying the subject within a treatment condition

j = level of the A variable that the subject receives

k = level of the B variable that the subject receives

For example, X_{311} is the score of the third person in the A_1B_1 treatment condition (80 in Table 11.2), X_{421} is the score of the fourth person in the A_2B_1 treatment condition (95), X_{212} is the score of the second subject in the A_1B_2 treatment condition (87), X_{522} is the score of the fifth subject in the A_2B_2 treatment condition (115), and so on. When it is not necessary to identify a specific person, we drop the ijk subscripts and simply use X. For each cell there are n_{AB} subjects with a total of N subjects in the experiment. For the example, $n_{AB} = 5$ and $N = 20$. The first step in data analysis begins with computing measures of central tendency, the sample means. Table 11.4 illustrates the cell and main effect means that may be calculated from the example scores.

Cell Means

Cell mean ▶ The mean of the n_{AB} scores for a treatment combination in a factorial design.

The **cell means**, symbolized by $\overline{X}_{A_1B_1}$, $\overline{X}_{A_1B_2}$, $\overline{X}_{A_2B_1}$, and $\overline{X}_{A_2B_2}$, or, in general, by $\overline{X}_{AB}$, are the means of the n_{AB} scores for a treatment combination (see Table 11.4a). A cell mean indicates the typical performance of subjects in a treatment condition. The numerical values of the cell means for the scores of Table 11.2 are presented in Table 11.5 with the standard deviations in parentheses. In a factorial design, the standard deviation typically is calculated only for the cell means.

TABLE

11.3

Notational representation of scores in a 2 × 2 between-subjects design with two levels of each independent variable and five subjects per cell.

		Factor A	
		A_1	A_2
	B_1	X_{111} X_{211} X_{311} X_{411} X_{511}	X_{121} X_{221} X_{321} X_{421} X_{521}
Factor B			
	B_2	X_{112} X_{212} X_{312} X_{412} X_{512}	X_{122} X_{222} X_{322} X_{422} X_{522}

TABLE 11.4

Cell and main effect means in a 2 × 2 between-subjects design.

(a) Cell means

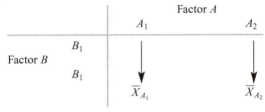

(b) Main effect means for factor A: $\overline{X}_{A_1}$ and $\overline{X}_{A_2}$

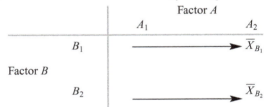

Ignore classification of scores by factor B to obtain main effect means for factor A. The difference between $\overline{X}_{A_1}$ and $\overline{X}_{A_2}$ is the main effect of factor A.

(c) Main effect means for factor B: $\overline{X}_{B_1}$ and $\overline{X}_{B_2}$

Ignore classification of scores by factor A to obtain main effect means for factor B. The difference between $\overline{X}_{B_1}$ and $\overline{X}_{B_2}$ is the main effect of factor B.

TABLE 11.5

Cell and main effect means for the data of Table 11.2. The numerical values are mathematics achievement test scores. Standard deviations of cell means are given in parentheses.

		Level of Math Identification (Factor A)		
		Low (A₁)	High (A₂)	Main Effect Means for Stereotype Threat ($\overline{X}_B$)
Stereotype Threat Condition (Factor B)	Threat Present (B₁)	90.8 (11.6)	84.6 (9.6)	87.7
	No Threat Present (B₂)	82.2 (9.1)	112.4 (11.2)	97.3
	Main Effect Means for Math Identification ($\overline{X}_A$)	86.5	98.5	Grand mean 92.5

Main Effect Means

Main effect mean ▷ The mean of all subjects given one level of an independent variable, ignoring the classification by the other independent variable in a factorial design.

A **main effect mean** indicates the typical performance of all subjects given one level of an independent variable, ignoring the classification by the other independent variable. Thus, there are two sets of main effect means, those for factor A and those for factor B.

Factor A

The *main effect means for factor A* are symbolized by $\overline{X}_{A_1}$ and $\overline{X}_{A_2}$. These means, sometimes called *column means*, are found for all subjects within either level A_1 or A_2, while disregarding the level of factor B that they received. Collapsing the data over levels of factor B to obtain main effect means for factor A is shown in Table 11.4b. For the example, in Table 11.2, the main effect means for factor A, level of math identification, are based on the 10 scores of subjects who are either low or high in math identification. Stereotype threat, factor B, is ignored when finding the main effect means of factor A. The values of $\overline{X}_{A_1}$ and $\overline{X}_{A_2}$ are presented in Table 11.5. The **main effect of factor A** is the difference between $\overline{X}_{A_1}$ and $\overline{X}_{A_2}$. If factor A has an effect on the dependent variable, then $\overline{X}_{A_1}$ and $\overline{X}_{A_2}$ will differ from each other, and the value of $\overline{X}_{A_1} - \overline{X}_{A_2}$ will become larger.

Main effect of factor A ▷ The difference between $\overline{X}_{A_1}$ and $\overline{X}_{A_2}$, symbolized by $\overline{X}_{A_1} - \overline{X}_{A_2}$.

Factor B

A similar logic applies to finding the main effect for independent variable B. The *main effect means for factor B* (sometimes called *row means*), symbolized as $\overline{X}_{B_1}$ and $\overline{X}_{B_2}$, are obtained by collapsing the data over factor A as shown in Table 11.4c. To find the main effect means for factor B in the example, stereotype threat, the categorization by level of math identification (factor A) is ignored. The numerical values of $\overline{X}_{B_1}$ and $\overline{X}_{B_2}$ also are presented in Table 11.5. The **main effect of factor B** is the difference $\overline{X}_{B_1} - \overline{X}_{B_2}$. If factor B has an effect on the dependent variable, then $\overline{X}_{B_1}$ and $\overline{X}_{B_2}$ will differ from each other, and the value of $\overline{X}_{B_1} - \overline{X}_{B_2}$ will become larger.

Main effect of factor B ▷ The difference between $\overline{X}_{B_1}$ and $\overline{X}_{B_2}$, symbolized by $\overline{X}_{B_1} - \overline{X}_{B_2}$.

Grand Mean

The **grand mean**, symbolized as $\overline{X}_G$, is the mean of all the scores in the table. For the data in Table 11.2, the grand mean of 92.5 is the mean of all 20 scores. The grand mean typically is not presented as a descriptive statistic, but it is needed in this chapter for developing an analysis of variance for this design.

Grand mean ▷ The mean of all the scores in a factorial design, symbolized by $\overline{X}_G$.

Interaction of the Independent Variables

Interaction ▷ A situation in a factorial design when the effect of one independent variable depends on the level of the other independent variable with which it is combined.

An **interaction** occurs in a factorial design when the effect of one independent variable (e.g., factor A) depends on the level of the other independent variable (e.g., either B_1 or B_2) with which it is combined. For example, if an interaction occurs in a 2×2 design, then the effect of factor A, the difference in behavior between treatments A_1 and A_2, depends on the level of factor B. Similarly, if an interaction occurs, the effect of factor B, the difference in behavior between treatments B_1 and B_2, depends on the level of factor A. An interaction often is symbolized as $A \times B$, which is read as "A by B" or the "A by B interaction."

The hypotheses we presented for our example experiment predicted an interaction. These hypotheses predicted that a female's mathematics achievement test performance would depend on two factors: how strongly she identified with mathematics and whether or not she experienced stereotype threat. It is predicted that females who identify with mathematics and who experience stereotype threat will perform poorly (the A_2B_1 cell mean) in comparison to females who identify with mathematics but do not experience

CHAPTER 11 Two-Factor Between-Subjects Analysis of Variance   **289**

stereotype threat (the A_2B_2 cell mean). For the low math identification subjects, however, no difference was expected between threat present (the A_1B_1 cell mean) and no threat present conditions (the A_1B_2 cell mean). Similarly, for a threat present condition, no difference was expected between low (the A_1B_1 cell mean) and high math identification subjects (the A_2B_1 cell mean). But, when no threat was given, the low math identification subjects (the A_1B_2 cell mean) were expected to perform more poorly than the high math identification subjects. (the A_2B_2 cell mean). Notice, then, that the occurrence of an interaction is analyzed by comparing differences among the cell means rather than among the main effect means. We discuss these comparisons more fully later in the chapter.

Testing Your Knowledge 11.1

1. Define: *a, b,* cell, cell mean, column mean, factor, factorial design, grand mean, interaction, level of an independent variable, main effect for factor A, main effect for factor B, main effect mean, n_{AB}, N, row mean, treatment condition, $\overline{X}_{AB}, \overline{X}_A, \overline{X}_B, \overline{X}_G$.

2. For each of the following factorial designs, identify how many independent variables are varied and indicate the number of levels for each factor. Then, assuming that the design is a between-subjects design, indicate how many subjects would be needed if 10 subjects were to be tested in each treatment combination.

   Type of design: (a) 3×3, (b) 3×2, (c) 2×3, (d) 6×2, (e) 4×4, (f) $2 \times 2 \times 2$, (g) $2 \times 4 \times 3$, (h) $3 \times 3 \times 2$.

3. Find cell means, main effect means, and the grand mean for the scores in each of the following tables:

<table>
<tr><th colspan="3" style="text-align:center">Table 1</th></tr>
<tr><td></td><td colspan="2" style="text-align:center">Factor A</td></tr>
<tr><td></td><td>A_1</td><td>A_2</td></tr>
<tr><td rowspan="6">B_1</td><td>10</td><td>17</td></tr>
<tr><td>13</td><td>23</td></tr>
<tr><td>8</td><td>17</td></tr>
<tr><td>17</td><td>21</td></tr>
<tr><td>12</td><td>19</td></tr>
<tr><td>20</td><td>24</td></tr>
<tr><td rowspan="6">B_1</td><td>19</td><td>27</td></tr>
<tr><td>13</td><td>21</td></tr>
<tr><td>10</td><td>16</td></tr>
<tr><td>20</td><td>19</td></tr>
<tr><td>22</td><td>30</td></tr>
<tr><td>17</td><td>24</td></tr>
</table>

Factor B

<table>
<tr><th colspan="3" style="text-align:center">Table 2</th></tr>
<tr><td></td><td colspan="2" style="text-align:center">Factor A</td></tr>
<tr><td></td><td>A_1</td><td>A_2</td></tr>
<tr><td rowspan="6">B_1</td><td>23</td><td>41</td></tr>
<tr><td>13</td><td>22</td></tr>
<tr><td>28</td><td>27</td></tr>
<tr><td>11</td><td>32</td></tr>
<tr><td>19</td><td>26</td></tr>
<tr><td>20</td><td>24</td></tr>
<tr><td></td><td>18</td><td>39</td></tr>
<tr><td rowspan="7">B_1</td><td>29</td><td>28</td></tr>
<tr><td>33</td><td>31</td></tr>
<tr><td>18</td><td>26</td></tr>
<tr><td>29</td><td>34</td></tr>
<tr><td>36</td><td>39</td></tr>
<tr><td>47</td><td>44</td></tr>
<tr><td>27</td><td>35</td></tr>
</table>

Factor B

Analysis of Variance of a Two-Factor Between-Subjects Design

The statistical analysis of a factorial design involves hypothesis testing to determine if the main effect means differ significantly from each other for each independent variable and to determine if the interaction of the independent variables is statistically significant. Again, this testing is done with an analysis of variance that partitions the total variation of scores into sources of variation that are independent of each other. The one-factor between-subjects analysis of variance (discussed in Chapter 10) partitions the total variation into two independent sources: that due to the effect of the independent variable (i.e., factor A) and that due to within-groups error variation. In a two-factor between-subjects design, the total variation of scores is partitioned into three between-groups sources and one within-group source. The between-groups sources of variation are the following:

▶ The variation due to the effect of factor A
▶ The variation due to the effect of factor B
▶ The variation due to the interaction of factors A and B, symbolized as $A \times B$

The within-groups source is the within-cells error variation.

The analysis of variance then uses these partitioned scores to generate four mean squares:

MS_A, which varies with the effect of factor A

MS_B, which varies with the effect of factor B

$MS_{A \times B}$, which varies with an interaction of factors A and B

MS_{Error}, which varies with the within-cells variation of the scores

Following this step, three separate F statistics are generated, one for each independent variable and one for interaction, as follows:

Source of Variation	F Statistic
Factor A	$MS_A \div MS_{Error}$
Factor B	$MS_B \div MS_{Error}$
Interaction of $A \times B$	$MS_{A \times B} \div MS_{Error}$

Each of the three F statistics is used in a statistical hypothesis test to find if the source of variation to which the F statistic corresponds is statistically significant.

To provide a conceptual understanding of a factorial analysis of variance, the next section derives the mean squares that enter into these F statistics. If you were to perform a factorial analysis of variance on an actual set of data, however, you would use a computer data analysis program such as SPSS or Minitab.

Partitioning a Score

The factorial analysis of variance finds the mean squares for the three F statistics by partitioning or separating the total variation of the scores in an experiment into parts varying with factor A (between groups), factor B (between groups), the $A \times B$ interaction (between groups), and error variation (within groups). This model for representing a score in a two-factor between-subjects design can be expressed as follows:

| Total variation in a subject's score | = | Variation due to factor *A* plus sampling error | + | Variation due to factor *B* plus sampling error | + | Variation due to interaction of factors *A* and B plus sampling error | + | Variation due to within-cells error | (11.1) |

In terms of scores, this equation can be written as

$$X - \overline{X}_G = (\overline{X}_A - \overline{X}_G) + (\overline{X}_B - \overline{X}_G) + (\overline{X}_{AB} - \overline{X}_A - \overline{X}_B + \overline{X}_G) + (X - \overline{X}_{AB})$$

| Difference of a subject's score from the grand mean | = | Difference of factor *A* main effect mean from the grand mean | + | Difference of factor *B* main effect mean from the grand mean | + | Interaction: Difference of a cell mean from the grand mean after the main effects of factors *A* and *B* have been removed | + | Difference of the subject's score from its cell mean | (11.2) |

We examine each part of equation 11.2.

Total Variation

Similar to the one-factor analysis of variance of Chapter 10, the difference of a score from the grand mean (i.e., $X - \overline{X}_G$ represents the total variation of that score. As equation 11.2 indicates, a part of this variation is due to the effect of each independent variable and the interaction of the independent variables, and a part of it is due to error variation.

Variation Due to the Effect of Factor *A* and Sampling Error

The difference between a main effect mean of factor *A* and the grand mean (i.e., $\overline{X}_A - \overline{X}_G$) varies with the effect of factor *A* and with sampling error among the main effect means of factor *A*. Its use in a two-factor design is identical to its use in the one-factor between-subjects design to measure the effect of the independent variable. Any effect of factor *A* is expected to affect all subjects within a level of this factor equally. Thus, an effect of factor *A* changes the value of the main effect means for factor *A*. These main effect means will then differ from the grand mean. Hence, the difference $\overline{X}_A - \overline{X}_G$ reflects any effect of factor *A* (the treatment effect for factor *A* in equation 11.1). In addition to any treatment effect, the main effect means for factor *A* will also differ from each other because of sampling error. Therefore, the value of any $\overline{X}_A - \overline{X}_G$ difference reflects both a treatment effect of factor *A* and sampling error affecting the values of $\overline{X}_A$. Accordingly, it enters into the computation of MS_A.

Variation Due to the Effect of Factor *B* and Sampling Error

The difference between a main effect mean of factor *B* and the grand mean (i.e., $\overline{X}_B - \overline{X}_G$) varies with the effect of factor *B* and sampling error among the main effect means of factor *B*. As with factor *A*, any effect of factor *B* is expected to affect all subjects within a level of this factor equally and, thus, change the value of the main effect means for factor *B*, which will then differ from the grand mean. Therefore, the difference $\overline{X}_B - \overline{X}_G$ reflects any effect of factor *B* (the treatment effect for factor *B* in equation 11.1). In addition, the main effect means for factor *B* will differ from each other because of sampling error. Hence, the difference $\overline{X}_B - \overline{X}_G$ reflects both a treatment effect of factor *B* and sampling error affecting the values of $\overline{X}_B$ and, thus, enters into the computation of MS_B.

Variation Due to the Interaction of Factors *A* and *B*

The interaction of factors *A* and *B* is the remaining difference of the cell means from the grand mean after the main effect of each independent variable has been removed. Symbolically, this statement may be represented as follows:

$$A \times B = (\overline{X}_{AB} - \overline{X}_G) \quad - (\overline{X}_A - \overline{X}_G) - (\overline{X}_B - \overline{X}_G),$$

$$\frac{\text{Interaction}}{\text{of } A \text{ and } B} = \frac{\text{Difference of}}{\text{cell mean from}} - \frac{\text{Main effect}}{\text{of factor } A} - \frac{\text{Main effect}}{\text{of factor } B}.$$

The equation indicates that the interaction represents the variation in cell means after the main effect of each independent variable has been removed. This remaining variation in the cell means is due to the interaction of the independent variables and any sampling error among the cell means.

Carrying out the subtractions indicated in the equation results in a simplified expression of the interaction:

$$\overline{X}_{AB} - \overline{X}_A - \overline{X}_B + \overline{X}_G.$$

The interaction is expressed in this form in equation 11.2. This part of the equation enters into the computation of $MS_{A \times B}$.

Variation Due to Within-Cells Error

The difference of a score from its cell mean (i.e., $X - \overline{X}_{AB}$) reflects only within-cells error variation in the experiment. This error is what is left over in the score after the main effects of both factors and their interaction have been taken into account. As in a one-factor analysis of variance, the error reflects the uniqueness of a person's score in a group of individuals, all of whom receive the same treatment. It enters into the computation of MS_{Error}.

Obtaining Mean Squares from Partitioned Scores

As discussed in Chapter 10, the partitioning equation provides the basis for obtaining the *SS* and *df* that produce the mean squares for the *F* ratio. The first step is to obtain the *SS* from the scores.

Obtaining Sums of Squares

Following the approach of Chapter 10, sums of squares (*SS*) are obtained by partitioning each score in the form of equation 11.2. To illustrate this partitioning, we use the score for the first person in the low math identification/threat present condition (i.e., X_{111}) of Table 11.2, which is 97.0. For this score, equation 11.2 becomes

$$X_{111} - \overline{X}_G = (\overline{X}_{A_1} - \overline{X}_G) + (\overline{X}_{B_1} - \overline{X}_G) + (\overline{X}_{A_1 B_1} - \overline{X}_{A_1} - \overline{X}_{B_1} + \overline{X}_G) + (X_{111} - \overline{X}_{A_1 B_1}).$$

Substituting numerical values, we obtain

$$97.0 - 92.5 = (86.5 - 92.5) + (87.7 - 92.5)$$
$$+ (90.8 - 86.5 - 87.7 + 92.5) + (97.0 - 90.8)$$

or, carrying out the arithmetic functions indicated,

$$+4.5 = (-6.0) + (-4.8) + (+9.1) + (+6.2).$$

This partitioning shows that this score differs from the grand mean as much as it does because of the systematic effect of the level of factor A received (reflected in $\overline{X}_{A_1} - \overline{X}_G = -6.0$), the systematic effect of the level of factor B received (reflected in $\overline{X}_{B_1} - \overline{X}_G = -4.8$), the inter-action of factors A and B (reflected in $\overline{X}_{A_1B_1} - \overline{X}_{A_1} - \overline{X}_{B_1} + \overline{X}_G = +9.1$), and because of the unsystematic influences of within-cells error variation (reflected in $X_{111} - \overline{X}_{A_1B_1} = +6.2$). A similar partitioning for each of the other scores in Table 11.2 is shown in step 1 of Table 11.6. The remaining steps in the table obtain sums of squares from these partitioned scores. Follow each of these steps carefully.

Step 1   The scores of all 20 subjects in the experiment are partitioned following equation 11.2.

Step 2   The numerical differences are found for each score.

Step 3   Each positive and negative difference found in step 2 is squared.

Step 4   The values of the squared differences are summed over all scores in the experiment. This summing is achieved by adding the 20 values in each of the columns. The result is five sums of squares:

$$SS_{\text{Total}} = 4567.000,$$
$$SS_A = 720.000,$$
$$SS_B = 460.800,$$
$$SS_{A \times B} = 1656.200,$$
$$SS_{\text{Error}} = 1730.000.$$

The SS_{Total} is the sum of its components; thus,

$$SS_{\text{Total}} = SS_A + SS_B + SS_{A \times B} + SS_{\text{Error}}. \tag{11.3}$$

This equation indicates that the total variation of the scores in the experiment (SS_{Total}) is the result of variation that occurs from four independent sources: factor A, factor B, the interaction of factors A and B, and the within-cells error.

Finding Degrees of Freedom

Mean squares (MS) are obtained by dividing each SS by its degrees of freedom. Recall that degrees of freedom are defined as the number of scores that are free to vary in the computation of a statistic. We use this definition to calculate the df for each SS of equation 11.3.

Total Degrees of Freedom.   To find the SS_{Total}, the grand mean $\overline{X}_G$ must be known. Because the total sum of squares is based on the difference of every score in the experiment from the grand mean (i.e., $X - \overline{X}_G$), then one less than the total number of scores is free to vary when calculating SS_{Total}. In notation,

$$\textbf{Total degrees of freedom} = df_{\textbf{Total}} = N - 1,$$

TABLE 11.6

Obtaining sums of squares for a two-factor analysis of variance based on the scores of Table 11.2

Step 1: Partition the scores for the 20 subjects using the following equation:

$$X - \bar{X}_G = (\bar{X}_A - \bar{X}_G) + (\bar{X}_B - \bar{X}_G) + (\bar{X}_{AB} - \bar{X}_A - \bar{X}_B + \bar{X}_G) + (X - \bar{X}_{AB})$$

	$X - \bar{X}_G$	=	$(\bar{X}_A - \bar{X}_G)$	+	$(\bar{X}_B - \bar{X}_G)$	+	$(\bar{X}_{AB} - \bar{X}_A - \bar{X}_B + \bar{X}_G)$	+	$(X - \bar{X}_{AB})$
Scores in A_1B_1	97.0 − 92.5	=	(86.5 − 92.5)	+	(87.7 − 92.5)	+	(90.8 − 86.5 − 87.7 + 92.5)	+	(97.0 − 90.8)
	90.0 − 92.5	=	(86.5 − 92.5)	+	(87.7 − 92.5)	+	(90.8 − 86.5 − 87.7 + 92.5)	+	(90.0 − 90.8)
	80.0 − 92.5	=	(86.5 − 92.5)	+	(87.7 − 92.5)	+	(90.8 − 86.5 − 87.7 + 92.5)	+	(80.0 − 90.8)
	107.0 − 92.5	=	(86.5 − 92.5)	+	(87.7 − 92.5)	+	(90.8 − 86.5 − 87.7 + 92.5)	+	(107.0 − 90.8)
	80.0 − 92.5	=	(86.5 − 92.5)	+	(87.7 − 92.5)	+	(90.8 − 86.5 − 87.7 + 92.5)	+	(80.0 − 90.8)
Scores in A_2B_1	70.0 − 92.5	=	(98.5 − 92.5)	+	(87.7 − 92.5)	+	(84.6 − 98.5 − 87.7 + 92.5)	+	(70.0 − 84.6)
	87.0 − 92.5	=	(98.5 − 92.5)	+	(87.7 − 92.5)	+	(84.6 − 98.5 − 87.7 + 92.5)	+	(87.0 − 84.6)
	81.0 − 92.5	=	(98.5 − 92.5)	+	(87.7 − 92.5)	+	(84.6 − 98.5 − 87.7 + 92.5)	+	(81.0 − 84.6)
	95.0 − 92.5	=	(98.5 − 92.5)	+	(87.7 − 92.5)	+	(84.6 − 98.5 − 87.7 + 92.5)	+	(95.0 − 84.6)
	90.0 − 92.5	=	(98.5 − 92.5)	+	(87.7 − 92.5)	+	(84.6 − 98.5 − 87.7 + 92.5)	+	(90.0 − 84.6)
Scores in A_1B_2	68.0 − 92.5	=	(86.5 − 92.5)	+	(97.3 − 92.5)	+	(82.2 − 86.5 − 97.3 + 92.5)	+	(68.0 − 82.2)
	87.0 − 92.5	=	(86.5 − 92.5)	+	(97.3 − 92.5)	+	(82.2 − 86.5 − 97.3 + 92.5)	+	(87.0 − 82.2)
	92.0 − 92.5	=	(86.5 − 92.5)	+	(97.3 − 92.5)	+	(82.2 − 86.5 − 97.3 + 92.5)	+	(92.0 − 82.2)
	80.0 − 92.5	=	(86.5 − 92.5)	+	(97.3 − 92.5)	+	(82.2 − 86.5 − 97.3 + 92.5)	+	(80.0 − 82.2)
	84.0 − 92.5	=	(86.5 − 92.5)	+	(97.3 − 92.5)	+	(82.2 − 86.5 − 97.3 + 92.5)	+	(84.0 − 82.2)
Scores in A_2B_2	114.0 − 92.5	=	(98.5 − 92.5)	+	(97.3 − 92.5)	+	(112.4 − 98.5 − 97.3 + 92.5)	+	(114.0 − 112.4)
	96.0 − 92.5	=	(98.5 − 92.5)	+	(97.3 − 92.5)	+	(112.4 − 98.5 − 97.3 + 92.5)	+	(96.0 − 112.4)
	127.0 − 92.5	=	(98.5 − 92.5)	+	(97.3 − 92.5)	+	(112.4 − 98.5 − 97.3 + 92.5)	+	(127.0 − 112.4)
	110.0 − 92.5	=	(98.5 − 92.5)	+	(97.3 − 92.5)	+	(112.4 − 98.5 − 97.3 + 92.5)	+	(110.0 − 112.4)
	115.0 − 92.5	=	(98.5 − 92.5)	+	(97.3 − 92.5)	+	(112.4 − 98.5 − 97.3 + 92.5)	+	(115.0 − 112.4)

Step 2: Perform the subtractions in step 1 to obtain numerical differences for each subject.

		=		+		+		+	
Scores in A_1B_1	+4.5	=	−6.0	+	−4.8	+	+9.1	+	+6.2
	−2.5	=	−6.0	+	−4.8	+	+9.1	+	−0.8
	−12.5	=	−6.0	+	−4.8	+	+9.1	+	−10.8
	+14.5	=	−6.0	+	−4.8	+	+9.1	+	+16.2
	−12.5	=	−6.0	+	−4.8	+	+9.1	+	−10.8
Scores in A_2B_1	−22.5	=	+6.0	+	−4.8	+	−9.1	+	−14.6
	−5.5	=	+6.0	+	−4.8	+	−9.1	+	+2.4
	−11.5	=	+6.0	+	−4.8	+	−9.1	+	−3.6
	+2.5	=	+6.0	+	−4.8	+	−9.1	+	+10.4
	−2.5	=	+6.0	+	−4.8	+	−9.1	+	+5.4
Scores in A_1B_2	−24.5	=	−6.0	+	+4.8	+	−9.1	+	−14.2
	−5.5	=	−6.0	+	+4.8	+	−9.1	+	+4.8
	−0.5	=	−6.0	+	+4.8	+	−9.1	+	+9.8
	−12.5	=	−6.0	+	+4.8	+	−9.1	+	−2.2
	−8.5	=	−6.0	+	+4.8	+	−9.1	+	+1.8

TABLE 11.6 (Continued)

Scores in A_2B_2					
+21.5	=	+6.0 +	+4.8 +	+9.1 +	+1.6
+3.5	=	+6.0 +	+4.8 +	+9.1 +	−16.4
+34.5	=	+6.0 +	+4.8 +	+9.1 +	+14.6
+17.5	=	+6.0 +	+4.8 +	+9.1 +	−2.4
+22.5	=	+6.0 +	+4.8 +	+9.1 +	+2.6

Step 3: Square each difference.

	$(X - \bar{X}_G)^2$	$(\bar{X}_A - \bar{X}_G)^2$	$(\bar{X}_B - \bar{X}_G)^2$	$(\bar{X}_{AB} - \bar{X}_A - \bar{X}_B + \bar{X}_G)^2$	$(X - \bar{X}_{AB})^2$
Scores in A_1B_1	20.25	36.00	23.04	82.81	38.44
	6.25	36.00	23.04	82.81	0.64
	156.25	36.00	23.04	82.81	116.64
	210.25	36.00	23.04	82.81	262.44
	156.25	36.00	23.04	82.81	116.64
Scores in A_2B_1	506.25	36.00	23.04	82.81	213.16
	30.25	36.00	23.04	82.81	5.76
	132.25	36.00	23.04	82.81	12.96
	6.25	36.00	23.04	82.81	108.16
	6.25	36.00	23.04	82.81	29.16
Scores in A_1B_2	600.25	36.00	23.04	82.81	201.64
	30.25	36.00	23.04	82.81	23.04
	0.25	36.00	23.04	82.81	96.04
	156.25	36.00	23.04	82.81	4.84
	72.25	36.00	23.04	82.81	3.24
Scores in A_2B_2	462.25	36.00	23.04	82.81	2.56
	12.25	36.00	23.04	82.81	268.96
	1190.25	36.00	23.04	82.81	213.16
	306.25	36.00	23.04	82.81	5.76
	506.25	36.00	23.04	82.81	6.76

Step 4: Sum the squared differences for each partition over all subjects.

4567.000	720.000	+ 460.800	+ 1656.200	+ 1730.000
SS_{Total}	= SS_A	+ SS_B	+ $SS_{A \times B}$	+ SS_{Error}

where N is the total number of scores in the experiment. With $N = 20$, $df_{\text{Total}} = 20 - 1 = 19$.

Degrees of Freedom for SS$_A$. The SS_A is computed from the differences of the main effect means of factor A (i.e., $\overline{X}_{A_1}$ and $\overline{X}_{A_2}$ for the example) from $\overline{X}_G$. For a factorial design with two levels of factor A, if $\overline{X}_G$ is known, then only one main effect mean for factor A is free to vary. In general, the df for SS_A (df_A) are equal to one less than the number of levels of factor A, or

$$\text{Degrees of freedom for } SS_A = df_A = a - 1,$$

where a is the number of levels of independent variable A. For the example, $a = 2$; thus, $df_A = 2 - 1 = 1$.

Degrees of Freedom for SS$_B$. The SS_B is computed from the differences of the main effect means of factor B (i.e., $\overline{X}_{B_1}$ and $\overline{X}_{B_2}$ in the example) from $\overline{X}_G$. For a factorial design with two levels of factor B, if $\overline{X}_G$ is known, then only one main effect mean for factor B is free to vary. Thus, the df for SS_B (df_B) are equal to one less than the number of levels of factor B, or

$$\text{Degrees of freedom for } SS_B = df_B = b - 1,$$

where b is the number of levels of independent variable B. For the example, $b = 2$; thus, $df_B = 2 - 1 = 1$.

Degrees of Freedom for SS$_{A \times B}$. The $SS_{A \times B}$ is found by subtracting the appropriate main effect means from each cell mean. For a 2×2 design, if each main effect mean is known, then only one cell mean is free to vary. Given one cell mean, and knowing the main effect means for factors A and B, you can find the other three cell means. In general,

$$\text{Degrees of freedom for } SS_{A \times B} = df_{A \times B} = (a - 1)(b - 1).$$

In the 2×2 design, $a = 2$ and $b = 2$; thus,

$$df_{A \times B} = (2 - 1)(2 - 1) = 1.$$

Degrees of Freedom for SS$_{\text{Error}}$. The SS_{Error} is found by subtracting each $\overline{X}_{AB}$ from each score within that cell, for all the cells in the experiment. Thus, for each treatment condition, after $\overline{X}_{AB}$ is found, only $n_{AB} - 1$ scores are free to vary within that cell. For example, in Table 11.2, only four of the five scores are free to vary within each cell if each $\overline{X}_{AB}$ is known. Because there are four cells and four scores free to vary within each cell, there are 16 df for the SS_{Error}. In general, where a is the number of levels of factor A, b the levels of factor B, and n_{AB} the number of scores within each cell,

$$\text{Degrees of freedom for } SS_{\text{Error}} = df_{\text{Error}} = ab(n_{AB} - 1).$$

Additivity of Degrees of Freedom. The degrees of freedom for a factorial analysis are additive in the same manner as they are for the one-factor analysis of variance. Thus,

$$df_{\text{Total}} = df_A + df_B + df_{A \times B} + df_{\text{Error}}. \tag{11.4}$$

This relationship holds in the example, for $df_{\text{Total}} = 19$, $df_A = 1$, $df_B = 1$, $df_{A \times B} = 1$, and $df_{\text{Error}} = 16$.

Obtaining *MS* from *SS* and *df*

Dividing each *SS* in equation 11.3 by its corresponding *df* produces the four mean squares needed for the two-factor between-subjects analysis of variance:

$$MS_A = \frac{SS_A}{df_A},$$

$$MS_B = \frac{SS_B}{df_B},$$

$$MS_{A \times B} = \frac{SS_{A \times B}}{df_{A \times B}},$$

$$MS_{\text{Error}} = \frac{SS_{\text{Error}}}{df_{\text{Error}}}.$$

We do not obtain MS_{Total} because it is not used for any *F* ratios in this analysis.

For the scores in Table 11.2, we have found $SS_A = 720.000$, $SS_B = 460.800$, $SS_{A \times B} = 1656.200$, and $SS_{\text{Error}} = 1730.000$. Furthermore, $df_A = 1$, $df_B = 1$, $df_{A \times B} = 1$, and $df_{\text{Error}} = 16$. Consequently,

$$MS_A = \frac{720.000}{1} = 720.000,$$

$$MS_B = \frac{460.800}{1} = 460.800,$$

$$MS_{A \times B} = \frac{1656.200}{1} = 1656.200,$$

$$MS_{\text{Error}} = \frac{1730.000}{16} = 108.125.$$

Computing the *F* Statistics

An *F* statistic is formed by the ratio of two mean squares, one *MS* varying with the effect of an independent variable, as well with sampling error, and the other *MS* varying only with error variation in the experiment. In the two-factor between-subjects analysis of variance, MS_A varies with factor *A*, MS_B varies with factor *B*, $MS_{A \times B}$ varies with the interaction of factors *A* and *B*, and MS_{Error} varies only with the within-cells error variation. Thus, three *F* statistics are formed, one for each systematic source of variation in the experiment:

Source of Variation	F
Factor *A*	$\dfrac{MS_A}{MS_{\text{Error}}}$
Factor *B*	$\dfrac{MS_B}{MS_{\text{Error}}}$
Interaction of $A \times B$	$\dfrac{MS_{A \times B}}{MS_{\text{Error}}}$

TABLE 11.7

Summary of formulas for a two-factor between-subjects analysis of variance

Source	SS	df^{a}	MS	F
Factor A	$\sum\sum(\overline{X}_A - \overline{X}_G)^2$	$a - 1$	$\dfrac{SS_A}{df_A}$	$\dfrac{MS_A}{MS_{Error}}$
Factor B	$\sum\sum(\overline{X}_B - \overline{X}_G)^2$	$b - 1$	$\dfrac{SS_B}{df_B}$	$\dfrac{MS_B}{MS_{Error}}$
Interaction of A and B	$\sum\sum(\overline{X}_{AB} - \overline{X}_A - \overline{X}_B + \overline{X}_G)^2$	$(a-1)(b-1)$	$\dfrac{SS_{A\times B}}{df_{A\times B}}$	$\dfrac{MS_{A\times B}}{MS_{Error}}$
Error	$\sum\sum(X - \overline{X}_{AB})^2$	$ab(n_{AB} - 1)$	$\dfrac{SS_{Error}}{df_{Error}}$	
Total	$\sum\sum(X - \overline{X}_G)^2$	$N - 1$	Not calculated	

^{a}a = number of levels of factor A; b = number of levels of factor B; n_{AB} = number of scores in each cell; N = total number of scores.

Substituting numerical values for the mean squares, we obtain the following F statistics:

Source of Variation	F
Factor A	$\dfrac{720.000}{108.125} = 6.66$
Factor B	$\dfrac{460.800}{108.125} = 4.26$
Interaction of $A \times B$	$\dfrac{1656.200}{108.125} = 15.32$

We discuss how to use and interpret each F shortly.

Table 11.7 provides a summary of the sources of variance in a two-factor between-subjects analysis of variance and the definitional formulas for each df, MS, and F statistic. A numerical summary of the analysis of variance on the data of Table 11.2 is presented in Table 11.8.

TABLE 11.8

Numerical summary of the analysis of variance on the hypothetical scores of Table 11.2

Source	SS	df	MS	F
Level of math identification (A)	720.000	1	720.000	6.66*
Stereotype threat condition (B)	460.800	1	460.800	4.26
$A \times B$	1656.200	1	1656.200	15.32**
Error	1730.000	16	108.125	
Total	4567.000	19		

*$p < .05$.
**$p < .01$.

Testing Your Knowledge 11.2

1. Identify the sources of variation in scores from a two-factor between-subjects design.

2. Write the equation to partition a score for the two-factor between-subjects analysis of variance.

3. Explain why the value of $\overline{X}_A - \overline{X}_G$ varies with the effect of factor A in a factorial experiment.

4. Explain why the value of $\overline{X}_B - \overline{X}_G$ varies with the effect of factor B in a factorial experiment.

5. Explain why the value of $\overline{X}_{AB} - \overline{X}_A - \overline{X}_B + \overline{X}_G$ varies with the effect of the interaction of factors A and B in a factorial experiment.

6. Explain why the value of $X - \overline{X}_{AB}$ varies only with within-cells error variation in a factorial experiment.

7. Complete the following equations for a two-factor between-subjects analysis of variance.

   a. $df_A =$

   b. $df_B =$

   c. $df_{A \times B} =$

   d. $df_{Error} =$

   e. $df_{Total} =$

   f. $MS_A =$

   g. $MS_B =$

   h. $MS_{A \times B} =$

   i. $MS_{Error} =$

8. What is the value of SS_{Total} if $SS_A = 40.00$, $SS_B = 70.00$, $SS_{A \times B} = 30.00$, and $SS_{Error} = 100.00$?

9. What is the value of SS_A if $SS_{Total} = 224.00$, $SS_B = 14.00$, $SS_{A \times B} = 64.00$, and $SS_{Error} = 101.00$?

10. What is the value of $SS_{A \times B}$ if $SS_{Total} = 302.00$, $SS_A = 75.00$, $SS_B = 19.00$, and $SS_{Error} = 153.00$?

11. What is the value of SS_{Error} if $SS_{Total} = 98.00$, $SS_A = 14.00$, $SS_B = 7.00$, and $SS_{A \times B} = 17.00$?

12. Find df_A, df_B, $df_{A \times B}$, df_{Error}, and df_{Total} for a 2×3 between-subjects analysis of variance with six subjects in each cell.

13. Find df_A, df_B, $df_{A \times B}$, df_{Error}, and df_{Total} for a 3×2 between-subjects analysis of variance with 13 scores in each treatment condition.

14. What is the value of df_{Total} if $df_A = 3$, $df_B = 1$, $df_{A \times B} = 3$, and $df_{Error} = 72$?

15. Find the numerical values of mean squares for the following SS and df: $SS_A = 14.00$, $SS_B = 26.00$, $SS_{A \times B} = 44.00$, $SS_{Error} = 480.00$, $df_A = 1$, $df_B = 2$, $df_{A \times B} = 2$, and $df_{Error} = 60$.

16. You conducted a 2×2 factorial experiment with three subjects in each cell and obtained the following scores:

		Factor A	
		A_1	A_2
	B_1	30	34
		32	36
		28	32
Factor B			
		28	38
	B_2	30	34
		26	36

a. Partition these scores following the approach illustrated in Table 11.6. Obtain the SS_{Total}, SS_A, SS_B, $SS_{A \times B}$, SS_{Error}, and the corresponding degrees of freedom for each partition. Then complete a numerical summary table with values of MS and F.

b. Why is SS_B equal to zero in this example?

17. Tables 1 and 2 below are incomplete summary tables for a factorial between-subjects analysis of variance. Assume an equal number of scores in each cell. Fill in the missing values in each table by using the relationships among SS and df given in equations 11.3 and 11.4, respectively. Then answer these questions for each table.

a. How many levels of factor A were used?

b. How many levels of factor B were used?

c. How many subjects were measured in each cell?

d. How many subjects participated in the study?

Table 1				
Source	SS	df	MS	F
Factor A	—	2	16.00	—
Factor B	24.00	1	—	3.00
$A \times B$	—	—	12.00	—
Error	—	—	—	
Total	560.00	65		

Table 2				
Source	SS	df	MS	F
Factor A	—	2	—	4.50
Factor B	24.00	4	—	1.50
$A \times B$	160.00	—	—	5.00
Error	—	—	4.00	
Total	—	224		

Statistical Hypothesis Testing with the Two-Factor Between-Subjects Analysis of Variance

To understand statistical hypothesis testing using the F statistics obtained from a factorial analysis of variance, we must know what affects MS_A, MS_B, $MS_{A \times B}$, and MS_{Error} in an experiment.

Factors Affecting the Value of Mean Squares in a Factorial Analysis of Variance

Each MS in a factorial analysis is affected by a different source of variation in the experiment. If neither of the independent variables has an effect on the dependent variable and there is no interaction of the independent variables, then each MS estimates only error variation. Under these circumstances, all four mean squares should be approximately equal in value and reflect only the effects of sampling error. But if either or both of the independent variables have a main effect or if they interact, then the effect increases the value of the corresponding MS. For example, if factor A produces a main effect, then MS_A, will increase relative to MS_{Error}, but MS_B, $MS_{A \times B}$, and MS_{Error} will not be affected by this main effect. A similar situation holds if factor B has a main effect. If factor B produces a main effect, then MS_B will increase relative to MS_{Error}, but MS_A, $MS_{A \times B}$, and MS_{Error} will not be affected by this main effect. If the independent variables interact, then $MS_{A \times B}$ increases, but MS_A, MS_B, and MS_{Error} will not be affected. The MS_{Error} is not affected by either main effects or interaction of the independent variables. It reflects only within-cells error variance in the experiment. Thus, the value of each MS is independent of the value of the other mean squares.

The four mean squares and the sources of variation affecting them may be summarized as follows:

Mean Square	Affected by:
MS_A	Systematic variance due to factor A Sampling error
MS_B	Systematic variance due to factor B Sampling error
$MS_{A \times B}$	Systematic variance due to the interaction of factors A and B Sampling error
MS_{Error}	Within-cell error variance

To relate this understanding of the factors affecting each MS to the three F statistics of Table 11.8, notice that each F uses MS_{Error} as the denominator and the appropriate MS for the independent variable or the interaction as the numerator. If the independent variable affecting the MS in the numerator of a particular F ratio does not have an effect, then that F ratio should equal about 1.00, for both the numerator and denominator MS will measure only error variation in the experiment. But if the independent variable does have an effect, then the value of the MS for that variable increases and the value of F for that factor becomes greater than 1.0. This reasoning is identical to that expressed in Chapter 10 for the one-factor analysis of variance.

Statistical Decision Making from the *F* Statistics

With this understanding of the factors affecting each value of F, we are ready to use each F in a statistical hypothesis test. The steps followed are identical to those discussed in Chapter 10.

▶ A null hypothesis, H_0, and an alternative hypothesis, H_1, are formulated for each F statistic.

▶ The sampling distribution of F, assuming that H_0 is true, is obtained for each F value. This distribution is given in Appendix C.3.

▶ A significance level is selected.

▶ A critical value of F, identified as F_{crit}, is found for each of the F statistics from the sampling distribution of F given in Appendix C.3.

▶ A rejection region is located in the sampling distribution of F for each F.

▶ The three F values, identified as F_{obs}, are calculated from the sample data.

▶ A decision to reject or not reject H_0 for each F_{obs} is made on the basis of whether or not F_{obs} falls into the rejection region.

▶ The results of the statistical decisions are related to the research hypotheses.

Statistical Hypotheses

For a two-factor between-subjects analysis of variance, three different null hypotheses are tested, one for each F_{obs}. For a 2×2 factorial analysis of variance, the null (H_0) and alternative hypotheses (H_1) for each F are as follows:

F for:	Statistical Hypotheses
Factor *A*	H_0: $\mu_{A_1} = \mu_{A_2}$ H_1: The μ_A's are not equal
Factor *B*	H_0: $\mu_{B_1} = \mu_{B_2}$ H_1: The μ_B' s are not equal
A × *B*	H_0: All $(\mu_{AB} - \mu_A - \mu_B + \mu_G) = 0$ H_1: Not all $(\mu_{AB} - \mu_A - \mu_B + \mu_G) = 0$

Main Effects.   The null and alternative hypotheses for the main effects of factors A and B are identical in form to the statistical hypotheses for a one-factor analysis. For the main effect of an independent variable, the factorial analysis of variance is treating the data as if they were obtained from a one-factor design, as illustrated in Table 11.4. The number of population means identified in H_0 for either factor A or B corresponds to the number of levels of that factor in the experiment. For example, if an experiment involves three levels of factor A, then H_0 for factor A is written as

$$H_0: \mu_{A_1} = \mu_{A_2} = \mu_{A_3}$$

and H_1 as

$$H_1: \text{The } \mu_A\text{'s are not all equal.}$$

The null hypothesis for each factor represents the situation that exists if the independent variable has no effect. If the null hypothesis is true, then any observed difference between the corresponding main effect means is due only to sampling error.

The alternative hypothesis states that the population means are not equal to each other, a situation that exists if the independent variable does have an effect.

Interaction.   The null hypothesis for the interaction states that in the population, if no interaction occurs, then the difference of a cell mean, μ_{AB}, from the grand mean, μ_G, will be equal to zero after the main effects of each independent variable [i.e., $(\mu_A - \mu_G)$ and $(\mu_B - \mu_G)$] have been subtracted from it. In other words, this H_0 states that with no interaction of the independent variables, the value of each cell mean may be exactly predicted from the main effects of the independent variables. The alternative hypothesis states that this relation is not the case and that the variation in cell means is not predictable from the main effects alone.

Decision Making from the *F* Value

Making decisions about each of the three sets of hypotheses from the values of F_{obs} is identical to the process followed in a one-factor analysis of variance. A value of α defining the size of the rejection region is chosen prior to conducting the analysis. The sampling distribution of F under H_0 is then determined for each of the three values of F_{obs}, and a rejection region is located in each sampling distribution. This step requires looking up three values of F_{crit} with the appropriate numerator and denominator *df* in Appendix C.3a or b, depending on the value of α selected. Then, for each F_{obs}, if F_{obs} is equal to or larger than its corresponding F_{crit} value, the H_0 for that F_{obs} is rejected and H_1 accepted. The difference between the means entering into that value of F_{obs} is statistically significant. If F_{obs} is less than its F_{crit} value, then the decision is to fail to reject H_0 and to not accept H_1 for that source of variance. The difference between the means entering into that value of F_{obs} is nonsignificant. The two sets of decisions for each F_{obs} in a two-factor analysis of variance are summarized in Table 11.9.

TABLE 11.9   Summary of statistical decisions in a two-factor analysis of variance

F Ratio for:	Value of F_{obs}	Statistical Decision	
Factor *A*	Less than F_{crit}	Fail to reject H_0 Do not accept H_1	The main effect of factor *A* is nonsignificant.
	Equal to or greater than F_{crit}	Reject H_0 Accept H_1	The main effect of factor *A* is statistically significant.
Factor *B*	Less than F_{crit}	Fail to reject H_0 Do not accept H_1	The main effect of factor *B* is nonsignificant.
	Equal to or greater than F_{crit}	Reject H_0 Accept H_1	The main effect of factor *B* is statistically significant.
$A \times B$	Less than F_{crit}	Fail to reject H_0 Do not accept H_1	The interaction of factors *A* and *B* is nonsignificant.
	Equal to or greater than F_{crit}	Reject H_0 Accept H_1	The interaction of factors *A* and *B* is statistically significant.

We illustrate decision making with the analysis of variance on the example data of Table 11.2, which is summarized in Table 11.8. In this table, each F_{obs} has 1 df for its numerator and 16 df for its denominator. Hence, each F_{obs} has the same value of F_{crit} and, thus, the same rejection region. This relationship is not necessarily the case in all factorial analyses of variance. Depending on the number of levels of each independent variable, it is possible for each F_{obs} to have a different df for the numerator and, thus, a different rejection region.

For $\alpha = .05$, F_{crit} with 1, 16 df is 4.49 (obtained from Appendix C.3a). Hence, for each F_{obs} in Table 11.8, the rejection region consists of values of F_{obs} equal to or greater than 4.49. Accordingly, we make the following decisions from this analysis of variance:

Source	F_{obs}	Falls into Rejection Region	Statistical Decision	
Factor A	6.66	Yes	Reject H_0 Accept H_1	The main effect of factor A is statistically significant.
Factor B	4.26	No	Fail to reject H_0 Do not accept H_1	The main effect of factor B is nonsignificant.
$A \times B$	15.32	Yes	Reject H_0 Accept H_1	The interaction of A and B is statistically significant.

Assumptions of Factorial Between-Subjects Analysis of Variance

The factorial between-subjects analysis of variance is based on the same three assumptions about the scores obtained in an experiment as is the one-factor between-subjects analysis.

1. Each subject in the experiment is randomly selected from a population, and each subject is independent of every other subject.

2. The scores on the dependent variable in the populations sampled are normally distributed.

3. The variances of scores in the populations are equal.

As we pointed out with a one-factor analysis, the first assumption of independence of scores must be met for a between-subjects analysis of variance to be used. Each subject may contribute only one score in the experiment. The second and third assumptions, however, may not always be met by the data of an experiment. Again, violations of the normality and equality of variance assumptions are more likely to have minimal effects on the probability of making a Type I error when the following conditions are met:

▶ The number of subjects in each cell is the same.

▶ The shape of the distributions of the scores for each treatment condition is about the same, and the distributions are neither very peaked nor very flat.

▶ The significance level is set at .05.

Testing Your Knowledge 11.3

1. Identify the factors affecting the value of each *MS* in a between-subjects factorial analysis of variance.

2. Explain why MS_A increases in value if factor *A* has an effect in a factorial experiment.

3. Explain why MS_B increases in value if factor *B* has an effect in a factorial experiment.

4. Explain why $MS_{A \times B}$ increases in value if factors *A* and *B* interact in a factorial experiment.

5. Explain why the value of MS_{Error} is not affected by either factors *A* or *B* or their interaction in a factorial experiment.

6. What is expected to happen to the value of F_{obs} for factor *A* if factor *A* has an effect in an experiment?

7. What is expected to happen to the value of F_{obs} for $A \times B$ if the independent variables interact in an experiment?

8. Identify the steps in statistical testing with a factorial analysis of variance.

9. Write the statistical hypotheses for the following:

   a. A 2 $\times$ 4 between-subjects analysis of variance

   b. A 3 $\times$ 2 between-subjects analysis of variance

   c. A 3 $\times$ 3 between-subjects analysis of variance

10. This exercise provides a brief analysis of variance summary tables for several two-factor between-subjects designs. For each F_{obs}, find F_{crit} for a .05 significance level from Appendix C.3a and indicate whether F_{obs} falls into the rejection region. Then indicate your decision with respect to H_0 and H_1. If the exact *df* are not tabled for df_{Error}, use the next lower value in the table.

Table 1		
Source	*df*	F_{obs}
Factor *A*	1	4.63
Factor *B*	3	2.11
A $\times$ *B*	3	3.97
Error	56	
Total	63	

Table 2		
Source	*df*	F_{obs}
Factor *A*	3	1.42
Factor *B*	2	3.51
A $\times$ *B*	6	2.37
Error	144	
Total	155	

Table 3		
Source	*df*	F_{obs}
Factor *A*	2	4.12
Factor *B*	4	2.83
A $\times$ *B*	8	1.87
Error	150	
Total	164	

11. Identify the assumptions underlying the use of the factorial between-subjects analysis of variance.

Interpreting a 2 $\times$ 2 Factorial Analysis of Variance

The final step in statistical testing with the analysis of variance is to relate the decisions about H_0 and H_1 to the research hypotheses. With a factorial design, this step requires interpreting both the possible main effects of the independent variables and the possible interaction of the independent variables. We begin discussion of the interpretation of the results of a factorial design with the steps needed to interpret a statistically significant interaction. We then turn to the interpretation of statistically significant main effects.

The Simple Effect of an Independent Variable

An interaction of two independent variables occurs when the effect of one independent variable depends on the level of the other independent variable with which it is combined. Consequently, a statistically significant interaction in the analysis of variance is interpreted by comparing differences among the cell means in the experiment. The differences between the cell means reveal the simple effects of the independent variables. The **simple effect of an independent variable** (sometimes called a *simple main effect*) in a factorial design is the effect of that independent variable at only one level of the other independent variable. Table 11.10 illustrates the four simple effects as well as the two main effects in a 2×2 design. The simple effects for each independent variable are identified in the rectangular boxes between cells. In a 2×2 design there are only two simple effects for each independent variable.

> **Simple effect of an independent variable** ▷ The effect of one independent variable at only one level of the other independent variable in a factorial design.

Simple Effects of Factor A

The simple effect of factor A at level B_1 of factor B is given by the difference between the $\overline{X}_{A_1B_1}$ and $\overline{X}_{A_2B_1}$ cell means (i.e., $\overline{X}_{A_1B_1} - \overline{X}_{A_2B_1}$). This difference reveals the effect of factor A at level B_1 of factor B. Similarly, the simple effect of factor A at level B_2 of factor B is

---

TABLE 11.10   Simple and main effects in a 2×2 between-subjects analysis of variance

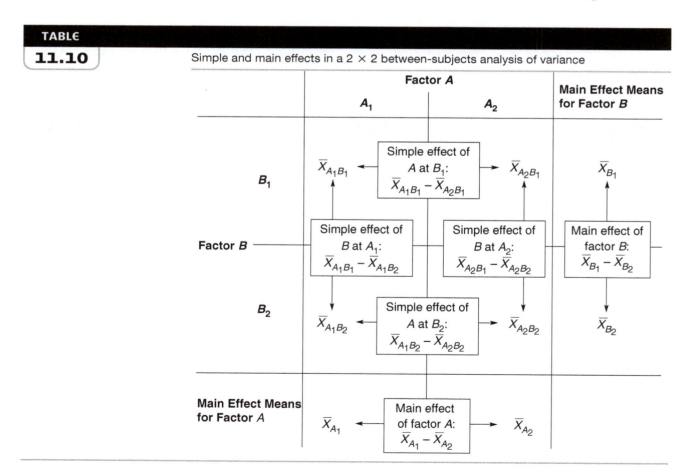

given by the difference between the $\overline{X}_{A_1B_2}$ and $\overline{X}_{A_2B_2}$ cell means (i.e., $\overline{X}_{A_1B_2} - \overline{X}_{A_2B_2}$). This difference reveals the effect of factor A at level B_2. In finding the numerical values of the simple effects, it is important to maintain a consistency of direction in the comparisons and to retain the sign ($+$ or $-$) of the effect.

Simple Effects of Factor *B*

The simple effect of factor B at level A_1 of factor A is given by the difference between the $\overline{X}_{A_1B_1}$ and $\overline{X}_{A_1B_2}$ cell means (i.e., $\overline{X}_{A_1B_1} - \overline{X}_{A_1B_2}$), and the simple effect of factor B at level A_2 of factor A is given by the difference between the $\overline{X}_{A_2B_1}$ and $\overline{X}_{A_2B_2}$ cell means (i.e., $\overline{X}_{A_2B_1} - \overline{X}_{A_2B_2}$). Each simple effect indicates the effect of factor B at only one level of factor A.

A Numerical Example of Simple and Main Effects.   The numerical values of the simple and main effect differences from the means of Table 11.5 are presented in Table 11.11. The main effect and simple effect differences between means are shown in the rectangular boxes. For example, the simple effect of level of math identification for the threat present condition (the simple effect of factor A at B_1) is $\overline{X}_{A_1B_1} - \overline{X}_{A_2B_1}$, which equals $90.8 - 84.6$, or $+6.2$. Likewise, the simple effect of stereotype threat condition for the low math identification subjects (the simple effect of B at A_1) is $\overline{X}_{A_1B_1} - \overline{X}_{A_1B_2}$, which equals $90.8 - 82.2$, or $+8.6$.

TABLE

11.11

Main effect and simple effect differences of performance on a test of mathematical ability for level of math identification and stereotype threat condition in the example experiment.

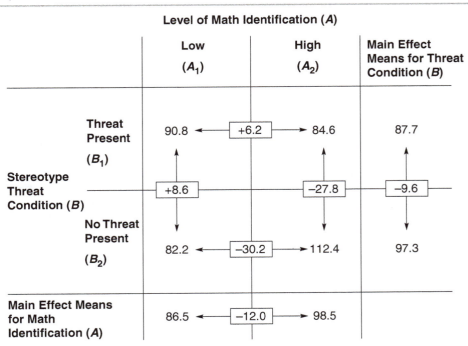

Interpreting Simple Effects When a Statistically Significant Interaction Occurs

If a statistically significant interaction of the independent variables occurs in an analysis of variance, then the two simple effects for a factor are not equal to each other or to the main effect for that factor. Thus, if there is a statistically significant interaction, the simple effect of factor A at level B_1, $\overline{X}_{A_1B_1} - \overline{X}_{A_2B_1}$, is not equal to the simple effect of factor A at level B_2, $\overline{X}_{A_1B_2} - \overline{X}_{A_2B_2}$. In addition, neither simple effect of factor A is equal to the main effect of factor A given by $\overline{X}_{A_1} - \overline{X}_{A_2}$.

Applying this relationship to the example results in Table 11.11, we find that the simple effect of level of math identification for the threat present condition (an effect of $+6.2$) is not equal to the simple effect of level of math identification for the no threat present condition (an effect of -30.2), and neither simple effect is equal to the main effect for level of math identification (an effect of -12.0).

A similar relationship applies to the simple effects of factor B. If a statistically significant interaction occurs, then the simple effect of factor B at level A_1, $\overline{X}_{A_1B_1} - \overline{X}_{A_1B_2}$, is not equal to the simple effect of B at level A_2, $\overline{X}_{A_2B_1} - \overline{X}_{A_2B_2}$. And neither simple effect equals the main effect of factor B given by $\overline{X}_{B_1} - \overline{X}_{B_2}$.

Applying this relationship to the example results in Table 11.11 indicates that the simple effect of stereotype threat condition for the low math identification subjects (an effect of $+8.6$) is not equal to the simple effect of stereotype threat condition for the high math identification subjects (an effect of -27.8), and neither simple effect is equal to the main effect for stereotype threat condition (an effect of -9.6).

Multiple Comparison Tests for a Statistically Significant Interaction.   Each simple effect comparison in Tables 11.10 and 11.11 is a pairwise comparison; two cell means are compared with each other. To determine if the two cell means differ significantly from each other, a multiple comparison test is used to find a **critical difference** (*CD*) for the simple effect. If the observed value of the simple effect is equal to or exceeds the *CD*, then the difference between the cell means is statistically significant.

Again, the **Tukey HSD test** is frequently used for post hoc comparisons of simple effects. The *CD* for this test is given by

$$CD = q\sqrt{\frac{MS_{\text{Error}}}{n_{AB}}}.$$

The value of q is found from Appendix C.4 and depends on the number of simple effect comparisons to be made and the df_{Error}. Because Appendix C.4 was constructed for a one-factor design, we use the following conversion to enter the table:

Type of Design	Use *q* from Appendix C.4 Found in the Column for ___ Levels of the Independent Variable:
2×2	3
2×3	5
3×2	5
3×3	7
3×4	8
4×3	8
4×4	10

The MS_{Error} is the value of MS_{Error} calculated in the factorial analysis of variance, and n_{AB} is the number of scores in each cell.

To illustrate this computation for the 2×2 experiment on the effects of level of math identification and stereotype threat, we use the column for $a = 3$ in Appendix C.4 to find q. With 16 df for MS_{Error} (from Table 11.8) and $\alpha = .05$, the value of q (3, 16) is 3.65. $MS_{\text{Error}} = 108.125$ from Table 11.8, and n_{AB}, the number of scores entering into each cell mean, is 5. Hence, the numerical value of the Tukey CD is

$$CD = 3.65\sqrt{\frac{108.125}{5}} = 17.0.$$

Any simple effect in Table 11.11 equal to or greater than 17.0 points on the mathematics achievement test in absolute value is statistically significant at the .05 level. The simple effect of level of math identification for the no threat present condition (i.e., -30.2), and the simple effect for the stereotype threat condition for high math identification (i.e., -27.8) are greater in absolute value than the CD of 17.0. These simple effects reveal statistically significant differences between the cell means involved. The simple effect for level of math identification for the threat present condition (i.e., $+6.2$) and the simple effect for stereotype threat condition in the low math identification subjects (i.e., $+8.6$) are less in absolute value than the CD of 17.0. These simple effects are nonsignificant, and the cell means involved differ only because of sampling error.

Interpreting Main Effects When an Interaction Occurs

When a statistically significant interaction occurs, the main effects for the independent variables may not lend themselves to meaningful interpretation. This outcome happens because the main effect of an independent variable is the mean of the simple effects for that variable. For example, with an equal number of scores in each cell, the main effect for level of math identification (-12.0) in Table 11.11 is the mean of the simple effects for level of math identification for the threat present condition and the no threat present condition (i.e., $[(+6.2) + (-30.2)]/2 = -12.0$). A similar relationship holds for the main effect for stereotype threat condition (-9.6). This main effect is the mean of the simple effects for stereotype threat condition for the low math identification subjects ($+8.6$) and the high math identification subjects (-27.8). Accordingly, when an interaction occurs so that the simple effects of an independent variable are not equal to each other, the main effect of that independent variable may not accurately represent the effect of the variable. Such main effects are artifacts of the interaction and do not provide meaningful information about the results of the experiment. An **artifactual main effect**, then, is a main effect that does not give meaningful information about the effect of an independent variable, for it occurs only because of the specific pattern of interaction observed. It is an artificial result of the pattern of simple effects for that variable. Consequently, an important note of caution about interpreting main effects in a factorial design is in order:

> **Artifactual main effect** ▶ A main effect that does not give meaningful information about the effect of an independent variable in a factorial design.

▶ If a statistically significant interaction occurs in a factorial design, then main effects for either factor A or factor B may be artifactual and may not present meaningful results about the effect of that independent variable.

▶ If the interaction in a factorial design is nonsignificant, then main effects for either factor A or factor B will present meaningful results about the outcome of that independent variable.

A statistically significant interaction in an analysis of variance does not ensure that the main effects will be artifactual, but it is a warning to examine any significant main effect to find whether it provides meaningful results about the effect of the independent variable.

Table 11.12a summarizes these relationships among simple and main effects when a statistically significant interaction occurs.

Interpreting Simple and Main Effects When No Statistically Significant Interaction Occurs

If no statistically significant interaction of the independent variables occurs, then the effect of one independent variable does not depend on the level of the other independent variable. Thus, if no interaction occurs, the simple effect of factor A at level B_1 will be

---

TABLE	
11.12	Interaction and interpretation of simple effects and main effects in a 2 $\times$ 2 factorial analysis of variance.

(a) **If F_{obs} for the $A \times B$ interaction falls into the rejection region, then:**
  - The F ratio for interaction is statistically significant.
  - The effect of one independent variable depends on the level of the other independent variable.
  - The simple effect of factor A at B_1 (i.e., $\overline{X}_{A_1B_1} - \overline{X}_{A_2B_1}$) is not equal to the simple effect of factor A at B_2 (i.e., $\overline{X}_{A_1B_2} - \overline{X}_{A_2B_2}$). The observed difference between the two simple effects for factor A is due to the interaction of the independent variables and not simply due to sampling error.
  - The simple effect of factor B at A_1 (i.e., $\overline{X}_{A_1B_1} - \overline{X}_{A_1B_2}$) is not equal to the simple effect of factor B at A_2 (i.e., $\overline{X}_{A_2B_1} - \overline{X}_{A_2B_2}$). The observed difference between the two simple effects for factor B is due to the interaction of the independent variables and not simply due to sampling error.
  - The simple effects of factor A are not equal to the main effect of factor A.
  - The simple effects of factor B are not equal to the main effect of factor B.
  - Each simple effect should be compared to a Tukey CD to find which cell means differ significantly from each other.
  - The main effects for either factor A or factor B may be artifactual and may not present meaningful results about the effect of the independent variable.

(b) **If F_{obs} for the $A \times B$ interaction does not fall into the rejection region, then:**
  - The F ratio for interaction is nonsignificant.
  - The effect of one independent variable does not depend on the level of the other independent variable.
  - The main effects for factor A and factor B will present meaningful results about the outcome of the experiment.
  - The simple effect of factor A at B_1 (i.e., $\overline{X}_{A_1B_1} - \overline{X}_{A_2B_1}$) does not differ significantly from the simple effect of factor A at B_2 (i.e., $\overline{X}_{A_1B_2} - \overline{X}_{A_2B_2}$). The observed difference between the two simple effects for factor A is due to sampling error.
  - The simple effect of factor B at A_1 (i.e., $\overline{X}_{A_1B_1} - \overline{X}_{A_1B_2}$) does not differ significantly from the simple effect of factor B at A_2 (i.e., $\overline{X}_{A_2B_1} - \overline{X}_{A_2B_2}$). The observed difference between the two simple effects for factor B is due to sampling error.
  - The simple effects of factor A do not differ from the main effect of factor A. The main effect of factor A provides the best description of the effect of factor A.
  - The simple effects of factor B do not differ from the main effect of factor B. The main effect of factor B provides the best description of the effect of factor B.
  - There is no need to analyze the simple effects with a multiple comparison test.

equivalent to the simple effect of factor A at level B_2. Any observed difference between these simple effects is due only to sampling error. Furthermore, if the simple effects of factor A are equivalent to each other, they are also equivalent to the main effect of factor A, and the main effect of factor A provides the best description of the effect of this independent variable.

A similar relationship holds for the simple effects of factor B. If no interaction occurs, then the simple effect of factor B at level A_1 will be equivalent to the simple effect of factor B at level A_2. Any observed difference between these simple effects is due only to sampling error. The simple effects of factor B also are equivalent to the main effect of factor B, and the main effect of factor B provides the best description of the effect of this independent variable. These relationships are summarized in part (b) of Table 11.12.

Putting It All Together: Interpreting the Analysis of Variance on the Example Experiment

Understanding the results of a factorial experiment requires looking at each main effect and their interaction and interpreting them with respect to the decisions made in the analysis of variance. Whenever a statistically significant interaction occurs, as in the example experiment (see Table 11.8), interpretation of the results should start with the interaction.

Interpreting the Interaction of Level of Math Identification and Stereotype Threat Condition
The value of F_{obs} for interaction = 15.32 in Table 11.8 is greater than the F_{crit} value of 4.49 and, thus, falls into the rejection region. Consequently, H_0 for the interaction of factors A and B,

$$H_0: \text{All } (\mu_{AB} - \mu_A - \mu_B + \mu_G) = 0,$$

is rejected and

$$H_1: \text{Not all } (\mu_{AB} - \mu_A - \mu_B + \mu_G) = 0$$

is accepted. To interpret this interaction, we first apply the Tukey HSD critical difference to the simple effects in Table 11.11. The Tukey CD is 17.0; thus, any simple effect in Table 11.11 equal to or greater than 17.0 in absolute value is statistically significant at the .05 level.

Turning to Table 11.11, we first examine the simple effects of factor A, the level of math identification. The simple effect of factor A at B_1, a difference of +6.2, is less than the CD of 17.0; this simple effect is nonsignificant. Math identification is not related to achievement test performance when a stereotype threat is present. The difference between the low math identification and high math identification means for stereotype threat (90.8 and 84.6, respectively) is due only to sampling error. The simple effect of factor A at B_2, a difference of -30.2, however, is greater in absolute value than the CD of 17.0. This simple effect is statistically significant. Mathematics achievement test performance is significantly higher for females with high math identification and no threat present (at 112.4) than for females with a low level of math identification and no threat present (at 82.2).

We now turn to the simple effects of factor B, stereotype threat condition. The simple effect of factor B at A_1, a difference of +8.6, is less in absolute value than the CD of 17.0; this simple effect is nonsignificant. When the subject does not identify with mathematics, her performance on a mathematics test does not differ significantly for the threat present and no threat present conditions. The difference between the threat present and no threat present cell means for the females with low math identification (90.8 and 82.2, respectively) is treated as due only to sampling error. The simple effect of factor B at A_2, a difference of -27.8, is greater in absolute value than the CD of 17.0; thus, this simple effect is a significant difference. Females with high math identification perform better on a test of mathematics achievement with no threat present (at 112.4) than when experiencing a stereotype threat (at 84.6).

This analysis leads to the following summary of the outcome of this interaction of level of math identification and stereotype threat.

► The relationship of level of math identification to achievement test performance depends on whether females do or do not experience stereotype threat.

   a. For females experiencing a stereotype threat, there was no significant difference in mathematics achievement test performance for low and high math identification subjects (90.8 and 84.6, respectively).

   b. For females with no stereotype threat present, the mathematics achievement test performance of high math identification females (112.4) was significantly better than the performance of the low math identification females (82.2).

► The effect of stereotype threat on mathematics achievement test performance depends on whether females identify with mathematics.

   a. For females with a low level of math identification, there was no significant difference between the threat present and no threat present conditions; mathematics achievement was not related to whether a female experienced stereotype threat or not (90.8 and 82.2, respectively).

   b. For females with a high level of math identification, mathematics achievement was significantly greater in the no threat present compared to the threat present condition (112.4 versus 84.6, respectively).

These outcomes are in agreement with the predictions we expressed when we introduced this experiment that stereotype threat is detrimental to mathematics achievement test performance for females with high math identification but not for females with low math identification.

Graphic Presentation of the Results of the Example Experiment.   In published results of factorial designs, cell means frequently are presented graphically in a figure, rather than in a table such as Table 11.5, for a figure often provides a clearer portrayal of an interaction.

The cell means from Table 11.5 are plotted in Figure 11.1. Each cell mean is identified in this figure, but in published articles the cell means are represented only by a symbol such as filled or open circles, which are labeled in a legend on the figure. When plotting a figure, one of the independent variables is placed on the abscissa (i.e., horizontal axis), and the second independent variable is represented as a function on the figure. The measure of the dependent variable is represented on the ordinate (i.e., vertical axis). Which of the two independent variables is placed on the abscissa? The rule generally followed is that the independent variable that is more quantitative in nature or with a more continuous underlying dimension is plotted on the abscissa. In the example experiment, this variable is factor B, stereotype threat. Stereotype threat may vary over the dimension from extremely threatening to not at all threatening in a continuous manner; some situations may be extremely threatening from a stereotypical perspective, other situations may not contain stereotype threats, and some situations will fall between these two extremes. Thus, the stereotype threat condition was placed on the abscissa. The second independent variable, level of math identification, is represented by the two functions within the figure. The filled

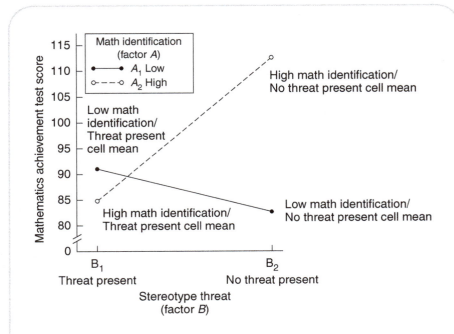

Figure 11.1 Mathematics achievement test performance in the example experiment as a function of level of math identification (low versus high) and stereotype threat condition (threat present versus no threat present). This figure plots the cell means of Table 11.5.

circles connected by the solid line represent the low math identification subjects (A_1), and the open circles connected by the dashed line indicate the high math identification subjects (A_2). The dependent variable is represented on the ordinate. Because the lowest mathematics score is 82.2, the axis is broken by the hatch marks between scores of 0 and 80, and the first labeled value begins at 80.

Figure 11.1 portrays the differing simple effects for each of the two independent variables. When a statistically significant interaction occurs, the effect of one independent variable depends on the level of the other independent variable with which it is combined. This "it depends" nature of an interaction becomes clear from this figure. If you were asked, "What is the relationship of level of math identification to mathematics achievement test performance?", your answer would be, "It depends on whether or not a female experiences a stereotype threat. For the threat present condition there is a nonsignificant difference between the low and high math identification subjects, but for the no threat present condition, high math identification females score significantly higher than low math identification females." Likewise, if you were asked, "What is the effect of stereotype threat condition on female's performance on tests of mathematics achievement?", your answer would take the form, "It depends on whether a female is low or high on math identification level. For females with low math identification, there is no significant difference in mathematics achievement performance between the threat present and no threat present conditions. Females with high math identification, however, score significantly higher on a test of mathematics achievement when in a no threat present condition than in a threat present condition."

The lines connecting data points in Figure 11.1 are nonparallel, a distinguishing characteristic of a figure of a statistically significant interaction. Because an interaction indicates that the simple effects of an independent variable are not equal to its main effect, the plot of a statistically significant interaction must show nonparallel lines. But the lines need not cross as they do in Figure 11.1; they will only do so when the simple effects for an independent variable have opposite signs, as in this example.

In practice, it is rare for any two lines in a figure to be exactly parallel. Because of sampling error, the lines will not be precisely parallel, even when there is no statistically significant interaction. Thus, visual inspection alone is not adequate to determine whether an interaction has occurred. An interaction is present in data *only* if a statistically significant F_{obs} is found for the interaction term in an analysis of variance.

Interpreting the Main Effect for Independent Variable *A*: Level of Math Identification

The value of F_{obs} (1, 16) = 6.66 for the main effect of factor A in Table 11.8 is greater than F_{crit} (1, 16) = 4.49. This F_{obs} falls into the rejection region; thus H_0: $\mu_{A_1} = \mu_{A_2}$ for level of math identification is rejected, and H_1: The μ_A's are not equal is accepted. This decision implies that the main effect of level of math identification (the difference of -12.0 between the main effect means of 86.5 and 98.5 for low and high identification subjects, respectively) is statistically significant. This main effect indicates that females with high math identification score higher on tests of mathematics achievement than females with low math identification. However, this relationship does not hold true for females in the threat present condition; mathematics achievement performance between the low and high math identification females does not differ significantly. Thus, although the main effect for math identification indicates a higher mathematics achievement test performance for females with high math identification, this difference is not seen when females experience stereotype threat.

Interpreting the Main Effect for Independent Variable *B*: Stereotype Threat Condition

The value of F_{obs} for factor B, stereotype threat, is 4.26. This value of F_{obs} is less than F_{crit} of 4.49 and, hence, H_0: $\mu_{B_1} = \mu_{B_2}$ is not rejected and H_1: The μ_B's are not equal is not accepted. This decision implies that the main effect of stereotype threat (the difference of -9.6 between 87.7 and 97.3 for threat present and no threat present, respectively) is nonsignificant. From this nonsignificant main effect alone, we would conclude that stereotype threat does not affect the mathematics achievement score of a subject; the -9.6 main effect difference between the stereotype threat present and no threat present conditions is due to sampling error. But does this conclusion accurately describe the effect of stereotype threat? Again, examination of the simple effects indicates that it does not; stereotype threat does have an effect, but the effect depends on the level of math identification. When the subject has low math identification, there is no significant difference in the mathematics achievement test performance between the threat present and no threat present conditions (i.e., the difference between 90.8 and 82.2 is due to sampling error); but for high math identification females, subjects in the no threat present condition score higher on the mathematics achievement test ($\overline{X}_{A_2B_2} = 112.4$) than subjects in the threat present condition ($\overline{X}_{A_2B_1} = 84.6$). The statistically significant interaction has made it inappropriate to interpret the nonsignificant main effect for stereotype threat.

Patterns of Interaction

The relationship among the cell means in the example experiment is only one of many that may result in a statistically significant interaction. A statistically significant interaction in the analysis of variance indicates only that the simple effect and main effect differences for an independent variable will not be equal. It alone does not provide any further information about the numerous ways in which this result may occur. The exact nature of the interaction can be determined only by carefully analyzing the relationships among the cell means, as we have done for the example experiment.

Measuring the Effect Size in a Factorial Analysis of Variance

As with the one-factor analysis of variance, the size of a statistically significant effect in a factorial design may be measured by η^2. Because there are tests for two main effects and the interaction, we obtain three different values of η^2 as follows:

$$\eta^2 = \frac{SS_A}{SS_{\text{Total}}} \quad \text{for a statistically significant main effect of factor } A.$$

$$\eta^2 = \frac{SS_B}{SS_{\text{Total}}} \quad \text{for a statistically significant main effect of factor } B.$$

$$\eta^2 = \frac{SS_{A \times B}}{SS_{\text{Total}}} \quad \text{for a statistically significant interaction of factors } A \text{ and } B.$$

To illustrate the use of η^2 for the example, the interaction provided the only meaningful information in the experiment; thus, η^2 for the interaction based on the SS values from Table 11.8 is

$$\eta^2 = \frac{SS_{A \times B}}{SS_{\text{Total}}} = \frac{1656.200}{4567.000} = .36.$$

This value indicates that 36 percent of the variance in the mathematics achievement test scores can be accounted for by the interaction of level of math identification and stereotype threat.

Testing Your Knowledge 11.4

1. Define: artifactual main effect, main effect, simple effect.

2. Each of the following tables and Figures 11.2 and 11.3 present cell means obtained in an experiment. A summarized analysis of variance is included for each set of means. In the summarized analysis, a statistically significant F_{obs} is indicated by $p < .05$. A nonsignificant F_{obs} is indicated by $p > .05$. When a significant interaction occurs, the Tukey HSD CD for the simple effects is given at the bottom of the analysis of variance summary. Assume that factor A is a teaching method with two levels, online assisted (A_1) and traditional teaching (A_2). Factor B is type of material to be learned, mathematics (B_1) or social studies (B_2). The dependent variable is test score. Interpret

each set of means by finding the simple and main effects for each independent variable and relating these effects to the summarized analysis of variance. Then, answer these questions for each example:

a. Do the main effect means of factor A differ significantly from each other?

b. Do the main effect means of factor B differ significantly from each other?

c. Is there a statistically significant interaction of factors A and B?

d. What is the effect of teaching method (factor A) on test scores?

e. What is the effect of type of material (factor B) on test scores?

f. Do the main effects provide useful information about the results of the experiment?

Table 1

		Factor A A_1	A_2	ANOVA Summary	
Factor B	B_1	91	85	Factor A	$p < .05$
				Factor B	$p > .05$
	B_2	92	87	$A \times B$	$p > .05$

Table 2

		Factor A A_1	A_2	ANOVA Summary	
Factor B	B_1	89	90	Factor A	$p > .05$
				Factor B	$p < .05$
	B_2	81	80	$A \times B$	$p > .05$

Table 3

		Factor A A_1	A_2	ANOVA Summary	
Factor B	B_1	85	94	Factor A	$p < .05$
				Factor B	$p < .05$
	B_2	78	86	$A \times B$	$p > .05$

Table 4

		Factor A A_1	A_2	ANOVA Summary	
Factor B	B_1	88	75	Factor A	$p > .05$
				Factor B	$p > .05$
	B_2	76	90	$A \times B$	$p < .05$
				Tukey $CD = 4$	

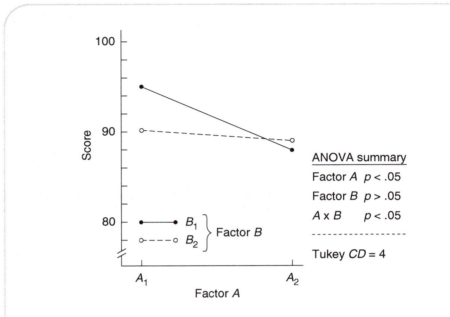

Figure 11.2 Outcome of an experiment involving manipulation of factors *A* and *B*.

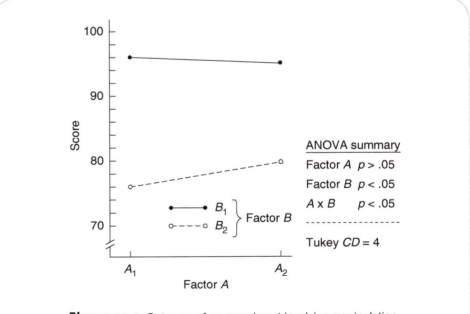

Figure 11.3 Outcome of an experiment involving manipulation of factors *A* and *B*.

Table 5			
	Factor A		
	A_1	A_2	ANOVA Summary
Factor B B_1	87	88	Factor A $p < .05$
			Factor B $p < .05$
B_2	74	80	$A \times B$ $p < .05$
			Tukey $CD = 4$

Table 6			
	Factor A		
	A_1	A_2	ANOVA Summary
Factor B B_1	90	80	Factor A $p < .05$
			Factor B $p < .05$
B_2	81	82	$A \times B$ $p < .05$
			Tukey $CD = 4$

EXAMPLE PROBLEM

11.1

Analyzing a 2 × 2 Design with a Statistically Significant Interaction and Nonsignificant Main Effects

Problem: Let's return to the example given at the beginning of this chapter, where we discussed that the effect of disclosing a personal situation on feelings of emotional intimacy in couples depended upon whether the person was male or female. Mitchell et al. (2008) found these results with a sample of heterosexual couples, the majority of whom were married and in a cohabiting relationship of six months or longer. Suppose we were interested in testing this to see if this relationship holds for heterosexual romantic couples in a newly formed relationship of two to four weeks in length. Our research design will be a 2 × 2 between-subjects design with two independent variables: disclosure condition, either partner disclosure or self disclosure (factor A), and the gender of the partner who is rating the emotional intimacy of the relationship (factor B). Couples will be randomly assigned to one of two disclosure conditions: level A_1, partner disclosure, where the partner of the person rating the intimacy of the relationship is asked to disclose a painful situation that has happened in his or her past, or level A_2, self-disclosure, where the person rating the intimacy of the relationship discloses a painful situation that has happened in his or her past. For example, a disclosure of a painful situation might be, "When I was little, I was very fond of my grandfather. I was very sad when he died." In addition, couples will be either assigned to one of two conditions for the evaluating the emotional intimacy of the relationship: level B_1, the male partner of the couple will rate emotional intimacy of the relationship, or level B_2, the female partner of the couple will rate the emotional intimacy of the relationship. Twenty-four couples were used, with six couples randomly assigned to each treatment condition. The table below summarizes the design of the study.

	Disclosure Condition (A)	
	Partner Disclosure (A_1)	Self Disclosure (A_2)
Male (B_1) Gender of Subject (B) Female (B_2)	Six couples with the male rating emotional intimacy after disclosure of his partner Six couples with the female rating emotional intimacy after disclosure of her partner	Six couples with the male rating emotional intimacy after his own disclosure Six couples with the female rating emotional intimacy after her own disclosure

Emotional intimacy of the relationship was measured by having subjects rate three statements similar to "This disclosure makes me feeler closer to my partner" on a seven-point scale from 1, "not at all," to 7, "very much." Thus, scores could range from 3 to 21, with higher scores indicating greater emotional intimacy. Assume that the following hypothetical scores were obtained from the 24 couples.

	Disclosure Condition (A)	
	Partner Disclosure (A_1)	Self Disclosure (A_2)
Male (B_1)	4 5 7 6 10 4	16 14 17 19 16 20
Gender of Subject (B)		
Female (B_2)	12 15 18 13 16 16	5 9 7 6 10 5

There are three questions we must answer about these data:

1. Is there an effect of disclosure condition on the emotional intimacy ratings?
2. Do males and females differ in the intimacy ratings given?
3. Is there an interaction of disclosure condition with gender of the subjects?

Use a .05 significance level.

Solution: The design used is a 2×2 between-subjects design. The first step is to perform a two-factor between-subjects analysis of variance on the scores to determine if either statistically significant main effects or statistically significant interaction exists.

Assumptions for Use:
1. The subjects were sampled randomly and independently from a population.
2. Intimacy ratings are normally distributed in the population.
3. The variances for the intimacy rating scores are equal in the populations sampled.

Statistical Hypotheses:

Factor A

H_0: $\mu_{A_1} = \mu_{A_2}$.

H_1: The μ_A's are not equal.

Factor B

H_0: $\mu_{B_1} = \mu_{B_2}$.

H_1: The μ_B's are not equal.

$A \times B$

H_0: All $(\mu_{AB} - \mu_A - \mu_B + \mu_G) = 0$.

H_1: Not all $(\mu_{AB} - \mu_A - \mu_B + \mu_G) = 0$.

Significance Level: $\alpha = .05$.

df:

$$df_A = a - 1 = 2 - 1 = 1$$
$$df_B = b - 1 = 2 - 1 = 1$$
$$df_{A \times B} = (a - 1)(b - 1) = (2 - 1)(2 - 1) = 1$$
$$df_{Error} = ab(n_{AB} - 1) = (2)(2)(6 - 1) = 20$$
$$df_{Total} = N - 1 = 24 - 1 = 23$$

Critical Value of F: Each F_{obs} has 1 df for the numerator and 20 df for the denominator; thus, $F_{crit}(1, 20) = 4.35$ from Appendix C.3a.

Rejection Region: Values of F_{obs} equal to or greater than 4.35.

Calculation: The analysis of variance was calculated with SPSS software to obtain the following summary table.

Source	df	SS	MS	F
Disclosure condition (A)	1	13.50	13.50	2.81
Gender of subject (B)	1	1.50	1.50	0.31
$A \times B$	1	541.50	541.50	112.81[*]
Error	20	96.00	4.80	
Total	23	652.50		

[*]$p < .01$.

Decisions: Three decisions must be made for the statistical hypotheses of this analysis, one for each F_{obs}.

▶ Disclosure condition (factor A): $F_{obs} = 2.81$. This F_{obs} does not fall into the rejection region; we fail to reject H_0 and do not accept H_1.

▶ Gender of subject (factor B): $F_{obs} = 0.31$. This F_{obs} does not fall into the rejection region; we fail to reject H_0 and do not accept H_1.

▶ Disclosure condition by gender of subject ($A \times B$): $F_{obs} = 112.81$. This F_{obs} falls into the rejection region; we reject H_0 and accept H_1.

Effect Size: η^2 for the statistically significant interaction equals $SS_{A \times B}/SS_{Total} = 541.50/652.50 = .83$.

Interpretation and Conclusions: To interpret the statistically significant inter-action, we find the Tukey HSD CD for the simple effects and then compare the simple effects to this CD. The numerical values needed for this test are found as follows:

▶ q is obtained from Table A.4. Using the conversion chart for a 2 × 2 design given with this table, the value of q is obtained for $a = 3$ and 20 df for MS_{Error}. This value is 3.58 for $\alpha = .05$.

▶ MS_{Error}, obtained from the analysis of variance, is 4.80.

▶ n_{AB}, the number of scores in each cell, is 6.

Substituting these numerical values into the formula,

$$CD = q\sqrt{\frac{MS_{\text{Error}}}{n_{AB}}} = 3.58\sqrt{\frac{4.80}{6}} = 3.2 \text{ rating points.}$$

Any simple effect equal to or larger than 3.2 rating points in absolute value is statistically significant at the .05 level.

Table 11.13 presents the cell and main effect means and the simple and main effects for the scores. Each simple effect in this table is larger in absolute value than the $CD = 3.2$ and, thus, is statistically significant. Notice, however, that for each indepen-dent variable, the simple effects are opposite in sign. The effect of disclosure condition clearly depends on the gender of the subject. Males rate the intimacy of the relationship

---

TABLE

11.13

Main effect and simple effect differences in ratings of intimacy as a function of disclosure condition and gender of subject

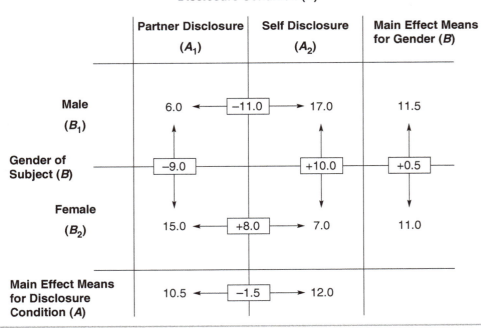

	Disclosure Condition (A)		
	Partner Disclosure (A₁)	Self Disclosure (A₂)	Main Effect Means for Gender (B)
Male (B₁)	6.0 ←—[−11.0]—→ 17.0		11.5
Gender of Subject (B)	[−9.0]	[+10.0]	[+0.5]
Female (B₂)	15.0 ←—[+8.0]—→ 7.0		11.0
Main Effect Means for Disclosure Condition (A)	10.5 ←—[−1.5]—→ 12.0		

significantly higher at 17.0 after their self disclosure compared to partner disclosure (i.e., 6.0). This rating pattern is reversed for females. Females rate the intimacy of the relationship significantly higher at 15.0 after hearing partner disclosure, whereas they rate the intimacy at 7.0 after self disclosure. The simple effects for disclosure condition (-11.0 for males, $+8.0$ for females) are not equal to each other, nor are they equal to the nonsignificant main effect of -1.5 for disclosure condition.

Similarly, the difference between males and females in rating emotional intimacy depends on the disclosure condition. Females listening to partner disclosure ($\overline{X}_{A_1B_2} = 15.0$) rate emotional intimacy significantly higher than do males ($\overline{X}_{A_1B_1} = 6.0$) listening to partner disclosure. But males after self disclosure ($\overline{X}_{A_2B_1} = 17.0$) rate intimacy as significantly higher than do females after self disclosure ($\overline{X}_{A_2B_2} = 7.0$). Thus, the simple effects for gender (-9.0 for partner disclosure, $+10.0$ for self disclosure) are not equal to each other or to the nonsignificant main effect of $+0.5$ for gender of the subjects.

The main effects do not provide useful information about the results of this study. From the main effects alone, we would conclude that there is no effect for disclosure condition and that males and females do not differ on their intimacy ratings. The analysis of the interaction, however, indicates that disclosure condition does have an effect on the intimacy ratings, but the direction of the effect depends on gender. Furthermore, males and females differ in their intimacy ratings, but the difference depends on the disclosure condition. The η^2 indicates that 83 percent of the variance in the ratings is determined by the interaction. Predicting scores from the cell means rather than the grand mean reduces the total variance by 83 percent in this sample.

EXAMPLE PROBLEM

11.2

Analyzing a 2 × 2 Design with a Statistically Significant Interaction and Main Effects

Problem: The keyword method is a memory-enhancement technique in which a person uses a visual image to form an association between two items. One use of this method is in helping to learn the vocabulary of a second language. Suppose that you are asked to learn a list of unfamiliar French words and their English equivalents, such as the French word *boue* and its English equivalent *mud*. Here, the keyword might be *boot*, an English word that sounds like the French *boue*. To use the technique, when you hear *boue*, you think of *boot* and then form an image of a person wearing boots and walking through *mud*. A number of studies have shown that the keyword technique enhances learning and immediate recall of a second language vocabulary (Wang, Thomas, & Ouellette, 1992). How long this improved recall lasts, however, is open to question. Wang et al. (1992) found that, although the keyword technique enhanced immediate retention in comparison to rote learning by simple repetition of the words, the keyword subjects also forgot at a greater rate over a one-week retention interval.

You are interested in finding out if this relationship holds for adult learners as well as for the college students tested by Wang et al. Accordingly, you use a 2 × 2 between-subjects design with learning method, either rote or keyword, as factor *A*, and retention interval, either immediate or delayed for one week, as factor *B*. You randomly assigned eight adult learners unfamiliar with French to each treatment condition. People in the rote learning method were told to simply repeat the French words and their English equivalents over and over in order to remember them. In the keyword method, subjects were taught the keyword method and given a keyword for each French–English pair. For the immediate-retention condition, recall of the English equivalents was tested 5 minutes after the list was learned. For the delayed-retention groups, subjects were tested for recall of the English equivalents one week after they had learned the list. The list of words was 25 items long, so a person's recall score could vary from 0 (no recall) to 25 (perfect recall). Assume that the accompanying hypothetical recall scores were given by the 32 subjects. Analyze and describe the results of this experiment.

	Learning Condition (A)	
	Rote (A_1)	Keyword (A_2)
Immediate (B_1)	12	25
	9	22
	11	19
	19	23
	16	17
	14	24
	13	20
	15	21
Retention Interval (B)		
	6	9
	7	4
	3	7
Delayed (B_2)	11	11
	5	5
	10	8
	5	12
	8	6

Solution: A two-factor between-subjects analysis of variance is needed to statistically analyze this experiment.

Assumptions for Use:

1. The subjects were sampled randomly and independently from a population.
2. Recall scores are normally distributed in the population.
3. The variances for the recall scores are equal in the populations sampled.

Statistical Hypotheses:

Factor A H_0: $\mu_{A_1} = \mu_{A_2}$.
           H_1: The μ_A's are not equal.

Factor B H_0: $\mu_{B_1} = \mu_{B_2}$.
           H_1: The μ_B's are not equal.

$A \times B$ H_0: All $(\mu_{AB} - \mu_A - \mu_B + \mu_G) = 0$.
           H_1: Not all $(\mu_{AB} - \mu_A - \mu_B + \mu_G) = 0$.

Significance Level: $\alpha = .05$.

df:

$$df_A = a - 1 = 2 - 1 = 1$$
$$df_B = b - 1 = 2 - 1 = 1$$
$$df_{A \times B} = (a - 1)(b - 1) = (2 - 1)(2 - 1) = 1$$
$$df_{Error} = ab(n_{AB} - 1) = (2)(2)(8 - 1) = 28$$
$$df_{Total} = N - 1 = 32 - 1 = 31$$

Critical Value of F: $F_{crit}(1, 28) = 4.20$ for each value of F_{obs}.

Rejection Region: Values of F_{obs} equal to or greater than 4.20.

Calculation: The analysis of variance was calculated with *SPSS* software to obtain the following summary table.

Source	SS	df	MS	F
Learning condition (*A*)	148.781	1	148.781	18.59*
Retention interval (*B*)	830.281	1	830.281	103.73*
A × *B*	94.531	1	94.531	11.81*
Error	224.125	28	8.004	
Total	1297.718	31		

*$p < .01$.

Decisions:

▶ Learning condition (factor *A*): $F_{obs} = 18.59$. This F_{obs} falls into the rejection region; we reject H_0 and accept H_1.

▶ Retention interval (factor *B*): $F_{obs} = 103.73$. This F_{obs} falls into the rejection region; we reject H_0 and accept H_1.

▶ Learning condition by retention interval (*A* × *B*): $F_{obs} = 11.81$. This F_{obs} falls into the rejection region; we reject H_0 and accept H_1.

Effect Size:

Learning condition: $\eta^2 = SS_A/SS_{Total} = 148.781/1297.718 = .11.$
Retention interval: $\eta^2 = SS_B/SS_{Total} = 830.281/1297.718 = .64.$
Learning condition × retention interval: $\eta^2 = SS_{A \times B}/SS_{Total} = 94.531/1297.718 = .07.$

Interpretation and Conclusions: We first interpret the interaction by finding the Tukey HSD *CD* for the simple effects and then comparing the simple effects to this *CD*. The numerical values needed for this test are found as follows:

▶ q is obtained from Appendix C.4 for $a = 3$ and 28 *df* for MS_{Error}. Because 28 *df* are not in the table for MS_{Error}, q for the next lower *df*, 24 was used. This value is 3.53 for $\alpha = .05$.

▶ MS_{Error} is 8.004.

▶ n_{AB} is 8.

Substituting these numerical values into the formula,

$$CD = q\sqrt{\frac{MS_{Error}}{n_{AB}}} = 3.53\sqrt{\frac{8.004}{8}}$$

$$= 3.5 \text{ words, rounded to one decimal place.}$$

Any simple effect equal to or larger than 3.5 words in absolute value is statistically significant at the .05 level. Table 11.14 presents the cell and main effect means and the simple and main effects for the scores. We first interpret the interaction for each independent variable and then the main effect of that variable.

Learning Condition: The simple effect of learning condition for immediate recall, −7.8, is greater in absolute value than the *CD* of 3.5 and is statistically significant. The keyword condition ($\overline{X}_{A_2B_1}$ = 21.4 words) results in significantly greater recall than does rote learning for immediate retention ($\overline{X}_{A_1B_1}$ = 13.6 words). For delayed retention, however, the simple effect of learning condition, −0.9, is smaller in absolute value than the *CD* of 3.5. This simple effect is nonsignificant. Thus, for delayed retention, rote ($\overline{X}_{A_1B_2}$ = 6.9 words) and keyword ($\overline{X}_{A_2B_2}$ = 7.8 words) conditions do not differ significantly. Learning condition has no effect on recall for delayed retention. The $F_{obs}(1, 28)$ = 18.59 for the main effect of learning condition is statistically significant, indicating that the main effect means for learning condition ($\overline{X}_{A_1}$ = 10.2 and $\overline{X}_{A_2}$ = 14.6) differ significantly. But this significant main effect does not provide meaningful information about the outcome of the experiment. This main effect indicates that people recall more words with the keyword condition, but the analysis of the simple effects for learning condition revealed that this relationship holds only for the immediate-recall interval; it does not hold for the delayed-retention interval. Hence, the main effect of learning condition does not provide a correct description of the effect of learning condition. We thus ignore it in the description of the results of the experiment.

TABLE 11.14	Main effect and simple effect differences in number of words correctly recalled as a function of learning condition and retention interval

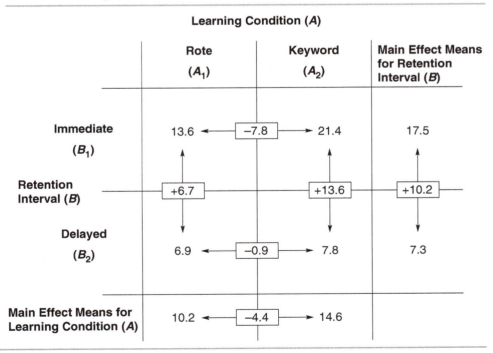

Retention Interval: The significant interaction indicates also that the effect of retention interval depends on learning condition. For both levels of learning condition, the simple effects of retention interval (+6.7 for rote learning, +13.6 for keyword learning) are larger in absolute value than the *CD* of 3.5. These statistically significant simple effects indicate that, for both rote and keyword learning, delayed recall results in significantly less recall than does immediate recall. Examination of the simple effects, however, reveals that the decrease in retention from immediate to delayed recall is greater for the keyword condition (13.6 words) than it is for the rote condition (6.7 words). The statistically significant main effect of retention interval [i.e., $F_{obs}(1, 28) = 103.73, p < .01$] indicates that the main effect means for retention interval ($\overline{X}_{B_1} = 17.5$ and $\overline{X}_{B_2} = 7.3$) differ significantly. From this significant main effect alone, we conclude that immediate recall leads to greater retention than does delayed retention. This conclusion is correct, for the relationship holds for both rote and keyword conditions. Hence, the main effect for retention interval is meaningful and provides useful information about the results of the experiment. The interpretation of this main effect must be qualified, however, by recognizing that the interaction indicates that the extent of the difference between immediate and delayed recall depends on learning condition.

The η^2 for the main effect of retention interval, .64, indicates that the retention interval accounts for a large proportion of the variance in recall scores. The η^2 for the interaction, .07, indicates that the interaction accounts for a smaller portion of the variance in the recall scores. Because the main effect of learning condition is artifactual, we do not use the eta squared for this factor.

Reporting the Results of a Factorial Analysis of Variance

The style of reporting the results of a factorial experiment follows that used for the one-factor design in Chapter 10. We illustrate by using the results of the example problem on the effects of level of math identification (low or high identification) and stereotype threat (threat present or no threat present) on mathematics achievement performance. Cell means for this experiment are presented in Table 11.5 and the analysis of variance summarized in Table 11.8. Because of the expense of printing tables, the results of an experiment, including cell means and the statistical analysis, are often reported in text format as illustrated here.

> An alpha level of .05 was used for all statistical tests. There was a significant interaction of level of math identification with stereotype threat condition, $F(1, 16) = 15.32$, $MSE = 108.125$, $p < .01$. The Tukey HSD test (critical difference = 17.0 with $\alpha = .05$) was used for testing the statistical significance of the simple effects. When a stereotype threat was present, the low and high math identification females did not differ in mathematics achievement ($M = 90.8$, $SD = 11.6$ for low identification, and $M = 84.6$, $SD = 9.6$ for high identification). For the no threat present condition, however, high math identification females ($M = 112.4$, $SD = 11.2$) scored significantly higher on the mathematics achievement test than did low math identification females ($M = 82.2$, $SD = 9.1$). The difference in mathematics achievement scores between the threat present and no threat present conditions for the low math identification females was nonsignificant. For the high math identification females, however, test performance for the no threat present condition was significantly higher than for the threat present condition. Eta squared for the interaction was .36. The main effect of level of math identification was

significant, $F(1, 16) = 6.66$, $p < .05$, with high math identification females scoring higher on the mathematics test ($M = 98.5$) than low math identification females ($M = 86.5$), but this effect is not meaningful because of the interaction. The main effect for stereotype threat was not statistically significant, $F(1, 16) = 4.26$, $p > .05$.

In this presentation:

$\alpha = .05$ Indicates the significance level selected for the statistical tests.

$F(1, 16)$ Identifies the test statistic as the F. The df for the numerator and denominator of each F_{obs} reported are shown in parentheses. Three values of F_{obs} are reported, one for each independent variable and one for the interaction of the independent variables. The order in which F_{obs} is reported is not necessarily factor A, factor B, and $A \times B$. Often, an experimenter has more interest in the interaction and will present this F_{obs} value first in the description of the results, as illustrated in the example.

$= 15.32$ Gives the value of F_{obs} (not the F_{crit} value found in Appendix C.3). In some instances, only two of the three F_{obs} obtained in the analysis of variance may be reported. In this case, you may assume that the unreported value of F_{obs} was nonsignificant.

$p < .01$ Indicates that

       a. The probability of F_{obs} if H_0 is true is less than or equal to .01. This value is the probability of F_{obs} or an even more extreme value of F_{obs} if H_0 is true; it may not be the same as the value of α selected.

       b. H_0 was rejected and H_1 was accepted.

       c. This F_{obs} was for the interaction term of the analysis of variance; thus, it indicates that the interaction of factors A and B is statistically significant.

       d. Something other than sampling error is responsible for the interaction of factors A and B.

$MSE = 108.125$ Gives the MS_{Error} for the F_{obs}. This value is a measure of the within-cells error variation in the scores.

$CD = 17.0$ Gives the critical difference for simple effect comparisons using the Tukey HSD test. The statistically significant simple effects are then described.

$\eta^2 = .36$ Indicates that 36 percent of the variance in the mathematics achievement test scores in this experiment is accounted for by the interaction of factors A and B. In this example, the interaction provides the only meaningful information about the outcome of the experiment; thus, η^2 is given only for this source of variance.

Testing Your Knowledge 11.5

Complete these problems using a two-factor between-subjects analysis of variance following the format illustrated in the example problems. Use a .05 significance level for each problem.

    1. A psychologist hypothesized that the effect of type of instructions on a person's performance on an anagram solution task would depend on that individual's perceived locus of control. To evaluate this hypothesis, she obtained 12 females who scored low on a locus of control scale (indicating an internal locus of control) and 12 females who scored high on the scale (indicating an external locus of control). Half the females in each group were randomly assigned to one of two instructional conditions, skill or chance instructions. In the skill instructions condition, subjects were told that their performance on an anagram solution task depended on their verbal ability and was under their control. The chance instructions indicated that performance on this task does not depend on verbal ability and is beyond a person's control. The subjects then solved a series of anagrams, and the amount of time devoted to the task was recorded. Suppose that the following amounts of time (in seconds) that each person worked on solving the anagrams were obtained:

	Locus of Control (A)	
	Internal (A_1)	External (A_2)
Skill (B_1)	175	115
	202	106
	193	87
	186	93
	150	99
	212	157
Instructions (B)		
Chance (B_1)	125	218
	100	202
	77	196
	101	244
	131	237
	152	180

a. Calculate the cell and main effect means. Then, analyze the scores to determine (1) if there is a main effect for either independent variable and (2) if there is an interaction of the independent variables.

b. Describe the effect of type of instructions. If needed, use the Tukey HSD test to determine the statistically significant simple effects.

c. Are you able to meaningfully interpret any statistically significant main effects, or are they artifactual?

d. What proportion of the variance in the dependent variable can be accounted for by the interaction of the independent variables?

2. In many jurisdictions, potential jurors are shown a film to acquaint them with the legal process and the nature of the jury system. A lawyer was interested in finding out whether the film alters a juror's behavior in comparison to standard oral instructions. Furthermore, the lawyer wanted to know if any effect of the film may depend on the type of crime the juror is to evaluate. To answer these questions, the lawyer conducted a 2 × 2 between-subjects factorial experiment with nine people in each treatment condition serving as mock jurors. Factor A was the type of instruction given to jurors: A_1, normal oral instructions by a court officer, and A_2, filmed instructions. Factor B was the type of crime that the juror was asked to evaluate; this variable was manipulated by having the subjects read a description of an auto theft case (level B_1) or of an aggravated assault case (level B_2). Each subject was then asked to assign a prison term to the defendant described in the case. The prison terms assigned (in months) are given in the accompanying table.

| | Type of Instruction (A) | |
	Normal (A₁)	Filmed (A₂)
Auto Theft (B₁)	15	13
	10	16
	10	9
	14	11
	17	14
	9	8
	8	10
	12	10
	10	12
Aggravated Assault (B₂)	25	30
	20	33
	23	26
	20	25
	19	30
	17	35
	18	30
	22	28
	20	32

Type of Crime (B)

a. Calculate the cell and main effect means. Then, analyze the scores to determine (1) if there is a main effect for either independent variable and (2) if there is an interaction of the independent variables.

b. Describe the effect of type of instructions.

c. Describe the effect of type of crime.

d. Are you able to meaningfully interpret any statistically significant main effects, or are they artifactual?

e. What proportion of the variance in the dependent variable can be accounted for by the type of crime and the interaction of the independent variables?

3. The following exercises present sample reports of two-factor between-subjects analyses of variance. Answer the following questions for each report.

a. How many levels of factor A were varied in this experiment?

b. How many levels of factor B were varied in this experiment?

c. How many subjects were used in the experiment?

d. What is the value of F_{crit} at the .05 significance level for each F_{obs} reported?

e. Is the value of F_{obs} for factor A statistically significant?

f. Is the value of F_{obs} for factor B statistically significant?

g. Is the value of F_{obs} for $A \times B$ statistically significant?

Report 1: An alpha level of .05 was used for all statistical tests. The main effect of drug level (factor A) was statistically significant, $F(2, 36) = 9.43$, $p < 0.1$, $MSE = 17.814$. There was also a main effect for retention interval (factor B), $F(1, 36) = 5.60$, $p < .05$. The interaction was nonsignificant, $F(2, 36) = 2.46$, $p > .05$.

Report 2: An alpha level of .05 was used for all statistical tests. There was a significant gender of athlete (factor *A*) by type of sport (factor *B*) interaction on self-esteem ratings, $F(3, 88) = 3.28$, $p < .05$, $MSE = 42.163$. In addition, males gave higher-rated self-esteem than females, $F(1, 88) = 4.82$, $p < .05$. There were no main effect differences among sport types, $F(3, 88) = 1.65$, $p > .05$.

Report 3: An alpha level of .05 was used for all statistical tests. There was a significant interaction of noise condition with personality type $F(1, 56) = 5.33$, $p < .05$, $MSE = 26.718$. Neither the main effect for noise condition, $F(1, 56) < 1.0$, nor personality type $F(1, 56) = 1.43$, $p > .05$, was significant.

 ## Summary

▶ Factorial designs are research designs in which two or more independent variables are varied simultaneously.

▶ Each cell or treatment condition of a factorial design represents a combination formed from one level of each independent variable.

▶ Main effect means indicate the typical performance of all individuals given one level of an independent variable, while ignoring the classification by the other independent variable.

▶ An interaction occurs in a factorial design when the effect of one independent variable depends on the level of the other independent variable with which it is combined.

▶ Three *F* statistics are obtained in the two-factor between-subjects analysis of variance.

Source of Variation	F
Factor *A*	MS_A/MS_{Error}
Factor *B*	MS_B/MS_{Error}
Interaction of $A \times B$	$MS_{A \times B}/MS_{\text{Error}}$

▶ The steps in statistical testing with these *F* ratios are identical to those discussed in Chapter 10.

▶ The simple effect of an independent variable in a factorial design is the effect of that independent variable at only one level of the other independent variable.

▶ If a statistically significant interaction of the independent variables occurs, then the two simple effects for a factor are not equal to each other or to the main effect for that factor.

▶ An artifactual main effect is a main effect that cannot be meaningfully interpreted; it occurs only because of the specific pattern of interaction obtained.

▶ Follow-up tests are needed to statistically analyze the simple effects if a significant interaction is obtained. The Tukey HSD test is used for post hoc comparisons.

▶ η^2 is used as a measure of effect size for statistically significant main effects and interaction.

 ## Key Terms and Symbols

a (284)
artifactual main effect (309)
b (284)
cell or treatment condition (284)
cell mean ($\overline{X}_{AB}$) (286)
critical difference (*CD*) (308)

df_A (296)
df_B (296)
$df_{A \times B}$ (296)
df_{Error} (296)
df_{Total} (296)
factor *A* (283)

factor *B* (283)
factorial design (283)
grand mean ($\overline{X}_G$) (288)
interaction ($A \times B$) (288)
main effect of factor *A* (288)
main effect of factor *B* (288)

main effect mean (288)
MS_A (290)
MS_B (290)
$MS_{A \times B}$ (290)
MS_{Error} (290)
n_{AB} (286)

simple effect of an independent
variable (306)
SS_A (293)
SS_B (293)
$SS_{A \times B}$ (293)

SS_{Error} (293)
SS_{Total} (293)
Tukey HSD test (308)
$\overline{X}_A$ (288)
$\overline{X}_B$ (288)

Review Questions

Answer questions 1 to 3 by performing a two-factor between-subjects analysis of variance on the scores given.

1. In a study of environmental factors that influence food consumption, Wansink, Painter, and Lee (2006) examined the effects of placement of a candy dish and the visibility of the candy on candy consumption. One independent variable (factor A) was the proximity of the candy dish in relation to the subject. The candy dish was placed either on the desk of the subject (close, A_1) or approximately 9 feet (3 meters) from the desk (far, A_2). The second independent variable (factor B) was the visibility of the candy, either non-visible or visible. In both levels the candy was placed in a candy dish with a lid. In the non-visible condition (B_1), the candy dish was opaque, whereas in the visible condition (B_2), the candy dish was transparent. The dependent variable was how much candy was consumed. Suppose that you wanted to replicate this experiment with a 2 × 2 between-subjects design and eight subjects per cell. You obtained the following number of grams of candy consumed.

	Proximity of Candy Dish (A)	
	Close (A_1)	Far (A_2)
Not Visible (B_1)	75	61
	77	68
	68	71
	72	59
	83	74
	78	66
	70	67
	65	57
Candy Dish Visibility (B)		
Visible (B_2)	79	84
	82	79
	75	88
	77	90
	84	75
	72	75
	78	77
	69	85

a. Does the effect of proximity of the candy dish depend on visibility of the candy? If so, use the Tukey HSD test for the simple effect comparisons. Describe the relationship that you found.

    b. Does the effect of the visibility of the candy depend on the proximity of the candy? If so, use the Tukey HSD test for the simple effect comparisons. Describe the relationship that you found.

    c. Are you able to meaningfully interpret any main effects, or are they artifactual?

    d. What proportion of the variance in the dependent variable can be accounted for by the interaction of the independent variables?

    e. Describe the results of this experiment following the style illustrated in the Reporting the Results of a Factorial Analysis of Variance section of this chapter.

2. One personality dimension that seems well recognized by most people is that of introversion–extroversion. Extroverts are described as outgoing, sociable, and fun-loving, whereas introverts are described as reserved and less sociable. Because introverts seem more directed toward their own thoughts and ideas, we might suspect that introverts and extroverts may respond differently to external stimulation such as noise. To more fully investigate this issue, Standing, Lynn, and Moxness (1990) used a 2 × 2 between-subjects design to vary personality type (factor A), introverts (A_1) and extroverts (A_2), and background noise (factor B), quiet (B_1) and noisy (B_2), while subjects performed a reading comprehension task. Suppose you conducted a similar study with 12 subjects per cell, and each person completed a 15-item true–false reading comprehension task. A person's score was the number of items correctly answered. You obtained the following scores:

		Personality Type (A)	
		Introvert (A_1)	Extrovert (A_2)
Background Noise (B)	**Quiet (B_1)**	10	15
		8	14
		12	12
		15	15
		10	11
		9	8
		14	12
		13	8
		14	13
		7	10
		12	9
		11	11
	Noisy (B_2)	6	13
		8	8
		11	9
		4	14
		5	13
		8	12
		9	15
		10	11
		9	9
		10	11
		7	12
		11	10

a. What is the relationship between personality type and the effect of background noise? If an interaction occurred, use the Tukey HSD test for the simple effects. Describe the relationship that you found.

b. What is η^2 for the interaction?

c. Are you able to meaningfully interpret any main effects, or are they artifactual?

d. Describe the results of this experiment following the style illustrated in the Reporting the Results of a Factorial Analysis of Variance section of this chapter.

3. What is the best approach to teaching phonics to beginning readers? Joseph (2000) tested two new approaches to teaching phonics to first-graders, word box instruction and word sort instruction, as well as traditional phonics instruction. Word box instruction provides a child with a rectangle that is divided into sections for each phoneme in a word (a phoneme is the smallest speech sound). In the initial phases of this instruction, as a word is spoken, the child places a token in each section of the rectangle corresponding to the phoneme being sounded. Word sort instruction involves asking children to sort words into categories based on some common aspect such as spelling or sound. Traditional phonics teaching involves having students give choral readings of words sharing spelling patterns. Suppose you were also interested in the effect of phonics teaching methods but further wanted to know the effects of practice on the methods. Thus, you manipulated three methods of phonics instruction (factor A): traditional (A_1), word box (A_2), and word sort (A_3). You also manipulated amount of practice (factor B) over two levels: one week (B_1) and six weeks (B_2). Nine first-grade children were randomly assigned to each cell. At the end of the practice period, each child was tested on a 30-item spelling test, and the following scores were obtained (each score is the number of words correctly spelled):

| | Instructional Method (A) | | |
	Traditional (A_1)	Word Box (A_2)	Word Sort (A_3)
One Week (B_1)	10	16	21
	14	17	24
	16	23	23
	12	19	20
	14	20	23
	13	15	25
	15	19	21
	11	18	26
	13	21	22
Amount of Practice (B)			
Six Weeks (B_2)	15	18	21
	18	24	19
	22	19	20
	18	22	23
	21	21	24
	17	20	24
	18	20	22
	16	22	25
	16	23	20

a. Does the effect of instructional method depend on the amount of practice? If so, use the Tukey HSD test for the simple effects. Describe the relationship between instructional method and amount of practice that you found.

    b. What is η^2 for the interaction?

    c. Are you able to meaningfully interpret any main effects, or are they artifactual?

    d. Describe the results of this experiment following the style illustrated in the Reporting the Results of a Factorial Analysis of Variance section of this chapter.

4. A psychologist used a 2 × 3 between-subjects design with eight subjects in each cell.

    a. What are the values of a, b, n_{AB}, and N for this design?

    b. What are the values of df_A, df_B, $df_{A \times B}$, df_{Error}, and df_{Total} for this design?

5. The following tables are incomplete summary tables for between-subjects factorial analyses of variance. Assume an equal number of scores in each cell. Use the relationships among SS, df, and MS to provide the missing values in each table. Then, answer the following questions for each table.

    a. How many levels of factor A were varied?

    b. How many levels of factor B were varied?

    c. How many subjects were used in each cell?

    d. What was the total number of subjects in the experiment?

    e. Which values of F_{obs} are statistically significant at the .05 level?

    f. What decision do you make for each null and alternative hypothesis for this analysis?

Table 1

Source	SS	df	MS	F
Type of task (A)	—	3	5.00	—
Noise level (B)	16.00	—	—	—
$A \times B$	36.00	6	—	—
Error	—	60	2.00	
Total	—	—		

Table 2

Source	SS	df	MS	F
Training length (A)	40.00	—	10.00	—
Skill level (B)	—	3	40.00	—
$A \times B$	960.00	—	80.00	—
Error	3200.00	160	—	
Total	—	179		

Table 3

Source	SS	df	MS	F
Type of feedback (A)	200.00	—	50.00	—
Task difficulty (B)	—	—	—	—
$A \times B$	—	8	30.00	—
Error	—	—	20.00	
Total	3300.00	149		

6. Suppose that you had people learn a series of sentences and then recall the nouns in the sentences. You manipulated two levels of type of imagery (factor A), ordinary imagery and bizarre imagery, and two levels of the amount of elaboration (factor B), low and high elaboration, of the sentences. Each person had 30 sentences to learn; thus, a maximum of 30 nouns could be recalled. The cell means for number of nouns correctly recalled are shown in Table 1. An analysis of variance for these data is presented in Table 2. Assume a between-subjects design with five subjects per cell.

   A Tukey HSD yielded a $CD = 6.8$ words for the simple effects.

Table 1

Mean number of nouns correctly recalled as a function of type of imagery and amount of elaboration

		Type of Imagery (A)	
		Ordinary (A$_1$)	Bizarre (A$_2$)
Amount of Elaboration (B)	Low (B$_1$)	21.4	4.8
	High (B$_2$)	10.4	18.8

Table 2

Analysis of variance summary table for mean number of nouns recalled in Table 1

Source	SS	df	MS	F
Type of imagery (A)	84.050	1	84.050	4.91*
Amount of elaboration (B)	11.250	1	11.250	0.66
$A \times B$	781.250	1	781.250	45.62**
Error	274.000	16	17.125	

*$p < .05$

** $p < .01.$

   a. What is the effect of type of imagery on the recall of nouns?

   b. What is the effect of amount of elaboration on the recall of nouns?

7. A human factors psychologist was interested in the ability of pilots to read aircraft instruments after a period of sleep deprivation. She used two different types of gauges for the pilots to read, analog and digital, as illustrated in Figure 11.4.

   The psychologist obtained a sample of pilots, and half were randomly assigned to read the analog gauge and the other half, the digital gauge. For each group, half the pilots were tested after a normal night's sleep and the other half after they had been deprived of sleep for 24 hours. Thus, a 2 × 2 between-subjects design was used with type of gauge, analog or digital, as one independent variable, and amount of sleep deprivation, none or 24 hours, as the second independent variable. The dependent variable was the number of correct readings out of 100 trials. The cell means for the number of correct readings are given in Table 1. An analysis of variance for these data is presented in Table 2.

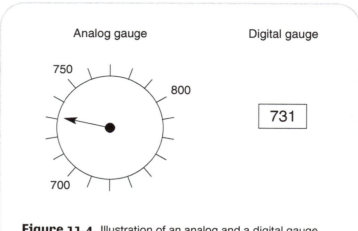

Figure 11.4 Illustration of an analog and a digital gauge.

<table>
<tr><td colspan="4" align="center">Table 1</td></tr>
</table>

Mean number of correct gauge readings as a function of type of gauge and amount of sleep deprivation.

		Type of Gauge (A)	
		Analog (A_1)	Digital (A_2)
Amount of Sleep Deprivation (B)	None (B_1)	89.0	91.0
	24 hours (B_2)	72.0	81.0

<table>
<tr><td colspan="5" align="center">Table 2</td></tr>
</table>

Analysis of variance summary for mean correct gauge readings in Table 1.

Source	SS	df	MS	F
Type of gauge (A)	211.750	1	211.750	11.71**
Amount of sleep deprivation (B)	1275.750	1	1275.750	70.56**
A × B	85.750	1	85.750	4.74*
Error	433.920	24	18.080	
Total	2007.170	27		

*$p < .05$
**$p < .01$.

The CD for simple effects using a Tukey HSD test is 5.7 correct readings.

    a. What is the effect of type of gauge on the number of correct readings?

    b. What is the effect of amount of sleep deprivation on the number of correct readings?

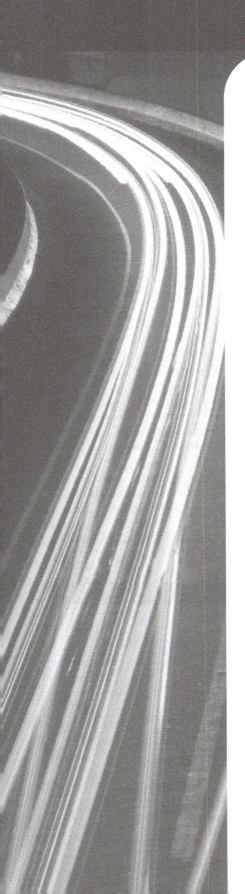

One-Factor Within-Subjects Analysis of Variance

At one time or another we have all looked at a friend or a family member's selected romantic interest and wondered, "What does he or she see in that person?" There is no question that different people find different physical and personal attributes appealing, and fortunately, there are many individual differences among people. There seem to be as many individual differences about what we find romantically appealing as there are people. Such large amounts of variability due to individual differences, however, can make it challenging to determine the effect of an independent variable when we are using a between-subjects design. Thus, if we were to conduct a between-subjects study on what attributes people find appealing in others, we may miss finding the effect of an independent variable because of individual differences among subjects. Recall from Chapter 9 (page 215) that one approach to increasing the power of a statistical test, that is, increasing the probability of detecting the effect of an independent variable, is to decrease the amount of variability in the scores of our sample. In that chapter, we saw that larger amounts of variability decrease the power of experiments, whereas smaller amounts of variability increase an experiment's power. One very effective approach to decreasing this variability is to use a **within-subjects design**. In a within-subjects design, a subject is tested in each level of the independent variable rather than testing different subjects in each treatment condition, as is done in the between-subjects design. We introduced within-subjects designs along with the t test for related scores in Chapter 9. However, the related t II test can be used only with two levels of a single independent variable. This chapter expands the discussion of within-subjects designs and introduces the analysis of variance for these designs when two or more levels of the independent variable are manipulated.

Within-subjects design ▶
A research design in which one group of subjects is exposed to and measured under each level of the independent variable.

In a one-factor within-subjects design, a single group of subjects is exposed to and measured in each level of the independent variable. Because subjects are measured repeatedly in a within-subjects design, this design also is called a **repeated measures design** or a **treatments-by-subjects design**, a reminder that each subject is tested under all levels of the independent variable.

Table 12.1 presents the notation for the scores of a one-factor within-subjects design with four levels of an independent variable and five subjects. The independent variable is identified as factor A with levels A_1, A_2, A_3, and A_4. The number of levels of factor A is represented by a; for Table 12.1, $a = 4$. A score for a subject is represented by X_{ij}, where the subscript i represents a number identifying the subject (e.g., X_{1j}, X_{2j}, ..., X_{5j}) and the

---

TABLE 12.1

Notational representation of scores from a one-factor within-subjects design with four levels of the independent variable and five subjects

Subject	Factor A				Means for Subject
	A_1	A_2	A_3	A_4	
S_1	X_{11}	X_{12}	X_{13}	X_{14}	$\overline{X}_{S_1}$
S_2	X_{21}	X_{22}	X_{23}	X_{24}	$\overline{X}_{S_2}$
S_3	X_{31}	X_{32}	X_{33}	X_{34}	$\overline{X}_{S_3}$
S_4	X_{41}	X_{42}	X_{43}	X_{44}	$\overline{X}_{S_4}$
S_5	X_{51}	X_{52}	X_{53}	X_{54}	$\overline{X}_{S_5}$
Means for Factor A	$\overline{X}_{A_1}$	$\overline{X}_{A_2}$	$\overline{X}_{A_3}$	$\overline{X}_{A_4}$	$\overline{X}_G$

subscript *j* represents a number identifying the level of the independent variable. Thus, X_{34} represents the score of subject 3 in level 4 of factor *A*. When it is not necessary to identify a specific subject, we drop the *ij* subscripts and simply use *X*. The means for each level of the independent variable are indicated by $\overline{X}_{A_1}$, $\overline{X}_{A_2}$, $\overline{X}_{A_3}$, and $\overline{X}_{A_4}$, or generally by $\overline{X}_A$. The number of scores in a level of the independent variable is represented by n_A. Notice that $\boldsymbol{n_A}$ is also the number of subjects in a within-subjects design. The total number of scores in the experiment is represented by *N*. For Table 12.1, $n_A = 5$ and $N = 20$. The mean for a subject over all levels of factor *A* is represented by $\overline{X}_S$. This mean represents the typical performance of a person over all levels of the independent variable.

An Example One-Factor Within-Subjects Experiment

To illustrate the design and analysis of a one-factor within-subjects experiment, we will use an example on subjective contours and the Ponzo illusion. Look at Figure 12.1. Although there are only partially filled circles present, it should appear that there are edges forming a triangle between the dots. These edges are called *subjective contours*, for they do not exist in the stimulus itself. Is it possible to use such subjective contours to induce an illusion in perception? Suppose that we decide to investigate this question by using several forms of the Ponzo illusion, as did Meyer (1986). Figure 12.2a illustrates the standard Ponzo illusion, named after the Italian psychologist, Mario Ponzo (1882–1960). This figure is an illusion because the two horizontal lines are physically equal in length, although they do not appear to be equal. The top line should appear longer to you than the bottom line. Figure 12.2b presents a subjective contours version of this illusion. The version in Figure 12.2c provides orientation information, but the solid dots do not introduce a subjective contour. Finally, Figure 12.2d presents a control condition in which no illusion should occur. Suppose that a person is asked to adjust the length of the bottom horizontal line so that it appears equal in length to the top horizontal line, and suppose further that the length of the top line is 14.0 centimeters (cm). If no illusion appears, then the bottom line also should be adjusted to 14.0 cm. If, however, an illusion appears, then the top line should appear to be longer than it really is (i.e., it should appear to be longer than 14.0 cm), and the bottom line should be adjusted to match its perceived length.

Figure 12.1 Subjective contours forming a triangle.

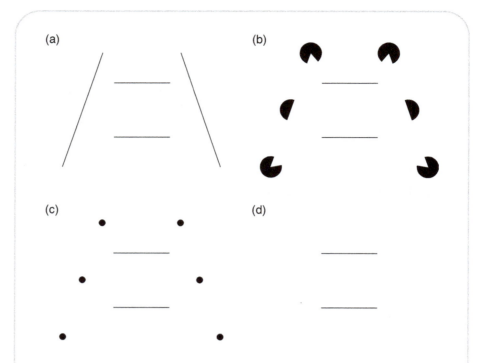

Figure 12.2 Four versions of the Ponzo illusion: (a) standard, (b) subjective contours, (c) solid dots, and (d) control (no illusion).

It is likely that the differences in the conditions illustrated in Figure 12.2 will be small. Moreover, just as there are differences in how we perceive others, there are individual differences in how we see illusions or how well we judge the length of lines. To create a more powerful experiment, we can decrease the variability due to individual differences among subjects by using a within-subjects design with the same subjects in each treatment condition. Hence, we use a one-factor within-subjects experiment with four levels of illusion type (factor A) and five subjects to test the effect of illusion condition on the perceived magnitude of the illusion. Each subject views each of the four stimuli shown in Figure 12.2 and adjusts the bottom horizontal line to look equal in length to the top horizontal line. The adjusted length of the bottom horizontal line, in centimeters, is the dependent variable. Suppose that the scores obtained are those presented in Table 12.2. Is the magnitude of the perceived illusion affected by the illusion condition?

As with between-subjects designs, the analysis of the data in Table 12.2 begins with the calculation of descriptive statistics. Thus, treatment means and standard deviations are shown at the bottom of each column in the table. If the independent variable does affect the perception of the illusion, then at least two of the four treatment means should differ from each other. But, as we know, any differences observed between treatment means must always be viewed against a background of error variation. How much might the means differ by sampling error alone? Again, a simple visual inspection of the means does not permit an answer to this question. As we have done for between-subjects designs, we resolve this decision-making problem by using a statistical test, the one-factor within-subjects analysis of variance.

TABLE						
12.2	Perceived equal line lengths (in cm) from five subjects viewing four versions of the Ponzo illusion.					

	Illusion Condition (A)				
Subject	Standard (A_1)	Subjective Contours (A_2)	Solid Dots (A_3)	Control (A_4)	Subject Means
1	16.6	15.8	14.7	14.4	15.38
2	16.9	15.6	15.1	13.8	15.35
3	17.1	16.1	14.8	13.9	15.48
4	17.2	16.3	15.2	14.1	15.70
5	16.8	15.7	15.3	14.3	15.53
$\overline{X}_A$	16.92	15.90	15.02	14.10	
s_A	0.24	0.29	0.26	0.25	

One-Factor Within-Subjects Analysis of Variance

The one-factor within-subjects analysis of variance is used to analyze one-factor multi-level within-subjects designs. It may also be used in place of t_{rel} if only two levels of an independent variable are manipulated. This analysis partitions the total variation of scores in an experiment into three sources:

▶ The variation due to the effect of **factor** A.

▶ The variation due to the effect of **factor** S, individual differences among subjects.

▶ The variation due to the interaction of the treatments with the subjects, symbolized as $A \times S$.

These three partitions are used to obtain three mean squares:

▶ MS_A, which varies with the effect of factor A and error variation.

▶ MS_S, which varies with differences among subjects.

▶ $MS_{A \times S}$, which varies with the interaction of treatments with subjects and provides a measure of the error variation in the experiment.

The F statistic used in the statistical hypothesis test is

$$F = \frac{MS_A}{MS_{A \times S}}.$$

Partitioning a Score and Obtaining Sums of Squares

In this section, we discuss the partitioning of scores and obtaining sums of squares for a within-subjects design. Because the approach followed is very similar to that for the between-subjects design, the presentation of the partitioning will be brief.

To understand how sources of variance from a within-subjects design are partitioned, it is useful to think of the within-subjects design as a two-factor design with the independent variable as one factor (factor A) and the subjects being tested as the second factor (factor S, where S represents the subject). Because each subject is tested under each level of the independent variable, a one-factor within-subjects design can be regarded as an $A \times S$ factorial design, with a levels of factor A and n_A levels of factor S. Thus, there are $a \times n_A$ conditions, or cells, and each cell represents one level of the independent variable combined with a particular subject. In Table 12.2, there are four levels of factor A and five subjects; therefore, the experiment can be viewed as a 4 (levels of illusion condition) $\times$ 5 (number of subjects) factorial design, producing a total of 20 different treatment-by-subject ($A \times S$) conditions. But only one score is obtained for each $A \times S$ condition.

Thinking of the one-factor within-subjects analysis of variance as a two-factor analysis of variance allows obtaining "main effect" means for factors A and S. Notice in Table 12.2 that means are given for each subject, as well as for each level of the independent variable. Each subject mean is the mean of the scores of a single subject over all the illusion conditions. These means reflect individual differences in the perception of illusions among the subjects in the experiment. Although the subject means are relevant to the analysis of variance, these means typically are not reported as descriptive statistics for experiments using a within-subjects design.

Conceptualizing a one-factor within-subjects analysis of variance as a two-factor analysis does not change the nature of the experiment; only one independent variable is manipulated, and its effect is analyzed. Thinking of the analysis as a two-factor design, however, helps us understand the introduction of the $A \times S$ interaction as the error term for the F statistic.

To obtain the F statistic, the analysis of variance for a within-subjects design takes the total amount by which a score differs from the grand mean and partitions this difference into three components, as follows:

Total variation in a subject's score	=	Variation due to factor A + error due to the interaction of factors A and S	+	Variation due to individual differences among subjects (factor S)	+	Variation due to interaction of factors A and S	12.1

In terms of scores this equation can be written as

$$X - \overline{X}_G = \overline{X}_A - \overline{X}_G + \overline{X}_S - \overline{X}_G + X - \overline{X}_A - \overline{X}_S + \overline{X}_G \qquad 12.2$$

Difference of a score from the grand mean	=	Difference of the treatment condition mean from the grand mean	+	Difference of the subject's mean from the grand mean	+	Difference of the subject's score from the grand mean after the effects of factor A and factor S have been removed

Following the basic approach of analysis of variance, each score is partitioned using Equation 12.2. The components of the partitioned scores are squared and summed over subjects and treatment conditions to obtain the sum of squares:

$$SS_{\text{Total}} = SS_A + SS_S + SS_{A \times S.} \qquad 12.3$$

These sums of squares indicate that the total variation of the scores in the experiment (given by SS_{Total}) is the result of variation that occurs from factor A (given by SS_A), factor S (given by SS_S), and the interaction of factors A and S (given by $SS_{A \times S}$). For the scores in Table 12.2, this process leads to the numerical values

$$SS_{\text{Total}} = 22.926,$$
$$SS_A = 21.830,$$
$$SS_S = 0.314,$$
$$SS_{A \times S} = 0.782.$$

SS_{Total}

The SS_{Total} represents the total variation of the scores in the experiment. As equation 12.3 indicates, a part of this variation is due to the effect of the independent variable, part is due to individual differences among subjects, and part is due to the treatments-by-subjects interaction.

SS_A

The SS_A varies with the effect of an independent variable and with treatments-by-subjects interaction. As with the one-factor between-subjects design, an effect of an independent variable increases the value of SS_A. In addition, the SS_A responds to any treatments-by-subjects interaction. In a within-subjects design, the treatments-by-subjects interaction is considered to be error variation.

SS_S

The SS_S varies with individual differences among the subjects in the experiment. We refer to these differences among subjects as factor S. Notice from Table 12.2 that subject 4 tends to see the largest amount of an illusion over all levels of the independent variable ($\overline{X}_{S4} = 15.70$ cm), whereas subject 2 perceives the least illusion ($\overline{X}_{S2} = 15.35$ cm). The more the subject means differ from each other in an experiment, the larger SS_S becomes.

$SS_{A \times S}$

Treatments-by-subjects interaction ($A \times S$) ▸
A situation in a one-factor within-subjects design where the effect of the independent variable depends on the subject.

The interaction of the treatment with the subjects is the remaining variation in a score and affects $SS_{A \times S}$. This **treatments-by-subjects interaction** can be seen in Figure 12.3, which depicts the hypothetical data of Table 12.2. The four types of illusion figures are represented on the abscissa. The functions within the figure depict the four scores obtained from each of the five subjects. The perceived equal line length is longest for all subjects at the standard illusion condition. Thus, there is an apparent effect-of-illusion condition on perceived line length. Because the five functions are not parallel, however, a treatments-by-subjects interaction is present as well. The difference in perceived line length between the illusion conditions is not the same for all subjects. For example, for subject 1, the difference in the standard condition and subjective contour condition scores is $16.6 - 15.8 = 0.8$ cm, but for subject 2 the difference is $16.9 - 15.6 = 1.3$ cm. Thus, the effect of illusion

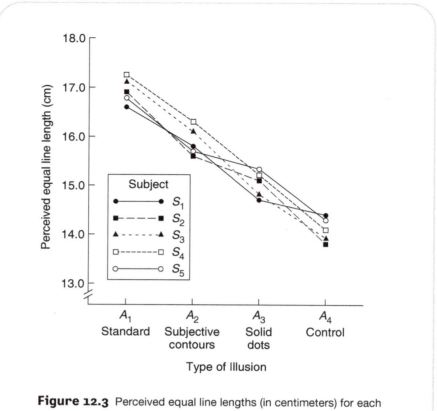

Figure 12.3 Perceived equal line lengths (in centimeters) for each subject as a function of type of illusion.

condition on perceived line length depends on the subjects. The $SS_{A \times S}$ provides a measure of the extent of the treatments-by-subjects interaction in a within-subjects experiment. However, because only one score is obtained from each person in each treatment condition, the treatments-by-subjects interaction cannot be separated from any error that may be affecting the score. Accordingly, $SS_{A \times S}$ is considered to be a measure of the error variation in a one-factor within-subjects design and is the basis for the error term of the F statistic for this analysis.

Finding Degrees of Freedom

To obtain the mean squares needed for the F statistic, each SS is divided by its corresponding degrees of freedom. The process of finding degrees of freedom is very similar to that for the between-subjects design.

Total Degrees of Freedom

$$df_{\text{Total}} = N - 1,$$

where N is the total number of scores in the experiment. For the example, $N = 20$; thus, $df_{\text{Total}} = 20 - 1 = 19$.

Degrees of Freedom for SS_A

$$df_A = a - 1,$$

where a is the number of levels of the independent variable A. For the four levels of factor A in the example, $a = 4$; hence, $df_A = 4 - 1 = 3$.

Degrees of Freedom for SS_S

$$df_S = n_A - 1.$$

There are five subjects in the example experiment; accordingly, $n_A = 5$ and $df_S = 5 - 1 = 4$.

Degrees of Freedom for $SS_{A \times S}$

$$df_{A \times S} = (a - 1)(n_A - 1).$$

In the example, $a = 4$ and $n_A = 5$; therefore,

$$df_{A \times S} = (4 - 1)(5 - 1) = 12.$$

Additivity of Degrees of Freedom

The degrees of freedom are additive, so

$$df_{\text{Total}} = df_A + df_S + df_{A \times S}.$$

This relationship holds for the example; for

$$df_{\text{Total}} = 19, df_A = 3, df_S = 4, \text{ and } df_{A \times S} = 12.$$

Finding Mean Squares and F

Three mean squares are obtained from the SS in equation 12.2 by dividing each SS by its df:

$$MS_A = \frac{SS_A}{df_A},$$

$$MS_S = \frac{SS_S}{df_S},$$

$$MS_{A \times S} = \frac{SS_{A \times S}}{df_{A \times S}}.$$

MS_{Total} is not calculated because it is not used in the analysis of variance.

For the scores in Table 12.2,

$$SS_A = 21.830,$$
$$SS_S = 0.314,$$
$$SS_{A \times S} = 0.782.$$

The degrees of freedom for these sums of squares are

$$df_A = 3,$$
$$df_S = 4,$$
$$df_{A \times S} = 12.$$

Therefore,

$$MS_A = \frac{21.830}{3} = 7.277,$$

$$MS_S = \frac{0.314}{4} = 0.078,$$

$$MS_{A \times S} = \frac{0.782}{12} = 0.065.$$

The F statistic for the one-factor within-subjects analysis of variance is given by

$$F = \frac{MS_A}{MS_{A \times S}}.$$

Thus, for the scores of Table 12.2,

$$F_{obs} = \frac{7.277}{0.065} = 111.95.$$

This F_{obs} is the only F computed in this analysis; no F is found for factor S. A numerical summary of the analysis of variance on the scores of Table 12.2 is presented in Table 12.3. Table 12.4 summarizes the sources of variance in a one-factor within-subjects analysis of variance, the SS, df, MS, and F.

TABLE 12.3	Analysis of variance summary table for hypothetical perceived equal line length scores of Table 12.2				
Source		SS	df	MS	F
Type of illusion (A)		21.830	3	7.277	111.95*
Subjects (S)		0.314	4	0.078	
$A \times S$		0.782	12	0.065	
Total		22.926	19		

*$p < .01$.

TABLE

12.4   Summary of formulas for a one-factor within-subjects analysis of variance

Source	SS	df*	MS	F
Factor A	$\Sigma\Sigma(\overline{X}_A - \overline{X}_G)^2$	$a - 1$	$\dfrac{SS_A}{df_A}$	$\dfrac{MS_A}{MS_{A \times S}}$
Factor S	$\Sigma\Sigma(\overline{X}_S - \overline{X}_G)^2$	$n_A - 1$	$\dfrac{SS_S}{df_S}$	
$A \times S$	$\Sigma\Sigma(X - \overline{X}_A - \overline{X}_S + \overline{X}_G)^2$	$(a - 1)(n_A - 1)$	$\dfrac{SS_{A \times S}}{df_{A \times S}}$	
Total	$\Sigma\Sigma(X - \overline{X}_G)^2$	$N - 1$	Not calculated	

*N = number of levels of factor A; n_A = number of scores in a treatment condition or, equivalently, the number of subjects; N = total number of scores.

Testing Your Knowledge 12.1

1. Define: $A \times S$ interaction, df_A, $df_{A \times S}$, df_S, df_{Total}, factor A, factor S, MS_A, $MS_{A \times S}$, MS_S, n_A, one-factor within-subjects design, repeated measures design, SS_A, $SS_{A \times S}$, SS_S, SS_{Total}, treatments-by-subjects design.

2. Identify the sources of variation in scores from a one-factor within-subjects design.

3. Complete the following equations for a one-factor within-subjects analysis of variance:
   a. $SS_{\text{Total}} =$
   b. $df_A =$
   c. $df_S =$
   d. $df_{A \times S} =$
   e. $MS_A =$
   f. $MS_S =$
   g. $MS_{A \times S} =$
   h. $F =$

4. What is the value of SS_{Total} if $SS_A = 74.00$, $SS_S = 29.00$, and $SS_{A \times S} = 96.00$?

5. What is the value of SS_A if $SS_{\text{Total}} = 426.00$, $SS_S = 92.00$, and $SS_{A \times S} = 301.00$?

6. What is the value of SS_S if $SS_{\text{Total}} = 96.00$, $SS_A = 15.00$, and $SS_{A \times S} = 56.00$?

7. What is the value of $SS_{A \times S}$ if $SS_{\text{Total}} = 173.00$, $SS_A = 41.00$, and $SS_S = 36.00$?

8. A psychologist used a one-factor within-subjects analysis of variance with five levels of factor A and 13 subjects. What are the values of df_A, df_S, $df_{A \times S}$, and df_{Total}?

9. What is the value of df_{Total} in a one-factor within-subjects analysis of variance if $df_A = 2$ and $df_S = 19$?

10. Find the numerical values of mean squares for the following SS and df: $SS_A = 22.00$, $SS_S = 18.00$, $SS_{A \times S} = 36.00$, $df_A = 2$, $df_S = 9$, and $df_{A \times S} = 18$.

11. Tables 1 and 2 are incomplete summary tables for a one-factor within-subjects analysis of variance. Fill in the missing values in each table by using the relationships

among SS and df given in Table 12.4. Then, answer the following questions for each table.

a. How many levels of the independent variable were manipulated?

b. How many scores were obtained in each treatment condition?

c. How many subjects participated in the study?

Table 1				
Source	SS	df	MS	F
Factor A	48.00	4	—	—
Factor S	27.00	9	—	
$A \times S$	72.00	—	—	
Total	—	—		

Table 2				
Source	SS	df	MS	F
Factor A	6.00	—	—	—
Factor S	36.00	12	3.00	
$A \times S$	—	24	—	
Total	78.00	—		

Statistical Hypothesis Testing with F_{obs}

$F_{obs} = MS_A/MS_{A \times S}$ is used to decide if the treatment condition means differ significantly. As the discussion of $SS_{A \times S}$ indicated, the denominator of F, $MS_{A \times S}$, represents the error variation in this analysis. The numerator of F, MS_A varies with the systematic effect of the independent variable and with any treatments-by-subjects interaction. If the independent variable has no effect and variation in the treatment means is due only to treatments-by-subjects interaction, then the value of MS_A should be about the same as $MS_{A \times S}$, and F_{obs} should be approximately 1.00. If factor A has an effect, however, and the treatment means differ because of both this effect and the treatments-by-subjects interaction, then MS_A will have a value larger than $MS_{A \times S}$, and F_{obs} becomes greater than 1.00.

No F ratio is constructed involving MS_S for individual differences. Although MS_S varies with the extent of the differences among the subjects in the experiment, there is no MS calculated in this analysis that provides an estimate of the chance variation expected among individuals. Therefore, the value of MS_S often is not included in a summary table.

The three mean squares and the sources of variation affecting them may be summarized as follows

Mean Square	Affected by
MS_A	Systematic variance due to factor A
	Treatments-by-subjects interaction (i.e., error variation)
MS_S	Systematic variance due to factor S
$MS_{A \times S}$	Treatments-by-subjects interaction (i.e., error variation)

Statistical testing with F follows the now familiar procedure:

▶ A null hypothesis, H_0, and an alternative hypothesis, H_1, are formulated.

▶ The sampling distribution of F, assuming that H_0 is true, is obtained. This distribution is given in Appendix C.3.

▶ A significance level is selected.

▶ A critical value of F, identified as F_{crit}, is found from the sampling distribution of F given in Appendix C.3.

▶ A rejection region is located in the sampling distribution of F.

▶ The F statistic, identified as F_{obs}, is calculated from the sample data.

▶ A decision to reject or not reject H_0 is made on the basis of whether or not F_{obs} falls into the rejection region.

▶ The statistical decisions are related to the research hypothesis.

Statistical Hypotheses

Null Hypothesis.   The null hypothesis for a within-subjects design with four levels of factor A is expressed as

$$H_0: \mu_{A_1} = \mu_{A_2} = \mu_{A_3} = \mu_{A_4}.$$

This null hypothesis represents the situation that exists if the independent variable has no effect. If H_0 is true, then any observed differences among the treatment means are due simply to error variation. As with the between-subjects design, the number of population means identified in the null hypothesis always corresponds to the number of levels of the independent variable.

Alternative Hypothesis.   The alternative hypothesis is

$$H_1: \text{The } \mu_A\text{'s are not all equal},$$

regardless of the number of population means involved in the null hypothesis. The alternative hypothesis states a situation that exists if the independent variable has an effect.

Decision Making from the *F*

The statistical decision-making process in a one-factor within-subjects design is identical to that followed in the one-factor between-subjects analysis of variance. A value of α defining the size of the rejection region for F_{obs} is selected prior to conducting the analysis.

TABLE 12.5	Summary of decisions and conclusions in statistical hypothesis testing using the analysis of variance for a one-factor within-subjects design. A .05 significance level is used.

If F_{obs} falls into the rejection region for $\alpha = .05$, then:	If F_{obs} does not fall into the rejection region for $\alpha = .05$, then:

▸ Probability of F_{obs} is less than or equal to .05 or $p \leq .05$.
▸ H_0 is rejected.
▸ H_1 is accepted.
▸ We found a statistically significant difference at the .05 level.
  ▻ The sample means are not all from the same population.
  ▻ At least one difference between the treatment means exists.
  ▻ Something, in addition to sampling error, is responsible for differences among the sample means.
  ▻ In a carefully designed experiment, changes in the independent variable are causing changes in the dependent variable.
▸ Multiple comparison tests are needed if the independent variable has three or more levels.
	▸ Probability of F_{obs} is greater than .05 or $p > .05$.
	▸ H_0 is not rejected.
	▸ H_1 is not accepted.
	▸ We failed to find a statistically significant difference at the .05 level.
	  ▻ Sampling error alone is the most plausible explanation for the differences among the sample means.
	  ▻ There is no evidence that the independent variable had an effect.
	▸ No multiple comparison tests are needed.

The value of F_{crit} with the appropriate numerator and denominator df is then found from Appendix C.3a or b. If F_{obs} is equal to or larger than F_{crit}, then F_{obs} falls into the rejection region. The null hypothesis is rejected and the alternative hypothesis accepted. There is at least one statistically significant difference among the treatment means. If F_{obs} is less than F_{crit}, then F_{obs} does not fall into the rejection region; the null hypothesis is not rejected, and the alternative hypothesis is not accepted. The treatment means do not differ significantly; the observed differences among the means are due to error variation. In such cases, we conclude that the independent variable did not have an effect. The decisions from F_{obs} and the conclusions that follow are summarized in Table 12.5.

To illustrate the decision process, we use the results summarized in Table 12.3 on the example scores of Table 12.2. In this analysis, F_{obs} has 3 (numerator) and 12 (denominator) df. Thus, for $\alpha = .05$, $F_{crit} = 3.49$ (obtained from Appendix C.3a). The $F_{obs} = 111.95$ is larger than F_{crit} and falls into the rejection region. We reject

$$H_0: \mu_{A_1} = \mu_{A_2} = \mu_{A_3} = \mu_{A_4}$$

and accept

$$H_1: \text{The } \mu_A\text{'s are not all equal.}$$

This decision indicates that there is at least one statistically significant difference among the four means of Table 12.2, but it does not indicate specifically which means differ from each other. To find which pairwise comparisons differ significantly and thus make a decision about the research hypothesis, multiple comparison tests are necessary.

Multiple Comparison Tests for Within-Subjects Analysis of Variance

The problems and issues of multiple comparison tests for the within-subjects analysis of variance are the same as those discussed in Chapter 10 for the between-subjects analysis of variance. For post hoc comparisons, the Tukey HSD test with a critical difference of

$$CD = q\sqrt{\frac{MS_{A \times S}}{n_A}}$$

may be used. Applying this test to the example experiment:

- $MS_{A \times S} = 0.065$ (obtained from Table 12.3).
- $n_A = 5$.
- q at the .05 level for four levels of the independent variable and 12 df for $MS_{A \times S}$ is 4.20 (obtained from Appendix C.4).

Substituting these values, we obtain

$$CD = 4.20\sqrt{\frac{0.065}{5}} = 4.20\sqrt{0.013} = 0.48 \text{ cm.}$$

For each pairwise comparison, a difference between the treatment means larger in absolute value than 0.48 cm is a statistically significant difference at the .05 level. The six pairwise comparisons, the absolute values of each comparison, the statistical hypothesis, and the decision for each hypothesis are shown in Table 12.6 (where $A_1 =$ standard illusion, $A_2 =$ subjective contours illusion, $A_3 =$ solid dots illusion, $A_4 =$ control condition).

The absolute value of each difference is larger than the CD of 0.48; thus, each comparison is statistically significant at the .05 level. The standard illusion creates the greatest illusion of the four conditions, the subjective contours create a significantly lesser amount of illusion, the solid dots significantly less illusion, and the control condition the least illusion.

Measuring the Effect Size

Eta squared may be used as a measure of effect size for a one-factor within-subjects design. The formula used is modified slightly from that for a between-subjects design,

$$\eta^2 = \frac{SS_A}{SS_A + SS_{A \times S}}.$$

Notice that with this formula, the variability due to individual differences, given by SS_S, is not included in the total variation of the experiment.

TABLE 12.6

Application of the Tukey HSD CD to the pairwise comparisons of the example experiment. The value of the $CD = 0.48$.

Comparison	Absolute Value of Comparison	Statistical Hypotheses	Decision
$\overline{X}_{A_1}$ vs. $\overline{X}_{A_2}$ $(16.92 - 15.90)$	1.02	$H_0: \mu_{A_1} = \mu_{A_2}$ $H_1: \mu_{A_1} \neq \mu_{A_2}$	Reject Accept
$\overline{X}_{A_1}$ vs. $\overline{X}_{A_3}$ $(16.92 - 15.02)$	1.90	$H_0: \mu_{A_1} = \mu_{A_3}$ $H_1: \mu_{A_1} \neq \mu_{A_3}$	Reject Accept
$\overline{X}_{A_1}$ vs. $\overline{X}_{A_4}$ $(16.92 - 14.10)$	2.82	$H_0: \mu_{A_1} = \mu_{A_4}$ $H_1: \mu_{A_1} \neq \mu_{A_4}$	Reject Accept
$\overline{X}_{A_2}$ vs. $\overline{X}_{A_3}$ $(15.90 - 15.02)$	0.88	$H_0: \mu_{A_2} = \mu_{A_3}$ $H_1: \mu_{A_2} \neq \mu_{A_3}$	Reject Accept
$\overline{X}_{A_2}$ vs. $\overline{X}_{A_4}$ $(15.90 - 14.10)$	1.80	$H_0: \mu_{A_2} = \mu_{A_4}$ $H_1: \mu_{A_2} \neq \mu_{A_4}$	Reject Accept
$\overline{X}_{A_3}$ vs. $\overline{X}_{A_4}$ $(15.02 - 14.10)$	0.92	$H_0: \mu_{A_3} = \mu_{A_4}$ $H_1: \mu_{A_3} \neq \mu_{A_4}$	Reject Accept

For the example, $SS_A = 21.830$ and $SS_{A \times S} = 0.782$. Thus,

$$\eta^2 = \frac{21.830}{21.830 + 0.782} = .97.$$

Ninety-seven percent of the variance in the length of line measures is accounted for by the illusion condition after the variability due to individual differences is removed, a very strong effect of the independent variable.

Assumptions of a Within-Subjects Analysis of Variance

The assumptions for the appropriate use of a one-factor within-subjects analysis are as follows:

1. Each subject is tested under each level of the independent variable.
2. The subjects in the sample are drawn randomly from a population.
3. The populations of scores for the different treatment conditions are normally distributed.
4. The population variances of scores for the different treatment conditions are equal.
5. The contribution of the individual differences of a subject remains the same for his or her scores over all treatment conditions.

The first assumption is necessary in order for the within-subjects analysis of variance to be the appropriate statistical test for the data; it cannot be violated. For the second assumption, remember that random selection has two components: every member of the population has an *equal chance of selection* and the subjects are *selected independently* of each other. Like the between-subjects analysis of variance, many within-subjects studies use convenience samples and thus violate the equal chance of selection assumption. As with between-subjects designs, however, the major impact of convenience sampling is to limit the extent to which the results can be generalized to a population. Nevertheless, the requirement that subjects be selected independently of each other cannot be violated for a within-subjects analysis of variance. The third and fourth assumptions are identical to assumptions for a between-subjects analysis of variance. They are sometimes violated in experiments, but the analysis of variance maintains some robustness toward such violations. The fifth assumption states that the person's behavior, independent of the treatment effect, remains stable over all levels of the independent variable. It is likely that this assumption is violated in many cases of behavioral research. The effect of such a violation is to increase the probability of making a Type I error above the value set by the significance level.

Several approaches have been offered for dealing with this increased error rate. The Geisser–Greenhouse correction changes the df used to obtain F_{crit} so that a larger F_{crit} will be used to evaluate F_{obs}. With this correction, F_{crit} is found using 1 df for the numerator and $(n_A - 1)$ df for the denominator in place of the $a - 1$, $(a - 1)$ (n_{A-1}) df normally used. Applying the Geisser–Greenhouse correction to the example, $F_{crit}(1, 4) = 7.71$. The $F_{obs}(3, 12) = 111.95$ still is larger than F_{crit} and H_0 is rejected; the same decision made using F_{crit} with 3, 12 df. This approach and others for reducing the error rate if assumption 5 is violated, are discussed in Keppel and Wickens (2004).

An alternative approach is to use the nonparametric Wilcoxon signed-ranks test or the Friedman analysis of variance in place of the within-subjects analysis of variance. The Wilcoxon test is presented in Chapter 15.

Testing Your Knowledge 12.2

1. Identify the factors affecting the value of each MS in a one-factor within-subjects analysis of variance.

2. Explain why MS_A increases in value if factor A has an effect in a one-factor within-subjects experiment.

3. Write the statistical hypotheses for a one-factor within-subjects analysis of variance with five levels of the independent variable.

4. Identify the assumptions underlying the use of the one-factor within-subjects analysis of variance.

EXAMPLE PROBLEM

12.1

Analyzing a One-Factor Within-Subjects Design with Four Levels of an Independent Variable

Problem: When reading *Discover Magazine*, you came across an article about Oliver Sacks, a physician who studies the impact of neurological malfunction on human behavior (Kruglinski, 2008). The article discussed his long-term fascination with the effects of music on people. Reading this article made you think about the role music plays in your life. Recognizing that when you listen to certain songs your mood often changes, you hypothesized this change of mood may also change how other situations are evaluated. To test this hypothesis, you decide to have a group of 13 subjects evaluate the pleasantness of photographs of natural scenes while listening to different types of music. You selected four

TABLE

12.7

Mean photograph pleasantness ratings as a function of music type for 13 subjects

	Music Type (A)			
Subject	Blues-like Emo (A_1)	Angry Metal Rock (A_2)	Calm Saxophone Jazz (A_3)	Physically Motivating Hip Hop (A_4)
1	6.2	6.7	7.4	7.8
2	5.9	4.8	6.1	6.9
3	8.4	8.7	9.9	10.3
4	7.6	7.8	8.7	8.9
5	4.1	4.7	5.4	6.6
6	5.4	5.3	5.9	7.1
7	6.6	6.7	7.2	7.5
8	6.1	5.8	6.4	6.7
9	4.9	5.1	5.2	6.8
10	8.2	8.6	9.3	10.4
11	5.7	5.7	6.5	7.2
12	5.9	6.4	6.9	7.6
13	6.9	6.6	7.1	7.5
$\overline{X}_A$	6.30	6.38	7.08	7.79
s_A	1.24	1.34	1.45	1.28

types of instrumental music: blues-like emo music, angry metal rock, calm saxophone jazz, and physically motivating hip hop. Each subject was told that the purpose of the study was to evaluate the pleasantness of photographs, but because the testing environment was noisy, you would play music in the background. Each subject heard the four types of music, but the order in which the types of music played was randomly determined for each subject. While listening to each type of music, each subject was presented with six photographs of emotionally neutral scenes, one photograph at a time, and asked to evaluate the pleasantness of each photograph using a 12-point rating scale, with 1 being completely unpleasant to 12 being perfectly pleasant. The mean ratings of the six photographs by each subject for each type of music are presented in Table 12.7. The score in each column represents the mean rating by a subject for the six photographs viewed in that type of music condition. Did the different types of music affect the pleasantness ratings of the photographs?

Solution: The design is a one-factor within-subjects design with four levels of the independent variable, the type of music. The first step in data analysis is to conduct a one-factor within-subjects analysis of variance on the scores. If F_{obs} is statistically significant, we will use the Tukey HSD test to find the statistically significant pairwise differences between the treatment means.

Statistic to Be Used: $F = MS_A/MS_{A \times S}$.

Assumptions for Use

1. Each subject is tested with each music type.
2. The subjects in the sample are drawn randomly from a population.

3. The populations of pleasantness ratings for each photograph are normally distributed.
4. The population variances of pleasantness ratings for each photograph are equal.
5. The contribution of the individual differences of a subject remains the same for his or her scores over all music types.

Statistical Hypotheses: H_0: $\mu_{A_1} = \mu_{A_2} = \mu_{A_3} = \mu_{A_4}$

H_1: The μ_A's are not all equal.

Significance Level: $\alpha = .05$.

df:

$$df_A = a - 1 = 4 - 1 = 3$$
$$df_S = n_A - 1 = 13 - 1 = 12$$
$$df_{A \times S} = (a - 1)(n_A - 1)$$
$$= (4 - 1)(13 - 1) = 36$$
$$df_{Total} = N - 1 = 52 - 1 = 51$$

Critical value of F: $F_{crit}(3, 36) = 2.92$. A value of 36 df for the denominator is not presented in Appendix C.3a. We used the critical value for the next lower tabled df for df_{Error}, 30.

Rejection Region: Values of F_{obs} equal to or greater than 2.92.

Calculation: We calculated the analysis of variance using SPSS software to obtain the following analysis of variance summary table.

Source	SS	df	MS	F
Music type (A)	18.985	3	6.328	60.85*
Subjects (S)	81.188	12	6.766	
$A \times S$	3.727	36	0.104	
Total	103.900	51		

*$p < .05$.

Decision: $F_{obs} = 60.85$ falls into the rejection region. We reject H_0: $\mu_{A_1} = \mu_{A_2} = \mu_{A_3} = \mu_{A_4}$ and accept H_1: The μ_A's are not all equal. Rejecting H_0 indicates that there is at least one statistically significant difference between the treatment condition means. To find the statistically significant pairwise differences, we use the Tukey HSD test.

Tukey Test: The numerical values needed for this test are found as follows:

▶ q is obtained from Appendix C.4. There are four levels of the independent variable and 36 df for $MS_{A \times S}$. However, 36 df is not given in Appendix C.4. Remember, when a specific df is not listed in a table, we always use the next lower df listed. Therefore, we use 30 df, the next lower tabled df from the 36 df for $MS_{A \times S}$ to find q. Thus, $q = 3.85$ for a .05 significance level.

▶ $MS_{A \times S}$, obtained from the analysis of variance, is 0.104.

▶ n_A, the number of scores in each of the means to be compared, is 13.

TABLE 12.8	Application of the Tukey HSD *CD* to the pairwise comparisons of the four music types. The value of the *CD* is 0.34.

Comparison	Absolute Value of Comparison	Statistical Hypotheses	Decision
$\overline{X}_{A_1}$ vs. $\overline{X}_{A_2}$ $(6.30 - 6.38)$	0.08	$H_0: \mu_{A_1} = \mu_{A_2}$ $H_1: \mu_{A_1} \neq \mu_{A_2}$	Fail to reject Do not accept
$\overline{X}_{A_1}$ vs. $\overline{X}_{A_3}$ $(6.30 - 7.08)$	0.78	$H_0: \mu_{A_1} = \mu_{A_3}$ $H_1: \mu_{A_1} \neq \mu_{A_3}$	Reject Accept
$\overline{X}_{A_1}$ vs. $\overline{X}_{A_4}$ $(6.30 - 7.79)$	1.49	$H_0: \mu_{A_1} = \mu_{A_4}$ $H_1: \mu_{A_1} \neq \mu_{A_4}$	Reject Accept
$\overline{X}_{A_2}$ vs. $\overline{X}_{A_3}$ $(6.38 - 7.08)$	0.70	$H_0: \mu_{A_2} = \mu_{A_3}$ $H_1: \mu_{A_2} \neq \mu_{A_3}$	Reject Accept
$\overline{X}_{A_2}$ vs. $\overline{X}_{A_4}$ $(6.38 - 7.79)$	1.41	$H_0: \mu_{A_2} = \mu_{A_4}$ $H_1: \mu_{A_2} \neq \mu_{A_4}$	Reject Accept
$\overline{X}_{A_3}$ vs. $\overline{X}_{A_4}$ $(7.08 - 7.79)$	0.71	$H_0: \mu_{A_3} = \mu_{A_4}$ $H_1: \mu_{A_3} \neq \mu_{A_4}$	Reject Accept

Substituting these numerical values into the formula,

$$CD = q\sqrt{\frac{MS_{A \times S}}{n_A}} = 3.85\sqrt{\frac{0.104}{13}} = 0.34.$$

Any difference between the mean ratings for type of music equal to or larger in absolute value than 0.34 is statistically significant at the .05 level. The pairwise comparisons, their absolute values, the statistical hypothesis tested, and the decision reached on the statistical hypothesis for each comparison are shown in Table 12.8 (where $A_1 =$ blues-like emo, $A_2 =$ angry metal rock, $A_3 =$ calm saxophone jazz, and $A_4 =$ physically motivating hip hop types of music).

Effect Size: $\quad \eta^2 = \dfrac{SS_A}{SS_A + SS_{A \times S}} = \dfrac{18.985}{18.985 + 3.727} = .84.$

Conclusion: The only comparison smaller than the $CD = 0.34$ is between the blues-like emo and angry metal rock music. Thus, there is no evidence that the blues-like emo music and angry metal rock music conditions differ in pleasantness evaluations of the photographs. All the other comparisons are larger than the CD. Consequently, the highest pleasantness evaluations of the four music types occur with hip hop music. Saxophone jazz results in higher pleasantness evaluations than either blues-like emo or angry metal rock music, but lower evaluations than hip hop. The $\eta^2 = .84$ indicates that the type of music a person is listening to accounts for a large proportion of the variance in the pleasantness ratings of neutral stimuli after individual differences variability has been removed from the experiment.

<table>
<tr><td>**EXAMPLE PROBLEM**

12.2</td><td>## Using the One-Factor Within-Subjects Analysis of Variance with Two Levels of an Independent Variable</td></tr>
</table>

Problem: The yawn of a student during class often is interpreted by an instructor as a sign of boredom. But is yawning actually such a sign? To explore this hypothesis, Provine and Hamernik (1986) designed an experiment to test if studying uninteresting material actually increases the frequency of yawning. In this experiment, students saw 30 minutes of rock music videos (A_1, the interesting stimulus) and 30 minutes of a color-bar test pattern without sound (A_2, the uninteresting stimulus) in two different sessions. The number of times a person yawned during the two sessions was observed and recorded. Assume we replicated this experiment using 11 subjects and observed the number of yawns for each session given in Table 12.9. Does the type of video affect the amount of yawning that occurs?

Solution: A one-factor within-subjects analysis of variance is an appropriate statistical test for these data. Because only two treatment conditions are involved, a t_{rel} also would be an appropriate statistical test.

Statistic to Be Used: $F = MS_A/MS_{A \times S}$.

Assumptions for Use

1. Each subject is tested under each type of video condition.
2. The subjects in the sample are drawn randomly from a population.
3. The populations of yawning scores for the different treatment conditions are normally distributed.

<table>
<tr><td>**TABLE**

12.9</td><td>Number of yawns observed as a function of type of video viewed for 11 subjects</td></tr>
</table>

Subject	Type of Video (A)	
	Interesting (A_1)	Uninteresting (A_2)
1	5	7
2	2	1
3	4	7
4	3	8
5	0	2
6	4	5
7	7	6
8	6	9
9	3	3
10	1	4
11	8	9
$\overline{X}_A$	3.9	5.5
s_A	2.5	2.8

4. The population variances of yawning scores for the different treatment conditions are equal.

5. The contribution of the individual differences of a subject remains the same for his or her scores over both video conditions.

Statistical Hypotheses: $H_0: \mu_{A_1} = \mu_{A_2}$.

H_1: The μ_A's are not equal.

Significance Level: $\alpha = .05$.

df:

$$df_A = a - 1 = 2 - 1 = 1$$
$$df_S = n_A - 1 = 11 - 1 = 10$$
$$df_{A \times S} = (a - 1)(n_A - 1)$$
$$= (2 - 1)(11 - 1) = 10$$
$$df_{Total} = N - 1 = 22 - 1 = 21$$

Critical Value of F: $F_{crit}(1, 10) = 4.96$

Rejection Region: Values of F_{obs} equal to or greater than 4.96.

Calculation: The summary of this analysis is as follows:

Source	SS	df	MS	F
Type of video (A)	14.728	1	14.728	8.53*
Subjects (S)	120.364	10	12.036	
A × S	17.272	10	1.727	
Total	152.364	21		

*$p < .05$.

Decision: F_{obs} falls into the rejection region; thus, we reject H_0 and accept H_1.

Effect Size: $\eta^2 = \dfrac{14.728}{14.728 + 17.272} = .46$.

Conclusion: The difference between the two treatment means of 3.9 and 5.5 yawns is statistically significant. When viewing the interesting video, individuals yawned less often than when watching the uninteresting video. Because only two means are involved, no multiple comparison test is necessary. The η^2 indicates that 46 percent of the variance in the dependent variable is accounted for by the type of video after individual differences variability has been removed from the experiment.

Reporting the Results of the Analysis of Variance

A description of the results of the analysis of the example experiment on illusion condition and perceived line length following the style of *The Publication Manual of the American Psychological Association* (American Psychological Association, 2001) might be written for the results section of an article as follows:

> The mean perceived equal line lengths for the standard, subjective contours, solid dots, and control illusion conditions were 16.92 ($SD = 0.24$), 15.90 ($SD = 0.29$), 15.02 ($SD = 0.26$), and 14.10 ($SD = 0.25$) cm, respectively. With an alpha level of .05, a one-factor within-subjects analysis of variance indicated that the means differed significantly, $F(3, 12) = 111.95$, $MSE = 0.065$, $p < .01$. A Tukey test on the pairwise comparisons revealed that each illusion condition differed significantly from each other illusion condition, $p < .05$ ($CD = 0.48$ cm). η^2 for the scores was .97.

Much of the information in this report is similar to that of a between-subjects design. We review this presentation briefly.

Sample means	The obtained values of the sample means and standard deviations are presented in the first sentence. Because only four means were obtained, they are presented in a sentence rather than in a table or a figure.
$\alpha = .05$	Indicates the significance level selected for the test.
$F(3, 12)$	Identifies the name of the test statistic as the F. The numbers shown in parentheses indicate the *df* for the numerator (3) and the denominator (12) of F_{obs}, respectively.
$= 111.95$	Gives the value of F_{obs}.
$p < .01.$	Indicates that:
	a. The probability of F_{obs} if H_0 is true is less than or equal to .01. This value is the probability of F_{obs} or an even more extreme value of F_{obs} if H_0 is true.
	b. H_0: $\mu_{A_1} = \mu_{A_2} = \mu_{A_3} = \mu_{A_4}$ was rejected. H_1: The μ_A's are not all equal was accepted.
	c. There is at least one statistically significant difference among the treatment means.
	d. Something other than sampling error alone is responsible for a difference in the treatment means.
$MSE = 0.065$	Gives the value of the $MS_{A \times S}$ for F_{obs}. This MS is the error term for the F ratio.
$CD = 0.48$ cm	Gives the critical difference for pairwise comparisons using the Tukey HSD test. The statistically significant pairwise comparisons are then described.
$\eta^2 = .97$	Indicates that 97 percent of the variance in the perceived equal line lengths in this experiment is accounted for by the illusion condition after variability due to individual differences has been removed.

Choice of Research Design: Between-Subjects or Within-Subjects

How does a behavioral scientist decide whether to use a between-subjects or within-subjects research design to evaluate a research hypothesis? Each type of design has its advantages and limitations. In general, there are three concerns when making this decision: (1) the number of subjects needed, (2) the anticipated effectiveness of the independent variable, and (3) the possibility of multiple treatment effects occurring.

Number of Subjects Needed

A subject in a within-subjects design is measured under each treatment condition; thus, fewer subjects are needed than would be required for a corresponding between-subjects design. In the example shown in Table 12.2, five scores are obtained under each of the four levels of illusion condition for a total of 20 scores. But only five people are required to obtain these 20 scores. For a corresponding between-subjects design, 20 different subjects would be needed to obtain the 20 scores. Thus, when subjects are difficult to obtain or where obtaining and instructing them requires considerably more time than actually performing the experimental task, the within-subjects design may be advantageous in comparison to a between-subjects design with respect to use of subjects.

Effectiveness of the Independent Variable

How easily the effect of an independent variable can be detected in an experiment depends partially on the effect size of that variable. A within-subjects design is often more sensitive to detecting the effect of an independent variable than is a between-subjects design. Therefore, a within-subjects design may be preferred when the anticipated effect of the independent variable is weak. The increased sensitivity of the within-subjects design occurs because each subject receives each level of the independent variable and is exposed to all treatment conditions. The within-subjects analysis of variance partitions out the variability due to individual differences among subjects (i.e., the variability due to factor S, MS_S) so that it does not contribute to the error term for the F (i.e., $MS_{A \times S}$). In a between-subjects design, this variation is included in the MS_{Error}. Thus, the error term in a within-subjects design will be smaller than the error term in a between-subjects design. A smaller error term leads to a larger value of F_{obs}, which is more likely to result in the rejection of H_0. Thus, in an experiment where there are large individual differences among subjects and the effect of the independent variable is not expected to be strong, a within-subjects design is more likely to detect the effect of the independent variable than is a between-subjects design.

Multiple Treatment Effects

Multiple treatment effects ▶
Changes in subjects' performance in a within-subjects design that are due to being tested in each level of the independent variable.

In a within-subjects design, a subject is given each level of the independent variable over a period of time. This sequence of treatments opens the within-subjects design to the possibility of **multiple treatment effects** occurring; the effect of a level of the independent variable may depend on the levels preceding it. Multiple treatment effects include both practice effects and treatment carry-over effects.

Practice effect ▶ A multiple treatment effect that occurs because subjects may become more practiced or fatigued on the experimental task.

Treatment carry-over effect ▶ A multiple treatment effect that occurs when the effect of one level of the independent variable carries over to affect performance in the next level of the independent variable.

Practice effects are changes in performance due simply to repeated practice in the experimental task. These changes may result either in improved or impaired performance as the experiment progresses. For instance, in the example experiment measuring the extent of an illusion in four different illusion conditions, subjects may become bored with the experiment as it progresses, or they may become more accurate with their estimates as they make more of them. In either case, a person's performance may change whether or not the illusion condition affects behavior.

Treatment carry-over effects are specific effects from one level of an independent variable that may carry over to affect performance on a subsequent level of the independent variable. For example, in the problem of the perception of illusions as a function of the illusion condition, if subjects always saw the control condition last, they may perceive an illusion because they had seen conditions creating illusions prior to the control condition. They have an expectation of seeing an illusion that carries over to the control condition. If they had seen the control condition first without the expectation of seeing an illusion, they would not have perceived it as an illusion.

Practice effects and treatment carry-over effects are important because, if they occur and are not controlled for, they confound an experiment. Control for these effects is usually obtained by giving each subject the treatments in a different order.

Each of the issues discussed, the number of subjects needed, the anticipated effectiveness of the independent variable, and the possibility of multiple treatment effects occurring must be considered when choosing a research design. The effective use of subjects and the greater sensitivity to detecting the effect of an independent variable are advantages of the within-subjects design. The potential for multiple treatment effects occurring, however, is a disadvantage of this design. Multiple treatment effects cannot occur in a between-subjects design, for each subject experiences only one level of the independent variable. Thus, when multiple treatment effects are likely to occur in an experiment and cannot be easily controlled through the ordering of treatments, a between-subjects design will likely be used. Because multiple treatment effects occur with many independent variables and cannot be easily controlled in a within-subjects design, behavioral scientists often choose to use between-subjects designs.

Testing Your Knowledge 12.3

1. Define: multiple treatment effects, practice effect, treatment carry-over effect.
2. When people think of geographical locations, their identification of areas is often affected by a superordinate bias. That is, geographical locations, such as cities, are located within larger geographical areas such as a state or country. The larger geographical areas (i.e., the superordinate locations) may affect how we think about locations within them. For example, Canada is located north of the United States, yet there are some Canadian cities that are located further south than some U.S. cities. But, most people would judge the U.S. cities to be more southerly simply because the United States is south of Canada. Indeed, Friedman and Brown (2000) found that people judged Seattle, Washington, United States, to be considerably south of St. Johns, Newfoundland, Canada, although both cities are at the same latitude. Suppose you are interested in this issue and asked subjects to estimate the latitudes of three cities located at essentially the same latitude: Dallas, Texas (United States); Tijuana, Mexico; and Tripoli, Libya. Each person is given instruction and brief practice on estimating latitude and asked to estimate the latitude for each city. The following estimates were obtained:

	City (A)		
Subject	Dallas (A_1)	Tijuana (A_2)	Tripoli (A_3)
1	33	18	20
2	29	27	24
3	35	21	26
4	28	17	19
5	30	18	27
6	40	26	23
7	32	25	25
8	31	19	24
9	30	23	17
10	25	20	21
11	27	20	20
12	36	24	23
13	26	22	18
14	29	23	29

Find the mean and standard deviation for each treatment condition. Then perform a one-factor within-subjects analysis of variance on these scores to determine if a superordinate bias exists in estimating latitudes, and answer the following questions.

a. State the statistical hypotheses for the F test for these scores.

b. What is the value of F_{obs}?

c. What are the df for F_{obs}?

d. What is F_{crit} at the .05 level?

e. What is the rejection region for F_{obs}?

f. Does F_{obs} fall into the rejection region?

g. What decisions do you make about the statistical hypotheses? Do you reject or fail to reject H_0? Accept or not accept H_1?

h. Do you conclude that the means are from the same or different populations?

i. Is there a statistically significant difference between at least one pair of means?

j. Are multiple comparison tests needed in this experiment? Give the reason for your answer.

k. What is the value of the Tukey CD?

l. Which pairwise differences are statistically significant?

m. What is η^2 for this experiment?

n. Describe the results of this experiment following the style illustrated in the Reporting the Results of an Analysis of Variance section of this chapter.

Exercises 3 and 4 below present sample reports of one-factor within-subjects analysis of variance. Answer the following questions for each exercise.

a. How many levels of the independent variable were used in this experiment?

b. How many subjects were used in this experiment?

c. What is the value of F_{obs}?

    d. What is the value of F_{crit} at the .05 significance level?

    e. Do you reject or fail to reject H_0?

    f. Do you accept or not accept H_1?

    g. Is there at least one statistically significant difference between the means?

    h. Which treatment conditions, if any, differ significantly?

3. The mean reaction time for the simple stimulus condition was 396 milliseconds (ms), whereas the mean for the complex stimulus condition was 412 ms. With alpha equal to .05, a one-factor within-subjects analysis of variance revealed a significant difference between the means, $F(1, 18) = 4.76$, $MSE = 510.924$, $p < .05$.

4. The mean number of faces correctly recognized was 13.9 on trial 1, 14.6 on trial 2, and 14.1 on trial 3. With alpha equal to .05, a one-factor within-subjects analysis of variance indicated no difference in the number of correct recognitions over trials, $F(2, 22) = 2.81$, $MSE = 0.555$, $p > .05$.

Summary

▶ In a one-factor within-subjects design, a single group of subjects is given each level of the independent variable.

▶ The one-factor within-subjects analysis of variance is used to analyze scores from a one-factor multilevel within-subjects design.

▶ Three mean squares are generated in a one-factor within-subjects analysis of variance: MS_A, which varies with the effect of the independent variable and treatments by subjects interaction; MS_S, which varies with differences among subjects; and $MS_{A \times S}$, which varies with the interaction of treatments with subjects and provides a measure of the error variation in the experiment.

▶ The F statistic used in the one-factor within-subjects analysis of variance is $F = MS_A/MS_{A \times S}$.

▶ Using the F statistic follows the usual steps of formulating statistical hypotheses, setting a significance level,

locating a rejection region, calculating F_{obs}, and making decisions concerning the statistical hypotheses.

▶ A statistically significant F when three or more levels of an independent variable are manipulated requires a multiple comparison test to find the statistically significant pairwise differences.

▶ The Tukey test is used for all possible pairwise post hoc comparisons.

▶ η^2 may be used as a measure of the effect size.

▶ Choosing between a between-subjects or a within-subjects design requires considering the number of subjects needed, the anticipated effectiveness of the independent variable, and the possibility of occurrence of multiple treatment effects.

Key Terms and Symbols

critical difference (*CD*) (351)
df_A (345)
df_S (345)
$df_{A \times S}$ (345)
df_{Total} (344)
eta squared (η^2) (351)
factor *A* (341)
factor *S* (341)

MS_A (341)
MS_S (341)
$MS_{A \times S}$ (341)
multiple treatment effects (360)
n_A (339)
practice effect (361)
repeated measures design (338)
SS_A (343)

SS_S (343)
$SS_{A \times S}$ (343)
SS_{Total} (343)
treatment carry-over effect (361)
treatments-by-subjects design (338)
treatments-by-subjects interaction
  ($A \times S$) (343)
within-subjects design (338)

Review Questions

1. You are interested in whether the type of mood reflected by a word (happy, neutral, or sad) affects how well the word is remembered from a list. Thus, you construct a list composed of six happy words (e.g., joyful, bright), six neutral words (e.g., derive, convey), and six sad words (e.g., gloomy, lonely). Each of eight subjects then learns the list to a criterion of two complete correct recitations. One week later, each subject attempts to recall the list. The number of items correctly recalled as a function of the type of word was as follows:

Subject	Type of Word		
	Happy	Neutral	Sad
1	5	4	3
2	6	3	4
3	4	5	2
4	5	3	1
5	3	1	2
6	6	3	4
7	2	2	3
8	5	3	1

   a. Find the mean and standard deviation for each type of word condition. Then, analyze the scores with a one-factor within-subjects analysis to answer the following question: Does the type of word affect recall? Use a .05 significance level. If needed, use the Tukey HSD test for multiple comparisons.

   b. What is the effect size of the independent variable of type of word?

   c. Describe the results following the style illustrated in the Reporting the Results of the Analysis of Variance section of this chapter.

2. In review question 5 of Chapter 9 (page 232), a group of students hypothesized that when people are upset or under stress, they are more likely to make errors in pronunciation of words. To test this hypothesis, they first recorded students talking about a non-stressful topic, then they recorded the same students talking about a stressful topic. The number of words that were not clearly enunciated for the first 100 words each subject uttered in each condition were recorded. The results from the 11 students participating in this study are presented below.

Student	Type of Topic (A)	
	Non stressful (A_1)	Stressful (A_2)
1	1	2
2	2	2
3	0	3
4	5	6
5	3	2

6	2	3
7	1	3
8	4	5
9	6	7
10	7	7
11	2	4

a. Find the mean and standard deviation for each type of topic condition. Then, analyze the scores with a one-factor within-subjects analysis to answer the question: Does discussing a stressful topic increase the number of errors a person makes when pronouncing words? Use a .05 significance level.

b. Compare F_{obs} to t_{obs} for Chapter 9 review question 5. Does $\sqrt{F_{obs}} = t_{obs}$?

c. Do you reach the same or different conclusions about the effect of the independent variable from the analysis of variance and the t_{rel} test?

d. Describe the results of this experiment following the style illustrated in the Reporting the Results of the Analysis of Variance section of this chapter.

3. Assume that you plan to conduct a one-factor within-subjects experiment with five levels of the independent variable and 12 subjects.

a. Write the statistical hypothesis tested by the analysis of variance on the scores that you would obtain.

b. Find the df for the analysis of variance of this design.

c. What is the value of F_{crit} at the .05 significance level for the analysis of variance of this design?

d. Suppose that the value of F_{obs} was larger than F_{crit}. What decision would you make about H_0 and H_1?

e. Suppose that you reject H_0 and accept H_1 for this experiment. What inference would you make about the treatment means from these decisions?

4. The following tables are incomplete summary tables for an analysis of variance. By using the relationships among SS, df, and MS, provide the missing values in each table. Then, answer the following questions for each table.

a. How many levels of the independent variable were manipulated?

b. How many scores were obtained in each level of the independent variable?

c. How many subjects participated in the study?

d. Is the value of F_{obs} statistically significant at the .05 level?

e. What decision do you make for H_0 and H_1 for each analysis?

Table 1				
Source	SS	df	MS	F
Factor A	—	—	11.00	—
Factor S	138.00	23	6.00	
$A \times S$	253.00	46	—	
Total	—	71		

Table 2				
Source	SS	df	MS	F
Factor A	60.00	—	—	—
Factor S	133.00	19	7.00	
$A \times S$	—	95	—	
Total	573.00	—		

5. Several experimenters recently investigated an infant's interest in unfamiliar faces in comparison to familiar faces. Each of 14 infants viewed photographs of familiar faces (e.g., photographs of the mother and father), unfamiliar faces (e.g., photographs of males and females unknown to the infant), and a blank oval the same size as a face. The experimenters recorded the amount of time each infant fixated on the face. The stimulus conditions and the mean duration of time fixated on the stimulus for each condition are presented in Table 1. An analysis of variance on these data is presented in Table 2.

Table 1		
Mean fixation time (in seconds) as a function of stimulus condition.		
Stimulus Condition		
Familiar Face (A_1)	Unfamiliar Face (A_2)	Blank Oval (A_3)
34.2	26.8	18.5

Table 2				
Analysis of variance summary for mean fixation times presented in Table 1.				
Source	SS	df	MS	F
Stimulus condition (A)	1727.32	2	863.66	15.99*
Subjects (S)	2047.37	13	157.49	
$A \times S$	1404.52	26	54.02	
Total	5179.21	41		

*$p < .01$.

A Tukey HSD gave a $CD = 6.9$ seconds at the .05 significance level.

a. What is the effect of the stimulus conditions on fixation time?

b. Describe the results of this experiment following the style illustrated in the Reporting the Results of the Analysis of Variance section of this chapter.

knowledge

PART A

A Look at a Problem   The movie *The Pursuit of Happyness* starring Will Smith attempted to capture the real life struggles of a man who went from being a single, homeless father to a multimillionaire through sheer determination. The movie captures pure moments of happiness even in the midst of great despair and challenges. To help understand what makes people happy, one study investigated happiness in 1280 young people (Associated Press, 2007). The subjects in the study were asked a series of questions on their current happiness and what types of activities and events made them happy. Forty percent of the subjects said that their relationship with their parents made them very happy, 49 percent said their relationships with their friends made them very happy, and 28 percent said their religious or spiritual life made them very happy.

1. Are these statistics descriptive or inferential statistics? Explain your answer.
2. What type of research method was used to collect these data?
3. From the results we have presented, can you conclude that relationships with friends make young people happier than their relationships with their parents? What additional information would you need to reach such a conclusion?
4. For many questions asked of the subjects, one of the alternatives was, "Does not apply." Why is it important to have such an alternative to certain questions?

PART B

Your Turn: Selecting Your Research Tools   After reading the findings of the survey on happiness, you became interested in further understanding differences in what college students perceive as bringing them happiness. Using the topics of relationships with parents, relationships with friends, and religious or spiritual life, think about how you would go about collecting and analyzing data to see if there was a statistically significant difference between how college students view the amount of happiness they obtain from these three activities.

1. What type of research method would you use for this study?
2. What would be the population from which you would select your subjects?
3. What type of a research design would you select so that you could compare subjects on their responses to these three activities?
4. How would you measure the dependent variable of "happiness"?
5. What statistical test would you use to compare the happiness scores for the three activities?

PART C

Using Your Statistical Tools   You decided to conduct a survey looking at three different types of activities and self-reported happiness in college students. You randomly selected 12 college students and asked them to rate their levels of happiness with regard to relationships with parents, relationships with friends, and religious or spiritual life. For each activity, subjects answered five questions with a 5-point rating scale for each question where 0 represents not at all happy and 4 represents extremely happy. Thus, the happiness scores for each activity can range from 0 to 20. Suppose you collected the data presented below.

	Type of Activity		
Subject	Relationships with Friends	Religious/Spiritual Life	Relationships with Parents
1	12	18	19
2	8	6	8
3	14	16	17
4	15	17	16
5	14	15	16
6	10	11	15
7	17	18	18
8	13	13	15
9	14	16	17
10	13	12	16
11	11	10	12
12	15	16	17

1. Find the mean and standard deviation for each type of activity. Then, analyze the scores with the appropriate analysis of variance to answer the question: Does the type of activity affect the happiness ratings? If needed, use the Tukey HSD test for multiple comparisons. Use a .05 significance level.

2. Write a brief summary of your results following the guidelines of *The Publication Manual of the American Psychological Association* (American Psychological Association, 2001). Include a measure of effect size in your description.

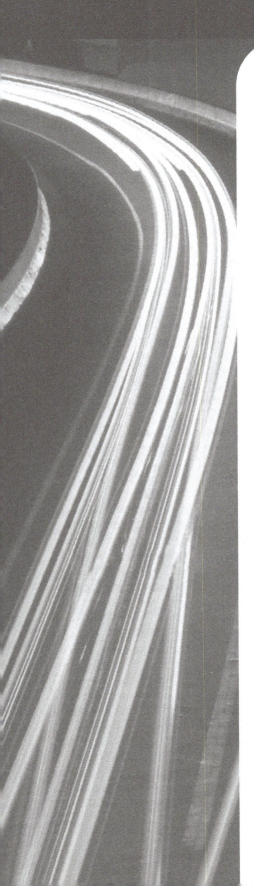

Correlation: Understanding Covariation

The discussion in Chapters 9–12 dealt with the design and analysis of experiments. We have seen that if we carefully manipulate an independent variable, avoid confounding, and measure the dependent variable, then, if a statistically significant difference is obtained, we can reach conclusions about the causal effect of the independent variable on the dependent variable. That is, we can reach conclusions that the independent variable is causing changes in the dependent variable. But, as we introduced in Chapter 1, there are many instances of research where we are unable to manipulate an independent variable. Consider the following example.

Students know that paying attention in class is critical for academic success, and there are likely many variables that affect how well you pay attention in class. The subject, time of day, and class activities could all be variables that impact your level of attention. In addition, how well you pay attention in class is likely related to how much you like the professor (Abrantes, Seabra, & Lages, 2007). We would like to investigate this possible relationship between liking a professor and paying attention in class, but how can we do it? Both the amount you like a professor and the amount of attention you pay in class are subject variables. Recall from Chapter 1 that we defined a **subject variable** as a characteristic or attribute of a person, such as gender, age, handedness, anxiety level, or a person's liking of another. In general, we cannot manipulate a subject variable as we can an independent variable. Clearly, it would be challenging to manipulate in-class attention or your liking of a professor. Although we cannot manipulate subject variables, we can determine if they covary. Two variables are said to **covary** if a change in one variable is related to a consistent change in the other variable. For example, if a subject's level of in-class attention is related to how much he or she likes a professor, such that high levels of attention are related to high levels of liking and low levels of attention are related to low levels of liking, then in-class attention and liking a professor covary.

To find if two variables covary, we measure a sample of people and obtain two scores from each person, such as a liking a professor score and an in-class attention score. Then a *correlation coefficient* is calculated. A **correlation coefficient** is a statistic that provides a numerical description of the extent of the relatedness of two sets of scores and the direction of the relationship. Values of this coefficient may range from -1.00 to 1.00.

Statistical hypothesis testing also enters into use with the correlation coefficient. There will always be some chance relationship between scores on two different variables. Thus, the question arises of whether an observed relation, given by the numerical value of the correlation coefficient, is greater than would be expected from chance alone. A statistical test on the correlation coefficient provides an answer for this question.

If the two sets of scores are related beyond chance occurrence, then we may be interested in attempting to predict one score from the other. If you knew a subject's liking of a professor score, could you predict his or her in-class attention score? And, if you could predict the in-class attention score, how accurate would your prediction be? Predicting a score on one variable from a score on a second variable involves using *regression analysis*. Correlation and regression analysis techniques are widely used in many areas of behavioral science to find relationships between variables and to find if one variable predicts another. This chapter introduces **correlational studies** and the statistics associated with them. Using correlated scores to predict one score from another is introduced in Chapter 14. Let us continue with our example of a possible relationship between liking a professor and in-class attention to introduce concepts of correlation and the correlation coefficient.

To study the relationship between liking a professor and in-class attention, we obtain a sample of 10 students and measure both their liking of a professor and their in-class attention level in the professor's class. Liking of a professor is measured by asking the student to respond to 10 statements similar to, "I like going to class because of the professor,"

Subject variable ▷ A characteristic or attribute of a subject that can be measured but not manipulated by the researcher.

Covary ▷ Two variables covary when a change in one variable is related to a consistent change in the other variable.

Correlation coefficient ▷ A statistic that provides a numerical description of the extent of the relatedness of two sets of scores and the direction of the relationship.

Correlational studies ▷ Studies in which two or more variables are measured to find the direction and degree to which they covary.

with never (0), rarely (1), sometimes (2), or often (3). The numbers in parentheses indicate the numerical weight assigned to the response. A subject who answers "never" to all 10 statements will receive a zero for liking of a professor, whereas someone who responds with "often" for all 10 statements will receive a 30 for liking of a professor. In-class attention is measured similarly with 10 statements, such as, "I think about what the professor is saying in class and attempt to relate the information to something I already know or have experienced." Again the subject responds with never (1), rarely (2), sometimes (3), or often (4). Notice in this scale the numerical values assigned to the responses differ from those assigned to the liking of a professor scale. The lowest score is 10, obtained by someone who answers "never" to all 10 statements, and the highest is 40, obtained by a subject who answers "often" to all 10 statements. Thus, for each subject two scores were obtained, one a score on liking of a professor and the other a score on in-class attention.

The liking of a professor scores (designated variable X) and the in-class attention scores (designated variable Y) obtained are those presented in Table 13.1. The designation of a variable as either X or Y is arbitrary. In general, however, a researcher asks the question, "What is the level of Y as a function of X?" This statement indicates the researcher is interested in predicting the value of one variable (Y) from the value of the other variable (X). The variable we wish to use as the predictor is usually designated the X variable and the predicted variable as Y. Thus, if a researcher asks the question, "What is the in-class attention score for a certain liking of a professor score?", she is attempting to predict the in-class attention (Y) from the level of liking of a professor (X). The details of using one score to predict another are presented in Chapter 14.

Bivariate distribution ▷ A distribution in which two scores are obtained from each subject.

The paired scores in Table 13.1 represent a **bivariate distribution** of scores. The prefix *bi* means "two"; thus, these scores are bivariate in that two scores are obtained from each student. Are these scores positively related? Are higher liking of a professor scores associated with higher in-class attention scores and lower liking of a professor scores related to lower scores on in-class attention? Or perhaps the relationship is negative; that is, higher liking of a professor scores are associated with lower in-class attention scores, and lower scores on liking of a professor are related to higher scores on in-class attention. It also is

TABLE 13.1	Hypothetical scores for 10 subjects on liking of a professor and in-class attention	
Subject	**Liking of a Professor Score: X**	**In-Class Attention Score: Y**
1	4	16
2	27	37
3	18	33
4	7	23
5	30	34
6	12	32
7	18	24
8	23	29
9	19	26
10	12	26

possible that the scores do not covary, that liking of a professor and in-class attention scores are independent of each other. To find if the scores are related we first construct a graph of the scores, called a *scatterplot;* then, we calculate a statistic called a *Pearson correlation coefficient* on the scores.

Scatterplots

Scatterplot ▶ A graph of a bivariate distribution in which the X variable is plotted on the horizontal axis and the Y variable is plotted on the vertical axis.

A scatterplot of the scores of Table 13.1 is presented in Figure 13.1. In a **scatterplot** (sometimes called a *scattergram* or a *scatter diagram*), the variable labeled X (in the example, the liking of a professor score) is plotted on the horizontal axis (the abscissa), and the Y variable (in the example, the in-class attention score) is plotted on the vertical axis (the ordinate). The score of a subject on each of the two measures is indicated by one point on the scatterplot. For example, in Figure 13.1, the scores for subject 1 are plotted at the point that intersects a value of 4 on the liking of a professor score and 16 on the in-class attention scale. To illustrate how the scatterplot was constructed, we have identified each score by placing the number of the subject from Table 13.1 next to the point that represents his or her scores on the scatterplot. Typically, however, subjects are not identified by name or number on a scatterplot.

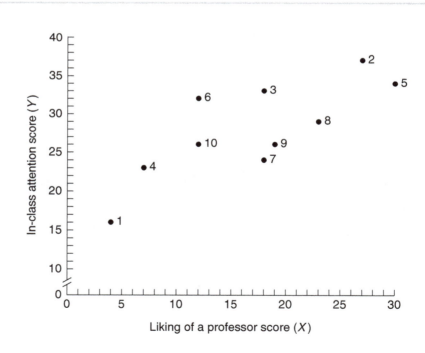

Figure 13.1 Scatterplot of liking of a professor scores and in-class attention scores for 10 subjects. The numbers next to the plotted scores identify the subjects. The scores are from Table 13.1.

Positive Relationships

The scatterplot indicates that the example scores tend to covary: higher in-class attention scores tend to be related to higher liking of a professor scores, and lower in-class attention scores tend to be related to lower liking of a professor scores. The relationship among the scores in Figure 13.1 is positive. In a **positive relationship** (also called a *direct relationship*), as the value of variable X increases, the value of variable Y tends to increase also. Thus, in Figure 13.1, as the liking of a professor scores increase, the in-class attention scores also tend to increase. Because both variables are measured and not manipulated, it is equally appropriate to state that as the in-class attention scores increase, the liking of a professor scores tend to increase also. But in Figure 13.1, the positive relationship is not perfect. Subject 9, for example, has a higher liking of a professor score than subject 10, but both have an in-class attention score of 26. Similarly, subjects 6 and 10 both have liking of a professor scores of 12, but in-class attention scores of 32 and 26, respectively.

A perfect positive relationship between in-class attention and liking of a professor scores is illustrated in Figure 13.2. A perfect positive relationship, such as the one shown in Figure 13.2, would seldom, if ever, occur between scores obtained in actual research. This figure, however, allows us to see that this scatterplot results in a straight line. Relationships between two variables that can be described by a straight line are called **linear relationships**. In a perfect positive relationship, such as that illustrated in Figure 13.2, for every value of X, there is only one corresponding value of Y. Thus, knowing the value

Positive relationship ▸ A relationship between two variables in which, as the value of one variable increases, the value of the other variable tends to increase also.

Linear relationship ▸ A relationship between two variables that can be described by a straight line.

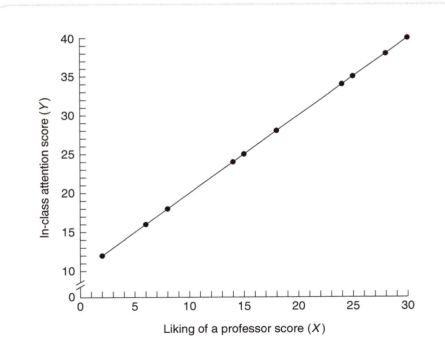

Figure 13.2 A perfect positive relationship between liking of a professor scores and in-class attention scores for 10 subjects.

of one score permits us to know or predict perfectly the score on the second variable. For example, a subject who obtained a liking of a professor score of 8 scored 18 on the in-class attention measurement. Or, a subject who scored 24 on in-class attention obtained a 14 on liking of a professor. There is no error in predicting one score from the other in a perfect relationship. Although in actual research scatterplots do not show perfect positive relationships, we will still try to describe them by a straight line. How we do so is discussed in Chapter 14.

Negative Relationships

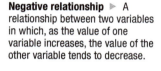

Negative relationship ▷ A relationship between two variables in which, as the value of one variable increases, the value of the other variable tends to decrease.

Suppose that the relationship obtained between liking a professor and in-class attention scores was that shown in Figure 13.3. This figure illustrates a **negative relationship** between the two variables: as the value of variable X increases, the value of variable Y tends to decrease. In Figure 13.3, you can see that low scores on liking a professor tend to be associated with high in-class attention scores, and high liking a professor scores are associated with low in-class attention scores. Negative relationships are sometimes identified as *inverse relationships* because the variables are oppositely related: low values on X are related to high values on Y, and high values on X are related to low values on Y.

The negative relationship illustrated in Figure 13.3 is not a perfect relationship between liking a professor and in-class attention scores. For example, two people have liking of a professor scores of 20, but in-class attention scores of 17 and 24, respectively. Similarly,

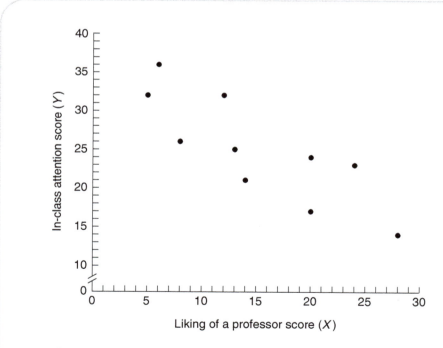

Figure 13.3 A negative relationship between liking of a professor scores and in-class attention scores for 10 subjects.

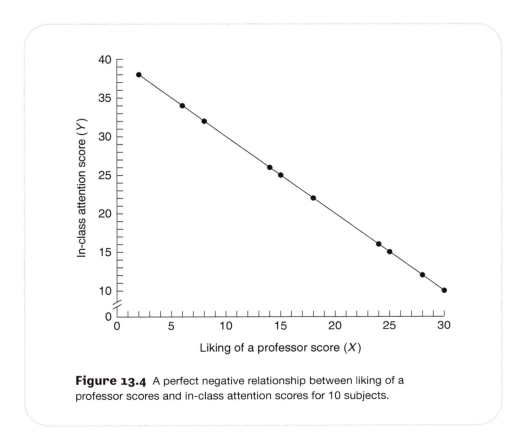

Figure 13.4 A perfect negative relationship between liking of a professor scores and in-class attention scores for 10 subjects.

two subjects have in-class attention scores of 32, but one has a liking of a professor score of 5 and the other a liking of a professor score of 12.

A perfect negative relationship between in-class attention and liking of a professor scores is illustrated in Figure 13.4. In this instance, the scatterplot again creates a straight line, and knowing one score allows a perfect prediction of the other score. For example, if we know that a subject obtained 8 on liking a professor, we know also that his or her in-class attention score was 32. Similarly, if we know someone obtained an in-class attention score of 22, then his or her liking a professor score was 18. As with perfect positive relationships, perfect negative relationships rarely, if ever, occur with actual scores. Notice that the description *positive* or *negative* applied to a scatterplot indicates only the direction, not the strength, of a relationship. For predicting one score from another, positive and negative relationships are equally useful.

Testing Your Knowledge 13.1

1. Define: bivariate distribution of scores, correlational study, covary, direct relationship, inverse relationship, linear relationship, negative relationship, positive relationship, scatterplot.

2. Reverse the designation of the X and Y variables for Table 13.1 (i.e., call the in-class attention score X and the liking of a professor score Y) and then construct a scatterplot of the scores similar to Figure 13.1. Does the designation of a variable as X or Y change the relationship between the scores?

3. Tables 1 and 2 present hypothetical liking of a professor and in-class attention scores for 10 subjects. For each table, construct a scatterplot of the scores on a sheet of graph paper, then answer the following questions.

   a. Does the relationship between the scores appear to be positive or negative, or is there no relationship between the scores?

   b. Is the relationship between the scores perfect or less than perfect?

   c. Would knowing the liking of a professor score of a subject increase the accuracy of predicting the in-class attention score for that subject?

Table 1		
Subject	Liking of a Professor	In-Class Attention
1	4	19
2	12	20
3	28	33
4	18	32
5	14	26
6	6	19
7	22	28
8	23	36
9	15	30
10	18	27

Table 2		
Subject	Liking of a Professor	In-Class Attention
1	5	29
2	11	31
3	23	23
4	17	17
5	28	16
6	13	21
7	12	26
8	4	28
9	21	14
10	16	25

4. The following scores represent the body weight in pounds and self-esteem scores from a sample of 10 subjects.

Subject	Body Weight	Self-Esteem
1	100	39
2	111	47
3	117	54
4	124	23
5	136	35
6	139	30
7	143	48
8	151	20
9	155	28
10	164	46

a. Plot a scatterplot of the scores on a sheet of graph paper. Does the relationship between the scores appear to be positive or negative, or is there no relationship between the scores?

b. Is the relationship between the scores perfect or less than perfect?

c. Would knowing the body weight of a person increase the accuracy of predicting the self-esteem score for that person?

The Pearson Correlation Coefficient

Pearson correlation coefficient ▶
A statistic, symbolized by r, that indicates the degree of linear relationship between two variables measured at the interval or ratio level.

An inspection of a scatterplot gives an impression of whether two variables are related and the direction of their relationship. However, a scatterplot alone is not sufficient to determine whether there is an association between two variables. The relationship depicted in the scatterplot must be described quantitatively. The descriptive statistic that expresses the degree of relation between two variables is called the *correlation coefficient*. A commonly used correlation coefficient for scores at the interval or ratio level of measurement is the **Pearson correlation coefficient** (sometimes called the *Pearson product-moment correlation coefficient*), symbolized as *r*. This statistic is named after Karl Pearson (1857–1936), a British statistician who devised the formula for its computation. The Pearson correlation coefficient provides a numerical value ranging from 0 to 1, which describes the extent to which the variables are related. It also provides a sign, + or −, which tells us if the relationship is positive or negative.

The Pearson correlation coefficient is defined as

$$\text{Pearson correlation coefficient} = r = \frac{\Sigma(X - \overline{X})(Y - \overline{Y})}{\sqrt{\left[\Sigma(X - \overline{X})^2\right]\left[\Sigma(Y - - \overline{Y})^2\right]}}$$

where X = score of a subject on the X variable.
$\overline{X}$ = mean of all scores on the X variable.
Y = score of a subject on the Y variable.
$\overline{Y}$ = mean of all scores on the Y variable.

This formula may be written using simpler notation as

$$r = \frac{CP_{XY}}{\sqrt{(SS_X)(SS_Y)}},$$

where $CP_{XY} = \Sigma(X - \overline{X})(Y - \overline{Y})$, the cross products of X and Y (the subscripts X and Y indicate that the cross products are calculated on variables identified as X and Y)

SS_X = sum of squares for the X scores [i.e., $\Sigma(X - \overline{X})^2$],
SS_Y = sum of squares for the Y scores [i.e., $\Sigma(Y - \overline{Y})^2$].

This definitional formula is not usually used to actually calculate r. Instead, either a standard score formula or a statistical software program such as Minitab or SPSS is used. The definitional formula, however, illustrates conceptually what the correlation coefficient is measuring. We will work through the derivation of this formula and then present the standard score formula.

Obtaining a Measure of Covariation: Cross Products

To see how r provides a measure of how much two variables covary, return to the scores of Table 13.1. The scatterplot of these scores (see Figure 13.1) indicated that the scores tend to be positively related: low scores on liking of a professor are related to low in-class attention scores, and higher scores on liking of a professor are related to higher in-class attention scores. We develop a statistic that indicates how much the two variables covary by using a difference score: how much a score differs from the mean of the scores, either $X - \overline{X}$ or $Y - \overline{Y}$. For example, the mean of the liking of a professor scores in Table 13.1 is 17. Subject 2 obtained a liking of a professor score of 27. If we find $X_2 - \overline{X}$, or $27 - 17 = +10$, we see that subject 2 obtained a liking of a professor score 10 points above the mean of the liking of a professor scores. Similarly, subject 4 obtained a liking of a professor score of 7. This subject's liking of a professor score could also be expressed as $X_4 - \overline{X}$; in this case, $7 - 17 = -10$, or 10 points below the mean liking of a professor score. Converting a score into a difference from the mean of the scores indicates both whether the score is above or below the mean and how far below or above it is.

The Y scores could be indexed similarly with respect to their mean, $\overline{Y}$. For example, the mean of the in-class attention scores is 28. Subject 2 obtained an in-class attention score of 37. Converting this score to a difference from the mean, we obtain $Y_2 - \overline{Y} = 37 - 28 = +9$. On the other hand, subject 4 obtained an in-class attention score of 23. Expressed as a difference from the mean, this score is $Y_4 - \overline{Y} = 23 - 28 = -5$, or 5 points below the mean in-class attention score.

From these difference scores we see that subject 2 was above the mean on both liking of a professor and in-class attention, whereas subject 4 was below the mean on both scores. The difference scores for both liking of a professor and in-class attention for all the subjects are shown in columns b and d, respectively, of Table 13.2. Notice that four of the six people who are above the mean on liking of a professor (column b, subjects 2, 3, 5, and 8) are also above the mean on in-class attention (column d). Likewise, three of the four subjects below the mean on liking of a professor (column b, subjects 1, 4, and 10) are also below the mean on in-class attention (column d).

A measure of how much the scores covary can be obtained by multiplying each subject's difference from the mean on the X variable by his or her difference from the mean on the Y variable and then summing the product of each multiplication over all the subjects. This process is illustrated in column e of Table 13.2. For example, for subject 4, $(X - \overline{X})(Y - \overline{Y}) = (-10)(-5) = +50$. The sum of the products in column e is +367.

The $\Sigma(X - \overline{X})(Y - \overline{Y})$ is called the **cross products of X and Y**, symbolized as CP_{XY}, and it forms the numerator of the formula for r. The CP_{XY} reflect the amount and direction of a relationship between two sets of scores. If the scores are positively related, as in

Cross products of X and Y ▶
The value of $\Sigma(X - \overline{X})(Y - \overline{Y})$ for variables X and Y.

TABLE
13.2

Calculation of the cross products of X and Y. Scores in columns a and c are the liking of a professor scores and in-class attention scores of Table 13.1, respectively.

	(a)	(b)	(c)	(d)	(e)
		Liking of a Professor		In-Class Attention	
Subject	X	$X - \overline{X}$	Y	$Y - \overline{Y}$	$(X - \overline{X})(Y - \overline{Y})$
1	4	−13	16	−12	+156
2	27	+10	37	+9	+90
3	18	+1	33	+5	+5
4	7	−10	23	−5	+50
5	30	+13	34	+6	+78
6	12	−5	32	+4	−20
7	18	+1	24	−4	−4
8	23	+6	29	+1	+6
9	19	+2	26	−2	−4
10	12	−5	26	−2	+10
$\overline{X}$	17		$\overline{Y}$ 28	Sum	+367

Table 13.2, the cross products take on a positive value; the more strongly the X and Y scores covary, the larger the CP_{XY} becomes. For negatively related scores, the CP_{XY} is negative and becomes larger as the negative relationship becomes stronger. The value of the CP_{XY} for a negative relationship of X and Y is illustrated in Table 13.3a with the scores of the negative relationship in Figure 13.3. The CP_{XY} is −399 for these scores.

TABLE
13.3a

(a) Cross products of X and Y for the negative relationship between liking of a professor and in-class attention scores shown in Figure 13.3.

		Liking of a Professor		In-Class Attention	
Subject	X	$X - \overline{X}$	Y	$Y - \overline{Y}$	$(X - \overline{X})(Y - \overline{Y})$
1	5	−10	32	+7	−70
2	24	+9	23	−2	−18
3	20	+5	17	−8	−40
4	12	−3	32	+7	−21
5	14	−1	21	−4	+4
6	20	+5	24	−1	−5
7	28	+13	14	−11	−143
8	13	−2	25	0	0
9	6	−9	36	+11	−99
10	8	−7	26	+1	−7
$\overline{X}$	15		$\overline{Y}$ 25	Sum	−399

TABLE 13.3b	(b) Cross products of X and Y for no relationship between the liking of a professor and in-class attention scores shown in Figure 13.5.

Subject	Liking of a Professor		In-Class Attention		$(X - \overline{X})(Y - \overline{Y})$
	X	$X - \overline{X}$	Y	$Y - \overline{Y}$	
1	24	+7	14	−12	−84
2	16	−1	36	+10	−10
3	4	−13	24	−2	+26
4	12	−5	16	−10	+50
5	22	+5	28	+2	+10
6	30	+13	26	0	0
7	10	−7	34	+8	−56
8	28	+11	30	+4	+44
9	14	−3	28	+2	−6
10	10	−7	24	−2	+14
	$\overline{X}$ 17		$\overline{Y}$ 26	Sum	−12

When the X and Y scores are not related, the CP_{XY} will be closer to zero. The CP_{XY} for an instance when X and Y are not related is presented in Table 13.3b. Figure 13.5 is a scatterplot of these scores. Notice that the X and Y scores do not covary: high scores on X are

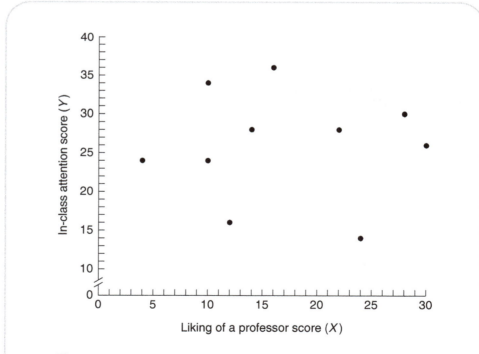

Figure 13.5 No relationship between liking of a professor scores and in-class attention scores for 10 subjects. The scores are from Table 13.3b.

not related consistently to either high or low scores on Y. Similarly, low scores on X are not related consistently to either high or low scores on Y. The $CP_{XY} = -12$ calculated in Table 13.3b corresponds to this lack of relationship.

r: Comparing the CP_{XY} with a Measure of the Total Variation in Scores

The CP_{XY} indicates the direction of a relationship between two variables, but the numerical value of the CP_{XY} depends on the units of measurement of X and Y and the number of scores obtained. Two different sets of scores may have the same degree of relationship but different values of CP_{XY} because the scores measure different units or because one set of scores involves a larger sample than the other. To be useful as a measure of the covariation of X and Y, CP_{XY} must be put into a form that will take on a common range of values regardless of the unit of measurement used or the number of scores obtained.

The cross products take on a common range of values when they are compared to a measure of the total variation in each set of scores. One measure of variation we have consistently used is the sum of squares (SS). For scores identified as the X variable, $SS_X = \Sigma(X - \overline{X})^2$, and for the scores identified as the Y variable, $SS_Y = \Sigma(Y - \overline{Y})^2$. To put the SS into the same units as the cross products, we take the square root of each SS. Then, by multiplying the square root of SS_X by the square root of SS_Y, we obtain a measure of the total variation in the two sets of scores, $\sqrt{(SS_X)(SS_Y)}$. The Pearson correlation coefficient, r, is a ratio of the CP_{XY} to this measure of the total variation. Accordingly, we see that the two definitional formulas for r,

$$r = \frac{\Sigma(X - \overline{X})(Y - \overline{Y})}{\sqrt{\left[\Sigma(X - \overline{X})^2\right]\left[\Sigma(Y - \overline{Y})^2\right]}}$$

and

$$r = \frac{CP_{XY}}{\sqrt{(SS_X)(SS_Y)}},$$

use identical numerical values to obtain r.

Notice that because the denominator of the formula for r involves squared differences, it always takes on positive values. Hence, the sign of the correlation coefficient, either positive ($+$) or negative ($-$), is determined by the sign of the numerator. The computation of r on the 10 scores of Table 13.1 using the definitional formula is illustrated in Table 13.4. For each subject,

▶ Column a is the liking of a professor score.
▶ Column b is the difference between the liking of a professor score and the mean of the liking of a professor scores (i.e., $X - \overline{X}$).
▶ Column c is the squared value of column b.
▶ Column d is the in-class attention score, Y.
▶ Column e is the difference between the in-class attention score and the mean of the in-class attention scores (i.e., $Y - \overline{Y}$).
▶ Column f is the squared value of column e.
▶ Column g presents column b multiplied by column e [i.e., $(X - \overline{X})(Y - \overline{Y})$], or the CP_{XY}.

The SS_X is obtained by summing the values of column c, the SS_Y by summing the values of column f, and the CP_{XY} by summing the values of column g. These sums are then

TABLE 13.4	Calculating r on the liking of a professor and in-class attention scores of Table 13.1 using the definitional formula

Step 1. Finding $SS_X = \Sigma(X - \bar{X})^2$, $SS_Y = \Sigma(Y - \bar{Y})^2$, $CP_{XY} = \Sigma(X - \bar{X})(Y - \bar{Y})$

	(a)	(b)	(c)	(d)	(e)	(f)	(g)
	Liking of a Professor			**In-Class Attention**			
Subject	X	$X - \bar{X}$	$(X - \bar{X})^2$	Y	$Y - \bar{Y}$	$(Y - \bar{Y})^2$	$(X - \bar{X})(Y - \bar{Y})$
1	4	−13	169	16	−12	144	+156
2	27	+10	100	37	+9	81	+90
3	18	+1	1	33	+5	25	+5
4	7	−10	100	23	−5	25	+50
5	30	+13	169	34	+6	36	+78
6	12	−5	25	32	+4	16	−20
7	18	+1	1	24	−4	16	−4
8	23	+6	36	29	+1	1	+6
9	19	+2	4	26	−2	4	−4
10	12	−5	25	26	−2	4	+10
	$\bar{X}$ 17		SS_X 630	$\bar{Y}$ 28		SS_Y 352	CP_{XY} + 367

Step 2. Calculating r:

$$\Sigma(X - \bar{X})^2 = SS_X = 630,$$
$$\Sigma(Y - \bar{Y})^2 = SS_Y = 352,$$
$$\Sigma(X - \bar{X})(Y - \bar{Y}) = CP_{XY} = +367,$$

and

$$r = \frac{\Sigma(X - \bar{X})(Y - \bar{Y})}{\sqrt{\left[\Sigma(X - \bar{X})^2\right]\left[\Sigma(Y - \bar{Y})^2\right]}}$$

or

$$r = \frac{CP_{XY}}{\sqrt{(SS_X)(SS_Y)}}.$$

Substituting numerical values,

$$r_{obs} = \frac{+367}{\sqrt{(630)(352)}} = +.779 = +.78.$$

substituted into the formula to obtain a numerical value of r, identified as r_{obs} (see step 2 of Table 13.4). For the scores of Table 13.1, $r_{obs} = +.78$. Before we discuss the interpretation of r_{obs}, however, we present a standard score formula frequently used to calculate the correlation coefficient.

Standard Scores Formula for *r*

The definitional formula for *r* may be rewritten separating the denominator into its two separate sums of squares as follows:

$$r = \frac{\Sigma(X - \overline{X})(Y - \overline{Y})}{\sqrt{\left[\Sigma(X - \overline{X})^2\right]}\sqrt{\left[\Sigma(Y - \overline{Y})^2\right]}}$$

or

$$r = \frac{\Sigma(X - \overline{X})(Y - \overline{Y})}{\left(\sqrt{SS_X}\right)\left(\sqrt{SS_Y}\right)}.$$

Notice that $(X - \overline{X})/\sqrt{SS_X}$ is very similar to a standard score, $z = (X - \overline{X})/S$, introduced in Chapter 6. All that is needed to make this expression a standard score is to divide the SS_X by N, the number of scores entering into SS_X, to obtain S_X, the sample standard deviation of the X scores. A similar argument follows for $(Y - \overline{Y})/\sqrt{SS_Y}$. Accordingly, the **standard score formula** for *r* is

$$r = \frac{\Sigma(z_X z_Y)}{N_{\text{pairs}}},$$

where $z_X = (X - \overline{X})/S_X.$
$z_Y = (Y - \overline{Y})/S_Y.$
$N_{\text{pairs}} = $ number of pairs of scores.

The sample standard deviation for the X scores, S_X, is found by

$$S_X = \sqrt{\frac{\Sigma(X - \overline{X})^2}{N}}$$

and S_Y, the sample standard deviation for the Y scores, by

$$S_Y = \sqrt{\frac{\Sigma(Y - \overline{Y})^2}{N}}.$$

Table 13.5 illustrates the use of this formula for finding r_{obs} on the scores of Table 13.1. The first step is to obtain S_X and S_Y needed to find the z scores. The values of $\Sigma(X - \overline{X})^2 = 630$ and $\Sigma(Y - \overline{Y})^2 = 352$ in this step were obtained from Table 13.4. From these calculations, we find that to convert X scores into standard scores $z_X = (X - 17)/7.937$. Similarly, for the Y scores, $z_Y = (Y - 28)/5.933$ (see step 2 of the table).

The third step is to convert each raw score into a standard score using the z formulas. Column a of step 3 in Table 13.5 presents the X score for each subject. Column b presents the $X - \overline{X}$ differences for each subject and column c the z score for each X. Similarly, column d presents the Y score for each subject. Column e presents the $Y - \overline{Y}$ differences for each subject, and column f the z score for each Y. The z_X and z_Y scores of each subject are multiplied in column g, and the sum of this column, $+7.794$, provides the value of $\Sigma(z_X z_Y)$ needed for the numerator of the formula for *r*. Step 4 of the table illustrates substituting $\Sigma(z_X z_Y)$ and N_{pairs} into the formula. The $r_{\text{obs}} = +.78$, the same value obtained using the definitional formula in Table 13.4. We recommend the standard score method when you have data expressed as standard scores.

TABLE 13·5

Calculating r on the liking of a professor and in-class attention scores of Table 13.1 using the standard score formula

Step 1: Obtaining S_X and S_Y

$$S_X = \sqrt{\frac{\Sigma(X - \overline{X})^2}{N_{pairs}}}, \qquad S_Y = \sqrt{\frac{\Sigma(Y - \overline{Y})^2}{N_{pairs}}}.$$

From Column c of Table 13.4	From Column f of Table 13.4
$\Sigma(X - \overline{X})^2 = 630$	$\Sigma(Y - \overline{Y})^2 = 352$
$N_{pairs} = 10$	$N_{pairs} = 10$
$S_X = \sqrt{\dfrac{630}{10}} = 7.937$	$S_Y = \sqrt{\dfrac{352}{10}} = 5.933$

Step 2: Finding z_X, z_Y, and $\Sigma z_X z_Y$:

To convert X scores to standard scores:	To convert Y scores to standard scores:
$\overline{X} = 17, \qquad S_X = 7.937.$	$\overline{Y} = 28, \qquad S_Y = 5.933.$
Thus,	Thus,
$z_X = \dfrac{X - 17}{7.937}.$	$z_Y = \dfrac{Y - 28}{5.933}.$

Step 3: Converting raw scores to z scores:

	(a)	(b)	(c)	(d)	(e)	(f)	(g)
	Liking of a Professor			In-class Attention			
Subject	X	$X - \overline{X}$	z_X	Y	$Y - \overline{Y}$	z_Y	$z_X z_Y$
1	4	−13	−1.638	16	−12	−2.023	+3.314
2	27	+10	+1.260	37	+9	+1.517	+1.911
3	18	+1	+0.126	33	+5	+0.843	+0.106
4	7	−10	−1.260	23	−5	−0.843	+1.062
5	30	+13	+1.638	34	+6	+1.011	+1.656
6	12	−5	−0.630	32	+4	+0.674	−0.425
7	18	+1	+0.126	24	−4	−0.674	−0.085
8	23	+6	+0.756	29	+1	+0.169	+0.128
9	19	+2	+0.252	26	−2	−0.337	−0.085
10	12	−5	−0.630	26	−2	−0.337	+0.212
	$\overline{X}$ 17			$\overline{Y}$ 28		Sum	+7.794

Step 4: Calculating r:

$\Sigma(z_X z_Y) = +7.794$ (see column g),

$N_{pairs} = 10,$

$r = \dfrac{\Sigma(z_X z_Y)}{N_{pairs}}.$

Substituting numerical values,

$$r_{obs} = \frac{+7.794}{10}$$

$$= +.779$$

$$= +.78.$$

TABLE

13.6

Summary of formulas for r.

Definitional formula

$$r = \frac{\Sigma(X - \overline{X})(Y - \overline{Y})}{\sqrt{\left[\Sigma(X - \overline{X})^2\right]\left[\Sigma(Y - \overline{Y})^2\right]}}$$

Definitional formula expressed as CP_{XY} and SS_X, SS_Y

$$r = \frac{CP_{XY}}{\sqrt{(SS_X)(SS_Y)}}$$

Standard scores formula

$$r = \frac{\Sigma(z_X z_Y)}{N_{\text{pairs}}}$$

Summary of Formulas for *r*

The three formulas for r are summarized in Table 13.6. All the formulas produce the same value of r_{obs} when applied to a set of scores.

Testing Your Knowledge 13.2

1. Define: cross product, CP_{XY}, r, SS_X, SS_Y.
2. Explain why the cross products provide a measure of the covariation of two sets of scores.
3. Given the following scores:

Subject	Liking of a Professor	In-Class Attention
1	4	19
2	12	20
3	28	33
4	18	32
5	14	26
6	6	19
7	22	28
8	23	36
9	15	30
10	18	27

  a. Find r_{obs} for these scores.
  b. The scores for this question were drawn from Testing Your Knowledge 13.1, question 3, Table 1. Compare r_{obs} to the scatterplot of the scores constructed for that question. Use this comparison to visualize the relationship a value of r_{obs} describes.

4. Given the following scores:

Subject	Liking of a Professor	In-Class Attention
1	5	29
2	11	31
3	23	23
4	17	17
5	28	16
6	13	21
7	12	26
8	4	28
9	21	14
10	16	25

a. Find r_{obs} for these scores.

b. The scores for this question were drawn from Testing Your Knowledge 13.1, question 3, Table 2. Compare r_{obs} to the scatterplot of the scores constructed for that question. Use this comparison to visualize the relationship a value of r_{obs} describes.

5. Given the following scores:

Subject	Body Weight	Self-Esteem
1	100	39
2	111	47
3	117	54
4	124	23
5	136	35
6	139	30
7	143	48
8	151	20
9	155	28
10	164	46

a. Find r_{obs} for these scores.

b. The scores for this question were drawn from Testing Your Knowledge 13.1, question 4. Compare r_{obs} to the scatterplot of the scores constructed for that question. Use this comparison to visualize the relationship a value of r_{obs} describes.

Characteristics of r

The correlation coefficient reveals both the direction and the degree of linear relationship between two variables. The direction of the relationship is indicated by the positive or negative sign of the correlation coefficient. The degree to which the points on the scatterplot lie on a straight line is given by the absolute value of r, a value that may vary from .00 to 1.00.

Combining the sign (+ or −) with the numerical values of r allows r to vary from −1.00 through .00 to +1.00.

Direction of Relationship

Earlier we discussed positive and negative relationships among the scores in a scatterplot. The correlation coefficient indicates the direction of the relationship by the plus or minus sign of the coefficient. A positive r (e.g., $r_{obs} = +.86$) indicates a positive relationship between variables X and Y; as the scores on variable X increase, the scores on variable Y tend to increase also. The scores in Figures 13.1 and 13.2 illustrate positive relationships; $r_{obs} = +.78$ for Figure 13.1 and $r_{obs} = +1.00$ for Figure 13.2.

A negative r (e.g., $r_{obs} = -.86$) indicates an inverse relationship between the variables; as scores increase on variable X, they tend to decrease on variable Y. A negative relation is illustrated in Figures 13.3 and 13.4. Here $r_{obs} = -.83$ for Figure 13.3 and −1.00 for Figure 13.4.

Degree of Relationship

The numerical value of r indicates how well the relationship between variables X and Y is described by a straight line. An r of 1.00 means that the relationship is perfectly linear; all points in the scatterplot lie in a straight line. Figure 13.2 portrays a scatterplot showing a perfect positive correlation, $r_{obs} = +1.00$, for liking of a professor and in-class attention scores. A perfect negative correlation, $r_{obs} = -1.00$, is illustrated in Figure 13.4. When r equals either plus or minus 1.00, for every value of X there is only one corresponding value of Y. You can see this relationship in either Figure 13.2 or 13.4. For every liking of a professor score there is only one in-class attention score. This relation allows us to predict perfectly the Y scores from the X scores. In either Figure 13.2 or 13.4, if you are given a liking of a professor score, then you can predict perfectly the in-class attention score associated with that liking of a professor score.

At the other extreme, if the variables are unrelated, then the value of the correlation coefficient approaches zero. When r is about zero, a value of one score is not systematically associated with a value of the other score. Such an instance is shown in Figure 13.5, where $r_{obs} = -.02$.

Values of the correlation coefficient less than 1.00 indicate that there is some, but not a perfect, relationship between X and Y. To illustrate, we notice in Figure 13.1, for which $r = +.78$, that the X and Y variables are not perfectly related. As the liking of a professor scores increase, the in-class attention scores tend to increase, but knowing a liking of a professor score does not allow perfect prediction of the in-class attention score. For example, two people obtained a liking of a professor score of 12, but one subject had an in-class attention score of 32 and the other an in-class attention score of 26.

An analogous negative correlation is demonstrated in Figure 13.3, for which $r_{obs} = -.83$. Here, as liking of a professor scores increase, in-class attention tends to decrease. But again, the relationship is not perfect; knowing the liking of a professor score does not allow us to perfectly predict the associated in-class attention score. For example, notice that two people obtained a score of 20 on liking of a professor, but one subject had a 17 on in-class attention, and the other had a 24.

It is often difficult to visualize what a value of r might look like if the scores were placed on a scatterplot. This ability is gained only by comparing values of r to a scatterplot of the scores that produced the correlation. Figure 13.6 presents several scatterplots exhibiting different values of r. Panels (a) to (e) of this figure illustrate correlations

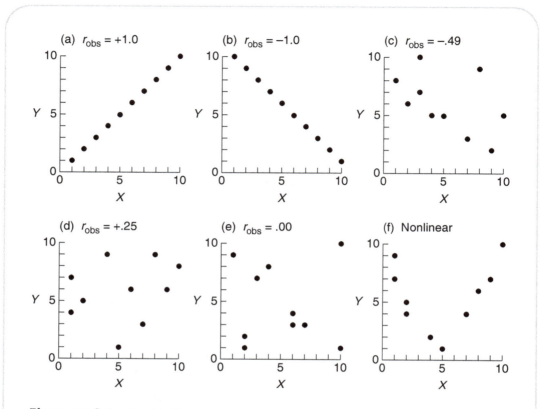

Figure 13.6 Scatterplots illustrating various correlations between scores on variable X and variable Y for 10 scores. The value of the Pearson correlation coefficient between the sets of scores is given by r_{obs}.

decreasing from 1.00 to .00. Notice that as r decreases, the linear relationship between X and Y becomes weaker, until $r_{obs} = .00$ and there is no relationship remaining.

The Pearson r is a measure of the linear or straight-line relationship between variables X and Y. Figure 13.6f presents a nonlinear, U-shaped relationship between the X and Y variables. In this relation, low values of X are associated with high values of Y. As X increases, Y decreases to a point; then, further increases in X are associated with increases in Y. This relationship between X and Y cannot be represented by a straight line, and r should not be used to describe such a relationship. This example illustrates an important point: any value of r should always be compared against a scatterplot of the scores that generated it to ensure that the scores are linearly related.

Restriction of Range and the Value of r

The value of r is sensitive to the range of values that either the X or Y variable may take on. As the range of values for one or both of the variables becomes smaller or restricted, the value of r also becomes smaller. To illustrate this relationship, consider the scores in Figure 13.1 with $r_{obs} = +.78$. Suppose that we want to examine the relationship of liking of a professor and in-class attention on only the six subjects scoring highest on liking a professor. These are liking of a professor scores that range from 18 to 30 (i.e., scores from subjects 2, 3, 5, 7, 8, and 9). The range of in-class attention scores for these 6 people is from 24 to 37. In comparison to the range of liking of a professor and in-class attention scores for the full 10 subjects, the range of both the liking of a professor and in-class attention scores for the top 6 people has become restricted or truncated (i.e., shortened). The r_{obs} of these six scores is +.69, less than the r_{obs} of +.78 on the full set of scores.

The implication of this illustration is clear. Correlation coefficients calculated on scores that have a restricted range may lead us to believe that there is no relationship between two variables, when, had a larger range of scores been used, a relationship would have been found. Accordingly, before calculating a correlation coefficient, carefully examine the scores obtained to determine if they represent a limited range of values.

Outliers and the Value of *r*

Outlier ▶ A set of scores that differ substantially from the other sets of scores in a bivariate distribution.

In Chapter 4, we defined an *outlier* as an extreme score that is not typical of the other scores in the distribution. In a bivariate distribution, an **outlier** is a set of scores that differ substantially from the other sets of scores in the distribution. If outliers exist in a bivariate distribution, they can dramatically affect the value of *r*. Consider the following example illustrated in Tables 13.7a and b. Let the scores represent students' scores on two very difficult statistics exams. For each exam, assume the maximum score was 30. Notice in Table 3.7a that all the scores are near the lower end of the possible distribution of scores and differ little from each other. The r_{obs} for this set of scores is .00. There is no correlation between the two sets of scores.

Now look at Table 13.7b. This table contains a set of outlier scores for Jenna. Jenna did very well on both exams, with scores considerably higher than the other six students who took the exam. The r_{obs} for this set of scores is +.89, a statistically significant value of *r*. What happened between these two distributions to so dramatically affect the value of r_{obs}?

Recall that *r* is a statistic that takes into account how much the two variables covary by finding how much a score differs from the mean of the scores, either $X - \overline{X}$ or $Y - \overline{Y}$. In Table 13.7a, none of the scores on either exam differs by much from the mean of that exam. Furthermore, the two sets of scores do not differ consistently in the direction they are away

---

TABLE 13.7

Example scores without an outlier (Table 13.7a) and with an outlier (Table 13.7b)

a. No Outliers			b. Outlier Scores for Jenna Added		
Student	Exam 1	Exam 2	Student	Exam 1	Exam 2
Kayla	9	10	Kayla	9	10
Alexis	11	8	Alexis	11	8
Ricardo	10	7	Ricardo	10	7
Molly	7	11	Molly	7	11
Makayla	12	11	Makayla	12	11
Ian	11	13	Ian	11	13
$\overline{X}$	10.0	10.0	Jenna	24	24
			$\overline{X}$	12.0	12.0

from the mean. For example, Alexis has an exam 1 score of 11, slightly above the mean of 10 for the exam 1 scores, but an exam 2 score of 8, below the mean of exam 2. On the other hand, Ian also has an exam 1 score of 11, but an exam 2 score of 13, above the mean of the exam 2 scores. You will notice from an examination of Table 13.7a, knowing an exam 1 score doesn't help us to know whether the exam 2 score is above or below the mean of the exam 2 scores. The value of $r_{obs} = .00$ for this set of scores reflects this lack of relationship.

In Table 13.7b, however, the addition of the outlier scores has increased the mean of each exam. An inspection of this table reveals that for Kayla, Alexis, Ricardo, and Molly, both exam scores now fall below the mean of each exam. Likewise, both exam scores for Jenna fall above the mean for each exam. If you were now told that a student's exam 1 score was below the mean and asked what you expect her or his exam 2 score to be, your answer would be that exam 2 would be below the mean, and this answer would apply for four of the six students whose exam 1 score was below the mean of exam 1. Similarly, if you were told that a student's exam 1 score was above the mean, then you would predict her or his exam 2 score to also be above the mean of the exam 2 scores and you would be correct for Jenna, the only student to have scores above the mean on both exams. The value of $r_{obs} = +.89$ for this set of scores reflects this changed relationship.

A scatterplot of the scores illustrates this change in the correlation. Figure 13.7 presents a scatterplot of these scores. The six scores of Table 13.7a are enclosed within the

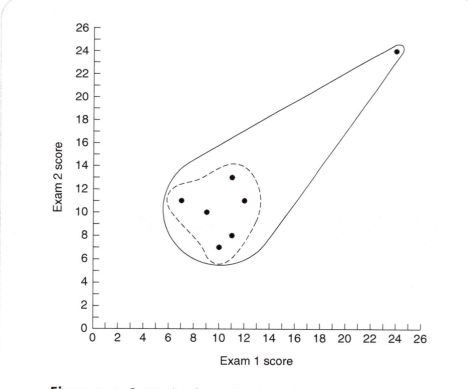

Figure 13.7 Scatterplot of exam 1 and exam 2 scores of Tables 13.7a and b.

dashed lines. It is easy to note that these scores do not covary. When Jenna's score of Table 13.7b is included, however, the scores appear to be correlated, as illustrated by the solid line enclosing the distribution.

The point is clear; an outlier can dramatically affect the value of r_{obs}, particularly if the correlation is on a small set of scores, such as we have illustrated here. With a larger set of scores, a single outlier will have less effect on the mean and thus have less effect on r_{obs}. Nevertheless, this example reiterates the importance of preparing and examining a scatterplot of the scores before calculating a correlation coefficient.

Coefficient of Determination

Coefficient of determination ▶
The value of r^2 indicating the common variance of variables X and Y.

In Chapter 9, we introduced η^2 as a measure of the strength of the effect of an independent variable on a dependent variable in an experiment. In correlational studies, the **coefficient of determination**, r^2 (the squared value of r), provides an analogous measure of the strength of association between X and Y.

The interpretation of r^2 is similar to that of η^2. That is, r^2 indicates the proportion of variance in one set of scores that is related to the variance in the other set of scores. To illustrate, for the scores of Table 13.1, $r_{obs} = +.78$; thus, r^2_{obs} is equal to $(+.78)^2$, or .61. This value means that these pairs of scores have 61 percent of their variance in common. In other words, 61 percent of the variance in scores for liking of a professor is associated with the variance of in-class attention scores.

Correlation and Causality

Many variables are highly correlated, but the existence of a correlation between variables X and Y does not imply that one causes the other. If variables X and Y are correlated, then at least three possibilities exist with respect to a causal relation between the variables:

▶ X causes Y.

▶ Y causes X.

▶ Neither X nor Y causally affect each other, but both are caused by a third variable, Z.

Consider the example of the correlation between liking a professor (variable X) and in-class attention (variable Y). The example resulted in a correlation of +.78, indicating that students who like a professor more tend also to pay more attention in class. Which variable, if either, causally affects the other? Does liking a professor cause in-class attention? Or does in-class attention cause liking of a professor? Or does neither of these relationships apply, and a third variable, Z, such as a student's interest in the course material, cause a subject to both like a professor and pay attention in class? These three possible causal relationships are illustrated in Table 13.8. A correlation between two variables indicates only that they are linearly related; it does not provide any information about what causes them to be related.

As another example, smoking (variable X) and stress levels (variable Y) are positively correlated; cigarette smokers typically report higher stress levels than do nonsmokers (Parrott, 1999). This relationship is correlational, found simply by questioning individuals on both their smoking habits and stress levels. The relationship itself is not in question, but the cause of the relationship is (see Kassel, Stroud, & Paronis, 2003, for a review). One explanation proposed for this relationship is that smokers have higher stress levels for multiple reasons (variable Z), such as higher job or family stresses than nonsmokers, and

TABLE 13.8	Possible causal relationships from an observed correlation of two variables, liking of a professor (*X*) and in-class attention (*Y*)

A. *The observed correlation:*

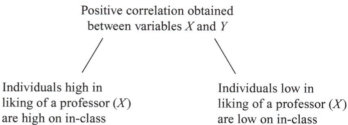

Positive correlation obtained
between variables *X* and *Y*

Individuals high in
liking of a professor (*X*)
are high on in-class
attention (*Y*)

Individuals low in
liking of a professor (*X*)
are low on in-class
attention (*Y*)

B. *Possible causal relationships that may explain the observed relationship:*

Possibility 1

variable *X* causes variable *Y*

Liking of a professor (*X*) causes a student to pay attention in class (*Y*).

Possibility 2

variable *Y* causes variable *X*

Paying attention in class (*Y*) causes a student to like a professor (*X*).

Possibility 3

variable *Z* causes both variables *X* and *Y*

The course content (variable *Z*) causes a student
to both like a professor (*X*) and pay attention in class (*Y*).

smoking is a method used to reduce this stress. A second explanation that has been offered is that the higher stress level is actually caused by the smoking itself, a product of nicotine dependency. A simple correlational finding, however, cannot answer the question of which, if either, explanation is correct.

Other research studies have indicated a negative correlation between the reported amount of sleep per night (variable *X*) and energy levels during the day (variable *Y*); people who sleep less also report higher daytime energy levels. Should you conclude from this relationship that if you lack energy during the day, then you should sleep less during the night? The answer is no, for a correlational relationship does not permit a researcher to make such a causal conclusion. Probably a third variable, such as a physiological condition (variable *Z*) that affects both daytime energy level and the amount of sleep needed, accounts for the observed relationship. These examples illustrate that we must always be aware that a correlational relationship only indicates that two variables are related, but it does not tell us about the cause of the relationship.

Testing Your Knowledge 13.3

1. What does the plus or minus sign of r tell you about the relationship of variables X and Y?

2. What does the numerical value of r tell you about the relationship of variables X and Y?

3. What effect may restricting the range of scores on either the X or Y variable have on the value of r?

4. Calculate the coefficient of determination for the following values of r_{obs}:

   a. +.12   **b.** −.74   **c.** −.59

   d. −.36   **e.** +.23   **f.** +.19

5. You observe a correlation between variables X and Y. Identify the three possible causal relationships that may explain the correlation.

6. Various researchers have reported the following correlations. Identify a third variable that may be responsible for the observed correlation.

   a. A negative correlation between income and blood pressure.

   b. A positive correlation between coffee drinking and cigarette smoking.

   c. A positive correlation between exposure to violence on television and aggressive behavior in children.

Testing the Statistical Significance of the Pearson r

The Population Correlation, ρ

ρ ▶ Rho, the symbol for the population correlation coefficient.

The Pearson r describes the linear relationship between the X and Y scores of a sample. As with any set of scores, the sample is drawn from a larger population of scores, and we may wish to test if a correlation exists among the X and Y scores in the population. In a population, a linear correlation between X and Y scores is represented by the parameter ρ (the seventeenth letter of the Greek alphabet, *rho*, pronounced "row"). In the example problem of the correlation between liking of a professor and in-class attention, $r_{obs} = +.78$ provides an estimate of ρ. As with any statistic, r_{obs}, because it is obtained from a sample, will vary from sample to sample, even though the samples are from the same population; thus, it is unlikely that r_{obs} will be equal to ρ. Accordingly, we may test a statistical hypothesis that r_{obs} represents a sample from a population with a specific ρ. Although it is possible to test hypotheses concerning any value of ρ, the most commonly tested hypothesis is that ρ equals zero in the population sampled.

Testing for a Nonzero Correlation in the Population

The statistical test to determine if r is a chance difference from a zero correlation in the population is straightforward. The familiar steps of statistical hypothesis testing are followed:

▶ A null hypothesis, H_0, and an alternative hypothesis, H_1, are formulated.

▶ The sampling distribution of r, assuming that H_0 is true, is obtained. This distribution is given in Appendix C.5.

▶ A significance level is selected.

▶ A critical value of r, identified as r_{crit}, is found from the sampling distribution of r given in Appendix C.5.

▶ A rejection region is located in the sampling distribution of r.

▶ The correlation coefficient, identified as r_{obs}, is calculated from the sample data.

▶ A decision to reject or not reject H_0 is made on the basis of whether or not r_{obs} falls into the rejection region.

▶ The statistical decisions are related to the research hypothesis.

Statistical Hypotheses

Null Hypothesis.   The null hypothesis is

$$H_0: \rho = 0.$$

This hypothesis states that the correlation between the X and Y variables is zero in the population.

Alternative Hypothesis.   The alternative hypothesis is

$$H_1: \rho \neq 0.$$

This hypothesis states that the correlation between the X and Y variables is not zero in the population.

Sampling Distribution of r and Critical Values

Because r may take on values only between .00 to 1.00, its sampling distribution under $H_0: \rho = 0$ may be determined readily. As is the case with most other statistical tests, however, the sampling distribution of r depends on its degrees of freedom. The df for r are equal to $N_{pairs} - 2$, where N_{pairs} is the number of pairs of scores from which r is calculated. Critical values of r, identified as r_{crit}, from sampling distributions of r with df ranging from 1 to 100 are presented in Appendix C.5 for $\alpha = .05$ and .01.

Locating a Rejection Region

If H_1 is true, we expect to obtain values of r greater than zero. Accordingly, the rejection region for r_{obs} is a value of r equal to or greater than r_{crit}. An r_{obs} equal to or larger than r_{crit} in absolute value (that is, ignoring the $+$ or $-$ sign of r_{obs}), falls into the rejection region. The probability of such an r_{obs} is equal to or less than the value of alpha if H_0 is true.

Decision Rules

The decision rules for the statistical hypotheses follow the common pattern:

▶ If r_{obs} falls into the rejection region, then:

Reject $H_0: \rho = 0.$

Accept $H_1: \rho \neq 0.$

▶ If r_{obs} does not fall into the rejection region, then:

Do not reject H_0.

Do not accept H_1.

We illustrate this process in the example problems that follow. Table 13.9 summarizes the decisions and conclusions reached from a statistical test on r.

TABLE 13.9	Summary of decisions and conclusions in statistical hypothesis testing with r. A .05 significance level is used.

If r_{obs} falls into the rejection region for $\alpha = .05$, then:	If r_{obs} does not fall into the rejection region for $\alpha = .05$, then:
▶ Probability of r_{obs} is less than or equal to .05, or $p \le .05$.	▶ Probability of r_{obs} is greater than .05, or $p > .05$.
▶ $H_0: \rho = 0$ is rejected.	▶ H_0 is not rejected.
▶ $H_i: \rho \ne 0$ is accepted.	▶ H_1 is not accepted.
▶ The r_{obs} is treated as estimating a population ρ different from zero.	▶ The r_{obs} is treated as estimating a population ρ of zero.
▷ r_{obs} is statistically significant at the .05 level.	▷ r_{obs} is not statistically significant at the .05 level.
▷ It is decided that the X and Y variables are correlated in the population from which the sample was selected.	▷ It is decided that the X and Y variables are not correlated in the population from which the sample was selected.

Assumptions of the Test for Statistical Significance of r

The test for statistical significance of r assumes that X and Y form a bivariate normal distribution in the population.

Bivariate normal distribution ▶
A distribution of X and Y variables in which (1) the X scores are normally distributed in the population sampled; (2) the Y scores are normally distributed in the population sampled; (3) for each X score the distribution of Y scores in the population is normal; and (4) for each Y score the distribution of X scores in the population is normal.

A **bivariate normal distribution** possesses the following characteristics:

▶ The X scores, liking of a professor scores in the example, are normally distributed in the population sampled.

▶ The Y scores, in-class attention scores in the example, are normally distributed in the population sampled.

▶ For each X score, the distribution of Y scores in the population is normal. Using the example, this assumption means that for each liking of a professor score in the population, there is a normal distribution of in-class attention scores.

▶ For each Y score, the distribution of X scores in the population is normal. This assumption is similar to the previous assumption, except now for each in-class attention score in the population there is a normal distribution of liking of a professor scores.

For many paired measures of behavior, we may assume that they form a bivariate normal distribution in the population and thus test for a nonzero correlation of the scores in the population.

EXAMPLE PROBLEM

13.1

Testing the Statistical Significance of r_{obs} Between Liking of a Professor and In-Class Attention

Problem: The Pearson correlation for the liking of a professor and in-class attention scores of Table 13.1 was found to be $r_{obs} = +.78$. Does this sample value indicate the presence of a nonzero correlation between liking a professor and in-class attention scores in the population from which the subjects were sampled? Use a .05 significance level.

Solution: The problem requires that we test the statistical hypothesis that the population correlation, ρ, for liking of a professor and in-class attention scores is zero.

Statistic to Be Used: $r_{obs} = +.78$.

Assumptions for Use: Liking of a professor and in-class attention scores possess a bivariate normal distribution in the population from which the scores were sampled.

Statistical Hypotheses: H_0: $\rho = 0$.
H_1: $\rho \neq 0$.

Significance Level: $\alpha = .05$.

df: $df = N_{pairs} - 2 = 10 - 2 = 8$.

Critical Value of r: $r_{crit}(8) = .632$ from Appendix C.5.

Rejection Regions: Values of r_{obs} equal to or greater in absolute value than .632.

Decision: The $r_{obs} = +.78$ is greater in absolute value than $r_{crit} = .632$. Accordingly, it falls into the rejection region. Therefore, we

Reject H_0: $\rho = 0$.
Accept H_1: $\rho \neq 0$.

Conclusion: Liking of a professor and in-class attention scores are significantly correlated in the population; the $r_{obs} = +.78$ is not simply a chance difference from a true population correlation of zero. The best estimate we have of the population correlation is provided by $r_{obs} = +.78$. Liking of a professor is positively related to paying attention in class. The coefficient of determination $r_{obs}^2 = (+.78)^2 = .61$, indicating that liking of a professor and in-class attention have 61 percent of their variance in common.   ▬▬▬

EXAMPLE PROBLEM

13.2

Is Exhaustion Related to GPA?

Problem: Not getting enough sleep and attending college often go hand in hand, but does lack of sleep affect our perceptions of how well we will succeed at a task? Law (2007) hypothesized that physical exhaustion and perceived academic success in college students is negatively correlated; that is, the more physically exhausted a student is, the lower they expect their grade point average (GPA) to be. Suppose that you test this hypothesis by measuring 16 college students on their perceived level of physical exhaustion and the GPA they expect to obtain. Exhaustion is measured using an eight-item exhaustion measure from Maslach's Burnout Inventory (Maslach, Jackson, & Leiter, 1996). This measure includes questions similar to, "I feel like I have no energy at the end of the day." Each question uses a 7-point rating scale with 1 representing "never occurs" and 7 representing "occurs everyday." Accordingly, scores on this measure may range from 8 to 56, with higher scores indicating more physical exhaustion. Expected GPA is measured by having subjects estimate their GPA for the semester. GPA is reported in the standard 4-point scale (e.g., $A = 4$, $B = 3$, and so forth). You obtain the following scores on these two measures.

Subject	Physical Exhaustion: X	Expected GPA: Y
1	18	4.0
2	42	3.2
3	31	2.7
4	35	3.9
5	48	3.2
6	50	1.8
7	19	3.0
8	22	3.7
9	37	2.7
10	39	2.5
11	28	2.9
12	31	3.4
13	42	2.2
14	22	3.5
15	39	3.8
16	41	3.1

Is the reported physical exhaustion score related to expected GPA? Use a .05 significance level.

Solution: The problem requires testing a statistical hypothesis that the population correlation, ρ for exhaustion and estimated GPA, is zero.

Statistic to Be Used: r.

Assumption for Use: The physical exhaustion scores and estimated GPA possess bivariate normal distributions in the populations from which the scores were sampled.

Statistical Hypotheses: H_0: $\rho = 0$.
H_1: $\rho \neq 0$.

Significance Level: $\alpha = .05$.

df: $df = N_{pairs} - 2 = 16 - 2 = 14$.

Critical Value of r: $r_{crit}(14) = .497$ from Appendix C.5.

Rejection Regions: Values of r_{obs} equal to or greater in absolute value than .497.

Calculation: Using SPSS, we find $r_{obs} = -.52$ and $r^2 = .27$.

Decision: The value of $r_{obs} = -.52$ is greater in absolute value than $r_{crit} = .497$ and, thus, falls into the rejection region. The decisions with respect to H_0 and H_1 are

Reject H_0: $\rho = 0$,
Accept H_1: $\rho \neq 0$.

Conclusion: There is a significant negative correlation between reported physical exhaustion and expected GPA. People who scored higher on the exhaustion measure have lower expected GPAs than those who scored lower on the exhaustion measure. The coefficient of determination indicates that the exhaustion measure and expected GPA have 27 percent of their variance in common.

Reporting the Results of a Correlational Study

The report of a correlational study should include the value of r_{obs}, the df for r_{obs}, the significance level used, and whether or not r_{obs} was statistically significant. Often, the mean and standard deviation for each set of scores are included in the report. To illustrate, we use the example of the correlation between liking of a professor and in-class attention calculated in Example Problem 13.1.

> The liking of a professor and in-class attention scores were significantly positively related, $r(8) = +.78$, $p < .01$, $r^2 = .61$. The mean liking of a professor rating was 17.0 ($SD = 8.4$), and the mean in-class attention score was 28.0 ($SD = 6.3$).

In this report,

$r(8)$ Identifies the test statistic as the r; hence, a Pearson correlation was used to analyze the data. This r is r_{obs}; the subscript *obs* is not used. The df for r (i.e., 8) are shown in parentheses. From these df you can determine the number of scores involved in the correlation is 10, because $df = N_{pairs} - 2 = 10 - 2 = 8$.

$= +.78$ Gives the value and direction (positive or negative) of r_{obs} (not the r_{crit} value found in Appendix C.5).

$p < .01$ Indicates that

     a. The probability of r_{obs} if H_0 is true is less than or equal to .01. This value is the probability of r_{obs} or an even more extreme value of r_{obs} if H_0 is true; it may not be the same as the value of α selected.

     b. $H_0: \rho = 0$ was rejected:
     $H_1: \rho \neq 0$ was accepted.

     c. The correlation between the liking of a professor and in-class attention scores is statistically significant.

     d. Something other than sampling error is responsible for the observed correlation between the scores

     e. If $p > .05$ had been reported, then the greater than sign would indicate that H_0 was not rejected and the value of r_{obs} was not statistically significant at the .05 significance level. In this instance, we would conclude that the liking of a professor and in-class attention scores were not related in the sample.

$r^2 = .61$ Presents the coefficient of determination for r_{obs}, indicating that 61 percent of the variance in scores for liking of a professor is associated with the variance in in-class attention scores.

The Spearman Rank-Order Correlation Coefficient

Spearman rank-order correlation coefficient (r_s) ▶ A correlation coefficient used with ordinal measurements.

The Pearson r is appropriate when scores on the variables to be correlated are interval or ratio measures. Sometimes, however, measures represent rank ordering on both the X and Y variables. When ranked scores are obtained, the **Spearman rank-order correlation coefficient**, symbolized by r_s, is commonly used to quantify the relationship between the two sets of scores. The Spearman rank-order correlation coefficient is found from the formula

$$r_s = 1 - \left[\frac{6 \sum D^2}{(N_{\text{pairs}})(N_{\text{pairs}}^2 - 1)} \right],$$

where D = difference in a pair of ranked scores for a subject.
N_{pairs} = number of pairs of ranks in the study.

As with the Pearson r, values of r_s may be positive or negative and range from -1.00 through .00 to $+1.00$.

An Example of the Use of r_s

We have all observed that animals within a species behave differently from each other. To study differences in dog behaviors, DePalma et al. (2005) developed a method of measuring dog behaviors, such as playfulness, sociability to humans, sociability to other dogs, and dominance. An investigator using this technique hypothesizes that playfulness (X) and sociability to humans (Y) behaviors are related in dogs. Ten dogs are observed for a period of time in the same environment and ranked separately on playfulness and sociability to humans behaviors. The most playful dog receives a rank of 1, and the least playful a rank of 10. Similarly, the dog that is the most sociable to humans is ranked 1, and the dog that is the least sociable is ranked 10. Ranks of the 10 dogs on playfulness and sociability to humans are presented in columns a and b, respectively, of Table 13.10. Dogs 1 and 10 were judged to be equal in sociability to humans behavior. Therefore, both dogs were assigned the same rank, 6.5, which is the average of the two ranks, 6 and 7, that would be assigned to them if they were not tied.

The procedures involved in calculating r_s are illustrated in the remainder of Table 13.10. The first step is to find the difference, D, in each pair of ranks by subtracting one rank from the other. This step is shown in column c, where the sociability to humans rank (Y) is subtracted from the playfulness rank (X) for each dog. Then each D is squared, as shown in column d. The sum of this column, 80.50, provides the value of $\sum D^2$. The $\sum D^2$ and N_{pairs} are substituted into the formula, and r_s is calculated; $r_{s \text{ obs}} = +.51$.

Statistical Significance of the Spearman Rank-Order Correlation

The test for the statistical significance of r_s is similar to that for the Pearson r. The null hypothesis is that the rank-order correlation in the population, symbolized by ρ_s, is zero, or H_0: $\rho_s = 0$. The alternative hypothesis is that the population correlation is not zero, or H_1: $\rho_s \neq 0$. Critical values of r_s for the .05 and .01 levels are presented in Appendix C.6. The critical values are based on N_{pairs} rather than degrees of freedom. If $r_{s \text{ obs}}$ is equal to or larger in absolute value than the critical value, then the decision is to reject H_0 and accept H_1.

For the example, the critical value of r_s for $N_{\text{pairs}} = 10$ and $\alpha = .05$ is .648. Because $r_{s \text{ obs}} = +.51$ is smaller than the critical value, the null hypothesis is not rejected at the .05 level. The relationship between the ranks on playfulness and sociability to humans is not statistically significant; playfulness and sociability behaviors were not related in the sample observed.

TABLE 13.10

Calculating the Spearman rank-order correlation coefficient (r_s) on playfulness and sociability behavior of 10 dogs. Columns a and b present ranks of each dog on playfulness and sociability behavior, respectively.

Dog	(a) Playfulness: X	(b) Sociability: Y	(c) $D = (X - Y)$	(d) $D^2 = (X - Y)^2$
1	2	6.5	−4.5	20.25
2	6	8	−2	4.00
3	8	4	4	16.00
4	4	1	3	9.00
5	7	5	2	4.00
6	5	9	−4	16.00
7	10	10	0	0.00
8	3	2	1	1.00
9	1	3	−2	4.00
10	9	6.5	2.5	6.25
			Sum	80.50

The formula for r_s is

$$r_{s\ obs} = 1 - \left[\frac{6\Sigma D^2}{(N_{pairs})(N^2_{pairs} - 1)} \right].$$

Substituting the values of $\Sigma D^2 = 80.50$ and $N_{pairs} = 10$,

$$r_{s\ obs} = 1 - \left[\frac{(6)(80.50)}{(10)(10^2 - 1)} \right] = 1 - 0.488$$

$$= +.512 = +.51, \text{ rounded to two decimal places}.$$

Characteristics of r_s

The Spearman correlation coefficient shows the agreement of the ranks of two variables. If variables X and Y are ranked identically, then r_s will be +1.00. If the variables are ranked oppositely, so that a rank of 1 on variable X corresponds to the lowest rank on variable Y and the lowest rank on variable X corresponds to a rank of 1 on variable Y, then r_s will be −1.00. If there is no agreement on the rankings, then r_s will be about zero. When there is some, but not perfect, agreement on the ranks, then r_s will take on a value between .00 and 1.00. The direction of the relationship is indicated by the plus or minus sign of the correlation.

Testing Your Knowledge 13.4

1. Define: bivariate normal distribution, ρ, ρ_s.
2. Identify the statistical hypotheses needed to test if r_{obs} differs significantly from zero.

3. For each of the following values of N_{pairs}, determine the df and then find the r_{crit} for $\alpha = .05$ and $\alpha = .01$ from Appendix C.5. $N_{pairs} =$

a. 8   **b.** 15   **c.** 20

d. 32   **e.** 43   **f.** 75

4. For each of the following r_{obs} and N_{pairs}, identify the statistical null and alternative hypotheses; then, find r_{crit} at the .05 significance level. Indicate whether the r_{obs} falls into a rejection region and give your decisions with respect to the statistical hypotheses.

	r_{obs}	N_{pairs}
a.	+.580	12
b.	−.346	12
c.	−.682	20
d.	+.204	24
e.	+.249	80
f.	−.731	9

5. College professors often believe that class attendance and course grades are correlated. Suppose that a professor maintained attendance records and found the following number of absences from class and examination averages for 12 students:

Student	Absences	Exam Average
1	22	72
2	6	88
3	1	99
4	8	78
5	6	66
6	11	77
7	10	52
8	6	78
9	10	76
10	0	96
11	5	91
12	10	86

a. Find the value of r_{obs} for these scores.

b. Test to determine if r_{obs} differs significantly from a population correlation of zero.

c. What do you conclude about the relationship of absences and exam averages?

6. For each of the following observed values of r_s and N_{pairs}, identify the statistical null hypotheses; then, find r_{crit} at the .05 significance level. Indicate whether the observed

r_s falls into a rejection region and give your decisions with respect to the statistical hypotheses.

	r_s	N_{pairs}
a.	+.401	17
b.	−.620	12
c.	+.541	24
d.	−.366	10
e.	+.544	21
f.	−.377	30

Summary

▶ Correlational studies attempt to find the extent to which two or more variables are related.

▶ In a scatterplot, one of the two scores (variable X) is represented on the horizontal axis (the abscissa), and the other measure (variable Y) is plotted on the vertical axis (the ordinate). The score of a subject on each of the two variables is represented by one point on the scatterplot.

▶ In a positive or direct relationship, as the value of variable X increases, the value of variable Y also increases.

▶ In a negative or inverse relationship, as the value of variable X increases, the value of variable Y decreases.

▶ The Pearson correlation coefficient is defined as

$$r = \frac{\Sigma(X - \overline{X})(Y - \overline{Y})}{\sqrt{\left[\Sigma(X - \overline{X})^2\right]\left[\Sigma(Y - \overline{Y})^2\right]}}.$$

▶ The $\Sigma(X - \overline{X})(Y - \overline{Y})$ is the cross product of X and Y and is symbolized as CP_{XY}. Thus, the correlation coefficient also may be expressed as

$$r = \frac{CP_{XY}}{\sqrt{(SS_X)(SS_Y)}}.$$

▶ The value of r using standard scores is given by

$$r = \frac{\Sigma(z_X z_Y)}{N_{\text{pairs}}}.$$

▶ The direction of a relationship is indicated by the positive or negative sign of r.

▶ The degree to which the points on the scatterplot lie on a straight line is given by the absolute value of r, a value that may vary from .00 to 1.00.

▶ A linear correlation between variables X and Y is represented in a population by ρ.

▶ The statistical significance of r is tested using Appendix C.5.

▶ The coefficient of determination, r^2, indicates the proportion of variance in the X variable that is related to the variance in the Y variable.

▶ An outlier may cause uncorrelated variables to appear correlated.

▶ If variables X and Y are correlated, then at least three possibilities exist with respect to the causal relations among the variables:

X causally affects Y.

Y causally affects X.

Neither X nor Y causally affect each other, but both are causally affected by a third variable, Z.

The Spearman rank-order correlation coefficient is found by

$$r_s = 1 - \left[\frac{6\Sigma D^2}{(N_{\text{pairs}})(N_{\text{pairs}}^2 - 1)}\right].$$

▶ The statistical significance of r_s is tested using Appendix C.6.

Key Terms and Symbols

bivariate distribution (371)
bivariate normal distribution (395)
coefficient of determination (r^2) (391)
correlation coefficient (370)
correlational study (370)
covary (370)
cross products of X and Y (CP_{XY}) (378)
linear relationship (373)

negative relationship (374)
outlier (389)
Pearson correlation coefficient (r)
   (377)
positive relationship (373)
ρ (393)
$ρ_s$ (399)
r (377)

r_s (398)
r^2 (391)
scatterplot (372)
Spearman rank-order correlation
   coefficient (r_s) (398)
subject variable (370)
SS_X (381)
SS_Y (381)

Review Questions

1. Review Question 3 of Chapter 1 indicated that a recent study reported a relationship between anger levels and blood pressure for males. Assume an experimenter interested in this topic obtains anger level scores and systolic blood pressure in millimeters of mercury from 16 male subjects. Anger level scores were obtained using a rating scale in which scores could range from 10 to 100 with higher scores indicating higher levels of anger. The following scores were obtained.

Subject	Anger Level	Blood Pressure
1	64	170
2	30	132
3	37	129
4	39	144
5	17	145
6	29	122
7	36	124
8	34	145
9	44	137
10	32	115
11	37	127
12	47	148
13	50	148
14	41	144
15	46	133
16	61	158

a. Construct a scatterplot of the anger score (on the abscissa) and blood pressure (on the ordinate).

b. Does the relationship between the scores on the scatterplot appear to be positive or negative, or is there no relationship apparent?

c. Calculate r_{obs} and test to find if it differs significantly from a correlation of zero in the population at the .05 significance level.

d. What conclusion do you reach about the relationship of anger level and systolic blood pressure scores in the sample?

   e. Calculate r^2. What proportion of the variation in anger level and systolic blood pressure is common to the two measures?

   f. Report the results of your study following the example in the Reporting the Results of a Correlational Study section of this chapter.

2. Physical and verbal bullying has long been a problem in schools. With the advent of the Internet and text messaging, however, adolescent bullying has taken on a different mode of attack. Raskauskas and Stoltz (2007) investigated the relationship of traditional bullying, such as spreading rumors about someone, teasing, or exclusion, to electronic bullying, such as creating web sites about others on the Internet or sending bullying text messages to other. For 84 adolescents, they found an r_{obs} of $+.48$ between reports of being a victim to traditional rumors and being a victim of Internet bullying, an r_{obs} of $-.11$ between reports of being a victim of traditional teasing and behaving like a bully on the Internet, and an r_{obs} of $+.32$ between being a traditional bully by excluding others and being an electronic bully through text messaging.

   a. Test each correlation coefficient to find if it differs significantly at the .05 level from a correlation of zero in the population sampled.

   b. Calculate the coefficient of determination for each value of r_{obs}.

   c. What conclusion do you reach concerning the relationship between being a victim to traditional rumors and being a victim of Internet bullying?

   d. What conclusion do you reach concerning the relationship between reports of being a victim of traditional teasing and behaving like a bully on the Internet?

   e. What conclusion do you reach concerning the relationship between being a traditional bully by excluding others and being an electronic bully through text messaging?

3. Students are often interested in predicting their final examination grade from the grade received on a midterm examination. To make such predictions, grades on the midterm and final exam must be correlated. Suppose that for an elementary statistics class the following grades were obtained for 10 students on a midterm and final examination.

Student	Examination	
	Midterm: X	Final: Y
1	87	84
2	89	91
3	97	96
4	80	87
5	73	66
6	85	90
7	81	79
8	74	80
9	80	89
10	89	86

   a. Plot a scatterplot of the midterm exam (on the abscissa) and final exam (on the ordinate).

   b. Does the relationship between the scores on the scatterplot appear to be positive or negative, or is no relationship apparent?

   c. Calculate r_{obs} and test to find if it differs significantly from a correlation of zero in the population at the .05 significance level.

   d. What conclusion do you reach about the relationship of midterm exam grades and final exam grades in the sample?

4. Krantz (1987) found that physical attractiveness and popularity are positively correlated for kindergarten girls, but not for kindergarten boys. Suppose that you wanted to determine if this relationship still exists by conducting a similar study. You had an observer rank kindergarten children on physical attractiveness and popularity. Twelve girls and 14 boys were ranked, and you found the following rankings.

	Girls	
Child	Physical Attractiveness: X	Popularity: Y
1	3	1
2	6	7
3	2	3
4	9	10
5	12	11
6	1	3
7	7	8
8	8	7
9	4	5
10	10	9
11	5	6
12	11	12

	Boys	
Child	Physical Attractiveness: X	Popularity: Y
1	5	9
2	11	1
3	3	10
4	9	4
5	4	6
6	8	12
7	12	5
8	1	13
9	14	8
10	10	14
11	6	2
12	13	11
13	2	7
14	7	3

    a. Calculate $r_{s\ obs}$ on the scores of the girls and test to find if it differs significantly from a correlation of zero in the population at the .05 significance level.

    b. What conclusion do you reach about the relationship of physical attractiveness and popularity rankings for the girls?

    c. Calculate $r_{s\ obs}$ on the scores of the boys and test to find if it differs significantly from a correlation of zero in the population at the .05 significance level.

    d. What conclusion do you reach about the relationship of physical attractiveness and popularity rankings for the boys?

5. A study by Wong (1993) measured 76 college students with the Wechsler Adult Intelligence Scale-Revised and correlated the resulting IQ scores with the students' grade point averages. The range of IQ scores was from 83 to 133. The r_{obs} between IQ score and grade point average was $+.18$, which is nonsignificant at the .05 level. Identify one reason why there may be no correlation between the two variables in this study.

6. Eating disorders are often common occurrences on college campuses, particularly for females. One hypothesis is that problems with same sex peer relationships may be associated with bulimic behaviors (Schutz & Paxton, 2007). A psychologist wanted to test this hypothesis on your college campus by using the friend-trust subscale from the Inventory of Parent and Peer Attachment scale (Armsden & Greenberg, 1987) as a measure of the quality of peer relationships This 10-item summated rating scale includes statements similar to, "My friends respect my feelings" with responses on a 5-point rating scale ranging from 1 (never) to 5 (always). Thus, scores on the scale may range from 10 to 50. Bulimic symptoms were measured using the bulimic symptoms subscale from the Eating Disorder Inventory (Garner, Olmsted, & Polivy, 1983). This 7-item summated rating scale assesses bulimic behaviors using a 6-point rating scale with scores ranging from 1 (not at all symptomatic) to 6 (most symptomatic). Scores on this scale may thus range from 7 to 42. The psychologist obtained the scores shown in the following table from 13 females.

Subject	Friend Trust Score: X	Bulimic Symptoms Score: Y
1	44	8
2	42	17
3	41	10
4	40	15
5	37	16
6	36	22
7	36	8
8	33	24
9	29	11
10	29	24
11	28	30
12	18	35
13	42	24

a. Construct a scatterplot of friend-trust score (on the abscissa) and bulimic-symptoms score (on the ordinate).

b. Does the relationship between the scores on the scatterplot appear to be positive or negative, or is no relationship apparent?

c. Calculate r_{obs} and test to find if it differs significantly from a correlation of zero in the population at the .05 significance level.

d. What conclusion do you reach about the relationship of friendship trust scores and bulimic symptoms in the sample?

7. Huebner and McCullough (2000) investigated factors affecting adolescents' satisfaction with school. One of the variables studied was the number of negative daily events associated with school. Negative daily events include such aspects as worrying about performance in a class, having a bad teacher, or interacting with disliked people. Suppose an investigator interested in this problem asks 15 adolescents to keep a record of the negative daily events associated with school and to evaluate their school satisfaction on a summated rating scale in which scores may range from 6 (very low satisfaction) to 48 (very high satisfaction) and obtained the following scores:

Student	Negative Events	School Satisfaction
1	7	34
2	14	14
3	8	24
4	19	15
5	6	29
6	10	27
7	17	14
8	7	38
9	12	19
10	17	21
11	6	29
12	9	27
13	13	18
14	22	18
15	5	30

a. Construct a scatterplot of the number of negative events (on the abscissa) and school satisfaction (on the ordinate).

b. Does the relationship between the scores on the scatterplot appear to be positive or negative, or is there no relationship apparent?

c. Calculate r_{obs} and test to find if it differs significantly from a correlation of zero in the population at the .05 significance level.

d. What conclusion do you reach about the relationship between the number of negative events and school satisfaction in the sample?

8. You hypothesize that the amount of time a student spends computer gaming may be related to his or her exam grades. To test this hypothesis, you asked 17 of your friends to record the number of hours per week they spend playing computer games so you

could correlate it against their first exam grade in a course. From the scores, you obtained the following values: for the amount of time playing computer games, $SS_x = 652$; for first exam grade, $SS_Y = 2094$; and $CP_{XY} = -859$.

a. Use these values to find r_{obs} between computer gaming and exam grade.

b. Is the value of r_{obs} statistically significant at the .05 level?

c. Suppose one friend reported playing computer games for 4 hours per week whereas another friend reported playing computer games for 15 hours per week. What would the correlation you found lead you to predict about their first exam score?

9. A teacher interested in finding if a relationship exists between how well children are liked by others in their class and a child's participation in class activities ranked fifth-grade students on the two dimensions. Suppose the following ranks were obtained for 16 children:

Child	Liking Rank	Participation Rank
1	6	8
2	9	12
3	1	2
4	2	4
5	16	14
6	3	1
7	8	11
8	4	3
9	10	5
10	5	6
11	15	13
12	12	9
13	7	7
14	13	10
15	14	16
16	11	15

a. Find the value of r_s for these scores.

b. Test to determine if the observed r_s differs significantly from a population correlation of zero.

c. What do you conclude about the relationship of liking and class participation?

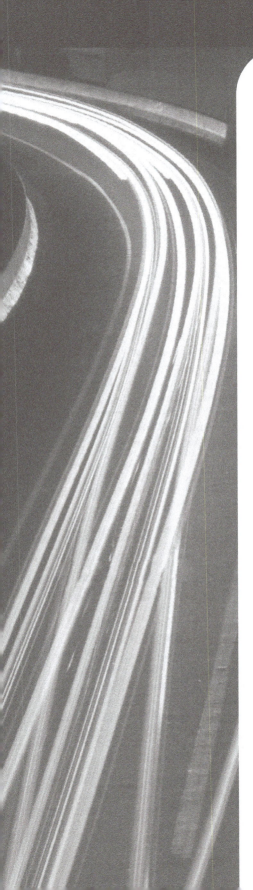

Regression Analysis: Predicting Linear Relationships

oogle the word *prediction* and you are likely to have over 40 million hits. Clearly, the concept of predicting events is popular among the public. Indeed, we all make predictions or use those made by others. You may try to predict a course grade from your first exam in a course. How you dress for the day often depends on the predicted weather. Scientists use research hypotheses to predict the effect of an independent variable on a dependent variable. College admission officers want to predict grade point averages from standardized achievement tests. Personnel managers may predict employee performance from employment test scores. Political pundits want to predict the outcomes of elections, and your doctor may predict your risk of developing a certain disease from the results of a medical test.

This chapter deals with the basic concepts of predicting one variable from another. We obviously cannot address all the forms of prediction identified above, some of which are quite complex. Many of the methods used for prediction were developed by Sir Francis Galton (1822–1911). Galton originated much of the study of individual differences, and in his work he noticed a curious phenomenon. When looking at the height of children, he found that the children of very tall parents were often not as tall as their parents, and the children of very short parents were often not as short as their parents. The children's height was closer to the mean of the population of heights than was that of the parents. Galton called this phenomenon *regression toward the mean*. The word *regression* means to go back or to return. Thus **regression toward the mean** denotes "to return to the mean." Following Galton's usage, the word *regression* is used today in statistics to refer to methods for predicting one variable from another.

Regression toward the mean ▶
The tendency of an extreme score to be less extreme on a second measurement.

The approach we take is limited to instances when the two variables are linearly related. We will learn how to fit a straight line, called a *linear regression line*, to a scatterplot of the two variables and use this regression line to predict one score from the other. Two variables may be related in a nonlinear way also, but our discussion is limited only to straight-line relationships. We begin with several simple examples of linear relationships; then, we introduce an example of predicting in-class attention scores from responses to a questionnaire on how much a professor is liked.

Linear Relations

Definition of a Linear Relation

A linear relationship between two variables is a straight-line relationship between the variables. Figure 14.1 illustrates two variables, X and Y, that are perfectly positively linearly related. This figure permits us to more completely define a linear relation. In a **linear relation**, each time one variable changes by 1 unit there is a constant change in the second variable. In Figure 14.1, for each 1-unit increase in X, Y increases by 0.5 unit. For example, as X increases from 2 to 3 (1 unit on the X measurement), Y increases from 1.0 to 1.5 (0.5 unit on the Y measurement). Similarly, as X increases from 4 to 5 (1 unit on the X measurement), Y increases from 2.0 to 2.5 (0.5 unit on the Y measurement). In this illustration, then, a change in X of 1 unit of its measurement results in a constant change of 0.5 unit on the Y measure.

Linear relation ▶ A relation between two variables such that each time that variable X changes by 1 unit, variable Y changes by a constant amount.

The requirement of a linear relationship that a change of 1 unit in the X variable be accompanied by a constant amount of change in the Y variable applies whether the relationship is positive or negative. Figure 14.2 illustrates a perfect negative linear relationship between X and Y. Each time X changes by 1 unit, Y also changes by a constant amount. For example, as X changes 1 unit from 2 to 3, Y changes from 9.4 to 8.6, a change of -0.8 on the Y measurement. Similarly, a change of X from 8 to 9 results in a change of Y from 4.6 to 3.8, again a change of -0.8 on the Y measurement. For the linear relationship in Figure 14.2, every change in X of 1 unit is accompanied by a corresponding and constant change of Y of -0.8 unit.

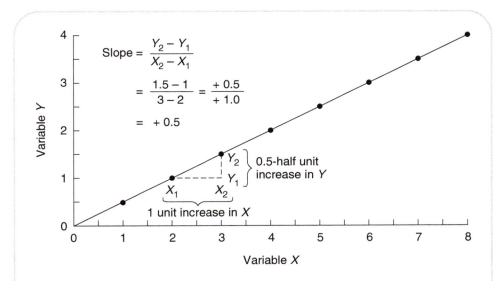

Figure 14.1 A perfect positive linear relationship between variable X and variable Y with a slope of $+0.5$.

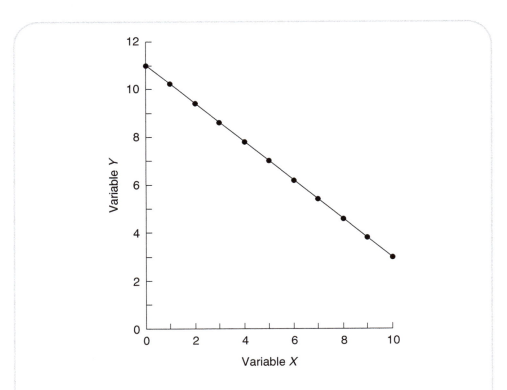

Figure 14.2 A perfect negative linear relationship between variable X and variable Y with a slope of -0.8 and a Y-intercept of $+11$.

General equation of a straight line ▸ $Y = bX + a$.

The **general equation of a straight line** is given by

$$Y = bX + a,$$

where $Y =$ Score on the Y variable.
$X =$ Score on the X variable.
$b =$ Slope of the line.
$a =$ Constant called the *Y-intercept*.

This equation is used to predict the value of variable Y from the value of variable X.

Slope of a Line

In Figures 14.1 and 14.2, every change in X by 1 unit of its measure is accompanied by a corresponding and constant change in the Y variable. The relationship of the change in the Y variable corresponding to a change in the X variable is the **slope of the straight line** relating the two variables. Specifically, the slope of a line relating variables X and Y is symbolized by **b** and defined as

Slope of a straight line ▸ The slope of a straight line is given by $b = \dfrac{\text{Change in value of } Y}{\text{Change in value of } X}$.

$$\textbf{Slope} = b = \frac{\textbf{Change in value of } Y}{\textbf{Change in value of } X}.$$

This relationship is expressed as

$$b = \frac{Y_2 - Y_1}{X_2 - X_1},$$

where X_1 and $X_2 =$ two values of X.
Y_1 and $Y_2 =$ values of Y corresponding to X_1 and X_2, respectively.

The numerical values presented in Figure 14.1 allow us to find the slope of the line relating X and Y using the values of $X_1 = 2$ and $X_2 = 3$. The values of Y corresponding to these X values are $Y_1 = 1$ and $Y_2 = 1.5$, respectively. Thus,

$$b = \frac{Y_2 - Y_1}{X_2 - X_1} = \frac{1.5 - 1}{3 - 2} = \frac{+0.5}{+1} = +0.5.$$

The slope of this straight line is $+0.5$; for every increase of 1 unit in X, Y increases by 0.5 unit. The slope of a straight line is constant over its length. Thus, regardless of the values of X used, b will be $+0.5$ for this example. For instance, suppose we use $X_1 = 3$ and $X_2 = 5$. For these values of X, the corresponding Y values are $Y_1 = 1.5$ and $Y_2 = 2.5$. Hence,

$$b = \frac{2.5 - 1.5}{5 - 3} = \frac{+1}{+2} = +0.5.$$

Knowing the slope of the line in Figure 14.1, we can write an equation relating the value of Y to X for this line. This equation is

$$Y = +0.5X.$$

For each value of X, this equation provides the corresponding value of Y, and we can solve $Y = +0.5X$ for different values of X as follows:

If $X =$ _____,	Then $Y =$ _____
0	0
1	0.5
2	1.0
3	1.5
4	2.0
5	2.5
6	3.0
7	3.5
8	4.0

Compare these values of Y with the values of Y plotted in Figure 14.1 for each X value. Notice that $Y = +0.5X$ provides the equation describing the linear relationship plotted in Figure 14.1. Thus, if we knew only this equation and the X score, we could predict the Y score perfectly.

The equation $Y = bX$ provides part of the general equation for a straight line and describes any linear relationship between X and Y, provided that $Y = 0$ when $X = 0$. But what if Y does not equal zero when $X = 0$? We turn to this problem next.

The *Y*-Intercept of a Line

Look at the relationship between variables X and Y presented in Figure 14.3. The slope of this line is also $+0.5$, because for every change of 1 unit in X, Y changes by $+0.5$ unit. But this line cannot be described by the equation $Y = +0.5X$, for this equation indicates that Y should equal zero when $X = 0$. But, looking at Figure 14.3, we see that $Y = 3$ when $X = 0$. Let us substitute another value for X, say $X = 10$, into the equation $Y = +0.5X$. Doing so, we find that Y should be 5 when $X = 10$. From Figure 14.3, however, we see that $Y = 8$ when $X = 10$. By comparing Y found from the equation $Y = +0.5X$ with the values of Y plotted in Figure 14.3, we find that the equation $Y = +0.5X$ gives a value of Y that is 3 units less than the Y plotted on the figure. Suppose, then, that we use the equation $Y = +0.5X$ and add 3 to each value of Y obtained from it. Then the equation is

$$Y = +0.5X + 3.$$

This equation now describes the relationship between X and Y in Figure 14.3. To demonstrate, solving $Y = +0.5X + 3$ for different values of X, we obtain the following:

If $X =$ _____,	Then $Y =$ _____
0	3.0
2	4.0
4	5.0
10	8.0
13	9.5
19	12.5
24	15.0
26	16.0
30	18.0

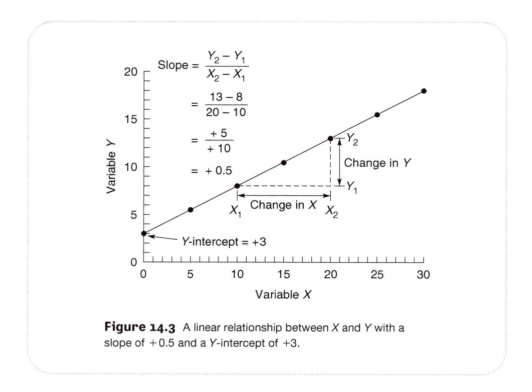

Figure 14.3 A linear relationship between X and Y with a slope of $+0.5$ and a Y-intercept of $+3$.

These values of Y for each value of X correspond perfectly with the values of Y plotted on Figure 14.3. Thus, $Y = 0.5X + 3$ is the equation describing the line shown in Figure 14.3.

This example provides a specific instance of the equation for a linear relationship between X and Y. To express the general equation for a straight line, we substitute the letter b for the slope of $+0.5$ and the letter a for the constant of 3 in the equation $Y = +0.5X + 3$. Doing so, we obtain $Y = bX + a$, the general equation of a straight line with slope b, and Y-intercept, a. The **Y-intercept** is the value of Y when $X = 0$. When $X = 0$, the line intercepts, or intersects, the Y axis, and the value of Y at this point is the Y-intercept. In Figure 14.3 the Y-intercept is $+3$, whereas in Figure 14.1 the Y-intercept is 0.

Y-intercept ▶ The value of Y when $X = 0$ in the equation $Y = bX + a$.

Example Linear Relations and Their Equations

To gain familiarity with linear relationships and the equations describing them, Figure 14.4 provides examples of both positive and negative linear relationships between X and Y. The equation of the straight line with the slope and Y-intercept is given for each relationship illustrated. For example, panel (b) presents the linear relationship used in Figure 14.2 to illustrate a negative relationship between X and Y. The equation for this relationship is $Y = -0.8X + 11$. Here we see that the slope is -0.8; the minus sign indicates the relationship is negative. For every increase of 1 unit in X, Y decreases by 0.8 unit. When X is zero, the line intercepts the Y-axis at a value of $+11$; thus, the Y-intercept for this equation is $+11$. Study each example and ensure that you can obtain the value of b and a for each relationship presented.

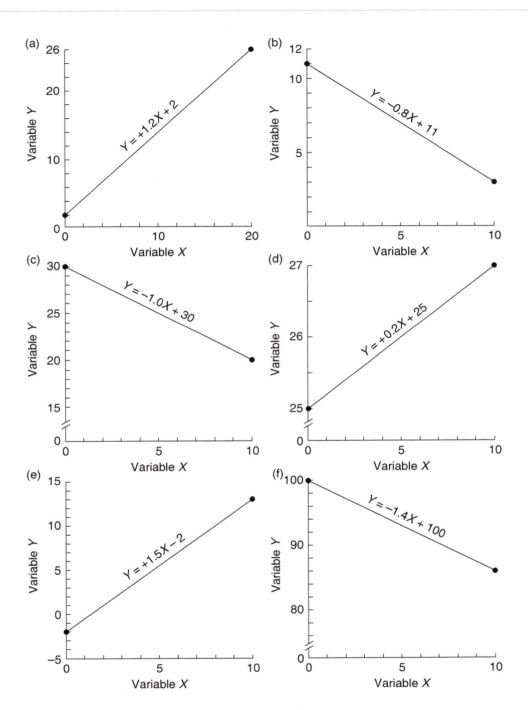

Figure 14.4 Various linear relationships between variables X and Y: (a) $Y = +1.2X + 2$; (b) $Y = -0.8X + 11$; (c) $Y = -1.0X + 30$; (d) $Y = +0.2X + 25$; (e) $Y = 1.5X - 2$; (f) $Y = -1.4X + 100$.

Testing Your Knowledge 14.1

1. Define: *a*, *b*, linear relation, slope of a straight line, *Y*-intercept.
2. Write the general equation for a straight line.
3. Write the equation for the slope of a straight line.
4. For each of the following graphs, find the slope and *Y*-intercept. Then write the equation for each line.

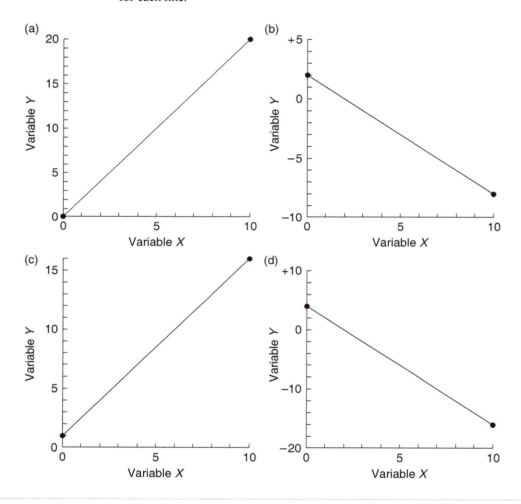

Finding a Linear Regression Line

An Example Problem

The previous examples involved variables identified simply as *X* and *Y* and the equation $Y = bX + a$ was used to predict *Y* from *X*. To introduce how we find the equation that describes the linear relationship of two sets of scores, we return to the problem introduced in Chapter 13, the relationship between liking a professor and in-class attention scores.

	Liking of a Professor	In-Class Attention
Subject	Score: X	Score: Y
1	6	16
2	15	25
3	28	38
4	2	12
5	24	34
6	8	18
7	25	35
8	30	40
9	14	24
10	18	28

TABLE 14.1 Hypothetical scores for 10 subjects on liking of a professor and in-class attention

Our goal is to develop an equation allowing us to predict in-class attention scores from liking of a professor scores.

Suppose, for a moment, that the scores in Table 14.1 were obtained from 10 students. These scores are perfectly positively related, $r_{obs} = +1.00$. Consequently, we expect a scatterplot to reveal that the scores fall on a straight line, as Figure 14.5 illustrates. We obtain the

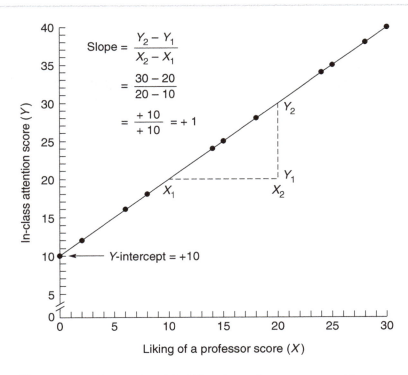

Figure 14.5 Scatterplot of the liking of a professor scores and in-class attention scores given in Table 14.1.

equation for the linear relationship between liking of a professor and in-class attention scores by finding the slope and Y-intercept of the line. Both values were found on the figure: $b = +1$ and $a = +10$. Thus, the equation relating the in-class attention scores (Y) to the liking of a professor scores (X) for Table 14.1 is

$$Y = +1X + 10$$

or

In-class attention score $= (+1)$ (liking of a professor score) $+ 10.$

Because the correlation of the scores is $+1.00$, we can use this equation to predict perfectly each subject's in-class attention score by knowing only his or her liking of a professor score. The predicted in-class attention scores are given in column b of Table 14.2. For example, subject 1 has a liking of a professor score of 6. Applying the equation,

Predicted in-class attention score $= (+1)$(liking of a professor score) $+ 10,$

we find

$$\text{Predicted in-class attention score} = (+1)(6) + 10$$
$$= 6 + 10 = 16.$$

The in-class attention score predicted from the liking of a professor score of 6 is 16. The in-class attention scores predicted from the other liking of a professor scores are presented

---

TABLE

14.2

In-class attention scores predicted from liking of a professor scores using the equation

In-class attention score $= (+1)$(liking of a professor score) $+ 10.$

Column a identifies the obtained liking of a professor score, column b the in-class attention score predicted from the equation, and column c the actual in-class attention score from Table 14.1.

Subject	(a) Liking of a Professor Score: X	(b) Predicted In-Class Attention: Y′	(c) Actual In-Class Attention: Y
1	6	16	16
2	15	25	25
3	28	38	38
4	2	12	12
5	24	34	34
6	8	18	18
7	25	35	35
8	30	40	40
9	14	24	24
10	18	28	28

Y' ▶ The value of Y predicted from X using a linear regression equation.

in column b of Table 14.2. These predicted scores are identified with the letter Y' (read as "Y prime" or "Y predicted") to indicate that they have been predicted from the X score of liking of a professor using the equation

$$Y' = 1X + 10.$$

The actual in-class attention score obtained by each subject (symbolized by Y) is presented in column c. Notice that the predicted and actual in-class attention scores are identical. Because $r_{obs} = +1.00$, Y' and Y are the same and there is no error in predicting in-class attention scores from liking of a professor scores.

A More Realistic Example Problem

From an applied perspective, the scores in Table 14.1 are unusual. Rarely, if ever, are two variables perfectly correlated as they are in Table 14.1. More realistically, scores on two variables will exhibit a less than perfect correlation, such as the scores presented in Table 14.3. These scores were used in Chapter 13 to present the Pearson correlation coefficient (see Table 13.1). The r_{obs} for these scores is $+.78$, which is statistically significant at the .05 level. The standard deviations given in this table will be used in additional computations, thus for accuracy in these computations, we are carrying them to three decimal places.

The scores of Table 14.3 are presented in a scatterplot in Figure 14.6. As $r_{obs} = +.78$ indicates, these scores are positively related: higher in-class attention scores are associated with higher scores on liking of a professor, and lower in-class attention scores are related to lower liking of a professor scores. Although the relationship between the liking of a professor and in-class attention scores in Figure 14.6 is not perfect, it does appear to be linear. But what would be the best straight line to describe these scores? Obviously, a number of straight

TABLE 14.3

Hypothetical scores for 10 subjects on liking of a professor and in-class attention. The mean and estimated population standard deviation are given for each set of scores.

Subject	Liking of a Professor Score: X	In-Class Attention Score: Y
1	4	16
2	27	37
3	18	33
4	7	23
5	30	34
6	12	32
7	18	24
8	23	29
9	19	26
10	12	26
	$\overline{X}$ 17.0	$\overline{Y}$ 28.0
	s_X 8.367	s_Y 6.254

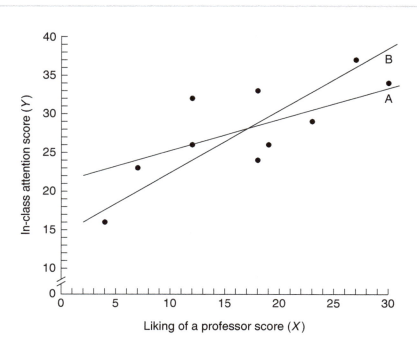

Figure 14.6 Scatterplot of the liking of a professor scores and in-class attention scores given in Table 14.3. Lines A and B were drawn arbitrarily on the scatterplot.

lines could be drawn on the scatterplot. For example, we have drawn two different straight lines labeled A and B on the figure. The lines were drawn arbitrarily, except that each line passes through $\overline{X} = 17$ and $\overline{Y} = 28$. Does line A appear to "fit" or describe the scores better or worse than line B? To answer this question, we need a criterion to decide how well a particular straight line fits a set of correlated scores.

The Least-Squares Criterion

Each line, A and B, in Figure 14.6 allows predicting a value of Y (that is, a Y') for each value of X. For example, for a liking of a professor score of 7, line A predicts a Y' of 24.0, and for a liking of a professor score of 27, a Y' equal to 32.0. On the other hand, line B predicts Y' equal to 20.0 for an X of 7 and Y' equal to 36.0 for a liking of a professor score of 27. These predicted Y scores are presented in column c of Table 14.4 for line A and in column f for line B. Each Y' score is in error in comparison with the Y score actually obtained, and the difference $Y - Y'$ is a measure of the error in prediction of the Y score from the X score. Table 14.4 illustrates the errors in prediction of each Y score from the X scores using either line A (see column d) or line B (see column g) of Figure 14.6.

Each line leads to errors in prediction. But does one line lead to smaller errors in prediction than the other? We might try to answer this question by adding up the errors in

TABLE
14.4

Error of prediction of Y scores from the X scores of Figure 14.6 using either line A or line B. The error is given by the difference between the obtained Y score and the Y′ score predicted from X, or Y − Y′. Columns a and b identify the obtained X and Y scores, respectively, column c the Y′ predicted from line A, columns d and e the error and squared error of the predicted score from line A, respectively, column f the Y′ predicted from line B, and columns g and h the error and squared error of the predicted score from line B, respectively.

	(a)	(b)	(c)	(d)	(e)	(f)	(g)	(h)
	Obtained Scores		Predicted from Line A			Predicted from Line B		
			Scores	Error		Scores	Error	
Subject	X	Y	Y'	$Y - Y'$	$(Y - Y')^2$	Y'	$Y - Y'$	$(Y - Y')^2$
1	4	16	22.8	−6.8	46.24	17.6	−1.6	2.56
2	27	37	32.0	+5.0	25.00	36.0	+1.0	1.00
3	18	33	28.4	+4.6	21.16	28.8	+4.2	17.64
4	7	23	24.0	−1.0	1.00	20.0	+3.0	9.00
5	30	34	33.2	+0.8	0.64	38.4	−4.4	19.36
6	12	32	26.0	+6.0	36.00	24.0	+8.0	64.00
7	18	24	28.4	−4.4	19.36	28.8	−4.8	23.04
8	23	29	30.4	−1.4	1.96	32.8	−3.8	14.44
9	19	26	28.8	−2.8	7.84	29.6	−3.6	12.96
10	12	26	26.0	0.0	0.00	24.0	+2.0	4.00
				Sum 0.0	159.20		0.0	168.00

columns d and g, respectively, of Table 14.4. But if we sum the columns, as we have done in Table 14.4, we find that the sum of the errors, $\Sigma(Y - Y')$, is zero for each line. Thus, the sum of the errors cannot be used as a criterion to determine the fit of a straight line to the points in a scatterplot; it will always be equal to zero. A similar problem occurred in Chapter 5 when attempting to find a measure of the variation of scores about the mean of a distribution. In that instance, we found that $\Sigma(X - \overline{X})$ was always equal to zero. The problem was resolved by squaring each $X - \overline{X}$ before the differences were summed. Then we used $\Sigma(X - \overline{X})^2$ to develop a measure of error variation in the scores.

The current problem may be resolved similarly by squaring each $Y - Y'$ difference and summing the squared $Y - Y'$ differences. Then we will use $\Sigma(Y - Y')^2$ to determine which line best fits the scatterplot. Table 14.4 illustrates obtaining $\Sigma(Y - Y')^2$ for each line, A and B in columns e and h, respectively. The $\Sigma(Y - Y')^2$ for line A is 159.20 (see column e), whereas for line B it is 168.00 (see column h). Based on $\Sigma(Y - Y')^2$ as a measure of error in prediction, line A produces less error than line B. However, although line A produces less error than line B, we cannot be sure it is the line that produces the least error; there may be other lines that would produce even less error. Our task, then, is to find the straight line relating the X and Y scores that produces the smallest value of $\Sigma(Y - Y')^2$.

A straight line that minimizes the value of $\Sigma(Y - Y')^2$ is called a **least-squares regression line**, for it minimizes the value of the sum of the squared differences of every predicted Y' score from the obtained Y score. Figure 14.7 illustrates a least-squares regression line for pre-

Least-squares regression line ▶
A straight line that minimizes the value of $\Sigma(Y - Y')^2$.

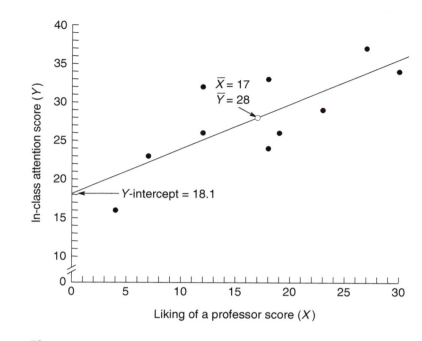

Figure 14.7 The least-squares regression line for the liking of a professor scores and in-class attention scores of Table 14.3.

dicting in-class attention scores from liking of a professor scores fitted to the scatterplot in Table 14.3. The equation for this line is $Y' = +0.583X + 18.1$. This line possesses the characteristic that $\sum(Y - Y')^2$ is a minimum; no other straight line fitted to the scores of Table 14.3 will produce a smaller value of $\sum(Y - Y')^2$. We now explain how to find the slope and Y-intercept for a least-squares regression line.

The Slope and *Y*-Intercept of a Least-Squares Regression Line for Predicting *Y* from *X*

To find a least-squares regression line to predict variable Y from variable X, we must determine the slope (b) and Y-intercept (a) of a straight line that minimizes the value of $\sum(Y - Y')^2$.

Slope of a Least-Squares Regression Line
There are several alternative formulas for finding the slope of a least-squares regression line; each formula produces the same value for b for a set of scores.

Deviational and Cross-Products Formula.   The slope of the least-squares regression line for two variables using deviations of scores from their mean is given by

$$\text{Slope} = b = \frac{\sum(X - \overline{X})(Y - \overline{Y})}{\sum(X - \overline{X})^2}.$$

Recall that the numerator of this formula, $\sum(X - \overline{X})(Y - \overline{Y})$, is the cross product of X and Y and is symbolized as CP_{XY}. The denominator of the formula,

$$\sum(X - \overline{X})^2,$$

is the sum of squares for X, or SS_X. Thus, we may also write an equation for b in cross products and sum-of-squares form as

$$\text{Slope} = b = \frac{CP_{XY}}{SS_X}.$$

Correlation Formula.   The value of b may also be obtained from the r between X and Y by using the equation

$$\text{Slope} = b = r\left(\frac{s_Y}{s_X}\right),$$

where $r = r_{obs}$ between two sets of scores.
s_Y = estimated population standard deviation for the Y scores.
s_X = estimated population standard deviation for the X scores.

Which Formula Should You Use to Find b?   Table 14.5 summarizes each of the preceding formulas for the slope. Each formula provides the same value of b when applied to a set of scores. In most instances, however, you will use a statistical software package such as SPSS or Minitab to calculate b. If, however, you choose to do the computations by hand, then the correlation formula is recommended, for it requires only that you find s_X and s_Y in addition to the value of r_{obs}. We illustrate its use next.

Finding b Using the Correlational Formula
The correlational formula requires that we know r_{obs}, s_X and s_Y. For the scores of Table 14.3, $r_{obs} = +.78$ (see page 382), $s_X = 6.254$, and $s_Y = 8.367$. Substituting these values into the formula for b, we obtain,

$$b = r\left(\frac{s_Y}{s_X}\right) = +.78\left(\frac{6.254}{8.367}\right) = +0.583.$$

The plus sign indicates that the slope is positive.

TABLE

14.5   Formulas for the slope of a least-squares regression line

Deviational formula

$$b = \frac{\sum(X - \overline{X})(Y - \overline{Y})}{\sum(X - \overline{X})^2}$$

Cross-products and sum-of-squares formula

$$b = \frac{CP_{XY}}{SS_X}$$

Correlation formula

$$b = r\left(\frac{s_Y}{s_X}\right)$$

Y-Intercept of a Least-Squares Regression Line

The Y-intercept of a least-squares regression line is calculated from the value of b by the formula

$$a = \overline{Y} - b\overline{X},$$

Where $\overline{Y}$ = mean of the Y scores.
$\overline{X}$ = mean of the X scores.
b = slope of the least-squares regression line obtained by using one of the formulas given in the previous section.

To illustrate the use of this formula for the scores of Table 14.3, $\overline{Y} = 28.0$, $\overline{X} = 17.0$, and $b = +0.583$. Thus,

$$a = 28.0 - (+0.583)(17.0) = 28.0 - 9.911 = 18.089 = 18.1$$

rounded to one decimal place. The least-squares regression line for these scores intersects the Y-axis at a value of $Y = 18.1$.

Equation for the Least-Squares Regression Line

When the values of b and a are substituted into the equation for a straight line,

$$Y' = bX + a,$$

we find

$$Y' = +0.583X + 18.1.$$

Hence, the least-squares regression line for the scores of Table 14.3 is described by the equation $Y' = +0.583X + 18.1$. To obtain predicted values of Y, a value of X is entered into the equation and the equation solved for Y'. Predicted values of Y for the scores of Table 14.3 are as follows:

Subject	If $X =$ _____,	Then $Y' =$ _____
1	4	20.4
2	27	33.8
3	18	28.6
4	7	22.2
5	30	35.6
6	12	25.1
7	18	28.6
8	23	31.5
9	19	29.2
10	12	25.1

The Y' values lie on the regression line illustrated in Figure 14.7.

Fitting a Least-Squares Regression Line to Scores

We now illustrate how the least-squares regression line given by $Y' = +0.583X + 18.1$ is fitted to the scores plotted in Figure 14.7. If any two points on a straight line are known, then we have sufficient information to plot the line on a figure. For the regression line, one point on the line is the Y-intercept, the value of Y' when $X = 0$. For the example, the Y-intercept is 18.1. Thus, one point on the line has the coordinates $X = 0$, $Y = 18.1$.

A second point may be obtained by substituting a different value of X and solving for Y'. Although we may substitute any value for X, we use the value of $\overline{X}$, where $\overline{X} = 17.0$, for the example. Substituting $\overline{X} = 17.0$, into the equation, we obtain

$$Y' = +0.583(17.0) + 18.1 = 28.0.$$

Consequently, when $\overline{X} = 17.0$, $Y' = 28.0$. Notice this predicted value of $Y' = 28.0$ is also the value of $\overline{Y}$. For any least-squares regression line, when the value of X is the mean of the X scores, Y' will be equal to the mean of the obtained Y scores. Therefore, a second point on the regression line will always be a point with coordinates of $\overline{X}$, $\overline{Y}$. For the scores in Figure 14.7, $\overline{X} = 17.0$, $\overline{Y} = 28.0$, and the regression line on Figure 14.7 passes through these coordinates.

Testing Your Knowledge 14.2

1. Define: least-squares regression line, Y'.
2. Write the general equation for predicting a value of Y from X with a straight line.
3. The slope and Y-intercept for the regression of Test 2 (Y) on Test 1 (X) grades are $b = +0.8$ and $a = 9$.
   a. Write the equation for the regression line of Test 2 on Test 1 grades.
   b. Find values of predicted Test 2 grades (i.e., Y') for the following Test 1 scores (i.e., X): 60, 65, 80, 85, 90.
   c. Plot the regression line on a sheet of graph paper. The value of $\overline{X} = 76$.
4. The slope and Y-intercept for the regression of Task 2 (Y) on Task 1 (X) scores are $b = -1.4$ and $a = 23$.
   a. Write the equation for the regression line of Task 2 on Task 1 scores.
   b. Find values of predicted Task 2 scores (i.e., Y') for the following Task 1 scores (i.e., X): 5, 8, 11, 14, 17.
   c. Plot the regression line on a sheet of graph paper. The value of $\overline{X} = 11$.

Error in Prediction

Residuals: A Measure of the Error in Prediction

Residual ▶ The value of $Y - Y'$.

As we saw from Figure 14.7, using variable X to predict variable Y leads to some error in prediction, unless, of course, X and Y are perfectly correlated. The difference between a score and its predicted value, $Y - Y'$, is a measure of this error and is called the **residual**.

		(a)	(b)	(c)	(d)	(e)
TABLE **14.6**	Subject	X	Y	Y'	Y − Y'	(Y − Y')²
	1	4	16	20.43	−4.43	19.6249
	2	27	37	33.84	+3.16	9.9856
	3	18	33	28.59	+4.41	19.4481
	4	7	23	22.18	+0.82	0.6724
	5	30	34	35.59	−1.59	2.5281
	6	12	32	25.10	+6.90	47.6100
	7	18	24	28.59	−4.59	21.0681
	8	23	29	31.51	−2.51	6.3001
	9	19	26	29.18	−3.18	10.1124
	10	12	26	25.10	+0.90	0.8100
					Sum	138.1597

Calculating the residual for the predicted in-class attention scores (Y', column c) from the liking of a professor scores (X, column a) of Table 14.3 using the regression equation $Y' = +0.583X + 18.1$. The residual, or error in prediction, is presented in column d, and the squared value of the residual is presented in column e.

The residual is used as the basis for a measure of the accuracy of prediction called the standard error of estimate. To develop the standard error of estimate, we turn to Table 14.6.

Table 14.6 presents the liking of a professor and in-class attention scores of Table 14.3 in columns a and b, respectively. Predicted in-class attention scores (i.e., Y') obtained from the regression equation $Y' = +0.583X + 18.1$ are shown in column c. For example, Y' for subject 6 with a liking of a professor score of 12 is

$$Y'_6 = (+0.583)(12) + 18.1 = 25.10.$$

To minimize rounding error in later calculations, the predicted values in column c were carried to two decimal places. You should calculate the remaining Y' values in column c to ensure that you are able to work with the regression equation for these scores.

The residual, $Y - Y'$, is shown in column d for each subject. The sum of these residuals is equal to zero (within the limits of rounding error), so we cannot use this sum as a measure of error in prediction. Therefore, to develop a measure of error in prediction, we square the residuals as shown in column e. Summing the squared values of $Y - Y'$ in column e results in a sum of squares called the **$SS_{Residual}$**, the sum of squared residuals. The $SS_{Residual}$ is equal to $\sum (Y - Y')^2$, or 138.1597 for the example.

$SS_{Residual}$ ▶ The value of $\sum (Y - Y')^2$.

The Standard Error of Estimate

In Chapter 5, we developed a measure of error variation for a set of scores, the standard deviation, s, by dividing the SS for a set of scores by its degrees of freedom and then taking the square root of the obtained value. We obtain a similar measure of error variation in the prediction of Y from X, the standard error of estimate, by finding the square root of the quotient of the $SS_{Residual}$ divided by its degrees of freedom. The df for $SS_{Residual}$ are $N_{pairs} - 2$,

Standard error of estimate ($s_{Y\cdot X}$) ▶

The value of $\sqrt{\dfrac{\Sigma(Y - Y')^2}{N_{\text{pairs}} - 2}}$.

where N_{pairs} is the number of pairs of scores. Accordingly, the **standard error of estimate**, symbolized as $s_{Y\cdot X}$ to indicate that Y is predicted from X, is defined as

$$\text{Standard error of estimate} = s_{Y\cdot X} = \sqrt{\frac{SS_{\text{Residual}}}{N_{\text{pairs}} - 2}},$$

or, equivalently,

$$\text{Standard error of estimate} = s_{Y\cdot X} = \sqrt{\frac{\Sigma(Y - Y')^2}{N_{\text{pairs}} - 2}}.$$

In the example, $SS_{\text{Residual}} = 138.1597$, and $N_{\text{pairs}} = 10$; thus, the standard error of estimate of predicting in-class attention scores from liking of a professor scores is

$$s_{Y\cdot X} = \sqrt{\frac{138.1597}{10 - 2}} = 4.16 \text{ rounded to two decimal places.}$$

The definition of $s_{Y\cdot X}$ as

$$s_{Y\cdot X} = \sqrt{\frac{\Sigma(Y - Y')^2}{N_{\text{pairs}} - 2}}$$

illustrates that it is a measure of error variation of the predicted scores compared with the actual scores. Because this formula requires finding $Y - Y'$ differences, however, it is both time consuming and open to computational error. Thus, a formula using r has been developed that can be applied to scores without obtaining $Y - Y'$ differences.

Calculating $s_{Y\cdot X}$ from r

The standard error of estimate may be calculated from the value of r_{obs} between X and Y and the standard deviation of the Y variable with the formula

$$s_{Y\cdot X} = s_Y \sqrt{\left[\frac{N_{\text{pairs}} - 1}{N_{\text{pairs}} - 2}\right](1 - r_{\text{obs}}^2)}.$$

For the scores of Table 14.3,

$$s_Y = 6.254,$$
$$r_{\text{obs}} = +.78,$$
$$N_{\text{pairs}} = 10.$$

Thus,

$$s_{Y\cdot X} = (6.254)\sqrt{\left[\frac{10 - 1}{10 - 2}\right][1 - (+.78)^2]} = (6.254)(0.6638) = 4.15,$$

which, within the limits of rounding error, is the same as the value found by the definitional formula.

When N_{pairs} is large, the ratio of $N_{pairs} - 1$ to $N_{pairs} - 2$ approaches 1.0, and the formula is often written as

$$s_{Y \cdot X} = s_Y \sqrt{1 - r_{obs}^2}.$$

Table 14.7 summarizes the formulas for calculating $s_{Y \cdot X}$.

Information Provided by the Standard Error of Estimate

To understand what information the standard error of estimate provides, we return briefly to a consideration of the standard deviation, s. The standard deviation for a set of scores provides a measure of error variation for those scores. If we know nothing about the scores other than the mean, then the best prediction we can make for any score is the mean. Of course, this prediction will likely be in error; and, on the average, the error will be the value of the standard deviation. For example, suppose that you are told that the mean in-class attention score for Table 14.3 is 28. If you are asked to predict an individual score knowing nothing other than $\overline{Y} = 28$, your best prediction is 28. But for any score in Table 14.3, this prediction is in error; no subject obtained an in-class attention score of 28. The average error in this prediction is the value of the standard deviation, $s_Y = 6.25$, for this set of scores.

Suppose now you are told that there is a linear relation between the liking of a professor and in-class attention scores given by

$$Y' = +0.583X + 18.1.$$

Furthermore, suppose that you are told that subject 1 has a liking of a professor score of 4. Using this score and applying the regression equation, you predict this subject's Y score to be 20.43. Although this prediction, too, is in error (the subject's actual score was 16), the prediction of 20.43 is closer to the actual score than is the prediction of 28.0 made from $\overline{Y}$. The standard error of estimate is the standard deviation of the error in the predicted scores.

TABLE 14.7   Formulas for the standard error of estimate, $s_{Y \cdot X}$

Residuals formula

$$s_{Y \cdot X} = \sqrt{\frac{SS_{Residual}}{N_{pairs} - 2}}$$

or

$$s_{Y \cdot X} = \sqrt{\frac{\Sigma (Y - Y')^2}{N_{pairs} - 2}}.$$

Formula using r_{obs}

$$s_{Y \cdot X} = s_Y \sqrt{\left[\frac{N_{pairs} - 1}{N_{pairs} - 2}\right](1 - r_{obs}^2)}$$

TABLE **14.8**	Relationship between $s_{Y \cdot X}$ and s_Y as a function of r	
	If r_{obs} = _____	Then $s_{Y \cdot X}$ = _____ s_Y.
	0	1.000
	.1	.995
	.2	.980
	.3	.954
	.4	.917
	.5	.866
	.6	.800
	.7	.714
	.8	.600
	.9	.436
	1.0	.000

Thus, $s_{Y \cdot X}$ indicates the average error in predictions from the linear regression line. Notice in the example that $s_{Y \cdot X} = 4.16$ is smaller than $s_Y = 6.25$. Accordingly, if we predict Y from X, the error in prediction typically will be less than if we simply used $\overline{Y}$ as a predictor for all the Y values. Table 14.8 presents the relationship between s_Y and $s_{Y \cdot X}$ as a function of the correlation between variables X and Y. The table was constructed by substituting values of r_{obs} into the formula

$$s_{Y \cdot X} = s_Y \sqrt{1 - r^2_{obs}}.$$

The first column of this table presents values of r_{obs} ranging from 0 to 1.0. The second column shows the proportion of s_Y that $s_{Y \cdot X}$ will be for the value of r_{obs}. Notice that when r_{obs} is zero, $s_{Y \cdot X} = s_Y$, and knowing the liking of a professor score for a subject does not improve the accuracy of prediction of the subject's in-class attention score. For small values of r (e.g., $r = .1, .2,$ or $.3$), knowing the X variable score does little to improve the accuracy of prediction of the Y variable score. On the other hand, large values of r (e.g., $r = .7, .8,$ or $.9$) improve the accuracy considerably. For example, if the correlation between X and Y is .8, then $s_{Y \cdot X}$ is only .6 of s_Y. When r is 1.00, then $s_{Y \cdot X} = 0$; prediction of the Y score from the X score is perfect and there is no error of prediction.

Predicting X from Y

The examples to this point have used the liking of a professor scores (X) to predict in-class attention scores (Y). But we could reverse the process and use the in-class attention scores to predict liking of a professor. This would result in a different regression equation from the one predicting in-class attention from liking of a professor. Table 14.9 presents the liking of a professor and in-class attention scores with the X and Y designation reversed from Table 14.3; in-class attention scores are now designated X (column a) and liking of a professor scores Y (column b). Columns c, d, e, and f present the values of $X - \overline{X}, (X - \overline{X})^2, Y - \overline{Y}$ and $(X - \overline{X})(Y - \overline{Y})$, respectively, needed to obtain the slope using the deviational formula as illustrated in Step 2 of the table. Step 3 obtains the value of the Y-intercept, a. The regression line for predicting liking of a professor from in-class attention is presented in Step 4. This

TABLE
14.9

Calculating the least-squares regression line, predicted scores, and residuals for liking of a professor scores from in-class attention scores.

Step 1. Finding $X - \overline{X}$, $(X - \overline{X})^2$, $Y - \overline{Y}$, and $(X - \overline{X})(Y - \overline{Y})$:

	(a)	(b)	(c)	(d)	(e)	(f)	(g)	(h)	(i)
Subject	In-class Attention (X)	Liking of a Professor (Y)	$X - \overline{X}$	$(X - \overline{X})^2$	$Y - \overline{Y}$	$(X - \overline{X})(Y - \overline{Y})$	Y'	$Y - Y'$	$(Y - Y')^2$
1	16	4	−12	144	−13	+156	4.488	−0.488	0.238
2	37	27	+9	81	+10	+90	26.391	0.609	0.371
3	33	18	+5	25	+1	+5	22.219	−4.219	17.800
4	23	7	−5	25	−10	+50	11.789	−4.789	22.935
5	34	30	+6	36	+13	+78	23.262	6.738	45.401
6	32	12	+4	16	−5	−20	21.176	−9.176	84.199
7	24	18	−4	16	+1	−4	12.832	5.168	26.708
8	29	23	+1	1	+6	+6	18.047	4.953	24.532
9	26	19	−2	4	−2	−4	14.918	4.082	16.663
10	26	12	−2	4	−5	−10	14.918	−2.918	8.515
Means	28	17	Sums	352		+367			247.362

Step 2. Calculating b using the deviational formula:

$$b = \frac{\Sigma(X - \overline{X})(Y - \overline{Y})}{\Sigma(X - \overline{X})^2}$$

$$= \frac{+367}{352}$$

$$= +1.043$$

Step 3. Calculating a:

$\overline{X} = 28$, $\overline{Y} = 17$

$a = \overline{Y} - b\overline{X}$

$\quad = 17 - 1.043(28) = -12.2$.

Step 4. Regression line:

$Y' = +1.043X - 12.2$.

Step 5. Calculating $s_{Y \cdot X}$ from the residuals:

$\Sigma(Y - Y')^2 = 247.362$

$N_{pairs} - 2 = 8$

$s_{Y \cdot X} = \sqrt{\Sigma(Y - Y')^2 \div (N_{pairs} - 2)}$

$\quad = \sqrt{247.362 \div 8} = 5.56$

regression line was used to calculate the Y' values shown in column g of the table. Residuals are presented in column h and the squared value of the residuals in column i. Step 5 illustrates calculating $s_{Y \cdot X}$ from the residuals.

Notice that the slope and Y-intercept of the regression line depend on which variable is designated as X and which as Y. If liking of a professor is designated as the X variable, then the regression line is $Y' = +0.583X + 18.1$. If, however, in-class attention is designated as the X variable, then the regression line is $Y' = +1.043X - 12.2$. Each line allows prediction of the variable designated Y with equal accuracy, however. This characteristic can be seen by comparing $s_{Y \cdot X}$ to s_Y for each line. If liking of a professor is the X variable, then $s_{Y \cdot X}$ is 4.16 and s_Y is 6.25. Here $s_{Y \cdot X}/s_Y$ equals 4.16/6.25, which equals .67. On the other hand, if in-class attention is the X variable, then $s_{Y \cdot X}$ is 5.56 and s_Y is 8.37. Here $s_{Y \cdot X}/s_Y$ equals 5.56/8.37, which equals .66. Within the limits of rounding error, each regression line allows a similar reduction in error in predicting scores. In most instances, however, a researcher will have a particular reason to designate a variable as X to be used to predict Y. Thus, for most data sets, only one regression line will be found.

Using a Linear Regression Line

Two conditions are required for appropriate use of linear regression. First, r_{obs} for the scores must be statistically significant. If the scores are not correlated, then the best prediction for a Y score is to use the mean of the Y scores. If the X and Y scores are not correlated, and you are given an X score and asked to predict a Y score, the best prediction of Y is simply $\overline{Y}$. The knowledge of X does not give you any information about the value of Y.

A second requirement is that the relationship between the X and Y scores must be linear. The least-squares regression line is a straight line. If the X and Y scores are not linearly related, then it is inappropriate to fit a least-squares regression line to them. For example, if X and Y are related in a U-shaped or an inverted U-shaped (i.e., ⌒) fashion, then constructing a least-squares regression line for the scores will not lead to accurate predictions, for the scores are not linearly related.

We must be cautious also not to predict beyond the range of scores encompassed in the sample from which the prediction equation was developed. The relationship may be nonlinear for values outside the range in the sample.

Testing Your Knowledge 14.3

1. Define: least-squares regression line, residual, $SS_{Residual}$, standard error of estimate, $s_{Y \cdot X}$, $Y - Y'$

2. Why is $\Sigma(Y - Y')$ not used as a measure of error for predicting Y from X?

3. Why may $\Sigma(Y - Y')^2$ be used as a measure of error for predicting Y from X?

4. Give the definitional formula for the standard error of estimate.

5. In a study attempting to predict examination grades (Y) from the number of hours devoted to studying for the examination (X), the $\Sigma(Y - Y') = 347.21$ for 16 pairs of scores. What is the value of $s_{Y \cdot X}$ for this study?

6. An exercise physiologist found a correlation of $r_{obs} = +.41$ between the amount of exercise and weight loss in a sample of 45 people over a three-month period. The value of s_Y was 5.2 pounds. What is the value of $s_{Y \cdot X}$ for this study?

7. An instructor attempting to predict final exam grades from midsemester exam grades for a class of 27 students found that $SS_{Residual} = 462.25$. What is the value of $s_{Y \cdot X}$ for this study?

EXAMPLE PROBLEM

14.1

Finding a Regression Line

Problem: Gratitude is a state of feeling appreciative or grateful for the benefits one has received in life. Psychologists believe that gratitude is a personality characteristic or trait and that people vary in the amount to which they experience and express gratitude (Wood, Joseph, & Linley, 2007b). Psychologists also believe that gratitude is related to psychological well-being and the ability to cope with difficult situations. For example, Wood, Joseph, and Linley (2007a) hypothesized that a person with higher levels of gratitude would be more likely to implement a type of social support coping in stressful situations. One type of social support coping is called instrumental social support, wherein a person in a stressful situation seeks out the advice of another person with the goal of attaining a solution to the problem at hand, thus reducing stress. As an example of instrumental social support, consider the following: a student unhappy with a test grade would seek out the advice of the professor on how to better prepare for upcoming exams. In one study testing this hypothesis, Wood et al. (2007a) found a correlation of +.35 between gratitude and the use of instrumental social support coping strategies. Imagine that you would like to replicate this finding with 15 college students. To measure gratitude, you ask the students to respond to the statement "I am grateful to many people for the things they have done for me" with a rating from 1 (strongly disagree) to 7 (strongly agree). Instrumental social support coping is measured by responding to the statement "I try to get advice from other people when I have a difficult situation to deal with," also using a rating from 1 (strongly disagree) to 7 (strongly agree). You found r_{obs} between gratitude and social support coping of +.58. For 13 df, $r_{crit} = .514$; thus, r_{obs} is statistically significant. The mean of the gratitude scores was $\overline{X} = 3.7$, with $s_X = 1.8$. For instrumental social support coping, $\overline{Y} = 3.8$ and $s_Y = 1.9$. Find (a) the least-squares regression line of instrumental social support coping on gratitude, (b) predicted social support coping scores as a function of gratitude scores, and (c) the standard error of estimate.

Solution: The problem requires finding values for the slope and Y-intercept of the regression line. Because r_{obs} is given, we find the slope using the correlational formula shown in Table 14.5.

Finding the Slope: The slope, b, of the regression line is found from r by

$$b = r\left(\frac{s_Y}{s_X}\right).$$

Substituting values of r_{obs} s_X, and s_Y, we obtain

$$b = +.58\left(\frac{1.9}{1.8}\right) = +0.61.$$

Finding the Y-Intercept: The Y-intercept is found from

$$a = \overline{Y} - b\overline{X} = 3.8 - (+0.61)(3.7) = 1.54.$$

Obtaining the Regression Equation: The regression equation of social support coping (Y) on gratitude (X) is given by

$$Y' = +0.61X + 1.54.$$

Obtaining Predicted Instrumental Social Support Coping Scores (Y'):
Social support coping scores (Y') predicted from gratitude scores (X) are obtained by solving the regression equation for a value of X. For example, for a gratitude rating score of 1, the regression equation becomes

$$Y' = +0.61(1) + 1.54 = 2.15.$$

The social support coping rating predicted from a gratitude rating of 1 is 2.15 or, rounding to one decimal place, 2.2.

Plotting the Regression Line: The regression line given by

$$Y' = +0.61X + 1.54$$

is plotted in Figure 14.8. Values of the predictor variable, gratitude (X), are placed on the abscissa, and values of the predicted variable, instrumental social support coping score (Y') are placed on the ordinate. The regression line is located on the graph by identifying the Y-intercept (1.54) and the coordinates of $\overline{X}, \overline{Y}$ (3.7 and 3.8, respectively), and drawing a straight line connecting these two points. The predicted social support coping scores for each value of X are identified by the dots on the line.

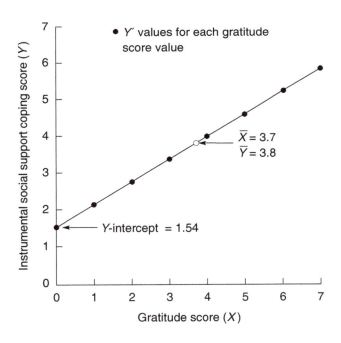

Figure 14.8 The least-squares regression line for gratitude and instrumental social support coping scores. Predicted values of the use of social support coping for each gratitude score are indicated by the dots on the regression line.

Finding the Standard Error of Estimate: The $s_{Y \cdot X}$ is found by

$$s_{Y \cdot X} = s_Y \sqrt{\left[\frac{N_{pairs} - 1}{N_{pairs} - 2}\right](1 - r_{obs}^2)}.$$

Substituting $s_Y = 1.9$, $N_{pairs} = 15$, and $r_{obs} = +.58$, we obtain

$$s_{Y \cdot X} = (1.9)\sqrt{\left[\frac{15 - 1}{15 - 2}\right][1 - (+.58)^2]} = 1.6 \text{ rounded to one decimal place.}$$

This $s_{Y \cdot X}$ is less than $s_Y = 1.9$. Knowing a person's gratitude score increases the accuracy of predicting instrumental social support coping in comparison to using $\overline{Y} = 3.8$ as a predicted value for all scores.

EXAMPLE PROBLEM

14.2

Predicting Job Performance with a Regression Equation

Problem: A major aspect of industrial psychology is predicting the work success of applicants to business and governmental organizations. Regression analysis is often used to make these predictions. Applicants may take a work-related test, and scores from the test are used to predict potential success on the job. Consider a simple example. Suppose that a business gives job applicants a work-sample test. A work-sample test is a miniature version of the job. Performance on the work-sample test (variable X) is used to predict actual job proficiency (Y') with the regression equation

$$Y' = +0.76X + 55.$$

Suppose 12 applicants are given the work-sample test, and the following scores were obtained.

Applicant	Work-Sample Test Score: X
Kevin	12
Luis	37
Mia	27
Jessica	34
Victor	17
Mackenzie	39
Jayden	24
Maya	40
Isabella	47
Allison	15
Juan	31
Grace	21

The company will not hire anyone whose predicted job proficiency is less than 75. Which applicants are eligible for hiring based on their work-sample test scores?

Solution: The solution requires applying the regression equation to each applicant's work-sample test score to obtain a predicted job-proficiency score. The predicted job-proficiency score for each applicant is shown next.

Applicant	Predicted Job-Proficiency Score: Y'
Kevin	64.1
Luis	83.1
Mia	75.5
Jessica	80.8
Victor	67.9
Mackenzie	84.6
Jayden	73.2
Maya	85.4
Isabella	90.7
Allison	66.4
Juan	78.6
Grace	71.0

The predicted scores of Kevin, Victor, Jayden, Allison, and Grace are below the required predicted score of 75; hence, these applicants would not be eligible for hiring. The scores of all other applicants are 75 or above; thus, these applicants are eligible for hiring. The regression line for $Y' = +0.76X + 55$ is illustrated in Figure 14.9. Notice that a predicted job-

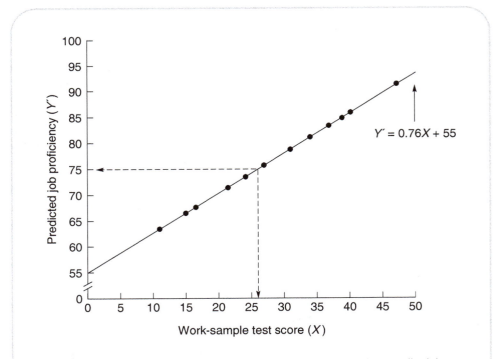

Figure 14.9 The regression line $Y' = +0.76X + 55$ used to predict job proficiency (Y') from a work-sample test (X). Predicted values of job proficiency for work-sample scores are indicated by dots on the regression line.

proficiency score of 75 corresponds to a work-sample score of 26.3. Any work-sample test score below 26.3 leads to a predicted job-proficiency score of less than 75. Accordingly, applicants with work-sample test scores less than 26.3 would not be hired.

A Further Look at Regression Toward the Mean

Earlier in the chapter, we introduced the concept of regression toward the mean. Although you may not have been familiar with this term, you are familiar with its implications. This concept implies that if two sets of scores are not perfectly correlated, then an extreme score on one measurement is likely to be associated with a less extreme score on the second measurement. Consider an example from sports. The performances of sports players are not perfectly correlated from one year to the next. For example, a baseball player's batting average from one year is not perfectly correlated with the average from the following year. In this instance, the concept of regression toward the mean implies that a player who has an outstanding year one year (i.e., has an extreme year) is likely to be closer to average the following year. Sports records provide considerable evidence for this occurrence. For the 28 years from 1980 to 2007, only four times has the same player won the American League batting championship in baseball in two consecutive years. Clearly, winning the batting championship is an extreme score, and the statistics indicate that the performance of a player the year after winning the title regresses toward the mean. Similarly, for the National Football League, no player has won the defensive player of the year award for two consecutive years in the 1980 to 2007 time period (World Almanac, 2007).

Regression toward the mean also applies to such things as test scores. For example, unless your test scores in a course are perfectly correlated, then if you score an extreme score (either low or high) on the first test in a course, you are likely to have a less extreme score on the second test, one closer to the mean. This principle applies also to research design and experimentation. Suppose a researcher selects a group of subjects who have scored very low on a test of reading comprehension, plans to give them instruction and practice on reading comprehension, and then test their reading comprehension a second time. The concept of regression toward the mean indicates that, because the subjects were selected from the very low test scores, we should expect their second test scores to be less extreme and closer to the mean of reading comprehension scores even if the instruction and practice had no effect. Obviously regression toward the mean increases the difficulty of interpreting results of research when we are using subjects who have been selected for their extreme performance on a variable. It applies also when we are using one score to predict another. Unless the r between the scores is 1.00, then extreme scores on the predictor variable (i.e., the X variable) will lead to predictions of less extreme scores on the predicted variable (i.e., Y').

Multiple Regression

Regression analysis is widely used in the behavioral sciences and in an array of practical settings. While the example problems have presented both X and Y variables, in practice, only the X variable and a regression equation for predicting Y from this X may be known, the regression equation having been developed from previous instances where both X and

Y were known. For example, a heating fuel dealer may predict how much fuel oil she needs to order for a subsequent week (variable Y) based on the mean daily temperature of the previous week (variable X). Or, a retailer may attempt to predict sales volume (variable Y) from the amount of money spent on advertising (variable X). Each of our examples used only one X variable to predict the Y variable. In practice, however, regression equations typically are more complex than those we introduced and use several X variables to predict Y. This approach is called **multiple regression** because multiple predictors are used. For example, an employer may want to predict potential employee performance as a function of an aptitude test score, a score on a standardized interview, and a score on a work-sample test. The general regression equation for representing this approach is

Multiple regression ▶ Predicting the value of Y scores using several X variables.

$$Y' = b_1X_1 + b_2X_2 + b_3X_3 + a,$$

where Y' is the predicted job performance; X_1, X_2, and X_3 are predictor variables (in this example, X_1 is the score on the aptitude test, X_2 is the score on the standardized interview, and X_3 is the score on the work-sample test); b_1, b_2, and b_3 are regression coefficients for X_1, X_2, and X_3, respectively; and a is the Y-intercept.

The regression coefficients weight each X variable in the prediction of Y. For example, if $b_1 = +0.18$, $b_2 = +0.10$, $b_3 = +0.34$, and $a = 30.3$, then the equation becomes

$$Y' = +0.18X_1 + 0.10X_2 + 0.34X_3 + 30.3.$$

If an applicant obtains an aptitude test score of 75, an interview score of 20, and a work-sample test score of 90, then

$$Y' = (0.18)(75) + (0.10)(20) + (0.34)(90) + 30.3$$
$$= 13.5 + 2.0 + 30.6 + 30.3 = 76.4.$$

Multiple regression equations are widely used for prediction in the behavioral sciences. Friedman et al. (1993), for example, used seven dimensions of childhood personality—sociability, physical energy, cheerfulness, conscientiousness, motivation, permanency of mood, and intelligence—to predict longevity. As another example, in an attempt to predict cigarette smoking among adolescents, Williams and Covington (1997) used the variables of race, age, peer involvement, family closeness, number of friends smoking, number of family members smoking, and an adolescent's perception of the health risks of smoking to develop a multiple regression equation. Obtaining the regression coefficients for these complex equations, however, requires knowledge beyond the scope of this introductory chapter.

Testing Your Knowledge 14.4

1. Personality attributes and performance of specific tasks are often related. For example, Gormly and Gormly (1986) correlated ratings of social introversion to performance on a block design test measuring spatial abilities. They found a statistically significant positive correlation: more socially introverted individuals created the required block designs more quickly. Suppose that you replicated this study rating subjects on a 9-point social introversion scale, where 1 indicates highly socially intro-

verted and 9 indicates not at all socially introverted. The amount of time in seconds each subject took to create a particular design with nine colored blocks was recorded. The scores obtained for 12 subjects were as follows:

Subject	Introversion: (X)	Block Design Times: (Y)
1	6	217
2	3	230
3	9	315
4	1	224
5	4	271
6	2	198
7	3	256
8	5	263
9	8	321
10	7	289
11	8	265
12	6	291

The mean block design time was 261.67 seconds, with $s_Y = 38.82$ seconds. The r_{obs} for these scores is statistically significant at the .05 level. Find the regression line of block design on introversion scores.

a. What is the slope of the regression line?

b. What is the Y-intercept of the regression line?

c. Write the equation for the regression line.

d. Plot a scatterplot of the introversion and block design scores. Place the regression line on this plot.

e. What is the predicted block design score (Y') for each introversion score?

f. Use the Y' given to find the residual for each subject.

g. Find the $SS_{Residual}$.

h. Find $s_{Y \cdot X}$ using the $SS_{Residual}$.

i. Compare $s_{Y \cdot X}$ to the s_Y, 38.82, for these scores. Does the use of the regression equation to predict block design scores from introversion scores reduce the error of prediction in comparison to using the mean block design score (i.e., 261.7 seconds) as the predicted value for all block design scores?

2. Bird-watchers notice that many species spend a great deal of time scanning the environment. Elgar, McKay, and Woon (1986) observed house sparrows to find the relationship between amount of scanning and feeding rate. They found a statistically significant negative correlation between the two variables. Suppose that you replicated this study observing 15 house sparrows. You recorded the number of scans of the environment each bird made per minute (variable X) and the number of pecks at food each bird made per minute (variable Y) and found the mean scan rate ($\overline{X}$) was 26.2 scans per minute with $s_X = 8.7$. The mean pecks per minute ($\overline{Y}$) was 13.3 with $s_Y = 4.5$. The r_{obs} between the two variables was $-.84$. Using the correlational formula to find b, construct the regression line of pecking rate (Y) on scans per minute (X).

    a. What is the slope of the regression line?

    b. What is the Y-intercept of the regression line?

    c. Write the equation for the regression line.

    d. What is the predicted pecking rate for a scan rate of 41 scans per minute? For 18 scans per minute?

3. Hannah obtained the highest grade on the first exam in your statistics class. What would you predict for her grade on the second exam. What principle leads you to this prediction?

Summary

▶ In a linear relation, each time that variable X changes by 1 unit, there is a constant change in variable Y.

▶ The general equation of a straight line is given by $Y = bX = a$.

▶ The slope, b, is defined as

$$b = \frac{\text{Change in value of } Y}{\text{Change in value of } X}.$$

▶ The Y-intercept, a, is the value of Y when $X = 0$.

▶ The general equation of a straight line may be used to predict Y scores from known X scores: $Y' = bX + a$. Y' represents the predicted value of Y.

▶ The residual, $Y - Y'$ is the difference between an obtained Y score and Y' predicted from X.

▶ A least-squares regression line minimizes the value of the sum of the squared residuals.

▶ The standard error of estimate is found by

$$s_{Y \cdot X} = \sqrt{\frac{SS_{\text{Residual}}}{N_{\text{pairs}} - 2}}$$

or

$$s_{Y \cdot X} = \sqrt{\frac{\sum (Y - Y')^2}{N_{\text{pairs}} - 2}}.$$

▶ The standard error of estimate indicates the average amount of error when predicting Y scores from X.

▶ Regression toward the mean is the tendency of an extreme score to be less extreme on a second measurement.

▶ Multiple regression involves using several X variables to predict variable Y.

Key Terms and Symbols

general equation of a straight line (412)
least-squares regression line (421)
linear relation (410)
multiple regression (437)

regression toward the mean (410)
residual $(Y - Y')$ (425)
slope of a straight line (b) (412)
SS_{Residual} (426)

standard error of estimate $(s_{Y \cdot X})$ (427)
Y-intercept (a) (414)
Y' (419)

Review Questions

1. Jamie received her midterm grade in her statistics class. Her instructor said that for a previous semester the following midterm and final examination grades were obtained by 10 students in the class.

| | Examination | |
Student	Midterm: X	Final: Y
1	87	84
2	89	91
3	97	96
4	80	87
5	73	66
6	85	90
7	81	79
8	74	80
9	80	89
10	89	86

a. Find the slope of the least-squares regression line for predicting final exam grades from midterm grades.

b. The r_{obs} for these scores is $+.781$, $s_X = 7.37$, and $s_Y = 8.34$. Find b using the correlational formula.

c. Find the equation of the least-squares regression line for predicting Y from X for these scores.

d. Jamie received a 77 on her midterm examination. Based on the regression line found in part c, what is her predicted final examination score?

e. What is the value of $s_{Y \cdot X}$ for this regression line?

2. An investigator observed 12 students regarding the amount of time playing computer games per week (variable X) and correlated this time with their semester grade point averages (variable Y). For a range of 0 to 15 hours per week of computer game playing, r_{obs} was $-.632$ ($p < .05$). The $s_X = 4.10$ hours, and $s_Y = 0.75$. The Y-intercept of the regression line was 3.23.

a. Find the least-squares regression line for predicting grade point average from computer game-playing time.

b. Brian plays computer games about 3 hours per week. What is his predicted grade point average?

c. The mean computer game-playing time in the sample observed was 5.1 hours per week. What is the mean grade point average for the sample?

3. Several studies have found an association between women who smoke during pregnancy and low-birth-weight infants (e.g., Centers for Disease Control and Prevention, 2001; 2004). Some research indicates a linear relationship between amount of smoking by a pregnant woman and the amount of weight loss of the neonate. This research indicates that for each cigarette smoked per day during pregnancy by the mother, the baby's birth weight is reduced by 4.3 ounces. Thus, if a mother smoked an average of two cigarettes per day during pregnancy, the baby's birth weight would be reduced by 8.6 ounces. Assume that if the pregnant mother does not smoke, the average weight of the neonate is 128 ounces.

a. Write the equation for the linear relationship for these data. (*Hint:* Both the slope and the Y-intercept are given.)

b. Plot the linear regression line on a sheet of graph paper. Place the number of cigarettes smoked (X) on the abscissa.

c. What is the predicted birth weight of a baby whose mother smoked the following number of cigarettes per day during pregnancy?

$$0 \quad 1 \quad 5 \quad 8 \quad 10 \quad 13 \quad 20$$

4. In Chapter 13, review question 1, we gave the following values of anger level scores and systolic blood pressure for 16 males.

Subject	Anger Level	Blood Pressure
1	64	170
2	30	132
3	37	129
4	39	144
5	17	145
6	29	122
7	36	124
8	34	145
9	44	137
10	32	115
11	37	127
12	47	148
13	50	148
14	41	144
15	46	133
16	61	158

a. Find the equation for the regression of blood pressure (Y) on anger level (X) for these scores.

b. What is the predicted blood pressure for each subject as a function of anger level?

c. Plot a scatterplot of anger level (on the abscissa) and blood pressure (on the ordinate). Place the regression line on this plot also.

d. What proportion of s_Y is $s_{Y \cdot X}$ for these scores?

5. Exercise 2 of Testing Your Knowledge 14.4 presented a study on the relationship of the number of scans per minute (X) and number of pecks per minute (Y) for 15 house sparrows. Suppose you made similar observations with 13 wrens and obtained the following scores.

Bird	Scans: X	Pecks: Y
1	29	12
2	34	8
3	24	14
4	14	20
5	37	11
6	22	13
7	11	23
8	33	9
9	24	11
10	30	14
11	36	9
12	20	23
13	32	7

a. What is the slope of the regression line?

b. What is the Y-intercept of the regression line?

c. Write the equation for the regression line.

d. Plot a scatterplot of the scans and pecks scores. Place the regression line on this plot.

e. Use the computational formula to find $s_{Y \cdot X}$ for this set of scores.

f. Compare $s_{Y \cdot X}$ to $s_Y = 5.41$ for these scores. Does use of the regression equation to predict pecks from scans reduce the error of prediction in comparison to using the mean number of scans (i.e., 13.4) as the predicted value for all scan scores?

6. A company uses a score on a standardized interview to predict work performance of job applicants. The regression equation used is $Y' = +1.2X + 18$, where Y' is the predicted job performance and X is the job applicant's score on the standardized interview. The company will hire only applicants whose predicted job performance is 60 or better. The standardized interview scores of eight applicants are as follows. Which of the applicants will the company hire?

Applicant	Standardized Interview Score: X
Dianne	31
Rodrigo	36
Colin	30
Maria	41
Ruben	39
Luke	29
Holly	27
Blythe	44

7. Review question 8 of Chapter 13 presented a study on the correlation of the number of hours of playing computer games per week and the first exam grade in a course for 17 students. The value of r_{obs} for the scores was $-.735$, the mean number of hours of computer gaming $(\overline{X})$ was 10.0, with s_X equal to 6.38, and the mean exam grade $(\overline{Y})$ was 76.0, with s_Y equal to 11.44. The SS_X was 652.0, and CP_{XY} was -859.0.

   a. Find the equation for the regression line for predicting exam grades from the number of hours of computer gaming for these scores.

   b. Find the predicted exam scores for students who play 4 and 15 hours of computer games per week, respectively.

   c. What is the value of $s_{Y.X}$ for these scores? What proportion of s_Y is $s_{Y.X}$ for these scores?

knowledge

PART A

A Look at a Problem   It's spring, the flowers are beginning to bloom, and the weather hits a pleasant 72 degrees. For students, such weather seems to make it harder to focus on schoolwork. This phenomenon even has an unscientific name, *spring fever*. We've all used it for an excuse when we would rather be outside than completing an assignment, attending class, studying, or working. Nicholson (2008) indicates that the "fever" of spring fever is not really a medical category, however. Nevertheless, there is evidence that spring fever is a real occurrence driven by a combination of the amount of daylight and physiological responses to sunlight. Of course, once we recognize that an event is real, the next research step is to understand the nature of that phenomenon.

Scientists try to explain an event by developing research hypotheses about the variables that may affect the occurrence of that event. Thus, suppose a psychologist hypothesized that a person's rated energy level and his or her rated mood state (happy or sad) is correlated with the amount of daylight, but is not related to the daily outdoor temperature. The psychologist found the following values of r_{obs} for each correlation. The N refers to the number of subjects on which the correlation is based.

	N	Rated Energy Level	Rated Mood State
Hours of Daylight	34	+.58	+.67
Daily Temperature	38	+.19	−.13

1. For the correlation between rated energy level and hours of daylight:
   a. Is this correlation statistically significant? How did you make this decision?
   b. If the hours of daylight increase, what does this correlation tell you about will happen with rated energy levels?
   c. What is the strength of association between rated energy levels and hours of daylight?
   d. Does this correlation support or not support the psychologist's research hypothesis about the relationship between rated energy level and hours of daylight?

2. For the correlation between rated mood state and hours of daylight:
   a. Is this correlation statistically significant? How did you make this decision?
   b. If the hours of daylight increase, what does this correlation tell you about will happen with rated mood state?
   c. What is the strength of association between rated mood state and hours of daylight?
   d. Does this correlation support or not support the psychologist's research hypothesis about the relationship between rated mood state and hours of daylight?

3. For the correlation between rated energy levels and daily temperature:
   a. Is this correlation statistically significant? How did you make this decision?
   b. If the daily temperature increases, what does this correlation tell you about will happen with rated energy levels?
   c. What is the strength of association between rated energy levels and daily temperature?

    d. Does this correlation support or not support the psychologist's research hypothesis about the relationship between rated energy level and daily temperature?

4. For the correlation between rated mood state and daily temperature:

    a. Is this correlation statistically significant? How did you make this decision?

    b. If the daily temperature increases, what does this correlation tell you about will happen with rated mood state?

    c. What is the strength of association between rated mood state and daily temperature?

    d. Does this correlation support or not support the psychologist's research hypothesis about the relationship between rated mood state and daily temperature?

PART B

Your Turn: Selecting Your Research Tools   You would like to do a study that would allow you to predict a person's rated mood state from the number of hours of daylight. With this task in mind answer the following questions.

1. What research method would you use?

2. What two sets of observations would you obtain?

3. How would you measure a person's mood state? What level of measurement would you be using?

4. What level of measurement is the number of hours of daylight in a day?

5. What statistic would you use to determine if hours of daylight and rated mood state are related?

6. If you did find that hours of daylight and rated mood state are related, what statistical method would you use to allow you to predict a person's rated mood state from the number of hours of daylight?

PART C

Using Your Statistical Tools   You conducted your study with 30 subjects who rated their mood state on a 1 to 50 scale (from very sad to very happy) and obtained the scatterplot show in Figure 14.10 for the relationship between hours of daylight and rated mood state.

1. Does there appear to be a relationship between the two variables? If you think there is a relationship, does it appear to be positive or negative? Does it seem like you might be able to predict rated mood state from the number of hours of daylight?

2. What would you estimate the r_{obs} to be between the two variables?

The following values are based on the scores presented in the scatterplot in Figure 14.10.

$N_{pairs} = 30$.

$\sum X = 348.50$.

$\sum Y = 736.00$.

$SS_X = 65.92$.

$SS_Y = 2273.47$.

$SS_{residual} = 1359.02$.

$CP_{XY} = 245.53$.

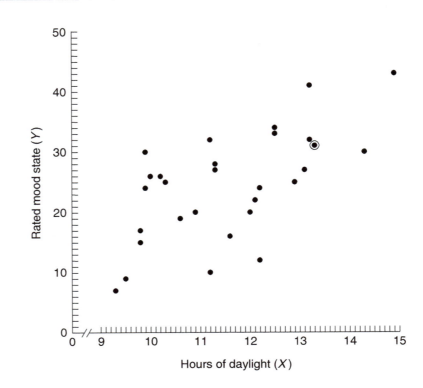

Figure 14.10 Scatterplot of the number of hours of daylight and rated mood state.

3. Use these values to calculate $\overline{X}$, $\overline{Y}$, s_X, s_Y, and $s_{Y \cdot X}$.

4. If you knew only $\overline{X}$ and $\overline{Y}$ for the scores in the scatterplot, what would you predict a person's rated mood state to be? What is the average error associated with this prediction?

5. What is r_{obs} between rated mood state and the number of hours of daylight? Is this r_{obs} statistically significant?

6. Calculate the least-squares regression line for predicting rated mood state from hours of daylight.

   a. What is the slope of this line?

   b. What is the Y-intercept for this line?

   c. If a day has 10 hours of daylight, what is the predicted rated mood state? What is the average error associated with this prediction?

   d. If a day has 14 hours of daylight, what is the predicted rated mood state? What is the average error associated with this prediction?

   e. How much does knowing the regression equation allow you to reduce the error in your prediction of rated mood state?

CHAPTER

15

Nonparametric Statistical Tests

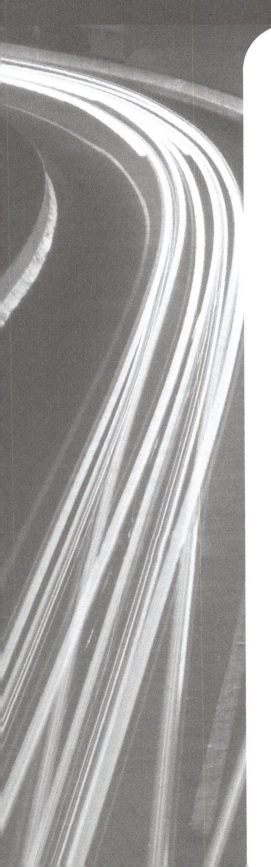

I n Chapter 11, we discussed research on the interaction of gender and self- or partner-disclosure with emotional intimacy in a romantic couple. Of course, before a couple can become emotionally intimate, they must begin with the first date. So, what does a first date look like? Are there some activities that you expect on a first date, such as getting something to eat? Are there other activities that you would find really strange for a first date, perhaps meeting your date's extended family, all 24 of them? Are there differences in what a male or female expects on a first date? This type of research poses interesting questions, but the results of such research might leave us with simply a set of categories of first-date activities, a nominal measurement. Thus, these results could not be analyzed using a parametric statistical test such as the analysis of variance. Rather, a different type of statistical test, a nonparametric statistical test, is needed.

Chapters 8 to 12 developed statistical hypothesis testing emphasizing the *t* test and the analysis of variance. Both tests are **parametric tests**, for they use sample statistics, such as $\overline{X}$, to make inferences about population parameters, such as μ. **Nonparametric statistical tests** involve hypotheses that do not state relationships about population parameters. They also make fewer assumptions about the shapes of populations than do parametric tests. For this reason, nonparametric tests are sometimes called **distribution-free tests**.

Nonparametric statistical test ▶
A statistical test involving hypotheses that do not state a relationship about a population parameter.

Recall that parametric tests assume the following:

▶ The scores in the populations sampled are normally distributed.

▶ The variances of scores in the populations are equal.

In practice, the data collected in a study may not meet these assumptions. Yet, because parametric tests are thought to be robust, researchers may use the *t* test or analysis of variance on the data even if the assumptions are not fully met.

In some instances, however, these assumptions are not met sufficiently to allow using a parametric test. For example, in measuring the reaction time of an individual, most times are likely to be short (e.g., perhaps about a half second or less). No reaction time can be less than 0 seconds, but there is no upper limit on the maximum time that may be measured. A few individuals may have very long reaction times compared to other people. Thus, a frequency distribution of reaction-time measures is likely to be positively skewed; most reaction times are very short, and a few may be much longer. Such a distribution clearly is not a normal distribution.

Parametric tests also assume that it is appropriate to compute $\overline{X}$ on the scores obtained. This requirement implies that the scores are either an interval or ratio scale of measurement. But often an experimenter simply may count the number of people displaying a certain behavior, thus obtaining frequencies of occurrence of the behavior, a nominal measurement. Or the scores obtained may represent an ordinal scale, such as rank ordering individuals on a certain personality trait. Because parametric tests require $\overline{X}$ to be calculated, they are not appropriate for use if the scores represent nominal or ordinal measurements. Thus, nonparametric tests are used when:

▶ The assumptions of parametric tests are not met, or

▶ Scores are at either the nominal or ordinal level of measurement.

Table 15.1 presents parametric tests and corresponding nonparametric tests for one-factor designs. We discuss the chi-square, Mann–Whitney *U*, and the Wilcoxon signed-ranks tests in this chapter. A nonparametric test of correlation, the Spearman rank-order correlation coefficient, was presented in Chapter 13.

TABLE 15.1	Parametric and nonparametric tests for one-factor designs as a function of type of design and scale of measurement.

		Type of Design			
		Between Subjects		**Within Subjects**	
	Scale of Measure of Data	**Two Levels**	**Three or More Levels**	**Two Levels**	**Three or More Levels**
Parametric tests	Ratio or interval	t_{ind} or between-subjects ANOVA	Between-subjects ANOVA	t_{rel} or within-subjects ANOVA	Within-subjects ANOVA
Nonparametric tests	Ordinal	Mann–Whitney U	Kruskal–Wallis ANOVA by ranks	Wilcoxon signed ranks	Friedman ANOVA by ranks
	Nominal	Chi square	Chi square		

Analysis of Frequency Data: The Chi-Square Test

Chi-square test ▶ A statistical test used to analyze nominal level of measurement scores where frequencies of occurrence of the various categories are obtained.

Many studies lead to scores that indicate only whether a behavior occurred or not. For example, when observing animals in the wild, a scientist may record only whether an animal does or does not behave in a certain way. These scores represent nominal measurements; they simply represent the occurrence of different categories of behavior. The frequency of occurrence of responses in the various categories may be counted, but an individual score indicates only whether a behavior occurred or not; it conveys no numerical information about the response. A nonparametric test, the **chi-square test** (the word *chi* rhymes with *pie*) provides an appropriate test for these scores when a between-subjects design is used and the scores are nominal measures representing only the frequency of occurrence of a response. We discuss two forms of the chi-square test, the chi-square test of independence and the chi-square test for goodness of fit.

The Chi-Square Test of Independence

Chi-square test of independence ▶ The chi square used when a score is categorized on two independent dimensions.

The **chi-square test of independence** (also called a *two-way chi square*) is used when a score is categorized on two independent dimensions. The example of first-date activities we introduced above illustrates its use. College is often a time for students to date others. What does a typical first date look like for college students? Is there a difference between what men think of as typical first-date activities compared to women? Let's suppose that we were interested in designing a study that tested whether there was a difference between how men and women view a typical first date with regard to building a future relationship. Following a method similar to Bartoli and Clark (2006), a total of 180 first-year college students, 96 females and 84 males, were asked to write down activities they considered typical of a first date with someone. The activities each student listed were then coded based on whether the activity would aid directly in further building a relationship or not. For example, activities such as talking about common interests or talking about future aspirations would be considered activities toward building a future relationship, whereas activities such as eating or watching a movie or TV would not be considered activities toward building a relationship. We hypothesize that mentioning relationship-building activities is related to gender; females will be more likely to list such activities than will males. Hypothetical results for this proposed study are presented in Table 15.2. The responses of each subject are categorized on two dimensions in this table: (1) the absence or presence of the mention of relationship-building activities and (2) the gender of the subject. The values in this table designated by O (for *observed frequency*) represent the frequency of observations in each category. For example, of the 96 females who participated, 24 of them did not mention relationship-building activities in their responses, whereas 72 did include such activities in their responses. Each subject contributed only one response to the table, the subject was either male or female, and relationship-building activities were either absent or present in their list of first-date activities.

Contingency Tables

Rows-by-columns contingency table ▶ A rows-by-columns table presenting the frequency of each category formed by the intersection of the row and column variables in the table.

Table 15.2 is called a **rows-by-columns contingency table** or a *two-way frequency table*. The rows of the table (symbolized by r) represent one category into which the subjects may be placed, either male or female in this example. The columns (symbolized by c) provide a second category, either the absence or presence of relationship-building activities in their responses. Table 15.2 is, thus, 2 rows (r = two categories of gender, male or female) by 2 columns (c = two categories of mentioning relationship-building activities, absent or present). It is called a contingency table because we are trying to find if mentioning relationship-building activities on a first date depends on the gender of the subject, either male or female. The **marginal frequencies** shown in the table are the row totals (i.e., the *row marginals*) and the column totals (i.e., the *column marginals*) of the obtained frequencies.

Marginal frequencies ▶ The row totals and the column totals of the observed frequencies in a contingency table.

Expected Frequencies

The column marginals of Table 15.2 indicate there were 60 subjects who did not mention relationship-building activities as typical first-date activities (the *absent* column marginal)

TABLE
15.2

Hypothetical data for categorization of the mention of relationship-building activities by gender for a typical first date. The values given for O are the observed frequencies, and the values given for E are the expected frequencies obtained from the marginal frequencies.

		Mention of Relationship-Building Activities		
		Absent	Present	(Marginal)
	Male	$O = 36$ $E = 28$	$O = 48$ $E = 56$	84
Gender				
	Female	$O = 24$ $E = 32$	$O = 72$ $E = 64$	96
	(Marginal)	60	120	(Total) 180

and 120 subjects who did mention such activities (the *present* column marginal). Of the total of 180 subjects, 84, or 46.7 percent (i.e., 84/180) were males (the *male* row marginal) and 96, or 53.3 percent (i.e., 96/180), were females (the *female* row marginal). If gender is not related to mentioning relationship-building first-date activities, then we expect that about 46.7 percent of the 60 people who did not mention relationship-building activities on a first date, or 28 subjects, to be male. Similarly, we expect about 53.3 percent of the 60 people who did not mention relationship-building activities on a first date, or 32 subjects, to be female. A similar expectation holds for people who mention relationship-building activities for a typical first date if there is no relation to gender. In this instance, we expect about 46.7 percent of the 120 students who mentioned relationship-building activities, or 56 students, to be male and about 53.3 percent of the 120 students who mentioned relationship-building activities, or 64 students, to be female. These values are called **expected frequencies**, the frequencies of response expected if mention of relationship-building activities on a typical first-date activity is not related to gender. Expected frequencies are indicated by the value of E (for *expected frequency*) in each cell of the table. Expected frequencies are obtained assuming there is no relationship between the two dimensions on which the subject is categorized. In this example, the expected frequencies assume that mention of relationship-building activities and gender of the student are independent of each other.

Expected frequencies ▷ The frequencies in a contingency table obtained assuming that the two dimensions of the table are independent.

The chi-square test uses expected and observed frequencies to develop a test statistic. If there is no relation between the categories in the population sampled, then the observed frequencies should be about the same as the expected frequencies. Large differences between the observed and the expected frequencies should occur only rarely by chance if the column and row variables are not associated. But if the column and row variables are related in the population sampled, then the observed frequencies should differ from the expected frequencies by larger amounts. For example, if the frequency of mention of relationship-building activities on a typical first date is related to gender as hypothesized, then it is likely that there will be fewer males mentioning relationship-building activities on a typical first date than the 56 expected by chance and more males who do not mention them than the 28 expected by chance. Similarly, if the hypothesized relationship exists, then it is also likely that more females will mention relationship-building activities as a typical first-date activity than the 64 expected and fewer than the 32 expected by chance to not mention such activities.

The χ^2 Statistic

The chi-square (symbolized as χ^2) test measures the difference of the obtained frequencies from the expected frequencies with the test statistic:

$$\chi^2 = \sum_{r=1}^{r} \sum_{c=1}^{c} \frac{(O_{rc} - E_{rc})^2}{E_{rc}},$$

where $\chi = chi$, the twenty-second letter of the Greek alphabet.

       O_{rc} = observed frequency in the rc cell, where r represents the row number and c the column number.

       E_{rc} = expected frequency of the rc cell.

       r = number of categories of the row variable ($r = 2$, gender in this example).

       c = number of categories of the columns variable ($c = 2$, absence or presence of mention of relationship-building activities in this example).

The double summation signs and limits (i.e., $\sum\limits_{r=1}^{r}\sum\limits_{c=1}^{c}$) indicate that the $(O_{rc} - E_{rc})^2/E_{rc}$ values are summed over all rows and columns of the contingency table. Thus, we can simplify this formula to

$$\chi^2 = \sum \frac{(O - E)^2}{E},$$

realizing that the χ^2 is always summed over all the rows and columns in the contingency table. We will use this formula for all the example problems.

Assumptions for the Use of the Chi-Square Test

A chi-square test of independence may be used on a contingency table of any size (e.g., 2×3, 3×4, or 4×4). Several assumptions apply to its use, however.

▶ Each subject may contribute only one response to the contingency table.

▶ The number of responses obtained should be large enough so that no expected frequency is less than 10 in a 2×2 contingency table or less than 5 in a contingency table larger than 2×2. If this condition is not met, then either more responses should be collected or an alternative test, such as the Fisher exact test, should be used.

Further details regarding use of alternative tests for frequency data may be found in most advanced statistics texts.

Statistical Hypothesis Testing with χ^2

Using χ^2 to determine whether expectations on relationship-building activities on a first date and gender are related requires statistical hypothesis testing following the familiar steps:

▶ A null hypothesis, H_0, and an alternative hypothesis, H_1, are formulated. The null hypothesis provides the sampling distribution of the χ^2 statistic.

▶ A significance level is selected.

▶ A critical value of χ^2, identified as χ^2_{crit}, is found from the sampling distribution of χ^2 in Appendix C.7.

▶ Using the value of χ^2_{crit}, a rejection region is located in the sampling distribution of χ^2.

▶ χ^2_{obs} is calculated from the frequencies in the contingency table.

▶ A decision to reject or not reject H_0 is made on the basis of whether χ^2_{obs} falls into the rejection region.

▶ The statistical decisions are related to the research hypothesis.

Statistical Hypotheses

Null Hypothesis. The null hypothesis under which the sampling distribution of χ^2 is developed and under which expected frequencies for each cell are found is

H_0: The row variable and the column variable are independent in the population.

For the example study, H_0 may be stated specifically as

H_0: The mention of relationship-building activities on a first date is independent of the gender of the subject.

Alternative Hypothesis.   The alternative hypothesis is

H_1:   The row and column variables are related in the population.

For the example study, H_1 may be stated specifically as

H_1:   The mention of relationship-building activities on a first date is related to the gender of the subject.

Selecting a Significance Level
The process of selecting a significance level is identical to that discussed in earlier chapters. In line with common practice, we choose $\alpha = .05$.

Finding χ^2_{crit} and Locating a Rejection Region

Degrees of Freedom of χ^2.   The specific sampling distribution of χ^2 and, thus, the value of χ^2_{crit} depends on the degrees of freedom of the statistic. The *df* for χ^2 are given by

$$\textbf{Degrees of freedom} = (r - 1)(c - 1),$$

where r represents the number of rows and c represents the number of columns in the contingency table. For the example, $r = 2$ and $c = 2$; thus, $df = (2 - 1)(2 - 1)$, which equals 1. Values of χ^2_{crit} for $\alpha = .05$ and $.01$ from the sampling distribution of χ^2 at various *df* are given in Appendix C.7. The critical value of χ^2 for 1 *df* and $\alpha = .05$ from Appendix C.7 is 3.84146, or 3.84, rounded to two decimal places.

Locating a Rejection Region.   If the null hypothesis is true and mention of relationship-building activities is independent of gender, then χ^2_{obs} should be relatively small; the expected and observed frequencies for each cell of the contingency table should be much alike. On the other hand, if H_1 is true and the row variable is related to the column variable, then χ^2_{obs} should become larger because the expected and observed frequencies will differ from each other. Consequently, relatively large values of χ^2_{obs} should be rare if the null hypothesis is true, but common if the alternative hypothesis is true. Thus, a value of χ^2_{obs} equal to or greater than χ^2_{crit} is statistically significant at the value of α selected. Accordingly, for the example, if χ^2_{obs} is equal to or greater than 3.84, it falls into the rejection region and will lead to rejection of H_0 and acceptance of H_1.

Calculating χ^2_{obs}
Calculating χ^2_{obs} requires knowing both the observed and expected frequencies of responses. The expected frequencies for each cell of a contingency table are obtained from the marginal frequencies by

$$\textbf{Expected frequency of a cell} = \frac{\textbf{(Row marginal for cell)(Column marginal for cell)}}{\textbf{Total number of responses}}.$$

For example, the expected frequency for the males/absence of relationship-building activities (row 1, column 1) is found by:

$$E_{11} = \frac{\text{(Row 1 marginal)(Column 1 marginal)}}{\text{Total}} \quad \text{or}$$

$$E_{11} = \frac{(84)(60)}{180} = \frac{5040}{180} = 28.$$

This expected frequency is the E in the males/absence of relationship-building activities cell of Table 15.2.

After expected frequencies for each cell are obtained, χ^2_{obs} is found using the statistic

$$\chi^2_{obs} = \sum \frac{(O - E)^2}{E}.$$

To calculate χ^2_{obs}:

▶ Subtract the expected frequency (E) from the observed frequency (O) for each cell.
▶ Square each $O - E$ difference.
▶ Divide each squared $O - E$ difference by the expected frequency of the cell.
▶ Sum the resulting $(O - E)^2/E$ values over all cells in the contingency table to obtain χ^2_{obs}.

The numerical value of χ^2_{obs} for the frequencies shown in Table 15.2 is calculated as follows:

$$
\begin{aligned}
\chi^2_{obs} &= \left[\frac{(36 - 28)^2}{28}\right] + \left[\frac{(24 - 32)^2}{32}\right] + \left[\frac{(48 - 56)^2}{56}\right] + \left[\frac{(72 - 64)^2}{64}\right], \\
&= \frac{8^2}{28} + \frac{(-8^2)}{32} + \frac{(-8^2)}{56} + \frac{8^2}{64}, \\
&= 2.286 + 2.000 + 1.143 + 1.000, \\
&= 6.43 \text{ rounded to two decimal places.}
\end{aligned}
$$

Decisions About the Statistical Hypotheses

The χ^2_{obs} of 6.43 is larger than χ^2_{crit} of 3.84 and, thus, falls into the rejection region. Accordingly, H_0 is rejected and H_1 is accepted. There is a statistically significant relationship between the row and column variables.

Conclusion from the Test

The rejection of H_0 indicates that mention of first-date relationship-building activities is associated with gender. The nature of the relationship is seen by examining Table 15.2: a greater than chance frequency of females mention relationship-building activities during a first date, and a greater than chance frequency of males do not mention such activities.

EXAMPLE PROBLEM

15.1

Using the Chi-Square Test with a 3 × 2 Contingency Table

Problem: Being a firstborn often appears to confer certain advantages to a child. Several studies from the past have indicated that firstborn children typically perform better on academic-type measures than do later-born children, and Eisenman (1987) found a relationship between birth order and creativity among college males. Firstborn males' scores were more frequently above the median on creativity, and later-born males' creativity scores were more frequently below the median in his sample. Suppose you want to see if what Eisenman found is still true today by testing 100 firstborn and 100 later-born

10-year-old children by asking them for creative uses of common objects. You categorize their responses as being either in the top, middle, or bottom one-third of the scores for creativity. The categorization by birth order and creativity test score resulted in the following observed frequencies.

		Birth Order	
		Firstborn	Later Born
Creativity Test Score	Top One-third	47	29
	Middle One-third	29	35
	Bottom One-third	24	36

Is there a relationship between birth order and creativity in children? Use a .05 significance level.

Solution: One categorization of a subject in this study is birth order with two levels, firstborn and later born. The second categorization was based on the creativity test score being in the top, middle, or bottom one-third of scores for creativity. Each subject contributes only one score or count to the frequency; hence, the chi-square test is an appropriate statistical test for these data.

Statistic to Be Used: χ^2.

Assumptions for Use:

1. Each subject contributes only one response to the contingency table.
2. No expected frequency will be less than 5. This minimum expected frequency applies because the contingency table, a 3×2, is greater than a 2×2.

Statistical Hypotheses:
H_0:   Birth order and creativity are independent in the population sampled.
H_1:   Birth order and creativity are related in the population sampled.

Significance Level: $\alpha = .05$.

df: $df = (r - 1)(c - 1) = (3 - 1)(2 - 1) = 2$.

Critical Value: $\chi^2_{\text{crit}}(2) = 5.99146$ from Appendix C.7 or 5.99 rounded to two decimal places.

Rejection Region: Values of χ^2_{obs} equal to or greater than 5.99.

Calculation: The formula for χ^2_{obs} requires finding expected frequencies; to do so we must find the marginal frequencies. The observed frequencies (indicated by O), the expected frequencies (indicated by E), and the marginal frequencies are provided in the following contingency table:

| | | Birth Order | | |
		Firstborn	Later Born	(Row Marginals)
	Top One-third	$O = 47$	$O = 29$	76
		$E = 38$	$E = 38$	
Creativity	Middle One-third	$O = 29$	$O = 35$	64
Test		$E = 32$	$E = 32$	
Score	Bottom One-third	$O = 24$	$O = 36$	60
		$E = 30$	$E = 30$	
	(Column Marginals)	100	100	(Total) 200

Column marginals are obtained by summing the observed frequencies in each column. Row marginals are obtained analogously by summing the observed frequencies in each row. Given the marginal frequencies, expected frequencies are found using

$$\text{Expected frequency of a cell} = \frac{(\text{Row marginal for cell})(\text{Column marginal for cell})}{\text{Total number of responses}}.$$

Expected frequencies for each cell of the table are then as follows:

$$\text{Firstborn—top } \tfrac{1}{3} \text{ cell:} \quad E_{11} = \frac{(76)(100)}{200} = \frac{7600}{200} = 38,$$

$$\text{Later born—top } \tfrac{1}{3} \text{ cell:} \quad E_{12} = \frac{(76)(100)}{200} = \frac{7600}{200} = 38,$$

$$\text{Firstborn—middle } \tfrac{1}{3} \text{ cell:} \quad E_{21} = \frac{(64)(100)}{200} = \frac{6400}{200} = 32,$$

$$\text{Later born—middle } \tfrac{1}{3} \text{ cell:} \quad E_{22} = \frac{(64)(100)}{200} = \frac{6400}{200} = 32,$$

$$\text{Firstborn—bottom } \tfrac{1}{3} \text{ cell:} \quad E_{31} = \frac{(60)(100)}{200} = \frac{6000}{200} = 30,$$

$$\text{Later born—bottom } \tfrac{1}{3} \text{ cell:} \quad E_{32} = \frac{(60)(100)}{200} = \frac{6000}{200} = 30.$$

The value of χ^2_{obs} is found by

$$\chi^2_{\text{obs}} = \sum \frac{(O - E)^2}{E}.$$

Substituting numerical values,

$$\chi^2_{\text{obs}} = \frac{(47 - 38)^2}{38} + \frac{(29 - 38)^2}{38} + \frac{(29 - 32)^2}{32} + \frac{(35 - 32)^2}{32} + \frac{(24 - 30)^2}{30} + \frac{(36 - 30)^2}{30},$$

$$= 2.13 + 2.13 + 0.28 + 0.28 + 1.20 + 1.20,$$

$$= 7.22.$$

Decision: The $\chi^2_{obs} = 7.22$ is greater than $\chi^2_{crit} = 5.99$; thus, it falls into the rejection region. We reject H_0 and accept H_1.

Conclusion: Birth order and creativity are related in the population of children sampled. By examining the table of observed and expected frequencies, we see that firstborn children's scores occur more frequently and later-born children's scores occur less frequently in the top one-third of the scores than expected by chance. We notice also that firstborn children's scores occur less frequently and later-born children's more frequently in the bottom one-third of scores than a chance hypothesis predicts.

The Chi-Square Test for Goodness of Fit

Chi-square test for goodness of fit ▶ The chi square used when a score is categorized on only one dimension.

In the chi-square test of independence, subjects were categorized on two different dimensions, for example whether there was a difference between male and female college students on mentioning relationship-building activities on a first date. With the **chi-square test for goodness of fit**, scores are categorized on only one dimension or variable. Consider an example.

Many people believe that unusual behavior is more likely to occur during a full moon. As a test for empirical evidence to support this belief, suppose that you categorized the visits of new clients to a community health unit over a one-year period by lunar phases and found the following distribution of visits.

Lunar Phase			
Full Moon	New Moon	First Quarter	Third Quarter
62	50	60	56

Do new visits vary with the phase of the moon? The chi-square goodness of fit test may be used to answer this question.

The observed frequencies categorize behavior only by lunar phase. To use a chi-square test, we need to find expected frequencies of visits for each lunar phase. Because we do not have row and column marginals to obtain expected frequencies, we must have some other basis for predicting expected frequencies. For this example, we use the following reasoning to obtain the expected frequencies. If visits to a community health unit are unrelated to phase of the moon, then the frequency of new visits should be equal in each phase, with any observed differences reflecting only sampling error. This reasoning may be expressed in the null hypothesis:

H_0:   New visits to a community health unit and phase of the moon are independent in the population sampled.

The alternative hypothesis, then, is

H_1:   New visits to a community health unit and phase of the moon are related in the population sampled.

If this alternative hypothesis is true, then new visits should not be equal among the lunar phases. But if H_0 is true, then one-fourth of the new visits should occur in each lunar phase.

Hence, expected frequencies of new visits may be obtained by dividing the total frequency of new visits by 4, the number of lunar phases. Applying this reasoning to our example, there are 228 total new visits, so the expected frequency for each phase is $\frac{228}{4}$ or 57. The observed and expected frequencies for each lunar phase are then as follows:

Lunar Phase			
Full Moon	New Moon	First Quarter	Third Quarter
$O = 62$	$O = 50$	$O = 60$	$O = 56$
$E = 57$	$E = 57$	$E = 57$	$E = 57$

Chi square may be obtained from these data by

$$\chi^2_{obs} = \sum \frac{(O - E)^2}{E}.$$

Accordingly, applying the formula to each cell of the contingency table and summing over all cells, we obtain

$$\chi^2_{obs} = \frac{(62 - 57)^2}{57} + \frac{(50 - 57)^2}{57} + \frac{(60 - 57)^2}{57} + \frac{(56 - 57)^2}{57},$$

$$= \frac{(5)^2}{57} + \frac{(-7)^2}{57} + \frac{(3)^2}{57} + \frac{(-1)^2}{57},$$

$$= \frac{25}{57} + \frac{49}{57} + \frac{9}{57} + \frac{1}{57},$$

$$= \frac{84}{57} = 1.47.$$

The degrees of freedom for this χ^2_{obs} are $c - 1$, where c represents the number of categories used. For the example, $c = 4$; thus, $df = 4 - 1 = 3$. The critical value of χ^2 for 3 df and $\alpha = .05$ is given in Appendix C.7; $\chi^2_{crit} (3) = 7.81$ rounded to two decimal places. $\chi^2_{obs} = 1.47$ is less than χ^2_{crit} and does not fall into the rejection region. We fail to reject the null hypothesis. There is no evidence that the frequency of new visits to a community health unit is related to phases of the moon in the population sampled.

The assumptions for the chi-square goodness of fit test are similar to those for the chi-square test of independence; each subject must contribute only one observation to the data, and the expected frequencies should not be less than 10 if there are only two categories or not less than 5 if there are three or more categories.

Reporting the Results of the Chi-Square Test

The *Publication Manual of the American Psychological Association* (American Psychological Association, 2001) requires that a report of the chi-square test include the *df* and the sample size on which χ^2_{obs} is based. To illustrate, we use the example of the chi-square test for independence on the dating activity example.

Table 1 presents the observed frequencies for the absence or presence of mention of relationship-building dating activities on a first date by gender. With alpha equal to .05, a chi-square test on these frequencies was statistically significant, χ^2 (1, N = 180) = 6.43, p < .05. Females were more likely to mention relationship-building activities for a typical first date than were males.

Table 1

Hypothetical Data for Categorization of the Mention of Relationship-Building Activities by Gender for a Typical First Date

Gender	Mention of relationship-building activities	
	Absent	Present
Male	36	48
Female	24	72

In this report:

Table 1	Provides the observed frequencies of the responses.
α = .05	Indicates the significance level selected for the test.
χ^2 (1, N = 180)	Identifies the test statistic as the chi square. The 1 in parentheses indicates the test was based on 1 *df*, and the N = 180 gives the total sample size.
= 6.43	Gives the value of χ^2_{obs} (not the χ^2_{crit} value of Appendix C.7).
p < .05	Indicates that

    a. the probability of χ^2_{obs} if H_0 is true is less than or equal to .05. This value is the probability of χ^2_{obs} or an even more extreme value of χ^2_{obs} if H_0 is true; it may not be the same as the value of α selected.

    b. "H_0: The mention of relationship-building activities is independent of the gender of the subject" was rejected.

       "H_1: The mention of relationship-building activities on a first date is related to the gender of the subject" was accepted.

Testing Your Knowledge 15.1

1. Define: c, chi-square test, expected frequencies, marginal frequencies, nonparametric test, observed frequencies, parametric test, r, rows-by-columns contingency table, two-way frequency table.

2. Under what circumstances is a nonparametric test used to analyze data from an experiment?

3. What form of data is suitable for analysis by the chi-square test?

4. What is represented by the columns of a rows-by-columns contingency table?

5. What is represented by the rows of a rows-by-columns contingency table?

6. The following are values of χ^2_{obs} for various degrees of freedom (given in parentheses).

$$\chi^2_{obs}(2) = 7.26 \qquad \chi^2_{obs}(4) = 8.33$$
$$\chi^2_{obs}(7) = 14.19 \qquad \chi^2_{obs}(20) = 26.94$$

For each value of χ^2_{obs} and df, find the value of χ^2_{crit} at the .05 level. Then indicate whether χ^2_{obs} falls into the rejection region and the decisions you make concerning H_0 and H_1.

7. For each of the following contingency tables, calculate expected frequencies; then χ^2_{obs} and indicate whether it is statistically significant at the .05 level. The values in each cell represent observed frequencies.

a.

		Column	
		1	2
Row	1	12	32
	2	16	38

b.

		Column	
		1	2
Row	1	27	22
	2	17	46

c.

		Column	
		1	2
Row	1	33	66
	2	27	14

8. Complete the following problem using the chi-square test following the format illustrated in the example problem. Use a .05 significance level. Have you ever run a traffic stop sign while driving? Perhaps not, but no doubt you have seen others do so. How frequently do drivers fail to stop for stop signs, and does the frequency of occurrence of such behaviors depend on the time of day or day of the week? Suppose that a researcher investigated this problem by observing the number of vehicles not stopping for a stop sign at an intersection. He observed traffic from 10:00 A.M. to 11:00 A.M. and from 2:00 P.M. to 3:00 P.M. on Tuesday, Wednesday, and Thursday of one week. Car licenses were noted, and each car was counted only on its first trip through the intersection for the week. Suppose that the investigator reported the following frequency of vehicles ignoring the stop sign during the two times on each of the days of the week observed.

	Day of Week		
	Tuesday	Wednesday	Thursday
Time 10:00 to 11:00 A.M.	38	46	58
2:00 to 3:00 P.M.	46	54	63

Is there a relationship between day of the week and time of day with respect to drivers ignoring stop signs?

9. Complete the following problem using the chi-square test following the format illustrated in the example problem. Use a .05 significance level. For quite some time, psychologists have hypothesized that one cause for eating disorders among females is the many cues that stress thinness as desirable for females. Smith, Waldorf, and Trembath (1990) investigated one form of cue, the personal ad, to see if these ads indicated weight as an important characteristic of a desired partner. They hypothesized that ads placed by males seeking females would more likely indicate a weight requirement than would an ad placed by a female seeking a male. To test this hypothesis, they examined a set of personal ads from newspapers and categorized them by gender of the person placing the ad and whether or not the ad expressed a weight preference. The hypothesized relationship was found. A psychologist was interested in seeing if similar findings are true with Internet personal ads and found the following hypothetical frequencies from an Internet dating site. Does the hypothesized relationship exist in these scores?

	Preference for Weight Indicated	
	Yes	No
Ad Placed by Male	89	186
Ad Placed by Female	6	219

Mann–Whitney *U* Test

Mann–Whitney *U* test ▶
A nonparametric test for a between-subjects design using two levels of an independent variable with scores representing at least ordinal measurement.

The **Mann–Whitney *U* test** is a nonparametric test for a between-subjects design using two levels of an independent variable with scores representing at least ordinal measurement. We develop the Mann–Whitney *U* test using an example of research on perceiving reversible figures (Strueber & Stadler, 1999).

Reversible figures are stimuli that offer two or more possible perceptual organizations. For example, Figure 15.1 illustrates the Schroeder staircase. This figure has two possible perceptual organizations: in one, a set of stairs appears normal; in the other, the stairs seem upside down. The stairs will reverse perceptually if you view them for a while. If attention and memory are required to reverse the perception from one organization to the other, then an additional task that occupies attention and memory should lengthen the time

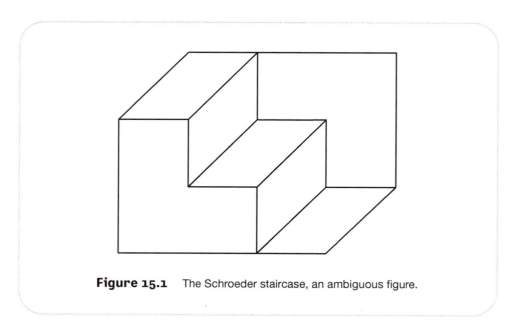

Figure 15.1   The Schroeder staircase, an ambiguous figure.

needed to reverse the perception. To test this hypothesis, suppose we created two equivalent groups of subjects. Both groups viewed the Schroeder staircase and reported when they had seen both organizations of the stimulus. The independent variable was the type of interfering task. Subjects in the control group (A_1) simply viewed the figure and reported the reversal. Subjects in the experimental group (A_2) counted backward by threes from a three-digit number, a task requiring both attention and memory, while they viewed the stimulus. If perceiving reversal of the figure also requires attention and memory, then counting backward should interfere with perception of the figure and delay the reports of a reversal. The amount of time it took each subject to report a reversal was recorded. This time is called the *latency* of a response. If a subject did not report a reversal at the end of 2 minutes, the test was stopped and the subject assigned an infinite (∞) latency.

Table 15.3 presents hypothetical data for this experiment, with nine people in each of the two groups. The scores are shown in order of increasing latency in each group, although they would not occur in this order as they actually were recorded from subjects. Notice that for the experimental group, one subject did not report a reversal within 2 minutes. This subject was assigned an infinite latency without a numerical value. Because both the t test and the analysis of variance require numerical values from each subject, they cannot be used to analyze these data if this subject's score is included. The Mann–Whitney U test, however, only requires that scores be ranked, and an infinite latency can be ranked. Thus, the scores are analyzed with the Mann–Whitney U test.

Assumptions of the Mann–Whitney *U* Test

The assumptions applying to the U test are the following:

▸ Each subject contributes only one score to the data. This assumption is met by the scores of our example problem.

▸ Scores are at least ordinal measurement and represent a continuous variable. In many instances, as in the example problem, scores will be either interval or ratio measurements, and these measures will be converted to ranks for application of the U test.

TABLE
15.3

Hypothetical perceptual reversal latencies (in seconds) of the Schroeder staircase figure. Subjects in the control group simply viewed the figure. Subjects in the experimental group counted backward by threes while viewing the figure.

Group	
Control (A_1)	Experimental (A_2)
2	4
5	10
6	11
8	12
9	14
13	17
15	85
21	98
42	∞^a

For ease of discussion, the scores are presented in order of increasing latency in each treatment group.

[a]This score represents an infinite reversal latency; this subject did not see the reversal within the two-minute time limit.

Statistical Hypothesis Testing with the Mann–Whitney U

We first present a conceptual overview of the U test and then a computational format. Both approaches require ranking scores to develop a test statistic and a sampling distribution of that statistic. This ranking is done even if the scores represent an interval or ratio measurement; the scores are converted to ordinal measurement by ranking them.

Ranking Scores

The first step in ranking the scores is to combine the scores of both groups (for a total of N scores) and then place the scores in order of increasing magnitude from smallest to largest. This procedure is shown in row 1 of Table 15.4 for the data of Table 15.3. In performing the

TABLE	
15.4	Rank ordering scores of Table 15.3

1.	Latency scores ordered from smallest to largest	2	4	5	6	8	9	10	11	12	13	14	15	17	21	42	85	98	∞
2.	Group identity*	1	2	1	1	1	1	2	2	2	1	2	1	2	1	1	2	2	2
3.	Rank	1	2	3	4	5	6	7	8	9	10	11	12	13	14	15	16	17	18
4.	Number of times an A_1 score precedes A_2 scores	9		8	8	8	8				5		4		3	3			
5.	Number of times an A_2 score precedes A_1 scores		8					4	4	4		3		2					

*A 1 indicates the score is from group A_1 control; 2 indicates the score is from group A_2, experimental.

ranking, the group identity of the scores, that is, whether the score is from the control or experimental group, is maintained (see row 2 of Table 15.4). Then, the ranks from 1 to N are assigned to the scores, giving the smallest score the rank of 1 and the largest score the rank of N. This ranking is shown in row 3 of Table 15.4. Often, there may be tied scores, such as two people obtaining a latency of 12 seconds. Table 15.5 describes the procedure for dealing with such ties, and example problem 15.2 illustrates this procedure.

The *U* Statistic

The *U* statistic is the number of times that the rank of a score in one group precedes the rank of a score in the other group. This calculation is illustrated in rows 4 and 5 of Table 15.4. For example, the score of 2 (shown in row 1) from the A_1 group (identified in row 2) precedes all the A_2 scores in rank (given in row 3). Thus, this score precedes nine of the A_2 scores in rank. Scores of 5, 6, 8, and 9 from the A_1 group each precede eight of the scores in the A_2 group in rank. Row 4 of Table 15.4 presents the number of times that an A_1 score precedes an A_2 score in rank. Examine the numerical values in this row to be sure you understand how they were obtained. The total number of times that an A_1 score precedes an A_2 score in rank is 56, the total of the values in row 4 (i.e., $9 + 8 + 8 + 8 + 8 + 5 + 4 + 3 + 3 = 56$). Thus, the value of $U_{A_1 \text{ obs}}$ (for the U observed on group A_1) is 56.

There is also a value of U for the A_2 group. This value represents the number of times that the rank of an A_2 score precedes the rank of an A_1 score. Row 5 of Table 15.4 indicates the number of times that an A_2 score precedes an A_1 score in rank. The sum of the values in this row (i.e., $8 + 4 + 4 + 4 + 3 + 2 = 25$) provides $U_{A_2 \text{ obs}} = 25$.

Characteristics of the *U* Statistic

If a treatment has no effect, then it is expected that, when the scores are combined and ordered as they are in Table 15.4, scores from each group will be approximately equally distributed over the rankings. We do not expect the scores from one group to be represented exclusively among the lower ranks and the scores of the other condition to be exclusively among the higher ranks. Consequently, the value of $U_{A_1 \text{ obs}}$ should be about equal to $U_{A_2 \text{ obs}}$. For example, if the treatment had no effect in the example, then $U_{A_1 \text{ obs}}$ and $U_{A_2 \text{ obs}}$ would each equal about 40. If the treatment had an exceptionally strong effect, however, and all the A_1 scores had lower ranks than the A_2 scores, then $U_{A_1 \text{ obs}}$ would be 81 and $U_{A_2 \text{ obs}}$ would be equal to 0. The values of $U_{A_1 \text{ obs}}$ and $U_{A_2 \text{ obs}}$ are perfectly inversely related. As $U_{A_1 \text{ obs}}$ increases, $U_{A_2 \text{ obs}}$ decreases by an equal amount. Hence, only one value of U, the smaller value, is used in a statistical test. We can easily determine if the smaller value has been calculated by using the relation

$$U_{A_2 \text{ obs}} = n_{A_1} n_{A_2} - U_{A_1 \text{ obs}},$$

where n_{A_1} is the number of scores in group A_1 and n_{A_2} is the number of scores in group A_2. In the example, $U_{A_2 \text{ obs}}$ is found from $U_{A_1 \text{ obs}}$ by

$$U_{A_2 \text{ obs}} = (9)(9) - 56 = 81 - 56 = 25,$$

and 25 is the smaller of the two values of U for the data of Table 15.3. Thus, $U_{\text{obs}} = 25$.

This U statistic is used in a statistical hypothesis test by following the steps of statistical hypothesis testing.

Statistical Hypotheses

Null Hypothesis.   The null hypothesis under which the sampling distribution of U is developed is

H_0:   The population distribution of A_1 scores is identical to the population distribution of A_2 scores.

If H_0 is true, then the value of $U_{A_1 \text{ obs}}$ should be about the same as $U_{A_2 \text{ obs}}$.

Alternative Hypothesis.   The alternative hypothesis for the U test is

H_1:   The population distribution of A_1 scores is not identical to the population distribution of A_2 scores.

If H_1 is true, then $U_{A_1 \text{ obs}}$ and $U_{A_2 \text{ obs}}$ should differ from each other.

Sampling Distributions and Critical Values of *U*

The sampling distribution of U varies with n_{A_1} and n_{A_2}. To simplify the use of the U statistic, tables of its sampling distribution and critical values of U at the .01 and .05 levels have been developed for various sizes of n_{A_1} and n_{A_2}. Because the maximum value of U is determined by n_{A_1} and n_{A_2}, tables of the sampling distribution of U present only the smaller of the two values of U that may be obtained from a study. The sampling distribution for the smaller value of U for groups ranging in size from 1 to 20 for $\alpha = .01$ and $\alpha = .05$ is presented in Appendix C.8. The values in this table present the critical value of U, identified as U_{crit}, for the smaller U_{obs}. Values of the smaller U_{obs} *less than or equal to* U_{crit} are statistically significant for the value of α selected. Notice that, in contrast to the t, F, and χ^2 statistics, the rejection region for U_{obs} consists of values of the smaller U_{obs} that are less than or equal to U_{crit}. For the example data, $n_{A_1} = 9$ and $n_{A_2} = 9$; thus, $U_{\text{crit}} = 17$ at the .05 significance level.

Decisions about the Statistical Hypotheses

Decisions about the statistical hypotheses are made using the smaller of the two values of U_{obs}, as follows:

Value of Smaller U_{obs}	Statistical Decision
Less than or equal to U_{crit}	Reject H_0 Accept H_1
Greater than U_{crit}	Do not reject H_0 Do not accept H_1

For our example of the reversal latency scores of Table 15.3, $U_{A_1 \text{ obs}} = 56$ and $U_{A_2 \text{ obs}} = 25$. $U_{A_2 \text{ obs}}$ is the smaller of the two values, and this value is used as U_{obs} for the statistical hypothesis test. $U_{\text{obs}} = 25$ is larger than $U_{\text{crit}} = 17$. Accordingly, the value of U_{obs} does not fall into the rejection region; we fail to reject H_0, and we do not accept H_1.

Conclusion from the Test

Failing to reject H_0 leads to the conclusion that there is no evidence to indicate that the population distribution of the control group scores differs from the population distribution of experimental group scores in the example. Counting backward did not change the latency of a reversal in comparison to the control condition.

Computational Formulas for U

The approach taken in Table 15.4 to obtain U_{A_1} and U_{A_2} is cumbersome, but it illustrates what U_{A_1} and U_{A_2} represent. For computational purposes, however, simplified formulas have been developed.

$U_{A_1 \text{ obs}}$

The value of $U_{A_1 \text{ obs}}$ is found from the formula

$$U_{A_1 \text{ obs}} = n_{A_1}n_{A_2} + \frac{n_{A_1}(n_{A_1} + 1)}{2} - \Sigma R_{A_1},$$

where n_{A_1} = number of scores in group A_1.
n_{A_2} = number of scores in the A_2 group.
ΣR_{A_1} = sum of the ranks assigned to scores in group A_1.

The ΣR_{A_1} is obtained by adding the ranks assigned to the A_1 scores in row 3 of Table 15.4. For the example, the ranks of the scores in the A_1 group are 1, 3, 4, 5, 6, 10, 12, 14, and 15. The sum of these ranks is 70; thus, $\Sigma R_{A_1} = 70$. Substituting values into the equation for U_{A_1} provides

$$U_{A_1 \text{ obs}} = (9)(9) + \frac{9(9 + 1)}{2} - 70 = 56.$$

$U_{A_2 \text{ obs}}$

The value of $U_{A_2 \text{ obs}}$ is obtained from the formula

$$U_{A_2 \text{ obs}} = n_{A_1}n_{A_2} + \frac{n_{A_2}(n_{A_2} + 1)}{2} - \Sigma R_{A_2},$$

where ΣR_{A_2} is the sum of the ranks assigned to scores in A_2. For the example, the ranks of the scores in the A_2 group are 2, 7, 8, 9, 11, 13, 16, 17, and 18 (see row 3 in Table 15.4). The sum of these ranks is 101; thus, $\Sigma R_{A_2} = 101$. Substituting into the formula,

$$U_{A_2 \text{ obs}} = (9)(9) + \frac{9(9 + 1)}{2} - 101 = 25.$$

| TABLE 15.5 | | Using the Mann–Whitney U test with computational formulas |

Step 1		Rank order the combined scores of both groups from the smallest score (rank $= 1$) to the largest score (rank $= N$). Maintain the group designation (A_1 or A_2) of each score. Assign tied scores the mean of the ranks they would have been assigned if they were not tied.
Step 2		Find $\sum R_{A_1}$ and $\sum R_{A_2}$.
Step 3		Compute $U_{A_1 \text{ obs}}$.

$$U_{A_1 \text{ obs}} = n_{A_1} n_{A_2} + \frac{n_{A_1}(n_{A_1} + 1)}{2} - \sum R_{A_1}.$$

Step 4		Compute $U_{A_2 \text{ obs}}$.

$$U_{A_2 \text{ obs}} = n_{A_1} n_{A_2} + \frac{n_{A_2}(n_{A_2} + 1)}{2} - \sum R_{A_2}$$

or

$$U_{A_2 \text{ obs}} = n_{A_1} n_{A_2} - U_{A_1}.$$

Step 5		Choose the smaller of the two values of U_{obs}. This U_{obs} is compared with the U_{crit}.

Alternatively, if $U_{A_1 \text{ obs}}$ is known, $U_{A_2 \text{ obs}}$ may be obtained from the formula given earlier:

$$U_{A_2 \text{ obs}} = n_{A_1} n_{A_2} - U_{A_1 \text{ obs}}.$$

Each formula provides the same value of $U_{A_2 \text{ obs}}$.

Table 15.5 summarizes the U test using these computational formulas. This table also includes the procedure to be followed if ranks are tied. Example problem 15.2 illustrates the steps in this table.

| EXAMPLE PROBLEM 15.2 | **Using the Mann–Whitney U Test** |

Problem: At many colleges and universities, the major drug-use problem of students is alcohol abuse. In response to this problem, a counselor developed an alcohol education program for students. At the beginning of an academic year, the counselor randomly selected 8 first-year males and presented the educational program to them. Six weeks after presenting the program, she gave the students a questionnaire on their alcohol consumption. At the same time she randomly chose 10 other first-year males who had not been given the alcohol education program and also gave them the questionnaire. The estimated daily alcohol consumption of the two groups in ounces of pure alcohol was as follows:

Educational Program Condition	
Program Given (A₁)	No Program Given (A₂)
0.31	0.41
0.53	0.63
0.58	1.14
0.14	0.21
0.16	0.89
0.52	0.55
0.53	0.89
0.02	0.91
	0.08
	0.59

Because these scores are estimates of a behavior, the counselor believed that they do not meet the requirements of interval measurement. Consequently, she treated them as presenting ordered information only. Did the educational program condition affect the estimated alcohol consumption of those students exposed to it? Use a .05 significance level.

Solution: The research design is a between-subjects design with two levels of the independent variable, educational program condition. The dependent variable, estimated alcohol consumption, is considered an ordinal measure. Accordingly, the Mann–Whitney U test is an appropriate statistical test for these data.

Statistic to Be Used: Smaller U_{obs}.

Assumptions for Use:

1. Each subject is measured in only one treatment condition.
2. The dependent variable is at least ordinal measurement and represents a continuous variable.

Statistical Hypotheses:

H_0: The population distribution of the educational program given (A_1) scores is identical to the population distribution of the no-educational program given (A_2) scores.

H_1: The population distribution of the educational program given (A_1) scores is not identical to the population distribution of the no-educational program given (A_2) scores.

Significance Level: $\alpha = .05$.

Critical Value of U: For $n_{A_1} = 8$, $n_{A_2} = 10$, and $\alpha = .05$, $U_{crit} = 17$ from Appendix C.8.

Rejection Region: Values of the smaller U_{obs} equal to or less than 17.

Calculation: The steps of Table 15.5 are followed to calculate U_{obs}.

Step 1   Rank order the combined scores of both groups from smallest to largest.

Ordered scores:	0.02	0.08	0.14	0.16	0.21	0.31	0.41	0.52	0.53	0.53	0.55	0.58	0.59	0.63	0.89	0.89	0.91	1.14
Group identity:	1	2	1	1	2	1	2	1	1	1	2	1	2	2	2	2	2	2
Rank:	1	2	3	4	5	6	7	8	9.5	9.5	11	12	13	14	15.5	15.5	17	18

Two sets of scores are tied, 0.53 and 0.89. For 0.53, the scores occupy the ranks of 9 and 10; hence, each score was assigned the mean (i.e., 9.5) of the two ranks. Similarly, the two scores of 0.89 occupy the ranks of 15 and 16; thus, each score was assigned the mean (i.e., 15.5) of the two ranks.

Step 2   Obtain the sum of the ranks for each group.

$$\Sigma R_{A_1} = 1 + 3 + 4 + 6 + 8 + 9.5 + 9.5 + 12 = 53.$$
$$\Sigma R_{A_2} = 2 + 5 + 7 + 11 + 13 + 14 + 15.5 + 15.5 + 17 + 18 = 118.$$

Step 3   Compute $U_{A_1 \, obs}$.

$$U_{A_1 \, obs} = (8)(10) + \frac{8(8 + 1)}{2} - 53$$
$$= 80 + (72/2) - 53$$
$$= 80 + 36 - 53 = 63.$$

Step 4   Compute $U_{A_2 \, obs}$.

$$U_{A_2 \, obs} = (8)(10) + \frac{10(10 + 1)}{2} - 118$$
$$= 80 + (110/2) - 118$$
$$= 80 + 55 - 118 = 17.$$

Step 5   Choose the smaller U_{obs}.

$$U_{A_2 \, obs} = 17 \text{ is the smaller } U_{obs}.$$

Decision: $U_{obs} = 17$ is equal to $U_{crit} = 17$. Thus, it falls into the rejection region; H_0 is rejected and H_1 is accepted.

Conclusion: Rejection of H_0 indicates that the distribution of estimates from the educational program group is different from the distribution of estimates of the no-educational program group. The alcohol education program reduced the amount of alcohol consumed as measured by students' estimates of daily alcohol consumption.

Reporting the Results of the Mann–Whitney U Test

The journal presentation of the U test follows the general guidelines for statistical presentations. We illustrate using the example problem on the effect of counting backward on the perception of reversals in the Schroeder staircase figure.

A Mann–Whitney U test was used to compare the distributions of the reversal latencies of the control ($n = 9$) and experimental groups ($n = 9$). With an alpha level of .05, the distributions did not differ significantly, $U = 25, p > .05$.

This presentation provides the typical information about the test used. The value of $U = 25$ is the smaller U_{obs}, and the $p > .05$ indicates that this U is nonsignificant at the .05 level. The group size information ($n_{A_1} = n_{A_2} = 9$) provides the information needed to look up U_{crit} in Appendix C.8.

Testing Your Knowledge 15.2

1. Combine the following scores of groups A_1 and A_2 and rank order from 1 to N. Maintain the group identity of each score. Then find $U_{A_1\,obs}$ the number of times an A_1 score precedes an A_2 score, and $U_{A_2\,obs}$, the number of times an A_2 score precedes an A_1 score.

Group	
A_1	A_2
15	7
23	26
10	14
19	16

    a. Which value of U_{obs} is the smaller value?

    b. Is the smaller U_{obs} statistically significant at the .05 level?

2. Find $U_{A_1\,obs}$ and $U_{A_2\,obs}$ for the scores of question 1 using the computational formulas for U.

    a. Do the values of $U_{A_1\,obs}$ and $U_{A_2\,obs}$ obtained with the computational formulas agree with those obtained in question 1?

3. Write the statistical hypotheses for the Mann–Whitney U test.

4. If H_0 is true, then what should be the relation of $U_{A_1\,obs}$ to $U_{A_2\,obs}$?

5. If H_1 is true, then what should be the relation of $U_{A_1\,obs}$ to $U_{A_2\,obs}$?

6. Given in the following table are the smaller values of U_{obs} for various group sizes. For each set of U_{obs} and group sizes, find the value of U_{crit} at the .01 level. Then, indicate whether U_{obs} falls into the rejection region and the decisions you make concerning H_0 and H_1.

	U_{obs}	n_{A_1}	n_{A_2}
a.	3	6	4
b.	12	10	10
c.	28	16	9
d.	21	7	19
e.	4	13	19
f.	126	18	19

7. Complete the following problem using the Mann–Whitney U test, following the format illustrated in the example problem. Use a .05 significance level. The use of music to induce relaxation in dental patients is becoming more widespread. A dentist tested the effectiveness of music in relaxing patients by randomly assigning patients to one of two groups. Thirteen patients in a music condition listened to music while dental procedures were performed; 12 patients in a no-music condition did not listen to music while similar dental procedures were performed. Midway through the appointment, each patient was asked to estimate his or her anxiety on a scale of 1 (not at all anxious) to 100 (extremely anxious). The anxiety estimates obtained were as follows:

Music Condition	
No Music	**Music**
52	44
75	21
66	66
33	54
17	37
78	84
94	30
89	29
27	54
49	49
53	33
78	10
	78

Do the groups differ in their distributions of anxiety estimates?

The Wilcoxon Signed-Ranks Test

Wilcoxon signed-ranks test ▷
A nonparametric test for within-subjects designs with two levels of an independent variable.

The **Wilcoxon signed-ranks test** is a nonparametric test for within-subjects designs with two levels of an independent variable. Thus, it is a nonparametric analog of the t_{rel}. The Wilcoxon test assumes only that the underlying dimension of behavior measured is continuous and that scores may be placed in rank order.

To illustrate the Wilcoxon signed-ranks test, we introduce an experiment on the expression of emotion in voice patterns (Cosmides, 1983). Suppose a psychologist hypothesized that vocal frequencies will change with different emotional states. To test this hypothesis, she uses a one-factor within-subjects design with two levels of an independent variable: the type of script a person is to read, either a script reflecting a happy scene (A_1) or a script reflecting a sad scene (A_2). The purpose of the script is to induce either a happy or sad emotion in the subject. In each condition, the person's task is to read the script silently and, on a signal from the experimenter, say aloud the words, "I'm still reading." The frequency span of the vocal expression of "I'm still reading" is the dependent variable for each subject and is measured in cycles per second (cps, or hertz). Thus, a score is the range of the highest vocal frequency minus the lowest vocal frequency in a subject's expression of the three words.

Suppose that the frequency spans for 10 people tested under both script conditions are those presented in Table 15.6. The means, standard deviations, and variances for these scores are also shown here. Notice that not only do the mean frequency ranges appear to differ, but there is a large difference in the variability of the two conditions. Recall that t_{rel} requires the variances of the two populations to be equal. In this example, however, the two variances differ considerably (702.3 and 10,282.0 for the happy and sad scripts, respectively). Thus, one of the assumptions of t_{rel} is violated by these data. The Wilcoxon signed-ranks test does not make assumptions about the variances; accordingly, it is an appropriate test for these scores.

Assumptions of the Wilcoxon Signed-Ranks Test

The assumptions applying to the Wilcoxon signed-ranks test are the following:

▶ Each subject is measured on both levels of the independent variable.

▶ The dependent variable is measured at least at the ordinal level.

TABLE

15.6

Hypothetical scores for vocal-frequency span (in hertz) as a function of type of script read

| | Type of Script | |
Subject	Happy (A_1)	Sad (A_2)
1	305	214
2	275	385
3	360	519
4	299	307
5	317	483
6	326	454
7	284	501
8	347	463
9	331	382
10	314	297
$\overline{X}_A$	315.8	400.5
s_A	26.5	101.4
s_A^2	702.3	10,282.0

Statistical Hypothesis Testing with the Wilcoxon Signed-Ranks Test

The *T* Statistic
The Wilcoxon test uses ranked scores to obtain a test statistic called the *T*, which is the smaller sum of the ranks from the two treatment conditions.

Statistical Hypotheses

Null Hypothesis.   The null hypothesis tested with the *T* is

H_0:   The population distributions of the related A_1 and A_2 scores are identical.

Alternative Hypothesis.   The alternative hypothesis is

H_1:   The population distributions of the related A_1 and A_2 scores are not identical.

Sampling Distribution and Critical Values of *T*
Values of T_{crit} for $\alpha = .05$ and $\alpha = .01$ are presented in Appendix C.9 for samples from 6 to 50. This table is entered with the value of N_{pairs}, the number of pairs of scores or, equivalently, the number of subjects. Values of T_{obs} less than or equal to T_{crit} fall into the rejection region and are statistically significant for the value of α selected. In the example with $N_{pairs} = 10$ and $\alpha = .05$, $T_{crit} = 8$. The rejection region is thus defined by values of T_{obs} less than or equal to 8.

Calculating *T*
The computations for obtaining T_{obs} involve the following steps. The result of each step is shown in Table 15.7 using the example vocal-frequency-span scores.

Step 1   Find $d = X_{A_1} - X_{A_2}$, the difference between the A_1 and A_2 scores for each subject as shown in column a of Table 15.7. Maintain the $+$ or $-$ sign of the difference.

Step 2   Find the absolute value of each difference ($|d|$, the value without regard to sign) as shown in column b.

Step 3   Rank the absolute differences from smallest (rank $= 1$) to largest (rank $= N$) as shown in column c. Differences of zero are not ranked, and the value of N used to find T_{crit} is reduced by the number of zero differences occurring. Tied values of d are assigned the mean of the ranks that would have been assigned had no tie occurred.

Step 4   Give each rank in column c the sign of the difference in column a. The signed ranks are shown in column d.

Step 5   Sum the ranks of like sign (i.e., the sum of the positive-signed ranks and the sum of the negative-signed ranks) in column d. For example, the sum of the positive-signed ranks in column d equals 6 [i.e., $(+4) + (+2)$], and the sum of the negative-signed ranks equals -49 [i.e., $(-5) + (-8) + (-1) + (-9) + (-7) + (-10) + (-6) + (-3)$].

Step 6   Find the absolute value of each sum of the ranks. Then, choose the smaller of the two sums of the ranks. In this case it is 6, the sum of the positive ranks. This sum is T_{obs}; thus, $T_{obs} = 6$.

TABLE

15·7

Computation of the Wilcoxon T on the scores of Table 15.6.

| | Type of Script | | (a) | (b) | (c) | (d) |
| | Happy | Sad | | | Ranked | Signed |
Subject	(A_1)	(A_2)	d	$|d|$	$|d|$	Rank
1	305	214	+91	91	4	+4
2	275	385	−110	110	5	−5
3	360	519	−159	159	8	−8
4	299	307	−8	8	1	−1
5	317	483	−166	166	9	−9
6	326	454	−128	128	7	−7
7	284	501	−217	217	10	−10
8	347	463	−116	116	6	−6
9	331	382	−51	51	3	−3
10	314	297	+17	17	2	+2

Decisions about the Statistical Hypotheses

The $T_{obs} = 6$ is less than $T_{crit} = 8$; accordingly, T_{obs} falls into the rejection region. We reject H_0 and accept H_1.

Conclusion from the Test

Rejection of H_0 and acceptance of H_1 lead to the conclusion that the two distributions of scores differ; the type of script produced differences in the vocal-frequency span. The vocal-frequency span for a sad script is larger than for a happy script.

EXAMPLE PROBLEM

15·3

Using the Wilcoxon Signed-Ranks Test

Problem: It has been found that music affects the behaviors and attitudes of people dining in a restaurant, with people staying longer and spending more money when they enjoy the music (Caldwell & Hibbert, 2002). However, when Caldwell and Hibbert examined the effect of music tempo on restaurant dining behaviors and attitudes, they failed to find a relationship. Yet, other studies have found that fast-tempo music increases the speed with which a behavior may occur (McElrea & Standing, 1992; Roballey et al., 1985). Let's imagine that a researcher formulated a hypothesis that states that fast-tempo music will be associated with taking more bites of food than slow-tempo music. To investigate this hypothesis, the researcher conducted the following study. Eleven cafeteria patrons were observed eating on two different days with two different background music conditions, slow music on day 1 (A_1) and fast music on day 2 (A_2). The same people were observed unobtrusively on both days. The number of bites per minute taken by each person under each music condition was recorded. Suppose that the following median bites per minute were observed for each person under the two music tempo conditions.

| | Music Tempo | |
Subject	Slow (A_1)	Fast (A_2)
1	3	4
2	4	6
3	2	3
4	3	3
5	3	8
6	4	2
7	1	4
8	5	4
9	3	6
10	5	9
11	2	8

The experimenter treated the scores as ordinal measurements. Does music tempo affect biting rate? Use a .05 significance level.

Solution: The research design is a one-factor within-subjects design with two levels of the independent variable, music tempo. The dependent variable is measured at least at the ordinal level; thus, the Wilcoxon signed-ranks test is an appropriate statistical test for these data.

Statistic to Be Used: T, the smaller sum of the ranks.

Assumptions for Use:

1. Each subject is measured on both levels of the independent variable.
2. The dependent variable is measured at least at the ordinal level.

Statistical Hypotheses:

H_0: The population distributions of the related A_1 and A_2 scores are identical.

H_1: The population distributions of the related A_1 and A_2 scores are not identical.

Significance Level: $\alpha = .05$.

Critical Value of T: For $N_{pairs} = 11$ and $\alpha = .05$, $T_{crit} = 10$. In the calculation of T, however, subject 4 shows a zero change between the music conditions. This subject is dropped from the analysis. Accordingly, N_{pairs} becomes 10, and T_{crit} for $N = 10$ is 8 from Appendix C.9.

Rejection Region: Values of T_{obs} less than or equal to 8.

TABLE 15.8	Computation of the Wilcoxon T on the number of bites taken as a function of music tempo

| | Music Tempo | | (a) | (b) | (c) | (d) |
Subject	Slow (A_1)	Fast (A_2)	d	$|d|$	Ranked $|d|$	Signed Rank
1	3	4	−1	1	2	−2
2	4	6	−2	2	4.5	−4.5
3	2	3	−1	1	2	−2
4	3	3	0	0	—	—
5	3	8	−5	5	9	−9
6	4	2	+2	2	4.5	+4.5
7	1	4	−3	3	6.5	−6.5
8	5	4	+1	1	2	+2
9	3	6	−3	3	6.5	−6.5
10	5	9	−4	4	8	−8
11	2	8	−6	6	10	−10

Calculation

Step 1 The value of $d = X_{A_1} - X_{A_2}$ is found for each subject (column a of Table 15.8).

Step 2 Absolute values of d are obtained (column b of Table 15.8).

Step 3 The absolute values of d are ranked from 1 to 10; $d = 0$ is not included in the ranking (column c). Notice the ranking of the several sets of tied d values. Tied scores are given the mean of the ranks that they occupy. For example, there are three differences of $|d| = 1$ in column b. These values occupy the ranks 1, 2, and 3. The mean of these ranks is 2; thus, each value of $|d| = 1$ is assigned a rank of 2.

Step 4 The sign of each d (from column a) is attached to the rank of d (column d).

Step 5 Like-signed ranks are summed. The absolute value of the sum of the positive-signed ranks = 6.5 [i.e., $(+4.5) + (+2) = 6.5$]. The absolute value of the sum of the negative-signed ranks = 48.5 [i.e., $(-2) + (-4.5) + (-2) + (-9) + (-6.5) + (-6.5) + (-8) + (-10) = 48.5$].

Step 6 The absolute value of the sum of the positive-signed ranks is the smaller sum of the ranks; hence, $T_{obs} = 6.5$.

Decision: $T_{obs} = 6.5$ is less than $T_{crit} = 8$ and falls into the rejection region; H_0 is rejected and H_1 accepted.

Conclusion: The distributions of the number of bites taken per minute differ significantly under the two music tempos; more bites are taken per minute under a fast tempo than under a slow tempo.

Reporting the Results of the Wilcoxon Signed-Ranks Test

We illustrate the reporting of the Wilcoxon signed-ranks test using the example manipulating the type of script and measuring the vocal-frequency span of subjects.

> A Wilcoxon signed-ranks test was used to compare the vocal-frequency spans of the happy and sad script conditions. With an alpha level of .05, the script conditions differed significantly, $T = 6$ ($N = 10$), $p < .05$. There was a significantly greater range of frequencies in the sad-script condition compared to the happy-script condition.

Again, this presentation provides the information needed to interpret the value of T_{obs}. Knowing the value of N_{pairs}, we can look up the value of T_{crit} if necessary.

Using Nonparametric Tests

As we have seen, nonparametric tests do not make assumptions about the population distribution of scores for a sample. Furthermore, they usually require only that we be able to rank order the scores obtained. Parametric tests, such as the t or analysis of variance, require stronger assumptions about the nature of scores in an experiment, assumptions that sometimes may be questionable for the scores collected in a study. Nevertheless, nonparametric statistical tests are less widely used in behavioral science research than are parametric statistical tests. Why?

There are several answers to this question. In general, if the assumptions for a parametric test are met by the scores being analyzed, then a nonparametric test is less likely to detect an effect of the independent variable than its corresponding parametric test. That is, nonparametric tests typically are less powerful and, thus, more likely to lead to Type II errors than parametric tests when the assumptions for parametric tests are met by the data. Because most parametric tests are considered robust with respect to violation of assumptions, many researchers routinely analyze their data with parametric tests.

Nonparametric tests also provide different information than do parametric tests. For example, the t_{ind} leads to conclusions about the equality or inequality of the population means, but conclusions with the U test concern the equality or inequality of the population distributions. In addition, for more complex designs, such as the factorial designs discussed in Chapter 11, there are no nonparametric tests that provide as much information as the factorial analysis of variance.

As we have suggested, there are no hard and fast rules about when a nonparametric test should be used. The perception of reversals in the Schroeder staircase example presented to introduce the U test in this chapter provides an unusually clear-cut instance when a nonparametric statistical test is necessary. One of the scores in this experiment was an infinite value. With such a value, a mean or standard deviation of scores cannot be computed. Obviously, then, a parametric test cannot be used on these data.

Other instances are often not so straightforward. For example, how much must the underlying distribution of a population of scores differ from a normal distribution before the use of a parametric test is inappropriate? When are the variances of two or more populations considered to be unequal? Behavioral scientists are not in agreement on the answers to these questions; consequently, they may not agree on whether a parametric or nonparametric test should be used to analyze a set of scores.

Testing Your Knowledge 15.3

1. For what type of research design is the Wilcoxon signed-ranks test appropriate?

2. What is the test statistic used by the Wilcoxon signed-ranks test?

3. Write the statistical hypotheses for the Wilcoxon signed-ranks test.

4. Given next are the smaller absolute values of the sum of the signed ranks for experiments of different group sizes. For each smaller rank and value of N_{pairs}, identify the value of T_{obs}. Then, find T_{crit} for the .05 significance level and indicate whether T_{obs} falls into the rejection region. Finally, identify the decisions you make concerning H_0 and H_1.

	Smaller Rank	N_{pairs}
a.	2	8
b.	9	10
c.	17	13
d.	40	19
e.	98	25

5. Complete the following problem using the Wilcoxon signed-ranks test following the format illustrated in the example problem. Use a .05 significance level.

Problem: Sport psychologists are interested in the relationship of anxiety to performance in sports competition. For example, Cottyn, De Clercq, Pannier, Cromber, and Lenoir (2006) measured anxiety in gymnasts during a practice session and in competition on the balance beam. You attempted a similar study and found the following anxiety scores for the first practice of a new routine on the balance beam compared to a competition performance of the balance beam routine. The range of possible scores is from 12 (very low reported anxiety) to 84 (very high reported anxiety).

Subject	Balance Beam Activity	
	Practice	Competition
1	68	72
2	56	65
3	78	77
4	49	54
5	66	64
6	43	53
7	77	70
8	68	78
9	28	29
10	69	75
11	75	78
12	80	72
13	75	75
14	65	76
15	71	70

It is likely that the population distribution of these anxiety scores is negatively skewed (most players reporting high anxiety, a few reporting very low anxiety levels); thus, you plan to use a nonparametric statistical analysis for these scores. Do the distributions of anxiety scores differ from the initial practice of a new routine to competition?

Summary

▶ The chi-square test is used for scores that represent the frequency of occurrence of a response.

▶ The chi-square test of independence is used to test for a relationship between categories on two independent dimensions.

▶ The chi-square test of independence is obtained by

$$\chi^2_{obs} = \sum \frac{(O - E)^2}{E}.$$

▶ The chi-square goodness of fit test is used to determine how well scores categorized on one dimension agree with theoretically derived expected frequencies for those categories.

▶ The chi-square test for goodness of fit is obtained by

$$\chi^2_{obs} = \sum \frac{(O - E)^2}{E}.$$

▶ The Mann–Whitney U test is a nonparametric test for a between-subjects design using two levels of an independent variable and scores at least at an ordinal level.

▶ The U statistic is the number of times that the rank of a score in one group precedes the rank of a score in the other group.

▶ The value of $U_{A_1 \, obs}$ is found from

$$U_{A_1 \, obs} = n_{A_1} n_{A_2} + \frac{n_{A_1}(n_{A_1} + 1)}{2} - \sum R_{A_1}$$

and the value of $U_{A_2 \, obs}$ from

$$U_{A_2 \, obs} = n_{A_1} n_{A_2} + \frac{n_{A_2}(n_{A_2} + 1)}{2} - \sum R_{A_2}.$$

The smaller U_{obs} is used as the test statistic.

▶ The Wilcoxon signed-ranks test is a parametric test for within-subjects designs with two levels of an independent variable.

▶ The test statistic used in the Wilcoxon signed-ranks test is the T, the smaller sum of the ranks from the two treatment conditions.

▶ When the assumptions for a parametric test are met by the data being analyzed, a parametric test is more powerful than its corresponding nonparametric test.

Key Terms and Symbols

chi-square test (449)
chi-square test for goodness of fit (457)
chi-square test of independence (449)
χ^2 (451)
χ^2_{crit} (452)
χ^2_{obs} (452)
distribution-free tests (448)
expected frequencies (E) (451)

Mann–Whitney U test (461)
marginal frequencies (450)
nonparametric statistical test (448)
parametric test (448)
rows-by-columns contingency
   table (450)
T (473)

T_{crit} (473)
T_{obs} (473)
U (464)
U_{crit} (465)
$U_{A_1 \, obs}$ (464)
$U_{A_2 \, obs}$ (464)
Wilcoxon signed-ranks test (471)

Review Questions

1. Identify the appropriate statistical test for each of the following one-factor designs with two levels of the independent variable and the level of measurement of the scores indicated.

   a. Within-subjects, ratio measurement.

   b. Between-subjects, nominal measurement.

   c. Between-subjects, ratio measurement.

   d. Between-subjects, ordinal measurement.

   e. Within-subjects, ordinal measurement.

2. Many individuals in psychotherapy terminate the therapy before its scheduled completion. These people (known as psychotherapy dropouts) appear to make up a substantial minority of those in psychotherapy (Ogrodniczuk, Joyce, & Piper, 2005). To gain more knowledge of this problem you obtain the records of several community mental health centers and categorize dropouts and nondropouts by gender and severity of the problem that they exhibit.

   a. You obtained the following frequencies of dropouts and non-dropouts for males and females.

	Gender	
	Male	Female
Non-dropout	99	130
Dropout	75	78

   Is the dropout frequency related to gender at the .05 significance level? If so, what is the relationship?

   b. The clients were then categorized by the severity of their psychological problem: mild, moderate, and severe. The following frequencies were obtained:

	Severity of Psychological Problem		
	Mild	Moderate	Severe
Non-dropout	51	66	112
Dropout	64	54	35

   Is the dropout rate related to severity of the psychological problem at the .05 significance level? If so, what is the relationship?

3. Example problem 12.2 introduced a study testing whether yawning is a sign of boredom. Using a one-factor within-subjects design, subjects saw a 30-minute rock music video (the interesting video) and 30 minutes of a color-bar test pattern without sound (the uninteresting video). The number of times a subject yawned during the two sessions was observed and recorded. Suppose that we replicated this experiment using 11 subjects and observed the following number of yawns for each session:

	Type of Video	
Subject	Interesting	Uninteresting
1	5	7
2	2	1
3	4	7
4	3	8
5	0	2
6	4	5
7	7	6
8	6	23
9	3	3
10	1	4
11	8	9

a. Use the Wilcoxon signed-ranks test and a .05 significance level to find if the type of task affects the amount of yawning that occurs.

b. Why might the Wilcoxon signed-ranks test be more appropriate for these data than t_{rel}? (*Hint:* Examine the distribution of the scores.)

c. What conclusions do you reach from the Wilcoxon test?

4. Chapter 9, review question 1 presented a study to determine the effect of noise on blood pressure. Two groups of subjects were formed. Subjects in the quiet group relaxed in a comfortable chair for 30 minutes, and at the end of the 30 minutes their systolic blood pressure was measured. Subjects in the noise group also sat in the same chair for 30 minutes. During the 30-minute wait, however, they listened to a recording of traffic noise from a large city during rush hour. After listening to the noise for 30 minutes, the systolic blood pressure of these individuals was also recorded. Suppose that the following blood pressure measures (in millimeters of mercury) were obtained:

Group	
Quiet	Noise
106	141
117	136
124	124
129	139
115	121
147	119
121	147
115	128
128	115
136	134
127	140

Use the U test and a .05 significance level to find if the distributions differ. Describe your conclusions.

5. To find if sex differences exist in trait anxiety, a researcher gave an anxiety inventory to 9 females and 13 males. The scores on the inventory may range from 20 (low anxiety) to 80 (high anxiety). Suppose that the following scores were obtained.

Gender	
Female	Male
36	54
25	70
47	34
39	53
55	41
41	56
29	32
59	44
38	40
	61
	50
	30
	37

Use the Mann–Whitney U test and a .05 significance level to find if the distribution of female anxiety scores differs from that of the males. Describe your conclusions.

6. John, Meyer, Rumpf, Hapke, and Schumann (2006) found a relationship between weight gain in certain populations who stop smoking cigarettes. Let's imagine we replicated this study with a group of college students. The weights of eight college students were measured at the time they entered a smoking cessation program and one year after they had stopped smoking. The following weights were obtained.

	Time of Weight Measurement	
Subject	Entering Program	One Year after Stopping
1	122.4	127.9
2	117.1	119.4
3	127.8	127.1
4	123.2	126.5
5	112.5	114.6
6	118.7	125.3
7	121.4	119.8
8	131.7	134.2

Analyze the scores with the Wilcoxon signed-ranks test to see if the distributions differ at the .05 level. Describe your conclusions.

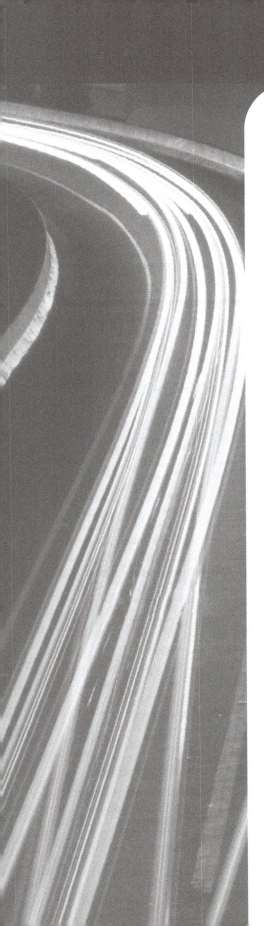

Appendixes

Mathematics Review

This review briefly covers the mathematics needed to understand the statistics presented in this text.

Statistical Symbols

A **symbol**, sometimes called a **sign**, is a letter or character used to represent something. The following table presents the common symbols used in statistics.

Symbol and Example	Description
X or X_i	X is used to represent a score or a measurement obtained from a subject. The subscript i, when used, indicates the score of a particular subject. For example, X_1 represents the score of subject number 1.
$=$	Equals sign.
$X_1 = 3$	The score of subject 1 equals 3.
$X_5 = 27$	The score of subject 5 equals 27.
$a = 2$	The value of a equals 2.
$\neq$	Does not equal sign.
$6 \neq 3$	6 is not equal to 3.
$+$	Plus sign. This sign indicates that the numbers joined by the $+$ should be added. The result of addition is called the *sum*. A statement such as "The sum of 5 and 1" indicates that the numbers are to be added together.
$5 + 1 = 6$	The sum of 5 plus 1 equals 6.
$5 + 1 + 6 = 12$	The sum of 5 plus 1 plus 6 equals 12.
$a + b$	a plus b: The value of b is to be added to the value of a.
$-$	Minus sign. This sign indicates that the number that follows the $-$ should be subtracted from the number preceding the $-$ sign. The result of subtraction is called the *difference*. A statement such as "The difference of 5 and 1" indicates that one number is to be subtracted from the other.
$5 - 1 = 4$	The difference of 5 minus 1 is 4.
$a - b$	a minus b: The value of b is to be subtracted from the value of a.
$(\,)(\,)$ or $\times$	Multiplication or times sign. The values in parentheses or separated by the $\times$ are multiplied. The result of multiplication is called a *product*.

$(2)(3) = 6$	The product of 2 multiplied by 3 is 6.
$2 \times 3 = 6$	The product of 2 multiplied by 3 is 6.
$(a)(b)$ or $a \times b$	a times b: The value of a is to be multiplied by the value of b.
	Exception to the rule: In a factorial design the interaction of factors A and B is indicated by $A \times B$. In this instance, the term should be read as "the A by B interaction." It does not mean that A is multiplied by B.
$\div$ or $/$ or —	Division sign. The number preceding the $\div$ or the $/$ or the number above the — (the *numerator*) is divided by the number following the $\div$ or the $/$ or the number below the — (the *denominator*), respectively. The result of division is called the *quotient*.
$6 \div 2 = 3$	The quotient of 6 divided by 2 is 3.
$6/2 = 3$	The quotient of 6 divided by 2 is 3.
$\frac{6}{2} = 3$	The quotient of 6 divided by 2 is 3.
$a \div b$, or a/b, or $\frac{a}{b}$	The quotient of a divided by b.
$<$	Less than symbol. The number preceding the $<$ is less than the number following the $<$.
$2 < 3$	2 is less than 3.
$a < b$	The value of a is less than the value of b.
$X_3 < 10$	The score of subject 3 is less than 10.
$>$	Greater than symbol. The number preceding the $>$ is greater than the number following the $>$.
$3 > 2$	3 is greater than 2.
$a > b$	The value of a is greater than the value of b.
$X_3 > 10$	The score of subject 3 is greater than 10.
$\leq$	Less than or equal to symbol. The number preceding the $\leq$ is less than or equal to the number following the $\leq$.
$2 \leq 3$	2 is less than or equal to 3.
$4 \leq 4$	4 is less than or equal to 4.
$a \leq b$	The value of a is less than or equal to the value of b.
$X_3 \leq 10$	The score of subject 3 is less than or equal to 10.
$\geq$	Equal to or greater than symbol. The number preceding the $\geq$ is equal to or greater than the number following the $\geq$.
$3 \geq 2$	3 is equal to or greater than 2.
$4 \geq 4$	4 is equal to or greater than 4.
$a \geq b$	The value of a is equal to or greater than the value of b.
$X_3 \geq 10$	The score of subject 3 is equal to or greater than 10.
$5 < X_1 < 10$	The greater than and less than symbols may be placed in one term as illustrated. This term is read as "The score of subject 1 is greater than 5 and less than 10."

$5 \le X_1 \le 10$	The equal to or greater than and less than or equal to symbols may also be placed in one term as illustrated. This term is read as "The score of subject 1 is equal to or greater than 5 and equal to or less than 10."
$\| \|$	Absolute value symbol. This symbol indicates that we ignore the $+$ or $-$ sign attached to a number.
$\|-6\| = 6$	The absolute value of negative 6 is 6.
$\|+6\| = 6$	The absolute value of positive 6 is 6.
$(\ )^2$	The number enclosed in parentheses is squared, or multiplied by itself. Sometimes the parentheses are not used, and the square indicator, ^{2}, simply follows the number to be squared.
$(5)^2 = 25$	5 squared, which is 5×5, equals 25.
$5^2 = 25$	5 squared equals 25.
$\sqrt{}$	Square root symbol. The $\sqrt{}$ indicates finding the number that, when multiplied by itself (i.e., when squared), equals the number under the $\sqrt{}$ symbol.
$\sqrt{25} = 5$	The square root of 25 equals 5, for 5 multiplied by itself (i.e., 5×5) equals 25.
$\sqrt{36} = 6$	The square root of 36 equals 6, for 6 multiplied by itself (i.e., 6×6) equals 36.
Σ	Summation symbol. The numbers following the Σ should be added together.
$\Sigma\,(3 + 2) = 5$	The sum of 3 plus 2 is 5.
$\Sigma\,(3 + 2 + 4) = 9$	The sum of 3 plus 2 plus 4 is 9.
ΣX or ΣX_i	The sum of X. Add all the scores that are represented by X. For example, if the scores of three subjects are $X_1 = 3$, $X_2 = 6$, and $X_3 = 4$, then $\Sigma X = 3 + 6 + 4 = 13$. Sometimes limits are placed on the summation sign, such as $\sum_{i=1}^{3} X_i$. These limits indicate the scores of subjects 1 to 3 should be added. If limits are not used, then ΣX means all the scores designated by X should be added.

Mathematical Operations

Negative Numbers

A negative number may occur as a result of subtraction, such as $6 - 8 = -2$. The 8, which is larger than the 6 by 2, results in a difference of -2 when it is subtracted from the 6. Negative numbers occur often in statistics and then are used in basic mathematical operations. If a number is not preceded by a minus sign, it is assumed to be positive.

Adding Negative Numbers

$6 + (-4) = 2$ Adding a negative number to a positive number is equivalent to subtracting the negative number from the positive number. Thus, $6 + (-4) = 6 - 4 = 2$.

$(-6) + (-4) = -10$ In this instance, the -4 is subtracted from the -6, or $(-6) + (-4) = -6 - 4 = -10$

Subtracting Negative Numbers

$6 - (-4) = 10$ Subtracting a negative number is equivalent to adding the absolute value of the negative number. Thus, $6 - (-4) = 6 + |-4| = 6 + 4 = 10$.

Multiplying Negative Numbers

$(-6)(-4) = 24$ If both numbers to be multiplied are negative, then the product is positive.

$(6)(-4) = -24$ If only one of the two numbers is negative, then the product is negative.

$(-6)(4) = -24$

Dividing Negative Numbers

$-10 \div 5 = -2$ If either the numerator or the denominator is negative, then the quotient is negative.

$10 \div -5 = -2$

$-10 \div -5 = 2$ If both the numerator and the denominator are negative, then the quotient is positive.

Fractions

The easiest approach to working with fractions is to convert the fraction to a decimal by dividing the numerator by the denominator, for example, $\frac{1}{4} = 0.25$, $\frac{2}{4} = 0.50$, and $\frac{3}{4} = 0.75$. If the decimal is to be involved in further calculations, then it should be carried to at least three decimal places (e.g., $\frac{4}{11} = 0.364$). Thus, $\frac{2}{5} + \frac{1}{8} + \frac{1}{3}$ equals $0.400 + 0.125 + 0.333 = 0.858$.

Proportions and Percents

Proportion

A proportion is a part of a whole. For example, if 100 people answer a questionnaire and 45 of them are males, then the proportion of male respondents is $\frac{45}{100}$ or .45. The proportion of female respondents is $\frac{55}{100}$ or .55.

Percent

A percent is formed when a proportion is multiplied by 100. Thus, a proportion of .45 equals $.45 \times 100$ or 45 percent. A proportion of .55 equals $.55 \times 100 = 55$ percent.

Order of Mathematical Operations

The following examples illustrate the order in which mathematical operations are performed with common statistical terms.

Term	Order of Mathematical Operations
$\Sigma(X - \overline{X})$	**1.** The mean is subtracted from each score in a set of scores.
	2. The differences are summed.
$\Sigma(X - \overline{X})^2$	**1.** The mean is subtracted from each score in a set of scores.
	2. Each difference is squared.
	3. The squared differences are summed.
ΣX^2	**1.** Each X value is squared.
	2. The squared X values are summed.
$(\Sigma X)^2$	**1.** The X values are summed.
	2. The sum of the X values (i.e., ΣX) is squared.
ΣXY	**1.** The corresponding X and Y values are multiplied for the set of scores.
	2. The multiplied XY values are summed for the set of scores.
$(\Sigma X)(\Sigma Y)$	**1.** The X values are summed to obtain ΣX.
	2. The Y values are summed to obtain ΣY.
	3. The sum of the X values (i.e., ΣX) is multiplied by the sum of the Y variables (i.e., ΣY).

Rounding Rules

There are several rules that are commonly used when numerical computations require rounding.

Rounding: Answers to Computations

Suppose that you obtained three scores on a task of recalling a list of words: 4, 4, and 3. To describe the typical response, you found the sum of these numbers, 11, and divided it by 3, or $\frac{11}{3} = 3.666\overline{6}$. The bar (–) over the last 6 indicates that the 6s continue endlessly. How many decimal places should you present in your answer?

One convention is that the final value of a computation should be rounded to two decimal places beyond the value to which the original scores were measured. In the example, the scores were given to the ones (or units) place; a person could obtain 3 correct answers or 4 correct answers, but not 3.2 or 4.6. Following this rule, the final value of the computation is rounded to two decimal places beyond the ones place, or to 3.67.

Others follow a convention of rounding the final value of a computation to one decimal place beyond the value to which the original scores were measured. Following this approach, the final value of the computation for the example is rounded to one decimal place beyond the ones place, or to 3.7. We follow this approach in text examples.

Rounding: Intermediate Steps in Computations

If computations require a number of steps prior to obtaining the final answer, then intermediate numerical values should be carried to at least two decimal places beyond the number of decimal places needed for the final answer. For example, if the value of $\frac{11}{3}$ were to enter into further computations, we would not round its value to 3.67. Rather, we carry it to 3.667 for the computations. This approach minimizes rounding error in computations.

Rounding Rules

Suppose that we have an answer to a computation such as $3.6AB$, where the A and B are possible numerical values. For example, if $A = 2$ and $B = 9$, then $3.6AB = 3.629$. We wish to round this number to two decimal places.

Several rules typically are followed when rounding numbers:

▶ If the number represented by the letter B is greater than 5, increase A by 1 and drop the B value. Following this rule, 3.629 (here $A = 2$ and $B = 9$) is rounded to 3.63.

▶ If the number represented by the letter B is less than 5, leave the A value as is and drop the B value. Following this rule, 3.623 (here $A = 2$ and $B = 3$) is rounded to 3.62.

▶ If the number represented by the letter B is exactly 5, increase A by 1 if A is an odd number, but leave its value as is if it is an even number; then drop B. Following this rule, 3.635 (here $A = 3$ and $B = 5$) is rounded to 3.64, but 3.625 (here $A = 2$ and $B = 5$) is rounded to 3.62. Notice, however, that if the number is 3.6251 it is rounded to 3.63, not 3.62.

Statistical Symbols

A — Factor A, the independent variable in an experiment.

A_1, A_2, A_3 — Levels of factor A in a factorial design.

α — Alpha, the probability of a Type I error.

$A \times B$ — The representation of the interaction of factors A and B in a factorial design.

a — (1) Number of levels of factor A or
(2) Y-intercept of an equation for a straight line in a regression analysis.

B — Factor B, the second independent variable in a factorial design.

B_1, B_2, B_3 — Levels of factor B in a factorial design.

b — (1) Number of levels of factor B or
(2) slope of a straight line in a regression analysis.

β — Beta, the probability of a Type II error.

χ^2 — Chi-squared statistic.

χ^2_{crit} — Critical value of χ^2.

χ^2_{obs} — Value of χ^2 statistic obtained from data.

CD — Critical difference in a multiple comparison test.

CP_{XY} — Cross products of X and Y in a correlational study.

$cum\ f$ or cf — Cumulative frequency of a score.

cf_L — Cumulative frequency of scores up to the lower real limit of an interval in a grouped frequency distribution.

$cum\ rf$ or crf — Cumulative relative frequency of a score.

$cum\ \%f$ or $c\%f$ — Cumulative percentage frequency of a score.

D — (1) Difference in a pair of ranked scores for an individual; used in Spearman rank-order correlation coefficient; or
(2) Difference between two scores obtained from a subject in a within-subjects design.

df — Degrees of freedom. In an analysis of variance, the df are usually subscripted, such as df_A, df_B, $df_{A \times B}$, df_{Error}, or df_{Total}, to indicate to which source of variance they correspond.

η^2 — Eta squared.

E_{rc} — Expected frequency of a score in row r, column c, of a chi-square test contingency table.

f — Frequency of a score.

f_i — Frequency of scores in an interval of a grouped frequency distribution.

F — The F statistic in the analysis of variance.

F_{crit} — Critical value of F.

F_{obs} — Value of F obtained from data.

H_0 — Statistical null hypothesis.

H_1 — Statistical alternative hypothesis.

i — Size or width of the class interval in a grouped frequency distribution.

M — Sample mean. The symbol used in publications following the editorial style of the *Publication Manual of the American Psychological Association* (American Psychological Association, 2001).

Mdn — Median.

MS — Mean square, a variance estimate in the analysis of variance. Mean squares typically are subscripted, such as MS_A, MS_B, $MS_{A \times B}$, or MS_{Error}, to indicate which source of variance they represent.

MSE — Mean square error. The symbol used to identify the MS_{Error} for an analysis of variance in publications following the editorial style of the *Publication Manual of the American Psychological Association* (American Psychological Association, 2001).

μ — Mu, the population mean.

$\mu_{\overline{X}}$ — Mean of the theoretical sampling distribution of the mean.

N — Total number of scores in a sample or the total number of scores in an experiment.

N_{pairs} — Number of pairs of scores.

n — Number of scores in a subgroup of a larger sample.

n_1, n_2 — Number of scores in a level of a one-factor design.

n_{AB} — Number of scores in a cell of a two-factor design.

O_{rc} — Observed frequency of a score in row r, column c of a chi-square test contingency table.

$\%f$ — Percentage frequency of a score.

P — A percentile point expressed as a proportion. Used to obtain the score at a specified percentile point.

P_X — Percentile rank of score of X.

p	Probability.
q	Studentized range statistic used in the Tukey HSD test.
r	Pearson correlation coefficient for a sample.
r_{crit}	Critical value of Pearson correlation coefficient.
r_{obs}	Observed value of a Pearson correlation between variables X and Y.
rf	Relative frequency of a score.
ρ	Rho, the population correlation coefficient.
ρ_S	Population Spearman rank-order correlation coefficient.
r_S	Spearman rank-order correlation coefficient.
r^2	Coefficient of determination.
σ	Sigma, the population standard deviation.
σ^2	Population variance.
$\sigma_{\overline{X}}$	Standard error of the mean.
$\sigma_{\overline{X}_1 - \overline{X}_2}$	Standard error of the difference between means.
$\sum$	Summation
$\sum\limits_{i=1}^{N}$	Summation notation from $i = 1$ to N.
S	Sample standard deviation.
s	Estimated population standard deviation.
SD	Standard deviation. The symbol used in publications following the editorial style of the *Publication Manual of the American Psychological Association* (American Psychological Association, 2001).
S^2	Sample variance.
s^2	Estimated population variance.
s^2_{pooled}	Pooled variance estimate for the difference between two population means.
$s_{\overline{X}}$	Estimated standard error of the mean.
SE	Standard error of the mean. The symbol used in publications following the editorial style of the *Publication Manual of the American Psychological Association* (American Psychological Association, 2001).
$s_{\overline{X}_1 - \overline{X}_2}$	Estimated standard error of the difference between means.
$s_{Y \cdot X}$	Standard error of estimate when predicting Y from X.
$\sum R$	Sum of ranks.
SS	Sum of squares. In an analysis of variance, a SS is usually subscripted, such as SS_A, SS_B, $SS_{A \times B}$, SS_{Error}, or SS_{Total}, to indicate which source of variation it represents.
$SS_{Residual}$	The value of $\sum(Y - Y')^2$.
SS_X	Sum of squares of the X variable in a correlation.

SS_Y	Sum of squares of the Y variable in a correlation.
t	t statistic in the t test.
t_{crit}	Critical value of t.
t_{ind}	t statistic obtained in the t test for independent groups.
t_{obs}	Value of t obtained from data.
t_{rel}	t statistic obtained in the t test for related measures.
T	Wilcoxon T statistic.
T_{crit}	Critical value of T.
T_{obs}	Value of T obtained from data.
U	Mann–Whitney U statistic.
U_{crit}	Critical value of U.
U_{obs}	The smaller value of U obtained from data.
X	A subject's score on the variable identified as the X variable. Depending on the design used, a score may be represented by X_i, X_{ij}, or X_{ijk}.
$X_{highest\ URL}$	Upper real limit for the highest score in a distribution of scores.
$X_{lowest\ LRL}$	Lower real limit for the lowest score in a distribution.
X_L	Lower real limit of an interval containing the score X in a frequency distribution.
X_P	Score at the P percentile point in a distribution.
X_{50}	Score corresponding to the median of a distribution.
$\overline{X}$	X bar, the sample mean.
$\overline{X}_{A_1}, \overline{X}_{A_2}, \overline{X}_{A_3}$	Main effect means for levels of factor A.
$\overline{X}_{B_1}, \overline{X}_{B_2}, \overline{X}_{B_3}$	Main effect means for levels of factor B.
$\overline{X}_{AB}$	Cell mean in a two-factor design.
$\overline{X}_G$	Grand mean.
$\overline{X}_S$	Subject mean in a within-subjects design.
$\overline{X}_{\overline{X}}$	Mean of the empirical sampling distribution of the mean.
$\overline{X}_{\overline{X}_1 - \overline{X}_2}$	Mean of an empirical sampling distribution of the difference between means.
Y	A subject's score on the variable identified as the Y variable.
$\overline{Y}$	Y bar. The sample mean for scores identified as the Y variable.
Y'	Predicted value of Y from a linear regression line.
z	Value of a score obtained from using the z transformation.

Statistical Tables

TABLE C.1

Proportions of area under the standard normal distribution

(a) Value of +z/−z	(b)	(c)	(a) Value of +z/−z	(b)	(c)	(a) Value of +z/−z	(b)	(c)
.00	.0000	.5000	.28	.1103	.3897	.56	.2123	.2877
.01	.0040	.4960	.29	.1141	.3859	.57	.2157	.2843
.02	.0080	.4920	.30	.1179	.3821	.58	.2190	.2810
.03	.0120	.4880	.31	.1217	.3783	.59	.2224	.2776
.04	.0160	.4840	.32	.1255	.3745	.60	.2257	.2743
.05	.0199	.4801	.33	.1293	.3707	.61	.2291	.2709
.06	.0239	.4761	.34	.1331	.3669	.62	.2324	.2676
.07	.0279	.4721	.35	.1368	.3632	.63	.2357	.2643
.08	.0319	.4681	.36	.1406	.3594	.64	.2389	.2611
.09	.0359	.4641	.37	.1443	.3557	.65	.2422	.2578
.10	.0398	.4602	.38	.1480	.3520	.66	.2454	.2546
.11	.0438	.4562	.39	.1517	.3483	.67	.2486	.2514
.12	.0478	.4522	.40	.1554	.3446	.68	.2517	.2483
.13	.0517	.4483	.41	.1591	.3409	.69	.2549	.2451
.14	.0557	.4443	.42	.1628	.3372	.70	.2580	.2420
.15	.0596	.4404	.43	.1664	.3336	.71	.2611	.2389
.16	.0636	.4364	.44	.1700	.3300	.72	.2642	.2358
.17	.0675	.4325	.45	.1736	.3264	.73	.2673	.2327
.18	.0714	.4286	.46	.1772	.3228	.74	.2704	.2296
.19	.0753	.4247	.47	.1808	.3192	.75	.2734	.2266
.20	.0793	.4207	.48	.1844	.3156	.76	.2764	.2236
.21	.0832	.4168	.49	.1879	.3121	.77	.2794	.2206
.22	.0871	.4129	.50	.1915	.3085	.78	.2823	.2177
.23	.0910	.4090	.51	.1950	.3050	.79	.2852	.2148
.24	.0948	.4052	.52	.1985	.3015	.80	.2881	.2119
.25	.0987	.4013	.53	.2019	.2981	.81	.2910	.2090
.26	.1026	.3974	.54	.2054	.2946	.82	.2939	.2061
.27	.1064	.3936	.55	.2088	.2912	.83	.2967	.2033

(continued)

TABLE C.1 (continued)

(a) Value of +z (−z)	(b)	(c)	(a) Value of +z (−z)	(b)	(c)	(a) Value of +z (−z)	(b)	(c)
.84	.2995	.2005	1.53	.4370	.0630	2.22	.4868	.0132
.85	.3023	.1977	1.54	.4382	.0618	2.23	.4871	.0129
.86	.3051	.1949	1.55	.4394	.0606	2.24	.4875	.0125
.87	.3078	.1922	1.56	.4406	.0594	2.25	.4878	.0122
.88	.3106	.1894	1.57	.4418	.0582	2.26	.4881	.0119
.89	.3133	.1867	1.58	.4429	.0571	2.27	.4884	.0116
.90	.3159	.1841	1.59	.4441	.0559	2.28	.4887	.0113
.91	.3186	.1814	1.60	.4452	.0548	2.29	.4890	.0110
.92	.3212	.1788	1.61	.4463	.0537	2.30	.4893	.0107
.93	.3238	.1762	1.62	.4474	.0526	2.31	.4896	.0104
.94	.3264	.1736	1.63	.4484	.0516	2.32	.4898	.0102
.95	.3289	.1711	1.64	.4495	.0505	2.33	.4901	.0099
.96	.3315	.1685	1.65	.4505	.0495	2.34	.4904	.0096
.97	.3340	.1660	1.66	.4515	.0485	2.35	.4906	.0094
.98	.3365	.1635	1.67	.4525	.0475	2.36	.4909	.0091
.99	.3389	.1611	1.68	.4535	.0465	2.37	.4911	.0089
1.00	.3413	.1587	1.69	.4545	.0455	2.38	.4913	.0087
1.01	.3438	.1562	1.70	.4554	.0446	2.39	.4916	.0084
1.02	.3461	.1539	1.71	.4564	.0436	2.40	.4918	.0082
1.03	.3485	.1515	1.72	.4573	.0427	2.41	.4920	.0080
1.04	.3508	.1492	1.73	.4582	.0418	2.42	.4922	.0078
1.05	.3531	.1469	1.74	.4591	.0409	2.43	.4925	.0075
1.06	.3554	.1446	1.75	.4599	.0401	2.44	.4927	.0073
1.07	.3577	.1423	1.76	.4608	.0392	2.45	.4929	.0071
1.08	.3599	.1401	1.77	.4616	.0384	2.46	.4931	.0069
1.09	.3621	.1379	1.78	.4625	.0375	2.47	.4932	.0068
1.10	.3643	.1357	1.79	.4633	.0367	2.48	.4934	.0066
1.11	.3665	.1335	1.80	.4641	.0359	2.49	.4936	.0064
1.12	.3686	.1314	1.81	.4649	.0351	2.50	.4938	.0062

z			z			z		
1.13	.3708	.1292	1.82	.4656	.0344	2.51	.4940	.0060
1.14	.3729	.1271	1.83	.4664	.0336	2.52	.4941	.0059
1.15	.3749	.1251	1.84	.4671	.0329	2.53	.4943	.0057
1.16	.3770	.1230	1.85	.4678	.0322	2.54	.4945	.0055
1.17	.3790	.1210	1.86	.4686	.0314	2.55	.4946	.0054
1.18	.3810	.1190	1.87	.4693	.0307	2.56	.4948	.0052
1.19	.3830	.1170	1.88	.4699	.0301	2.57	.4949	.0051
1.20	.3849	.1151	1.89	.4706	.0294	2.58	.4951	.0049
1.21	.3869	.1131	1.90	.4713	.0287	2.59	.4952	.0048
1.22	.3888	.1112	1.91	.4719	.0281	2.60	.4953	.0047
1.23	.3907	.1093	1.92	.4726	.0274	2.61	.4955	.0045
1.24	.3925	.1075	1.93	.4732	.0268	2.62	.4956	.0044
1.25	.3944	.1056	1.94	.4738	.0262	2.63	.4957	.0043
1.26	.3962	.1038	1.95	.4744	.0256	2.64	.4959	.0041
1.27	.3980	.1020	1.96	.4750	.0250	2.65	.4960	.0040
1.28	.3997	.1003	1.97	.4756	.0244	2.66	.4961	.0039
1.29	.4015	.0985	1.98	.4761	.0239	2.67	.4962	.0038
1.30	.4032	.0968	1.99	.4767	.0233	2.68	.4963	.0037
1.31	.4049	.0951	2.00	.4772	.0228	2.69	.4964	.0036
1.32	.4066	.0934	2.01	.4778	.0222	2.70	.4965	.0035
1.33	.4082	.0918	2.02	.4783	.0217	2.71	.4966	.0034
1.34	.4099	.0901	2.03	.4788	.0212	2.72	.4967	.0033
1.35	.4115	.0885	2.04	.4793	.0207	2.73	.4968	.0032
1.36	.4131	.0869	2.05	.4798	.0202	2.74	.4969	.0031
1.37	.4147	.0853	2.06	.4803	.0197	2.75	.4970	.0030
1.38	.4162	.0838	2.07	.4808	.0192	2.76	.4971	.0029
1.39	.4177	.0823	2.08	.4812	.0188	2.77	.4972	.0028
1.40	.4192	.0808	2.09	.4817	.0183	2.78	.4973	.0027
1.41	.4207	.0793	2.10	.4821	.0179	2.79	.4974	.0026
1.42	.4222	.0778	2.11	.4826	.0174	2.80	.4974	.0026
1.43	.4236	.0764	2.12	.4830	.0170	2.81	.4975	.0025
1.44	.4251	.0749	2.13	.4834	.0166	2.82	.4976	.0024
1.45	.4265	.0735	2.14	.4838	.0162	2.83	.4977	.0023
1.46	.4279	.0721	2.15	.4842	.0158	2.84	.4977	.0023
1.47	.4292	.0708	2.16	.4846	.0154	2.85	.4978	.0022
1.48	.4306	.0694	2.17	.4850	.0150	2.86	.4979	.0021
1.49	.4319	.0681	2.18	.4854	.0146	2.87	.4979	.0021
1.50	.4332	.0668	2.19	.4857	.0143	2.88	.4980	.0020
1.51	.4345	.0655	2.20	.4861	.0139	2.89	.4981	.0019
1.52	.4357	.0643	2.21	.4864	.0136	2.90	.4981	.0019

(continued)

TABLE C.1

(continued)

(a) Value of +z/−z	(b)	(c)	(a) Value of +z/−z	(b)	(c)	(a) Value of +z/−z	(b)	(c)
2.91	.4982	.0018	3.18	.4993	.0007	3.45	.4997	.0003
2.92	.4982	.0018	3.19	.4993	.0007	3.46	.4997	.0003
2.93	.4983	.0017	3.20	.4993	.0007	3.47	.4997	.0003
2.94	.4984	.0016	3.21	.4993	.0007	3.48	.4997	.0003
2.95	.4984	.0016	3.22	.4994	.0006	3.49	.4998	.0002
2.96	.4985	.0015	3.23	.4994	.0006	3.50	.4998	.0002
2.97	.4985	.0015	3.24	.4994	.0006	3.51	.4998	.0002
2.98	.4986	.0014	3.25	.4994	.0006	3.52	.4998	.0002
2.99	.4986	.0014	3.26	.4994	.0006	3.53	.4998	.0002
3.00	.4987	.0013	3.27	.4995	.0005	3.54	.4998	.0002
3.01	.4987	.0013	3.28	.4995	.0005	3.55	.4998	.0002
3.02	.4987	.0013	3.29	.4995	.0005	3.56	.4998	.0002
3.03	.4988	.0012	3.30	.4995	.0005	3.57	.4998	.0002
3.04	.4988	.0012	3.31	.4995	.0005	3.58	.4998	.0002
3.05	.4989	.0011	3.32	.4995	.0005	3.59	.4998	.0002
3.06	.4989	.0011	3.33	.4996	.0004	3.60	.4998	.0002
3.07	.4989	.0011	3.34	.4996	.0004	3.61	.4998	.0002
3.08	.4990	.0010	3.35	.4996	.0004	3.62	.4999	.0001
3.09	.4990	.0010	3.36	.4996	.0004	3.63	.4999	.0001
3.10	.4990	.0010	3.37	.4996	.0004	3.64	.4999	.0001
3.11	.4991	.0009	3.38	.4996	.0004	3.65	.4999	.0001
3.12	.4991	.0009	3.39	.4997	.0003	3.66	.4999	.0001
3.13	.4991	.0009	3.40	.4997	.0003	3.67	.4999	.0001
3.14	.4992	.0008	3.41	.4997	.0003	3.68	.4999	.0001
3.15	.4992	.0008	3.42	.4997	.0003	3.69	.4999	.0001
3.16	.4992	.0008	3.43	.4997	.0003	3.70	.4999	.0001
3.17	.4992	.0008	3.44	.4997	.0003			

Source: Values calculated by the authors using Microsoft Excel Normsdist(value) − .5 (column b); 1 − Normsdist(value) (column c). All values rounded to four decimal places.

C.2

Critical values of the t distribution for $\alpha = .05$ and $\alpha = .01$. A value of $t_{obs}(df)$ equal to or greater than the tabled value is statistically significant at the α level selected.

	Two-Tailed Test			One-Tailed Test	
df	$\alpha = .05$	$\alpha = .01$	df	$\alpha = .05$	$\alpha = .01$
1	12.706	63.657	1	6.314	31.821
2	4.303	9.925	2	2.920	6.965
3	3.182	5.841	3	2.353	4.541
4	2.776	4.604	4	2.132	3.747
5	2.571	4.032	5	2.015	3.365
6	2.447	3.707	6	1.943	3.143
7	2.365	3.499	7	1.895	2.998
8	2.306	3.355	8	1.860	2.896
9	2.262	3.250	9	1.833	2.821
10	2.228	3.169	10	1.812	2.764
11	2.201	3.106	11	1.796	2.718
12	2.179	3.055	12	1.782	2.681
13	2.160	3.012	13	1.771	2.650
14	2.145	2.977	14	1.761	2.624
15	2.131	2.947	15	1.753	2.602
16	2.120	2.921	16	1.746	2.583
17	2.110	2.898	17	1.740	2.567
18	2.101	2.878	18	1.734	2.552
19	2.093	2.861	19	1.729	2.539
20	2.086	2.845	20	1.725	2.528
21	2.080	2.831	21	1.721	2.518
22	2.074	2.819	22	1.717	2.508
23	2.069	2.807	23	1.714	2.500
24	2.064	2.797	24	1.711	2.492
25	2.060	2.787	25	1.708	2.485
26	2.056	2.779	26	1.706	2.479
27	2.052	2.771	27	1.703	2.473
28	2.048	2.763	28	1.701	2.467
29	2.045	2.756	29	1.699	2.462
30	2.042	2.750	30	1.697	2.457
40	2.021	2.704	40	1.684	2.423
60	2.000	2.660	60	1.671	2.390
120	1.980	2.617	120	1.658	2.358
∞	1.960	2.576	∞	1.645	2.326

Source: Reprinted from Table 12, Percentage points of the *t*-distribution. E. S. Pearson and H. O. Hartley, *Biometrika Tables for Statisticians,* Volume 1, Copyright 1976, Cambridge University Press. Reprinted by permission of the Biometrika Trustees.

TABLE

C-3a

Critical values of the F distribution for α = .05. A value of F_{obs} ($df_{numerator}$, $df_{denominator}$) equal to or greater than the tabled value is statistically significant at the .05 significance level

Degrees of Freedom for the Numerator

	1	2	3	4	5	6	7	8	9	10	12	15	20	24	30	40	60	120	∞
1	161.4	199.5	215.7	224.6	230.2	234.0	236.8	238.9	240.5	241.9	243.9	245.9	248.0	249.1	250.1	251.1	252.2	253.3	254.3
2	18.51	19.00	19.16	19.25	19.30	19.33	19.35	19.37	19.38	19.40	19.41	19.43	19.45	19.45	19.46	19.47	19.48	19.49	19.50
3	10.13	9.55	9.28	9.12	9.01	8.94	8.89	8.85	8.81	8.79	8.74	8.70	8.66	8.64	8.62	8.59	8.57	8.55	8.53
4	7.71	6.94	6.59	6.39	6.26	6.16	6.09	6.04	6.00	5.96	5.91	5.86	5.80	5.77	5.75	5.72	5.69	5.66	5.63
5	6.61	5.79	5.41	5.19	5.05	4.95	4.88	4.82	4.77	4.74	4.68	4.62	4.56	4.53	4.50	4.46	4.43	4.40	4.36
6	5.99	5.14	4.76	4.53	4.39	4.28	4.21	4.15	4.10	4.06	4.00	3.94	3.87	3.84	3.81	3.77	3.74	3.70	3.67
7	5.59	4.74	4.35	4.12	3.97	3.87	3.79	3.73	3.68	3.64	3.57	3.51	3.44	3.41	3.38	3.34	3.30	3.27	3.23
8	5.32	4.46	4.07	3.84	3.69	3.58	3.50	3.44	3.39	3.35	3.28	3.22	3.15	3.12	3.08	3.04	3.01	2.97	2.93
9	5.12	4.26	3.86	3.63	3.48	3.37	3.29	3.23	3.18	3.14	3.07	3.01	2.94	2.90	2.86	2.83	2.79	2.75	2.71
10	4.96	4.10	3.71	3.48	3.33	3.22	3.14	3.07	3.02	2.98	2.91	2.85	2.77	2.74	2.70	2.66	2.62	2.58	2.54
11	4.84	3.98	3.59	3.36	3.20	3.09	3.01	2.95	2.90	2.85	2.79	2.72	2.65	2.61	2.57	2.53	2.49	2.45	2.40
12	4.75	3.89	3.49	3.26	3.11	3.00	2.91	2.85	2.80	2.75	2.69	2.62	2.54	2.51	2.47	2.43	2.38	2.34	2.30
13	4.67	3.81	3.41	3.18	3.03	2.92	2.83	2.77	2.71	2.67	2.60	2.53	2.46	2.42	2.38	2.34	2.30	2.25	2.21
14	4.60	3.74	3.34	3.11	2.96	2.85	2.76	2.70	2.65	2.60	2.53	2.46	2.39	2.35	2.31	2.27	2.22	2.18	2.13
15	4.54	3.68	3.29	3.06	2.90	2.79	2.71	2.64	2.59	2.54	2.48	2.40	2.33	2.29	2.25	2.20	2.16	2.11	2.07
16	4.49	3.63	3.24	3.01	2.85	2.74	2.66	2.59	2.54	2.49	2.42	2.35	2.28	2.24	2.19	2.15	2.11	2.06	2.01
17	4.45	3.59	3.20	2.96	2.81	2.70	2.61	2.55	2.49	2.45	2.38	2.31	2.23	2.19	2.15	2.10	2.06	2.01	1.96
18	4.41	3.55	3.16	2.93	2.77	2.66	2.58	2.51	2.46	2.41	2.34	2.27	2.19	2.15	2.11	2.06	2.02	1.97	1.92
19	4.38	3.52	3.13	2.90	2.74	2.63	2.54	2.48	2.42	2.38	2.31	2.23	2.16	2.11	2.07	2.03	1.98	1.93	1.88
20	4.35	3.49	3.10	2.87	2.71	2.60	2.51	2.45	2.39	2.35	2.28	2.20	2.12	2.08	2.04	1.99	1.95	1.90	1.84
21	4.32	3.47	3.07	2.84	2.68	2.57	2.49	2.42	2.37	2.32	2.25	2.18	2.10	2.05	2.01	1.96	1.92	1.87	1.81
22	4.30	3.44	3.05	2.82	2.66	2.55	2.46	2.40	2.34	2.30	2.23	2.15	2.07	2.03	1.98	1.94	1.89	1.84	1.78
23	4.28	3.42	3.03	2.80	2.64	2.53	2.44	2.37	2.32	2.27	2.20	2.13	2.05	2.01	1.96	1.91	1.86	1.81	1.76
24	4.26	3.40	3.01	2.78	2.62	2.51	2.42	2.36	2.30	2.25	2.18	2.11	2.03	1.98	1.94	1.89	1.84	1.79	1.73
25	4.24	3.39	2.99	2.76	2.60	2.49	2.40	2.34	2.28	2.24	2.16	2.09	2.01	1.96	1.92	1.87	1.82	1.77	1.71
26	4.23	3.37	2.98	2.74	2.59	2.47	2.39	2.32	2.27	2.22	2.15	2.07	1.99	1.95	1.90	1.85	1.80	1.75	1.69
27	4.21	3.35	2.96	2.73	2.57	2.46	2.37	2.31	2.25	2.20	2.13	2.06	1.97	1.93	1.88	1.84	1.79	1.73	1.67
28	4.20	3.34	2.95	2.71	2.56	2.45	2.36	2.29	2.24	2.19	2.12	2.04	1.96	1.91	1.87	1.82	1.77	1.71	1.65
29	4.18	3.33	2.93	2.70	2.55	2.43	2.35	2.28	2.22	2.18	2.10	2.03	1.94	1.90	1.85	1.81	1.75	1.70	1.64
30	4.17	3.32	2.92	2.69	2.53	2.42	2.33	2.27	2.21	2.16	2.09	2.01	1.93	1.89	1.84	1.79	1.74	1.68	1.62
40	4.08	3.23	2.84	2.61	2.45	2.34	2.25	2.18	2.12	2.08	2.00	1.92	1.84	1.79	1.74	1.69	1.64	1.58	1.51
60	4.00	3.15	2.76	2.53	2.37	2.25	2.17	2.10	2.04	1.99	1.92	1.84	1.75	1.70	1.65	1.59	1.53	1.47	1.39
120	3.92	3.07	2.68	2.45	2.29	2.17	2.09	2.02	1.96	1.91	1.83	1.75	1.66	1.61	1.55	1.50	1.43	1.35	1.25
∞	3.84	3.00	2.60	2.37	2.21	2.10	2.01	1.94	1.88	1.83	1.75	1.67	1.57	1.52	1.46	1.39	1.32	1.22	1.00

Degrees of Freedom for the Denominator

Source: Reprinted from Table 18, Percentage points of the F-distribution (variance ratio). Upper 5% points. E. S. Pearson and H. O. Hartley, *Biometrika Tables for Statisticians*, Volume 1, Copyright 1976, Cambridge University Press. Reprinted by permission of the Biometrika Trustees.

TABLE C.3b

Critical values of the F distribution for $\alpha = .01$. A value of $F_{obs}(df_{numerator}, df_{denominator})$ equal to or greater than the tabled value is statistically significant at the .01 significance level

Degrees of Freedom for the Numerator

df denom	1	2	3	4	5	6	7	8	9	10	12	15	20	24	30	40	60	120	∞
1	4052	4999.5	5403	5625	5764	5859	5928	5981	6022	6056	6106	6157	6209	6235	6261	6287	6313	6339	6366
2	98.50	99.00	99.17	99.25	99.30	99.33	99.36	99.37	99.39	99.40	99.42	99.43	99.45	99.46	99.47	99.47	99.48	99.49	99.50
3	34.12	30.82	29.46	28.71	28.24	27.91	27.67	27.49	27.35	27.23	27.05	26.87	26.69	26.60	26.50	26.41	26.32	26.22	26.13
4	21.20	18.00	16.69	15.98	15.52	15.21	14.98	14.80	14.66	14.55	14.37	14.20	14.02	13.93	13.84	13.75	13.65	13.56	13.46
5	16.26	13.27	12.06	11.39	10.97	10.67	10.46	10.29	10.16	10.05	9.89	9.72	9.55	9.47	9.38	9.29	9.20	9.11	9.02
6	13.75	10.92	9.78	9.15	8.75	8.47	8.26	8.10	7.98	7.87	7.72	7.56	7.40	7.31	7.23	7.14	7.06	6.97	6.88
7	12.25	9.55	8.45	7.85	7.46	7.19	6.99	6.84	6.72	6.62	6.47	6.31	6.16	6.07	5.99	5.91	5.82	5.74	5.65
8	11.26	8.65	7.59	7.01	6.63	6.37	6.18	6.03	5.91	5.81	5.67	5.52	5.36	5.28	5.20	5.12	5.03	4.95	4.86
9	10.56	8.02	6.99	6.42	6.06	5.80	5.61	5.47	5.35	5.26	5.11	4.96	4.81	4.73	4.65	4.57	4.48	4.40	4.31
10	10.04	7.56	6.55	5.99	5.64	5.39	5.20	5.06	4.94	4.85	4.71	4.56	4.41	4.33	4.25	4.17	4.08	4.00	3.91
11	9.65	7.21	6.22	5.67	5.32	5.07	4.89	4.74	4.63	4.54	4.40	4.25	4.10	4.02	3.94	3.86	3.78	3.69	3.60
12	9.33	6.93	5.95	5.41	5.06	4.82	4.64	4.50	4.39	4.30	4.16	4.01	3.86	3.78	3.70	3.62	3.54	3.45	3.36
13	9.07	6.70	5.74	5.21	4.86	4.62	4.44	4.30	4.19	4.10	3.96	3.82	3.66	3.59	3.51	3.43	3.34	3.25	3.17
14	8.86	6.51	5.56	5.04	4.69	4.46	4.28	4.14	4.03	3.94	3.80	3.66	3.51	3.43	3.35	3.27	3.18	3.09	3.00
15	8.68	6.36	5.42	4.89	4.56	4.32	4.14	4.00	3.89	3.80	3.67	3.52	3.37	3.29	3.21	3.13	3.05	2.96	2.87
16	8.53	6.23	5.29	4.77	4.44	4.20	4.03	3.89	3.78	3.69	3.55	3.41	3.26	3.18	3.10	3.02	2.93	2.84	2.75
17	8.40	6.11	5.18	4.67	4.34	4.10	3.93	3.79	3.68	3.59	3.46	3.31	3.16	3.08	3.00	2.92	2.83	2.75	2.65
18	8.29	6.01	5.09	4.58	4.25	4.01	3.84	3.71	3.60	3.51	3.37	3.23	3.08	3.00	2.92	2.84	2.75	2.66	2.57
19	8.18	5.93	5.01	4.50	4.17	3.94	3.77	3.63	3.52	3.43	3.30	3.15	3.00	2.92	2.84	2.76	2.67	2.58	2.49
20	8.10	5.85	4.94	4.43	4.10	3.87	3.70	3.56	3.46	3.37	3.23	3.09	2.94	2.86	2.78	2.69	2.61	2.52	2.42
21	8.02	5.78	4.87	4.37	4.04	3.81	3.64	3.51	3.40	3.31	3.17	3.03	2.88	2.80	2.72	2.64	2.55	2.46	2.36
22	7.95	5.72	4.82	4.31	3.99	3.76	3.59	3.45	3.35	3.26	3.12	2.98	2.83	2.75	2.67	2.58	2.50	2.40	2.31
23	7.88	5.66	4.76	4.26	3.94	3.71	3.54	3.41	3.30	3.21	3.07	2.93	2.78	2.70	2.62	2.54	2.45	2.35	2.26
24	7.82	5.61	4.72	4.22	3.90	3.67	3.50	3.36	3.26	3.17	3.03	2.89	2.74	2.66	2.58	2.49	2.40	2.31	2.21
25	7.77	5.57	4.68	4.18	3.85	3.63	3.46	3.32	3.22	3.13	2.99	2.85	2.70	2.62	2.54	2.45	2.36	2.27	2.17
26	7.72	5.53	4.64	4.14	3.82	3.59	3.42	3.29	3.18	3.09	2.96	2.81	2.66	2.58	2.50	2.42	2.33	2.23	2.13
27	7.68	5.49	4.60	4.11	3.78	3.56	3.39	3.26	3.15	3.06	2.93	2.78	2.63	2.55	2.47	2.38	2.29	2.20	2.10
28	7.64	5.45	4.57	4.07	3.75	3.53	3.36	3.23	3.12	3.03	2.90	2.75	2.60	2.52	2.44	2.35	2.26	2.17	2.06
29	7.60	5.42	4.54	4.04	3.73	3.50	3.33	3.20	3.09	3.00	2.87	2.73	2.57	2.49	2.41	2.33	2.23	2.14	2.03
30	7.56	5.39	4.51	4.02	3.70	3.47	3.30	3.17	3.07	2.98	2.84	2.70	2.55	2.47	2.39	2.30	2.21	2.11	2.01
40	7.31	5.18	4.31	3.83	3.51	3.29	3.12	2.99	2.89	2.80	2.66	2.52	2.37	2.29	2.20	2.11	2.02	1.92	1.80
60	7.08	4.98	4.13	3.65	3.34	3.12	2.95	2.82	2.72	2.63	2.50	2.35	2.20	2.12	2.03	1.94	1.84	1.73	1.60
120	6.85	4.79	3.95	3.48	3.17	2.96	2.79	2.66	2.56	2.47	2.34	2.19	2.03	1.95	1.86	1.76	1.66	1.53	1.38
∞	6.63	4.61	3.78	3.32	3.02	2.80	2.64	2.51	2.41	2.32	2.18	2.04	1.88	1.79	1.70	1.59	1.47	1.32	1.00

Degrees of Freedom for the Denominator (row labels at left)

Source: Reprinted from Table 18, Percentage points of the F-distribution (variance ratio), Upper 1% points. E. S. Pearson and H. O. Hartley, *Biometrika Tables for Statisticians*, Volume 1, Copyright 1976, Cambridge University Press. Reprinted by permission of the Biometrika Trustees.

TABLE

C.4a   Values of the studentized range statistic, q, for $\alpha = .05$

Number of Means Being Compared

		2	3	4	5	6	7	8	9	10
	1	17.97	26.98	32.82	37.08	40.41	43.12	45.40	47.36	49.07
	2	6.08	8.33	9.80	10.88	11.74	12.44	13.03	13.54	13.99
	3	4.50	5.91	6.82	7.50	8.04	8.48	8.85	9.18	9.46
	4	3.93	5.04	5.76	6.29	6.71	7.05	7.35	7.60	7.83
	5	3.64	4.60	5.22	5.67	6.03	6.33	6.58	6.80	6.99
	6	3.46	4.34	4.90	5.30	5.63	5.90	6.12	6.32	6.49
	7	3.34	4.16	4.68	5.06	5.36	5.61	5.82	6.00	6.16
Degrees of	8	3.26	4.04	4.53	4.89	5.17	5.40	5.60	5.77	5.92
Freedom	9	3.20	3.95	4.41	4.76	5.02	5.24	5.43	5.59	5.74
for MS_{Error}	10	3.15	3.88	4.33	4.65	4.91	5.12	5.30	5.46	5.60
	11	3.11	3.82	4.26	4.57	4.82	5.03	5.20	5.35	5.49
	12	3.08	3.77	4.20	4.51	4.75	4.95	5.12	5.27	5.39
	13	3.06	3.73	4.15	4.45	4.69	4.88	5.05	5.19	5.32
	14	3.03	3.70	4.11	4.41	4.64	4.83	4.99	5.13	5.25
	15	3.01	3.67	4.08	4.37	4.59	4.78	4.94	5.08	5.20
	16	3.00	3.65	4.05	4.33	4.56	4.74	4.90	5.03	5.15
	17	2.98	3.63	4.02	4.30	4.52	4.70	4.86	4.99	5.11
	18	2.97	3.61	4.00	4.28	4.49	4.67	4.82	4.96	5.07
	19	2.96	3.59	3.98	4.25	4.47	4.65	4.79	4.92	5.04
	20	2.95	3.58	3.96	4.23	4.45	4.62	4.77	4.90	5.01
	24	2.92	3.53	3.90	4.17	4.37	4.54	4.68	4.81	4.92
	30	2.89	3.49	3.85	4.10	4.30	4.46	4.60	4.72	4.82
	40	2.86	3.44	3.79	4.04	4.23	4.39	4.52	4.63	4.73
	60	2.83	3.40	3.74	3.98	4.16	4.31	4.44	4.55	4.65
	120	2.80	3.36	3.68	3.92	4.10	4.24	4.36	4.47	4.56
	∞	2.77	3.31	3.63	3.86	4.03	4.17	4.29	4.39	4.47

Source: Reprinted from Table 29, Percentage points of the studentized range, $q = (x_n - x_1)/s_v$. Upper 5% points. E. S. Pearson and H. O. Hartley, *Biometrika Tables for Statisticians,* Volume 1, Copyright 1976, Cambridge University Press. Reprinted by permission of the Biometrika Trustees.

If Appendix C.4 is used to find q for the *CD* of a test of simple effects in a factorial design, use the following conversion to find the column to be used.

Type of Design	Use q from Table C.4 Found in the Column for ___ Levels of the Independent Variable
2 × 2	3
2 × 3	5
3 × 2	5
3 × 3	7
3 × 4	8
4 × 3	8
4 × 4	10

TABLE

c.4b   Values of the studentized range statistic, q, for $\alpha = .01$

		Number of Means Being Compared								
		2	3	4	5	6	7	8	9	10
	1	90.03	135.0	164.3	185.6	202.2	215.8	227.2	237.0	245.6
	2	14.04	19.02	22.29	24.72	26.63	28.20	29.53	30.68	31.69
	3	8.26	10.62	12.17	13.33	14.24	15.00	15.64	16.20	16.69
	4	6.51	8.12	9.17	9.96	10.58	11.10	11.55	11.93	12.27
	5	5.70	6.98	7.80	8.42	8.91	9.32	9.67	9.97	10.24
	6	5.24	6.33	7.03	7.56	7.97	8.32	8.61	8.87	9.10
	7	4.95	5.92	6.54	7.01	7.37	7.68	7.94	8.17	8.37
Degrees of	8	4.75	5.64	6.20	6.62	6.96	7.24	7.47	7.68	7.86
Freedom	9	4.60	5.43	5.96	6.35	6.66	6.91	7.13	7.33	7.49
for MS_{Error}	10	4.48	5.27	5.77	6.14	6.43	6.67	6.87	7.05	7.21
	11	4.39	5.15	5.62	5.97	6.25	6.48	6.67	6.84	6.99
	12	4.32	5.05	5.50	5.84	6.10	6.32	6.51	6.67	6.81
	13	4.26	4.96	5.40	5.73	5.98	6.19	6.37	6.53	6.67
	14	4.21	4.89	5.32	5.63	5.88	6.08	6.26	6.41	6.54
	15	4.17	4.84	5.25	5.56	5.80	5.99	6.16	6.31	6.44
	16	4.13	4.79	5.19	5.49	5.72	5.92	6.08	6.22	6.35
	17	4.10	4.74	5.14	5.43	5.66	5.85	6.01	6.15	6.27
	18	4.07	4.70	5.09	5.38	5.60	5.79	5.94	6.08	6.20
	19	4.05	4.67	5.05	5.33	5.55	5.73	5.89	6.02	6.14
	20	4.02	4.64	5.02	5.29	5.51	5.69	5.84	5.97	6.09
	24	3.96	4.55	4.91	5.17	5.37	5.54	5.69	5.81	5.92
	30	3.89	4.45	4.80	5.05	5.24	5.40	5.54	5.65	5.76
	40	3.82	4.37	4.70	4.93	5.11	5.26	5.39	5.50	5.60
	60	3.76	4.28	4.59	4.82	4.99	5.13	5.25	5.36	5.45
	120	3.70	4.20	4.50	4.71	4.87	5.01	5.12	5.21	5.30
	∞	3.64	4.12	4.40	4.60	4.76	4.88	4.99	5.08	5.16

Source: Reprinted from Table 29, Percentage points of the studentized range, $q = (x_n - x_1)/s_v$. Upper 1% points. E. S. Pearson and H. O. Hartley, *Biometrika Tables for Statisticians*, Volume 1, Copyright 1976, Cambridge University Press. Reprinted by permission of the Biometrika Trustees.

If Appendix C.4 is used to find q for the *CD* of a test of simple effects in a factorial design, use the following conversion to find the column to be used.

Type of Design	Use q from Table C.4 Found in the Column for ___ Levels of the Independent Variable
2×2	3
2×3	5
3×2	5
3×3	7
3×4	8
4×3	8
4×4	10

TABLE

C.5

Critical values of r for $\alpha = .05$ and $\alpha = .01$ (two-tailed test). A value of r_{obs} equal to or greater than the tabled value is statistically significant at the α level selected.

df[a]	$\alpha = .05$	$\alpha = .01$
1	.99692	.999877
2	.9500	.99000
3	.878	.9587
4	.811	.9172
5	.754	.875
6	.707	.834
7	.666	.798
8	.632	.765
9	.602	.735
10	.576	.708
11	.553	.684
12	.532	.661
13	.514	.641
14	.497	.623
15	.482	.606
16	.468	.590
17	.456	.575
18	.444	.561
19	.433	.549
20	.423	.537
25	.381	.487
30	.349	.449
35	.325	.418
40	.304	.393
45	.288	.372
50	.273	.354
60	.250	.325
70	.232	.302
80	.217	.283
90	.205	.267
100	.195	.254

[a]df are equal to $N_{pairs} - 2$ where N_{pairs} is the number of paired observations.

Source: Reprinted from Table 13, Percentage points for the distribution of the correlation coefficient, r, when $\rho = 0$. E. S. Pearson and H. O. Hartley, *Biometrika Tables for Statisticians,* Volume 1, Copyright 1976, Cambridge University Press. Reprinted by permission of the Biometrika Trustees.

TABLE C.6

Critical values of r_s for $\alpha = .05$ and $\alpha = .01$ (two-tailed test). A value of $r_{s\ obs}$ equal to or greater than the tabled value is statistically significant at the α level selected.

N_{pairs}	$\alpha = .05$	$\alpha = .01$
5	—	—
6	.886	—
7	.786	.929
8	.738	.881
9	.700	.833
10	.648	.794
11	.618	.818
12	.591	.780
13	.566	.745
14	.545	.716
15	.525	.689
16	.507	.666
17	.490	.645
18	.476	.625
19	.462	.608
20	.450	.591
21	.438	.576
22	.428	.562
23	.418	.549
24	.409	.537
25	.400	.526
26	.392	.515
27	.385	.505
28	.377	.496
29	.370	.487
30	.364	.478

Source: E. G. Olds, Distribution of sums of squares of rank differences for small numbers of individuals. *Annals of Mathematical Statistics,* Volume 9, 1938, 133–148, and E. G. Olds. The 5% significance levels for sums of squares of rank differences and a correction. *Annals of Mathematical Statistics,* Volume 20, 1949, 117–118. Reprinted with permission from *Annals of Mathematical Statistics.*

	TABLE
	C.7

Critical values of the chi-square distribution for $\alpha = .05$ and $\alpha = .01$. A value of $\chi^2_{obs}(df)$ equal to or greater than the tabled value is statistically significant at the α level selected.

df	$\alpha = .05$	$\alpha = .01$
1	3.84146	6.63490
2	5.99146	9.21034
3	7.81473	11.3449
4	9.48773	13.2767
5	11.0705	15.0863
6	12.5916	16.8119
7	14.0671	18.4753
8	15.5073	20.0902
9	16.9190	21.6660
10	18.3070	23.2093
11	19.6751	24.7250
12	21.0261	26.2170
13	22.3620	27.6882
14	23.6848	29.1412
15	24.9958	30.5779
16	26.2962	31.9999
17	27.5871	33.4087
18	28.8693	34.8053
19	30.1435	36.1909
20	31.4104	37.5662
21	32.6706	38.9322
22	33.9244	40.2894
23	35.1725	41.6384
24	36.4150	42.9798
25	37.6525	44.3141
26	38.8851	45.6417
27	40.1133	46.9629
28	41.3371	48.2782
29	42.5570	49.5879
30	43.7730	50.8922
40	55.7585	63.6907
50	67.5048	76.1539
60	79.0819	88.3794
70	90.5312	100.425
80	101.879	112.329
90	113.145	124.116
100	124.342	135.807

TABLE c.8a

Critical values of U in the Mann–Whitney U test for $\alpha = .05$ (two-tailed test). If the group sizes are unequal, n_1 is the smaller group. A value of U_{obs} equal to or less than the tabled value is statistically significant at the .05 significance level.

n_1 \ n_2	1	2	3	4	5	6	7	8	9	10	11	12	13	14	15	16	17	18	19	20
1																				
2								0	0	0	0	1	1	1	1	1	2	2	2	2
3					0	1	1	2	2	3	3	4	4	5	5	6	6	7	7	8
4				0	1	2	3	4	4	5	6	7	8	9	10	11	11	12	13	13
5			0	1	2	3	5	6	7	8	9	11	12	13	14	15	17	18	19	20
6			1	2	3	5	6	8	10	11	13	14	16	17	19	21	22	24	25	27
7			1	3	5	6	8	10	12	14	16	18	20	22	24	26	28	30	32	34
8		0	2	4	6	8	10	13	15	17	19	22	24	26	29	31	34	36	38	41
9		0	2	4	7	10	12	15	17	20	23	26	28	31	34	37	39	42	45	48
10		0	3	5	8	11	14	17	20	23	26	29	33	36	39	42	45	48	52	55
11		0	3	6	9	13	16	19	23	26	30	33	37	40	44	47	51	55	58	62
12		1	4	7	11	14	18	22	26	29	33	37	41	45	49	53	57	61	65	69
13		1	4	8	12	16	20	24	28	33	37	41	45	50	54	59	63	67	72	76
14		1	5	9	13	17	22	26	31	36	40	45	50	55	59	64	67	74	78	83
15		1	5	10	14	19	24	29	34	39	44	49	54	59	64	70	75	80	85	90
16		1	6	11	15	21	26	31	37	42	47	53	59	64	70	75	81	86	92	98
17		2	6	11	17	22	28	34	39	45	51	57	63	67	75	81	87	93	99	105
18		2	7	12	18	24	30	36	42	48	55	61	67	74	80	86	93	99	106	112
19		2	7	13	19	25	32	38	45	52	58	65	72	78	85	92	99	106	113	119
20		2	8	13	20	27	34	41	48	55	62	69	76	83	90	98	105	112	119	127

Source: D. Auble, Critical values of U in the Wilcoxon (Mann–Whitney) two-sample statistic, Institute of Educational Research, Indiana University, Bloomington, Indiana, Volume 1, Number 2, 1953. Reprinted with permission from Institute of Educational Research, Indiana University, Bloomington, Indiana.

TABLE

c.8b

Critical values of U in the Mann–Whitney U test for $\alpha = .01$ (two-tailed test). If the group sizes are unequal, n_1 is the smaller group. A value of U_{obs} equal to or less than the tabled value is statistically significant at the .01 significance level.

n_1	n_2=1	2	3	4	5	6	7	8	9	10	11	12	13	14	15	16	17	18	19	20
1																				
2																			0	0
3									0	0	0	1	1	1	2	2	2	2	3	3
4					0	0	0	1	1	2	2	3	3	4	5	5	6	6	7	8
5				0	0	1	1	2	3	4	5	6	7	7	8	9	10	11	12	13
6				0	1	2	3	4	5	6	7	9	10	11	12	13	15	16	17	18
7				0	1	3	4	6	7	9	10	12	13	15	16	18	19	21	22	24
8				1	2	4	6	7	9	11	13	15	17	18	20	22	24	26	28	30
9			0	1	3	5	7	9	11	13	16	18	20	22	24	27	29	31	33	36
10			0	2	4	6	9	11	13	16	18	21	24	26	29	31	34	37	39	42
11			0	2	5	7	10	13	16	18	21	24	27	30	33	36	39	42	45	48
12			1	3	6	9	12	15	18	21	24	27	31	34	37	41	44	47	51	54
13			1	3	7	10	13	17	20	24	27	31	34	38	42	45	49	53	56	60
14			1	4	7	11	15	18	22	26	30	34	38	42	46	50	54	58	63	67
15			2	5	8	12	16	20	24	29	33	37	42	46	51	55	60	64	69	73
16			2	5	9	13	18	22	27	31	36	41	45	50	55	60	65	70	74	79
17			2	6	10	15	19	24	29	34	39	44	49	54	60	65	70	75	81	86
18			2	6	11	16	21	26	31	37	42	47	53	58	64	70	75	81	87	92
19		0	3	7	12	17	22	28	33	39	45	51	56	63	69	74	81	87	93	99
20		0	3	8	13	18	24	30	36	42	48	54	60	67	73	79	86	92	99	105

Source: D. Auble, Critical values of U in the Wilcoxon (Mann–Whitney) two-sample statistic, Institute of Educational Research, Indiana University, Bloomington, Indiana, Volume 1, Number 2, 1953. Reprinted with permission from Institute of Educational Research, Indiana University, Bloomington, Indiana.

TABLE
C.9

Critical values of T in the Wilcoxon test for $\alpha = .05$ and $\alpha = .01$ (two-tailed test). A value of T_{obs} equal to or less than the tabled value is statistically significant at the α level selected. Dashes indicate that statistical significance cannot be attained at this level for this group size.

N_{pairs}	$\alpha = .05$	$\alpha = .01$	N_{pairs}	$\alpha = .05$	$\alpha = .01$
6	0	—	29	126	100
7	2	—	30	137	109
8	3	0	31	147	118
9	5	1	32	159	128
10	8	3	33	170	138
11	10	5	34	182	148
12	13	7	35	195	159
13	17	9	36	208	171
14	21	12	37	221	182
15	25	15	38	235	194
16	29	19	39	249	207
17	34	23	40	264	220
18	40	27	41	279	233
19	46	32	42	294	247
20	52	37	43	310	261
21	58	42	44	327	276
22	65	48	45	343	291
23	73	54	46	361	307
24	81	61	47	378	322
25	89	68	48	396	339
26	98	75	49	415	355
27	107	83	50	434	373
28	116	91			

Source: Robert L. McCornack, Extended Tables of the Wilcoxon Matched Pair Signed Rank Statistic. *Journal of the American Statistical Association,* 1965, *60,* 864–871. Reprinted with permission from *The Journal of the American Statistical Association*. Copyright 1965 by the American Statistical Association. All rights reserved.

APPENDIX D

Commonly Used Formulas

Frequency Distributions

Ungrouped Frequency Distributions

rf of a score $= f$ of a score$/N$

$\%f$ of a score $= (rf$ of a score$) \times 100$

Grouped Frequency Distributions

size of class interval $= i = \dfrac{X_{\text{highest}} - X_{\text{lowest}}}{\text{number of intervals}}$

rf of scores in an interval $= \dfrac{f \text{ of scores in interval}}{N}$

$\%f$ of scores in an interval $= (rf$ of scores in interval$) \times 100$

Percentile Rank

$P_X = \dfrac{cf_L + [(X - X_L)/i]f_i}{N} \times 100$

Percentile of a Score

$X_p = X_L + \left(\dfrac{P(N) - cf_L}{f_i}\right)i$

Measures of Central Tendency

Median

$Mdn = X_{.50} = X_L + \left(\dfrac{.50(N) - cf_L}{f_i}\right)i$

Population Mean

$\mu = \dfrac{\Sigma X}{N_{\text{population}}}$

Sample Mean

$\overline{X} = \dfrac{\Sigma X}{N}$

Measures of Variability

Range

$$\text{Range} = X_{\text{highest URL}} - X_{\text{lowest LRL}}$$

Variance

Population Variance

$$\sigma^2 = \frac{\Sigma(X - \mu)^2}{N_{\text{population}}}$$

Variance of a Sample

$$S^2 = \frac{\Sigma(X - \bar{X})^2}{N}$$

Estimated Population Variance

Definitional formula: $s^2 = \dfrac{\Sigma(X - \bar{X})^2}{(N - 1)}$

Sum of squares formula: $s^2 = \dfrac{SS}{(N - 1)}$

Standard Deviation

Population Standard Deviation

$$\sigma = \sqrt{\sigma^2}$$

Standard Deviation of a Sample

$$S = \sqrt{S^2} = \sqrt{\frac{\Sigma(X - \bar{X})^2}{N}}$$

Estimated Population Standard Deviation

Definitional formula: $s = \sqrt{\dfrac{\Sigma(X - \bar{X})^2}{(N - 1)}}$

Sum of squares formula: $s = \sqrt{\dfrac{SS}{(N - 1)}}$

Standard Error of the Mean

σ Known

$$\sigma_{\bar{X}} = \frac{\sigma}{\sqrt{N}}$$

Estimated from s

$$s_{\bar{X}} = \frac{s}{\sqrt{N}}$$

Standard Error of the Difference between Means

σ Known

$$\sigma_{\overline{X}_1 - \overline{X}_2} = \sqrt{\frac{\sigma_1^2}{n_1} + \frac{\sigma_2^2}{n_2}}$$

Estimated from s_1^2 and s_2^2

$$s_{\overline{X}_1 - \overline{X}_2} = \sqrt{\left[\frac{(n_1 - 1)s_1^2 + (n_2 - 1)s_2^2}{n_1 + n_2 - 2}\right]\left[\frac{1}{n_1} + \frac{1}{n_2}\right]}$$

Probability

Probability (p) of Occurrence of an Event

$$p(\text{event}) = \frac{\text{Number of outcomes composing the event}}{\text{Total number of possible outcomes}}$$

z Scores and Standard Scores

Single Score

$$z = \frac{X - \mu}{\sigma}$$

Standard Score

$$z = \frac{X - \overline{X}}{S} \quad \text{or} \quad z = \frac{X - \overline{X}}{\sqrt{\frac{\Sigma(X - \overline{X})^2}{N}}}$$

Sample Mean

$$z = \frac{(\overline{X} - \mu)}{\sigma_{\overline{X}}}$$

t Tests

One-Sample t Test

$$t = \frac{\overline{X} - \mu}{s_{\overline{X}}} \quad \text{or} \quad t = \frac{\overline{X} - \mu}{s/\sqrt{N}}, \quad df = N - 1$$

t Test for Independent Groups

Definitional formula: $t_{\text{ind}} = \dfrac{\overline{X}_1 - \overline{X}_2}{s_{\overline{X}_1 - \overline{X}_2}}, \quad df = N - 2$

Computational formula: $t_{\text{ind}} = \dfrac{\overline{X}_1 - \overline{X}_2}{\sqrt{\left[\dfrac{(n_1 - 1)s_1^2 + (n_2 - 1)s_2^2}{n_1 + n_2 - 2}\right]\left[\dfrac{1}{n_1} + \dfrac{1}{n_2}\right]}}, \quad df = N - 2$

t Test for Related Scores

$$t_{\text{rel}} = \frac{\overline{X}_1 - \overline{X}_2}{s_{\overline{D}}}, df = N_{\text{pairs}} - 1, \text{ or}$$

$$t_{\text{rel}} = \frac{\overline{X}_1 - \overline{X}_2}{\sqrt{\dfrac{s_{\overline{D}}^2}{N_{\text{pairs}}}}}, df = N_{\text{pairs}} - 1$$

Analysis of Variance

One-Factor Between-Subjects Design

Source	SS	df [a]	MS	F
Factor A	$\sum\sum(\overline{X}_A - \overline{X}_G)^2$	$a - 1$	SS_A/df_A	MS_A/MS_{Error}
Error	$\sum\sum(X - \overline{X}_A)^2$	$N - a$	$SS_{\text{Error}}/df_{\text{Error}}$	
Total	$\sum\sum(X - \overline{X}_G)^2$	$N - 1$	Not calculated	

[a] a = number of levels of factor A, N = total number of scores.

Two-Factor Between-Subjects Design

Source	SS	df [a]	MS	F
Factor A	$\sum\sum(\overline{X}_A - \overline{X}_G)^2$	$a - 1$	$\dfrac{SS_A}{df_A}$	$\dfrac{MS_A}{MS_{\text{Error}}}$
Factor B	$\sum\sum(\overline{X}_B - \overline{X}_G)^2$	$b - 1$	$\dfrac{SS_B}{df_B}$	$\dfrac{MS_B}{MS_{\text{Error}}}$
Interaction of A and B	$\sum\sum(\overline{X}_{AB} - \overline{X}_A - \overline{X}_B + \overline{X}_G)^2$	$(a-1)(b-1)$	$\dfrac{SS_{A\times B}}{df_{A\times B}}$	$\dfrac{MS_{A\times B}}{MS_{\text{Error}}}$
Error	$\sum\sum(X - \overline{X}_{AB})^2$	$ab(n_{AB} - 1)$	$\dfrac{SS_{\text{Error}}}{df_{\text{Error}}}$	
Total	$\sum\sum(X - \overline{X}_G)^2$	$N - 1$	Not calculated	

[a] a = number of levels of factor a; b = number of levels of factor B; n_{AB} = number of scores in each cell; N = total number of scores.

One-Factor Within-Subjects Design

Source	SS	df*	MS	F
Factor A	$\sum\sum(\overline{X}_A - \overline{X}_G)^2$	$a - 1$	$\dfrac{SS_A}{df_A}$	$\dfrac{MS_A}{MS_{A\times S}}$
Factor S	$\sum\sum(\overline{X}_S - \overline{X}_G)^2$	$n_A - 1$	$\dfrac{SS_S}{df_S}$	
$A \times S$	$\sum\sum(X - \overline{X}_A - \overline{X}_S + \overline{X}_G)^2$	$(a-1)(n_A - 1)$	$\dfrac{SS_{A\times S}}{df_{A\times S}}$	
Total	$\sum\sum(X - \overline{X}_G)^2$	$N - 1$	Not calculated	

*a = number of levels of factor A; n_A = number of scores in a treatment condition or, equivalently, the number of subjects; N = total number of scores.

Tukey HSD Multiple Comparison Tests

For One-Factor Between-Subjects Designs

$$CD = q\sqrt{\frac{MS_{\text{Error}}}{n_A}}$$

For One-Factor Within-Subjects Designs

$$CD = q\sqrt{\frac{MS_{A \times S}}{n_A}}$$

For Simple Effects in a Factorial Between-Subjects Design

$$CD = q\sqrt{\frac{MS_{\text{Error}}}{n_{AB}}}$$

Effect Size Measures

Eta Squared for *t* Test

$$\eta^2 = \frac{t_{\text{obs}}^2}{t_{\text{obs}}^2 + df}$$

Eta Squared for One-Factor Between-Subjects Analysis of Variance

$$\eta^2 = \frac{SS_A}{SS_{\text{Total}}}$$

or

$$\eta^2 = \frac{(df_A)(F_{\text{obs}})}{(df_A)(F_{\text{obs}}) + df_{\text{Error}}}$$

Eta Squared for One-Factor Within-Subjects Analysis of Variance

$$\eta^2 = \frac{SS_A}{SS_A + SS_{A \times S}}$$

Eta Squared for Two-Factor Between-Subjects Analysis of Variance

$$\eta^2 = \frac{SS_A}{SS_{\text{Total}}} \quad \text{for factor } A$$

$$\eta^2 = \frac{SS_B}{SS_{\text{Total}}} \quad \text{for factor } B$$

$$\eta^2 = \frac{SS_{A \times B}}{SS_{\text{Total}}} \quad \text{for the interaction of factors } A \text{ and } B$$

Correlation

Pearson Correlation Coefficient

Definitional formula: $r = \dfrac{\sum(X - \overline{X})(Y - \overline{Y})}{\sqrt{[\sum(X - \overline{X})^2][\sum(Y - \overline{Y})^2]}}$

Cross products formula: $r = \dfrac{CP_{XY}}{\sqrt{(SS_X)(SS_Y)}}$

Standard score formula: $r = \dfrac{\sum(z_X z_Y)}{N_{\text{pairs}}}$,

$df = N_{\text{pairs}} - 2$ for all formulas

Coefficient of Determination

r^2

Spearman Rank-Order Correlation Coefficient

$r_s = 1 - \left[\dfrac{6\sum D^2}{(N_{\text{pairs}})(N^2_{\text{pairs}} - 1)}\right]$

Regression

Equation of a Straight Line

$Y = bX + a$

Slope of a Straight Line

$b = \dfrac{\text{Change in value of } Y}{\text{Change in value of } X} = \dfrac{Y_2 - Y_1}{X_2 - X_1}$

Equation of Least-Squares Linear Regression Line

$Y' = bX + a$

Slope of Least-Squares Linear Regression Line

Deviational formula: $b = \dfrac{\sum(X - \overline{X})(Y - \overline{Y})}{\sum(X - \overline{X})^2}$

Cross products formula: $b = \dfrac{CP_{XY}}{SS_X}$

Correlation formula: $b = r\left(\dfrac{s_Y}{s_X}\right)$

Y-Intercept of Least-Squares Linear Regression Line

$a = \overline{Y} - b\overline{X}$

Standard Error of Estimate

Definitional formula: $s_{Y \cdot X} = \sqrt{\dfrac{SS_{\text{Residual}}}{N_{\text{pairs}} - 2}}$ or $s_{Y \cdot X} = \sqrt{\dfrac{\sum(Y - Y')^2}{N_{\text{pairs}} - 2}}$

Correlation formula: $s_{Y \cdot X} = s_Y \sqrt{\left[\dfrac{N_{\text{pairs}} - 1}{N_{\text{pairs}} - 2}\right](1 - r_{\text{obs}}^2)}$

Nonparametric Tests

Chi-Square Test for Independence

$\chi^2 = \sum\sum \dfrac{(O_{rc} - E_{rc})^2}{E_{rc}}, \quad df = (r - 1)(c - 1)$, or simplified formula,

$\chi^2 = \sum \dfrac{(O - E)^2}{E}, \; df = (r - 1)(c - 1)$

Expected frequency of a cell $= \dfrac{(\text{Row marginal for cell})(\text{Column marginal for cell})}{\text{Total number of responses}}$

Chi-Square Test for Goodness of Fit

$\chi^2 = \sum \dfrac{(O - E)^2}{E}, \; df = c - 1$

Mann–Whitney U Test

$U_{A_1} = n_{A_1} n_{A_2} + \dfrac{n_{A_1}(n_{A_1} + 1)}{2} - \sum R_{A_1}$

$U_{A_2} = n_{A_1} n_{A_2} + \dfrac{n_{A_2}(n_{A_2} + 1)}{2} - \sum R_{A_2}$

or

$U_{A_2} = n_{A_1} n_{A_2} - U_{A_1}$

Wilcoxon Signed-Ranks Test

$T = $ smaller of $\sum(-R)$ or $\sum(+R)$

Answers for Computational Problems

Solutions are given for most of the numerical problems in the "Testing Your Knowledge," "Chapter Review," and "Integrating Your Knowledge" sections. For formulas and explanations, see the relevant sections of the text.

Chapter 1

Testing Your Knowledge 1.1
2. **a.** Math anxiety ratings.
   b. Yes.
   c. See text.
   d. 37 percent.
   e. Why students have math anxiety.

Testing Your Knowledge 1.2
2. **b.** From a sample statistic of 52 percent to a population parameter of 52 percent for Candidate A.
   d, e. Aspects of selecting the sample that may affect whether it is representative of the population from which it was selected.

Testing Your Knowledge 1.3
2. **a.** Learning words under relaxing conditions will lead to fewer recall errors than learning words under neutral conditions.
   b. The study involved the creation of two equivalent groups in a between-subjects design and the manipulation of an independent variable.
   c. Type of background learning condition.
   d. Number of recall errors.
   f. The average of 5.4 and 9.1 errors is a descriptive statistic; the analysis of variance is an inferential statistic.

Testing Your Knowledge 1.4
2. **a.** To find if the two measurements obtained, belief in paranormal phenomena and number of science courses taken, are related.
   b. Belief in paranormal phenomena; number of science courses taken.

Review Questions
3. **a.** Correlation and regression.
   c. Anger level; blood pressure.

4. **a.** Description and statistical hypothesis testing.
   b. Type of videotape viewed.
   c. Duration of time a subject kept his or her hand in the ice water.
5. **a.** Description.　　　　**c.** Percentage.
6. **a.** Descriptive statistic.　**b.** Inferential statistic.
   c. Descriptive statistic.　**d.** Inferential statistic.
7. **a.** Raw data.　　　　　**b.** Inference.
   c. Descriptive statistic.　**d.** Raw data.
   e. Inference.　　　　　**f.** Descriptive statistic.
9. An example might be to use your SAT score to predict how well you will do on a test for graduate school.

Chapter 2

Testing Your Knowledge 2.1
2. See text for definitions.

Research Method	Used For
Case study	Hypothesis building
Naturalistic observation	Hypothesis building & testing
Archival record	Hypothesis testing
Survey research	Hypothesis testing
Experiment	Causal hypothesis testing
Quasi-experiment	Hypothesis testing

3. **a.** Survey research.　　**b.** Experiment.
   c. Archival records.　　**d.** Naturalistic observation.
   e. Quasi-experiment.　　**f.** Case study.
4. **a.** Everyone who may conduct research.
   b. Information on the study's purpose, duration, and potential risk; the subject may select to leave the study at any point; all information will be kept confidential; anything else specified by the IRB.
   c. The IRB reviews and approves proposed research to assure the ethical treatment of subjects.

Testing Your Knowledge 2.2
2. People are assigned to the same category although they do not possess the same amount of the variable being measured.
4. **b.** No.

Testing Your Knowledge 2.3

2. **a.** Yes, the scale is interval.
   b. No, interval scales do not have a true zero.
   c. No. The zero is an arbitrary starting point for interval data.
3. **a.** Yes, the scale is ratio.
   b. Yes, a ratio scale has a true zero.
   c. Yes, ratio data have a true zero representing the absence of the attribute being measured.

Testing Your Knowledge 2.4

2. **a.** Continuous.   **b.** Continuous.
   c. Discrete.   **d.** Continuous.
   e. Continuous.   **f.** Discrete.
   g. Discrete.   **h.** Discrete.
3. **a.** 152.35 to 152.45 cm. **b.** 17.25 to 17.35 sec.
   c. 3.5 to 4.5.   **d.** 0.4365 to 0.4375 sec.
   e. 6.85 to 6.95 mm.   **f.** 67.805 to 67.815 lb.

Review Questions

1. **a.** Survey research.
   b. Archival records.
   c. Experiment.
   d. Naturalistic observation.
   e. Case study.
   f. Quasi-experiment.
3. **a.** Career orientation.
   b. Ordinal.
4. **a.** Body weight.
   b. Ratio.
   c. 134.55 to 134.65 lb.
5. **a.** Emotional stability.
   b. Interval scale.
   c. 7.5 to 8.5.
6. **a.** Ratio.
   b. 97.5 to 98.5 minutes.
   c. Yes, the scale is ratio.
7. Ordinal.
8. Nominal.
9. **a.** Discrete.
   b. Continuous.
   c. Discrete.
   d. Continuous.
10. **a.** 141.25 to 141.35 lb.
    b. 33.5 to 34.5 minutes.
    c. 175.55 to 175.65 yards.

d. 98.15 to 98.25°F.
e. 108.5 to 109.5 mm of mercury.
11. Interval. More information beyond ordinal is included, as we can assume patrons broke down the 5-point scale into equal intervals. However, there is no real zero, as the range was arbitrarily selected. It just as easily could have been −3 to +3.
12. **a.** Ordinal.   **b.** Ratio.

Chapter 3

Testing Your Knowledge 3.1

2. **a.**

Score	Tally	f	rf	$\%f$
19	/	1	.05	5
18		0	.00	0
17		0	.00	0
16		0	.00	0
15	/	1	.05	5
14	/	1	.05	5
13	/	1	.05	5
12	/	1	.05	5
11	/	1	.05	5
10	/	1	.05	5
9	//	2	.10	10
8	////	4	.20	20
7		0	.00	0
6	//	2	.10	10
5	//	2	.10	10
4	//	2	.10	10
3	/	1	.05	5
2		0	.00	0

b. Lowest = 3; highest = 19.
c. 8.

Testing Your Knowledge 3.2

2. 10 to 20.   3. 5.   4. 11.
6. **a.** 123, 125.   **b.** 129, 131.
   c. 122.5, 125.5.   **d.** 128.5 to 131.5.
   e. 121.   **f.** 3.
7. **a.** $i = 10$.

b. The large majority of stotting distances were 99 meters or less. Distances in the interval of 60 to 69 meters occurred most frequently. No distance was less than 10 meters or greater than 209 meters.
c. $P_{68} = 67$.   **d.** $X_{50} = 60.4$ meters.

Class Interval	Real Limits Lower	Real Limits Upper	Midpoint of Class	Tally	f	rf	$\%f$	cf	crf	$c\%f$
200–209	199.5	209.5	204.5	/	1	.02	2	50	1.00	100
190–199	189.5	199.5	194.5	/	1	.02	2	49	.98	98
180–189	179.5	189.5	184.5		0	.00	0	48	.96	96
170–179	169.5	179.5	174.5		0	.00	0	48	.96	96
160–169	159.5	169.5	164.5		0	.00	0	48	.96	96
150–159	149.5	159.5	154.5	/	1	.02	2	48	.96	96
140–149	139.5	149.5	144.5	/	1	.02	2	47	.94	94
130–139	129.5	139.5	134.5		0	.00	0	46	.92	92
120–129	119.5	129.5	124.5		0	.00	0	46	.92	92
110–119	109.5	119.5	114.5		0	.00	0	46	.92	92
100–109	99.5	109.5	104.5		0	.00	0	46	.92	92
90–99	89.5	99.5	94.5	//	2	.04	4	46	.92	92
80–89	79.5	89.5	84.5	///	3	.06	6	44	.88	88
70–79	69.5	79.5	74.5	//////	6	.12	12	41	.82	82
60–69	59.5	69.5	64.5	///////////	11	.22	22	35	.70	70
50–59	49.5	59.5	54.5	////////	8	.16	16	24	.48	48
40–49	39.5	49.5	44.5	//////	6	.12	12	16	.32	32
30–39	29.5	39.5	34.5	///////	7	.14	14	10	.20	20
20–29	19.5	29.5	24.5	//	2	.04	4	3	.06	6
10–19	9.5	19.5	14.5	/	1	.02	2	1	.02	2

Testing Your Knowledge 3.3
2. a.

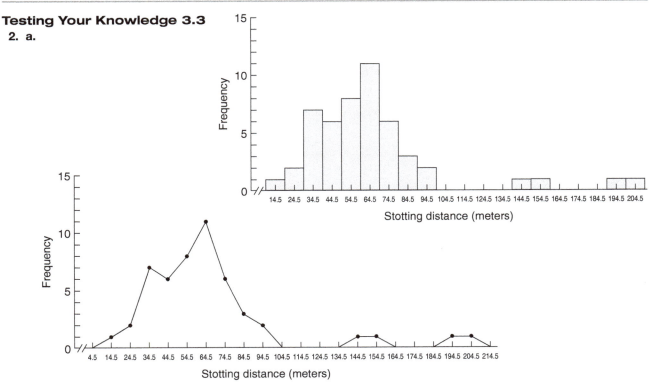

b. The distributions are similar to those in 2a except that relative frequencies are portrayed on the ordinate.

c. The majority of stotting distances were less than 104.5 meters. The most frequently occurring distances were in the interval with a midpoint of 64.5 meters. No distance was less than 9.5 meters or greater than 209.5 meters.

3. a. Symmetrical, unimodal.

    b. Asymmetrical, positively skewed, unimodal.

    c. Asymmetrical, positively skewed, bimodal.

    d. Asymmetrical, negatively skewed, unimodal.

Review Questions

1. a.

Amount of Time	Tally	f	rf	crf
6.0	/	1	.02	1.0
5.5	/	1	.02	.98
5.0	/	1	.02	.96
4.5	//	2	.04	.94
4.0	//	2	.04	.90
3.5	///	3	.06	.86
3.0	///	3	.06	.80
2.5	////	4	.08	.74
2.0	//////	6	.12	.66
1.5	/////	5	.10	.54
1.0	///////	7	.14	.44
0.5	/////	5	.10	.30
0.0	//////////	10	.20	.20

b. Lowest = 0.0; highest = 6.0.

c. 0.0.

d. $X_{.50} = 1.5$.

e. $P_{2.0} = 57$.

f.

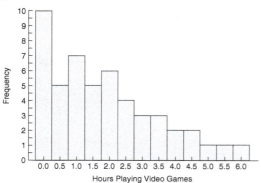

g. Positively skewed.

2. a.

Hours of Studying	Tally	f	rf	crf
12	/	1	.04	1.0
11	///	3	.12	.96
10	///	3	.12	.84
9	/////	5	.20	.72
8	////	4	.16	.52
7	///	3	.12	.36
6	///	3	.12	.24
5	//	2	.08	.12
4	/	1	.04	.04

b. $P_{10} = 78$. Miguel's study time is at the 78th percentile. Seventy-eight percent of the students study equal to or less than 10 hours.

c. $P_9 = 62$. Sixty-two percent of the students study equal to or less than 9 hours.

d. $X_{50} = 8$.

4. a.

Number of Days Absent	Reward-policy School	No-reward-policy School
More than 25	.02	.03
24–25	.00	.03
22–23	.02	.005
20–21	.00	.04
18–19	.01	.00
16–17	.00	.02
14–15	.02	.11
12–13	.00	.05
10–11	.03	.09
8–9	.08	.10
6–7	.04	.015
4–5	.13	.07
2–3	.23	.17
0–1	.42	.27

b. $X_{50} = 2.2$ 5.2

c. $P_4 = 68$ 46

d. For the reward-policy school, 78 percent of the students are absent 5 days or less, with a 50th percentile absence of 2.2 days. For the no-reward policy school, only 51 percent of the students are absent 5 days or less, and the 50th percentile absence is 5.2 days.

5. a. Lowest score = 6; highest score = 24.
   b. 18.   **c.** 76.

6. a. $i = 30$.   **b.** 209.5; 239.5.
   c. 224.5.   **e.** 340 minutes.
   f. $P_{264} = 53$.

7. a. 40.   **c.** $P_{78} = 69$.
   d. 79.3 minutes.

8. a.

Recall Errors	Tally	f	rf	$\%f$	cf	crf	$c\%f$
7	/	1	.02	2	50	1.00	100
6	///	3	.06	6	49	.98	98
5	/////	5	.10	10	46	.92	92
4	/////	5	.10	10	41	.82	82
3	///////	7	.14	14	36	.72	72
2	////////	8	.16	16	29	.58	58
1	/////////	9	.18	18	21	.42	42
0	////////////	12	.24	24	12	.24	24

   b. The distribution is negatively skewed, with a majority of subjects making 3 or fewer errors.
   c. $P_3 = 65$.
   d. $X_{50} = 2$.

Integrating Your Knowledge

A. 1. Survey.
   2. The average rating on the terms "happy," "enjoying myself," and "warm/friendly."
   3. Interval.
   4. Quantitative data.
   5. Summated rating scale.

Chapter 4

Testing Your Knowledge 4.1

3. a. $\overline{X} = 88.0$.   **c.** 262.
4. a. 41.7.   **b.** 39.5.
   c. 37.7.

Testing Your Knowledge 4.2

2. a. 49.   **b.** Unimodal.
3. a. 27.   **b.** Unimodal.
4. a. 24, 27, 49.   **b.** Multimodal.
6. 46.   **7.** 42.   **8.** 46.

Testing Your Knowledge 4.3

1. a. Median.   **b.** Mean.
   c. Mode.   **d.** Mean.

2. Smaller than median.
3. Positively skewed.
4. b. Positively skewed. The mean is considerably larger than the median.

Review Questions

1. Approximately symmetrical because the mean and the median are almost the same.
2. Actors: Positively skewed because the mean is considerably larger than the median.
Floral designers: Approximately symmetrical because the mean and the median are almost the same.
3. Approximately symmetrical because the mean and the median are almost the same.
5. *Set 1*
   b. Mode = 38, $Mdn = 38$, $\overline{X} = 38.6$.
   c. Approximately symmetrical; all measures of central tendency are about the same.
   Set 2
   b. Mode = 28, $Mdn = 29$, $\overline{X} = 33.5$.
   c. Positively skewed; mean is larger than the median.
   d. Median.
   Set 3
   b. Mode = 52, $Mdn = 50$, $\overline{X} = 46.7$.
   c. Negatively skewed; mean is less than the median.
   d. Median.
   Set 4
   b. Mode = bimodal, 26, 52; $Mdn = 40$; $\overline{X} = 38.6$.
   c. Approximately symmetrical, bimodal.
   d. Because the distribution is bimodal, neither the Mdn nor the $\overline{X}$ represents the typical score of a subject very well.

6. a.

	$\overline{X}$	Mdn	Mode	
Roberto	64.0	65	90	Mode
Dimitrios	58.0	65	None	Median
Karen	71.0	67	56	Mean

7. b. The median debt because the large difference between the mean and median debt indicates that each of the distributions is positively skewed by some students who had very large amounts of credit card debt.

8. a. Mode or median.
   b. Mode = 793, $Mdn = 832$.

Chapter 5

Testing Your Knowledge 5.1
2. **a.** 45.
3. 288 ms.

Testing Your Knowledge 5.2
3. **a.**

	Talking on Cell Phone	Not Talking on Cell Phone
$\overline{X}$	4.0	8.0
s^2	0.8	2.0
s	0.9	1.4
Range	3	5

   b. Not talking on cell phone group.
   c. 0.9 items.

4. **a.**

	Male	Female
$\overline{X}$	14.0	6.0
s^2	48.4	6.5
s	7.0	2.5

   b. Males.
   c. 7.0 minutes.
   d. Females; the s is smaller for females than for males.

Testing Your Knowledge 5.3
1. **a.** Mdn, Range.   **b.** Mdn, Range.
   c. $\overline{X}$, s.   **d.** Mdn, Range.
   e. $\overline{X}$, s.   **f.** Mdn, Range.
   g. Mdn, Range.

Review Questions
1. **a.** $Mdn = 55$, $\overline{X} = 53.0$, Range $= 29$, $s^2 = 60.6$, $s = 7.8$.
   b. The median. The distribution is negatively skewed because of the outlier of a score of 30.
2. **a.** $Mdn = 45$, $\overline{X} = 44.0$, Range $= 29$, $s^2 = 117.8$, $s = 10.9$.
   b. The median, but the distribution is only slightly negatively skewed in this example.
   c. The range is determined only by the highest and lowest scores in a distribution and both distributions have the same high and low scores.
3. **a.** Range.   **b.** s^2.
   c. Range.   **d.** s^2.
   e. s.   **f.** Range.
   g. s^2.   **h.** s.
   i. σ.   **j.** σ^2.
   k. s^2.   **l.** s.
4. **a.** $4127.
   b. Large.
   c. The large standard deviations indicate that the distributions were positively skewed. Some students had a very large credit card debt and inflated the value of s. This result indicates that the median would be a better measure of central tendency for the scores.
5. **a.**

	Men	Women
Mdn	28	28
$\overline{X}$	25.0	28.0
Range	22	8
s^2	46.0	5.4
s	6.8	2.3

   b. The median is larger than the mean; this relationship indicates the distribution is negatively skewed. The median is the preferred measure of central tendency for describing the scores.
   c. Men: 10; women: no outlier.
   e. The men are more variable. All the measures of variability are larger for the men than for the women.

Integrating Your Knowledge
A. 1. The student's report of a death in the family.
   2. 1.57.
   3. 0.06.
   4. Ratio.
   6. The FDRs for all grade levels when the midterm exam was scheduled for next week.
   7. It appears that the FDR increases when exams are scheduled. The largest increase is for students with an F grade.
   8.

	Student's Current Grade at Time of Reported Death				
	A	B	C	D	F
Mean FDR Rate	0.063	0.230	0.500	0.827	1.163

C. 1. The mode. No missed exam or assignments: 0.00. Missed assignment, no missed exam: 0.01. Missed exam, no missed assignment: 0.02.
   2. All ranges $= 0.04$.

3.

	Exam Condition		
	No Missed Exam or Assignments	Missed Assignment; No Missed Exam	Missed Exam; No Missed Assignment
$\overline{X}$	0.010	0.013	0.020
s	0.011	0.009	0.007

Any definitive answer to a question of whether means differ requires a statistical hypothesis test (see Chapter 9). In this example, however, when rounded to two decimal places, the means do not differ from each other.

Chapter 6

Testing Your Knowledge 6.1

4. **a.** .3413. **b.** .4772.
   c. .4987. **d.** .3413.
   e. .4772. **f.** .4987.
   g. .8400. **h.** .9544.
   i. .9974. **j.** .1359.
   k. .1574. **l.** .0215.

Testing Your Knowledge 6.2

2.

	z	Area 0 to z	Area beyond z
a.	+1.90	.4713	.0287
b.	−0.52	.1985	.3015
c.	+0.77	.2794	.2206
d.	−1.83	.4664	.0336
e.	+1.75	.4599	.0401
f.	−1.26	.3962	.1038

3. **a.** .0401. **b.** .1465.
   c. .3345. **d.** Approximately 58.8 to 85.2 using $z = +$ or -1.65.

Testing Your Knowledge 6.3

3. .0014.

4.

	z	p
a.	+1.90	.0287
b.	−0.52	.6985
c.	+0.77	.2206
d.	−1.83	.9664
e.	+1.75	.0401
f.	−1.26	.8962

5. **a.** .0668.
   b. .1865.
   c. .2426.
6. The probability of being drafted in any of the sports is small, but of the sports listed, baseball has the highest probability of this occurring, $p = .004$.

Review Questions

3. **a.** .1587. **b.** .0228.
   c. .0038. **d.** .4082.
   e. .4525.
   f. Approximately 80.8 to 119.2 using $z = +$ or -1.28.
   g. .6568. **h.** .0918.
   i. .0475. **j.** .0038.
4. **a.** .016. **b.** .018.
5. **a.** $p = .06$. **b.** $p = .08$.
   c. $p = .54$.
6. **a.** .1587. **b.** .4013.
   c. .7888.
7. **a.** .0668. **b.** .0401.
   c. .9544. **d.** .8664.
   e. .2266. **f.** .3085.

8.

	Video Games	GPA
$\overline{X}$	8.0	2.7
S	5.86	0.87
Alex	−0.34	−0.23
Lauren	0.00	−0.80
Yvonne	−1.37	+1.38
Laval	+1.19	+0.80
Bonnie	−0.85	+0.46
Jason	+1.37	−1.61

b. That she is at the mean of the group for video game playing.

c. That she is 1.38 standard deviations above the mean GPA of the group.

d. That the person's GPA is below the mean of the group.

e. That the person's video game playing time is above the mean of the group.

9.

English Literature	World History
$z = +0.83$	$z = +1.00$

World history, where your score is one standard deviation above the class mean.

10. a. $p = .146$. **b.** $p = .036$.
11. a. $p = .549$. **b.** $p = .419$.
12. a. $p = .162$ **b.** $p = .098$.

Chapter 7

Testing Your Knowledge 7.2

2. Unbiased.

3. Biased; slightly underestimates.

6. a. .6826. **b.** .1587.
c. .0228. **d.** .0475.
e. .4525.

7. a. 9, 6, 3 seconds, respectively.
b. As N increases, $s_{\overline{X}}$ decreases.

8. a. $s = 10, s_{\overline{X}} = 2; s = 15, s_{\overline{X}} = 3; s = 20, s_{\overline{X}} = 4$.
b. As s increases, $s_{\overline{X}}$ also increases.

9. Population A_2, because it has a larger value of σ.

Testing Your Knowledge 7.3

2. a. 73.0.
b. 69.1 to 76.9.
c. 67.8 to 78.2.
d. 73.0.
e. 71.0 to 75.0.
f. 70.4 to 75.6.
g. The value of $\sigma_{\overline{X}}$ becomes smaller as N increases.

Review Questions

1. a. σ. **b.** μ.
c. σ^2. **d.** $\sigma_{\overline{X}}$.

3. $N = 24$, because $\overline{X}$ is a consistent estimator.

4.

	Type of Distribution	
	Population	Sampling Distribution of the Mean
b. Mean	$\mu = 50.0$	$\mu_{\overline{X}} = 50.0$
c. Standard Deviation	$\sigma = 5.0$	$\sigma_{\overline{X}} = 0.5$

7. a. 9.0 cigarettes per day.
b. 7.5 to 10.5 cigarettes per day.
8. a. 0.3. **b.** .0013.
c. .1587. **d.** .9544.

10.

Sample	a.	b.	d.
A	1.250	.2119	.4452
B	0.833	.1151	.4918
C	0.625	.0559	.4993
D	0.500	.0228	>.4999.
E	0.250	<.0001	>.4999

Integrating Your Knowledge

A. 2. a. -3.1 to 6.5 incidents. It includes negative incidents, which cannot occur.
b. The distribution is positively skewed.
c. Yes.

C. 1. a. .39. **b.** .15.
c. .64. **d.** .10.

2. 0, mode.

3. 1.5, median.

5. Program A: 0.0 to 1.2; Program B: 0.6 to 1.8; Program C: 1.4 to 2.6.

6. The confidence intervals overlap; the treatment conditions do not differ.

7. The confidence intervals do not overlap; the treatment conditions differ.

Chapter 8

Testing Your Knowledge 8.1

4. a. $H_0: \mu = 100$.
$H_1: \mu \neq 100$.
b. $H_0: \mu = 4.4$ hours.
$H_1: \mu \neq 4.4$ hours.
c. $H_0: \mu = 423.0$ milliseconds.
$H_1: \mu \neq 423.0$ milliseconds.

5.

	z_{obs}	Decision
a.	-2.13	Falls into rejection region; reject H_0 accept H_1.
b.	-1.20	Does not fall into rejection region; do not reject H_0 do not accept H_1.
c.	$+2.25$	Falls into rejection region; reject H_0 accept H_1.
d.	$+1.72$	Does not fall into rejection region; do not reject H_0 do not accept H_1.

6. a. $z = (\overline{X} - \mu)/\sigma_{\overline{X}}$.
   b. $H_0: \mu = 100$; $H_1: \mu \neq 100$.
   c. $\alpha = .05$.
   d. $z_{crit} = 1.96$.
   e. Values of z_{obs} more extreme than $z = -1.96$ or $+1.96$.
   f. $z_{obs} = +2.50$.
   g. Reject H_0 accept H_1.
   h. The sample mean differs significantly from the population mean.

Testing Your Knowledge 8.2
3. a. 7.   **b.** 6.
   c. 6.
4. a. 9.   **b.** 15.
   c. 6.   **d.** 53.
   e. 119.   **f.** 29.
5. The distribution with 13 df.
6. When the $df = \infty$.

Testing Your Knowledge 8.3
1. a. $H_0: \mu = 493$; $H_1: \mu \neq 493$.
   b. $H_0: \mu = 36.1$; $H_1: \mu \neq 36.1$.
   c. $H_0: \mu = 100$; $H_1: \mu \neq 100$.
2. a. 2.447.   **b.** 2.898.
   c. 2.069.   **d.** 2.042.
   e. 2.042.   **f.** 2.660.
   g. 2.000.   **h.** 1.980.

3.

	Falls into Rejection Region	Decision
a.	Yes	Reject H_0 Accept H_1
b.	No	Fail to reject H_0 Do not accept H_1
c.	Yes	Reject H_0 Accept H_1
d.	No	Fail to reject H_0 Do not accept H_1
e.	Yes	Reject H_0 Accept H_1
f.	Yes	Reject H_0 Accept H_1
g.	No	Fail to reject H_0 Do not accept H_1
h.	Yes	Reject H_0 Accept H_1
i.	Yes	Reject H_0 Accept H_1
j.	Yes	Reject H_0 Accept H_1
k.	Yes	Reject H_0 Accept H_1

5. a. $t = (\overline{X} - \mu)/s_{\overline{X}}$.   **b.** See text.
   c. $H_0: \mu = 7.0$; $H_1: \mu \neq 7.0$.
   d. $\alpha = .05$.   **e.** $t_{crit}(10) = 2.228$.
   f. Values of t_{obs} more extreme than -2.228 or $+2.228$.
   g. $t_{obs} = -4.979$.   **h.** Reject H_0; accept H_1.
   i. The sample mean of 5.8 minutes differs significantly from the population mean of 7.0 minutes.
6. *Report 1*
   a. 70.4 kg.   **b.** 7.6 kg.
   c. One-sample t.
   d. $H_0: \mu = 75$ kg; $H_1: \mu \neq 75$ kg.
   e. 6.   **f.** -1.48.
   g. 5.   **h.** 2.571.
   i. Fail to reject H_0.
   j. Do not accept H_1.
   k. The sample mean does not differ significantly from the population mean.
   Report 2:
   a. 10.4 days.   **b.** 2.3 days.
   c. One-sample t.

d. H_0: $\mu = 8.7$ days; H_1: $\mu \neq 8.7$ days.
e. 25. **f.** +3.70.
g. 24. **h.** 2.064.
i. Reject H_0. **j.** Accept H_1.
k. The sample mean differs significantly from the population mean; 10.4 days is significantly longer than the hypothesized mean of 8.7 days.

Testing Your Knowledge 8.4

2. b. $p = \alpha$.
  c. A Type I error cannot occur if H_0 is false.
  e. No.
4. 80.1 to 113.9 minutes.

Review Questions

5. a. Reject H_0; accept H_1.
  b. Fail to reject H_0; do not accept H_1.
7. a. The sample mean differs significantly from the population mean.
  b. The sample mean does not differ significantly from the population mean.
8. Rejection region consists of values of z_{obs} more extreme than $z = -2.58$ or $+2.58$.

z_{obs}	Falls into Rejection Region	Decision
+3.71	Yes	Reject H_0 Accept H_1
-2.60	Yes	Reject H_0 Accept H_1
+1.74	No	Fail to reject H_0 Do not accept H_1
-3.05	Yes	Reject H_0 Accept H_1
-1.96	No	Fail to reject H_0 Do not accept H_1
+2.58	Yes	Reject H_0 Accept H_1

9. $z_{obs} = -1.52$; nonsignificant; fail to reject H_0.
11. a. The sample mean differs significantly from the population mean.
  b. The sample mean does not differ significantly from the population mean.

12.

	Falls into Rejection Region	Decision
a.	Yes	Reject H_0 Accept H_1
b.	No	Fail to reject H_0 Do not accept H_1
c.	Yes	Reject H_0 Accept H_1
d.	Yes	Reject H_0 Accept H_1
e.	No	Fail to reject H_0 Do not accept H_1
f.	No	Fail to reject H_0 Do not accept H_1

13. a. $t_{obs}(8) = -2.924$; significant at the .05 level; reject H_0, accept H_1.
  c. Yes. **d.** No.
  e. 6.8 to 7.6 hours; $\mu = 7.7$ is not included in this interval.
14. a. $t_{obs}(11) = +3.22$; significant at the .05 level; reject H_0, accept H_1.
  b. No.
15. a. Type I error.
  b. Type II error.
  c. Correct decision.
  d. Correct decision.

Chapter 9

Testing Your Knowledge 9.1

6. a. Extraneous variable = age; groups differ systematically in average age as well as noise condition.
  b. Extraneous variable = experimenter's encouragement; groups differ systematically in encouragement as well as noise condition.
  c. Extraneous variable = gender; groups differ systematically in gender as well as noise condition.
  d. Extraneous variable = college major; groups differ systematically in college major as well as noise condition.
  e. Extraneous variable = time of day when the experiment was conducted; groups differ systematically in time of day as well as noise condition.

Testing Your Knowledge 9.2

3. a. 3.77. **b.** 3.56.
  c. 3.81. **d.** 2.25.

Testing Your Knowledge 9.3

6.

Sample Set	df	t_{crit}	Falls into Rejection Region	Decision
1.	18	2.101	Yes	Reject H_0 Accept H_1
2.	18	2.101	No	Fail to reject H_0 Do not accept H_1
3.	28	2.048	Yes	Reject H_0 Accept H_1
4.	28	2.048	Yes	Reject H_0 Accept H_1
5.	68	2.000	Yes	Reject H_0 Accept H_1
6.	33	2.042	No	Fail to reject H_0 Do not accept H_1
7.	127	1.980	Yes	Reject H_0 Accept H_1
8.	148	1.980	Yes	Reject H_0 Accept H_1

9. *Problem 1*
  a. H_0: $\mu_1 = \mu_2$; H_1: $\mu_1 \neq \mu_2$.
  b. $t_{obs}(34) = -3.656$.
  c. 34.   **d.** 2.042.
  e. Values of t_{obs} more extreme than -2.042 or $+2.042$.
  f. Yes.   **g.** Reject H_0; accept H_1.
  h. Different populations.
  i. Yes.
  j. Yes; the control group estimated a statistically significant shorter time interval than the experimental group.
  Problem 2
  a. H_0: $\mu_1 = \mu_2$; H_1: $\mu_1 \neq \mu_2$.
  b. $t_{obs}(28) = -1.742$.
  c. 28.   **d.** 2.048.
  e. Values of t_{obs} more extreme than -2.048 or $+2.048$.
  f. No.
  g. Fail to reject H_0; do not accept H_1.
  h. There is no evidence that they are not from the same population.
  i. No; it is nonsignificant.
  j. No; the difference between the group means is treated as a chance difference.

Testing Your Knowledge 9.4

2. a. Set 2.   **b.** Set 2.
  c. Set 1.
3. $n_1 = n_2 = 20$ expected to have a smaller $s_{\overline{X}_1 - \overline{X}_2}$ and lead to a more powerful statistical test.
4. a. .42.   **b.** .27.
  c. .19.   **d.** .23.
  e. .08.
7. *Report 1*
  a. 2.   **b.** 62.
  c. 79.7; 73.0.   **d.** 8.57; 5.85.
  e. 3.60.   **f.** 2.000.
  g. Reject H_0.   **h.** Accept H_1.
  i. Statistically significant.
  j. The effect of the treatment.
  Report 2
  a. 2.   **b.** 30.
  c. 22.78; 24.33.   **d.** 5.23; 5.14.
  e. -0.82.   **f.** 2.048.
  g. Fail to reject H_0.   **h.** Do not accept H_1.
  i. Nonsignificant.   **j.** Sampling error.

Testing Your Knowledge 9.5

2. a. One-factor within-subjects design.
  b. H_0: $\mu_1 = \mu_2$; H_1: $\mu_1 \neq \mu_2$.
  c. $t_{obs}(10) = -3.148$.
  d. 10.
  e. 2.228.
  f. Values of t_{obs} more extreme than -2.228 or $+2.228$.
  g. Yes.
  h. Reject H_0; accept H_1.
  i. Different populations.
  j. Yes.
  k. Yes; the control group responded with statistically significant shorter reaction times than the experimental group.
  l. .50.
  m. -41.8 to -7.2 ms.

Review Questions

1.

	Group	
	Quiet	Noise
$\overline{X}$	122.6	131.3
s	8.8	10.5

a. One-factor between-subjects design.

b. $t_{obs}(20) = -2.099$, $p < .05$. The mean blood pressure of the quiet group is significantly lower than that of the noise group.

c. $\eta^2 = .18$; 18 percent of the variance in the dependent variable.

d. 0.1 to 17.2.

2.

	Group	
	Quiet	Noise
$\overline{X}$	113.1	115.3
s	4.6	6.5

$t_{obs}(20) = -0.913$, $p > .05$. The mean blood pressures of the two groups do not differ significantly.

3. a. One-factor within-subjects design.

b.

	Message From	
	Female	Male
$\overline{X}$	16.0	13.5
s	2.3	2.8

$t_{obs}(7) = +3.208$, $p < .05$. Messages from a male are perceived as less emotional than messages from a female.

c. $\eta^2 = .60$.

d. 0.7 to 4.3.

4 a. One-factor between-subjects design.

b.

	Learning Condition	
	Distributed	Massed
$\overline{X}$	7.0	5.5
s	1.2	1.5

$t_{obs}(22) = +2.691$, $p < .05$. Distributed learning leads to greater recall than massed learning.

c. $\eta^2 = .25$.

d. 0.3 to 2.7.

5. a. One-factor within-subjects design.

b.

	Type of Topic	
	Nonstressful	Stressful
$\overline{X}$	3.0	4.0
s	2.2	1.9

$t_{obs}(10) = -3.028$, $p < .05$. More errors occur for stressful topics than for nonstressful topics.

c. $\eta^2 = .48$.

d. -1.7 to -0.3.

6. a. One-factor between-subjects design.

b. $t_{obs}(69) = +0.543$, $p > .05$; The nonsignificant t indicates that the group means do not differ significantly at the .05 level.

d. -1.1 to 2.5.

7. a. One-factor between-subjects design.

b. $t_{obs}(32) = -0.818$, $p > .05$. The nonsignificant t indicates that the group means do not differ significantly at the .05 level.

8. a. One-factor between-subjects design.

b.

	Immediacy Condition	
	No Immediacy Behaviors	Immediacy Behaviors
$\overline{X}$	4.8	6.8
s	1.4	1.4

$t_{obs}(24) = -3.744$, $p < .05$. The mean trustworthiness rating of the speaker demonstrating immediacy behaviors is significantly higher than the rating of the speaker in the no immediacy behavior conditions.

c. $\eta^2 = .37$.

d. -3.223 to -0.931.

Integrating Your Knowledge

A. 1. First-year students underestimate the cost of textbooks. An instructional activity will change students estimates of textbook costs.

2. Two.

3. Student estimates of textbook costs before they had purchased any.

B. 1. Survey method.

2. Sample.

3. Random sampling.

4. a. Ratio.   **b.** Quantitative.

c. Discrete.

5. Median; it is likely that the distribution of estimates will be skewed. If it is not skewed, the mean is appropriate. If the median is used as the measure of central tendency, then the range is the appropriate measure of variability.

6. Population.   **7.** z; both μ and σ are known.

8. One-factor within-subjects design.

9. Presentation of the instructional activity.

10. Student's estimates of textbook costs.   **11.** t_{rel}.

C. 1. $\mu = \$455.00$; $\sigma = \$155.33$;   parameters;   these values represent the population of 432 first-year students at the college.

  2. $\overline{X}_1 = \$341.55$; $s_1 = \$112.37$; statistics, these values were obtained from the sample of 100 first-year students at the college.

  3. $z_{obs} = -15.18, p < .001$. Both μ and σ are known.

  4. $\overline{X}_2 = \$408.15$; $s_2 = \$126.35$.

  5. $t_{obs.} = -4.82, p < .05$.

Chapter 10

Testing Your Knowledge 10.1

  6. $a = 4, n_A = 11, N = 44$.

11. 150.00.

12. 25.00.

13. 79.

14. 25.00.

15. 10.00.

16. $df_A = 3, df_{Error} = 40, df_{Total} = 43$.

17.

Source	SS	df	MS	F
Factor A	24.00	1	24.00	6.00
Error	16.00	4	4.00	
Total	40.00	5		

18.

Source	SS	df	MS	F
Factor A	42.00	2	21.00	5.25
Error	24.00	6	4.00	
Total	66.00	8		

19.

Table 1				
Source	SS	df	MS	F
Factor A	50.00	1	50.00	5.00
Error	260.00	26	10.00	
Total	310.00	27		

  a. 2.   **b.** 14.

  c. 28.

Table 2				
Source	SS	df	MS	F
Factor A	18.00	3	6.00	3.00
Error	152.00	76	2.00	
Total	170.00	79		

  a. 4.   **b.** 20.   **c.** 80.

Testing Your Knowledge 10.2

  6. Approximately 1.00.

  7. It becomes greater than 1.00.

  8. a. H_0: $\mu_{A_1} = \mu_{A_2}$
      H_1: The μ_A's are not equal.

    b. H_0: $\mu_{A_1} = \mu_{A_2} = \mu_{A_3} = \mu_{A_4}$
      H_1: The μ_A's are not all equal.

    c. H_0: $\mu_{A_1} = \mu_{A_2} = \mu_{A_3} = \mu_{A_4} = \mu_{A_5} = \mu_{A_6}$
      H_1: The μ_A's are not all equal.

  9. The independent variable has no effect.

10. The independent variable has an effect.

11. Zero.

12. No upper limit.

13.

Experiment	F_{crit}	Falls into Rejection Region	Decision
1.	4.96	Yes	Reject H_0 Accept H_1
2.	3.40	No	Fail to reject H_0 Do not accept H_1
3.	4.26	Yes	Reject H_0 Accept H_1
4.	3.15	Yes	Reject H_0 Accept H_1
5.	3.89	Yes	Reject H_0 Accept H_1
6.	3.68	No	Fail to reject H_0 Do not accept H_1
7.	2.61	No	Fail to reject H_0 Do not accept H_1
8.	3.10	No	Fail to reject H_0 Do not accept H_1
9.	2.25	Yes	Reject H_0 Accept H_1
10.	2.53	No	Fail to reject H_0 Do not accept H_1

Testing Your Knowledge 10.3

1.

	Group	
	Control	Idealized Image
$\overline{X}$	8.8	7.1
s	1.5	1.3

a. $H_0: \mu_{A_1} = \mu_{A_2}$.
   H_1: The μ_A's are not equal.
b. $F_{obs}(1, 20) = 8.51$.
c. $df_A = 1$, $df_{Error} = 20$.
d. $F_{crit}(1, 20) = 4.35$.
e. Values of $F_{obs} \geq 4.35$.
f. Yes.
g. Reject H_0; accept H_1.
h. Different populations.
i. Yes.
j. They differ; the control group ate more junk food.
k. No, because only two levels of the independent variable were manipulated.
l. $\eta^2 = .30$.
m. 30 percent.

2.

	Grade		
	2nd	4th	6th
$\overline{X}$	565.8	530.6	501.0
s	32.4	29.0	24.4

a. $H_0: \mu_{A_1} = \mu_{A_2} = \mu_{A_3}$.
   H_1: The μ_A's are not all equal.
b. $F_{obs}(2, 39) = 17.76$.
c. $df_A = 2$, $df_{Error} = 39$.
d. $F_{crit}(2, 39) = 3.32$ (critical value for 2, 30 df).
e. Values of F_{obs} equal to or greater than 3.32.
f. Yes.
g. Reject H_0; accept H_1.
h. There is at least one significant difference among the means.
i. Yes; because F_{obs} is statistically significant and there are three means being compared in the experiment.
j. $CD = 26.86$.
k. Each group differs significantly from each other group.
l. The sleep periods from longest to shortest are 2nd graders, 4th graders, 6th graders.
m. $\eta^2 = .48$.   **n.** 48 percent.

Problem 1
a. 2.   **b.** 62.
c. 14.15.   **d.** 4.00.
e. Reject H_0.   **f.** Accept H_1.
g. Yes.
h. The familiar and unfamiliar poetry passage group means.

Problem 2
a. 4.   **b.** 40.
c. 1.13.   **d.** 2.92.
e. Fail to reject H_0.   **f.** Do not accept H_1.
g. No.
h. There are no significant differences among the means.

Problem 3
a. 3.   **b.** 39.
c. 33.94.   **d.** 3.32.
e. Reject H_0.   **f.** Accept H_1.
g. Yes.
h. The Tukey CD indicates that the mean for the hard rock music (29.9) was significantly higher than the mean for either classical music (18.5) or the mean for the no-music control group (17.5). The classical and no-music control group means did not differ significantly.

Review Questions

1. a. One-factor between-subjects design.
b.

	Treatment Group		
	No Music	Oldies	Hard Rock
$\overline{X}$	36.0	35.6	22.9
s	3.7	3.5	3.6

$F_{obs}(2, 21) = 34.39$, $p < .01$. Tukey $CD = 4.6$. The hard rock music group detected significantly fewer errors than did either the no music or the oldies music groups. The no music and oldies music groups means do not differ significantly.
c. $\eta^2 = .77$.

2. a. One-factor between-subjects design.
b.

	Payment Condition		
	None	$1	$20
$\overline{X}$	−0.5	1.5	0.0
s	0.9	1.1	1.3

$F_{obs}(2, 21) = 7.00$, $p < .05$. Tukey $CD = 1.4$. The $1 payment condition produces a significantly more favorable rating of the task than either the no payment or $20 payment. The no payment and $20 payment means do not differ significantly.

b. $\eta^2 = .40$.

3. a.

	Group	
	Quiet	Noise
$\overline{X}$	122.6	131.3
s	8.8	10.5

$F_{obs}(1, 20) = 4.41$, $p < .05$. The mean for the quiet group is significantly lower than the mean for the noise group.

b. Yes, $t = \sqrt{F} = \sqrt{4.41} = 2.10$.

4. a. $a = 6$, $n_A = 7$, $N = 42$.

b. $df_A = 5$, $df_{Error} = 36$, $df_{Total} = 41$.

5.

Table 1				
Source	SS	df	MS	F
Factor A	50.00	2	25.00	2.50
Error	270.00	27	10.00	
Total	320.00	29		

a. 3. **b.** 10.

c. 30.

d. $F_{crit}(2, 27) = 3.35$; F_{obs} is nonsignificant.

e. Fail to reject H_0; do not accept H_1.

Table 2				
Source	SS	df	MS	F
Factor A	60.00	5	12.00	4.00
Error	216.00	72	3.00	
Total	276.00	77		

a. 6. **b.** 13.

c. 78.

d. $F_{crit}(5, 72) = 2.37$; F_{obs} is statistically significant.

e. Reject H_0; accept H_1.

Table 3				
Source	SS	df	MS	F
Factor A	45.00	3	15.00	3.00
Error	320.00	64	5.00	
Total	365.00	67		

a. 4. **b.** 17.

c. 68.

d. $F_{crit}(3, 64) = 2.76$; F_{obs} is statistically significant.

e. Reject H_0; accept H_1.

7. $F_{obs}(1, 18) = 4.00$.

8. $t_{obs}(22) = 3.00$.

10. The statistically significant $F_{obs}(3, 64) = 21.64$ indicates that there is at least one significant difference between the groups. Applying the $CD = 5.0$ minutes to the pairwise comparisons reveals that the Behavior Modification and Cigarettes Anonymous Club have significantly longer mean times between smoking cigarettes than either the control group or the Smoke-Stop gum group. The Behavior Modification and Cigarettes Anonymous means do not differ significantly from each other, and the Control group and Smoke-Stop Gum group means also do not differ significantly from each other.

Chapter 11

Testing Your Knowledge 11.1

2.

	Number of Independent Variables	Levels	Number of Subjects Needed
a.	2	$A = 3$; $B = 3$	90
b.	2	$A = 3$; $B = 2$	60
c.	2	$A = 2$; $B = 3$	60
d.	2	$A = 6$; $B = 2$	120
e.	2	$A = 4$; $B = 4$	160
f.	3	$A = 2$; $B = 2$ $C = 2$	80
g.	3	$A = 2$; $B = 4$ $C = 3$	240
h.	3	$A = 3$; $B = 3$ $C = 2$	180

3.

Table 1			
		Factor A	Main Effect Means for Factor B
		A_1 $\quad$ A_2	
Factor B	B_1	13.3 $\quad$ 20.2	16.8
	B_2	16.8 $\quad$ 22.8	19.8
Main Effect Means for Factor A		15.1 $\quad$ 21.5	$\overline{X}_G = 18.3$

Table 2			
	Factor A		Main Effect Means for Factor B
	A_1	A_2	
Factor B B_1	18.9	30.1	24.5
Factor B B_2	31.3	33.9	32.6
Main Effect Means for Factor A	25.1	32.0	$\overline{X}_G = 28.6$

Testing Your Knowledge 11.2

8. 240.00.
9. 45.00.
10. 55.00.
11. 60.00.
12. $df_A = 1, df_B = 2, df_{A\times B} = 2, df_{Error} = 30, df_{Total} = 35.$
13. $df_A = 2, df_B = 1, df_{A\times B} = 2, df_{Error} = 72, df_{Total} = 77.$
14. 79.
15. $MS_A = 14.00/1 = 14.00.$
$MS_B = 26.00/2 = 13.00.$
$MS_{A\times B} = 44.00/2 = 22.00.$
$MS_{Error} = 480.00/60 = 8.00.$

16. a.

Source	SS	df	MS	F
Factor A	108.00	1	108.00	27.00
Factor B	0.00	1	0.00	0.00
A × B	12.00	1	12.00	3.00
Error	32.00	8	4.00	
Total	152.00	11		

b. Both main effect means for factor B are equal to 32.0.

17.

Table 1				
Source	SS	df	MS	F
Factor A	32.00	2	16.00	2.00
Factor B	24.00	1	24.00	3.00
A × B	24.00	2	12.00	1.50
Error	480.00	60	8.00	
Total	560.00	65		

a. 3.   **b.** 2.
c. 11.   **d.** 66.

Table 2				
Source	SS	df	MS	F
Factor A	36.00	2	18.00	4.50
Factor B	24.00	4	6.00	1.50
A × B	160.00	8	20.00	5.00
Error	840.00	210	4.00	
Total	1060.00	224		

a. 3.   **b.** 5.
c. 15.   **d.** 225.

Testing Your Knowledge 11.3
10.

Table 1					
Source	df	F_{obs}	F_{crit}	F_{obs} Falls into Rejection Region	Decision
Factor A	1	4.63	4.08	Yes	Reject H_0 Accept H_1
Factor B	3	2.11	2.84	No	Fail to reject H_0 Do not accept H_1
A × B	3	3.97	2.84	Yes	Reject H_0 Accept H_1

Table 2				
Source	df	F_{obs}	F_{crit}	F_{obs} Falls into Rejection Region	Decision
Factor A	3	1.42	2.68	No	Fail to reject H_0 Do not accept H_1
Factor B	2	3.51	3.07	Yes	Reject H_0 Accept H_1
$A \times B$	6	2.37	2.17	Yes	Reject H_0 Accept H_1

Table 3				
Source	df	F_{obs}	F_{crit}	F_{obs} Falls into Rejection Region	Decision
Factor A	2	4.12	3.07	Yes	Reject H_0 Accept H_1
Factor B	4	2.83	2.45	Yes	Reject H_0 Accept H_1
$A \times B$	8	1.87	2.02	No	Fail to reject H_0 Do not accept H_1

Testing Your Knowledge 11.4

2. *Figure 11.2*
   a. Yes.   b. No.
   c. Yes.
   d. Because of the statistically significant interaction, the effect of the type of teaching method depends on the type of material, factor B. For mathematical material (B_1), computer-assisted teaching (A_1) leads to significantly higher test scores than does noncomputer-assisted teaching (A_2). For social studies material (B_2), however, the teaching methods do not differ from each other.
   e. The statistically significant interaction indicates that the effect of type of material depends on the type of teaching, factor A. For computer-assisted teaching (A_1), mathematical material (B_1) leads to significantly higher test scores compared to social studies material (B_2). For noncomputer-assisted teaching (A_2), there is no difference between the types of materials.
   f. No; the main effect for factor A indicates an overall superiority for computer-assisted teaching, but computer-assisted teaching leads to significantly higher test scores only with mathematical material.

Thus the main effect for factor A is an artifact of the interaction; it conveys no meaningful information about the effect of factor A on test scores.

Figure 11.3
   a. No.   b. Yes.
   c. Yes.
   d. The statistically significant interaction indicates that the effect of type of teaching depends on the type of material, factor B. For mathematical material (B_1), the teaching methods do not differ significantly. For social studies material (B_2), noncomputer-assisted teaching (A_2) leads to significantly higher test scores than does computer-assisted teaching (A_1).
   e. The statistically significant interaction indicates that the effect of type of material depends on the type of teaching, factor A. Both types of teaching lead to higher test scores for mathematical material, but the difference between mathematical and social studies material is larger for computer-assisted teaching than it is for noncomputer-assisted teaching.
   f. Yes; the main effect for factor B indicates an overall superiority for mathematical material, and

mathematical material leads to significantly higher test scores for both types of teaching. The interaction, however, indicates that the difference between mathematical and social studies material depends on the type of teaching method.

2. *Table 1*

a. Yes.   **b.** No.

c. No.

d. Computer-assisted teaching (A_1) leads to significantly higher test scores than does noncomputer-assisted teaching (A_2).

e. No effect.

f. Yes; there is no interaction of A and B.

Table 2

a. No.   **b.** Yes.

c. No.   **d.** No effect.

e. Mathematical material (B_1) leads to significantly higher test scores than does social studies material (B_2).

f. Yes; there is no interaction of A and B.

Table 3

a. Yes.   **b.** Yes.

c. No.

d. Noncomputer-assisted teaching (A_2) leads to significantly higher test scores than does computer-assisted teaching (A_1).

e. Mathematical material (B_1) leads to significantly higher test scores than does social studies material (B_2).

f. Yes; there is no interaction of A and B.

Table 4

a. No.   **b.** No.

c. Yes.

d. Because of the statistically significant interaction, the effect of teaching method depends on the type of material, factor B. For mathematical material (B_1), computer-assisted teaching (A_1) leads to significantly higher test scores than does noncomputer-assisted teaching (A_2). For social studies material (B_2), however, noncomputer-assisted teaching (A_2) leads to significantly higher test scores than does computer-assisted teaching (A_1).

e. Because of the statistically significant interaction, the effect of the type of material depends on the type of teaching, factor A. For computer-assisted teaching (A_1), mathematical material (B_1) leads to significantly higher test scores than social studies material. For noncomputer-assisted teaching (A_2),

social studies material (B_2) leads to significantly higher test scores than mathematical material.

f. No; the main effect for each independent variable indicates no overall effect of the independent variable. However, each independent variable does have an effect, but the effect of each independent variable depends on the level of the other independent variable.

Table 5

a. Yes.   **b.** Yes.

c. Yes.

d. Because of the statistically significant interaction, the effect of the type of teaching method depends on the type of material. For mathematical material (B_1), the difference between computer-assisted (A_1) and noncomputer-assisted (A_2) teaching is nonsignificant. For social studies material, however, noncomputer-assisted teaching (A_2) leads to significantly higher test scores compared to computer-assisted teaching (A_1).

e. Because of the statistically significant interaction, the effect of the type of material depends on the type of teaching. For both computer-assisted (A_1) and noncomputer-assisted (A_2) teaching, mathematical material (B_1) leads to significantly higher test scores than does social studies material (B_2). However, the difference between mathematical and social studies scores is greater for computer-assisted teaching (A_1) than it is for noncomputer-assisted teaching (A_2).

f. The main effect of factor A, teaching method, is artifactual because it indicates an overall superiority for noncomputer-assisted teaching. But noncomputer-assisted teaching leads to significantly higher performance only with social studies material. The main effect of factor B, type of material, is meaningful; mathematical material leads to significantly higher performance for both computer-assisted and noncomputer-assisted teaching.

Table 6

a. Yes.   **b.** Yes.

c. Yes.

d. Because of the statistically significant interaction, the effect of the type of teaching method depends on the type of material. For mathematical material (B_1), computer-assisted teaching (A_1) leads to significantly higher test scores compared to noncomputer-assisted teaching (A_2). For social studies material, however, there is no effect of teaching method.

e. The effect of type of material depends on the type of teaching. For computer-assisted teaching (A_1), mathematical material (B_1) leads to significantly higher test scores than does social studies material (B_2). For noncomputer-assisted teaching (A_2), the difference between mathematical material (B_1) and social studies material (B_2) scores is non-significant.

f. The main effects for both factor A, teaching method, and factor B, type of material, are arti-factual.

Testing Your Knowledge 11.5

1. Analysis of variance summary.

Source	SS	df	MS	F
Locus of control (A)	704.167	1	704.167	1.15
Instructions (B)	1,472.667	1	1,472.667	2.41
$A \times B$	46,112.666	1	46,112.666	75.39*
Error	12,233.000	20	611.650	
Total	60,522.500	23		

*$p < .01$.

a. 1. No significant main effect for either indepen-dent variable.
   2. Significant interaction.
b. ($CD = 36.15$). The statistically significant inter-action indicates that the effect of instructions de-pends on the locus of control. For internal locus of control subjects, skill instructions led to signif-icantly more time spent on the task than did chance instructions. For external locus of control subjects, however, chance instructions led to sig-nificantly more time spent on the task than did skill instructions.
c. Because of the interaction, the nonsignificant main effects do not provide useful information for interpreting the outcome.
d. $\eta^2 = .76$ for the interaction of factors A and B.

2. Analysis of variance summary.

Source	SS	df	MS	F
Instruction (A)	191.361	1	191.361	23.61*
Crime (B)	1667.361	1	1667.361	205.75*
$A \times B$	210.250	1	210.250	25.94*
Error	259.333	32	8.104	
Total	2328.305	35		

*$p < .01$.

a. 1. Significant main effects for both factors A and B.
   2. Significant interaction.
b. ($CD = 3.31$). The statistically significant interac-tion indicates that the effect of type of instructions depends on the type of crime; the difference be-tween the filmed and normal instructions for auto theft is nonsignificant, but a significantly longer term is assigned with filmed instruction compared to normal instructions for aggravated assault.
c. The statistically significant interaction indicates that the effect of type of crime depends on the type of instructions. For both types of instructions, aggravated assault leads to significantly longer prison terms than does auto theft. However, the difference between the prison terms for auto theft and aggravated assault is larger for filmed instruc-tions than it is for normal instructions.
d. The statistically significant main effect for type of crime is meaningful; significantly longer terms are assigned for aggravated assault under both normal and filmed instructions. The main effect for type of instruction is artifactual; there is no difference between the filmed and normal instruc-tions for auto theft, but a significantly longer term is assigned with filmed instruction for aggravated assault.
e. $\eta^2 = .72$ for type of crime. $\eta^2 = .09$ for the inter-action of factors A and B.

Report 1

a. 3.   b. 2.
c. 42.
d.

	F_{crit}
A	3.32
B	4.17
$A \times B$	3.32

e. Yes.   **f.** Yes.

g. No.

Report 2

a. 2.   **b.** 4.

c. 96.

d. ▅▅▅▅▅▅▅▅▅▅

	F_{crit}
A	4.00
B	2.76
$A \times B$	2.76

e. Yes.   **f.** No.

g. Yes.

Report 3

a. 2.   **b.** 2.

c. 60.

d. ▅▅▅▅▅▅▅▅▅▅

	F_{crit}
A	4.08
B	4.08
$A \times B$	4.08

e. No.   **f.** No.

g. Yes.

Review Questions

1. Analysis of variance summary.

Source	SS	df	MS	F
Proximity (A)	24.500	1	24.500	0.76
Dish visibility (B)	780.125	1	780.125	24.17*
$A \times B$	325.125	1	325.125	10.07*
Error	903.750	28	32.277	
Total	2033.500	31		

*$p < .01$.

a. Yes; there is a significant interaction of factors A and B (Tukey $CD = 7.1$). For the candy dish not visible conditions, the close proximity mean is significantly higher than the far proximity mean. For the candy dish visible conditions, the close and far proximity means do not differ significantly.

b. For the close proximity condition, there is no significant difference between the non-visible and visible candy dish conditions. For the far proximity condition, however, the visible candy dish leads to significantly greater candy consumption than does the non-visible dish.

c. The statistically significant main effect for candy dish visibility condition is artifactual; there is no significant difference between the visibility conditions in the close proximity condition, but in the far proximity condition, the visible dish cell mean is significantly higher than the non-visible dish cell mean.

d. $\eta^2 = .16$ for the interaction of factors A and B.

2. Analysis of variance summary.

Source	SS	df	MS	F
Personality type (A)	36.750	1	36.750	6.58*
Background noise (B)	30.083	1	30.083	5.38*
$A \times B$	27.000	1	27.000	4.83*
Error	245.833	44	5.587	
Total	339.666	47		

*$p < .05$.

a. The analysis of variance reveals a statistically significant interaction; thus, a Tukey CD for simple effects is necessary. This CD for 3, 44 df equals 2.35. The analysis of the simple effects indicates that the mean for the introverts in the noisy background condition ($M = 8.2$ items correct) is significantly lower than the mean for the introverts in the quiet condition ($M = 11.3$ items correct) and also significantly lower than the mean for the extroverts in the noisy condition ($M = 11.4$ items correct). The mean for the introverts in the quiet background condition did not differ significantly from the mean of the extroverts in the quiet condition ($M = 11.5$ items correct), and the mean of the extroverts in the quiet background did not differ significantly from the mean of the extroverts in the noisy background condition.

b. $\eta^2 = .08$.

c. Both main effects are statistically significant, but are artifactual and cannot be meaningfully interpreted.

3. Analysis of variance summary.

Source	SS	df	MS	F
Instructional method (A)	436.594	2	218.297	47.78*
Practice (B)	60.168	1	60.168	13.17*
$A \times B$	69.777	2	34.888	7.64*
Error	219.332	48	4.569	
Total	785.871	53		

*$p < .01$.

a. There is a statistically significant interaction; thus, the effect of instructional method depends on the level of practice. For the traditional method, the one-week practice mean ($M = 13.1$ words correct) was significantly less than the six-week practice mean ($M = 17.9$ words correct; $CD = 2.9$). However, there was no significant difference between the one- and six-week practice conditions for either the word box ($M = 18.7$ words correct, $M = 21.0$ words correct, respectively) or word sort ($M = 22.8$ words correct, $M = 22.0$ words correct, respectively) methods. In addition, the differences between instructional methods depend on the amount of practice. For the one-week practice condition, each instructional method group differed significantly from the others; the word sort subjects obtained the highest score, the word box method the next highest score, and the traditional method the lowest score. For the six-week practice condition, the traditional method mean was significantly less than either the word box or word sort mean. The word box and word sort means did not differ significantly, however.

b. $\eta^2 = .09$.

c. Both main effects are artifactual.

4. a. $a = 2, b = 3, n_{AB} = 8, N = 48$.

   b. $df_A = 1, \quad df_B = 2, \quad df_{A \times B} = 2, \quad df_{\text{Error}} = 42, \quad df_{\text{Total}} = 47$.

5.

Table 1				
Source	SS	df	MS	F
Type of task (A)	15.00	3	5.00	2.50
Noise level (B)	16.00	2	8.00	4.00*
$A \times B$	36.00	6	6.00	3.00*
Error	120.00	60	2.00	
Total	187.00	71		

*$p < .05$.

a. 4.   b. 3.
c. 6.   d. 72.
e. Fobs for factor A and the $A \times B$ interaction are statistically significant.
f. Factor A: Fail to reject H_0
                Do not accept H_1
   Factor B: Reject H_0
                Accept H_1
   $A \times B$: Reject H_0
                 Accept H_1

Table 2				
Source	SS	df	MS	F
Training length (A)	40.00	4	10.00	0.50
Skill level (B)	120.00	3	40.00	2.00
$A \times B$	960.00	12	80.00	4.00*
Error	3200.00	160	20.00	
Total	4320.00	179		

*$p < .01$.

a. 5.   b. 4.
c. 9.   d. 180.
e. F_{obs} for the $A \times B$ interaction is statistically significant.
f. Factor A: Fail to reject H_0
                Do not accept H_1
   Factor B: Fail to reject H_0
                Do not accept H_1
   $A \times B$: Reject H_0
                 Accept H_1

Table 3				
Source	SS	df	MS	F
Type of feedback (A)	200.00	4	50.00	2.50*
Task difficulty (B)	160.00	2	80.00	4.00*
$A \times B$	240.00	8	30.00	1.50
Error	2700.00	135	20.00	
Total	3300.00	149		

*$p < .05$.

a. 5.   b. 3.
c. 10.   d. 150.
e. F_{obs} for factor A and factor B are statistically significant.

f. Factor A: Reject H_0
                    Accept H_1
      Factor B: Reject H_0
                    Accept H_1
      $A \times B$:   Fail to reject H_0
                    Do not accept H_1

6. a. Because of the statistically significant interaction, the effect of type of imagery depends on the amount of elaboration. For low elaboration, ordinary imagery leads to significantly greater recall than does bizarre imagery. For high elaboration, however, ordinary imagery leads to significantly less recall than does bizarre imagery. The main effect of type of imagery is artifactual.

b. Again, because of the statistically significant interaction, the effect of amount of elaboration depends on the type of imagery. For ordinary imagery, low elaboration leads to significantly higher recall than does high elaboration. For bizarre imagery, an opposite relation holds; low elaboration leads to significantly lower recall than does high elaboration.

7. a. The statistically significant interaction indicates that the effect of type of gauge depends on the amount of sleep deprivation. For no sleep deprivation, the difference between the number of correct readings for analog and digital gauges is nonsignificant. For 24 hours of sleep deprivation, digital gauges result in significantly more correct readings than do analog gauges. The main effect of type of gauge is artifactual.

b. Again, the statistically significant interaction indicates that the effect of amount of sleep deprivation depends on the type of gauge. For both analog and digital gauges, 24 hours of sleep deprivation results in significantly fewer correct readings than does no sleep deprivation. However, the difference between the number of correct readings for no sleep deprivation and 24 hours of sleep deprivation is greater for analog gauges than it is for digital gauges. Because 24 hours of sleep deprivation results in fewer correct readings for both analog and digital gauges, the main effect of amount of sleep deprivation is meaningful.

Chapter 12

Testing Your Knowledge 12.1

4. 199.00.
5. 33.00.
6. 25.00.
7. 96.00.
8. $df_A = 4$, $df_S = 12$, $df_{A \times S} = 48$, $df_{Total} = 64$.
9. 59.
10. $MS_A = 11.00$, $MS_S = 2.00$, $MS_{A \times S} = 2.00$.
11.

Table 1				
Source	SS	df	MS	F
Factor A	48.00	4	12.00	6.00
Factor S	27.00	9	3.00	
$A \times S$	72.00	36	2.00	
Total	147.00	49		

a. 5.   **b.** 10.
c. 10.

Table 2				
Source	SS	df	MS	F
Factor A	6.00	2	3.00	2.00
Factor S	36.00	12	3.00	
$A \times S$	36.00	24	1.50	
Total	78.00	38		

a. 3.   **b.** 13.
c. 13.

Testing Your Knowledge 12.2

3. H_0: $\mu_{A_1} = \mu_{A_2} = \mu_{A_3} = \mu_{A_4} = \mu_{A_5}$.
H_1: The μ_A's are not all equal.

Testing Your Knowledge 12.3

2.

	City (A)		
	Dallas	Tijuana	Tripoli
$\overline{X}$	30.8	21.6	22.6
s	4.1	3.2	3.6

a. H_0: $\mu_{A_1} = \mu_{A_2} = \mu_{A_3}$
H_1: The μ_A's are not all equal.

b.

Source	SS	df	MS	F
City (A)	709.000	2	354.500	37.52*
Subjects (S)	269.333	13	20.718	
A × S	245.667	26	9.449	
Total	1224.000	41		

*$p < .01$.

c. 2, 26.

d. $F_{crit}(2, 26) = 3.37$.

e. Values of F_{obs} equal to or greater than 3.37.

f. Yes.

g. Reject H_0; accept H_1.

h. Different populations.

i. Yes.

j. Yes, because the F_{obs} is statistically significant and three levels of the independent variable are varied.

k. Tukey $CD = 2.90$.

l. The mean estimated latitude for Dallas is significantly higher than the means for either Tijuana or Tripoli. The means for Tijuana and Tripoli do not differ significantly.

m. $\eta^2 = .74$.

3. a. 2.   **b.** 19.

  c. 4.76.   **d.** 4.41.

  e. Reject H_0.   **f.** Accept H_1.

  g. Yes.

  h. The simple and complex stimulus conditions.

4. a. 3.   **b.** 12.

  c. 2.81.   **d.** 3.44.

  e. Fail to reject H_0.   **f.** Do not accept H_1.

  g. No.

  h. No treatment conditions differ significantly.

Review Questions

1. a.

	Type of Word		
	Happy	Neutral	Sad
$\overline{X}$	4.5	3.0	2.5
s	1.4	1.2	1.2

Source	SS	df	MS	F
Type of word (A)	17.333	2	8.666	7.00*
Subjects (S)	16.667	7	2.381	
A × S	17.333	14	1.238	
Total	51.333	23		

*$p < .05$.

Tukey $CD = 1.5$. The mean for happy words is significantly greater than the mean for either neutral or sad words. The neutral and sad words means do not differ significantly.

b. $\eta^2 = .50$.

2.

	Type of Topic	
	Nonstressful	Stressful
$\overline{X}$	3.0	4.0
s	2.2	1.9

a.

Source	SS	df	MS	F
Type of Topic (A)	5.500	1	5.500	9.167
Subjects (S)	82.000	10	8.200	
A × S	6.000	10	0.600	
Total	93.500	21		

F_{obs} is significant at the .05 level. Stressful topics lead to more enunciation errors than nonstressful topics.

b. $t_{obs}(10) = 3.028$. $\sqrt{F_{obs}} = \sqrt{9.167} = 3.028$.

b. Same conclusions.

3. a. $H_0: \mu_{A_1} = \mu_{A_2} = \mu_{A_3} = \mu_{A_4} = \mu_{A_5}$.
  H_1: The μ_A's are not all equal.

b. $df_A = 4$, $df_S = 11$, $df_{A \times S} = 44$, $df_{Total} = 59$.

c. $F_{crit}(4, 44) = 2.61$.

d. Reject H_0; accept H_1.

e. There is at least one significant difference among the means. A Tukey HSD test is necessary to locate the specific significant differences.

4.

Table 1				
Source	SS	df	MS	F
Factor A	22.00	2	11.00	2.00
Factor S	138.00	23	6.00	
A × S	253.00	46	5.50	
Total	413.00	71		

a. 3.   b. 24.
c. 24.   d. No.
e. Fail to reject H_0; do not accept H_1.

Table 2			
Source	SS	df	MS	F
Factor A	60.00	5	12.0	3.00
Factor S	133.00	19	7.0	
$A \times S$	380.00	95	4.0	
Total	573.00	119		

a. 6.   c. 20.
b. 20.   d. Yes.
e. Reject H_0; accept H_1.
5. The statistically significant $F_{obs}(2, 26) = 15.99$ indicates that there is at least one significant difference among the means. Pairwise comparisons with the Tukey CD indicate that each mean differs significantly from each other mean. Consequently, infants fixated on the familiar face for the longest duration. The duration of fixation on the unfamiliar face was significantly less than the fixation on the familiar face, and the duration of fixation on the blank oval was significantly less than the fixation on either the familiar or unfamiliar face.

Integrating Your Knowledge
A. 1. Descriptive.   2. Survey.
   3. No. A statistical hypothesis test is needed to determine if the values differ significantly.
C.

	Type of Activity		
	Relationships with Friends	Religious/Spiritual Life	Relationships with Parents
$\overline{X}$	13.0	14.0	15.5
s	2.5	3.7	2.9

Source	SS	df	MS	F
Type of activity (A)	38.00	2	19.00	11.38
Subjects (S)	272.33	11	24.76	
$A \times S$	36.67	22	1.67	
Total	347.00	35		

$CD = 1.3$, $\eta^2 = .51$. The mean happiness rating for relationships with parents is significantly higher than either the ratings for relationships with friends or religious/spiritual life. The relationships with friends and religious/spiritual life ratings do not differ significantly.

Chapter 13

Testing Your Knowledge 13.1
2. No, the relationship between the two scores does not change.
3. *Table 1*
   a. Positive relationship.
   b. Less than perfect.
   c. Yes. Knowing the liking of a professor score allows better prediction of in-class attention than can be achieved without knowing it.
   Table 2
   a. Negative relationship.
   b. Less than perfect.   c. Yes.
4. a. Weak negative relationship.
   b. Less than perfect.
   c. No, it would do little to increase the accuracy of the prediction.

Testing Your Knowledge 13.2
3. a. $r_{obs} = +.870$.
4. a. $r_{obs} = -.764$.
5. a. $r_{obs} = -.277$.

Testing Your Knowledge 13.3
4. r^2
   a. .01
   b. .55
   c. .35
   d. .13
   e. .05
   f. .04

Testing Your Knowledge 13.4
2. H_0: $\rho = 0$; H_1: $\rho \neq 0$.
3.

		Critical Value	
	df	.05	.01
a.	6	.707	.834
b.	13	.514	.641
c.	18	.444	.561
d.	30	.349	.449
e.	41	.304	.393
f.	73	.232	.302

4.

	Statistical Hypotheses	Critical Value	Falls into Rejection Region	Decision
a.	$H_0: \rho = 0$ $H_1: \rho \neq 0$	.576	Yes	H_0: Reject H_1: Accept
b.	$H_0: \rho = 0$ $H_1: \rho \neq 0$	.576	No	H_0: Fail to reject H_1: Do not accept
c.	$H_0: \rho = 0$ $H_1: \rho \neq 0$	.444	Yes	H_0: Reject H_1: Accept
d.	$H_0: \rho = 0$ $H_1: \rho \neq 0$	.423	No	H_0: Fail to reject H_1: Do not accept
e.	$H_0: \rho = 0$ $H_1: \rho \neq 0$	.232	Yes	H_0: Reject H_1: Accept
f.	$H_0: \rho = 0$ $H_1: \rho \neq 0$	.666	Yes	H_0: Reject H_1: Accept

5. a. $r_{obs} = -.550$.

   b. $r_{crit}(10) = .576$; r_{obs} is nonsignificant.

   c. There is no evidence for a relationship between absences and test scores for the population from which these scores were sampled.

6.

	Statistical Hypotheses	Critical Value	Falls into Rejection Region	Decision
a.	$H_0: \rho_s = 0$ $H_1: \rho_s \neq 0$	.490	No	H_0: Fail to reject H_1: Do not accept
b.	$H_0: \rho_s = 0$ $H_1: \rho_s \neq 0$	.591	Yes	H_0: Reject H_1: Accept
c.	$H_0: \rho_s = 0$ $H_1: \rho_s \neq 0$	.409	Yes	H_0: Reject H_1: Accept
d.	$H_0: \rho_s = 0$ $H_1: \rho_s \neq 0$	.648	No	H_0: Fail to reject H_1: Do not accept
e.	$H_0: \rho_s = 0$ $H_1: \rho_s \neq 0$	.438	Yes	H_0: Reject H_1: Accept
f.	$H_0: \rho_s = 0$ $H_1: \rho_s \neq 0$	.364	Yes	H_0: Reject H_1: Accept

Review Questions

1. b. Positive.

   c. $r_{obs} = +.655$; $r_{crit}(14) = .497$; r_{obs} is statistically significant.

   d. There is a positive relationship between anger level and systolic blood pressure. Higher anger levels are associated with higher systolic blood pressure.

   e. $r^2 = .43$.

2. a. $r_{obs} = +.48$ for being a victim of traditional rumors and being a victim on the Internet; $r_{crit}(82) = .217$; r_{obs} is statistically significant. $r_{obs} = -.11$ for being a victim of teasing and behaving like a bully on the Internet; $r_{crit}(82) = .217$; r_{obs} is nonsignificant. $r_{obs} = +.32$ for being a bully by excluding others and being a bully through text messaging; $r_{crit}(82) = .217$; r_{obs} is statistically significant.

   b. $r^2 = .23$ for being a victim of traditional rumors and being a victim on the Internet; $r^2 = .01$ for being a victim of teasing and behaving like a bully; $r^2 = .10$ for being a bully by excluding others and being a bully through text messaging.

   c. There is a positive relationship between being a victim of traditional rumors and being a victim on the Internet and between being a bully by excluding others and being a bully through text messaging, but there is no relationship for being a victim of teasing and behaving like a bully.

3. **b.** Positive.
   c. $r_{obs} = +.781$; $r_{crit}(8) = .632$; r_{obs} is statistically significant.
   d. They are positively related; the higher the midterm grade, the higher the final exam grade tends to be.

4. **a.** $r_{s\,obs} = +.937$; $r_{crit}(12) = .591$; $r_{s\,obs}$ is statistically significant.
   b. Popularity and physical attractiveness are positively related in the population of girls from which the sample was drawn.
   c. $r_{s\,obs} = -.134$; $r_{crit}(14) = .545$; $r_{s\,obs}$ is nonsignificant.
   d. There is no relationship between popularity and physical attractiveness of boys in the population from which the sample was drawn.

5. The IQ of college students involves a restricted range of that variable. Very low and very high IQ scores were not included in the sample. It is also possible that the grade point averages are similarly restricted in range.

6. **b.** Negative relationship.
   c. $r_{obs} = -.667$; $r_{crit}(11) = .553$; r_{obs} is significant.
   d. Higher Friend Trust scores are associated with lower bulimic symptoms scores.

7. **b.** The relationship appears to be negative.
   c. $r_{obs} = -.807$; $r_{crit}(13) = .514$. r_{obs} is statistically significant.
   d. The number of negative daily events and school satisfaction are negatively related. More negative daily events are associated with lower school satisfaction.

8. **a.** $r_{obs} = -.735$.
   b. $r_{crit}(15) = .482$. r_{obs} is statistically significant.
   c. A negative correlation indicates that higher scores on variable X are associated with lower scores on variable Y. Thus, you expect a lower grade for the friend who plays 15 hours of video games per week than you do for the friend who plays video games 4 hours per week.

9. **a.** $r_{s\,obs} = +.847$.
   b. $r_{s\,crit}(16) = .507$. $r_{s\,obs}$ is statistically significant.
   c. There is a positive correlation between liking rank and participation rank. Higher liking ranks are associated with higher participation ranks.

Chapter 14

Testing Your Knowledge 14.1
4. **a.** $b = +2$; $a = 0$; $Y = +2X$.
   b. $b = -1$; $a = +2$; $Y = -1X + 2$.
   c. $b = +1.5$; $a = +1$; $Y = +1.5X + 1$.
   d. $b = -2$; $a = +4$; $Y = -2X + 4$.

Testing Your Knowledge 14.2
3. **a.** $Y' = +0.8X + 9$.
   b.

X	Y'
60	57
65	61
80	73
85	77
90	81

   c. $\overline{Y} = 69.8$. The regression line passes through the points $X = 0$, $Y = 9$; $\overline{X} = 76$, $\overline{Y} = 69.8$.

4. **a.** $Y' = -1.4X + 23$.
   b.

X	Y'
5	16.0
8	11.8
11	7.6
14	3.4
17	-0.8

   c. $\overline{Y} = 7.6$. The regression line passes through the points $X = 0$, $Y = 23$; $\overline{X} = 11$, $\overline{Y} = 7.6$.

Testing Your Knowledge 14.3
5. 4.98.
6. 4.80.
7. 4.30.

Testing Your Knowledge 14.4
1. **a.** +11.507.
   b. 202.215.
   c. $Y' = +11.507X + 202.215$.
   d. The regression line passes through the points $X = 0$, $Y = 202.215$; $\overline{X} = 5.17$, $\overline{Y} = 261.71$.

e.

X	Y′
6	271.3
3	236.7
9	305.8
1	213.7
4	248.2
2	225.2
3	236.7
5	259.8
8	294.3
7	282.8
8	294.3
6	271.3

f.

Subject	Residual (Y − Y′)
1	−54.3
2	−6.7
3	+9.2
4	+10.3
5	+22.8
6	−27.2
7	+19.3
8	+3.2
9	+26.7
10	+6.2
11	−29.3
12	+19.7

g. 6824.43.

h. 26.12.

i. Yes; $s_{Y \cdot X}$ is smaller than s_Y.

2. a. $b = -0.43$.

   b. $a = 24.6$

   c. $Y' = -0.43X + 24.6$.

   d. 41 scans, $Y' = 7.0$.
      18 scans, $Y' = 16.9$.

Review Questions

1. a. +0.884.   **b.** +0.884.

   c. $Y' = +0.884X + 10.96$.

   d. 79.0.   **e.** 5.52.

2. a. $Y' = -0.116X + 3.23$.

   b. 2.88.   **c.** 2.64.

3. a. $Y' = -4.3X + 1.28$, where X = number of cigarettes smoked per day.

c.

Cigarettes per Day	Predicted Birth Weight (oz)
0	128.0
1	123.7
5	106.5
8	93.6
10	85.0
13	72.1
20	42.0

4. a. $Y' = +0.786X + 107.16$.

   b.

Subject	Predicted Blood Pressure
1	157.5
2	130.7
3	136.2
4	137.8
5	120.5
6	130.0
7	135.5
8	133.9
9	141.7
10	132.3
11	136.2
12	144.1
13	146.5
14	139.4
15	143.3
16	155.1

   d. $s_{Y \cdot X}$ is .78 of s_Y.

5. a. −0.562.

   b. 28.33.

   c. $Y' = -0.562X + 28.33$.

   e. 2.90.

6.

Applicant	Predicted Job Performance: Y′
Dianne	55.2
Rodrigo	61.2
Colin	54.0
Maria	67.2
Ruben	64.8
Luke	52.8
Holly	50.4
Blythe	70.8

The predicted job performance scores of Rodrigo, Maria, Ruben, and Blythe are greater than 60. Thus, these applicants will be hired.

7. **a.** $Y' = -1.317X + 89.17$.
   b. Y' for 4 hours = 83.9; Y' for 15 hours = 69.4.
   c. $s_{Y \cdot X} = 8.01$; $s_{Y \cdot X}$ is .70 of s_Y.

Integrating Your Knowledge

A. 1. a. Statistically significant.
   b. Increase.
   c. .34.
   d. Supports the research hypothesis.
2. a. Statistically significant.
   b. Increase.
   c. .45.
   d. Supports the research hypothesis.
3. a. Nonsignificant.
   b. There is no relationship.
   c. .04.
   d. Supports the research hypothesis.
4. a. Nonsignificant.
   b. There is no relationship.
   c. .02.
   d. Supports the research hypothesis.
C. (Values are to given two decimal places for use in intermediate computations)
3. $\overline{X} = 11.62$, $\overline{Y} = 24.53$, $s_X = 1.51$, $s_Y = 8.85$, $s_{Y \cdot X} = 6.97$.
4. 24.53; error = 8.85.
5. $r_{obs}(28) = +.634$, statistically significant.
6. a. $b = +3.72$.
   b. Y intercept $= -18.70$.
   c. 18.5; error = 6.97.
   d. 33.4; error = 6.97.
   e. 21 percent reduction in error.

Chapter 15

Testing Your Knowledge 15.1
6.

χ^2_{obs}	df	χ^2_{crit}	Falls into Rejection Region	Decisions
7.26	2	5.99	Yes	H_0: Reject H_1: Accept
8.33	4	9.49	No	H_0: Fail to reject H_1: Do not accept
14.19	7	14.1	Yes	H_0: Reject H_1: Accept
26.94	20	31.4	No	H_0: Fail to reject H_1: Do not accept

7. The values in each cell are expected frequencies.
   a.

	Column 1	Column 2
Row 1	12.6	31.4
Row 2	15.4	38.6

$\chi^2_{obs}(1) = 0.073$, $p > .05$; nonsignificant.

   b.

	Column 1	Column 2
Row 1	19.2	29.8
Row 2	24.8	38.2

$\chi^2_{obs}(1) = 9.256$, $p < .01$; statistically significant.

   c.

	Column 1	Column 2
Row 1	42.4	56.6
Row 2	17.6	23.4

$\chi^2_{obs}(1) = 12.442$, $p < .01$; statistically significant.

8. $\chi^2_{obs}(2) = 0.168$. This χ^2_{obs} is nonsignificant; there is no relationship between day of the week and time of day for cars passing stop signs in this example.
9. $\chi^2_{obs}(1) = 70.914$, $p < .01$; the hypothesized relationship exists.

Testing Your Knowledge 15.2
1.

Scores ordered from smallest to largest	7	10	14	15	16	19	23	26
Group identity	2	1	2	1	2	1	1	2
Rank	1	2	3	4	5	6	7	8
Number of times an A_1 score precedes A_2 scores			3		2		1	1
Number of times an A_2 score precedes A_1 scores			4		3		2	

$U_{A_1} = 7$; $U_{A_2} = 9$.
a. U_{A_1}.   **b.** No.
2. $U_{A_1} = 7$; $U_{A_2} = 9$.
a. Yes.

4. U_{A_1} should be about equal to U_{A_2}.
5. They should differ considerably.
6.

	U_{crit}	Falls into Rejection Region	Decision
a.	0	No	H_0: Fail to reject H_1: Do not accept
b.	16	Yes	H_0: Reject H_1: Accept
c.	27	No	H_0: Fail to reject H_1: Do not accept
d.	22	Yes	H_0: Reject H_1: Accept
e.	56	Yes	H_0: Reject H_1: Accept
f.	87	No	H_0: Fail to reject H_1: Do not accept

7. Smaller $U = U_{A_1} = 54.5$; $U_{\text{crit}} = 41$; U_{A_1} does not fall into the rejection region. There is no evidence that the groups differ in their anxiety estimates.

Testing Your Knowledge 15.3
4.

	T_{crit}	Falls into Rejection Region	Decision
a.	3	Yes	H_0: Reject H_1: Accept
b.	8	No	H_0: Fail to reject H_1: Do not accept
c.	17	Yes	H_0: Reject H_1: Accept
d.	46	Yes	H_0: Reject H_1: Accept
e.	89	No	H_0: Fail to reject H_1: Do not accept

5. $T_{\text{obs}}(14) = 27$; $T_{\text{crit}}(14) = 21$; T_{obs} is not statistically significant. The anxiety level did not change from practice to competition in this sample.

Review Questions
2. a. $\chi^2_{\text{obs}}(1) = 1.235$, $p > .05$. The frequency of drop out is not related to gender.
b. $\chi^2_{\text{obs}}(2) = 28.990$, $p < .01$. The frequency of drop out is related to the severity of the problem. A larger than expected number of individuals with mild problems drop out; fewer than expected individuals with severe problems drop out.
3. $\Sigma(-R) = 50$, $\Sigma(+R) = 5$; therefore, $T_{\text{obs}}(11) = 5$, $p < .01$. Reject H_0; the type of task affects yawning.
a. The uninteresting video condition scores are positively skewed.
b. The distributions of the number of yawns differ. More yawns occur with an uninteresting stimulus than with an interesting stimulus.
4. $U_{A_2} = 38.5$, $p > .05$. The distributions do not differ significantly.
5. $U_{A_2} = 44.5$, $p > .05$. The distributions do not differ significantly.
6. $T_{\text{obs}} = 3$; $T_{\text{crit}}(8) = 3$. T_{obs} falls into the rejection region; thus, H_0: The population distributions of the related A_1 and A_2 scores are identical is rejected.

Glossary

Additivity rule of mutually exclusive events: $p(A \text{ or } B) = p(A) + p(B)$.

Alpha or α: The value of the significance level stated as a probability.

Alternative hypothesis: A statement of what must be true if the null hypothesis for a statistical test is false.

Analysis of variance (ANOVA): A statistical test used to analyze multilevel designs.

Archival records: Research using existing records.

Arithmetic mean ($\overline{X}$): The sum of a set of scores divided by the number of scores summed.

Artifactual main effect: A main effect that does not give meaningful information about the effect of an independent variable in a factorial design.

Asymptotic distribution: A distribution for which the tails of the distribution never touch the X axis.

Bar graph: A graph used to present a frequency distribution when the variable measured is qualitative in nature. The frequency of occurrence of scores in a category is given by the height of the bar.

Beta (β): The probability of a Type II error.

Between-groups variance: The variance calculated using the variation of the group means about the grand mean.

Between-subjects design: An experiment in which two or more groups are created.

Bimodal distribution: A distribution with two modes.

Bivariate distribution: A distribution in which two scores are obtained from each subject.

Bivariate normal distribution: A distribution of X and Y variables in which (1) the X scores are normally distributed in the population sampled, (2) the Y scores are normally distributed in the population sampled, (3) for each X score the distribution of Y scores in the population is normal, and (4) for each Y score the distribution of X scores in the population is normal.

Case study: Research involving the study of a single person, animal, or situation.

Cell mean: The mean of the n_{AB} scores for a treatment combination in a factorial design.

Cell or treatment condition: A combination formed from one level of each independent variable in a factorial design.

Central limit theorem: A mathematical theorem stating that, as sample size increases, the sampling distribution of the mean approaches a normal distribution.

Chance difference: A difference between equivalent groups due to random variation.

Chi-square test: A statistical test used to analyze nominal level of measurement scores where frequencies of occurrence of the various categories are obtained.

Chi-square test for goodness of fit: The chi square used when a score is categorized on only one dimension.

Chi-square test of independence: The chi square used when a score may be categorized on two independent dimensions.

Class interval: The width of the interval used to group raw scores in a grouped frequency distribution. The size or width of the interval is represented by i.

Coefficient of determination: The value of r^2 indicating the common variance of variables X and Y.

Confidence interval: A range of score values expected to contain the value of mu with a certain level of confidence.

Confidence limits: The lower and upper scores defining the confidence interval.

Confound: An extraneous variable that is covarying with the independent variable, potentially masking the true effects of the independent variable on the dependent variable.

Confounded experiment: An experiment in which an extraneous variable is allowed to vary consistently with the independent variable.

Consistent estimator: A statistic for which the probability that the statistic has a value closer to the parameter increases as the sample size increases.

Continuous distribution: A distribution for which, if any two scores in the distribution are chosen, another score that lies between them can always be found.

Continuous variable: A variable that can take on an infinite set of values between the limits of the variable.

Convenience sampling: Obtaining subjects from among people who are accessible or convenient to the researcher.

Correlation coefficient: A statistic that provides a numerical description of the extent of the relatedness of two sets of scores and the direction of the relationship.

Correlational study: Study in which two or more variables are measured to find the direction and degree to which they covary.

Covary: Two variables covary when a change in one variable is related to a consistent change in the other variable.

Critical difference: The minimum numerical difference between two treatment means that is statistically significant.

Critical value: The specific numerical values that define the boundaries of the rejection region.

Cross products of X and Y: The value of $\sum(X - \overline{X})(Y - \overline{Y})$ for variables X and Y.

Cumulative frequency of a class interval: The frequency of occurrence of scores in that interval plus the sum of the frequencies of scores of lower class intervals.

Cumulative frequency of a score: The frequency of occurrence of that score plus the sum of the frequencies of all the scores of lower value.

Cumulative grouped percentage frequency of a class interval: The percentage frequency of the scores in that interval plus the sum of the percentage frequencies of all the class intervals of lower value.

Cumulative grouped relative frequency of a class interval: The relative frequency of the scores in that interval plus the sum of the relative frequencies of class intervals of lower value.

Data: The scores or numerical measurements of behavior or characteristics obtained from observations of a sample of people or animals.

Degrees of freedom: The number of scores free to vary when calculating a statistic.

Dependent variable: The variable in an experiment that depends on the independent variable. In most instances the dependent variable is some measure of a behavior.

Descriptive statistic or statistic: A single number used to describe data from a sample.

Deviation: The difference of a score in a set of scores from that mean of that set of scores.

Discrete outcomes: Outcomes in a distribution that have a countable set of values.

Discrete variable: A variable that can take on only a finite or countable set of values within its limits.

Distribution-free test: A statistical test involving hypotheses that do not state a relationship about a population parameter. Also known as a *nonparametric test*.

Effect size: The size of the effect of an independent variable.

Empirical data: Scores or measurements based on observation and sensory experience.

Empirical probability distribution: A probability distribution found by counting actual occurrences of an event.

Equivalent groups: Groups of subjects that are not expected to differ in any consistent or systematic way prior to receiving the independent variable of the experiment.

Error rate in an experiment: The probability of making at least one Type I error in the statistical comparisons conducted in an experiment.

Estimated population standard deviation (s): The square root of the estimated population variance. Also known as the *standard deviation*.

Estimated population variance (s^2): The variance obtained from a sample of scores that is used to estimate the population variance for those scores. Also known as the *variance*.

Estimated standard error of the difference between means ($s_{\overline{X}_1 - \overline{X}_2}$): The standard error of the difference between means obtained by using s^2 to estimate σ^2.

Estimated standard error of the mean ($s_{\overline{X}}$): The standard error of the mean obtained by using s to estimate σ.

Event: The occurrence of a specified set of outcomes in a probability distribution.

Expected frequencies: The frequencies in a contingency table obtained assuming that the two dimensions of the table are independent.

Experiment: A controlled situation in which one or more independent variables are manipulated to observe the effect on the dependent variable.

Extraneous variables: Any variables, other than the independent variable, that can affect the dependent variable in an experiment.

Factor: An alternative name for an independent variable.

Factorial design: A research design in which two or more independent variables are varied simultaneously.

Frequency distribution: A count of the number of times that each score occurs in a set of scores.

Frequency polygon: A graph constructed by placing the midpoints of each class interval of a frequency distribution on the abscissa and indicating the frequency of a class interval by placing a dot at the appropriate frequency above the midpoint. The dots are connected with straight lines.

General equation of a straight line: $Y = bX + a$.

Grand mean: The mean of all scores in an experiment.

Grouped frequency distribution: A frequency distribution in which scores are grouped together in class intervals and the frequency of scores occurring within each class is tabulated.

Grouped percentage frequency distribution: A grouped frequency distribution obtained by multiplying the relative frequency values by 100 to obtain percentages.

Grouped relative frequency distribution: A grouped frequency distribution obtained by dividing the frequency of scores in an interval by the total number of scores in the distribution.

Histogram: A form of bar graph in which the frequency of occurrence of scores in a class interval is given by the height of the bar, and the size of each class interval is represented by the width of the bar on the abscissa.

Independent variable: A variable manipulated in an experiment to determine its effect on the dependent variable.

Inference: A process of reasoning from something known to something unknown.

Informed consent: Informing a subject of all aspects of a research study, including the study's purpose, duration, and potential risk, that might influence a person's willingness to participate in the research.

Institutional Review Board: A group of at least five people experienced in research issues who must review and approve all research involving human or animal subjects occurring in an institution.

Interaction: A situation in a factorial design in which the effect of one independent variable depends on the level of the other independent variable with which it is combined.

Interval measurement: The amount of a variable is ordered along a dimension, and the differences between the assigned numbers represent equal amounts in the magnitude of the variable measured. The zero point of an interval scale is an arbitrary starting point.

Least-squares regression line: A straight line that minimizes the value of $\sum (Y - Y')^2$.

Level of an independent variable: One value of the independent variable. To be a variable, an independent variable must take on at least two different levels.

Linear relation: A relation between two variables such that each time variable X changes by one unit, variable Y changes by a constant amount.

Linear relationship: A relationship between two variables that can be described by a straight line.

Lower stated limit of a class interval: The lowest score that could fall into that class interval.

Lower real limit of a number: The point midway between a number and the next lower number.

Main effect of factor A: The difference between $\overline{X}_{A_1}$ and $\overline{X}_{A_2}$ in a factorial design, symbolized by $\overline{X}_{A_1} - \overline{X}_{A_2}$.

Main effect of factor B: The difference between $\overline{X}_{B_1}$ and $\overline{X}_{B_2}$ in a factorial design, symbolized by $\overline{X}_{B_1} - \overline{X}_{B_2}$.

Main effect mean: The mean of all subjects given one level of an independent variable, ignoring the classification by the other independent variable in a factorial design.

Mann–Whitney U test: A nonparametric test for a between-subjects design using two levels of an independent variable with the scores representing at least ordinal measurement.

Marginal frequencies: The row totals and the column totals of the observed frequencies in a contingency table.

Mean ($\overline{X}$): The sum of a set of scores divided by the number of scores summed.

Mean square: The name used for a variance in the analysis of variance.

Measurement: Assigning numbers to variables following a set of rules.

Measures of central tendency: Numbers that represent the average or typical score obtained from measurements of a sample.

Measures of variability: Numbers that indicate how much scores differ from each other and the measure of central tendency in a set of scores.

Median (mdn): A score value in the distribution with an equal number of scores above and below it. The median is the 50th percentile in a distribution.

Midpoint of a class interval: The point midway between the real limits of the class interval.

Mode: The most frequently occurring score in a distribution of scores.

Multimodal distribution: A distribution with more than two modes.

Multiple comparison tests: Statistical tests used to make pairwise comparisons to find which means differ significantly from one another in a one-factor multilevel design.

Multiple regression: Predicting the value of Y scores using several X variables.

Multiple treatment effects: Changes in subjects' performance in a within-subjects design that are due to being tested in each level of the independent variable.

Mutually exclusive outcomes: Outcomes that cannot occur at the same time.

Naturalistic observation: Research involving the observation of behaviors occurring in natural settings.

Negative relationship: A relationship between two variables in which, as the value of one variable increases, the value of the other variable tends to decrease.

Negatively skewed distribution: A distribution in which the tail occurs for the low scores at the left of the distribution.

Nominal measurement: A classification of the measured variable into different categories.

Nonparametric test: A statistical test involving hypotheses that do not state a relationship about a population parameter. Also known as a *distribution-free test*.

Nonsignificant difference: The observed value of the test statistic does not fall into a rejection region and the null hypothesis is not rejected.

Normal distribution: A theoretical mathematical distribution that specifies the relative frequency of a set of scores in a population.

Null hypothesis: A statement of a condition that a scientist tentatively holds to be true about a population. The null hypothesis is the hypothesis tested by a statistical test.

One-factor between-subjects design: A research design in which one independent variable is manipulated and two or more groups are created.

One-factor multilevel design: An experiment with one independent variable and three or more levels of that independent variable.

One-sample *t* test: A *t* test used to test the difference between a sample mean and an hypothesized population mean for statistical significance when $\sigma_{\overline{X}}$ is estimated by $s_{\overline{X}}$.

One-tailed test: A statistical test employing a rejection region in only one tail of the sampling distribution of the test statistic. Also called a *directional test*.

Operational definition: A specification of the operations used to make observations, to manipulate an independent variable, or to measure the dependent variable.

Ordinal measurement: The amount of a variable is placed in order of magnitude along a dimension.

Outcome: Each possible occurrence in a probability distribution.

Outlier: An extreme score in a distribution.

Pairwise comparisons: Statistical comparisons involving two means.

Parameter: A number that describes a characteristic of a population.

Parametric test: A statistical test involving hypotheses that state a relationship about a population parameter.

Pearson correlation coefficient (*r*): A statistic, symbolized by *r*, that indicates the degree of linear relationship between two variables measured at the interval or ratio level.

Percent: A proportion multiplied by 100.

Percentage: A proportion multiplied by 100.

Percentage frequency (%*f*): The relative frequency of a score multiplied by 100.

Percentage frequency distribution: The frequency of occurrence of a score expressed as a percentage of the total number of scores obtained.

Percentile: The score at or below which a specified percentage of scores in a distribution fall.

Percentile rank of a score: The percentage of scores in the distribution that are equal to or less than that score.

Placebo control: A simulated treatment condition.

Point estimation: Estimating the value of a parameter as a single point from the value of a statistic.

Population: A complete set of people, animals, objects, or events that share a common characteristic.

Population mean (μ): The sum of all the scores in a population divided by the number of scores summed.

Population standard deviation (σ): The square root of the population variance.

Population variance (σ^2): The variance obtained by measuring all scores in a population.

Positive relationship: A relationship between two variables in which, as the value of one variable increases the value of the other variable tends to increase also.

Positively skewed distribution: A distribution in which the tail occurs for the high scores at the right of the distribution.

Post hoc comparisons: Statistical tests that make all possible pairwise comparisons after a statistically significant F_{obs} has occurred for the overall analysis of variance.

Power: The probability of rejecting H_0 when H_0 is false and H_1 is true. The power of a statistical test is given by $1 - \beta$.

Practice effect: A multiple treatment effect that occurs because subjects may become more practiced or fatigued on the experimental task.

Probability of occurrence of an event (p):

$$p(\text{event}) = \frac{\text{Number of outcomes composing the event}}{\text{Total number of possible outcomes}}.$$

Qualitative data: Data obtained from a nominal measurement indicating the kind or the quality of a variable.

Quantitative data: Data obtained from ordinal, interval, or ratio measurements indicating how much of a variable exists.

Quasi-experiment: Research involving the use of subject variables as independent variables.

Random assignment: A method of assigning subjects to treatment groups so that any individual selected for the experiment has an equal probability of assignment to any of the groups and the assignment of one subject to a group does not affect the assignment of any other individual to that same group.

Random sample: A sample in which individuals are selected so that each member of the population has an equal chance of being selected for the sample, and the selection of one member is independent of the selection of any other member of the population.

Random sampling: A sampling method in which individuals are selected so that each member of the population has an equal chance of being selected for the sample, and the selection of one member is independent of any other member of the population.

Range: The numerical difference between the lowest and highest score in a distribution.

Ratio measurement: The amount of a variable is ordered along a dimension, the differences between the assigned numbers represent equal amounts in the magnitude of the variable measured, and a true zero point exists, which represents the absence of the characteristic measured.

Raw data or raw scores: The scores obtained from all the subjects before the scores have been analyzed statistically.

Real limit of a class interval: The point midway between the stated limit of a class interval and the stated limit of the next lower or upper class interval.

Real limits of a number: The points midway between the number and the next lower and the next higher numbers on the scale used to make the measurements.

Regression analysis: The use of statistical methods to predict one set of scores from a second set of scores.

Regression toward the mean: The tendency of an extreme score to be less extreme on a second measurement.

Rejection region: Values on the sampling distribution of the test statistic that have a probability equal to or less than α if H_0 is true. If the test statistic falls into the rejection region, H_0 is rejected.

Relative frequency distribution: The frequency of a score divided by the total number of scores obtained.

Repeated measures design: A research design in which one group of subjects is exposed to and measured under each level of an independent variable. In a repeated measures design, each subject receives each treatment condition. Also known as a *treatment-by-subjects design* or a *repeated measures design*.

Research hypothesis: A statement of an expected, or predicted, relationship between two or more variables. In an experiment, a research hypothesis is a predicted relationship between an independent variable and a dependent variable.

Research method: An approach scientists take to collect data in order to develop or evaluate a research hypothesis.

Residual: The value of $Y - Y'$.

Robustness: A term used to indicate that violating the assumptions of a statistical test has little effect on the probability of a Type I error.

Rows-by-columns contingency table: A rows-by-columns table presenting the frequency of each category formed by the intersection of the row and column variables in the table.

Sample: A subset, or subgroup, selected from a population.

Sample mean ($\overline{X}$): The sum of a set of scores divided by the number of scores summed.

Sampling distribution: A theoretical probability distribution of values of a statistic resulting from selecting all possible samples of size n from a population.

Sampling distribution of the difference between means: The distribution of $\overline{X}_1 - \overline{X}_2$ differences when all possible pairs of samples of size n are selected from a population and $\overline{X}_1 - \overline{X}_2$ found for each pair of samples.

Sampling distribution of the mean: The distribution of $\overline{X}$ values when all possible samples of size n are selected from a population.

Sampling distribution of t: The distribution of t values for all possible sample sizes.

Sampling error: The amount by which a sample mean differs from the population mean.

Scatterplot: A plot of a bivariate distribution in which the X variable is plotted on the horizontal axis and the Y variable is plotted on the vertical axis.

Score: The measurement obtained on the subject's performance of a task.

Significance level: A probability value that provides the criterion for rejecting a null hypothesis in a statistical test.

Simple effect of an independent variable: The effect of one independent variable at only one level of the other independent variable in a factorial design.

Simple random sampling: Selecting members from a population such that each member of the population has an equal chance of being selected for the sample, and the selection of one member is independent of the selection of any other member of the population.

Skewed distribution: A frequency distribution in which scores are clustered at one end of the distribution with scores occurring infrequently at the other end of the distribution.

Slope of a straight line: The slope of a straight line is given by

$$b = \frac{\text{Change in value of } Y}{\text{Change in value of } X}.$$

Spearman rank-order correlation coefficient (r_S): A correlation coefficient used with ordinal measures.

Standard deviation: The square root of the estimated population variance. Also known as the *estimated population standard deviation*.

Standard error of estimate: The value of

$$\sqrt{\frac{\Sigma(Y - Y')^2}{N_{\text{pairs}} - 2}}.$$

Standard error of the difference between means, or the standard error of the difference: The standard deviation of a theoretical sampling distribution of $\overline{X}_1 - \overline{X}_2$ values.

Standard error of the mean ($\sigma_{\overline{X}}$): The standard deviation of the sampling distribution of the mean found by dividing σ by the square root of the size of the sample.

Standard normal deviate: The value of z_{obs} when a score is transformed into a score on the standard normal distribution.

Standard normal distribution: A normal distribution with $\mu = 0$ and $\sigma = 1$.

Standard score: A score obtained by using the transformation $z = (X - \overline{X})/S$.

Stated limits of a class interval: The highest and lowest scores that could fall into that class interval.

Statistic: A single number used to describe a set of data from a sample or to analyze those data more fully.

Statistical hypothesis: A statement about a population parameter (for a parametric test).

Statistical hypothesis testing: Procedures used to determine the anticipated size of chance differences between groups.

Statistical inference: Estimating population values from statistics obtained from a sample.

Statistically significant difference: The observed value of the test statistic falls into a rejection region and H_0 is rejected.

Statistics: The methods or procedures used to summarize, analyze, and draw inferences from data.

Subject or participant: The person who participates in an experiment.

Subject variable: A characteristic or attribute of a subject that can be measured but not manipulated by the researcher.

Sum of squares: A numerical value obtained by subtracting the mean of a distribution from each score in the distribution, squaring each difference, and then summing the differences.

Sum of squares residual: The value of $\Sigma(Y - Y')^2$.

Survey research: Research involving obtaining data from either oral or written interviews with people.

Symmetrical frequency distribution: A frequency distribution that when folded at a midpoint produces two halves identical in shape.

Test statistic: A number calculated from the scores of the sample that allows testing a statistical null hypothesis.

Theoretical probability distribution: A probability distribution found from the use of a theoretical probability model.

Treatment carry-over effect: A multiple treatment effect that occurs when the effect of one level of the independent variable carries over to affect performance in the next level of the independent variable.

Treatments-by-subjects design: A research design in which one group of subjects is exposed to and measured under each level of an independent variable. In a treatment-by-subjects design, each subject receives each treatment condition. Also known as a *repeated measures design* or a *within-subjects design*.

Treatments-by-subject interaction: A situation in a one-factor within-subjects design where the effect of the independent variable depends on the subject.

Tukey HSD test: A statistical test used for post hoc comparisons between treatment means in a one-factor multilevel design or to test for differences between cell means in a factorial design.

Two-tailed test: A statistical test using rejection regions in both tails of the sampling distribution of the test statistic. Also called a *nondirectional test*.

Type I error: The error in statistical decision making that occurs if the null hypothesis is rejected when actually it is true of the population.

Type II error: The error in statistical decision making that occurs if H_0 is not rejected when it is false and the alternative hypothesis (H_1) is true.

Unbiased estimator: A statistic with a mean value over an infinite number of random samples equal to the parameter it estimates.

Ungrouped frequency distribution: A frequency distribution constructed by listing all possible score values between the lowest and highest scores obtained and then placing a tally mark (/) beside a score each time it occurs.

Unimodal distribution: A distribution with one mode.

Upper stated limit of a class interval: The highest score that could fall into that class interval.

Upper real limit of a number: The point midway between a number and the next larger number.

Variable: Any environmental condition or event, stimulus, personal characteristic or attribute, or behavior that can take on different values at different times or with different people.

Variability: How much scores differ from each other and the measure of central tendency in a distribution.

Variance: The variance obtained from a sample of scores that is used to estimate the population variance for those scores. Also known as the estimated population variance.

Wilcoxon signed-ranks test: A nonparametric test for within-subjects designs with two levels of an independent variable.

Within-groups error variance: The variance of the scores in a group calculated about the group mean.

Within-subjects design: A research design in which one group of subjects is exposed to and measured under each level of an independent variable. In a within-subjects design, each subject receives each treatment condition. Also known as a *repeated measures design* or a *treatment-by-subjects design*.

Y-intercept: The value of Y when $X = 0$ in the equation $Y = bX + a$.

Y':   The value of Y predicted from X using a linear regression equation.

References

Abelson, R. P. (1997). On the surprising longevity of flogged horses: Why there is a case for the significance test. *Psychological Science, 8*, 12–15.

Abrantes, J. L., Seabra, C., Lages, L. F. (2007). Pedagogical affect, student interest, and learning performance. *Journal of Business Research, 60*, 960–964.

Adams, J. B. (2005). What makes the grade? Faculty and student perceptions. *Teaching of Psychology, 32*, 21–24.

Adams, M. (1990). The Dead Grandmother/Exam Syndrome and the Potential Downfall Of American Society. Retrieved February 19, 2008, from http://www.easternct.edu/personal/faculty/adams/Resources/Grannies.pdf

American Association of Motor Vehicle Administrators (2007). AAMVA–LCNS2ROM™ Vanity License Plates Survey: U.S. (2007). Retrieved November 12, 2007, from http://www.aamva.org

American Psychological Association. (2001). *Publication Manual of the American Psychological Association* (5th ed.). Washington, DC: Author.

American Psychological Association Ethics Code. (2003). Retrieved February 19, 2008, from http://www.apa.org/ethics/homepage.html

American Sociological Association Code of Ethics. (1997). Retrieved February 19, 2008, from http://www.asanet.org/cs/root/leftnav/ethics/code_of_ethics_table_of_contents

Armsden, G. C., & Greenberg, M. T. (1987). The inventory of parent and peer attachment: Individual differences and their relationship to psychological well-being in adolescence. *Journal of Youth and Adolescence, 16*, 427–454.

Associated Press. (2007). The Associated Press—MTV poll conducted by Knowledge Networks. Retrieved March 13, 2008, from http://www.mtv.com/thinkmtv/about/pdfs/APMTV_happinesspoll.pdf

Balch, W. R. (2006). Encouraging distributed study: A classroom experiment on the spacing effect. *Teaching of Psychology, 33*, 249–252.

Bartoli, A. M., & Clark, M. D. (2006). The dating game: Similarities and differences in dating scripts among college students. *Sexuality and Culture: An Interdisciplinary Quarterly, 10*(4), 54–80.

Bower, G. H. (1981). Mood and memory. *American Psychologist, 36*, 129–148.

Bradley, J. V. (1980). Nonrobustness in classical tests on means and variances: A large-scale sampling study. *Bulletin of the Psychonomic Society, 15*, 275–278.

Bradley, J. V. (1984). The complexity of nonrobustness effects. *Bulletin of the Psychonomic Society, 22*, 250–253.

Caldwell, C., & Hibbert, S. A. (2002). The influence of music tempo and musical preference on restaurant patrons' behavior. *Psychology and Marketing, 19*, 895–917.

Carlson, R. A., Avraamides, M. N., Cary, M., & Strasberg, S. (2007). What do the hands externalize in simple arithmetic? *Journal of Experimental Psychology: Learning, Memory, and Cognition, 33*, 747–756.

Caro, T. M. (1986). The functions of stotting in Thompson's gazelles: Some tests of the predictions. *Animal Behaviour, 34*, 663–684.

Cassaday, H. J., Bloomfield, R. E., & Hayward, N. (2002). Relaxed conditions can provide memory cues in both undergraduates and primary school children. *British Journal of Educational Psychology, 72*, 531–547.

Centers for Disease Control and Prevention. (2001). 2001 Surgeon General's Report—Women and Smoking Tobacco Use and Reproductive Outcomes. Retrieved January 31, 2008, from http://www.cdc.gov/tobacco/data_statistics/sgr/sgr_2001/highlight_outcomes.htm

Centers for Disease Control and Prevention. (2004). 2004 Surgeon General's Report—The Health Consequences of Smoking. Retrieved January 31, 2008, from http://www.cdc.gov/tobacco/data_statistics/sgr/sgr_2004/index.htm

Cohen, J. (1994). The Earth is round ($p < .05$). *American Psychologist, 49*, 997–1003.

Cortina, J. M., & Dunlap, W. P. (1997). On the logic and purpose of significance testing. *Psychological Methods, 2*, 161–172.

Cosmides, L. (1983). Invariance in the acoustic expression of emotion during speech. *Journal of Experimental Psychology: Human Performance and Perception, 9*, 864–881.

Cottyn, J., De Clercq, D., Pannier, J., Cromber, G., & Lenoir, M. (2006). The measurement of competitive anxiety during balance beam performance in gymnasts. *Journal of Sports Sciences, 24*(2), 157–164.

DePalma, C., Viggiano, E., Barillari, E., Palme, R., Dufour, A., Fantini, C., et al. (2005). Evaluating the temperament in shelter dogs. *Behaviour, 142*, 1313–1334.

Dudycha, A. L., & Dudycha, L. W. (1972). Behavioral statistics. In R. E. Kirk (ed.) *Statistical issues: A reader for the behavioral sciences* (pp. 2–25). Monterey, CA: Brooks/Cole.

Dweck, C. S. (1999). *Self–theories: Their role in motivation, personality, and development*. New York: Psychological Press.

Dweck, C. S. (2006). *Mindset: The new psychology of success*. New York: Random House.

Edes, G. (2007, April 24). Talk about long shots. . . . *The Boston Globe*, p. C6.

Educational Testing Service. (2006). General test percentage distribution of scores within intended broad graduate major field based on seniors and nonenrolled college graduates. Data set retrieved February 4, 2008, from http://www.ets.org/Media/Tests/GRE/pdf/5_01738_table_4.pdf

Eisenman, R. (1987). Creativity, birth order, and risk taking. *Bulletin of the Psychonomic Society, 25*, 87–88.

Elgar, M. A., McKay, H., & Woon, P. (1986). Scanning, pecking, and alarm flights in house sparrows. *Animal Behaviour, 34*, 1892–1894.

Elliot, A. J., Maier, M. A., Moller, A. C., Friedman, R., & Meinhardt, J. (2007). Color and psychological functioning: The effect of red on performance attainment. *Journal of Experimental Psychology: General, 136*, 154–168.

Ellison, N. B., Steinfield, C., & Lampe, C. (2007). The benefits of Facebook "friends": Social capital and college students' use of online social network sites. *Journal of Computer–Mediated Communication, 12*(4), 1143–1168.

Festinger, L., & Carlsmith, J. M. (1959). Cognitive consequences of forced compliance. *The Journal of Abnormal and Social Psychology, 58*, 203–210.

Frick, R. W. (1996). The appropriate use of null hypothesis testing. *Psychological Methods, 1*, 379–390.

Friedman, A., & Brown, N. R. (2000). Reasoning about geography. *Journal of Experimental Psychology: General, 129*, 193–219.

Friedman, H. S., Tucker, J. S., & Tomlinson-Keasey, C. (1993). Does childhood personality predict longevity? *Journal of Personality and Social Psychology, 65*, 176–185.

Gaito, J. (1977). Directional and nondirectional alternative hypotheses. *Bulletin of the Psychonomic Society, 9*, 371–372.

Gardner, P. L. (1975). Scales and statistics. *Review of Educational Research, 45*, 43–57.

Garner, D. M., Olmsted, M. P., & Polivy, J. (1983). Comparison between weight-preoccupied women and anorexia nervosa. *Psychosomatic Medicine, 46*, 255–266.

Gormly, J., & Gormly, A. (1986). Social introversion and spatial abilities. *Bulletin of the Psychonomic Society, 24*, 273–274.

Green, B. A., Deptula, N., & Agnew, S. (2006). *Using information on implicit views of intelligence to decrease math anxiety.* Paper presented at Association of Psychological Sciences Conference, New York, NY.

Gupta, R., Deverensky, J. L., & Ellenbogen, S. (2006). Personality characteristics and risk-taking tendencies among adolescent gamblers. *Canadian Journal of Behavioral Science/Revue Canadienne des Sciences du Comportement, 38*(3), 201–213.

Gurari, I., Hetts, J. J., & Strube, M. J. (2006). Beauty in the "I" of the beholder: Effects of idealized media portrayals on implicit self-image. *Basic and Applied Social Psychology, 28*(3), 273–282.

Gurung, G. A. R. (2005) How do students really study (and does it matter)? *Teaching of Psychology, 32*, 239–241.

Gustafson, R. (1987). Alcohol and aggression: A test of an indirect measure of aggression. *Psychological Reports, 60*, 1241–1242.

Hack, M., Schluchter, M., Cartar, L., Rahman, M., Cuttler, L., & Borawski, E. (2003). Growth of very low birth weight infants to age 20 years. *Pediatrics, 112*, 30–38.

Hagen, R. L. (1997). In praise of the null hypothesis statistical test. *American Psychologist, 52*, 15–24.

Harris, R. J. (1997). Significance tests have their place. *Psychological Science, 8*, 8–11.

Healy, B. (2008, March 2). To be a champion. . . . *Boston Globe,* pp. K1, K5.

Heckert, T. M., Latier, A., Ringwald-Burton, A., & Drazen, C. (2006). Relations among student effort, perceived class difficulty, appropriateness, and student evaluation of teaching: Is it possible to "buy" better evaluations through lenient grading? *College Student Journal, 40*, 588–596.

Huebner, E. S., & McCullough, G. (2000). Correlates of school satisfaction among adolescents. *Journal of Educational Research, 93*, 331–335.

Human Subjects Research Issues. (2008). Retrieved February 19, 2008, from http://www.nimh.nih.gov/research–funding/grants/human–subjects–research–issues.shtml

Hunter, J. E. (1997). Needed: A ban on the significance test. *Psychological Science, 8*, 3–7.

Infoplease (2008). *Cigarette consumption, United States, 1900–2007.* Retrieved April 17, 2008, from http://www.infoplease.com/ipa/A0908700.html

Jacoby, S. (2000). The allure of money. *Modern Maturity, 43R*(4), 34–41.

Jansz J., & Tanis, M. (2007). Appeal of playing online first person shooter games. *CyberPsychology & Behavior, 10*(1), 133–136.

John, U., Meyer, C., Rumpf, H., Hapke, U., & Schumann, A. (2006). Predictors of increased body mass index following cessation of smoking. *The American Journal on Addictions, 15*(2), 192–197.

Joseph, L. M. (2000). Developing first graders phonemic awareness, word identification and spelling: A comparison of two contemporary phonic instructional approaches. *Reading Research and Instruction, 39*(2), 160–169.

Kahneman, D., Krueger, A. B., Schkade, D. A., Schwartz, N., & Stone, A. A. (2004). A survey method for characterizing daily life experiences: The day reconstruction method. *Science, 306*, 1776–1780.

Kassel, J. D., Stroud, L. R., & Paronis, C. A. (2003). Smoking, stress, and negative affect: Correlation, causation, and context across stages of smoking. *Psychological Bulletin, 129*, 270–304.

Keller, J. (2007). Stereotype threat in classroom settings: The interactive effect of domain identification, task difficulty, and stereotype threat on female students' math performance. *British Journal of Educational Psychology, 77*, 323–338.

Keppel, G., & Wickens, T. (2004). *Design and analysis: A researcher's handbook* (5th ed.). Englewood Cliffs, NJ: Prentice Hall.

Krantz, M. (1987). Physical attractiveness and popularity: A predictive study. *Psychological Reports, 60*, 723–726.

Kruglinski, D. (2008). The Discover interview: Oliver Sacks. *Discover, 29*(1), 72–74, 76, 78.

Law, D. W. (2007). Exhaustion in university students and the effect of coursework involvement. *Journal of American College Health, 55*(4), 239–245.

Los Angeles Business Journal. (2005, July 18). *Entertainment industry income averages: as of May 2004.* Retrieved July 25, 2007, from http://www.findarticles.com/p/articles/mi_m5072.is_29_27/ai_n14860796

Martin, R. A. (2002). Sense of humor and physical health: Theoretical issues, recent findings, and future directions. *Humor: International Journal of Humor Research, 17*(1–2), 1–19.

Maslach, C., Jackson, S. E., & Leiter, M. P. (1996). *The Maslach Burnout Inventory* (3rd ed.). Palo Alto, CA: Consulting Psychologists Press.

McElrea, H., & Standing, L. (1992). Fast music causes fast drinking. *Perceptual and Motor Skills, 75*, 362.

McGarva, A. R., Ramsey, M., & Shear, S. A. (2006). Effects of driver cell-phone use on driver aggression. *Journal of Social Psychology, 146*, 133–146.

Meyer, G. E. (1986). Interactions of subjective contours with the Ponzo, Müller-Lyer, and vertical-horizontal illusions. *Bulletin of the Psychonomic Society, 24*, 39–40.

Mitchell, A. E., Castellani, A. M., Herrington, R. L, Joseph, J. I., Doss, B. D., & Snyder, D. K. (2008). Predictors of intimacy in couples' discussion of relationship injuries: An observational study. *Journal of Family Psychology, 22*, 21–29.

National Collegiate Athletic Association. (2007). Estimated probability of competing in athletics beyond the high school interscholastic level. Retrieved February 18, 2008, from http://www.ncaa.org/research/

Nellie Mae (2007). Graduate students and credit cards Fall 2006: An analysis of usage, rates, and trends. Retrieved April 17, 2008, from: http://www.nelliemae.com/pdf/ccstudy_2006.pdf

Nelson, L. D., & Simmons, J. P. (2007). Moniker maladies: When names sabotage success. *Psychological Science, 18*, 1106–1112.

Nicholson, C. (2008, April). Fact or Fiction?: Does "spring fever" exist? *Scientific American, 298*, 116.

O'Brien, R. M., & Stockard, J. (2006). A common explanation for the changing age distributions of suicides and homicides in the United States, 1930 to 2000. *Social Forces, 84*, 1539–1557.

Ogletree, S. M., Turner, G. M., Vieira, A., & Brunotte, J. (2005). College living: Issues related to housecleaning attitudes. *College Student Journal, 39*, 729–733.

Ogrodniczuk, J. S., Joyce, A. S., & Piper, W. E. (2005). Strategies for reducing patient-initiated premature termination of psychotherapy. *Harvard Review of Psychiatry, 13*(2), 57–70.

Parrott, A. C. (1999). Does cigarette smoking *cause* stress? *American Psychologist, 54*, 817–820.

Provine, R. R., & Hamernik, H. B. (1986). Yawning: Effects of stimulus interest. *Bulletin of the Psychonomic Society, 24*, 437–438.

Raskauskas, J., & Stoltz, A. D. (2007). Involvement in traditional and electronic bullying among adolescents. *Developmental Psychology, 43*, 564–575.

Roballey, T. C., McGreevy, C., Rongo, R. R., Schwantes, M. L., Steger, P. J., Wininger, M. A., et al. (1985). The effect of music on eating behavior. *Bulletin of the Psychonomic Society, 23*, 221–222.

Roedinger, H. L., & Karpicke, J. D. (2006). The power of testing memory: Basic research and implications for educational practice. *Perspectives on Psychological Science, 1*(3), 181–210.

Sadeh, A., Raviv, A., & Gruber, R. (2000). Sleep patterns and sleep disruptions in school-age children. *Developmental Psychology, 36*, 291–301.

Schutz, H. K., & Paxton, S. J. (2007). Friendship quality, body dissatisfaction, dieting, and disordered eating in adolescent girls. *British Journal of Clinical Psychology, 46*(1), 67–83.

Scoville, W. B., & Milner, B. (1957). Loss of recent memory after bilateral hippocampal lesions. *Journal of Neurology, Neurosurgery, and Psychiatry, 20*, 11–21.

Senders, V. L. (1958). *Measurement and statistics.* New York: Oxford University Press.

Skotko, B. G., Kensinger, E. A., Locascio, J. J., Einstein, G., Rubin, D. C., Tupler, L. A., et al. (2004). Puzzling thoughts for H. M.: Can new semantic information be anchored to old semantic memories? *Neuropsychology, 18*, 756–769.

Smith, J. E., Waldorf, V. A., & Trembath, D. L. (1990). "Single white male looking for thin, very attractive. . . ." *Sex Roles, 23*, 675–683.

St. George, D. (2007). *Despite "Mommy guilt," time with kids increasing.* Retrieved April 5, 2007, from www.washingtonpost.com/wp-dyn/content/article/2007/03/19/AR2007031901972.html

Standing, L., Lynn, D., & Moxness, K. (1990). Effects of noise upon introverts and extroverts. *Bulletin of the Psychonomic Society, 28*, 138–140.

Stephenson, M. T., Hoyle, R. H., Palmgren, P., & Slater, M. D. (2003). Brief measures of sensation seeking for screening and large-scale surveys. *Drug and Alcohol Dependence, 72*, 279–286.

Stigler, S. M. (1986). *The history of statistics: The measurement of uncertainty before 1900.* Cambridge, MA: Harvard University Press.

Strayer, D. L. & Drews, F. A. (2007). Cell-phone-induced driver distraction. *Current Directions in Psychological Science, 16*(3), 128–131.

Strueber, D., & Stadler, M. (1999). Differences in top-down influences on the reversal rate of different categories of reversible figures. *Perception, 28*, 1185–1196.

Sturgeon, R., & Beer, J. (1990). Attendance reward and absenteeism in high school. *Psychological Reports, 66*, 759–762.

Tobacyk, J., Miller, M. J., & Jones, G. (1984). Paranormal beliefs of high school students. *Psychological Reports, 55*, 255–261.

Travel + Leisure. (2007). *America's favorite cities.* Retrieved October 10, 2007, from http://travelandleisure.com/afc/2007/category/3

Trinkaus, J. (1982). Stop sign compliance: An informal look. *Psychological Reports, 50,* 288.

Trinkaus, J. (1983). Stop sign compliance: Another look. *Psychological Reports, 57,* 922.

Trinkaus, J. (1988). Stop sign compliance: A further look. *Perceptual and Motor Skills, 67,* 670.

Trinkaus, J. (1993). Stop sign compliance: A follow-up look. *Perceptual and Motor Skills, 76,* 1218.

Trinkaus, J. (1997). Stop sign compliance: A final look. *Perceptual and Motor Skills, 85,* 217–218.

Trinkaus, J. (1999). Stop sign dissenters: An informal look. *Perceptual and Motor Skills, 89,* 1193–1194.

Trinkaus, J. (2001). Blocking the box: An informal look. *Psychological Reports, 89,* 315–316.

Turrisi, R., Mastroleo, N. R., Mallett, K. A., Larimer, M. E., and Kilmer, J. R. (2007). Examination of the mediational influence of peer norms, environmental influences, and parent communications on heavy drinking in athletes and nonathletes. *Psychology of Addictive Behaviors, 21,* 453–461.

U.S. Census Bureau (2005). *America's families and living arrangements: 2004.* Retrieved January 20, 2008, from http://www.census.gov/population/www/socdemo/hh-fam/cps2004.html

U.S. Census Bureau (2006). *Median age at first marriage.* Retrieved January 22, 2008, from http://www.census.gov/population/www/socdemo/hh-fam/cps2004.html

U.S. Census Bureau. (2007). *The 2007 Statistical abstract of the United States:* Retrieved June 28, 2007, from www.census.gov/compendia/statab

USA Today (2007). *Salaries database: Basketball.* Retrieved February 12, 2007, from http://content.usatoday.com/sports/basketball/nba/salaries/default.aspx

Wainer, H. (1999). One cheer for null hypothesis significance testing. *Psychological Methods, 4,* 212–213.

Wang, A. Y., Thomas, M. H., & Ouellette, J. A. (1992). Keyword mnemonic and retention of second language vocabulary words. *Journal of Educational Psychology, 84,* 520–528.

Wansink, B., Painter, J. E., & Lee, Y. K. (2006). The office candy dish: Proximity's influence on estimated and actual consumption. *International Journal of Obesity, 30*(5), 93–100.

Wertz, A. T., Wright, K. P., Ronda, J. M., & Czeisler, C. A. (2006). Effects of sleep inertia on cognition. *JAMA: Journal of the American Medical Association, 295*(2), 163–164.

Weyzig, F., & Schipper, I. (2006). *SOMO briefing paper on ethics in clinical trials: Examples of unethical Trials.* Retrieved April 11, 2008, from http://www.wemos.nl/Documents/clinical_%20trials_%20report.pdf

Wilkinson, L., & The Task Force on Statistical Inference. (1999). Statistical methods in psychology journals: Guidelines and explanations. *American Psychologist, 54,* 594–604.

Williams, J. G., & Covington, C. J. (1997). Predictors of cigarette smoking among adolescents. *Psychological Reports, 80,* 481–482.

Wong, J. L. (1993). Comparison of the Shipley versus WAIS-R subtests and summary scores in predicting college grade point average. *Perceptual and Motor Skills, 76,* 1075–1078.

Wood, A. M., Joseph, S., & Linley, P. A. (2007a). Coping style as a psychological resource of grateful people. *Journal of Social and Clinical Psychology, 26,* 1076–1093.

Wood, A. M., Joseph, S., & Linley, P. A. (2007b, January). Gratitude—Parent of all virtues. *The Psychologist, 20*(1) 18–20.

World Almanac and Book of Facts 2007. (2007). New York: World Almanac Books.

World Tourism. (2006). *UNWTO tourism highlights, edition 2006.* Retrieved July 18, 2007, from http://www.world-tourism.org/facts/highlights.htm

Zusne, L. (1986–87). Some factors affecting the birthday-deathday phenomenon. *Omega, 17,* 9–26.

Name Index

Subject Index

Research Methods

Research Method	Description	Common Statistic Used	Hypotheses Role	Page
Case study	Fully detailed examination of a single case. Used for rare or new conditions/situations.	None	Building	19
Naturalistic observation	Unobtrusive examination of organisms in their natural habitat. Used to find associations between variables.	Qualitative Chi square	Building and Testing	19–20
Archival research	Use of data collected at a different time for a different purpose to test a current non-causal hypothesis. Answering questions by examining data from existing records.	Descriptive Correlation Regression	Non-causal Testing	20
Survey	Obtaining data through oral interviews or paper and pencil tasks.	Descriptive Correlation Regression	Non-causal Testing	20–21
Experiment	Researcher has control over the independent variable. Subjects are randomly assigned to conditions of the independent variable.	Descriptive t test ANOVA	Testing of Causal Hypotheses	21
Quasi-experiment	Resembles an experiment. Used when you have subject variables and not independent variables that can be manipulated.	Dependent upon design	Non-causal Testing	21–22

Measurement

Scales	Description	Qualitative/ Quantitative	Description	Variable	Description
Nominal	Classification of measured variable into different categories.	Qualitative	Provide information on kind or quality of variable instead of on amount.	Discrete	Variable that can take on only a finite or countable set of values within its limits.
Ordinal	Amount of a variable is placed in order of magnitude along a dimension.	Quantitative	Data indicates how much of a variable exists.		
Interval	Amount of a variable is ordered along a dimension. Differences between the assigned numbers represent equal amounts in the magnitude of the variable measured. The zero point of an interval scale is an arbitrary starting point.			Continuous	Variable that can take on an infinite set of values between the limits of the variable.
Ratio	Amount of a variable is ordered along a dimension. Differences between the assigned numbers represent equal amounts in the magnitude of the variable measured. A true zero point, which represents the absence of the characteristic measured, exists.	Quantitative	Data indicates how much of a variable exists.		

Descriptive Statistics

Measures of Central Tendency

Statistic	Description
Mean	Sum of a set of scores divided by the number of scores summed. The arithmetic average.
Median	A score value in the distribution with an equal number of scores above and below it. The 50th percentile in a distribution.
Mode	Most frequently occurring score in a distribution of scores.

Measures of Variability

Statistic	Description
Range	The numerical difference between the lowest and highest scores in a distribution.
Variance	Average of the sum of the squared deviations.
Standard deviation	Square root of the variance.

Inferential Statistics

	Statistic Symbol and Formula for Estimating Parameter	Population Parameter Symbol and Formula	APA Symbol
Mean	$\overline{X} = \dfrac{\Sigma X}{N}$	$\mu = \dfrac{\Sigma X}{N_{\text{population}}}$	M
Variance	$s^2 = \dfrac{\Sigma (X - \overline{X})^2}{N-1} = \dfrac{SS}{N-1}$	$\sigma^2 = \dfrac{\Sigma (X - \mu)^2}{N_{\text{population}}}$	MS
Standard deviation	$s = \sqrt{\dfrac{\Sigma (X - \overline{X})^2}{N-1}} = \sqrt{\dfrac{SS}{N-1}} = \sqrt{s^2}$	$\sigma = \sqrt{\dfrac{\Sigma (X - \mu)^2}{N_{\text{population}}}} = \sqrt{\sigma^2}$	SD

Confidence Intervals

Type	Page	Formula	Standard Error
One sample mean when you know the population variance.	180	$\overline{X} \pm z_{\text{crit}}(\sigma_{\overline{X}})$	$\sigma_{\overline{X}} = \dfrac{\sigma}{\sqrt{N}}$
One sample mean when you only know the sample variance.	186	$\overline{X} \pm t_{\text{crit}}(s_{\overline{X}})$	$s_{\overline{X}} = \dfrac{s}{\sqrt{N}}$
Difference between two independent means.	217	$(\overline{X}_1 - \overline{X}_2) \pm t_{\text{crit}}(s_{\overline{X}_1 - \overline{X}_2})$	$s_{\overline{X}_1 - \overline{X}_2} = \sqrt{\dfrac{(n_1 - 1)s_1^2 + (n_2 - 1)s_2^2}{n_1 + n_2 - 2}\left[\dfrac{1}{n_1} + \dfrac{1}{n_2}\right]}$
Difference between two related means.	226	$(\overline{X}_1 - \overline{X}_2) \pm t_{\text{crit}}(s_{\overline{D}})$	$s_{\overline{D}} = \dfrac{s_D}{\sqrt{N_{\text{pairs}}}}$

Normal Distribution and Probability

Normal Distribution and Sampling Distribution of the Mean

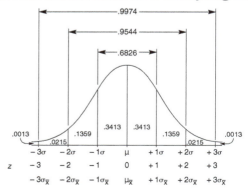

Important Formulas

Provides the location of a score on the standard normal distribution.

$$z = \frac{X - \mu}{\sigma}$$

Provides the location of a sample mean on the standard normal distribution.

$$z = \frac{\overline{X} - \mu}{\sigma_{\overline{X}}}$$

Provides the probability of an event.

$$p(\text{event}) = \frac{\text{Number of outcomes composing an event}}{\text{Total number of possible outcomes}}$$

Hypothesis Testing

t Tests

Type	Page	Description	Formula	Standard Error	*df*
One sample *t*	170	Compares one sample mean to a known or hypothesized population mean.	$t = \dfrac{\overline{X} - \mu}{s_{\overline{X}}}$	$s_{\overline{X}} = \dfrac{s}{\sqrt{N}}$	$N - 1$
Independent *t*	208	Compares the means of two independent samples from a between-subjects design.	$t = \dfrac{\overline{X}_1 - \overline{X}_2}{s_{\overline{X}_1 - \overline{X}_2}}$	$s_{\overline{X}_1 - \overline{X}_2} = \sqrt{\dfrac{(n_1 - 1)s_1^2 + (n_2 - 1)s_2^2}{n_1 + n_2 - 2}\left[\dfrac{1}{n_1} + \dfrac{1}{n_2}\right]}$	$N - 2$
Related *t*	224	Compares the means of two related samples from a within-subjects design.	$t = \dfrac{\overline{X}_1 - \overline{X}_2}{s_{\overline{D}}}$	$s_{\overline{D}} = \dfrac{s_D}{\sqrt{N_{\text{pairs}}}}$	$N_{\text{pairs}} - 1$

One-Factor Between-Subjects ANOVA

Source	SS	*df*[a]	MS	F
Factor A	$\sum\sum(\overline{X}_A - \overline{X}_G)^2$	$a - 1$	$\dfrac{SS_A}{df_A}$	$\dfrac{MS_A}{MS_{\text{Error}}}$
Error	$\sum\sum(X - \overline{X}_A)^2$	$N - a$	$\dfrac{SS_{\text{Error}}}{df_{\text{Error}}}$	
Total	$\sum\sum(X - \overline{X}_G)^2$	$N - 1$	Not Calculated	

Two-Factor Between-Subjects ANOVA

Source	SS	*df*[a]	MS	F
Factor A	$\sum\sum(\overline{X}_A - \overline{X}_G)^2$	$a - 1$	$\dfrac{SS_A}{df_A}$	$\dfrac{MS_A}{MS_{\text{Error}}}$
Factor B	$\sum\sum(\overline{X}_B - \overline{X}_G)^2$	$b - 1$	$\dfrac{SS_B}{df_B}$	$\dfrac{MS_B}{MS_{\text{Error}}}$
Interaction of A and B	$\sum\sum(\overline{X}_{AB} - \overline{X}_A - \overline{X}_B + \overline{X}_G)^2$	$(a - 1)(b - 1)$	$\dfrac{SS_{A \times B}}{df_{A \times B}}$	$\dfrac{MS_{A \times B}}{MS_{\text{Error}}}$
Error	$\sum\sum(X - \overline{X}_{AB})^2$	$ab(n_{AB} - 1)$	$\dfrac{SS_{\text{Error}}}{df_{\text{Error}}}$	
Total	$\sum\sum(X - \overline{X}_G)^2$	$N - 1$	Not Calculated	

[a] a = number of levels of factor A; b = number of levels of factor B; n_{AB} = number of scores in each cell; N = total number of scores.

One-Factor Within-Subjects ANOVA

Source	SS	*df*[a]	MS	F
Factor A	$\sum\sum(\overline{X}_A - \overline{X}_G)^2$	$a - 1$	$\dfrac{SS_A}{df_A}$	$\dfrac{MS_A}{MS_{A \times S}}$
Factor S	$\sum\sum(\overline{X}_S - \overline{X}_G)^2$	$n_A - 1$	$\dfrac{SS_S}{df_S}$	
AXS	$\sum\sum(X - \overline{X}_A - \overline{X}_S + \overline{X}_G)^2$	$(a - 1)(n_A - 1)$	$\dfrac{SS_{A \times S}}{df_{A \times S}}$	
Total	$\sum\sum(X - \overline{X}_G)^2$	$N - 1$	Not Calculated	

Effect Size

Statistic	Eta Squared	Page
t test	$\eta^2 = \dfrac{t_{\text{obs}}^2}{t_{\text{obs}}^2 + df}$	Independent *t*: 216 Related *t*: 226
One-factor between-subjects ANOVA	$\eta^2 = \dfrac{SS_A}{SS_{\text{Total}}}$ $\eta^2 = \dfrac{(df_A)(F_{\text{obs}})}{(df_A)(F_{\text{obs}}) + df_{\text{Error}}}$	264
One-factor within-subjects ANOVA	$\eta^2 = \dfrac{SS_A}{SS_A + SS_{A \times S}}$	356

Associations

Correlation

Correlation	Use	Type	Formula	Page
Pearson product moment	To find the degree of a linear relationship between two interval or ratio measurement variables.	Definitional formula	$r = \dfrac{\sum(X - \bar{X})(Y - \bar{Y})}{\sqrt{\left[\sum(X - \bar{X})^2\right]\left[\sum(Y - \bar{Y})^2\right]}}$	377
		Cross product/sum of squares formula	$r = \dfrac{CP_{XY}}{\sqrt{(SS_X)(SS_Y)}}$	377
		Standard score formula	$r = \dfrac{\sum(z_X z_Y)}{N_{\text{pairs}}}$	383
Spearman rank-order	To find the degree of a linear relationship between two ordinal measurement variables.		$r_s = 1 - \left[\dfrac{6\sum D^2}{(N_{\text{pairs}})(N_{\text{pairs}}^2 - 1)}\right]$	399

Linear Regression

Component	Formula	Component	Formula
Slope of a least squares regression line	$b = \dfrac{\sum(X - \bar{X})(Y - \bar{Y})}{\sum(X - \bar{X})^2}$ $b = \dfrac{CP_{XY}}{SS_X}$ $b = r\left(\dfrac{s_Y}{s_X}\right)$	Y-intercept	$a = \bar{Y} - b\bar{X}$
		Equation for least-squares regression line	$Y' = bX + a$
		Standard error of estimate	$s_{X \cdot Y} = \sqrt{\dfrac{\sum(Y - Y')^2}{N_{\text{pairs}} - 2}}$ $s_{X \cdot Y} = s_Y \sqrt{1 - r_{\text{obs}}^2}$

Nonparametric Statistics

Statistic	Use	Page	Formula
χ^2	Test of independence.	451	$\chi^2 = \sum \dfrac{(O - E)^2}{E}$ O is observed & E is expected frequency.
	Test of goodness of fit.	453	$\text{Expected Frequency of a cell} = \dfrac{\left(\begin{array}{c}\text{Row}\\\text{marginal}\\\text{for cell}\end{array}\right)\left(\begin{array}{c}\text{Column}\\\text{marginal}\\\text{for cell}\end{array}\right)}{\text{Total number of responses}}$ $df = (r - 1)(c - 1)$, where r is the number of rows and c is the number of columns.
Mann-Whitney U	Between-subjects design with 2 levels of an independent variable. Ordinal measurement or higher.	466	$U_{A_1} = n_{A_1} n_{A_2} + \dfrac{n_{A_1}(n_{A_1} + 1)}{2} - \sum R_{A_1}$ R is the rank for each group.
Wilcoxon Signed-ranks test T statistic	Ordinal measurement.	473	See pages 473–474 for the steps for finding a T statistic.